History in the Makin[illegible]

A History of the People of the United States of America to 1877

Edition 1, Version 3

Release Date: August 19, 2013

Written By:

Catherine Locks

Sarah Mergel, PhD

Pamela Roseman, PhD

Tamara Spike, PhD

Project Editor:

Marie Lasseter, EdD

BOARD OF REGENTS OF THE UNIVERSITY SYSTEM OF GEORGIA

"Creating A More Educated Georgia"
www.usg.edu
270 Washington Street, S.W.
Atlanta, GA 30334
U.S.A.

UNIVERSITY PRESS OF NORTH GEORGIA

"Local is Global"
www.upng.org
University of North Georgia
Dahlonega, GA 30598
U.S.A.

ISBN: 978-0-9882237-3-8

Produced by:
The University System of Georgia
www.usg.edu

Published by:
The University Press of North Georgia
Dahlonega, Georgia
upng@northgeorgia.edu

We invite you to contact the University Press of North Georgia directly with any feedback or comments regarding this book.

Cover Design:
Lacey Pyle

Layout and Format Design:
Lacey Pyle, Marie Lasseter, and April Loebick

ACKNOWLEDGEMENTS

The University System of Georgia would like to acknowledge the special efforts put forth by certain individuals, and their institutions, who worked on making this book possible. We extend a special thanks to Dr. Sarah Mergel, Dalton State College; Dr. Tamara Spike, University of North Georgia; Dr. Pamela Roseman, Georgia Perimeter College; and Ms. Catherine Locks, Fort Valley State University. This book would not have been possible without the support of these institutions and the dedication and generosity of these faculty authors.

Thanks to Dr. Marie Lasseter and Dr. Mike Rogers, from the University System of Georgia Academic Affairs office, who have long advocated for the use of open educational resources and open textbooks as one way to help ease the high cost of a college education for students and their families. Without their guidance and encouragement this book would not have materialized. Dr. Lasseter provided overall oversight and guidance for this project and provided years of experience of working with collaborative groups to develop and design educational materials. Her knowledge and experience in developing and using open educational resources was a valuable resource to the team.

We gratefully acknowledge the University Press of North Georgia, in particular Dr. Bonnie Robinson and Ms. April Loebick, for their role in guiding the publication process. Under Dr. Robinson's direction they worked tirelessly with the authors during all phases of the work, ensuring that this textbook achieves the high quality and scholarly standards our faculty and students expect.

We wish to extend a special thanks to eCore Administrative Services, especially Ms. Christy Talley Smith, for providing faculty authors, guidance, and support throughout the development process.

The guidance and support provided by all the members who contributed to this work was essential for the success of the project. Each of these individuals has engaged in open philanthropy, an act of generosity and a desire to contribute to, and encourage, the success of students everywhere. This is what educators do. As Thomas Jefferson said, "He who receives ideas from me receives instruction himself without lessening mine; as he who lights his taper at mine receives light without darkening me."

This is an open textbook, freely available for anyone to access, reuse, adapt, and redistribute. It is a dynamic entity that will continue to be updated and edited to suit the needs and the instructional goals of the users. We are grateful for the efforts of those who will continue this process.

AUTHOR BIOGRAPHIES

Catherine Locks: Catherine Locks is an instructor and also an instructional technologist/designer from Richmond, Virginia. She received her BS in history from Longwood University(1986) and her MA in history(2000) and MEd in instructional technology from Georgia College & State University(2002). She teaches online courses for the University System of Georgia's eCore program, and face-to-face courses for Fort Valley State University. Her areas of interest include pre-history, ancient Mesopotamia, Egypt and Rome, medieval English history, and colonial American history, particularly of the mid-Atlantic region.

As an instructional designer, Ms. Locks has built several online courses, including the first US History I course for Central Georgia Technical College. She is interested in usability and accessibility in the online environment, the impact of technology on education and improving the instructor and student online experience. She was drawn to this textbook project due to the goals of making a textbook that would be affordable, accessible in several formats, and written and organized in such a way as to be approachable for students.

Ms. Locks would like to first thank her co-authors, Tamara Spike, Pamela Roseman and especially the ever patient and ever available Sarah Mergel, as well as the others who made this project happen—Marie Lasseter, Mike Rogers, BJ Robinson, April Loebick, and Christy Talley Smith. She would also like to thank some very special people—Dr. Deborah Vess a pioneer who was putting history and technology together long before many in the field found it acceptable, Dr. Robert J. Wilson III who convinced Ms. Locks that American and Georgia history were actually fascinating, Dr. Frank Lowney a true innovator in the use of educational technology who taught Ms. Locks more than he'll ever know, Dr. Andrea Novak, the most generous mentor, friend and example of how to behave in meetings and Dr. Fred R. van Hartesveldt, who always has time to listen—even when he almost certainly has none. Finally and most importantly, Ms. Locks wants to thank her family for their never ending support and especially her son, Benjamin, who more than anyone else has had to put up with her throughout this marvelous madness.

AUTHOR BIOGRAPHIES

Sarah K. Mergel, PhD: Sarah Mergel received her BA in history and sociology from Boston College (1997) and her MA and PhD in history from The George Washington University (2002/2007). She works as an Assistant Professor of History at Dalton State College in Northwest Georgia teaching both face-to-face and online classes. She specializes in American political, intellectual, and diplomatic history since the end of the Civil War. Much of her work in *History in the Making: A History of the People of the United States of America to 1877* focuses on political and economic developments in the Colonial Era, the Federalist Era, the Jacksonian Era, and the Civil War Era.

Dr. Mergel has published several books and articles on twentieth century political figures and reform movements. *Conservative Intellectuals and Richard Nixon: Rethinking the Rise of the Right* (2009) examines how conservative intellectuals influenced and reacted to political and social developments during the Nixon administration. *A Biography of John M. Gillespie: A Teamster's Life* (2009) looks at an influential member of the International Brotherhood of Teamsters in the years before World War II. Her chapter for the *Chronology of the U.S. Presidency* (2012) was on Franklin Delano Roosevelt. Finally, she had published several encyclopedia articles on the populist movement, the origins of the New Deal, the Vietnamization program, the postwar conservative movement, the emergence of neoconservatism, and several political figures.

Dr. Mergel would like to thank her co-authors, Cathy Locks, Tam Spike, and Pam Roseman for their willingness share ideas and write together to complete this open textbook. She also wants to say how much she appreciates how diligently Marie Lasseter, BJ Robinson, and April Loebick worked on helping this open textbook come together. Moreover, she wants to thank Mary Nielsen, the Dean of Liberal Arts, and Judy Cornett, the Chair of Social Sciences, as well as Matthew Hipps, Seth Weitz and the other members of the Department of Social Sciences Dalton State for their support during the project. They helped clarify her thoughts on such varied things as mercantilism and the Bill of Rights and encouraged her to keep writing even when it seemed like the writing process would never end and. Finally, Dr. Mergel wants to thank her family, especially Carolyn Mergel (her mom), for their willingness to listen to her ramble on about all things history.

AUTHOR BIOGRAPHIES

Pamela Thomas Roseman, PhD: Born in Jacksonville, Florida, Pamela T. Roseman received her BA from Florida State University, did her MA work at Florida State and Georgia State Universities, and received her PhD from Georgia State University in 1980. Her fields of concentration include American Intellectual history, Renaissance and Reformation Europe, Tudor-Stuart England, and U.S. and Latin American colonial history. Her Master's Thesis explores Puritan motivation in the settlement of New England; her dissertation is entitled *Millennial Expectation Among Southern Evangelicals in the Mid-19th century.*

Dr. Roseman, a Professor of History at Georgia Perimeter College (GPC), has taught at the College since 1986, where from 1992-1999 she was also the Director of GPC's Center for Teaching and Learning. Dr. Roseman became involved in online course development and delivery in 2000 when she and five other historians from University System of Georgia (USG) institutions created the early American course for the University System's electronic CORE (eCore), an initiative of the USG Chancellor at the time. In 2002 this course won recognition as a *WebCT Exceptional Course.* Since 2000 she has developed and taught online courses in World History and currently teaches in the Online Program of Georgia Perimeter College.

Between 2004 and 2007 Dr. Roseman participated in two U.S. Department of Education Teaching American History grants in which six professors from the University System of Georgia taught, mentored, and developed instructional materials for high school teachers from three metropolitan Atlanta school districts. The work accomplished in the grant cycles came as the result of faculty collaboration; this was also true of developing the eCore early American history course and the current eText, *History in the Making: A History of the American People of the United States of America to 1877.*

Dr. Roseman has been a *Governor's Teaching Fellow,* a *Georgia Perimeter College Instructional Technology Scholar,* a *Georgia Perimeter College Fellow* and an *Academic Vice President's Teaching Scholar.* She has been active in the Georgia Association of Historians for many years, serving for a time on the Executive Board, in the Georgia Association for Women in Higher Education, for which she was Vice President and President, and as the Coordinator for the State of Georgia of the National Council of Staff and Organizational Development.

Dr. Roseman would like to thank the Board of Regents of the State of Georgia, and especially Mike Rogers, Assistant Vice Chancellor for Faculty Development, for making this project possible; project director, Marie Lasseter for her perseverance and patience in working with the historians; editors from the University of North Georgia, BJ Robinson and April Loebick, for their helpful comments, and her fellow writers. Most of all she thanks her family: daughter, Amanda Colbenson of Brooklyn, New York, and husband, Gary Roseman, for their encouragement, patience, humor and insights and especially to Gary for convincing her that U.S. history did not end in 1789.

With the support of family all things are possible.

Dr. Roseman lives in Decatur and on St Simons Island, Georgia.

AUTHOR BIOGRAPHIES

Tamara Spike, PhD: Tamara Spike is a historian of colonial Latin America and the indigenous peoples of the Americas. She is an Associate Professor in the Department of History, Anthropology, and Philosophy at the University of North Georgia. Dr. Spike earned her MA and PhD in History from Florida State University, and holds a dual BA in Anthropology and Classical Archaeology. She has worked as a professional archaeologist on historic and prehistoric digs throughout Florida. From 1999-2010, she was a staff member of the Guadalajara Census Project, a group which works to analyze censuses from the city spanning the years 1790-1930, and to digitize these censuses for use by scholars, genealogists, and the public (http://www.fsu.edu/~guadalaj/). She is the English language editor of both Volume I and II of the published databases of the Guadalajara Census Project. Dr. Spike's publications include "Making History Count: The Guadalajara Census Project (1791-1930)" in the *Hispanic American Historical Review*, "Si todo el mundo fuera Inglaterra: la teoría de Peter Laslett sobre la composición de las unidades domésticas vs. la realidad tapatía, 1821-1822," in *Estudios Sociales Nueva Época*, "St Augustine's Stomach: Indian Tribute Labor and Corn in Florida, 1565-1763" in *Florida's Labor and Working-Class Past: Three Centuries of Work in the Sunshine State, and* "Death and Death Ritual among the Timucua of Spanish Florida," in *From La Florida to La California*. Her research focuses on the ethnogenesis and cultural reconstruction of the Timucua Indians of Spanish Florida.

In addition to the people and organizations thanked in the acknowledgements, Tamara Spike would like to extend her thanks to her family and the members of her department for their support.

HISTORY IN THE MAKING: A HISTORY OF THE PEOPLE OF THE UNITED STATES OF AMERICA TO 1877

Chapter One:
United States History Before Columbus

Contents

Chapter One: United States History Before Columbus

1.1 INTRODUCTION

The history of the country that will eventually come to be called the United States begins long before the birth of the nation. Native Americans first inhabited the North American continent some 14,000 years ago, if not earlier. This earliest era is known as the Paleo-Indian era; it is closely identified with one of the most famous archaeological artifacts in the Americas, the Clovis point, which was used to hunt megafauna, the giant animals of the Pleistocene era, such as mammoth or mastodon. The eras following, the Archaic and Woodland, were marked by the development of plant domestication and incipient agriculture, one of the most important developments in human history. Two of the earliest centers for plant domestication were in Mesoamerica and the modern-day Southeastern United States. Finally, the period just before European contact is characterized by the development of many rich and diverse cultures. In the region that was to become the United States, there were some 500 groups, each with its own language, culture, and religion.

1.1.2 Learning Outcomes

After completing this chapter, you should be able to:

- Explain the various interpretations, scientific and religious, of the origins of indigenous peoples in the New World.
- Describe the political, cultural, and social differences between the major eras of the prehistoric United States.
- Describe the political, cultural, and social differences between the groups of the major regions of the prehistoric United States.

1.2 ORIGINS

When Columbus first encountered the Western hemisphere in 1492, it was inhabited by millions of people. Establishing a firm estimate of the population is troublesome; often such estimates are tinged with the ideological viewpoints of the authors, their cultures of origin, and the eras in which they wrote. Until recent decades, historians and scientists tended to make very low estimates of native populations, as conventional wisdom held that "inferior" indigenous peoples could not sustain the same kinds of dense populations as Europeans. More recently, estimates have soared for a variety of reasons; for example, some scholars speculate that estimates of population have become too inflated because of the desire to emphasize the devastation that European contact caused to the indigenous population.

Current estimates hold that as much as a fifth of the world's population—43-65 million people—inhabited the Western hemisphere at contact. Estimates of the North American population (excluding Mexico) vary from a low of seven million to a high of eighteen million people.[1]

A great deal of cultural diversity existed amongst this population; hundreds of groups spoke hundreds of languages, organized their society in a myriad of social and political ways, enacted innumerable rituals, and worshiped a multitude of gods.

Another problem we face in examining this early period in U.S. history is one of nomenclature. What do we call the indigenous peoples of the Americas? Every term has its advantages and flaws. Some terms have been dismissed as racist (Red Indian); others have become outdated (Eskimo). Some view terms like Native American or First Peoples (the preferred term in Canada) as so politically correct that they are meaningless. Terms like aboriginal and indigenous assert a global identity for native peoples. However, the term aboriginal has become so closely associated with Australian Aborigines that it seems to exclude others. Moreover, while the notion of a global identity for indigenous peoples is useful in some instances, it is far too broad an idea to be useful in others. In the U.S., many use the term "Native American," which first came into use in the 1980s as a means to indicate their primacy as the first peoples of the land. In general, the preference of native peoples is to self-identify as their own tribal affinity: Chickasaw, Ojibwa, Arapaho, etc. In terms of a larger, overarching term for the group as a whole, a 1995 survey of native peoples in the United States indicates that the first preference in nomenclature for native peoples is Indian.[2] For this reason, this term will be preferred here.

1.2.1 Origin Stories

Indigenous people throughout the Western hemisphere talk of their origins as a people in oral histories, stories, and myths that link them intimately to the places they inhabit. The land, the stories commonly assert, was made for "the people," and they were made to inhabit the land. Every group has an origin story, and they vary widely and are unique to the group. Sometimes, groups have multiple origin stories that tell differing versions of creation and the founding of the group. Origin stories often begin with a "First Person" (or First Peoples), a mythical man or woman who founded the group. These First People often are created from, or emerge from, the natural world itself. The first Iroquois fell from the

Figure 1.1 Spider Gorget | Ancient shell gorget from Fains Island, Tennessee, depicting a spider.

Author: Gates P. Thruston
Source: *The Antiquities of Tennessee*

sky; the first Lakota emerged from underground; the first Maya were created from corn. Sometimes, animals appear in origin stories as agents of creation. For example, in the Cherokee creation story, Water-Beetle dives deep into the ocean and brings up the mud that forms the earth. Buzzard then flies over the land, shaping it into mountains and valleys with the beat of his wings. These origin stories explained and shaped the worldview of each group, establishing their people's purpose in this world as well as their relationship to the gods and the world around them. In other words, origin stories are key to establishing a group identity and a deep connection with the region the people inhabit.

1.2.2 Scientific Theories Of Origin

Scientists and archaeologists hold several theories regarding the origins of Indians in the Americas. By far, the oldest and most widely accepted of these theories is the Bering Land Bridge migration model. This theory posits that during the last ice age (approximately 50,000-10,000 BP, or years before the present), humans were able to migrate from Siberia to Alaska, crossing over the land bridge between the continents that had been revealed by dropping sea levels as massive glaciers formed all over the world. During this time, as many as four distinct migrations occurred over the land bridge between about 10,000-14,000 BP. Peoples migrated from Siberia, Eurasia, and coastal Asia, following the megafauna of the Pleistocene, such as mammoth and mastodon. Other megafauna included giant species of animals that are familiar to us today, such as beavers and sloths.

The greatest supporting evidence of this theory is the extensive homogeneity of the North American Clovis culture, so named for the archaeological site at which it was first identified. Clovis peoples were long considered to be the first people to inhabit the Americas. Archaeologists theorize that Clovis peoples came over the land bridge and down a glacier pass to the east of the Rocky Mountains sometime between 12,000-11,000 BCE, eventually spreading through much of North America.

A second theory focuses on Pacific sea travel. The coastal migration theory suggests that some peoples arrived in the Americas through following the coast of land across Asia and the Bering Land Bridge, down the coast of North

Sidebar 1.1: Dating and Dates

This book employs three terms in conveying dates. BCE and CE stand for Before Common Era, and Common Era, respectively. These terms coincide exactly with the BC/AD dating system; therefore, 300 BC = 300 BCE, and 1976 AD = 1976 CE. The abbreviation BP stands for Before Present, and indicates "years ago" or years before the present. It is most commonly used by archaeologists in conjunction with radiocarbon dating, a means of determining the age of organic materials be measuring the amount of radioactive decay of carbon-14 in the material.

America, all the way to South America. The coastal migration theory is bolstered by the rich marine environment which would have supported maritime peoples well. Travel by boat would also have been much faster and easier than the route overland, thus allowing peoples to spread throughout the Americas much more quickly. The most compelling evidence supporting the coastal migration theory comes from archaeological sites in South America that predate the North American Clovis sites. Sites like Monte Verde in Chile, dated 14,800-12,500 BCE and Taima-Taima in western Venezuela, dated to 13,000 BCE, contradict the notion of "Clovis first." However, archaeological sites that support coastal migration theory number much fewer than Clovis sites, as the coastline of the Pleistocene era now lies under the Pacific Ocean, due to rising sea levels.

Although the two theories might seem to be at odds with each other, most historians and archaeologists now accept that both theories are probably correct, and that human migration to the Americas occurred over a very long span of time, over land and by boat. Linguistic evidence supports this combination of migration theory, as indigenous coastal languages are very different than interior languages throughout much of the Americas. The two theories also work together in that many South American sites date 500-1,000 years older than the oldest North American sites, a real problem for the Bering Land Bridge theory.

In more recent years, some archaeologists and historians have supported alternate migration theories. These theories are uniformly much more controversial than the Bering Land Bridge and coastal migration theories. One of the more notable theories is the Solutrean hypothesis, or the Atlantic coastal model. This model argues that Clovis peoples came not from Asia over the land bridge, but instead were descended from the Solutrean culture of Europe. Clovis peoples, it asserts, arrived in the Americas through coastal migration, hugging the ice sheet that spanned the ice age Atlantic. A handful of archaeologists support this theory, based on perceived similarities between Clovis and Solutrean points. However, the majority of archaeologists discount the theory, citing the lack of resources to support travelers on the ice sheet and the 5,000 years between the

Figure 1.2 Clovis Points | Examples of a Clovis Point from the Rummells-Maske Site (13CD15) Cedar County, Iowa. Clovis was once accepted as a defining characteristic of the first group of humans to come to the Americas, sometime between 10,000-14,000 BP. This assertion has been increasingly questioned as more and more well-documented archaeological sites with older dates have emerged.

Author: Bill Whittaker
Source: Wikimedia Commons

Solutrean and Clovis cultures. Genetic studies of indigenous peoples across the Americas also show the Solutrean hypothesis to be unlikely, as mitochondrial DNA (mtDNA) and DNA haplogroups show evidence of multiple migrations from Asia, starting at about 30,000 BP.[3] In contrast, no study has ever shown conclusive proof of European genetic markers among the Native American population before 1492.

Finally, a handful of sites across the Americas have unearthed portions dating 50,000-33,000 BCE, tens of thousands of years before the earliest coastal migration sites were established. These sites, including the earliest components of the Monte Verde site in Chile and the Topper site in South Carolina, are hotly contested by many archaeologists, who claim that the stone tools from the levels attributed to these early dates are not man-made, but natural formations. Moreover, 50,000 years BP stretches the boundaries of radiocarbon dating: as dates go further back in time, dating becomes less and less accurate, leading many more to call these early dates into further question. For now, these early radiocarbon dates are largely seen as aberrations, which offer no conclusive proof of human existence in the Americas before about 20,000 years ago.

1.2.3 Before You Move On...

Key Concepts

Current estimates hold that 43-65 million people inhabited the Western hemisphere at contact. There was a great deal of cultural diversity amongst this population, including languages, social and political structures, religious rituals, and deity worship. Each of these hundreds of groups had one or more creation or origin story explaining where they came from as a people as well as their relationship to the world around them. Origin stories help to define groups as a people and form an important part of the culture.

Scientific explanations of the origin of humans in the Americas focus on ways that the first people migrated to the Americas. The two most important and well-accepted of these theories are the Bering Land Bridge and the coastal migration. Most archaeologists now accept that both theories are correct, and date the earliest arrival of humans in the Americas to 20,000-14,000 BP. Each of these theories supports human migration from Asia. The Solutrean hypothesis, a more controversial theory, argues that the first humans of the Americas descended from the Solutrean culture of Europe. Genetic studies of indigenous peoples across the Americas, however, show the unlikelihood of this hypothesis.

Test Yourself

1. Origin stories

    a. explain where a group came from

    b. explain a group's place in the world and their relationship with it

    c. promote a common cultural identity

    d. all of the above

2. Clovis points are most closely identified with which migration theory?
    a. Bering Land Bridge Theory
    b. Coastal Migration Theory
    c. Solutrean Hypothesis
    d. European origin

See page 23 for answers

1.3 THE PALEO-INDIAN ERA THROUGH THE AGRICULTURAL REVOLUTION

This earliest period, from the time that humans entered the Americas until about 8,000 BCE, is known as the Paleo-Indian period. During this time, humans spread throughout the Western hemisphere, supporting themselves with similar subsistence patterns and technologies. Paleo-Indians, including the Clovis culture, were nomadic hunter/gatherers. They moved as frequently as once or twice a week, hunting the big game of the Paleolithic: the megafauna. As previously noted, well-known animals such as the mammoth and mastodon were included among the megafauna. Other North American megafauna included less well-known animals, such as the short-faced bear, and giant versions of animals such as sloth, moose, and beaver. Paleo-Indian technology included knapped, or chipped, stone tools such as scrapers, knives, and projectile points, such as the Clovis point. Throughout the Paleo-Indian era, the spear was the most common weapon. At first, humans used spears as thrusting weapons, which of course required very close range between the hunter and game, a dangerous prospect at best. Sometime during the Paleo-Indian era, humans developed new kinds of technology, including a lighter throwing spear and an implement to propel this spear much farther: the atlatl. The atlatl, or spear thrower, was one of the most important items in the late Paleo-Indian tool kit. It was a long, thin piece of wood with a notch at the end. This notch was designed to receive the end of a spear. The atlatl acted as an extension of the throwing arm, enabling the spear thrower to greatly increase the speed and range of the cast.

Paleo-Indians probably lived in groups that anthropologists call "bands," small groups of related individuals, typically no bigger than 100-150 people. This set-up allowed a simple leadership structure, probably with one individual at the head of the group, to be an effective means of control. It also allowed for easy mobility. In terms of possessions, hunter/gatherers such as Paleo-Indians lived with only easily transportable and reproducible possessions. One of the greatest problems of living in such a small group, however, was finding a suitable mate. Anthropologists theorize that regional Paleo-Indian groups came together yearly in the summer months to celebrate religious rituals, exchange news, and trade women to ensure genetic diversity amongst their groups.

Everything that we know about humans in the Americas from these early eras comes from the archaeological record. Perhaps the most famous Paleo-Indian site is the Blackwater Draw site near Clovis, New Mexico. Blackwater Draw is the archaeological site where the large,

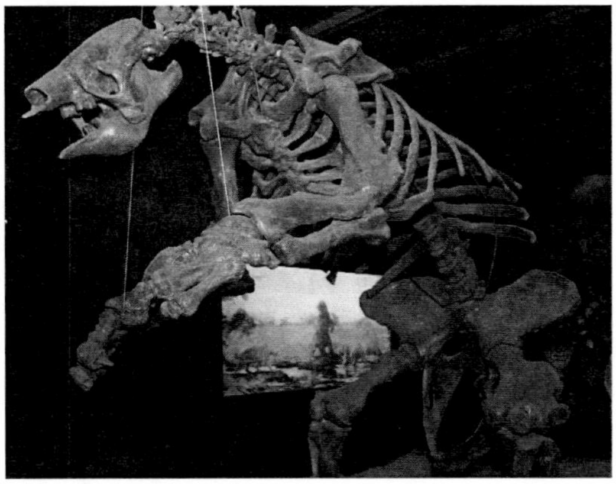

Figure 1.3 Giant Ground Sloth | The giant ground sloth was one of the many megafauna indigenous to the Americas during the Pleistocene.

Author: Flickr user "etee"
Source: Flickr
License: CC BY SA 2.0

leaf-shaped Clovis points were first identified. As many Clovis period sites were excavated in the mid-twentieth century, Clovis points came to be one of the defining artifacts for the Paleo-Indian era in North America, and anthropologists came to regard the Clovis culture as the first firmly established proof of human presence in the Americas. The "Clovis First" hypothesis held sway throughout much of the rest of the century, calling archaeological evidence that dated older than about 10,000 BCE unreliable. However, as more and more sites have produced reliable older dates and the coastal migration theory became more widely accepted, the Clovis First movement has lost favor.

One of the sites that first seriously challenged the Clovis First idea was the Monte Verde site in Chile, which consistently produced well-documented dates at and around 14,800-13,800 BP (12,800-11,800 BCE). Archaeological remains at this site include the evidence of wood and hide shelters, clay-lined fire pits, and dozens of plant materials used in the Paleo-Indian diet, a use supported by the appearance of coprolites, or fossilized human feces. Perhaps the most fascinating artifact from the Monte Verde site is a child's footprint, preserved in the soft clay surrounding a fire pit.

The Vero Man site, located outside of Vero Beach, Florida, is one of the few sites where human bones have been found alongside megafauna bones, including bison, mastodon, giant sloth, dire wolf, llama, and camel. More gracile, modern animals such as deer remains were also unearthed at the Vero Man site. The site dates roughly around 12,000-14,000 BP. In 2009, a bone with a carving of a mammoth on it was found; testing dates the bone to sometime between 13,000-20,000 BP. This artifact probably represents the oldest artwork ever found in the Americas.

1.3.1 The Archaic and Woodland Periods

From 8,000-7,000 BCE, the Earth's climate began to warm, and the North American environment changed. Paleo-Indians adapted to the world around them, learning to rely more and more on a diet rich in plant materials, and hunting smaller game such as bison as the megafauna began to die out. In this way, they began to more closely resemble typical hunter/gatherers, whose diet relies up to 90 percent on gathered food rather than on meat. Over the next 6,000-7,000 years, native cultures developed and diversified during the Archaic and the Woodland periods, 8,000-1,000 BCE and 1,000 BCE -1,000 CE respectively. During this era, the peoples of the Americas also began to domesticate plants, leading to one of the most important transformations in human history: the development of agriculture, known as the agricultural revolution.

In the Americas, the agricultural revolution began in Mesoamerica, the area between Central Mexico and Honduras. The process of domestication began some 10,000 years ago in Oaxaca, Mexico, when people began to tend squash plants in order to use the squash as containers. Eventually, more tender forms of squash became a food source. Following the domestication of beans at around 6,000 BP, Mesoamerican peoples began to become more sedentary. Finally, maize (or corn) was domesticated sometime around 5500 BP. Corn as we know it today originated as a wild grass called teosinte. Over thousands of years, the tiny teosinte seed pod, measuring about 4 cm long, was transformed though cultivation into much larger, nutritionally rich ears of corn. The domestication of maize completed the Mesoamerican triad, the three staple crops of the Americas. Native American agriculturalists all over the hemisphere grew corn, beans, and squash as the principal foods of their diet until many years after European contact. This combination proved ideally suited in several ways; first, the three foods grew well together. The corn grew tall and provided a "pole" for the beans to vine around and grow up, and the large squash leaves provided shade that retained moisture and inhibited the growth of weeds. Corn strips great quantities of nitrogen from the soil as it grows; beans are "nitrogen fixers" which put nitrogen back into the soil. From a dietary standpoint, the Mesoamerican triad provides an ideal diet, as long as the corn is processed in an alkaline solution. In Mesoamerica, this process involved soaking the corn kernels in a mixture of lime (calcium hydroxide, not the fruit) and ash. Processing the corn in this way unlocks certain proteins from the corn's endosperm, which allows the human body to digest it.

Agricultural knowledge and techniques spread from the region of Mesoamerica throughout the temperate parts of the Western hemisphere in a process called diffusion. Although corn and beans probably came from Mesoamerica, the eastern portions of North America might also have been an independent center of plant domestication; cultigens important to the regional diet, such as marshelder, chenopod, squash, and sunflower, appear to have been domesticated first in this region.[4]

One of the most famous Archaic period sites is the Windover site near Titusville, Florida. Windover was a burial site, dated 6,000-5,000 BCE. Individuals were wrapped in a textile and interred in the mucky bottom of a pond. The bog-like conditions of the pond helped to preserve the skeletons and grave goods, artifacts buried with the deceased, such as atlatls and projectile points. Of the 168 individuals excavated at Windover, 90 had preserved brain matter: the oldest preserved human brains. Several of the brains recovered at Windover have been DNA sequenced.

Figure 1.4 Teosinte | Teosinte, the ancestor of corn, is shown on the left. In the middle is a teosinte-maize hybrid. Modern corn is on the right.

Author: John Doebley
Source: teosinte.wisc.edu

The Head-Smashed-In buffalo jump site in Alberta, Canada first came into use at about 5,700 years ago. Archaic humans used it as a kill site, driving herds of buffalo and bison off of a 35 foot cliff, seriously injuring or killing the game. The bodies would then be drug to a nearby campsite and processed. The site remained in use for thousands of years, into the historic period, when Blackfoot, dressed as coyote and wolves, would drive buffalo along established "drive lanes" to the cliff. Excavations at Head-Smashed-In have unearthed a deposit of skeletons, primarily of buffalo and bison, measuring more than 10 meters (33 feet) deep.

The Poverty Point site in Louisiana (1650-700 BCE) is an important bridge between the Archaic and Woodland periods because it was one of the earliest sites to develop technologies and characteristics that came to define the Woodland period, including the development of pottery and manmade earthworks. Poverty Point has yielded some of the earliest known pottery in North America. Poverty Point is also important because it offers evidence of complex, far-reaching trade networks. Artifacts at the site, including shell, copper, and stone such as red jasper, came from all over the southeastern region. These materials would then be worked into finished, value-added objects and traded out again. Finally, Poverty Point is one of the first sites to exhibit evidence of monumental earthworks and a complex residential settlement, features that would come to define later peoples in the Southeast.

1.3.2 Early Agriculturalists in the Southeast and Southwest: The Mississippian and the Anasazi

The Southeastern portion of North America was an early agricultural center of development. This development fostered the growth of a large, long-lasting, and influential culture known as the Mississippian (ca. 500-1400 CE). This culture originated in the Mississippi River Valley and spread out to encompass an area which spread all the way to the lower Great Lakes region to the north, the Carolinas to the east, and northern Florida to the south. This culture emerged from the late Woodland Period as agriculturalists that practiced large-scale, corn-based agriculture. The excess agricultural product allowed them to support a dense population with a large group of specialized artisans.

Politically, Mississippians were organized as a chiefdom, a hierarchy of chiefs that pledged allegiance to the leader of the most important group. Within the chiefdom existed a high level of social stratification, with a noble class at the top. Socially, the Mississippians appear to have practiced matrilineal descent patterns. In matrilineal descent, familial relations focus on the mother's family, with property, status, and clan affiliation being conferred through the female line. A person's most important relations were his mother's parents and siblings. The father's relations were relatively unimportant. Boys looked to their mother's brother as an important male figure rather than to their father, and uncles passed political power and possessions to their nephews and maternal relatives rather than to their sons. This system's main advantage is that descent and clan affiliation was beyond a doubt; a child's paternity can be uncertain, but a clan can be sure of a child's maternity. Matrilineality is relatively common among indigenous peoples of North America, and came to be commonplace among Southeastern peoples.

The religion of the Mississippians is known as the Southeastern Ceremonial Complex. Important religious symbols for the culture included a snake (sometimes depicted as a horned serpent), a cross in circle motif, and Birdman, a warrior/falcon hybrid. These symbols were closely related to not only cosmology, but also the elite and warriors, giving the religion a socio-political aspect that reinforced the social status and authority of the elite—including the high chieftain, his lesser chiefs, and the priests of the cult. These symbols, along with a host of others, appeared multitudinously on a variety of artifacts such as cups and shell gorgets, a type of pendant. Archaeological evidence strongly indicates that only the elite were able to possess these objects, which may have been sacred and therefore viewed as powerful. Additionally, evidence suggests an exchange network of these sacred objects existed among the elite of the Mississippians, fostering not only political alliances, but also trade. Objects inscribed with symbols associated with the Southeastern Ceremonial Complex may have been produced by only a handful of artists; excavation of sites in Missouri and Oklahoma have turned up artifacts so similar that some archaeologists believe the same artist produced them. These sacred objects were buried as grave goods with their owners, indicating the status and power they carried into the afterlife.

Figure 1.5 Mississippian Cultures | The extent of the spread of Mississippian culture and the Southeastern Ceremonial Complex

Author: Herb Rowe
Source: Wikimedia Commons
License: CC BY-SA 3.0

One key feature of the Mississippian culture was that they were mound builders. They produced thousands of earthworks used in a variety of manners. Some earthworks were burial mounds for the elite. The chief, his family, and perhaps other members of the elite lived atop some of the mounds. Finally, some of the largest mounds appear to have been centers of worship. The largest and most important towns of the chiefdoms contained the greatest number of mounds.

Some of these chiefdoms produced large and complex settlements that rivaled and surpassed contemporary European cities. The largest and most important of these was Cahokia (ca 600-1400 CE) in southwestern Illinois, located just across the Mississippi River from St. Louis, Missouri. Cahokia was a walled complex made up of 120 mounds that housed perhaps as many as 30,000 people, making it a very large city for its day. Community plazas were located throughout the complex. A woodhenge was built for astrological observations; poles in the henge were marked to indicate the sun's rising point on the solstices and equinoxes. Cahokia's mounds took tremendous effort to build; laborers moved about 55 million cubic feet of earth in construction. The largest of the mounds, today called Monk's Mound, is approximately ten stories high and covers an area of 13.8 acres at the base. The top of the mound, the focal point of the city, housed a huge structure that may either have been a temple or the residence of the paramount chief of the Cahokia chiefdom.

Cahokia came to power in part because of its location near the confluence of the Mississippi, Illinois, and Missouri Rivers. This confluence allowed the chiefdom to control much of the regional trade, giving them access to a great variety of trade items from many regions. Cahokia participated in trade networks stretching as far as the Great Lakes to the north and the Gulf Coast to the south. Cahokia began to decline around 1300 CE and slowly dwindled in size and importance. Scholars have speculated that overhunting, deforestation, and the rise of the Moundville center in Alabama contributed to Cahokia's demise.

1.3.3 The Anasazi

Like the Mississippians, peoples of the southwestern region were also generally agriculturalists, supporting themselves by growing the Mesoamerican triad. One of the earliest Southwest groups was the Anasazi, who emerged in the Four Corners area of the modern United States (Colorado, Utah, Arizona, and New Mexico) around 700-1300 CE. They are also known as Ancient Puebloans because they are ancestors of the modern Pueblo peoples. The Anasazi grew and stored corn, a practice leading them to build large, complex, and beautiful towns.

These towns were carefully planned communities that provided for the changing needs of the society over time. Anasazi towns, such as the Pueblo Bonito site, were often organized around large, open plazas allowing for community gatherings. Structures were large and multi-storied apartment-like buildings that housed many people and provided a lot of room for storing their yearly harvest. The Ancient Puebloans later built similar structures high on canyon walls or atop mesas and became "cliff dwellers" to protect the population from nomadic raiding groups. Houses were often accessible only by ladder or rope so their inhabitants could easily cut off access.

Another important structure found at all Ancient Puebloan sites is the kiva, the ceremonial center of the village. Kivas, often circular in shape, were dug into the earth and entered from the roof via a ladder. At the center of the kiva lay a small hole in the floor called a sipapu. Modern Pueblo peoples hold that the sipapu symbolizes the navel of the Earth, the place where the ancestors first emerged. Much of what we know about Anasazi religion derives from modern Pueblo peoples, such as the Hopi and Zuni.

In modern Pueblo societies, kivas are associated with the kachina belief system. Kachinas are spirit beings, representations of the life force within all parts of the universe. They may represent a specific place or some aspect of nature: the sun, squash, and animals such as eagle or mountain lion. They may also represent an ancestor (or many ancestors), a historical event, or an idea, such as maidenhood. Kachinas are not worshipped, per se, but are spiritual forces that can use their power to benefit the population. The kachina cult was widespread in the Southwest. Religious ceremonies focused on venerating the kachina. Members of religious societies dressed as some of the more than 400 different kachina, enacting the spiritual being for ritual purposes. Some of the ceremonies took place inside the kiva, some outside in the plaza. Kivas were also put to secular use as gathering places for the community's men and probably houses for visitors to the community, such as traders.

Trade with outlying areas and other peoples through trade networks was central to the Anasazi economy. A large system of roads stretching some 180 miles into the countryside linked the Ancient Puebloan towns and connected the culture to the larger regional economy. Artifacts found at sites like Pueblo Bonito show that the Anasazi possessed many luxury items not found in their native southwest, including macaw feathers and obsidian from Mexico and marine shell from the Gulf Coast. Analysis of wood from the structures also attests to the economic importance of the road, as much of the timber originated at areas quite a distance from the Anasazis.

However, some modern Pueblo peoples, as well as some archaeologists, suggest that the roads also had religious significance for the Ancient Puebloans, as many roads seem to lead to areas of religious significance, such as lakes, mountains, and streams. Some of the major roads, like the Great North Road, were oriented along a north/south axis. This fact, combined with the north/south orientation of many of the kiva and religious structures, suggests a pattern of astrological observances. The Modern Pueblo also speak of the North Road as being the way to the sipapu, the place where the ancestors originated.

No clear reason suggests why the Ancient Puebloan cultures ended. Over the period from around 1150-1300 CE, the Ancient Puebloans underwent several changes and ultimately abandoned many of their towns. A variety of factors probably contributed to this abandonment. The period was one of dramatic climatic change for North America, the most prominent being the 300 year long Great Drought. During this period, the Anasazi appear to become more insular, engaging in less trade and practicing more intensive agriculture, aided by new irrigation techniques. Archaeological evidence indicates that new peoples were moving into the area, comprising an additional pressure. Finally, religious turmoil seems to have occurred amongst the Ancient Puebloans during this period, as many of the kiva and ceremonial structures at several sites evidence deliberately set fires and boarded up windows and doors. By 1300 CE, many of the towns and villages had been abandoned. While early historians held that the Anasazi "vanished," modern Pueblo peoples asserted that the Anasazi in fact migrated further south and joined groups that became the modern Pueblo cultures such as the Hopi and Zuni. Archaeological evidence has verified this account.

1.3.4 Before You Move On...

Key Concepts

The earliest period, from the time that humans entered the Americas until about 8,000 BCE, is known as the Paleo-Indian period. During this time, humans spread throughout the Western hemisphere, supporting themselves as nomadic hunter/gatherers. Native cultures developed and diversified during the Archaic (8,000-1,000 BCE) and the Woodland periods (1,000 BCE -1,000 CE). During this era, the peoples of the Americas also began to domesticate plants, leading to one of the most important events in human history: the development of agriculture, known as the agricultural revolution. Mesoamerica became one of the sites of early plant domestication: corn, beans, and squash, known as the Mesoamerican Triad, became the basis of many agriculturalists' diets.

The future Southeastern United States was another early site. Important domesticates from the region included marshelder, chenopod, squash, and sunflower. This development fostered the growth of a large, long-lasting, and influential culture, the Mississippian chiefdom (ca. 500-1400 CE), one of the most important in the region. The Mississippians produced thousands of earthworks used in a variety of manners, some as burial mounds, others as Mississippian religious centers, known as the Southeastern Ceremonial Complex.

Many of the peoples of the American Southwest were also agriculturalists. One of the earliest Southwestern groups was the Anasazi, who emerged in the Four Corners area of the modern United States (Colorado, Utah, Arizona, and New Mexico) around 700-1300 CE. The Anasazi produced large and multi-storied apartment-like buildings that housed many people and provided ample harvest storage space. Another important structure found at all Ancient Puebloan sites was the kiva, the ceremonial center.

Test Yourself

1. The Paleo-Indian era is most strongly associated with what type of artifact?

    a. Ceramic pottery

    b. The atlatl

    c. The Clovis point

    d. Basketry

2. The Mississippian culture is known for ____

 a. the kiva as the center of religious worship.

 b. moundbuilding.

 c. a tradition in whaling.

 d. hunting megafauna.

3. The region of the present-day Southeastern United States was likely one of the world's independent centers for plant domestication.

 a. True

 b. False

4. The _____ are ancestors of today's modern Pueblo peoples, and their cultures share much in common.

 a. Mississippians

 b. Clovis peoples

 c. Vero Man peoples

 d. Anasazi

See page 23 for answers

1.4 THE PRE-CONTACT ERA (1000-1492 CE)

In the period before European contact, more than 500 identifiable groups emerged in North America. A tremendous amount of diversity existed amongst these groups; the people of the West Coast had very little in common with the way that the peoples of the Southwest lived. However, groups within each region tended to have more commonalities. For instance, each region of the continent could be typified by the way in which peoples supported themselves, that is, their subsistence strategies. Other similarities might include kinship relations, political structure, and material culture, the objects and artifacts utilized by a people and having social significance to them.

1.4.1 The West Coast: The Pacific Northwest and California

Peoples in the Pacific Northeast supported themselves largely through hunting, gathering, and fishing, relying most heavily on salmon fishing. Consequently, the salmon became an important figure in the cosmology of groups like the Tlingit and Haida. The Pacific Northwest region was densely populated and culturally diverse because of the rich natural resources that allowed for a high "carrying capacity" of the land: that is, relatively reliable and plentiful food sources translated into a large population. Most groups lived in large, permanent towns in the winter. These towns formed the basis of the political structure for many Northwestern groups. People identified themselves by their town, and towns organized themselves into larger cultural and political groups through family and political alliances. Each town was led by a secular leader from one of the town's important clans. Clans are groups of families that recognize a common ancestor and a greater familial relationship amongst the group. Clans were often identified by a symbolic figure or idea important to the region. In the Pacific Northwest, for instance, clans were named for important animals such as raven, salmon, eagle, and killer whale. Society in Pacific Northwest groups was generally highly stratified in a complex system of hierarchy that ranked individuals, families, clans, and towns.

One of the most important ceremonies of the Pacific Northwest groups was the potlatch, a socio-political ceremony that gathered towns together to celebrate important events. Potlatches functioned as a demonstration of the host's status and importance. The hosts worked hard to ensure that all of the attendees were fed well, received gifts, and entertained; the hosts spent much of their wealth in demonstrating that they were deserving of their rank and societal status. In the Pacific Northwest, wealth was determined by how much individuals shared and gave away, not how much wealth they possessed. A successful potlatch could confer greater status on a person or a family.

One of the most diverse regions of North America was the region that came to be California. Politically, groups were divided into tribes led by chiefs whose title was passed down through families and clans. Economically, California peoples participated in large trade networks that linked much of the region and beyond. In general, they were hunter/gatherers. Acorns were a dietary staple, nutritious and able to be stored for long periods of time. However, they were a very labor-intensive crop, as they had to be pounded into flour and cooked in order to be edible. Agriculture was not completely unknown on the west coast; many groups cultivated tobacco as their sole agricultural crop. Contrary to popular opinion, the switch from hunter/gather to agriculturalist is not a measurement of "progress;" plentiful evidence suggests that hunter/gatherers often were able to live in semi-sedentary villages, complex societies, with even a better diet than agriculturalists. Religiously, the many of the peoples of Northern California participated in Kuksu, a religion that revolved around a male secret society that regulated the people's relationship with the sacred. The primary goal of this society and religion was to re-create the original, sacred, pure state of the world, in other words, to renew the world.

1.4.2 The Plains

Some of the earliest peoples of the Midwest/Great Plains region were agriculturalists, settling in the south and central areas. However, the reintroduction of the horse to North America at European contact transformed Plains life (the ancestor of modern horses was found throughout much of North America in the Pleistocene era, but died out and disappeared from the continent). Groups quickly adopted use of the horse in following and hunting the great bison herds, and many groups, such as the Sioux, comprising the Dakota, Lakota, and Nakota, were transformed from farmers to nomadic hunter/gatherers and emerged as one of the most important groups in the northern Plains region. Other important groups include the Crow in the north, the Cheyenne, Pawnee and Arapaho in the central plains area, and the Comanche in the south.

Warfare was endemic on the Plains. War was waged for three main reasons: for prestige, for obtaining goods, and for vengeance. The strategy and tactics of Plains warfare revolved around the concept of counting coup. Coup was an action that demonstrated bravery and skill. The most highly valued coup was to touch a live enemy and live to tell about it. Killing an enemy was coup, too, but demonstrated valor to a lesser degree; after all, the live man is still a threat, while a dead one can do you no harm. Touching a dead enemy was also a lesser form of coup. After a battle, warriors returned to the settlement to recount their stories, or "count coup." Demonstrations of skill also conferred honor to the warrior; a successful horse raid from a rival group, for example, showed great skill and bravery.

Politically, Plains groups were led by chiefs and councils. Most groups had a war and a peace chief. Peace chiefs held more power and tended to be older men with more experience. The war chiefs tended to be younger men. In this way, the war chiefs gained political experience that would lend future stability to the government as they aged and went on to become peace chiefs or members of the decision-making councils.

Religious beliefs on the Plains tended to hold the bison as a central figure of the sacred earth. Most groups kept "medicine bundles," a collection of sacred objects holding symbolic importance for the group. Often, religious celebrations center on the medicine bundle. For instance, the most important medicine bundle for the Cheyenne contains four sacred arrows given to the prophet Sweet Medicine by the Creator, Maheo. Each year, the medicine bundle was celebrated in a five-day ceremony which reenacted the creation of the world. During the ceremony, the arrows were cleansed and the world was renewed. The concept of world renewal was an important one in Plains religion. One of the important world renewal ceremonies celebrated by many Plains cultures was the Sun Dance. The Sun Dance was sponsored by an individual who wished to give to his tribe or to thank or petition the supernatural through the act of self-sacrifice for the good of the group. Celebration of the Sun Dance varied in detail from group to group, but a general pattern holds. The Sun Dance usually occurred in the summer and involved the erection of a large structure with a central pole, symbolizing the Tree of Life, as its dominant feature. Large groups would gather for the celebration, to give thanks, celebrate, pray, and fast. The individual sponsoring the Sun Dance would pray and fast throughout the celebration, which lasted up to a week in duration. He was the celebration's lead dancer, and the dance would continue until his strength was completely gone. Often, the dance involved some kind of bloodletting or self-torture. Participants might pierce the skin and/or muscle of the chest and attach themselves to the central pole, dancing around or hanging from it until the pins were pulled free. Another variation involved piercing the muscles of the back in a similar way and dragging buffalo skulls behind the dancer until the weight of the skull ripped the pins free. The scars that the dancers carried after the celebration were a mark of honor. At the end of the Sun Dance, the world was renewed and replenished. Finally, another kind of ceremony celebrated by many Plains groups was the smoking of the calumet, often called the "peace pipe." The smoking of the calumet bonded individuals and groups together. Smoking recognized alliances, formalized ceremonies, and established kin relations between individuals.

1.4.3 The Northeast

Northeastern groups were complex in many ways. Economically, they relied on both hunting/gathering and farming. Many participated in a system of exchange with shells as the medium. After the 1600s, groups began manufacturing wampum, made from white and purple shell beads, using them to record important events and to formalize agreements. Exact copies would be made for each party participating in an agreement. Wampum was very highly valued.

Politically, groups were led by men called sachems. Many towns organized themselves into tribes or nations; some tribes further allied to form political confederacies of affiliated nations. The Iroquois, or Haudenosaunee, made up of an association of the Mohawk, Oneida, Onondaga, Cayuga, and Seneca nations, was the largest and most successful of these northeastern confederacies. Confederacies were governed by councils made up of leaders from each of the member tribes; the most influential of these leaders often led the council itself. Among the Iroquois, the council was made up of fifty sachems from each of the Five Nations. Council members were chosen from among families designated to inherit the post.

Warfare played an important role in the Northeast, as it was the chief way to gain power and prestige. Revenge primarily motivated warfare in the region. A cycle of war was ensured because each group sought to avenge those killed in earlier wars or skirmishes in what became called the “Mourning Wars.” Acceptable outcomes of war could take several forms: killing the enemy, taking captives, and taking trophies of some sorts, often in the form of beheadings and/or scalping, a practice that may have been introduced to the region by the French. Captives would be taken back to the victors’ town, where they would be handed over to the women who had lost family members to war. These women led the torture of the captured, which often lasted for many hours or even days. The torture was quite brutal; prisoners were cut, beaten, mutilated, and burned. Ultimately, one of two fates awaited the prisoners. Either they would be tortured to death, or the women might decide that they be adopted by one of the families who had lost men to war. The captive who withstood the torture by showing strength, singing his death song so as to have a good death, would be held in high esteem and sometimes spared. Occasionally, the torturers would consume the flesh of these tortured after their deaths. This might have been a means of ingesting the strength of the enemy; some have suggested that the torture and sacrifice of prisoners was a way to maintain cosmic order through the ceremonies of warfare, torture, and sacrifice.

1.4.4 Before You Move On...

Key Concepts

During the Pre-contact Era (1000-1492 CE), more than 500 identifiable groups emerged in North America. Although tremendously diverse, the groups within each region of the continent shared many commonalities. Similarities included subsistence strategies, kinship relations, political structure, and material culture.

Peoples in the Pacific Northeast supported themselves largely through hunting, gathering, and fishing, relying most heavily on salmon fishing. The Pacific Northwest region was densely populated and culturally diverse because of the rich natural resources that allowed for a high "carrying capacity" of the land. Most groups lived in large, permanent towns in the winter; these towns formed the basis of many group's political structure. Society in Pacific Northwest groups was generally highly stratified. The practice of potlatch helped to maintain and reinforce this complex hierarchical structure.

The reintroduction of the horse to North America at European contact transformed the culture of many Plains peoples. Groups quickly adopted use of the horse in following and hunting the great bison herds, and many groups transformed from farmers to nomadic hunter/gatherers. Plains groups were led by chiefs and councils, with most having a war chief and a peace chief. Religious systems in the Plains region were often characterized by the centrality of the bison as an important figure and by the Sun Dance or other world renewal rituals as important ceremonies.

The peoples of the Northeast were both agriculturalists and hunter/gatherers. Many towns organized themselves into tribes or nations; some tribes further formed political confederacies of affiliated nations. An important example of such a confederacy is the Iroquois. Warfare played an important role in the Northeast, as it was the main way of gaining power and prestige. Revenge based warfare ensured a cycle of war as each group sought to avenge those killed in earlier wars or skirmishes in what became called the "Mourning Wars."

Test Yourself

1. The Mourning Wars were associated with what region?
    a. The Northeast
    b. California
    c. The Plains
    d. The Pacific Northwest

2. The practice of potlatch is associated with what region?
    a. The Northeast
    b. The Southwest
    c. The Plains
    d. The Pacific Northwest

3. Plains groups transformed from agriculturalists to nomadic hunter/gatherers in part because of

a. the death of the bison herds.

b. the reintroduction of the horse to North America.

c. a 100 year drought.

d. the European introduction of bison to North America.

See page 23 for answers

1.5 Conclusion

Prehistoric North America was home to a numerous and diverse array of peoples, languages, religions, and cultures. Scientific origin theories such as the Bering Land Bridge and the Solutrean hypothesis suggest that the ancestors of these groups arrived in the Western hemisphere at least 14,000 years ago. The origin stories of most of the groups take another view, stressing the intimate relationship between "the people" and the land they lived in; many origin stories state that the land was created exclusively for the group. The earliest groups in the Americas are referred to as Paleo-Indians. Clovis points are one of the most important and closely identified artifacts with the Paleo-Indian era. Changes in the global climate helped to bring the Paleo-Indian period to an end. The death of the megafauna meant that humans had to find new means of subsistence. The Archaic and Woodland periods, the archaeological periods following the Paleo-Indian, are characterized by the development of plant domestication and the beginnings of organized agricultural activities. Many of the groups of North America became agriculturalists, relying primarily on the Mesoamerican triad of corn, beans, and squash. The surplus of food from agriculture enabled the development of complex towns and cities such as the Mississippian Cahokia settlement. Regional geography also played a role in shaping groups; for instance, groups on the Plains came to be characterized by relying on the buffalo as a main source of food and resources for subsistence.

The Native American world that Europeans contacted after 1492 was complex, highly developed, and rich in oral history. The period of contact between Europeans and hundreds of native groups played an important role in shaping American colonies and nations, the United States among them. From the very beginning, Indians played a pivotal role in shaping the future of the nation.

1.6 CRITICAL THINKING EXERCISES

- What was the relationship between economic trade and political and social development in societies such as the Mississippian and Anasazi? What kinds of development does trade encourage?
- How are religion, politics, and social formation connected in groups such as the Cheyenne and Iroquois? Are there any kinds of discernible patterns? What are the ties between religion, politics, and social formation in our society?

1.7 KEY TERMS

- Agricultural Revolution
- Anasazi (Ancient Puebloans)
- Atlatl
- Bering Land Bridge
- Buffalo Jump
- Cahokia
- Clan
- Clovis
- Coastal Migration Theory
- Counting Coup
- Kachina
- Kiva
- Matrilineal
- Medicine Bundle
- Megafauna
- Mesoamerican Triad
- Mississippians
- Monk's Mound
- Monte Verde Site
- Mourning Wars
- Origin Story
- Paleo-Indian
- Potlatch
- Poverty Point
- Pre-contact Era
- Solutrean Hypothesis
- Southeastern Ceremonial Complex
- Sun Dance
- Vero Man Site
- Woodland Period

1.8 CHRONOLOGY

The following chronology is a list of important dates and events associated with this chapter.

Date	Event
14,800-13,800 BCE	Monte Verde site, Chile
14,000-10,000 BP	Bering land bridge migration
12,000-8,000 BCE	Paleo-Indian period
12,000-14,000 BP	Vero Man site
8,000-1,000 BCE	Archaic period
1,000 BCE-1,000 CE	Woodland Period
10,000-5,500 BP	Domestication of the Mesoamerican triad
500-1400 CE	Mississippian culture
700-1300 CE	Anasazi culture
1000-1492 CE	Pre-Contact era

1.9 END NOTES

1 Russell Thornton, American Indian Holocaust and Survival: A Population History since 1492 (Norman: University of Oklahoma Press, 1987); Henry Dobyns, Their Numbers Became Thinned: Native American Population Dynamics in Eastern North America (Knoxville: University of Tennessee Press, 1983).

2 Clyde Tucker, Brian Kojetin and Roderick Harrison, "A Statistical Analysis of the CPS Supplement on Race and Ethnic Origin" Bureau of Labor Statistics, Bureau of the Census. http://www.census.gov/prod/2/gen/96arc/ivatuck.pdf.

3 Jason A. Eshleman, Ripan S. Malhi, and David Glenn Smith. "Mitochondrial DNA Studies of Native Americans: Conceptions and Misconceptions of the Population Prehistory of the Americas" Evolutionary Anthropology 12 (2003), 7-18.

4 Bruce Smith, "Eastern North America as an independent center of plant domestication" Proceedings of the National Academy of Sciences, vol.103, no. 33 (August 15, 2006). http://www.pnas.org/content/103/33/12223.full.

ANSWER KEY FOR CHAPTER ONE: UNITED STATES HISTORY BEFORE COLUMBUS

Check your answers to the questions in the Before You Move On Sections for this chapter.

Correct answers are **BOLDED**

Section 1.2.3 - p. 6

1. Origin stories
    a. explain where a group came from
    b. explain a group's place in the world and their relationship with it
    c. promote a common cultural identity
    d. **ALL OF THE ABOVE**

2. Clovis points are most closely identified with which migration theory?
    a. **BERING LAND BRIDGE THEORY**
    b. Coastal Migration Theory
    c. Solutrean Hypothesis
    d. European origin

Section 1.3.4 - p. 14

1. The Paleo-Indian era is most strongly associated with what type of artifact?
    a. Ceramic pottery
    b. The atlatl
    c. **THE CLOVIS POINT**
    d. Basketry

2. The Mississippian culture is known for ____
    a. the kiva as the center of religious worship.
    b. **MOUNDBUILDING.**
    c. a tradition in whaling.
    d. hunting megafauna.

3. The region of the present-day Southeastern United States was likely one of the world's independent centers for plant domestication.
    a. **TRUE**
    b. False

4. The _____ are ancestors of today's modern Pueblo peoples, and their cultures share much in common.
    a. Mississippians
    b. Clovis peoples
    c. Vero Man peoples
    d. **ANASAZI**

Section 1.4.4 - p. 19

1. The Mourning Wars were associated with what region?
    a. **THE NORTHEAST**
    b. California
    c. The Plains
    d. The Pacific Northwest

2. The practice of potlatch is associated with what region?
    a. The Northeast
    b. The Southwest
    c. The Plains
    d. **THE PACIFIC NORTHWEST**

3. Plains groups transformed from agriculturalists to nomadic hunter/gatherers in part because of
    a. the death of the bison herds.
    b. **THE REINTRODUCTION OF THE HORSE TO NORTH AMERICA.**
    c. a 100 year drought.
    d. the European introduction of bison to North America.

Chapter Two:
The Global Context: Asia, Europe, and Africa in the Early Modern Era

Contents

Chapter Two: The Global Context: Asia, Europe, and Africa in the Early Modern Era

2.1 INTRODUCTION

The period before European contact with the Americas marked the beginning of globalization. During this time, the world became, in a sense, both larger and smaller. Voyages of exploration captured the immensity of the earth in maps, images, and the writings of travelers; simultaneously, emerging webs of connection between regions and peoples brought the world closer together. Thus, we often refer to this period as the "early modern era." For the first time, we see the emergence of a world that bears great similarity to ours of the twenty-first century, a world interconnected through trade, politics, culture, and religion. China took the lead in oceanic exploration in the early fifteenth century, but by mid-century leaders stopped seeking overseas markets. They preferred to let the trade come to them. Chinese efforts gave way to the much more aggressive Portugal and Spain who competed for control of the Atlantic in the fifteenth and sixteenth centuries. Both countries had engaged in overland trade with the Islamic world in the Middle Ages and hoped to find alternatives to the land routes used to conduct business with the Indies. Meanwhile, England and France largely ignored the trend of oceanic exploration in the sixteenth century. While their leaders witnessed the success the Portuguese and Spanish had, internal problems blunted their ability to sponsor expeditions. As the European nations expanded their presence in the Atlantic Ocean, they also drew many African kingdoms into their global web. The European exploration of the early sixteenth century set the stage for later colonization in the Americas.

2.1.1 Learning Outcomes

After completing this chapter, you should be able to:

- Analyze the roles the emergence of a more powerful monarchy and religious changes played in the development of England and France in the Age of Discovery.
- Compare the goals and outcomes of early Chinese and Iberian voyages during this era.
- Evaluate the development of early globalization through exploration and trade.
- Analyze the connections between new technologies and the growth of the Age of Discovery.
- Evaluate the role of Africa in the period before contact.

2.2 EUROPE IN THE AGE OF DISCOVERY: PORTUGAL AND SPAIN

Spain and Portugal led the European Age of Discovery, an era lasting from roughly 1450-1750, in technological advances, exploration, and colonization. Perhaps unsurprisingly, they emerged as leaders in this age; after all, the Iberian Peninsula protrudes out from Europe into the Atlantic Ocean, and rivers and harbors provided an ideal environment for sea trade as well as nurturing the art of boat building. Both countries had been incorporated into the Islamic world during much of the Middle Ages and emerged as newly reformulated kingdoms in the period leading into the Age of Discovery. Each sought to push forth from their geographic boundaries and, in so doing, enrich their kingdoms through exploration and trade.

2.2.1 Portugal Initiates the Age of Discovery

Portugal emerged as a nation in 1128 after the Battle of São Mamede with the defeat of the Moors, which is the Iberian name for the Muslims who invaded and controlled parts of the Iberian Peninsula from around 711 to 1492. After the re-conquest or *Reconquista* of Portugal was finalized in 1250 with the conquest of the south, Portugal began a period of great development in navigation. Instruments such as the compass and the astrolabe, which were Chinese and Arabian inventions respectively, allowed the Portuguese to successfully navigate the open sea above and below the equator. Improvements in cartography produced maps that were much more accurate than those of the Middle Ages. The Portuguese also developed the *caravel*, a ship with triangular sails and a square rig. A light, agile ship, the *caravel* could carry a large cargo with a small crew. Together, these advances allowed the Portuguese to begin establishing a maritime empire.

Under the sponsorship of Prince Henry the Navigator, Portugal began exploring the coast of Africa in order to trade and extend Christianity. Prince Henry the Navigator was the third son of John I, king of Portugal. He was called "the Navigator" because of his support of navigational studies in Portugal, where he established a school for it.

Like the Spanish and other Europeans, the chief desire of the Portuguese was to tap into the lucrative spice trade, including items such as cloves, pepper, and ginger. The spice trade, Europeans knew, originated somewhere in Asia and made its way through India before entering the hands of Muslim traders, who brought the product to European markets. Trade with Asia in spices would not only enrich the nation that established contact, but also would weaken the Muslim world and strengthen the Christian world by diverting the overland spice trade to a European sea trade. This promise of great wealth and sense of religious completion drove the Portuguese to explore the coast of Africa in search of a route to India. The same ideas motivated Columbus to seek a route to Asia and the spice trade by sailing west.

Figure 2.1 Caravel Boa Esperança of Portugal | The triangular sailed, square rigged caravel was quick, agile, and seaworthy.

Author: Navy of Brazil
Source: Wikimedia Commons

The Portuguese established trade networks along the coast of West Africa, trading for gold and, by 1441, for slaves. To facilitate trade, Portuguese captains negotiated relationships with African kingdoms and leaders in port cities, exchanging gifts and goods to secure permission to trade. They established stone fortresses known as *feitorias*, or factories, that served as trading posts and as holding areas for slaves. In later years, other nations such as the Dutch, Spanish, and British followed this pattern as the Trans-Atlantic slave trade emerged, driven by labor-intensive crops such as sugar, rice, and cotton.

The Portuguese explored the coast of Africa not only for profit and religious purpose, but also in search of the mythical kingdom of Prester John. The myth of Prester John emerged in Europe sometime in the twelfth century. Prester John was said to be a Christian monarch somewhere in the Orient—possibly India or Africa—that ruled in the midst of Muslims. Some said he was a descendant of one of the Three Magi; others claimed that the Fountain of Youth was to be found in his kingdom. In any case, Europeans viewed Prester John as a possible ally against the encroachment of Islam and as a powerful Christian figure in the Muslim world. In the late 1400s, Portugal sent ships in search of Prester John; eventually, a Portuguese captain made contact with the African Christian kingdom of Ethiopia. The Portuguese concluded that the Ethiopian monarch was in fact Prester John, even though such a figure would have been several hundred years old by 1500.

Portuguese exploration continued through the end of the fifteenth century. One of the most significant moments came in 1487, when Bartholomew Diaz rounded the Cape of Good Hope at the tip of Africa. A decade later, Vasco da Gama reached the subcontinent of India. This moment was particularly significant, for it marked the Portuguese entry into the lucrative spice trade which, until this time, had been dominated by Muslim traders. From India, the Portuguese continued east, following the spice trade to the so-called Spice Islands, today a part of Indonesia. In 1511, Admiral Alfonso de Albuquerque conquered the city and Strait of Malacca, which controlled all sea trade between China and India. This capture provided the Portuguese with a port of call at the heart of the spice trade while simultaneously breaking the Arab spice trade network. The conquest of Malacca marked the beginning of a period of great wealth, power, and prosperity for Portugal.

Columbus's 1492 voyage of discovery brought a new sense of competition to the race for the spice trade. In 1494, the Treaty of Tordesillas was negotiated and signed to preserve order and to effectively divide the world's trade routes into spheres of influence. The treaty imagined a line about halfway between the Portuguese-held Cape Verde islands off the coast of Africa and the islands discovered by Columbus, namely Hispaniola and Cuba. Lands and routes to the east belonged to Portugal; lands and routes to the west, to Spain.

2.2.2 The Spanish in the Age of Discovery

While 1492 is best known for Christopher Columbus's voyage to the New World, the year was also significant to the Spanish for reasons other than Columbus's "discovery." First and foremost, 1492 marked the end of the long *Reconquista* of the Spanish peninsula with Ferdinand and Isabella's conquest of Grenada, the last area to be held by Muslims. To consolidate their victory and to begin the process of "purifying" their kingdoms, the monarchs issued orders for all Jews and Muslims to make a choice: convert to Christianity or leave Spain. For many of the Spanish, the *Reconquista* had been as much a religious as a military re-conquest of the land. The Roman Catholic Church viewed the Spanish *Reconquista* as a great victory for Christianity; the pope marked the event by granting the monarchs the *Patronado Real*, which gave them powers to oversee the operation of the Church within their realm. The idea of religious conquest and the power of the Spanish monarch to oversee representatives of the Church in later years would play an important role in the New World as the Crown sent thousands of monks to convert Indians to Christianity. Proselytization was of course part of the Christian doctrine, and as good Catholics, the monarchs felt it their duty to convert the natives. Moreover, the Spanish had revisited their identity as Spaniards and as Christians in the wake of hundreds of years of Muslim rule and the *Reconquista*. The newly reformed Spanish identity was unquestionably Christian, and all subjects of the Crown were to belong to the Catholic fold. Thus, the religious conquest would be brought to the New World along with the military conquest.

For Spain, Columbus's voyage joined with the excitement of defeating the Muslims at Grenada. Isabella, Queen of Castile, agreed to support Columbus's enterprise in the hope of great gains for God and Castile. She promised him a title of nobility and 10 percent of the gold, silver, spices, and other valuables he obtained if he were successful. Columbus sailed in September of 1492 with three ships, fewer than ninety men, a year's provisions, and a fundamental misunderstanding of the size of the earth. Scholars all over Europe argued that Columbus grossly underestimated the distance to Asia. This, along with Columbus's egotistical demeanor and demands for great personal rewards from his expedition, ensured that Columbus failed to enlist other potential backers to finance the voyage.

On October 12, 1492, Columbus and his men sighted an island in the chain later named the Bahamas. Further exploration revealed Hispaniola and Cuba, the two largest islands in the Greater Antilles of the Caribbean. He established a settlement called La Navidad and left thirty-nine men to secure it. Columbus returned to Spain in 1493, convinced that he had reached Asia. He described a tropical paradise and brought back enough gold and valuables to secure permission for a second voyage.

The Caribbean quickly became the base for further Spanish exploration of the region. Within twenty-five years, European explorers and cartographers had sketched a remarkably accurate outline of the Caribbean and the eastern coasts of North, South, and Central America. For a time, Columbus himself served as Governor of the Indies, the name used by the Spanish for the Americas. He was accused of harsh rule and mistreatment of the colonists, who called him "the tyrant of the Caribbean." Columbus was arrested and returned to Spain in chains, where he was stripped of his titles and office for misrule.

Columbus went to his grave believing that his voyages had taken him to Asia. Others, however, argued that he had reached a previously unknown land mass, a so-called "New World." While the Spanish were busy establishing themselves in the Caribbean, Vasco da Gama had made contact with India and thus had "won" the race to tap into the spice trade. Columbus's mathematical errors and fundamental misunderstanding were confirmed in late 1520, when Ferdinand Magellan's fleet entered the Pacific Ocean. Magellan had been commissioned by the Spanish Crown to seek a trade route to Asia; however, what his voyage revealed was the immensity of South America and the Pacific Ocean. Although Magellan died mid-voyage, his fleet became the first to successfully circumnavigate the globe, returning to Spain in 1525. The voyage took an incredible toll on the fleet; of the original 237 men and five ships, only one ship and eighteen men survived.

The legacy of circumnavigation of the globe revealed itself politically, economically, and scientifically. The Treaty of Tordesillas had established that the world was to be divided into two zones of influence; this agreement lacked the exact divide between Portuguese and Spanish territory in the east. Since the Spanish fleet reached Asia and the Moluccas, or the Spice Islands, they claimed that the Portuguese were violating their territory, thus bringing the two nations once more into conflict. The matter was resolved in 1529 with the Treaty of Zaragoza, which gave the Moluccas to Portugal and the Philippines to Spain. Although Spain was disappointed not to have gained the Spice Islands, the Philippines quickly became an important base of Spanish operations for Asian trade. They obtained particular importance after Spain established mining operations in the colonies of New Spain and Peru, when silver became the basis for great wealth.

Scientifically, Magellan's voyage revealed the exact size of the earth's diameter. It also established the need for an International Date Line. Although the mariners kept strict track of dates over the voyage in a logbook, they found upon their return to Europe that they were one day behind the calendar. They had, in effect, lost a day while traveling westward, counter to the earth's rotation.

2.2.3 Before You Move On...

Key Concepts

Portugal was one of the leaders of the European Age of Discovery. The Portuguese were able successfully to navigate the open sea because of the compass, the astrolabe, and the *caravel*. Under the sponsorship of Prince Henry the Navigator, the Portuguese explored the coast of Africa and later established trading posts up and down the coast of West Africa. The Portuguese also established trading ports in India and, after the conquest of Malacca, in the Spice Islands. Portugal's entry into the Indian Ocean marked the beginning of a powerful sea empire.

The Spanish followed Portugal's lead after completing the *Reconquista* and sponsoring Columbus's 1492 voyage. Like the Portuguese, Columbus's goal had been to reach Asia to tap into the lucrative spice trade. Columbus instead reached a "New World," and the Spanish found themselves exploring vast new lands. Competition between Portugal and Spain was alleviated with the Treaty of Tordesillas, which divided the earth into two zones of influence. However, competition was reborn when the Spanish circumnavigated the globe in 1520-1525. The Treaty of Zaragosa established the antemeridian of the Treaty of Tordesillas, effectively extending the dividing line into the eastern half of the globe and completing the separation of the zones of influence.

Test Yourself

1. What important event(s) took place in 1492?

   a. Columbus's first voyage to the New World

   b. the expulsion of the Jews and Muslims from Spain

   c. the end of the Reconquista

   d. All of the above

   e. A and C

2. ______ enabled the Portuguese to enter the spice trade.

   a. Rounding the Cape of Good Hope

   b. The conquest of Malacca

   c. The discovery of the New World

   d. Making contact with Prester John

   e. The conquest of Goa

3. For the Spanish, reconquering the Iberian Peninsula was a military and religious action.

   a. True

   b. False

4. The mythical king Prester John was important to the Portuguese because

   a. he controlled the spice trade

   b. he would be an ally to the Spanish in reconquering the Iberian Peninsula

   c. he was a Christian king in an area dominated by Muslims

   d. he could direct them in how to cross the Indian Ocean

5. The Treaty of Tordesillas and the _____ worked in tandem to establish zones of influence for Portuguese and Spanish trade.

   a. Treaty of Nanking

   b. Treaty of Molucca

   c. Treaty of Zaragoza

   d. Treaty of Goa

See page 52 for answers

2.3 ASIA IN THE AGE OF DISCOVERY: CHINESE EXPANSION DURING THE MING DYNASTY

By the time Prince Henry, called "the Navigator," third son of John I of Portugal, established a school for navigational studies at Sagres, Portugal in the third decade of the fifteenth century (around 1433), the Chinese had been engaged in navigational exploration under the Ming Dynasty for more than thirty years. In 1369 the last of the Mongol invaders, who had controlled China since 1294, was defeated by the founder of the Ming Dynasty, Zhu Yuanzhang. Zhu chose the name "Ming" or "bright" for his dynasty rather than his family name, Zhu, which means "pig" and called himself "Hong Wu," which translates to "vast military."[1]

Hong Wu ruled China from 1368 to 1398, during which time he concentrated on defeating and controlling the last of the Mongols (they were driven out in 1420), expanding the military, and ruling over a diverse kingdom of Confucians, Muslims, and Christians. During the Ming dynasty, the Chinese expanded their rule into Mongolia and Central Asia, and for a brief time, Vietnam.[2] When Hong Wu died, the throne passed to his son, Shu Di, who took the name Yung Lo; he is also called the Yongle Emperor. Yung Lo had spent much of his youth undertaking expeditions against the remaining Mongol strongholds, and, when he became emperor, continued Chinese expansion, assisted by the Muslim eunuch, Zheng He, or Cheng Ho. After moving the capital city of his empire to Beijing, he constructed a new, splendid palace, the Forbidden City, the Temple of Heaven, and an impressive observatory. The construction of the Forbidden City took fourteen years to complete and employed 100,000 artisans and one million workers. Yung Lo also began dredging and reconstructing the Grand Canal. In 1417, the Emperor left Nanking for the last time, moving to his new capital city. The Court officially established itself there in 1421.[3]

Not only was Yung Lo intent on creating a splendid new capital city for his empire, he also wanted to expand China's military and economic control into the areas surrounding the Indian Ocean. Malacca, the third largest state in Malaysia, had become the center of a thriving Indian Ocean trading network in which porcelains, silks, and camphor from China, pepper, cloves, and other spices from the Moluccas, and cotton from India came into the port of Malacca. Yung Lo saw in this area an opportunity for Chinese expansion, and shortly after he became Emperor he chose Zheng He to lead a series of naval voyages from China into the Indian Ocean. Dispute exists among historians about his motivation in this endeavor. Historian John K. Fairbank maintains that "these official expeditions were not voyages of exploration in the Vasco da Gama or Columbian sense. They followed established routes of Arab and Chinese trade in the seas east of Africa."[4]

On the other hand, some historians of the twenty-first century have been influenced by the theories of Historian Gavin Menzies, whose best seller, *1421: The Year China Discovered America*, contends that the Chinese did indeed go well beyond the familiar trade routes, not only rounding the Cape of Good Hope, but also traveling to Australia and Central and South America. Menzies supports his theory with the diaries of fifteenth century Portuguese and Spanish conquistadors who encountered "Chinese people" when they arrived in the Americas, as well as with archaeological evidence, such as remains of

Figure 2.2 Zheng He's Ships | A comparison shows how Zheng He's treasure ships dwarfed Columbus's ships.

Author: Lars Plougmann
Source: Flickr
License: CC BY SA 2.0

the familiar blue and white Ming porcelain along the western coast of–South America. Menzies believes that Yung Lo's purpose was two-fold: "to sail the oceans of the world and chart them" in order to inspire awe in the countries of the world and to bring them "under China's tribute system."[5]

Although the theories of Menzies have created interest among historians, most scholars hold the view that the Chinese were mainly seeking new tributary nations, generally agreeing with Anatole Andro who comments in *The 1421 Heresy* that, though Menzies's theories are compelling, additional concrete evidence is needed before his contentions can be accepted as fact.

Whatever his motivation, Yung Lo did in fact commission the construction of a grand fleet. According to Andro Anatole, "The Ming maritime voyages were set in motion the very moment [Yung Lo] ascended the throne. Although the first ships did not set sail until 1405, more than two years into the new reign, preparations for the voyages were underway from day one."[6] He points out that the project was immense and complicated. Raw materials were not readily available and many were "procured from distant districts." Artisans came from all parts of the empire, and Zheng He himself had to be trained in navigational methods and cartography, or map reading.

One shipyard near Nanking alone built 2,000 vessels, including almost a hundred large treasure ships. The latter were approximately 400 feet long and almost 200 feet wide. Dragon eyes were carved on the prows to scare away evil spirits.[7] Anatole reminds us that "The large Chinese ships, majestic and impressive, and more than enough to fill with awe a country of lesser stature than the mighty Ming, were first and foremost built for military personnel transport."[8]

In addition to these large ships were junks belonging to merchants that were, in turn, protected by warships. As the Chinese flotilla progressed, the ships of other nations joined it, in order to secure the protection of the armada's war ships. By the time the armada reached India, seeking such spices as pepper, salt, ginger, and cinnamon, there were 800 ships in the flotilla. According to Fairbank, the armada of 1405-1407 set out with 317 ships. Of these, 62 were treasure ships. In comparison, the famous Spanish Armada that sailed against England in 1588 was made up of only 137 ships.[9]

Zheng He made seven voyages between 1405 and 1433, and, according to historian Louise Levathes's *When China Ruled the Seas: the Treasure Fleet of the Dragon Throne*, Yung Lo probably had in mind the expansion of the tributary system and the acquisition of information about distant lands and rare plants and animals. She comments that Zheng He went as far west as Egypt in order to gather herbs that might be used to fight a smallpox outbreak that plagued China.[10]

Although the Chinese were interested in the products of other cultures, and though Zheng He brought to China an Arab book on medical remedies, a giraffe, and "300 virgins," Yung Lo's successor, Zhu Zhanji, decided in 1433 to disband this naval effort and "never again were the expeditions resumed." Several possibilities explain this occurrence: the Chinese found nothing in the cultures visited that they could not obtain through trade; after Zheng He's death, no admiral rose to his stature as a sailor; or, according to Fairbank, "anti-commercialism and xenophobia won out."[11] Whatever the reason, the Chinese armada was allowed to fall into disrepair, service personnel were placed elsewhere, and a minister of war, Kiu Daxia, burned the navigational charts. Interestingly, the Chinese did not follow up on these voyages of trade and/or exploration, even though they were the inventors of gunpowder and the cannon, instruments necessary for European expansion as they struck out to find an all-water route to India.

What remains is this question: why did the Chinese take this approach, becoming in essence isolationists? Menzies suggests that superstition got the best of the culture as a series of natural disasters portended future catastrophe.[12] Historian Ray Huang blames it on the extravagances of Yung Lo, and Fairbank, on Neo-Confucian prejudice against expansion.[13] Historian L. Carrington Goodrich concedes that "the expeditions ceased as suddenly as they began, again for reasons only guessed at," though the expense and the "spirit of isolationism" that "penetrated the Court" were certainly factors.[14] Most scholars concede that, while various explanations exist, the "abrupt discontinuance" of China's outreach remains "one of the most fascinating enigmas in the history of the culture."[15] Whatever the reason, the Chinese did reap the benefits of expanded tribute, and the Chinese people participated in a "vast immigration" into Southeast Asia, taking with them Chinese knowledge and culture.[16]

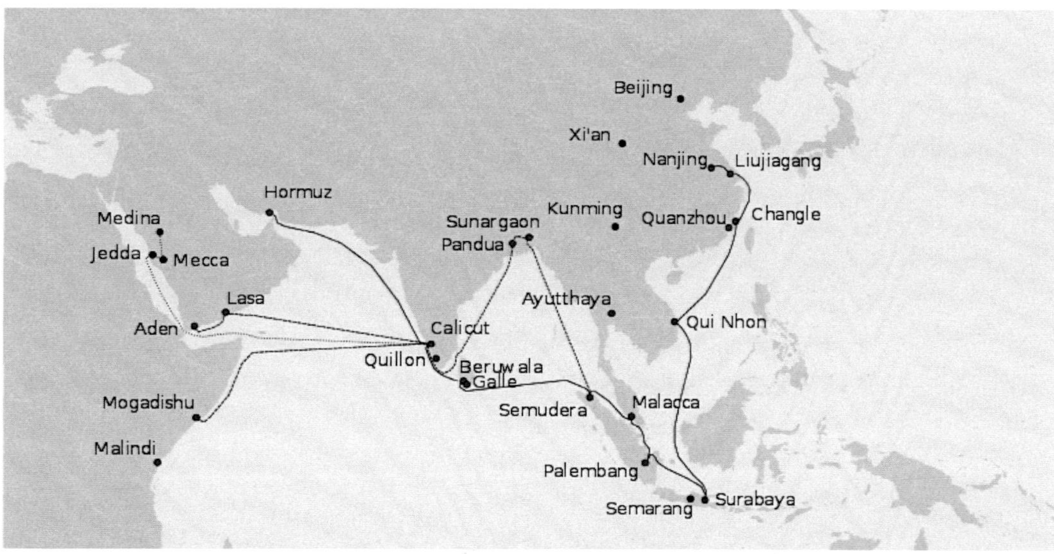

Figure 2.3 Zheng He's Seventh Expedition | This Map shows the route of the seventh voyage of Zheng He's fleet, 1431-1433.

Author: Vmenkov Menkov
Source: Wikimedia Commons

2.3.1 Before You Move On...

Key Concepts

The establishment of the Ming Dynasty in China in 1439 brought an end to Mongol rule and began a new era. The Forbidden City, the seat of Chinese rule in the following centuries and a lasting symbol of Chinese power, was built during this period. It was during this time also that the Chinese first undertook substantial oceanic voyages, far earlier than their European counterparts. Zheng He's massive fleet dwarfed European expeditions of the era, both in the number and the size of ships. The armadas explored much of the Indian Ocean region, as far as Africa, mapping, charting, trading, and incorporating a great part of the region into a Chinese tributary system. Although a few historians have suggested that Zheng He's fleet sailed as far as Australia and the Americas, compelling documentary evidence for this is lacking.

When the Ming Emperor Yung Lo died, Chinese participation in naval expansion died with him. The succeeding emperors did not follow up on the voyages of the early fifteenth century, and by the end of the century had begun a policy that would typify Chinese attitudes toward trade with overseas cultures: if foreign powers wanted to trade with China, they could bring their goods to her shores, in their own ships. And eventually, even this trade was limited to the port of Canton only.

Test Yourself

1. Zheng He's goals for exploring the Indian Ocean included
    a. exploring and mapping the region.
    b. establishing trade with port cities.
    c. incorporating new areas into the Chinese tribute system.
    d. all of the above.
    e. none of the above.

2. One possible reason for Zhu Zanji's decision to end the voyages of Zheng He was
    a. a spirit of isolationism in the Chinese court under Zhu Zanji.
    b. to save money and avoid the expense of the voyages.
    c. to end competition with the French, who were entering the Indian Ocean trade.
    d. A and B.
    e. all of the above.

See page 52 for answers

2.4 EUROPE IN THE AGE OF DISCOVERY: ENGLAND AND FRANCE

In the period before contact with the Americas, England and France, as they appear on the map today, had only recently taken shape. For much of the Middle Ages, both regions faced invasions by Germanic tribes (sometimes called the barbarians) from northern and central Europe. When those invasions ended, monarchs in England and France worked diligently to consolidate their power, between the twelfth century and the fifteenth century, which in turn led them to consider New World exploration and colonization. However, they lagged behind the Portuguese, the Spanish, and the Dutch because of the almost constant state of war between the two countries as well as the emergence of the Protestant Reformation in the early sixteenth century.

2.4.1 England and France at War

During the reign of Henry II of England (r. 1154-1189) and Phillip II of France (r. 1180-1223), the history of England and France became closely linked. The two countries fought for control over Normandy, a region in northern France directly across the channel from England. Henry's son, John, lost control of the province in 1204.[17] For the remainder of his reign, John tried to regain the lost territory. His actions upset the English nobility, who objected to his less-than-scrupulous means to finance the war, which included raising court fees and inheritance taxes beyond what most people could pay and selling government appointments. Several northern barons led a rebellion against the king that quickly spread to the rest of the country. In 1215, after several months of negotiations, John agreed to address the nobility's demands. The resulting Magna Carta tackled specific grievances and suggested that all English citizens, including the king, lived under the rule of law. Future generations of Englishmen based their concept of justice and liberty on the principles of the Magna Carta.[18] Political differences between England and France continued through the thirteenth and fourteenth centuries at a time when Europe also faced famine and disease.

While the Black Death (the plague) ravaged Europe in the fourteenth century, England and France descended into the Hundred Years' War (1337-1453) which was fought over who would succeed the childless Charles IV of France after he died in 1328. The lengthy war had a significant political impact for both sides. In England, it strengthened Parliament's role. Edward III (r. 1312-1377) and his successors had to call Parliament into session more frequently to raise funds to fight the French. As these meetings occurred, the House of Lords and the House of Commons began to take shape. After the war, the English began to see a representative government as the most enlightened form of government in the world. A corresponding national assembly did not appear in France because Phillip VI (r. 1328-1350) and his successors considered it repugnant. While the French people began to form a common identity because of the war, the nation's regional assemblies did not want to give up their power. Therefore, the French built their national government on a strong monarchy.[19]

The Hundred Years' War also brought on a period of domestic strife in England as the Duke of York and the Duke of Lancaster fought to control the young Henry VI who ascended to the throne in 1422. The War of the Roses finally ended when Henry Tudor defeated his rival in 1485. In the Tudor dynasty, the monarchy became the main political force in England. Henry VII (r. 1485-1508) preferred to rely on a royal council composed mostly of men from the middle class instead of on Parliament. He used diplomacy, not war, to smooth over problems with other nations. Therefore, he did not have to call Parliament into session to secure funds for his ventures. His actions undercut the influence of the English aristocracy. Henry VII's governing council also dealt with recalcitrant nobles by using the Star Chamber, which was a judicial body that undermined traditions of English common law, and by promoting the interests of the middle class. In the Tudor dynasty, the monarchy became the main political force in England.[20]

During Henry VII's reign, England made its first foray into overseas exploration. In May 1497, the king allowed John Cabot, a Venetian mariner living in London, to sail under the English flag in an attempt find a northern route to Asia. Cabot reached land, what he called Newfoundland, in June and claimed it on behalf of Henry VII. He made a second voyage in 1498, funded in part by the king because he expected to reap the financial rewards of the journey. However, after Cabot's death, his crew, led by his son Sebastian, failed to find any precious metals, so Henry VII lost interest in overseas exploration. Though Spain and Portugal began the process of colonization, England found itself in the midst of a political and a religious crisis for much of the sixteenth century. Events at home took precedence over any further state-sponsored oceanic voyages. However, Cabot's voyages gave England claim to the North American mainland when the English began to think about colonization in the New World.[21]

2.4.2 Religion and Politics in the Sixteenth Century

Through most of the medieval period, secular leaders in England and France had relied on a connection to the Roman Catholic Church to underscore their legitimacy. By the early sixteenth century, however, the church had come under fire. The intellectual currents of the Renaissance played a role in this change, but so too did the practices of the church, including clerical immorality, clerical ignorance, and clerical absenteeism. The church's failings led Martin Luther to touch off the Protestant Reformation in 1517. Luther, a Catholic priest in Germany, hoped to prompt a reform movement within the church when he posted his theses on Wittenberg's church door. In his early years, Luther struggled to grapple with the church's teachings about salvation, especially the idea that by doing good works, or purchasing *indulgences,* people could earn their salvation. In an effort to force the church to clarify its teachings on salvation, Luther wrote the ninety-five theses. He also called into question the authority of the pope. Church authorities subsequently sent Luther a letter giving him two months to recant his statements. Luther burned the letter, thus assuring his excommunication from the church. In spite of the church's hope that excommunication would quell the unrest, Protestant sects appeared throughout Europe, including in England and France. The decision to become Protestant or remain Catholic in many cases had as much to do with politics as it did with faith.[22]

The English Reformation began officially when Henry VIII (r. 1509-1549) asked Pope Clement VII to annul his marriage to Catherine of Aragon. To marry Catherine, his dead brother's wife, Henry had had to secure a special dispensation from Pope Julius. During the course of their marriage, Catherine had six children, but only one survived, a daughter named Mary. Henry convinced himself that marrying his brother's wife prevented him from having a male heir. Henry VIII's request put Clement in a bad situation because reversing Julius's decision would suggest papal fallibility. At a time when the church was already under fire from the Protestants, such a move would further weaken it. Moreover, Catherine's nephew, Charles V of Spain, had recently taken control of Rome, the papal seat of power.[23] Thus, Clement refused Henry's request. However, Thomas Cranmer, appointed the archbishop of Canterbury in 1532, harbored Protestant sympathies. He therefore granted the annulment in spite of the pope's previous decision. In 1533, Henry VIII married Anne Boleyn; their daughter, Elizabeth, was born the same year. When that marriage failed to produce a male heir, Henry tried again with Jane Seymour. She gave birth to Edward, in 1537. After Jane died in childbirth, Henry went on to have three more wives but no more children. Meanwhile, Parliament passed a series of succession acts, which made Edward the rightful heir followed by his older sisters, Mary and Elizabeth.[24]

While Henry VIII's quest to produce a male heir played out, he also moved to separate England from the Roman Catholic Church. Relying on the advice of Thomas Cranmer and Thomas Cromwell, Henry decided to break with the pope, a decision leading Parliament to pass the Act in Restraint of Appeals and the Act of Submission of the Clergy. The first measure made the king the head of the Church of England. The second measure required all priests in England to swear allegiance to the king's church. Doctrinally speaking, the Church of England, called the Anglican Church, made few changes. However, Henry VIII dissolved all the monasteries in England and confiscated their wealth as a means to build his treasury.[25]

The fate of Protestantism ebbed and flowed under Henry's children, Edward VI (r. 1547-1553), Mary I (r. 1553-1558), and Elizabeth I (r. 1558-1603). Edward was strongly Protestant and wanted to make significant changes that would mirror the religious changes on the continent. Mary, on the other hand, was strongly Catholic. She pushed Parliament to repeal the legislation that created the Church of England, and she executed several hundred Protestants. When Elizabeth succeeded Mary, she sought to achieve a balance between the Protestants and Catholics in England. Her policies leaned toward Protestantism, but she asked only for outward conformity from her subjects. The Church of England retained the ceremony of the Catholic service, but the priests said mass in the vernacular and could marry.[26] Her compromises brought a certain amount of stability to the country. They also led to the rise of the Puritans in England who would play an instrumental role in English colonization in the New World in the seventeenth century.

The French monarchy had little political reason to turn to Protestantism in the early sixteenth century. In 1516, Francis I (r. 1515-1547) and Pope Leo X signed the Concordat of Bologna. It made Catholicism the official religion of France but also gave the French king the right to appoint church authorities in his country. Unlike Henry VIII, Francis I did not need to break with Rome to exert his control over the church or its financial resources. In fact, given the religious stability in the 1520s, Francis looked for possible ways to catch up with the Spanish in the realm of overseas exploration and colonization.

In 1524, he sponsored a voyage by Giovanni da Verrazzano to stake a claim in the New World and discover the Northwest Passage. During his voyage, Verrazano explored the Atlantic coastline from modern-day South Carolina to New York. A decade later, Francis sponsored two voyages by Jacques Cartier. While he failed to find a northern route to Asia, Cartier surveyed the St. Lawrence River and made valuable contacts with the native population. Nevertheless, the discoveries did not inspire Francis to support a permanent settlement in Canada at that time.[27]

The connection between the state and the church established in 1516, however, did not prevent Protestant sentiments from growing in France during the tenure of Henry II (r. 1547-1559). The weakness of Henry II's sons led to a civil war in France that had religious undertones. Some members of the French nobility became Protestants in order to show their independence from the crown. The Catholic-Protestant split in France led to a series of religious riots, the worst of which occurred on St. Bartholomew's Day, August 24, 1572. Shortly after the marriage of Margaret of Valois to Henry of Navarre, Catholics led by Henry of Guise viciously attacked Protestants in Paris. After the so-called Saint Bartholomew's Day Massacre, three factions vied for control during the War of the Three Henrys—Henry III, Henry of Guise, and Henry of Navarre. A group of Catholic moderates finally ended the strife when they concluded that domestic tranquility was more important than religious doctrine. Moreover, the deaths of two of the Henrys left only the Protestant Henry of Navarre standing. After he ascended to the throne, Henry IV (r. 1589-1610) joined the Roman Catholic Church. Then, he issued the Edict of Nantes in 1598, which granted French Protestants, the Huguenots, the liberty of conscience and the liberty of worship. Henry IV's tentative nod to religious toleration brought stability to the country. Relative peace at home paved the way for future French exploration.[28]

2.4.3 Before You Move On...

Key Concepts

During the Middle Ages and the Early Modern Era, England and France took shape as nation states. When the barbarian invasions stopped in the twelfth century, English and French rulers sought to consolidate their control. While they managed to exert greater influence over their subjects, they also found themselves frequently at odds with one another and facing religious strife at home as the Protestant Reformation took hold in Europe. By the late sixteenth century, England and France, both of which had only flirted with overseas exploration to that point, had become sovereign states under the rule of strong monarchies. Thus, as the new century dawned, both seemed posed to start their colonial ventures and carry their rivalry to the New World.

Test Yourself

1. The principle implied in the Magna Carta (1215) was
   a. that democracy would replace monarchy.
   b. that the king was above the law.
   c. that the people ruled the monarch.
   d. that all people, even the king, were subject to the law.

2. Henry VIII's religious reformation in England occurred
   a. mostly for political reasons.
   b. strictly for economic reasons.
   c. mostly for diplomatic reasons.
   d. strictly for religious reasons.

See page 53 for answers

2.5 AFRICA AT THE OUTSET OF THE AGE OF DISCOVERY AND THE TRANS-ATLANTIC SLAVE TRADE

Africa takes a central role in any discussion of increasing globalization during the Age of Discovery. First, emerging European explorations and global trade networks began with European contact with and exploration of Africa. Early Portuguese exploration started trade networks in gold, ivory, and slaves that invigorated the European economy. Later, trade expanded to incorporate the Americas, transforming into the Triangle Trade that encompassed the Trans-Atlantic slave trade network. In many ways, contact and trade with Africa created the Atlantic World, the network of connections that linked the Americas, Europe, and Africa economically, politically, culturally, religiously, and environmentally. The transformations of the Age of Discovery began in Africa.

At the beginning of the sixteenth century, Africa was a continent of tremendous diversity and home to hundreds of cultures, languages, and political states. Different regions in Africa experienced the changes of the era in different ways. Western and Central Africa were greatly influenced by the changes wrought by the slave trade. Southern Africa was the first region to experience the phenomenon of European migration when the Dutch established Cape Colony in 1652. Northern and eastern Africa had been linked to the wider world through trade networks such as the Indian Ocean and Mediterranean, as well as through the spread of Islam and Christianity. However, the expansion of Europe through trade and political networks contested African control over their territory and European participation in the Indian Ocean trade.

2.5.1 Medieval West Africa: The Kingdoms of Ghana, Mali, and Songhay

In the mid-fifteenth century, European countries like Portugal and Spain sought an all-water route to the cultures of the Indian Ocean in order to enjoy their spices, silks, and cottons without having to pay the exorbitant rates of the Arab traders who controlled the overland routes; these routes began in Indonesia and wound their way along the coasts of southeast Asia and India and then up either the Persian Gulf or the Red Sea toward the eastern Mediterranean. Monarchs like Prince Henry the Navigator sponsored fleets along the western coast of Africa, rounding the Cape of Good Hope and sailing northward toward the Indian Ocean. Africa was not, however, just a way station on the route to the Indian Ocean; the continent was invaluable for the goods it contributed to world trade: ivory, tortoise shells, dried coconut, animal skins, cowrie shells, and porcelain from East Africa and from West and South Africa, gold, palm oil, and slaves.[29]

In the centuries before the Age of Discovery, Africa saw the rise to preeminence of a number of impressive kingdoms: Ghana, Mali, and Songhay in the west, the city states of the East African coast, and in the south, Great Zimbabwe. Located in West Africa, Ghana was inhabited by the Soninke people whose rulers were called "Ghana." Most of the territory called Wagadou by the Soninke was non-arable and thus unfit for agriculture. It was only the southern region that enjoyed measurable rainfall that enabled the growth of crops abundant enough to support a population of around 200,000. Ghana's monarchy was not unlike those of Europe during the same century. The king held all power, religious, judicial, military, and political, although unlike European monarchies, the crown was passed matrilineally though the eldest sister of the ruling monarch.

Much of what we know about Ghana comes from Al-Bakri, an eleventh century Spanish Muslim geographer whose *Book of Highways and Kingdoms* details the workings of the country. The king and his advisors were non-Muslims who practiced the animist religion of their ancestors, though by 1000 CE there was a large Muslim population, and many of the Ghana's advisors were Islamic.[30] Al-Bakri explains that the capital city of Ghana, Koumbi Saleh, consisted of "two towns lying on a plain." One of these cities was inhabited by Muslims and "possessed" twelve mosques, while the other, six miles from the Muslim town, was the "residence of the King;" it consisted of a "palace and a number of dome-shaped dwellings, all of them surrounded by a strong enclosure, like a city wall." The city also contained one mosque for "the convenience of those Muslims who came on diplomatic missions." In the judicial matters, over which the king presided, trial was by ordeal, not unlike the technique used by medieval European kings. As was also true of medieval European kingdoms, the monarch controlled all trade, and the social hierarchy placed the king, his court and Muslim administrators on the top rung, followed by a merchant class, and below them farmers, herders, and artisans. There is no doubt as to the wealth of the rulers of Ghana, as al-Bakri wrote: "When [the king] holds court...he sits in a pavilion around which stand ten horses wearing golden trappings; at his right are the sons of the chiefs of the country, splendidly dressed and with their hair sprinkled with gold."[31]

By 1200, the kingdom of Ghana was in decline as political disintegration saw the rise of several petty kingdoms led by warlords. Eventually one people, the Mandinka, asserted themselves over the others and created a new kingdom, Mali, built on the foundations of Ghana. Historians usually point out that the strength of Mali lay in part in the accession to the throne of two powerful leaders: Sundiata Keita and Mansa Musa. It was through the efforts and resourcefulness of these two men that a strong, vibrant kingdom was created.

The founder of Mali, Sundiata Keita (1230-1255), ruled over an empire that was larger, more agriculturally successful, and wealthier than Ghana. Technically, Mali was an Islamic state, though its religious practices mixed Islam and the more traditional African ceremonies; although the leaders participated in the pilgrimage and ritual prayers, they also followed ancient pagan practices of eating unclean meat, drinking strong beverages, self-abasement before the ruler, and "scanty female clothing."[32] Sundiata chose Niani as the capital of his empire and before his death had turned the city into an important trading center and had expanded his empire to include the trading cities of Gao, Jenne, and Walata.

The expansion of the empire of Mali continued under Sundiata's descendent, Mansa Musa (r. 1312-1337); *mansa* means emperor in the language of the Mandinka) to include Timbuktu and territory westward to the shores of the Atlantic Ocean. The empire Mansa Musa created was twice the size of Ghana and contained about 8,000,000 people. Mansa Musa was different from Sundiata in that he became a devout Muslim, though the majority of his subjects did not. Musa is perhaps best known for his fourteenth century pilgrimage to Mecca (1324-1325) on which he was accompanied by 500 slaves each carrying a six-pound staff of pure gold and 100 elephants bearing 100 pounds of gold.[33] He stopped in Egypt for three months before moving on to Mecca and Medina, during which his visit was recorded by al-Omari, the Egyptian sultan's scribe:

> This man, Mansa Musa, spread upon Cairo the flood of his generosity: there was not person, officer of the court or holder of any office of the Sultanate [of Egypt] who did not receive a sum of gold from him. The people of Cairo earned incalculable sums from him, whether by buying and selling or by gifts.[34]

During Mansa Musa's reign, Timbuktu became a center of international trade and education. The king brought Arab scholars to the city, as well as architects, astronomers, poets, lawyers, mathematicians, and theologians. Over one hundred schools and eighteen universities were established (for men only, of course) for Islamic studies.

Figure 2.4 Great Friday Mosque at Jenne | Mansa Musa established control over Jenne, and upon his return from the pilgrimage to Mecca, he brought an Egyptian architect by the name of al-Saheli whom Mansa Musa paid to create mosques at several cities; the Friday Prayers Mosque was one of these. Mansa Musa also built a royal palace (or Madugu) in Timbuktu. The mosque was completed in the late fourteenth/early fifteenth century.

Author: United States Department of Agriculture
Source: USDA.gov

The Muslim geographer, Ibn Battuta, visited Mali during the despotic reign of Mansa Musa's unpopular brother, Mansa Sulayman, remarking that in Mali there was "complete security in the land" as the *mansa* "shows no mercy to anyone guilty of the least act of [violence]." The inhabitants were pious Muslims:

> Another of their good qualities is their habit of wearing clean white garments on Fridays. Even if a man has nothing but an old worn shirt, he washes it and cleans it, and wears it to the Friday service. Yet another is their zeal for learning the Koran by heart. They put their children in chains if they show any

> backwardness in memorizing it, and they are not set free until they have it by heart. I visited [the emperor] in his house on the day of the festival. His children were chained up, so I said to him, 'Will you not let them loose?' He replied, 'I shall not do so until they learn the Koran by heart.'[35]

He remarks, however, that the practice of nakedness persisted among the women, which he, as a devout Muslim, looked upon with dismay:

> Among their bad qualities [is] the following: The women servants, slave-girls, and young girls go about in front of everyone naked, without a stitch of clothing on them. Women go into the sultan's presence naked and without coverings, and his daughters also go about naked.[36]

As was true of other empires in history, the empire of Mali was dependent on the strength and success of the *mansa*. When Mansa Musa died, he was followed by his unpopular and despotic brother, who was in turn followed by a series of weak rulers whose reigns were short-lived. During this period, the provinces began to break away and slowly the Mali Empire disintegrated; it was followed in the mid-fourteenth century by the third great empire of West Africa: the Songhay.

The empire of the Songhay people took in the territories that had been controlled by Ghana and Mali and extended them east and north to become one of the largest empires in African history. Basing their military success on armies of mounted horsemen, the Songhay warriors took one Mali city after another until by the mid-fifteenth century they controlled the important cities of Timbuktu and Jenna. As was true in Mali, the sources of income came from tribute, the royal farms, and tariffs on trade. The exports in greatest demand were similar to those of Mali: gold, ivory, and slaves. Politically, Songhay was more centralized than Mali, and with every territory taken, the local kings or chieftains were removed and replaced by governors appointed by the emperors. A young traveler calling himself "Leo Africanus" gave his readers an idea as to the wealth of one of the local governors, who had "many articles of gold and [keeps] a magnificent and well-furnished court. When he travels anywhere he rides upon a camel which is led by some of his noblemen...Attending him he has always three thousand horsemen, and a great number of footmen armed with poisoned arrows." Though generally, while the ruling classes were very wealthy, the majority of the citizens were "very poor."[37]

2.5.2 East and South Africa

By the mid-fifteenth century, the east African coast was dotted with city states which have left no written records of their history and society. The city states had served as trading depots as early as the fifth century, and after the death of Mohammed and the spread of Islam across North Africa, Arab traders established small cities, whose local peoples (called the "Zanj" by the Arabs) were ruled by local kings and practiced ancient animistic religions. As the centuries progressed, more and more Arabs and Indonesians settled along the coast, creating a culture called "Swahili." By the early fourteenth century, Kilwa had become the most important city in the region, whose culture was described in great detail by Ibn Battuta:

> [Kilwa] is a large city on the seacoast, most of whose inhabitants are Zinj [sic], jet black in colour. They have tattoo marks on their faces. Kilwa is a very fine and substantially built town, and all its buildings are of wood. Its inhabitants are constantly engaged in military expeditions, for their country is contiguous to the heathen Zanj. The sultan at the time of my visit was Abu'l-Muzaffar Hasan, who was noted for his gifts and generosity. He used to devote the fifth part of the booty made on his expeditions to pious and charitable purposes, as is prescribed in the Koran, and I have seen him give the clothes off his back to a mendicant who asked him for them.[38]

When the Portuguese made it around the Cape of Good Hope in the late fifteenth century and encountered the East African coastal societies, they were amazed at the wealth of these cities. Some of the cities created manufactures for export, while others focused on natural products like leopard skins, tortoise shell, ivory, and gold, as well as slaves.

Until the late nineteenth century, the society of South Africa known as Great Zimbabwe was unknown to the European world; in 1867 a German explorer named Adam Renders came across ruins that archaeologists consider the most impressive ruins south of the Nile Valley: Great Zimbabwe. The city was the capital of a vast empire stretching across South Africa by the first century CE; it continued to thrive as a gold producing area until the fifteenth century, when due to soil exhaustion it was unable to support its large population.

2.5.3 The Transatlantic Slave Trade

The Portuguese first traded for African slaves in 1441. They did not create the slave trade; Africans had held slaves and traded them long before the Europeans entered the market. African peoples throughout West Africa took captives in warfare and kept slaves as a means of incorporating foreigners into the society. African slavery therefore differed greatly from the European norms of slavery that became established in the New World. For instance, slaves in Africa were not property; they retained some rights as a person and as an individual. The condition of slavery was not inherited; if a slave had children, then the children were born free. Moreover, the condition of slavery might not last an entire lifetime but instead a period of years.

The Trans-Atlantic slave trade emerged with the colonization of the New World. As the need for labor grew, so too did the trade. At first, some Europeans tried to use force in acquiring slaves, but this method proved impracticable on any scale. The only workable method was acquiring slaves through trade with Africans, since they controlled all trade into the interior. Typically, Europeans were restricted to trading posts, or *feitorias,* along the coast. Captives were brought to the *feitorias*, where they were processed as cargo rather than as human beings. Slaves were kept imprisoned in small, crowded rooms, segregated by sex and age, and "fattened up" if they were deemed too small for transport. They were branded to show what merchant purchased them, that taxes had been paid, and even that they had been baptized as a Christian. The high mortality rate of the slave trade began on the forced march to the *feitorias* and in a slave's imprisonment within them; the mortality rate continued to climb during the second part of the journey, the Middle Passage.

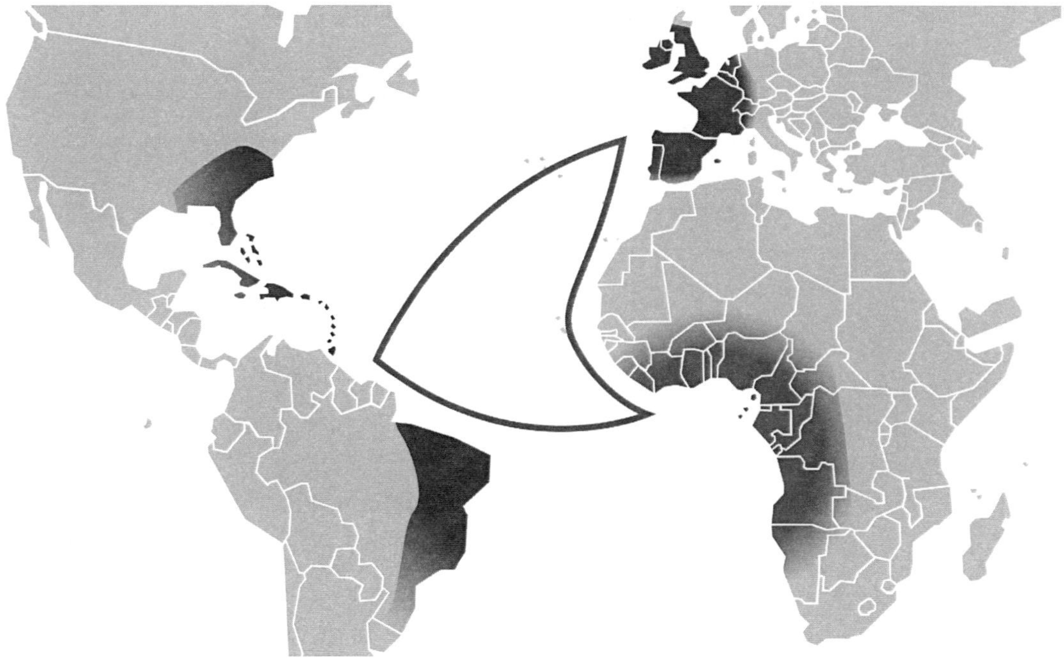

Figure 2.5 Atlantic Triangle Trade | The Triangle Trade linked Europe, Africa, and the Americas as part of a greater Atlantic World.

Author: Jon Chui
Source: Wikimedia Commons
License: CC BY-SA 3.0

The Middle Passage, the voyage across the Atlantic from Africa to the Americas, comprised the middle leg of the Atlantic Triangle Trade network, which traded manufactured goods such as beads, mirrors, cloth, and firearms to Africa for slaves. Slaves were then carried to the Americas, where their labor would produce items of the last leg of the Triangle Trade such as sugar, rum, molasses, indigo, cotton, and rice, to name a few. The Middle Passage itself was a hellish experience. Slaves were segregated by sex, often stripped naked, chained together, and kept in extremely tight quarters for up to twenty-three hours a day; as many as 12-13 percent died during this dehumanizing experience. Although we will likely never know the exact number of people who were enslaved and brought to the Americas, the number is certainly larger than ten million.[39]

2.5.4 The Kingdom of Dahomey

The Age of Discovery brought many changes to West Africa. In some areas, the slave trade had the effect of breaking down societies. For instance, in the early nineteenth century the great Yoruba confederation of states began to break down due to civil wars. Conflicts escalated as participants sold slaves to acquire European weapons; these weapons were then used to acquire more slaves, thus creating a vicious cycle. Other groups grew and gained power because of their role in the slave trade, perhaps the most prominent being the West African kingdom of Dahomey.

The Kingdom of Dahomey was established in the 1720s. Dahomey was built on the slave trade; kings used profits from the slave trade to acquire guns, which in turn were used to expand their kingdom by conquest and incorporation of smaller kingdoms. Most slaves were acquired either by trade with the interior or by raids into the north and west into

Nigeria; Dahomey took advantage of the civil wars among the Yoruba to gain access to a ready source of captives.

European trade agents were kept isolated in the main trade port of Whydah. Only a privileged few were allowed into the interior of the kingdom to have an audience with the king; as a result, only a few contemporary sources describe the kingdom. Like his European counterparts, the king of Dahomey was an absolute monarch, possessing great power in a highly centralized state. All trade with Europeans was a royal monopoly, jealously guarded by the kings. The monarchs never allowed Europeans to deal directly with the people of the kingdom, keeping all profits for the state, and allowing this highly militarized state to grow and expand.

2.5.5 Before You Move On...

Key Concepts

On the eve of the sixteenth century, Africa was a continent of tremendous diversity and home to hundreds of cultures, languages, and political states. Most of the empires of the past two centuries were in decline, though the demand for their goods continued and the city states of East Africa were viable trading depots. The trans-Saharan trade routes, in place since the earliest years of the Common Era, still linked East Africa, West Africa, and the Islamic sultanates in the North. It is not surprising, however, that the various regions in Africa experienced the changes brought by the Age of Discovery in different ways. Western and Central Africa were greatly influenced by the slave trade. The Kingdom of Dahomey provides an example of one of the ways that African groups were influenced by and participated in both the Age of Discovery and the Trans-Atlantic slave trade.

The Trans-Atlantic slave trade was the middle portion of the Atlantic Triangle Trade network. At least ten million Africans were enslaved and forced to make the Middle Passage across the Atlantic to the New World. Mortality rates for the Middle Passage averaged around 12-13 percent.

Test Yourself

1. The region of Africa most directly involved in the Trans-Atlantic slave trade was

   a. North Africa

   b. West Africa

   c. South Africa

   d. East Africa

2. The Middle Passage was a part of the Indian Ocean trade network.

   a. True

   b. False

3. Which of the following empires was not in West Africa?
   a.Great Zimbabwe
   b.Ghana
   c.Mali
   d.Songhay

4. Much of what we know about the cultures of East Africa comes from the writings of:
   a. Leo Africanus
   b. Sundiata Keita
   c. Mansa Musa
   d. Ibn Battuta

5. The empire of Mali was created by which of the following?
   a. Mansa Musa
   b. Sundiata Kieta
   c. Mansa Suleyman
   d. Leo Africanus

6. The Kingdom of Dahomey controlled the slave trade in their region by
   a. refusing to trade with anyone but the Dutch.
   b. keeping Europeans confined to the port at Whydah.
   c. making European merchants trade with only the king and no others.
   d. B and C.
   e. all of the above.

See page 53 for answers

2.6 Conclusion

The period before contact with the Americas marked the beginning of globalization. During this era, the world grew ever more interconnected through trade, politics, culture, and religion. In China, the rise of the Ming Dynasty in 1439 began a new era. Under the Ming Dynasty, the Forbidden City, the seat of Chinese rule in the following centuries and a lasting symbol of Chinese power, was built. The Chinese were the first to undertake substantial oceanic voyages in the Age of Discovery. Zheng He's massive fleet dwarfed European expeditions of the period, both in the numbers and size of the ships. The armada explored much of the Indian Ocean region as far as Africa, mapping, charting, trading, and incorporating a great part of the region into a Chinese tributary system. Although a few historians have suggested that Zheng He's fleet voyaged as far as Australia and the Americas, compelling documentary evidence for this is lacking.

In Europe, under the sponsorship of Prince Henry the Navigator, Portugal emerged as one of the leaders of the European Age of Discovery, in part because of technologies such as the compass, the astrolabe, and the *caravel*. The Portuguese established trading ports along the coast of West Africa as well as in India. After Columbus's 1492 voyage, the Spanish found themselves exploring vast new lands. Competition between Portugal and Spain was alleviated with the Treaty of Tordesillas and the Treaty of Zaragosa. These two agreements effectively divided the earth into two zones of influence. Meanwhile, England and France took shape as nation states, seeking to exert greater influence over their subjects. By the 1500s, England and France were sovereign states characterized by strong monarchies. These developments helped to pave the way for their overseas expansion in the seventeenth century; however, they had to deal with internal schisms caused by the Protestant Reformation before they could devote their attention to catching up with Portugal and Spain.

On the eve of the sixteenth century, Africa was a continent of tremendous diversity and home to hundreds of cultures, languages, and political states. In the centuries before the Age of Discovery, Africa saw the rise to pre-eminence of a number of impressive kingdoms: Ghana, Mali, and Songhay in the west, the city states of the East African coast, and in the south, Great Zimbabwe. Different regions in Africa experienced the changes of the era in different ways. Western and Central Africa were greatly influenced by the changes wrought by the slave trade. The Kingdom of Dahomey provides an example of one of the ways that African groups were influenced by and participated in both the Age of Discovery and the Trans-Atlantic slave trade. The Trans-Atlantic slave trade was the middle portion of the Atlantic Triangle Trade network. At least ten million Africans were enslaved and forced to make the Middle Passage across the Atlantic to the New World. Mortality rates for the Middle Passage averaged around 12-13 percent.

Voyages of exploration captured the immensity of the earth in maps and images and created webs of connection between regions and peoples, bringing the world closer together. It is for these reasons that this period is often referred to as the Early Modern Era. For the first time, we see the emergence of a world that bears great similarity to ours of the twenty-first century, a world interconnected through trade, politics, culture, and religion.

2.7 CRITICAL THINKING EXERCISES

- How might the Age of Discovery have been fundamentally changed if the Chinese had not abandoned their voyages of trade and exploration under Zheng He? Why, in your estimation, did Yung Lo's successor Zhu Zhanji decide to end the voyages in 1433?
- How did trade and the economy shape how each group or nation participated in the Age of Discovery? What are some other factors that shaped participation? Did religion or economy play a greater role in determining the actions of a nation during the Age of Discovery?
- Why do we know so little about the medieval empires of Africa? What sources do we depend on to instruct us in their history?

2.8 KEY TERMS

- *Caravel*
- Christopher Columbus
- Common law
- Edict of Nantes
- Kingdom of Ghana
- Great Zimbabwe
- Hong Wu
- Hundred Years' War
- Ibn Battuta
- Kingdom of Dahomey
- Magna Carta
- Kingdom of Mali
- Mansa Musa
- Martin Luther
- Middle Passage
- Prince Henry the Navigator
- Protestant Reformation
- Songhay
- Sundiata Kieta
- Timbuktu
- Spice Islands
- Strait of Malacca
- The Tudors
- Treaty of Tordesillas
- Treaty of Zaragoza
- Triangle Trade
- Yung Lo
- Zanj
- Zheng He

2.9 CHRONOLOGY

The following chronology is a list of important dates and events associated with this chapter.

Date	Event
642-800	Muslim conquest of Egypt and North Africa
650-1500	Slave trade from sub-Saharan Africa to Mediterranean
900-1100	Kingdom of Ghana created and flourished
1100-1400	Great Zimbabwe built and flourished
1154	Henry II became King of England, launching the Angevin dynasty
1180	Phillip II became the King of France and then expanded Capetian control over the continent
1194	Phillip II of France and Richard I of England began a war over Normandy
1215	King John of England accepted the Magna Carta
1250	End of Portuguese *Reconquista*
1300	Kilwa becomes the most power city state in East Africa
1312-1337	Reign of Mansa Musa in Mali
1324-1325	Mansa Musa's pilgrimage to Mecca
1337	Hundred Years' War between England and France broke out
1348	The Black Death (the Plague) spread across Europe
1369	Chinese defeated the Mongols and founded the Ming dynasty
1405-1433	Zheng He's seven voyages into the Indian Ocean region
1453	Wars of the Roses began in England
1485	Henry VII became King of England, ending the Wars of the Roses and launching the Tudor dynasty
1487	Bartlolmieu Dias rounded Cape of Good Hope

2.10 BIBLIOGRAPHY

Anatole, Andro. *The 1421 Heresy: An Investigation into the Ming Chinese Maritime Survey of the World.* Bloomington, Indiana: Author House, 2006.

Battutu, Ibn. *Travels in Asia and Africa.* Medieval Sourcebook, ed. Paul Halsall, November 12, 2012. http://www.fordham.edu/halsall/source/1354-ibnbattuta.asp.

Conrad, David C. *Empires of Medieval West Africa: Ghana, Mali, and Songhay.* New York: Facts on File, 2005.

Duiker, William J and Jackson J Spielvogel. *The Essential World History*, sixth edition. NY: Wadsworth Publishing, 2011.

Eltis, David. "A Brief Overview of the Trans-Atlantic Slave Trade," Voyages: The Trans-Atlantic Slave Trade Database, March 4, 2012. http://www.slavevoyages.org/tast/assessment/essays-intro-01.faces.

Fairbank, John King. *China: A New History.* Cambridge: Harvard University Press, 1992.

Goodrich, L. Carrington. *A Short History of the Chinese People.* Mineola, NY: Dover Publications, 1943.

Haine, W. Scott. *The History of France.* Westport, CT: Greenwood Press, 2000.

Huang, Ray: *China: A Macro History.* London: ME Sharpe, Inc., 1988.

Iliffe, John. *Africans: The History of a Continent.* Cambridge: Cambridge University Press, 1995.

Levathes, Louise. *When China Ruled the Seas: The Treasure Fleet of the Dragon Throne, 1405-1433.* New York: Oxford University Press, 1996.

McKay, John P, Bennett D. Hill, and John Buckler. *A History of Western Society*, vol. 1, fourth edition. Boston: Houghton Mifflin Company, 1991.

Menzies, Gavin. *1421: The Year China Discovered America.* New York: Harper Perennial, 2002.

Price, Roger. *A Concise History of France.* Cambridge: Cambridge University Press, 1993.

Shivington, Kevin. *History of Africa.* New York: Palgrave Macmillan, 1995.

Smith, Goldwin. *A History of England*, Fourth Edition. New York: Charles Scribner's Sons, 1974.

2.11 END NOTES

1 John K. Fairbank, *China: A New History* (Cambridge: Harvard University Press, 1992), 128.

2 Fairbank, *China: A New History*, 128.

3 Ray Huang, *China: A Macro History* (London: ME Sharpe, 1988), 155; Gavin Menzies, *1421: The Year China Discovered America* (New York: Harper Perennial, 2002), 56-59.

4 Fairbank, *China: A New History*, 138.

5 Menzies, 1421, 50-52.

6 Andro Anatole, *The 1421 Heresy: An Investigation into the Ming Chinese Maritime Survey of the World* (Bloomington, Indiana: Author House, 2006), 24.

7 Menzies, *1421*, 65; Fairbank, *China: A New History*, 137.

8 Anatole, *The 1421 Heresy*, 67-69.

9 Anatole, *The 1421 Heresy*, 67-68; Louise Levathes, *When China Ruled the Seas: The Treasure Fleet of the Dragon Throne, 1405-1433* (New York: Oxford University Press, 1996), 51.

10 Louise Levathes, *When China Ruled the Seas,* 47.

11 Fairbank, China: A New History, 140.

12 Menzies, *1421*, 67.

13 Huang, *China: A Macro History*, 157-165; Fairbank, *China: A New History,* 140-142.

14 L. Carrington Goodrich, *A Short History of the Chinese People* (Mineola, NY: Dover Publications, 1943), 195.

15 William J. Duiker and Jackson J. Spielvogel, *World History*, 5th ed. (United States: Thompson Wadsworth, 2007), 254.

16 Levathes, *When China Ruled the Seas*, 49-53.

17 Goldwin Smith, *A History of England*, fourth edition (New York: Charles Scribner's Sons, 1974), 51; John P. McKay, Bennett D. Hill, and John Buckler, *A History of Western Society*, vol. 1, 4th ed. (Boston: Houghton Mifflin Company, 1991), 324.

18 Smith, *The History of England*, 78-79; McKay, et al., *A History of Western Society*, 323-324.

19 W. Scott Haine, *The History of France* (Westport, CT: Greenwood Press, 2000), 44-45; McKay, et al., *A History of Western Society*, 368, 383.

20 McKay, et al., *A History of Western Society*, 412-413.

21 Hugh Chisholm, ed., *The Encyclopedia Britannica: A Dictionary of Arts, Sciences, Literature and General Information*, Eleventh Edition, Volume 4 (Cambridge: The University Press, 1910), 921-922.

22 McKay, et al., *A History of Western Society*, 424-428.

23 Smith, *The History of England*, 214-216, 220; McKay, et al., *A History of Western Society*, 440-441.

24 Smith, *The History of England*, 221, 224-228.

25 Smith, *The History of England*, 220-222; McKay, et al., *A History of Western Society*, 442-443.

26 McKay, et al., *A History of Western Society*, 443-444.

27 McKay, et al., *A History of Western Society*, 468-470; Adolph Caso, "GIOVANNI DA VERRAZZANO (1485-1527): Born in Florence; Died in Spain," *They Too Made America Great* (January 1978): 34-36; *History Reference Center*, EBSCO*host* (accessed November 11, 2012); Daniel E. Harmon, "The Voyages of Jacques Cartier," *Early French Explorers of North America* (January 2003): 14; *History Reference Center*, EBSCO*host* (accessed November 11, 2012).

28 McKay, et al., *A History of Western Society*, 470-472.

29 *Periplus of the Erythraean Sea*, excerpt in McKay, Hill, Buckler, et. al., *A History of World Societies*, 9th ed., vol. 1, (Boston: Bedford/St. Martins, 2012), 287.

30 John Iliffe, *Africans: the History of a Continent* (Cambridge: Cambridge Uni. Press, 1995), 51.

31 al-Bakri, *Book of Highways and Kingdoms* quoted in McKay, *History of World Societies*, 279.

32 Iliffe, *History of a Continent*, 53.

33 Iliffe, History of a Continent, 90.

34 al-Omari quoted in Kevin Shillington, *History of Africa* (New York: Palgrave Macmillan, 1995), 98-99.

35 Ibn Battutu, *Travels in Asia and Africa*, in *Medieval Sourcebook*, ed. Paul Halsall, November 12, 2012, http://www.fordham.edu/halsall/source/1354-ibnbattuta.asp.

36 ibid.

37 Leo Africanus quoted in Shillington, History of Africa, 105-106.

38 Ibn Battuta, *Travels*.

39 David Eltis, "A Brief Overview of the Trans-Atlantic Slave Trade," Voyages: The Trans-Atlantic Slave Trade Database, March 4, 2012, http://www.slavevoyages.org/tast/assessment/essays-intro-01.faces.

ANSWER KEY FOR CHAPTER TWO: THE GLOBAL CONTEXT: ASIA, EUROPE, AND AFRICA IN THE EARLY MODERN ERA

Check your answers to the questions in the Before You Move On Sections for this chapter.

Correct answers are **BOLDED**

Section 2.2.3 - p. 30

1. What important event(s) took place in 1492?
   a. Columbus's first voyage to the New World
   b. the expulsion of the Jews and Muslims from Spain
   c. the end of the Reconquista
   D. ALL OF THE ABOVE
   e. A and C

2. The _______ enabled the Portuguese to enter the spice trade.
   a. rounding the Cape of Good Hope
   B. THE CONQUEST OF MALACCA
   c. the discovery of the New World
   d. making contact with Prester John
   e. the conquest of Goa

3. True/False: For the Spanish, reconquering the Iberian Peninsula was a military and religious action.
   A. TRUE
   b. False

4. The mythical king Prester John was important to the Portuguese because
   a. he controlled the spice trade
   b. he would be an ally to the Spanish in reconquering the Iberian Peninsula
   C. HE WAS A CHRISTIAN KING IN AN AREA DOMINATED BY MUSLIMS
   d. he could direct them in how to cross the Indian Ocean

5. The Treaty of Tordesillas and the ______ worked in tandem to establish zones of influence for Portuguese and Spanish trade.
   a. Treaty of Nanking
   b. Treaty of Molucca
   C. TREATY OF ZARAGOZA
   d. Treaty of Goa

Section 2.3.1 - p. 34

1. Zheng He's goals for exploring the Indian Ocean included
   a. exploring and mapping the region.
   b. establishing trade with port cities.
   c. incorporating new areas into the Chinese tribute system.
   D. ALL OF THE ABOVE.
   e. none of the above.

2. One possible reason for Zhu Zanji's decision to end the voyages of Zheng He was
   a. a spirit of isolationism in the Chinese court under Zhu Zanji.
   b. to save money and avoid the expense of the voyages.
   c. to end competition with the French, who were entering the Indian Ocean trade.
   D. A AND B.
   e. all of the above.

Section 2.4.3 - p. 39

1. The principle implied in the Magna Carta (1215) was
   a. that democracy would replace monarchy.
   b. that the king was above the law.
   c. that the people ruled the monarch.
   D. THAT ALL PEOPLE, EVEN THE KING, WERE SUBJECT TO THE LAW.

2. Henry VIII's religious reformation in England occurred
    A. MOSTLY FOR POLITICAL REASONS.
    b. strictly for economic reasons.
    c. mostly for diplomatic reasons.
    d. strictly for religious reasons.

Section 2.5.5 - p. 45
1. The region of Africa most directly involved in the Trans-Atlantic slave trade was
    a. North Africa
    B. WEST AFRICA
    c. South Africa
    d. East Africa

2. True/False: The Middle Passage was a part of the Indian Ocean trade network.
    a. True
    B. FALSE

3. Which of the following empires was not in West Africa?
    A.GREAT ZIMBABWE
    b.Ghana
    c.Mali
    d.Songhay

4. Much of what we know about the cultures of East Africa comes from the writings of:
    a. Leo Africanus
    b. Sundiata Keita
    c. Mansa Musa
    D. IBN BATTUTA

5. The empire of Mali was created by which of the following?
    a. Mansa Musa
    B. SUNDIATA KIETA
    c. Mansa Suleyman
    d. Leo Africanus

6. The Kingdom of Dahomey controlled the slave trade in their region by
    a. refusing to trade with anyone but the Dutch.
    b. keeping Europeans confined to the port at Whydah.
    c. making European merchants trade with only the king and no others.
    D. B AND C.
    e. all of the above.

Chapter Three: Initial Contact and Conquest

Contents

Chapter Three: Initial Contact and Conquest

3.1 INTRODUCTION

The discovery of the New World in 1492 was one of the most important events in world history. Over the next two hundred years, the world underwent a rapid transformation in various areas of knowledge: geography, demographics, botany, anthropology, and history. European nations were also changed and challenged politically as they attempted to exert their control over these new lands. Although what would become the United States of America came to be dominated by English colonies, English models of colonialism were not the earliest or most powerful models of colonial control to emerge in the Americas. This chapter will explore the experience of first contact between the hemispheres in the forms of interactions between Europeans and Indians, developing and differing models of colonial control under the Spanish, Portuguese, French, and Dutch, and the process known as the Columbian Exchange: the exchange of people, plants, animals, and diseases that forever changed both the Old and New Worlds.

In the earliest era of contact and conquest, the Spanish dominated the New World. Their experiences largely defined early European knowledge of the Americas and its native inhabitants, the Indians, a group unknown to Europeans. In the fifty years after Christopher Columbus discovered the Americas in 1492, the Spanish expanded throughout the Caribbean, Mesoamerica, and the Andes, establishing the basis for a powerful hemispheric empire. Two of the main challenges the Spanish faced in establishing and administering their new empires were distance and time; the vast expanse of the Atlantic Ocean separating colony and mother country, and the long journey between the two, meant that communication was difficult. The distance between Europe and the Americas played a very important role in shaping colonial administration as well as patterns and methods of imperial control.

The first challenge to Spanish hegemony in the New World came with the Treaty of Tordesillas, which divided the known non-European world between Spain and Portugal. Part of Brazil fell within the Portuguese area of claim, leading to a growing struggle for control in the region between the powers. Later, France and the Netherlands entered the Americas. These two nations took a primarily economic interest in the American hemisphere, shaping their models of colonial administration largely around trade. The French spent much of their energy in conjunction with their political and economic capital building a fur trade in the North American frontier. The Dutch established their foothold in the Caribbean, engaging in both legitimate trade and smuggling under the aegis of the Dutch West Indies Company. Politically, both France and the Netherlands wanted to weaken the Iberian hold on the Americas. The French actively contested Spanish power by trying to establish a colony in Spanish Florida. The Dutch were much less overt in their contestation of Iberian power; instead of establishing large, rival colonies, they concentrated on weakening the Spanish economically through piracy. However, the Dutch took on the Portuguese much more directly, conquering small but important lands in Brazil, wresting these areas from Portuguese control.

3.1.1 Learning Outcomes

After completing this chapter, you should be able to:

- Analyze the motives of such explorers as Christopher Columbus, Pedro Cabral, Hernán Cortés, and Francisco Pizarro in venturing to Meso and South America and the motives of European monarchs in their efforts to reach the Indian Ocean by an all-water route.
- Explain the receptions extended to the Spanish explorers by the Indians of Mexico, Peru, and Brazil and the tactics employed by the Spanish as they attempted to conquer the Aztec and Inca Empires.
- Describe the complexities of the encounter of the Old World and the New, including the exchange of crops, animals, and diseases, as well as the experiences of the conquistadores and Native American as they interacted.
- Explain the dimensions of the Native American Holocaust and Transculturation.
- Discuss the impact of the Columbian Exchange on both the Old and New Worlds.

3.2 THE IMPACT OF "DISCOVERY": THE COLUMBIAN EXCHANGE

Most historians in the twenty-first century insist that the merits of Columbus and his experience must be measured in terms of fifteenth and sixteenth century standards and values, and not in terms of those of the twenty-first century. Columbus was a product of the crusading zeal of the Renaissance period, a religious man, whose accomplishments were remarkable. He sailed west and though he did not make it to the East Indies, he did encountered continents previously unknown to the Europeans. The subsequent crop and animal exchange revolutionized the lifestyle of Europeans, Asians, and Africans. Historians refer to this process as the "Columbian Exchange." The Exchange introduced (or in the case of the horse, reintroduced) into the New World such previously unknown commodities as cattle, horses, sugar, tea, and coffee, while such products as tobacco, potatoes, chocolate, corn, and tomatoes made their way from the New World into the Old World. Not all exchanges were beneficial, of course; European diseases such as smallpox and influenza, to which the Native Americans had no resistance, were responsible for the significant depopulation of the New World.

Because of such crops as the potato, the sweet potato, and maize, however, Europeans and later the East Asians were able to vary their diets and participate in the technological revolution that would begin within 200 years of Columbus's voyage.

The biological exchange following the voyages of Columbus was even more extensive than originally thought. Europeans discovered llamas, alpacas, iguana, flying squirrels, catfish, rattlesnakes, bison, cougars, armadillos, opossums, sloths, anacondas, electric eels, vampire bats, toucans, condors, and hummingbirds in the Americas. Europeans introduced goats and crops such as snap, kidney, and lima beans, barley, oats, wine grapes, melons, coffee, olives, bananas, and more to the New World.

3.2.1 From the New World to the Old: The Exchange of Crops

Corn (or maize) is a New World crop, which was unknown in the Old World before Columbus's voyage in 1492. Following his four voyages, corn quickly became a staple crop in Europe. By 1630, the Spanish took over commercial production of corn, overshadowing the ancient use of maize for subsistence in Mesoamerica. Corn also became an important crop in China, whose population was the world's largest in the early modern period. China lacked flat lands on which to grow crops, and corn was a hearty crop which grew in many locations that would otherwise be unable to be cultivated. Today corn is produced in most countries of the world and is the third-most planted field crop (after wheat and rice).

Both the white and the sweet potato were New World crops that were unknown in the Old World before Columbus. The white potato originated in South America in the Andes Mountains where the natives developed over 200 varieties and pioneered the freeze-dried potato, or *chuño,* which can be stored for up to four years. Incan units of time were based on how long it took for a potato to cook to various consistencies. Potatoes were even used to divine the truth and predict weather. It became a staple crop in Europe after Columbus and was brought to North America by the Scots-Irish immigrants in the 1700s. The white potato is also known as the "Irish" potato as it provided the basic food supply of the Irish in the early modern period. The potato is a good source of many nutrients. When the Irish potato famine hit in the nineteenth century, many Irish immigrated to the Americas.

The sweet potato became an important crop in Europe as well as Asia. Because China has little flat land for cultivation, long ago its people learned to terrace its mountainous areas in order to create more arable land. During the Ming (1398-1644) and Qing (1644-1911) Dynasties, China became the most populous nation on Earth. The sweet potato grew easily in many different climates and settings, and the Chinese learned to harvest it in the early modern period to supplement the rice supply and to compensate for the lack of flat lands on which to create rice paddies.

Tobacco was a New World crop, first discovered in 1492 on San Salvador when the Arawak gave Columbus and his men fruit and some pungent dried leaves. Columbus ate the fruit but threw away the leaves. Later, Rodrigo de Jerez witnessed natives in Cuba smoking tobacco in pipes for ceremonial purposes and as a symbol of good will.

By 1565, tobacco had spread throughout Europe. It became popular in England after it was introduced by Sir Walter Raleigh, explorer and national figure. By 1580, tobacco usage had spread from Spain to Turkey, and from there to Russia, France, England, and the rest of Asia. In 1614, the Spanish mandated that tobacco from the New World be sent to Seville, which became the world center for the production of cigars. In the same year, King James I of England created a royal monopoly on tobacco imports, though at the same time calling it "that noxious weed" and warning of its adverse effects.

Peppers have been found in prehistoric remains in Peru, where the Incas established their empire. They were grown in Central and South America. Spanish explorers first carried pepper seeds to Spain in 1493, and the plants then spread throughout Europe. Peppers are now cultivated in the tropical regions of Asia and in the Americas near the equator.

Tomatoes originated in the coastal highlands of western South America and were later cultivated by the Maya in Mesoamerica. The Spanish took them to Europe, where at first the Europeans believed them to be poisonous because of the pungent odor of their leaves. The *Physalis pubescens*, or husk tomato, was called *tomatl* by the natives, whereas the early common tomato was the *xitomatl.* The Spaniards called both fruits tomatoes. The use of tomatoes in sauces became known as "Spanish" cuisine. American tomatoes gradually made their way into the cuisine of Portugal, North Africa, and Italy, as well as the Germanic and Slavic regions held by the Spanish and Austrian Habsburgs. By the late seventeenth century, tomatoes were included in southern Italian dishes, where they were known as also *poma d'oro*. Raw and cooked tomatoes were eaten in the Caribbean, Philippines, and southeastern Asia.

The peanut plant probably originated in Brazil or Peru. Inca graves often contain jars filled with peanuts to provide food for the dead in the afterlife. When the Spanish arrived in the New World, peanuts were grown as far north as Mexico. The explorers took peanuts back to Spain, where they are still grown. From Spain, traders and explorers took peanuts to Africa and Asia. Africans believed the plant possessed a soul, and they brought peanuts to the southern part of North America when they were brought there as slaves. The word "goober" comes from the Congo name for peanuts, *nguba*.

The wonderful commodity we know as chocolate is a product of the cacao tree. This tree requires the warm, moist climate which is found only within fifteen or twenty degrees of the equator. The first written records of chocolate date to the sixteenth century, but this product of cacao trees was likely harvested as long as three or four thousand years ago. This product consists of pods containing a pulpy mass, inside of which are seeds. The cacao bean is a brown kernel inside the seed.

The Olmec used cacao beans as early as 400 BCE; later the Mayans, Aztecs, and Toltecs also cultivated the crop. Eventually, the Indians learned how to make a drink from grinding the beans into a paste, thinning it with water, and adding sweeteners such as honey. They called the drink *xocolatl* (pronounced shoco-latle). The Aztecs used cacao beans as currency, and in 1502, Columbus returned from one of his expeditions with a bag full of cacao beans as a sample of the coins being used in the New World. In 1519, Cortés observed the Aztec Emperor Montezuma and his court drinking chocolate. In 1606, Italians reached the West Indies and returned with the secret of this splendid potion. The drink became popular in Europe, and in 1657, the first chocolate house opened in London.

The Exchange of Diseases

Although the origin of syphilis has been widely debated and its exact origin is unknown, Europeans like Bartolomé de las Casas, who visited the Americas in the early sixteenth century, wrote that the disease was well known among the natives there. Skeletal remains of Native Americans from this period and earlier suggest that here, in contrast to other regions of the world, the disease had a congenital form. Skeletons show "Hutchinson's Teeth", which are associated with the congenital form of the disease. They also show lesions on the skull and other parts of the skeleton, a feature associated with the late stages of the disease.

A second explanation which has received a good deal of support in the twenty-first century is that syphilis existed in the Old World prior to the voyages of Columbus, but that it was unrecognized until it became common and widely spread in the years following the discovery of the New World.

The eighteenth century writer Voltaire called syphilis the "first fruits the Spanish brought from the New World." The disease was first described in Europe after Charles VIII of France marched his troops to Italy in 1494; when his men returned to France, they brought the disease with them and from there it spread to Germany, Switzerland, Greece, and other regions. When Vasco da Gama sailed around the tip of Africa in 1498, he carried the disease to India. In the 1500s, it reached China; in 1520 it reached Japan, where fifty percent of the population in Edo (modern Tokyo) was infected within one hundred years. Hernán Cortés contracted the disease in Haiti as he made his way to Mesoamerica. So widespread was the disease in the sixteenth century, it was called the "Great Pox" or, in a reflection of politics associated with the development of nation states, the disease was called the "French Pox," the "Italian Pox," or whatever name reflected the antagonisms of the time.

The Europeans brought smallpox, influenza, measles, and typhus to the New World, devastating the Native American population. Although Europeans had resistance to these diseases, the Native Americans did not. In Europe, measles was a minor irritant; in the New World, it killed countless natives. In the twenty-five years after Columbus landed on Hispaniola, the population there dropped from 5,000,000 to 500.

Some scholars estimate that between fifty to ninety percent of the Native American population died in the wake of the Spanish voyages. If these percentages are correct, they would represent an epidemic of monumental proportions to which there are no comparisons. For example, during the fourteenth century, the Black Death ravaged Europe, killing about fourteen million people, or between thirty to fifty percent of the population. By contrast, in Mexico alone, eight million people died from the diseases brought by the Spanish; there is really no accurate count as to how many other natives died in other regions of the Americas. The impact of smallpox on the native population continued for many centuries after Columbus. During the westward expansion of the United States, pioneers and the army often gave Native Americans blankets laced with smallpox germs in order to more quickly "civilize" the West.

The Exchange of Animals

Fossil evidence shows that turkeys were in the Americas ten million years ago. Wild turkeys are originally native to North and Central America. Mesoamericans domesticated the turkey, and the Spanish took it to Europe. By 1524 the turkey reached England, and by 1558, it was popular at banquets in England and in other parts of Europe. Ironically, English settlers brought the domesticated turkey back to North America and interbred it with native wild turkeys. In 1579, the English explorer Martin Frobisher celebrated the first formal Thanksgiving in the Americas with a ceremony in Newfoundland to give thanks for surviving the long journey. The pilgrims who settled in Plymouth, Massachusetts in 1621 celebrated their first harvest in the New World by eating wild turkey.

Although the horse very likely originated in the Americas, it migrated to Asia over the Bering Strait land bridge and became extinct in the Americas after prehistoric times. The horse was completely unknown to the Native Americans prior to the Spanish conquest. In 1519, Hernán Cortés wrote: "Next to God, We Owe Our Victory to Our Horses." Cortés had brought only sixteen horses, but because the Aztecs fought primarily on foot, the Spaniards had a decided advantage. After their victory over the Aztecs, the Spanish brought more horses. In 1519, Coronado had 150 horses when he went to North America, and de Soto had 237 horses in 1539. By 1547, Antonio de Mendoza, the first governor of New Spain (Mexico), owned over 1,500 horses. The Spanish forbade Native Americans to ride horses without permission.

Cattle were unknown in the Americas before the arrival of the Europeans. The Vikings brought European cattle to the Americas in 1000 CE. When their colony disappeared, so did their cattle. Columbus brought cattle to Hispaniola in 1493. In 1519, Cortés brought cattle to Central America. These cattle sported very long horns, hence the term "longhorns." Spanish missionaries brought longhorns to Texas, New Mexico, and California; the breed also thrived in South America, especially near modern Brazil and Argentina. The Jamestown colony got its first cattle from England in 1611, and other European powers later brought cattle to their colonies. As the westward expansion began in the nineteenth century, the eastern cattle supplanted the longhorn, as they were better for meat and proved to be hardy in difficult weather. Today, there are few longhorns in North America.

Pigs were unknown in the Americas before Hernán do de Soto brought thirteen of these animals to the Florida mainland. Columbus brought red pigs to the Americas on his second voyage. They were also brought into the United States from the Guinea coast of Africa on early slave-trading vessels. Today, the state of Kansas alone produces enough pigs every year to feed ten million people.

Sheep were first introduced in the southwestern United States by Cortés in 1519 to supply wool for his soldiers. Navajo sheep are descended from the multi-colored sheep from the Spanish. During the westward expansion of the nineteenth century, there would be great conflict between cattle and sheep owners over grazing land.

3.2.2 From the Columbian Exchange to Transculturation

The economic and cultural exchange in the wake of Columbus's voyages brought about a profound shift in the world view of Europeans; the trading empires that resulted from the discovery of the Americas created a new, global economy in which many different peoples interacted. The economic exchange had a profound effect on society and politics and the Americas were a microcosm of these changes.

Silver from the mines in the Americas flooded the European markets. From 1503-1650, the Spanish brought 6 million kilograms of silver and 185,000 kilograms of gold into Seville. Although the influx of New World silver has often been blamed for the rampant inflation which hit Spain and later Europe in the sixteenth century, prices had already risen sharply before 1565, while silver imports did not reach their peak until 1580-1620. However, Phillip II of Spain paid his armies and foreign debts with New World silver and transmitted the rising prices and inflation in Spain to the rest of Europe. This surge in prices is known as the Price Revolution. In Saxony in 1517, the year Martin Luther posted his Ninety-Five Theses, prices had risen by one hundred percent over what they were in 1492, the year of Columbus's first voyage.

The Voyages of Exploration also created a global economy through sea trade. The Portuguese reached India and then went on to Japan and China. They brought back spices to Lisbon and often paid for these goods with textiles from India along with gold and ivory from East Africa. From the Portuguese outpost at Macao, they took Chinese silk to the Philippines and Japan, where they traded silk for Spanish silver. Spanish silver from the New World had a dramatic effect on the Chinese economy; the Single Whip Reform united the taxation system of China through a single tax payable in silver.

The Portuguese also brought horses to India from Mesopotamia and copper from Arabia, and carried hawks and peacocks from India to China and Japan. The Portuguese traded in African slaves; African slave labor produced the sugar on their plantations in Brazil, which produced the bulk of Europe's sugar supply in the sixteenth and seventeenth centuries. Portuguese became the language of trade in East Africa and Asia. The legacy of the Portuguese trading empire continued until the late twentieth century.

The Spanish and Dutch also established large maritime empires during the Age of Exploration. Miguel López de Legazpi established Spanish control over the Philippine Islands, linking Spanish trade in the Americas with trade in the East. Similarly, the Dutch established a trading empire based on spices, and in 1599, a Dutch fleet brought over 600,000 pounds of pepper and other spices to Amsterdam.

The interaction among Europeans, Native Americans, and Africans in the sixteenth century illustrated the clash of cultures that arose as European motives were at odds with the ethos and lifestyle of the indigenous civilizations of the Americas. This process, transculturation, occurred especially in the cities, where the different ethnicities lived in closer proximity than in the provinces, and where African slaves were allowed greater freedom of movement and association. Transculturation was also obvious on the plantations of Brazil and the larger estates, known as *haciendas*, in Spanish America; on both, African slaves and indigenous peoples worked side by side with *mestizos*, who were usually "sharecroppers."

New ethnicities appeared: the *mestizos* were created by intermarriage between Europeans and Indians; *mulattoes* were the offspring of whites and Africans. Similarly, religion reflected the fact that traditional Indian religions adapted and adopted elements of Catholicism. An example of this can be found in the patron saint of Mexico, the Virgin of Guadalupe. The figure was placed on a site sacred to Aztec religion, and at times, her face is depicted as dark, at other times, light. The Nahuatl-speaking Mexicans gave her the name of the Aztec earth goddess, Tonantzin. The same melding of religious traditions is evident in the tendency of Mexican crucifixion figures to be covered in blood, a bow to the Aztec belief that blood was needed to keep the sun burning and thus was a symbol of a life-giving force.[1]

In looking at the story of the conquest and its impact on both conquistadors and the monarchs of Spain, it is interesting to compare the views of Philip II of Spain, writing in 1559, with those of Lope de Aguirre, a Spanish adventurer in Peru, just two years later. Philip II's thoughts turned entirely to the wealth that the Indies had brought to the Spanish monarchy (and indeed this wealth helped fund the famous Spanish Armada), while the conquistador chided the king for his indifference to the plight of those who had done so much to secure this wealth. Philip explained:

> [F]rom New Spain are obtained gold and silver, cochineal [little insects like flies], from which crimson dye is made, leather, cotton, sugar and other things; but from Peru nothing is obtained except minerals. The fifth part of all that is produced goes to the king, but since the gold and silver is brought to Spain and he has a tenth part of that which goes to the mint and is refined and coined, he eventually gets one-fourth of the whole sum.[2]

He was also aware that the supply of precious metals would not last forever because "great quantities of gold and silver are no longer found upon the surface of the earth, as they have been in past years; and to penetrate into the bowels of the earth requires greater effort."[3] The effort would not come from the Crown, of course.

A very different picture is painted by Lope de Aguirre, who actually scolded the King by saying,

> Look here, King of Spain! Do not be cruel and ungrateful to your vassals, because while your father and you stayed in Spain without the slightest bother, your vassals, at the price of their blood and fortune, have given you all the kingdoms and holding you have in these parts. Beware, King and lord, that you cannot take, under the title of legitimate king, any benefit from this land where you risked nothing, without first giving due gratification to those who have labored and sweated in it.[4]

These two writings came in the mid-sixteenth century, just a few decades after the conquest of the Aztec Empire and not long after the fall of the Incas to Pizarro. Great wealth had come to the Spanish monarchy, great suffering to those who actually went to or already lived in the New World.

3.2.3 Before You Move On...

Key Concepts

The significance of the exchange and sharing of cultures that resulted from the discovery of the Americas and their colonization by the Spanish and Portuguese can hardly be overstated. A profound economic revolution shook both hemispheres as the influx of crops, diseases, animals, and metals to the Old World changed patterns of trade, the medium of exchange, and ideas about the use and distribution of wealth.

Similarly, traditional ideas about the structure and inhabitants of the world were put aside as Europeans and Indians encountered and ultimately learned from each other. Ethnicities were intertwined as Europeans, Africans, Indians, and their children created a complicated hierarchy of race and class in the colonies. The world had been turned upside down, perhaps for the first, if not for the last, time.

Test Yourself

1. Which of the following animals did **not** originate in the Old World of Europe, Africa, or Asia?

   a. Llamas

   b. Cattle

   c. Sheep

   d. Pigs

2. Which of the following crops originated in the New World?

a. Oats

b. Peanuts

c. Barley

d. Coffee

3. What crop was so controversial that monarchs in Europe and China attempted to ban its use?

a. Tobacco

b. Rice

c. Potato

d. Wheat

4. Which of the following crops did **not** originate in the New World?

a. Tobacco

b. Maize

c. Potato

d. Wheat

5. Which of the following European diseases was responsible for the greatest number of Amerindian deaths in the late fifteenth and early sixteenth centuries?

a. Measles

b. Influenza

c. Bubonic Plague

d. Smallpox

See page 86 for answers

3.3 THE IBERIAN COUNTRIES IN THE NEW WORLD

The countries of the Iberian Peninsula in Western Europe, Spain, and Portugal were the first to arrive and establish settlements in the New World. Being established almost a century before the permanent English settlement at Jamestown in 1607, the Iberian colonies were not originally intended to be permanent; rather, the explorers and conquistadors came to the Americas as the conquistador Hernán Cortés said, "for gold and glory" and not to "work the fields like a peasant."[5] Portugal, long an insignificant player in world affairs, was the first European country to sponsor voyages of exploration along the coast of Africa. In 1488, four years before the first voyage of Christopher Columbus, the Portuguese sailor Bartholomew Diaz rounded the Cape of Good Hope at the southern tip of the African continent. The Portuguese, like the Spanish, sought an all-water route to the

Indian Ocean in order to trade directly with India, China, the East Indies, and Japan. The purpose of Columbus's voyages, the first of which came in 1492, was similar to that of the Portuguese; he sought a route that would allow Spain to trade directly with the countries bordering the Indian and Western Pacific Oceans. The Spanish in 1492, and the Portuguese eight years later, were the first European countries to encounter the indigenous peoples of the Americas. The Spanish dominated the exploration, conquest, and colonization of the Americas in the sixteenth century as Hernán Cortés conquered the Aztec Empire, 1519-1521, and Francisco Pizarro the Inca Empire a decade later.

3.3.1 Early Relations in the Caribbean, Mesoamerica, and Peru

When Christopher Columbus sailed west in 1492, he had no idea that he would encounter a world and a people never before seen by Europeans. He had no expectations about the people who actually swam out to meet his ships; he thought, after all, that he had reached the shores of the East Indies. Columbus kept a journal of his travels in which he recorded his first impressions of the peoples of the Caribbean Islands. According to this journal, the natives who greeted the three caravels,

> were very friendly to us, and [we] perceived that they could be much more easily converted to our holy faith by gentle means than by force. I presented them with some red caps, and strings of beads to wear upon the neck, and many other trifles of small value, wherewith they were much delighted, and became wonderfully attached to us. Afterwards they came swimming to the boats, bringing parrots, balls of cotton thread, javelins, and many other things which they exchanged for articles...which trade was carried on with the utmost good will. But they seemed on the whole to me, to be a very poor people.[6]

Columbus went on to remark that the people were "mostly naked" even the women, though he admitted that he had seen only one woman. The natives appeared to have few weapons and, in fact, lived a very simple life. Not only had they no weapons, they apparently had not seen any, as Columbus remarked that when he "showed them swords... they grasped by the blades, and cut themselves through ignorance. They have no iron, their javelins being without it, and nothing more than sticks, though some have fish-bones or other things at the ends."[7] The experience of the Spaniards on the other islands in the Caribbean was similar. In his entry of October 13, 1492, Columbus recalled that "The natives are an inoffensive people, and so desirous to possess anything they saw with us, that they kept swimming off to the ships with whatever they could find."[8]

The experience of Álvar Núñez Cabeza de Vaca and his men in North America mirrored the experiences of his countrymen in Meso- and South America. Writing in 1542, he praised the hospitality of the Indians of Florida:

> AS THE SUN ROSE next morning, the Indians appeared as they promised, bringing an abundance of fish and of certain roots which taste like nuts, some bigger than walnuts, some smaller, mostly grubbed from the water with great labor.
>
> That evening they came again with more fish and roots and brought their women and children to look at us. They thought themselves rich with the little bells and beads we gave them, and they repeated their visits on other days.[9]

Not surprisingly, Bartholomew de las Casas, an outspoken proponent of fair treatment of the Indians, echoed the comments of Columbus and Cabeza de Vaca in describing his early encounters on the Caribbean islands: "On one occasion they came out ten leagues from a great settlement to meet us, bringing provisions and gifts, and when we met them they gave us a great quantity of fish and bread and other victuals."[10]

Hernán Cortés, who would ultimately kidnap Moctezuma II, the emperor of the Aztec Empire, and raze the capital city of Tenochtitlan, was warmly greeted by the Mexica ruler. According to Cortés, Moctezuma remarked: "We believe that the King of Spain is our natural lord..."[11] In his second letter to Charles V, Cortés remarked that the people of the Aztec Empire appeared willing to accept Christianity as the true religion, saying, "if I would instruct them in these matters, and make them understand the true faith, they would follow my directions, as being for the best."[12] Furthermore, the natives were evidently passive when Cortés "purified" the temples by "removing the old idols and replacing them with symbols of Christianity." He forbade the natives to continue the practice of human sacrifice to Huitzilopochtli, a primary god, and was somewhat surprised when they complied. He wrote: "[D]uring the whole period of my abode in that city, they were never seen to kill or sacrifice a human being."[13]

An Aztec Account of the Conquest of Mexico describes the first encounter of Cortés and Moctezuma this way:

> Then he [Moctezuma] stood up to welcome Cortés; he came forward, bowed his head low and addressed him in these words: "Our lord, you are weary. The journey has tired you, but now you have arrived on the earth. You have come to your city, Mexico. You have come here to sit on your throne, to sit under its canopy."
>
> According to this same account, on another occasion Moctezuma remarked: "The kings who have gone before, your representatives, guarded [the Empire] and preserved it for your coming."[14]

Cortés Conquers the Aztec Empire

Hernán Cortés landed on the coast at Veracruz on Good Friday, April 22, 1519; just over two years later, on August 13, 1521, the Aztec capital of Tenochtitlan surrendered to him. The events that took place during these two short years were documented in a number of chronicles, of which the best known are the letters Cortés wrote to King Charles I of Spain, who was also Charles V, the Holy Roman Emperor, and the *True History of the Conquest of Mexico* by Bernal Díaz del Castillo. Until recently these two works, along with a few others also written by Spaniards, were almost the only basis on which historians have judged the conquest of one of the greatest civilizations in pre-Columbian America. These documents tell the story only from the point of view of the Spanish, but now another source has been added to the mix. *Broken Spears: An Aztec Account of the Conquest of Mexico*, draws from indigenous accounts to present a different picture of the Spanish and their relations with the Indians.

It was not surprising that the Aztec Empire would fall to the Spanish, despite the fact that the Spanish soldiers under Cortés numbered 600 and were faced by an Aztec army of thousands. One reason for the Spanish success was due to their military tactics and weaponry. The Mexica people, of whom Moctezuma was the head, and their allies fought with bows and arrows and spears, while the Spanish were protected by steel armor, wielded steel swords, and had the advantage of attacking on horseback. In addition, the Spanish found unexpected allies in the tribes that were previously forced to pay tribute to the Aztec Empire. At least one group, the Totonacs, greeted the Spanish as liberators. No small part of Spanish success came from the inadvertent introduction of smallpox into Tenochtitlan resulting in the deaths of thousands in the city in 1521.

For many decades, historians argued that another factor could be found in Aztec religious beliefs that Quetzalcoatl, a white-skinned god, would, at an undisclosed time, arrive in the Empire.[15] Indeed, according to Cortés, when Moctezuma first encountered the conquistador, he remarked, "We have always held that those who are descended from [Quetzalcoatl] would come and conquer this land and take us as his vassals."[16] Many observers at the time remarked that Mesoamerican natives, like those of the Caribbean Islands, believed the white men to be gods. Bernal Díaz offered an explanation about the origin of this belief when he commented in his *True History of the Conquest of Spain*, "The Indians thought the rider and the horse were the same body, as they had never seen a horse."[17]

However, over the last twenty years, Latin American historians have largely discredited this "white god" theory. The myth appears to have originated about forty years after the conquest in documents such as the Florentine Codex, an Aztec history produced by young Aztec men in Spanish schools. In these documents, the Spanish are referred to as *teotls*, a word that can mean either god or demon in Nahuatl, the spoken language of the Mexica.[18]

In 1519, Hernán Cortés entered the Aztec capital city of Tenochtitlan, awed by its splendor. It was, he remarked, "so big and so remarkable [as to be]...almost unbelievable, for the city is much larger than Granada and very much stronger...with many more people than Granada had when it was taken...[It] is as large as Seville or Cordova."[19] Cortés was aided in his communication with Moctezuma and his nobility by a slave presented to him by the natives of Tabasco in 1519, La Malinche, who was fluent in the Nahuatl language spoken by the Aztecs.

Figure 3.1 Moctezuma II and Hernán Cortés | Hernán Cortés, the Spanish conquistador, is famous for his conquest of the Aztecs of Mexico and the execution of the emperor Moctezuma II.

Author: Unknown
Source: Library of Congress

Despite their advantages, the Spanish did not defeat the Aztec coalition outright; rather they experienced a resounding defeat at the hands of the Indians in 1520 and were forced to flee the capital city. Those who were captured by the Aztecs were sacrificed at the pyramid of Huitzilopochtli; this occurred on the night of June 30-July 1, 1520, called *La Noche Triste* (The Sad Night) by the Spaniards.

But this defeat was only a temporary setback for the Spanish, who received aid from an unexpected source: in 1521, smallpox struck Tenochtitlan. Miguel León-Portilla includes an Aztec account in which a native bemoaned the condition of the city's inhabitants: "We were covered with agonizing sores from head to foot. The illness was so dreadful that no one could walk or move."[20] The disease had been introduced into the city by a Spanish slave, left behind when the Europeans retreated. Those struck by the disease were too weak to move, and even if they survived, were in no condition to cultivate food. The inhabitants of the city were literally starving to death.

Figure 3.2 Ritual Sacrifice | Ritual sacrifice was widely practiced by the Indians of Mesoamerica. According to Spanish accounts, the Aztecs ripped out the hearts of war captives in an effort to appease such gods as Huitzilopochtli. Such sacrifice took place on La Noche Triste, according to Spanish sources.

Author: Codex Magliabechiano, artist unknown
Source: Library of Congress

On August 21, 1521, the Spanish re-entered the city, overwhelmed its last defenses, declared victory, and accepted the surrender of the remaining native warriors. The conditions they encountered were horrifying. Bernal Díaz wrote some years later that the Spaniards "...found the houses full of corpses, and some poor Mexicans still in [the houses] who could not move away...The city looked as though it had been ploughed up. The roots of any edible greenery had been dug out, boiled and eaten, and they had even cooked the bark of some of the trees."[21]

After the defeat of the Aztecs, Cortés proceeded to execute Moctezuma, level Tenochtitlan, and begin to build what is now Mexico City. So thorough was the destruction of the city that few Aztec ruins remain today.

The wanton destruction of Tenochtitlan symbolized the Spanish attitude toward the Americas, which were for conquest, ownership, and exploitation. The contemporary accounts of Cortés, Bernal Díaz, and the Spanish historian Francisco López de Gómara reflected the attitude of the Crown: the Americas were a new Spanish Empire and the natives, Spanish vassals.

The Spanish and the Incas of Peru

The first Spanish to meet the Incas of Peru were impressed by their social and economic system, which some historians describe as an early form of socialism. Pedro de Cieza de León, Spanish conquistador and chronicler of Peru, commented on the Inca practice of tribute and crop sharing: "As this kingdom was so vast, in each of the many provinces there were storehouses that were filled during years of plenty and opened in time of need." He went on to explain:

> No one [was tolerated] who was lazy or tried to live by the work of others; everyone had to work. Thus on certain days each lord went to his lands and took the plow in hand and cultivated the earth, and did other things. Even the Incas [the rulers] themselves did this to set an example. And under their system there was none [who did not work] in all the kingdom, for, if he had his health, he worked and lacked for nothing; and if he was ill, he received what he needed from the storehouses.

The economic system was both well organized and egalitarian; each village was required to contribute grain to support the whole and "no rich man could deck himself out in more finery than the poor, or wear different clothing, except the rulers and the headmen, who, to maintain their dignity, were allowed great freedom and privilege."[22] Unlike the case in Mexico and the Caribbean, there was no honeymoon period in the relations between Francisco Pizarro, who eventually conquered the Inca Empire, and the natives of Peru; the relationship between the Spanish and Incas was antagonistic from the outset.[23]

Francisco Pizarro Conquers the Inca Empire

Long before the Inca enterprise was undertaken by Francisco Pizarro and his men, word had come to the Spanish in Mesoamerica about the wealth and riches of cultures in the South. In 1529, Francisco Pizarro, who had already undertaken two unsuccessful expeditions to South America in 1524 and 1526, was appointed governor of Peru by Charles V in an agreement known as the *Capitulación de Toledo*. Pizarro arrived in Peru in 1532 with 168 men, sixty-two of whom were horse soldiers. Hernán do de Soto was sent as an envoy from Pizarro to Atahualpa, the Inca emperor, to assure him that the Spanish meant no harm and came in friendship and with the best of intentions. Atahualpa agreed to meet Pizarro and his forces the following day at Cajamarca in the highlands of Peru.

On November 16, 1532, when Atahualpa and his 7,000-man, unarmed escort arrived, the Spanish, who were positioned around the town square, opened fire and 2,000 Inca were killed outright. Pizarro then rounded up and killed the Inca nobles. The Spaniards on horses rode through the carnage, swinging steel swords, and decapitating the bodies. Atahualpa was taken prisoner, and though the Incas came to Pizarro with mounds of gold for his ransom (which Pizarro gleefully accepted), Pizarro had Atahualpa executed, which was similar to the approach Cortés practiced in Mexico.

Once the conquest was complete, Pizarro appointed a nominal ruler of the Inca Empire, and in 1535, with his control of Peru consolidated, he established a new capital city now known as Lima. He was assassinated in 1541 by the son of a long-time associate Diego de Almagro. He was laid to rest in the Lima Cathedral.

Figure 3.3 Fransisco Pizarro | Francisco Pizarro, using trickery and deceit, conquered the Incas of Peru in 1532 and executed the Inca emperor, Atahualpa.

Author: D.M. Kelsey
Source: *Columbus and the New World Heroes of Discovery and Conquest*

The Portuguese in Brazil

The first Portuguese to reach the Americas were the men accompanying Pedro Cabral, who, when he sailed from Portugal in 1500, was headed to India. He and his ships were blown off course and ended up on the shores of Brazil, which he claimed for the King of Portugal, Manuel I. Cabral named the new land "The Island of the True Cross", but remained in Brazil only ten days before heading on to India. Cabral's claim of Brazil on behalf of the Portuguese Crown was facilitated by the *Treaty of Tordesillas* created by Pope Alexander VI in 1494 to settle competing claims to Atlantic discoveries. An imaginary line was drawn through the Americas; land west of the line went to Spain and east of the line to Portugal.

Although there were some commonalities between the Spanish experience in Mexico and Peru, and the Portuguese experience in Brazil, in the latter there were no wealthy, urbanized cultures like Tenochtitlan and the Inca cities of Cuzco and Quito. Rather, many of the 2.4 million Brazilian natives were either nomadic or semi-sedentary. According to some historians, the initial contacts were "generally peaceful." However, others point out that when the Portuguese came in contact with the forest peoples of the interior, like the Tupi, the Portuguese "attacked and enslaved each tribal group of several hundreds, one by one, in bloody skirmishes" because the only way to subdue the natives was to kill them all.[24]

After the Brazilian natives were subdued, sugar plantations sprang up along the coast of Brazil, but their numbers were not significant. However, while the Portuguese presence in Brazil remained small, the Spanish settled in large numbers in Mexico and Peru, which remained the wealthiest and most-populous areas in the New World for 300 years.[25]

3.3.2 Before You Move On...

Key Concepts

Spain and Portugal were the first countries in the new wave of exploration of the fifteenth and sixteenth centuries to arrive and establish settlements in the New World. Coming almost a century before the first permanent English settlement at Jamestown in 1607, the colonies of the Iberian countries were not originally intended to be permanent. Eventually, these settlements did in fact become permanent and, with the success in mining gold and silver, their European populations increased in size. But in the course of establishing control, the Spanish had to contend with two well-established New World empires: the Aztec Empire in Mesoamerica and the Inca Empire in Peru. The conquest of the Aztecs established patterns of conquest that were later utilized in the defeat of the Incas. Recruiting native allies and kidnapping local leaders allowed the Spanish to control power from within as they focused their efforts on the strongest group in the area, rather than fighting multiple wars against many groups. In addition, the Spanish inadvertently introduced European diseases like smallpox, which greatly weakened local groups.

Test Yourself

1. Which of the follow was well known for his criticism of the Europeans' treatment of the Indians of Meso- and South America?

    a. Álvar Núñez Cabeza de Vaca

    b. Hernán Cortés

    c. Bartholomew de las Casas

    d. Pedro Cabral

2. The *Treaty of Tordesillas*

a. Divided the New World between the Spanish and the Portuguese.

b. Specified that the *encomienda* system should be disbanded.

c. Allowed the use of Incas in the mines of Peru.

d. Formally recognized the conquest of the Aztec Empire by Cortés and his soldiers.

3. The majority of the natives killed in the exploration period were slaughtered by the Europeans who possessed superior weapons.

a. True

b. False

4. The first explorer to reach Brazil and claim it for the throne of Portugal was:

a. Christopher Columbus

b. Pedro Cabral

c. Ferdinand Magellan

d. Jacques Cartier

5. Recruiting native allies played an important role in the Spanish conquest of the Aztec.

a. True

b. False

6. The myth of Quetzalcoatl relies on sources that are contemporaneous with the conquest of the Aztec.

a. True

b. False

See page 86 for answers

3.4 CONTROL: THE IBERIAN NATIONS MANAGE THEIR NEW WORLD TERRITORIES

Three decades after Columbus's "discovery" of the New World, the Spanish Crown began centralizing its control of the new territories. In 1524, the Council of the Indies was created, which oversaw developments in New Spain until the close of the colonial period. The Council was located in the mother country.[26]

New Spain was divided into four viceroyalties: New Spain (Mexico, Central America, and California, Arizona, New Mexico, and Texas), whose capital was Mexico City; Peru (Peru, Chile, Bolivia, and Ecuador), whose capital city was Lima; New Granada (Venezuela, Colombia, Panama, and later Ecuador), whose capital city was Bogota; and La Plata (Argentina, Uruguay, and Paraguay) whose capital was Buenos Aires.

Each viceroyalty was overseen by a viceroy, who exercised ultimate power over his viceroyalty in a manner reminiscent of a European monarch. The viceroy was also in charge of the *Audiencia*, a twelve to fifteen judge advisory council and court of law. At the end of each term, the viceroy was subjected to a *Residencia*, or a judicial review of his term in office. All appeals went directly to the Council of the Indies.

The provinces were under the control of royal officials, the *corregidores (*governors whose territory was known as a *corregimiento),* the *captains general (*whose provinces were known as *captaincies general),* or *alcaldes mayores,* who held political and judicial power. The first governors of the provinces were the conquistadores themselves; this system did not last past the first decade. Most towns had a *cabildo* or town council, though these units did not represent democracy in the sense of the New England town meetings, as power was lodged in the hands of the royal officials. *Adelantados* were commanders of units of conquest or the governors of a frontier or newly-conquered province.[27]

The economic systems of Spanish America were also strictly-controlled hierarchical and economic endeavors. Spanish holdings were divided into mining zones when gold and silver was discovered and subsequently became extremely important to the Spanish economy. The rule known as the *quinto* specified that one-fifth of all precious metals mined in the colonies was to go to the Spanish Crown. Similar restrictions were placed on trade when there were only two designated ports through which colonial trade could go.

Native laborers were provided through the *encomienda* system (called the *mita* in Portuguese areas), which was a grant from the King of Spain given to an individual mine or plantation (*hacienda*) owner for a specific number of natives to work in any capacity in which they were needed; the *encomenderos,* or owners, had total control over these workers. Ostensibly, the purpose was to protect the natives from enemy tribes and instruct them in Christian beliefs and practices. In reality, the *encomienda* system was hard to distinguish from chattel slavery. The *Repartimiento,* which granted land and/or Indians to settlers for a specified period of time, was a similar system.

3.4.1 The Portuguese Settlements

In Brazil, economic development centered on sugar rather than silver and gold; thus, the main money maker for the Crown of Portugal was taxes on sugar. As the Indians were subdued, increasing numbers of sugar plantations emerged along the Atlantic coast. Those Portuguese who were wealthy enough to own a sugar mill as well as a plantation, the *senhores de engenho* or "lords of the mill," were at the apex of the social system. They oversaw production by the slaves and freemen who lived in and around the mill, which was the social center of any area.

Probably because the sugar taxes did not generate a large amount of revenue, the Portuguese Crown did not put forth an effort to create a similar highly-centralized system in New Spain until the mid-sixteenth century. Portuguese kings in the early sixteenth century, like John II in the fifteenth century, gave "captaincies," or administrative units, to wealthy Portuguese who were willing to settle in the New World. Those who held captaincies were known as "proprietors" or *donatários.*

Most of the labor on the sugar plantations came from African and Indian slaves, though the latter were especially resistant to control by the Europeans. In fact, many of the captaincies failed in part because of the resistance of the Indians. Because of ongoing rebellions, the Portuguese king in 1549 created a royal governor, or captain general, for Brazil; the powers of the *donatários* were consequently limited. The captain general was an office similar to the viceroys in New Spain.

During the Iberian Union (1580-1640, a period when Portugal and Spain were ruled by a single dynasty), the Spanish created a *Conselho da India* (similar to the Spanish Council for the Indies) to regulate the Portuguese colonies. After Portugal regained its independence from Spain in 1640, this structure was maintained.

The local provinces were under the control of governors, who were appointed for three-year terms; their military and political power was absolute. Before assuming the position of governor, a candidate had to present his qualifications to the *Senado da Câmara*, or town council. Judicial affairs were conducted by the *Ouvidor* and *Juiz de Fora,* who, like the governors, were appointed to three-year terms. Seven officials made up the *Junta*, or council, which decided the policies of the individual captaincy. The *Junta* consisted of the governor, the judicial officials, an attorney general, the secretary of the treasury, and two ports officials.

Except for the sugar-holding areas along the northeast coast, most of the remainder of Brazil was sparsely settled through the sixteenth century. The Amazon was surrounded by rainforests, and the areas beyond the sugar coast were considered "dirt-poor cattle country."[28] Despite the efforts of the Jesuits to improve the treatment and conditions of the indigenous people, disease was rampant; the Indians, who had no resistance to smallpox and influenza, died in droves. By 1600, Africans, who had developed immunity to European diseases over centuries of interaction between the two continents, were replacing indigenous peoples as slaves on the sugar plantations.

3.4.2 The Indians in the Iberian Colonies

There was a good deal of mistreatment of the American natives by both the Spanish and the Portuguese. Because the Catholic Church followed the adventurers, it was inevitable that attention would be drawn to the plight of the "pobres Indios" (as Bartholomew de las Casas referred to them). De las Casas is perhaps the most famous of the reformers, though he came to the New World originally as an adventurer and received an *encomienda* from the Spanish Crown. By 1514, however, he had had a change of heart and became an advocate for the fair treatment of the natives. Mainly as the result of his activities, in 1537, Pope Alexander VI issued a dictate stressing that the indigenous people were just that—people—who were not inferior to any other group. In 1542, the Spanish Crown issued the *New Laws of the Indies for the Good Treatment and Preservation of the Indians,* which limited and eventually ended the *encomienda* system.

Similarly, in Brazil, because the expanding plantation economy demanded a greater and greater supply of cheap labor, slave hunting became a lucrative profession. As the supply of coastal natives depleted, the *bandeirantes* (or "men of the banner") pushed further west and south in search of new sources of labor. As was the case in New Spain, one of the voices that spoke out against the exploitation of the natives was that of a Jesuit, Father Joseph de Anchieta, who wrote:

> The *bandeirantes* go into the interior and deceive these people [the Indians], inviting them to go to the coast, where they would live in villages as they did in their present lands...On arrival at the coast, [the Portuguese] would divide the Indians among themselves, some taking the women, others their husbands and still others the children, and they sell them.[29]

In 1549, as part of its effort to tighten control and to clarify relations with the American natives, the Portuguese Crown stipulated that military campaigns to "pacify" or subdue the natives would be accompanied by "evangelical campaigns of conversion."[30] In the 1570s the Portuguese Crown released a series of law intended to define the legal status of Indians in its colonies. Indians could still be enslaved, but only as the result of a "just war or for practicing cannibalism."[31]

Figure 3.4 Bartholomew de las Casas | Bartholomew de las Casas, though originally a conquistador himself, became an ardent proponent of fair treatment of "los pobres Indios" (the poor Indians) and wrote widely on their behalf.

Author: Constantino Brumidi
Source: USCapitol Photostream (Flickr)

3.4.3 Before You Move On...

Key Concepts

The years immediately following the conquest of the Aztec and Inca empires were a time of figuring things out and exploring options for the Spanish and Portuguese. They faced great challenges in ruling over colonies far from the mother country, and the time and distance involved in governance necessitated the establishment of institutions of rule and a colonial bureaucracy. Labor quickly became a defining need in the colonies, and many of the emerging policies and laws focused on the issue of the indigenous peoples. As the sixteenth century progressed, Portugal and Spain, now under one rule, began to officially address the status of the Indians and to recognize that the abuse of the earliest years must be rectified if peace were to be attainable in the Iberian colonies.

Test Yourself

1. The system that helped provide labor for the Spanish mines and sugar plantations was the:
   a. *Quinto*
   b. *Audiencia*
   c. *Encomienda*
   d. *Residencia*

2. The Brazilian economy was largely based on

a. Sugar

b. Coffee

c. Silver

d. Indigo

3. The ____________ was part of the bureaucracy of Spanish rule and oversaw developments in New Spain until the close of the colonial period.

a. *Encomienda*

b. *Mita*

c. Council of the Indies

d. *Donatários*

See page 87 for answers

3.5 ALTERNATE MODELS OF CONTROL: THE FRENCH AND DUTCH IN THE AMERICAS

Because Spain and Portugal were the first to establish colonies in the Americas, the patterns that they established served as the first models of colonization and control of American colonies. The biggest challenge that they faced in administering their colonial holdings were those of time and space. Communication between colony and mother country was difficult, and it took months for messages, orders, and news to travel across the Atlantic. The distance between Europe and the Americas played a very important role in shaping colonial administration along with patterns and methods of imperial control. The ways in which the Iberian powers politically and economically administered their colonial holdings were also a reflection of the relationship between mother country and colony. The American holdings were settlement colonies that would be shaped in the image of Spain and Portugal. Spaniards and Portuguese came from the mother country to populate the colonies; they desired to recreate their homeland in their new land, and so sought (sometimes unsuccessfully) to live in a Spanish or Portuguese manner. As a result, they set up a direct system of governance that exerted tight control of the colonies. The American colonies were to economically benefit the mother country; thus, colonial trade was also tightly controlled.

When other European powers became active in the colonization of the American hemisphere, political and economic models of control were similarly a result of time, distance, and the relationship between mother country and colony. The French and Dutch both provide very different models of control in the Americas than their Iberian counterparts. Both of these nations took a primarily economic interest in the American hemisphere; both shaped their models of colonial administration largely around trade. For the French, this meant engaging in the fur trade in the North American frontier in the Great Lakes region and later along the Mississippi River. The Dutch established their foothold in the Caribbean, a move which proved to be very lucrative.

Politically, both France and the Netherlands wanted to weaken the Spanish (and to a lesser extent, the Portuguese) hold on the Americas. The French actively contested Spanish power by trying to establish a colony in Florida, a strategic area which would allow them to interrupt Spanish shipping lanes coming north out of the Caribbean. The Dutch were much less overt in their contestation of Iberian power; instead of establishing large, rival colonies that encroached on the Spanish, they instead concentrated on weakening their Spanish competitors through piracy. The Dutch took on the Portuguese more directly, conquering small but important lands in Brazil, wresting these areas from Portuguese control.

3.5.1 The French in the Americas: Canada and Florida

The French were most active in North America as participants in a thriving fur trade. However, French activity in the New World did not begin as successfully; the earliest French expeditions to North America, and particularly in Canada, were largely unsuccessful ventures. The first voyages, led by Jacques Cartier between 1534 and 1542, established contact with local peoples, including the Huron and Iroquois. They were eager to trade with Cartier; in fact, on Cartier's second voyage, the headman of the Iroquoian town of Stadacona tried to prevent Cartier from leaving so that his village, through control of Cartier, could by extension control and dominate the French-Indian trade. For the French, these early voyages established that the area contained no natural or human resources that proved to be valuable to them at the time. As a result, the French retreated from Canada and spent much of the next fifty years trying to establish themselves elsewhere in the Americas, most notably in Florida in 1564. Eventually, the French came back to Canada to participate in the developing trade in beaver pelts, and came to successfully dominate much of the interior trade.

The French Struggle to Control Florida

The French next turned their attention to the south and towards taking action to weaken the Spanish political hold on the Americas. In 1564, René Goulaine de Laudonnière led an expedition to Florida, establishing Fort Caroline at the mouth of the St. John's River in modern Jacksonville. Florida was a strategic and valuable area for its proximity to the rich Spanish Caribbean. The French hoped to establish a successful settlement in Florida, and thus a stepping-off point to contest Spanish power in the Caribbean. A foothold in Florida could also provide the opportunity to weaken the Spanish Crown through piracy; the prevailing currents and winds of the Caribbean and Atlantic ensured Spanish shipping lanes, including the transport of the treasure fleets, traveled up along the Florida coast before venturing out across the Atlantic. The settlement at Fort Caroline was also a reflection of French concerns at home; religious tensions between Catholics and Huguenots (Protestants) had intensified. Many of the Huguenots had been cast out of France; some came to Fort Caroline to seek refuge.

The Spanish, hearing of the French incursion into Spanish territory, established their own colony slightly south of Fort Caroline at San Agustín (St. Augustine). The expedition was led by Pedro Menéndez de Avilés, who later became *adelantado* (the governing official) of *la Florida,* which encompassed much of North America, from the Chesapeake Bay south to the tip of the mainland and west to modern-day New Mexico. Spanish attempts to establish a settlement in Florida had been ineffective in the past, but the St. Augustine settlement proved successful, in part because of the relationship the Spaniards cultivated with the Timucua Indians. As a result, St. Augustine is the oldest continuously-settled European settlement in the continental United States.

Figure 3.5 Pedro Menéndez de Avilés | Pedro Menéndez de Avilés, founder of St. Augustine.

Artist: Francisco de Paula Martí
Source: Library of Congress

In September of 1565, Menéndez de Avilés led a force against the French settlement at Fort Caroline. The Spanish quickly overwhelmed the French forces, killing many of the men, but sparing most of the women and children. Twenty-five of the Frenchmen escaped, making their way along the Florida coast. The Spanish caught up to them about fifteen miles outside of St. Augustine, where Menéndez de Avilés ordered the men executed, securing Spanish dominance in Florida. The Catholic Spanish offered the Protestant Huguenots the chance to renounce their "apostate" faith and embrace Catholicism; their refusal was part of what sealed their fate. The massacre of the French settlers and soldiers marked the end of the French experiment in Florida and their attempts to undermine Spanish political control in the area.

Back to Canada—Control and the Fur Trade

Defeated in Florida, the French turned their efforts back to Canada at the turn of the century. In 1603, Samuel de Champlain established the colony of New France in modern-day Quebec. Champlain was well aware of the value of trade with local groups, and established alliances with groups such as the Algonquin and the Huron. This alliance shaped local patterns over the long term; when Champlain allied himself with the Huron, their long-standing enemies, the Iroquois, allied themselves with the British.

Few French came to the settlement at New France. In part, this was because New France was primarily a trading operation rather than a settlement intended to establish a new, growing colony. Champlain was very conscious of how his traders interacted with local peoples, and established many rules of conduct that focused on French traders fitting into indigenous groups. For example, traders were to rely on Indians for food and support, living by the cultural rules of the local Indians, and were to fully honor indigenous ritual and ceremonial practices. Champlain, too, was held to this standard. For example, the Huron and other Northeastern groups did not see the French/Indian relationship as merely economic; it was a relationship that was both economic and political. Champlain found himself drawn into a war with the Iroquois after a year of trading with the Huron.

The powerful local groups were eager to exploit the Europeans and their technology to their own ends in their own wars.

Although the French mission in Canada was primarily economic, they did try to Christianize some groups of Indians, most notably the Huron. In 1615, the first Jesuits (a monastic order of the Catholic Church) arrived in New France to go out among the Indians—particularly the Huron—to Christianize them. Over the next fifty years, the Jesuits worked among the Huron, learning their language and their culture. The efforts to Christianize the Huron were largely unsuccessful, with very few converts: perhaps less than ten converts in fifty years. However, The Jesuit experience in Canada is very significant as they wrote copious amounts of letters back to the Order in France, detailing the practices and beliefs of the Huron. Much of the information we have about the Huron and other groups in the Quebec area come from these letters.

3.5.2 The Dutch in the Americas

The Netherlands won independence from Spain at the end of the European Thirty Years' War. During the war and its aftermath, the Netherlands had emerged as the most important trading center in Europe, bringing great power and riches to the new nation. The Dutch had a long history in seafaring, mapmaking, and boatbuilding, and quickly entered the global spice trade competition. In 1602, the Dutch East India Company (DEIC) was founded. The DEIC was financed by shares that established the first modern stock exchange, making it the first multinational corporation. The company was granted a two decade long monopoly to carry out colonial activities in Asia on behalf of the Dutch government. As a result, the DEIC possessed quasi-governmental powers, including the powers to wage wars, coin money, negotiate treaties, and establish colonies. The DEIC also possessed judicial powers, and was allowed to imprison and execute convicts.

The DEIC was by far the most successful European operator in Asian trade. They established colonies throughout the Malaccas, including the modern-day city of Jakarta, Indonesia. These port colonies allowed them to dominate the trade from within. Outside of the spice trade, the DEIC began a trade monopoly with Japan in 1640 at the trading post of Dejima, further empowering the Netherlands.

In 1652, the DEIC established an African colony near the Cape of Good Hope. The settlement of Cape Town was originally intended to be a way station for ships to resupply on the way to and from the Spice Islands. Instead, Cape Town quickly transformed into a permanent and growing colony known as Cape Colony. It grew into a sizable colony, and became one of the most developed European colonies outside of the Americas. Dutch farmers displaced local groups such as the pastoralist Khoikhoi. The colony's strategic location meant that almost every ship travelling from Europe to Asia stopped in Cape Town to resupply.

The Dutch were involved in the Americas in two main areas: the Caribbean and modern-day New York. By far, the Caribbean was the more important, richer area because of its sugar production. In the 1620s and 1630s, large fleets employed by the Dutch West Indies Company (DWIC) dominated the Caribbean. During these decades, the company was an instrument of war as well as a business; it waged war, but tried to turn a profit in the meantime. In the 1620s, much of Europe, including the Netherlands, was at war. The Republic of the Netherlands set up the DWIC in 1621 primarily to carry this European war into the Caribbean through piracy and conquest.

Much like the Dutch East India Company (DEIC), the DWIC was authorized to carry out trade and set up colonies. Unlike the DEIC, the DWIC focused on naval and military ambitions. The two companies were set up to function in tandem; the state assigned the DWIC a twenty-five year monopoly in every territory not given to the DEIC, including the Caribbean and the Americas. Like the DEIC, the DWIC's stock was listed on the Amsterdam exchange; this reflects that the Dutch colonial experience was primarily an economic one. Through the activities of the DEIC and the DWIC, the Netherlands sought to empower their nation through control of markets on a global scale, from Indonesia to the Caribbean.

In 1624, the DWIC launched large-scale attacks in the Caribbean with three goals in mind. First, they sought to occupy the rich Portuguese sugar plantations in Brazil. Second, they tried to conquer the Portuguese slave-trading ports in West Africa, another lucrative trade. Finally, they sought to seize the treasure fleets that carried Peruvian and Mexican gold from Havana to Seville.

In all these efforts, the DWIC enjoyed initial victories but later failed. The Dutch conquered large parts of Brazil in the early 1630s and captured Portuguese slave-trading forts in Africa in the late 1630s. For a brief time, the DWIC successfully controlled the international sugar trade and the Atlantic slave trade. However in 1645, Portuguese Catholics in Brazil rose up in revolt and swept the Protestant Dutch out. While they were busy in Brazil, the Dutch were likewise busy in the Caribbean. They plundered Spanish merchant shipping, tried to capture the Spanish treasure fleets, and ran highly-successful smuggling operations in Spanish ports. The Dutch became the economic powerhouse of the Caribbean; the Spanish feared them, and English and French colonists often would prefer to trade with Dutch merchants (for their prices and reliability) than with their own mother countries. The Dutch, in great part because of the success of the DWIC, successfully contested Spain's economic hold over the Caribbean. Politically, the Dutch were less successful, able to maintain only six small islands of the Lesser Antilles as colonies.

The greatest economic victory for the Dutch came in 1628 when DWIC ships managed to trap the entire Mexican treasure fleet in Matanzas Bay off Cuba. They took an enormous treasure in gold, silver, and goods, and the company paid its shareholders a cash dividend of seventy percent in 1629. Until 1635, the company continued to mount large and costly expeditions to pillage Spanish settlements and shipping in the West Indies. Overall, the DWIC sent out 800 ships with 67,000 men between 1621 and 1637. But, the take was meager, and the shares sank on the Amsterdam exchange. However, the company's attacks, together with those of smaller fleets of Dutch, French, and English pirates did succeed in destroying Spanish commerce and communications. From 1625 to 1635, the Dutch maritime force changed the balance of power in the Caribbean, making it possible for Dutch traders to control most of the region's commerce for decades.

3.5.3 Before You Move On...

Key Concepts

Both the French and Dutch provided alternate models of colonial control in the Americas. Each of these countries sought to establish a foothold in the Americas through trade and commerce. Both sought to weaken the Spanish hold on the American hemisphere. After experimenting with colonization in Canada, the French attempted to directly contest Spain's claim on *la Florida* (and thus their political control of North America) by establishing the colony of Fort Caroline, a move which proved to be a dismal failure. In the wake of their failure to secure Florida, the French established their main foothold in the New World in New France in Canada. French activities in the New World focused mostly on trade with groups such as the Huron and Algonquin in the fur trade. Because there were relatively few French in the colony, Samuel de Champlain's policies for French traders encouraged them to closely associate themselves with local groups.

The Dutch became the most important force in the spice trade under the aegis of the Dutch East India Company. Established in 1602, the DEIC was the first multinational company, and possessed quasi-governmental powers. The DEIC established trading posts and colonies in modern-day Indonesia and South Africa (Cape Colony). These ports established seats of power for the Dutch to take control and amass great wealth from the lucrative spice trade. The Dutch established their presence in the Caribbean through the Dutch West Indies Company, an institution that was authorized to carry out trade and set up colonies. They approached the Caribbean with three goals in mind: occupy the Portuguese sugar plantations in Brazil, conquer the Portuguese slave-trading ports in West Africa, and seize the treasure fleets that carried Peruvian and Mexican gold from Havana to Seville. The Dutch were able to control parts of Brazil's sugar trade and the West African slave ports for only a short time. They proved much more successful in controlling both legitimate and black market Caribbean trade, becoming the most powerful shipping empire in the Americas. The Dutch also practiced piracy in the Caribbean, and captured a Spanish treasure fleet in 1628, a major blow to the Spanish.

Test Yourself

1. __________'s expeditions in Canada established the local Indians' interest in French trade when the leader of Stadacona tried to detain him in order to control French and Indian trade networks.

   a. Samuel de Champlain

   b. Stadacona

   c. Jacques Cartier

   d. René Goulaine de Laudonnière

2. The French settlement in Florida was settled by Protestants unwelcome in France known as ______.

a. Huguenots

b. Anabaptists

c. Apostates

d. Catholics

3. The Jesuits

a. were a group of missionaries.

b. were largely unsuccessful in converting local Indians.

c. were a great source of knowledge about the Indians of New France.

d. all of the above

4. The Dutch practiced which of the following in establishing themselves as an economic powerhouse in the Caribbean?

a. legitimate trade

b. piracy

c. smuggling

d. all of the above

5. The Dutch East India Company possessed the power to

a. establish colonies

b. punish criminals

c. negotiate treaties

d. wage war

e. all of the above

See page 87 for answers

3.6 Conclusion

The significance of the Columbian Exchange and sharing of foordways, technology, and cultures that resulted can hardly be overstated. A profound economic revolution shook both hemispheres as the influx of crops, diseases, animals, and metals to the Old World changed patterns of trade, the medium of exchange, and ideas about the use and distribution of wealth.

Similarly, traditional ideas about the structure and inhabitants of the world were put aside as Europeans and Indians encountered and ultimately learned from each other.

Ethnicities were intertwined as Europeans, Africans, Indians, and their children created a complicated hierarchy of race and class in the colonies. The world had been turned upside down, perhaps for the first, if not for the last, time

Early Spanish control of the American hemisphere developed from their discovery and early exploration of the region. During this period, Spanish experiences largely defined early European knowledge of the Americas and Indians. The Spanish empire grew rapidly in the first fifty years after 1492, expanding throughout the Caribbean, Mesoamerica, and the Andes. Time and distance constituted two of the main challenges the Spanish faced in establishing and administering their new empires. The distance between Europe and the Americas played a very important role in shaping colonial administration as well as patterns and methods of imperial control for not only the Spanish, but for all European imperial powers.

Over the next hundred years, the Portuguese, the French, and the Dutch established colonies and areas of influence in the American hemisphere. Portugal, like Spain, sought to establish a settlement colony, controlled through direct political ties. Culturally, religiously, and socially, the colonies were deeply influenced by the mother country. The French and Dutch established very different models of colonial control. Both of these nations took a primarily economic interest in the American hemisphere, and shaped their models of colonial administration largely around trade. Politically, both France and the Netherlands wanted to weaken the Iberian hold on the Americas. The French actively contested Spanish power by trying to establish a colony in Spanish Florida. The Dutch were much less overt in their contestation of Iberian power; instead of establishing large, rival colonies, they concentrated on economically weakening the Spanish through piracy.

3.7 CRITICAL THINKING EXERCISES

- Read the description of the experience of the Spanish adventurer Lope de Aguirre. Compare this narrative to the letter written by Philip II just two years later. How did the views of these two men differ when it came to the Spanish enterprise in the New World? Why do you think the accounts differed as much as they did?
- The treatment of the Indians by the Europeans and such systems as the *encomienda* was decried by reformers beginning in the early sixteenth century. What reforms were advocated by Bartholomew de las Casas? Was reform even possible, or were the conditions imposed on the Natives inevitable?
- Which of the crops that originated in the New World had the greatest impact on the diets of those in the Old World of Europe, Asia, and Africa? Support your answer with specifics on nutrition, degree of spread, and ease of growing.

3.8 KEY TERMS

- Arab Middle Men
- Atahualpa
- *Audiencia*
- Aztecs/Mexica
- *Bandeirantes*
- Jacques Cartier
- Bartholomew de las Casas
- Samuel de Champlain
- Christopher Columbus
- *Corregidores*
- Hernán Cortés
- Councils of the Indies
- *Donatários*
- Dutch West Indies Company
- *Encomienda/encomenderos*
- Francisco Pizarro
- René Goulaine de Laudonnière
- *Haciendas*
- Huguenots
- Huitzilopochtli
- Huron
- Incas
- Jesuit
- La Malinche
- Pedro Menéndez de Avilés
- *Mestizos*
- *Mita*
- Moctezuma; Tenochtitlan
- Nahuatl
- Quetzalcoatl
- *Quinto*
- *Repartimiento*
- *Senado da Câmara*
- *Senhores de engenho*
- The Columbian Exchange
- Transculturation
- Treaty of Tordesillas

3.9 CHRONOLOGY

The following chronology is a list of important dates and events associated with this chapter.

Date	Event
1477-1495	Reign of John II of Portugal
1492-1503	Voyages of Columbus to the New World
1492	Columbian Exchange began between the Old and New Worlds
1494	Treaty of Toresillas signed
1500	Pedro Cabral claimed Brazil for the Portuguese Crown
1518	Atlantic Slave Trade began

Date	Event
1516-1556	Reign of Charles I of Spain (Charles V of the Holy Roman Empire)
1534-1542	Voyages of Jacques Cartier
1564	René Goulaine de Laudonnière led French expedition to Florida, founded Fort Caroline
1565	Pedro Menéndez de Avilés founded St. Augustine, invaded and destroyed Fort Caroline settlement
1556-1598	Reign of Philip II of Spain
1519	Spanish Conquest of Tenochtitlan began
1520	*La Noche Triste*
1521	Tenochtitlan fell to the Spanish under Cortés
1533	Pizarro conquered the Inca Empire
1552	De Las Casas publishes *A Short Account of the History of the Indies*
1588	The Spanish Armada sailed against England
1603	Samuel de Champlain established the colony of New France
1615	First Jesuits arrived in New France
1624	Dutch West India Company active in Caribbean
1628	Dutch West India Company captured Spanish treasure fleet

3.10 BIBLIOGRAPHY

Aguirre, Lope. *Letter to Philip II of Spain*, 1561. *Modern History Sourcebooks*, ed. Paul Halsall. *www.fordham.edu*/halsall.

An Aztec Account of the Conquest of Mexico in *Modern History Sourcebooks*, ed. Halsall, *www.fordham.edu*.

Burkholder, Mark A. and Lyman L. Johnson. *Colonial Latin America*. New York: Oxford University Press, 1998.

Chasteen, John Charles. *Born in Blood and Fire*. NY: WW Norton, 2002.

Cieza de Léon, Pedro. *Chronicles of the Incas*, 1540, *Modern History Sourcebooks*, ed. Paul Halsall.

Columbus, Christopher. *Journal* in *Modern History Sourcebooks,* ed. Paul Halsall, www.fordham.edu.

Cortés, Hernán. *Second Letter to Charles V* in *Modern History Sourcebooks*, ed. Paul Halsall, www.fordham.edu/halsall.

De La Casas, Bartolomé. *A Short Account of the Destruction of the Indies*, 1542, *Modern History Sourcebooks*, ed. Paul Halsall .

Diaz, Bernal. *True History of the Conquest of Spain*, ed. RB Cunninghame-Graham. Internet Archives. http://www.archive.org/stream/bernaldiaz.txt.

Fitch, Nancy. *Bibliography of Aztec and Maya Law*. University of Texas, Austin: Tarlton Law School. http://tarlton.law.utexas.edu/exhibits/aztec/links.html.

Keen, Benjamin, ed. *Latin American Civilization: History and Society, 1492 to the Present* (Boulder, Colorado, Westview Press, 2000).

Leon Portilla, Miguel. *The Broken Spears: The Aztec Account of the Conquest of Mexico* (Boston: Beacon Press, 1962).

The New Laws of the Indies. Modern History Sourcebooks, ed. Paul Halsall.

Núñe-beza de Vaca, Álvar. *Adventures in the Unknown Interior of America*, 1542, translated and annotated by Cyclone Covey.

Phillip II of Spain (1527-1598): Two Letters on the Gold of the Indies, 1559, at *ThenAgain* http://www.thenagain.info/Classes/Sources/PhilipII.html.

Whitehead, Laurence. *Latin America: A New Interpretation*. New York: Palgrave-McMillan, 2006.

3.11 END NOTES

1 Chasteen, 75.

2 Phillip II of Spain, *Two Letters on the Gold of the Indies*, 1559, at Then Again, http://www.thenagain.info/Classes/Sources/PhilipII.html.

3 Philip II, *Two Letters.*

4 *Letter of Lope Aguirre to Philip II of Spain*, 1561, in *Modern History Sourcebooks.*

5 Cortés quoted in McKay, Hill, Buckler, A History of World Societies, v. 1, 9th edition (New York: Bedford, St. Martins, 466.

6 Columbus, Journal, October, 1492 in The History Guide, http://www.historyguide.org/earlymod/columbus.html. *It should be remembered that each type of original document contains the bias of the writer. Europeans came to the New World convinced of their own innate superiority and intelligence. Thus they were preconditioned to see the people they encountered as subordinate and subservient. Moreover, they approached Indian lives with the idea that life in Europe was "civilized" and the way in which the natives of the New World lived was something less. It was not uncommon for Europeans to see the Indians as open, affable and innocent.*

7 Columbus, Journal, October, 1492.

8 Columbus, Journal, October 1492.

9 Cabeza de Vaca, *Adventures in the Unknown Interior of America, in Modern History Sourcebooks*, ed. Paul Halsall, www.fordham.edu/halsall.

10 Bartolomé de las Casas quoted *Latin American Civilization*, ed. Benjamin Keen, Boulder, Colorado, Westview Press, 2000), 67.

11 Cortés, quoted in Mark A Burkholder and Lyman L. Johnson. *Colonial Latin America*. New York: Oxford University Press, 1998, 4.

12 Cortés, *Second Letter to Charles V*, in *Modern History Sourcebooks*, ed. Paul Halsall.

13 Cortés, *Second Letter to Charles V.*

14 *An Aztec Account of the Conquest of Mexico* in *Modern History Sourcebooks.*

15 John Charles Chasteen, *Born in Blood and Fire* (NY: WW Norton, 2001), 50.

16 Quoted in Burkholder, 44.

17 Bernal Diaz, *True History of the Conquest of Spain*, ed. RB Cunninghame-Graham. Internet Archive, http://www.archive.org/stream/bernaldiaz.txt), 22.

18 Camilla Townsend, "Burying the White Gods: New Perspectives on the Conquest of Mexico," *American Historical Review*, vol. 108 (June 2003), 659-687.

19 Cortés, *Letter to Charles V.*

20 Leon Portilla, *Broken Spears: The Aztec Account of the Conquest of Mexico*, http://ambergriscaye.com/pages/mayan/aztec.html.

21 Qtd. in Burkhart, 49.

22 *Aztec Account.*

23 Cieza de Léon, Pedro. *Chronicles of the Incas*, 1540, *Modern History Sourcebooks*, ed. Paul Halsall.

24 Burkholder, 66; Chasteen, 42.

25 Chasteen, 48.

26 Chasteen, 51.

27 Chasteen, 66-70.

28 Keen, 67.

29 Anchieta in *Latin American Civilization*, 164.

30 Qtd. in Laurence Whitehead. *Latin America: A New Interpretation*. New York: Palgrave-McMillan, 2006, 58.

31 Whitehead, 58-60.

ANSWER KEY FOR CHAPTER THREE: INITIAL CONTACT AND CONQUEST

Check your answers to the questions in the Before You Move On Sections for this chapter.

Correct answers are **BOLDED**

Section 3.2.3 - p62

1. Which of the following animals did **not** originate in the Old World of Europe, Africa, or Asia?
   A. LLAMAS
   b. Cattle
   c. Sheep
   d. Pigs

2. Which of the following crops originated in the New World?
   a. Oats
   B. PEANUTS
   c. Barley
   d. Coffee

3. What crop was so controversial that monarchs in Europe and China attempted to ban its use?
   A. TOBACCO
   b. Rice
   c. Potato
   d. Wheat

4. Which of the following crops did **not** originate in the New World?
   a. Tobacco
   b. Maize
   c. Potato
   D. WHEAT

5. Which of the following European diseases was responsible for the greatest number of Amerindian deaths in the late fifteenth and early sixteenth centuries?
   a. Measles
   b. Influenza
   c. Bubonic Plague
   D. SMALLPOX

Section 3.3.2 - p69

1. Which of the follow was well known for his criticism of the Europeans' treatment of the Indians of Meso- and South America?
   a. Álvar Núñez Cabeza de Vaca
   b. Hernán Cortés
   C. BARTHOLOMEW DE LAS CASAS
   d. Pedro Cabral

2. The *Treaty of Tordesillas*
   A. DIVIDED THE NEW WORLD BETWEEN THE SPANISH AND THE PORTUGUESE.
   b. Specified that the *encomienda* system should be disbanded.
   c. Allowed the use of Incas in the mines of Peru.
   d. Formally recognized the conquest of the Aztec Empire by Cortés and his soldiers.

3. The majority of the natives killed in the exploration period were slaughtered by the Europeans who possessed superior weapons.
   a. True
   B. FALSE

4. The first explorer to reach Brazil and claim it for the throne of Portugal was:
   a. Christopher Columbus
   B. PEDRO CABRAL
   c. Ferdinand Magellan
   d. Jacques Cartier

5. Recruiting native allies played an important role in the Spanish conquest of the Aztec.
   A. TRUE
   b. False

6. The myth of Quetzalcoatl relies on sources that are contemporaneous with the conquest of the Aztec.
   a. True
   B. FALSE

Section 3.4.3 - p73

1. The system that helped provide labor for the Spanish mines and sugar plantations was the:
   a. *Quinto*
   b. *Audiencia*
   C. ENCOMIENDA
   d. *Residencia*

2. The Brazilian economy was largely based on
   A. SUGAR
   b. Coffee
   c. Silver
   d. Indigo

3. The ____________ was part of the bureaucracy of Spanish rule and oversaw developments in New Spain until the close of the colonial period.
   a. *Encomienda*
   b. *Mita*
   C. COUNCIL OF THE INDIES
   d. *Donatários*

Section 3.5.3 - p79

1. _________'s expeditions in Canada established the local Indians' interest in French trade when the leader of Stadacona tried to detain him in order to control French and Indian trade networks.
   a. Samuel de Champlain
   b. Stadacona
   C. JACQUES CARTIER
   d. René Goulaine de Laudonnière

2. The French settlement in Florida was settled by Protestants unwelcome in France known as _____.
   A. HUGUENOTS
   b. Anabaptists
   c. Apostates
   d. Catholics

3. The Jesuits
   A. WERE A GROUP OF MISSIONARIES.
   b. were largely unsuccessful in converting local Indians.
   c. were a great source of knowledge about the Indians of New France.
   d. all of the above

4. The Dutch practiced which of the following in establishing themselves as an economic powerhouse in the Caribbean?
   a. legitimate trade
   b. piracy
   c. smuggling
   D. ALL OF THE ABOVE

5. The Dutch East India Company possessed the power to
   a. establish colonies
   b. punish criminals
   c. negotiate treaties
   d. wage war
   E. ALL OF THE ABOVE

Chapter Four:
The Establishment Of English Colonies Before 1642 And Their Development Through The Late Seventeenth Century

Contents

Chapter Four: The Establishment Of English Colonies Before 1642 And Their Development Through The Late Seventeenth Century

4.1 INTRODUCTION

Beginning in the late sixteenth century, England joined Spain and France in creating a new world empire. Late getting started, when compared to Spain, the English monarchy sponsored its first voyages to the New World under Sir Humphrey Gilbert in the 1580s. The first English colony was established on Roanoke Island in 1585 but was unsuccessful; what happened to its residents has remained one of history's great mysteries. However, beginning in 1607, a series of permanent colonies were created under the English flag: Jamestown, Plymouth, Massachusetts Bay, Maryland, Connecticut, Rhode Island, and New Hampshire.

The English came to the New World for many different reasons. Some, like the founders of Jamestown, were adventurers, looking for gold and hoping not to escape from English ideals, but rather to transplant those ideals to a new setting. Historian Daniel Boorstin comments that in the early years of Virginia it was not uncommon "to rise into the ranks of gentry," a goal of those who "believed in the mystique of the gentleman."[1] On the other hand, the New England colonies and Maryland were founded by religious groups, Pilgrims and Puritans in the case of New England, and in Maryland, Catholics, all escaping persecution in the mother country.

When England became embroiled in a civil war and experienced a period of republicanism in the 1640s and 1650s, colonizing efforts stopped; they began again when Charles II was restored to the throne in 1660. Most of the English colonies established between 1585 and 1642 were created by charter companies like the London and Plymouth Companies; only Maryland was proprietary.

The purpose of this chapter is to trace English colonization from the late sixteenth century until the outbreak of Civil War in England in 1642, and to follow the evolution of these colonies through the late seventeenth century.

4.1.1 Learning Outcomes

After completing this chapter, you should be able to:

- Explain the motivation of the English Crown in sponsoring voyages of exploration and colonization in the new world.
- Compare the attitudes of Maryland and New England on the issue of religious toleration and explain why the Calverts of Maryland did not want an official church for their colony.
- Analyze the differences in how the New England and Chesapeake Bay colonists interacted with the Indians.
- Explain the motivation behind the creation of Roanoke Island and analyze why Roanoke Island became a "lost colony."

- Analyze the impact of Puritanism, including Puritan ideas about predestination and election, on the government and social structure of the Massachusetts Bay Colony and Plymouth, and on the development of other colonies such as Rhode Island and Connecticut; compare the relationship of religion and society in Massachusetts Bay to that in Rhode Island.
- Analyze the differences in political, social, and religious structure between the New England and Chesapeake Bay colonies.
- Analyze sources of labor in the English colonies created before 1642 and explain why slavery did not become as entrenched in New England as it did in the Chesapeake colonies.
- Explain the major issues that affected the New England and Chesapeake colonies through the end of the seventeenth century.

4.2 THE ENGLISH BACKGROUND

In 1559, Elizabeth I, youngest daughter of Henry VIII, continued the Tudor dynasty when she came to the throne of England. In a departure from the strict Catholicism of her sister Mary I, known as Bloody Mary, Elizabeth reflected the atmosphere of religious diversity in which she had been raised. Many historians believe that Elizabeth's mother, Anne Boleyn, secretly followed the theology of Martin Luther, who broke with the Catholic Church in the late 1510s and early 1520s.

When Elizabeth took the throne, hundreds of Protestants, called the "Marian exiles" because they had left England when Mary intensified persecution of non-Catholics, began to return to their motherland. These exiles had spent the 1550s mainly in Geneva, which was under the control of the ardent Protestant John Calvin; he was more radical in his intent on spreading Protestantism than Martin Luther had been. The Marian exiles were determined to force a religious settlement on Elizabeth that would take the Church of England away from the Catholicism of Mary toward a more Protestant, or Calvinist, direction. Most of the exiles believed that all people were predestined to be saved or damned no matter what they did during their lifetimes, a concept known as predestination; that individuals did not have free will and could not earn salvation through "good works," which was an important Catholic doctrine; that priests should be allowed to marry; and, finally, that "high church," or Catholic, practices like genuflecting, the use of incense and music during services, and kneeling at the sign of the cross, should be removed from church liturgy. According to these Protestants, priests were simply men; they could not perform miracles, could not convert bread into wine during the Eucharist, and should be allowed to marry. All of these reforms, of course, were anathema to orthodox Catholics.

In 1559, pressured by the Marian exiles, Elizabeth agreed to the "Settlement" whose prayer book is still the basis of the Anglican worship in the twenty-first century. The Settlement consisted of two acts of Parliament, one that conferred upon Elizabeth the title Supreme Head of the Church, and a second, the Act of Uniformity, which created the Anglican prayer book and defined the new Church of England. The theology reflected in the *Book of Common Prayer* is a compromise between the Catholicism of Henry VIII, Mary I, and Calvinist theology; it is neither strictly Catholic nor strictly Calvinist. Stained glass, genuflecting, incense, and music during church services were remnants of Catholic liturgy; on the other hand, priests were allowed to marry, they were not thought to be able to perform miracles during the Eucharist or Lord's Supper, free will was modified, and predestination was given credence. In typical Anglican fashion, the *Articles of Religion* stressed the importance of the two Protestant sacraments of baptism and communion, but also acknowledged the remaining five Catholic sacraments: ordination, confirmation, marriage, the last rites, and penance. Transubstantiation, or the conversion of the elements during the Eucharist by the priest, was put aside. The Eucharist became, in the Calvinist tradition, simply commemorative of the Last Supper.

The Elizabethan Settlement, however, did not go far enough in the direction of fundamental Calvinism to suit the Puritans. This group of reformers insisted that the Anglican church should be "purified" (hence the name) of all Catholic trappings. Puritan protests grew more strident in the early decades of Elizabeth's reign. Because these reformers also were being elected regularly to the House of Commons, they quickly became a thorn in her side. In addition to the Puritans' demands, Elizabeth was faced with challenges by her first cousin, Mary, Queen of Scots of the Stuart line. Mary had issues with the Presbyterian leadership in the Church of Scotland. While Elizabeth was a moderate in religion, Mary was a strict Catholic who plotted to take the English crown away from Elizabeth and unite England and Scotland under her own control. Mary was accused of treason, found guilty, and decapitated in 1587, the year before the defeat of the Spanish Armada.

As if conditions in the British Isles were not pressing enough, Philip II of Spain, the avowed leader of European Catholicism and widower of Mary I, Tudor, raised an armada against England in the hopes of ending Protestantism in Europe once and for all. Unfortunately for Phillip, the fleet he raised—and paid for with income from the silver mines of the new world—failed. In the view of Elizabeth, God had come down on the side of the Protestants; a "Protestant wind" had blown, insuring victory against Catholic Spain and the preservation of the Protestant faith.

England's earliest experience with colonization began in 1578 when Elizabeth gave a grant of land to Sir Humphrey Gilbert; the purpose for colonizing was "to discover, search, find out and view such remote heathen and barbarous lands, countries and territories not actually possessed of any Christian people."[2] She was no doubt encouraged in her continuing patronage by the publication four years later of Richard Hakluyt's *Divers Voyages Touching the Discovery of America and the Islands Adjacent*. Hakluyt's consideration was exhaustive and madc much of the advantages to any who either sponsored or participated in voyages of exploration. He insisted that "lasting riches do waite upon them who are zealous for the advancement of the kingdome of Christ and enlargement of our glorious Gospell."[3] The grant to Gilbert excluded lands already controlled by Spain, Portugal, or the Dutch. Gilbert led three expeditions to the Americas; after he was lost at sea during the third, Elizabeth, in 1584, passed the grant to Gilbert's half-brother, Sir Walter Raleigh. The first English colony, the "lost colony" of Roanoke, was founded the same year.

4.2.1 The Stuarts of Scotland and England: James I and Charles I

Elizabeth I never married, and her two siblings, Edward VI and Mary I, both childless, had predeceased her. On her death in 1603, the throne therefore went to her nearest living male relative, her first cousin, James VI (Stuart), king of Scotland. James I, as he was known in England, was an unfortunate monarch whose character was, according to Historian J.P. Kenyon, "complex, extensive and shallow."[4] James came to England thinking that he would be independent of Parliament and automatically receive a generous annual allowance to do with as he wished. A firm believer in the "divine right of kings" as put forth in his book *The Trew Law of Free Monarchies,* James made the mistake of lecturing Parliament, insisting that "there are no privileges or immunities that can stand against the divinely appointed King."[5]

Upon hearing of James's succession, English Puritans at first looked forward to his arrival. James after all was the leader of a country, Scotland, whose official religion was Presbyterianism, based, like Puritanism, on the theology of John Calvin. They were convinced that James would no doubt take seriously their complaints about the remaining Catholic practices of the Church of England. The Puritans could not have been more wrong. Shortly after James came to the throne, a delegation of Puritan clergy presented him with the Millenary Petition. The Petition urged, among other things, that the term "priest" should not be used when referring to the clergy and that confirmation no longer be practiced in the Church. James bluntly refused to consider the petition, commenting that "no Bishops" would mean "no King." He was resolute in enforcing uniformity.[6]

James I, like his cousin Elizabeth, was interested in the developments taking place in the new world, and in 1606 granted a group of wealthy merchants, who had formed the Virginia Company of London, the right to settle in Virginia or in any area "not now actually possessed by any Christian prince or people." The purpose of those who participated in the venture would be finding gold and "propagating of Christian religion to such people as yet live in darkness and miserable ignorance of the true knowledge and worship of God and may in time bring the infidels and savages living in those parts to humane civility and to a settled and quiet government."[7] The *First Virginia Charter* granted land to two branches of the Company: the London branch, which was granted land to establish a colony near the Chesapeake Bay, and the Plymouth branch, which was given land in the New England area. The Company was a stock company whose shares cost £12, 10 shillings.

Charles I followed his father to the throne in 1625 and was equally unsuccessful with the English people in general and Parliament and the Puritans in particular. He made errors that alienated Puritans both in and outside of Parliament. First, he married a Catholic princess, Henrietta Maria, sister of Louis XIII of France, and, second, he allowed the Archbishop of Canterbury, William Laud, to introduce additional Catholic liturgy and theology into the Church of England. Laud even went so far as to deny predestination, a doctrine mentioned in the *Articles of Religion* and a cornerstone of Puritan ideology; this action on the part of the Archbishop was anathema to the Puritans. Charles, whom many of the English, especially the Puritans, thought was an undeclared Catholic, tried to avoid Puritan influence in Parliament by dismissing the body in 1629 and attempting to rule England on his own; thus he created what historians call the "eleven-year tyranny."[8] During this period, Charles imposed taxes, many of them not used for hundreds of years, in an effort to give economic support to the Crown. He had little success in this endeavor; the rule without Parliament was fiscally disastrous, and, in 1640, he was forced to reconvene the body.

The Long Parliament, the English Civil War, and the Republic

Known as the "Long Parliament," the meeting convened by Charles sat from 1640 until 1660. One of its first actions was to present Charles with a list of grievances and demands, including a Triennial Act that would force a king to call Parliament at least once every three years, whether he wanted to or not. The year before Parliament drafted the *Triennial Act*, William Laud, who was responsible in the eyes of Puritans for all of the problems in the Church, was tried for treason, found guilty, and sent to the Tower of London. Charles, fearing further retaliation from Parliament, reluctantly accepted the act and agreed to address the remainder of their grievances.

Relations between king and Parliament did not improve over the succeeding two years, however. In 1642, both sides raised troops, and the English Civil War broke out between Royalists and Parliamentarians. By 1648, the Royalists were on the defensive; the next year, 1649, Charles was captured, tried for treason, and executed. It marked the first time that a reigning monarch had been brought before a legislative body and indicted for treason. The army of Parliament, known as the New Model Army, was led by a popular figure, Oliver Cromwell, whom historians credit for its decisive victory over the Royalists.

The eleven year period that followed the execution of Charles I is usually called the "Interregnum," a period "between kings." During this time, England was actually a republic ruled by Parliament, a Council of State, and a Lord Protector in the person of Oliver Cromwell. In addition to being militarily talented, Cromwell was a devout Puritan who supported religious toleration. Religious policies were outlined in the *Instrument of Government,* which gave all Christians except Catholics the right to practice the religion of their choice. Many historians point out that England under Cromwell was in reality a military dictatorship. There was not much immigration to the English colonies during the Interregnum, nor were new colonies created.

By 1655, the republic was clearly a fiscal failure, and, when Cromwell died, he was followed only briefly by his ineffectual son, Richard. In 1660, the republic ended and the monarchy restored. Lacey Baldwin Smith comments that the failure of republican England was due to the fact that Oliver Cromwell had been caught between opposing forces: the army, the nobility, the Puritans, and Parliament. He, and all of England, had learned an important lesson: "Parliament could no more exist without the Crown than the Crown without Parliament."[9] Oliver Cromwell had not objected to monarchy and had even suggested in 1650 that Charles I be replaced by his son, also Charles, who had taken refuge in France. Therefore, it was not completely unexpected that within two years of his death, Parliament extended an invitation to the man who would become Charles II, the third Stuart King of England. Monarchy was restored, and the republican experiment was at an end.

4.3 ROANOKE, RALEIGH'S LOST COLONY

Under the rule of Elizabeth I, Sir Humphrey Gilbert was an Englishman of vision who saw the potential for English colonization in North America. He understood that, for his island nation to grow strong enough to stand against other European countries such as Spain, its territory had to expand. Colonizing North America would benefit the English in numerous ways. It would give them possible access to untold riches, such as the Spanish enjoyed in their colonies, as well natural resources like timber needed for fleets of ships. It would also give closer access to the best fishing grounds in the North Atlantic, a launch point for a search for the Northwest Passage, and safe harbors on both sides of the Atlantic. A man of influence with important connections at Court, Gilbert raised the funds for an expedition and was granted the letters allowing him to lay claim to land in the name of the English Crown and set out in 1583. He reached Newfoundland, which had a mixed temporary population of various European fishers as well as Indians. Gilbert claimed it for England and then sailed on. His little ship, the *Squirrel,* and its larger partner, the *Golden Hind,* were caught in a particularly fierce North Atlantic storm. Gilbert refused to transfer to the larger and somewhat safer ship, as he would not abandon his ship or its crew; instead, he stayed on the *Squirrel* even as its decks were awash with the sea. The crew of the *Golden Hind* watched helplessly as the lights of the *Squirrel* vanished beneath the waves. The *Golden Hind* survived and brought the news back to England that the *Squirrel* went down with all hands, including Sir Humphrey.

Gilbert's dream of a North American English colony was shared by his half-brother, Sir Walter Raleigh who, like Gilbert, was an adventurer and man of many talents. Raleigh was one of the most famous courtiers of Queen Elizabeth I, who made him a man of wealth and power. Raleigh was a devout Protestant who harbored a great enmity for Catholic Spain. He also saw Spain as a source of wealth for anyone with ships capable of attacking the Spanish galleons filled with gold that sailed across the Atlantic from the Americas to Spain. When sailors such as Raleigh attacked a Spanish fleet, they brought wealth back for England, keeping a large portion for themselves. These privateers enriched themselves and England at Spanish expense. They also kept England diplomatically neutral, as they did not sail Crown ships but their own.

To be an effective base, an English settlement would have to be close enough to the Spanish territory to target their ships bound for Spain yet far enough away not to be easily found and destroyed by the Spanish. Newfoundland was too far north for Raleigh's purpose, and, by this time, the Spanish had been in Florida for almost twenty years. Both the French and Spanish had attempted to colonize Florida: the French at Fort Caroline in 1564, and the Spanish at St. Augustine in 1565. The Spanish destroyed Fort Caroline and drove the French out of Florida, securing their hold on the area. Raleigh opted to look for a location in the mid-Atlantic coastal area, far enough south to avoid harsh winters, yet far enough north to stay clear of Spanish warships.

Raleigh took great care in planning his first exploratory expedition. He did not go himself; instead, in 1584, he sent two ships, one large, one smaller, with a company of soldiers, good provisions, and experienced officers and crews. The ships arrived safely at the Outer Banks in July, 1584. The region was inhabited by two main groups of Indians, each united by a common language group yet divided into several tribes. The first, the Algonquian, were the larger of the two and occupied the Outer Banks and nearby mainland coast; the other, the Iroquois, lived further inland. It should be noted that the Iroquois tribe, which gave its name to the Iroquois group, did not inhabit the Carolinas; rather, they lived to the northeast. The Algonquian first encountered by the English were friendly and curious about the visitors. They had seen ships sail by before and may have seen Europeans up close or at least heard stories of them from the Indians further south. These were probably the first English they had met. Raleigh's men had brought items for trade: beads and metal items such as plates and cooking pots. Other Indians were not friendly, however, and killed some of Raleigh's men. Nevertheless, the English had found a good place for a settlement, Roanoke Island, which was inhabited by the Secotan, an Algonquian tribe; it had plentiful wildlife, fresh water, and other natural resources to help a new colony survive. Raleigh's men returned to England, taking with them two Indians, Manteo and Wanchese, with the encouraging report of what they had found.

Raleigh had not been idle while his ships were away. He had been working to raise the funds for his main expedition, one that would actually create a permanent English settlement in North America. For this expedition, Raleigh outfitted a small fleet of ships. He had intended to lead the voyage himself, but Elizabeth I would not allow it. Instead, Sir Richard Grenville, Raleigh's cousin, sailed with the fleet and 600 men on April 9, 1585; the ships were soon beset by storms. Grenville on the *Tiger*, the largest ship in the fleet, lost contact with the other ships, the *Roebuck*, the *Lion*, the *Elizabeth,* and the *Dorothy*. One of their smaller boats was lost as well. The *Tiger* made its way to the closest port on Puerto Rico and was soon joined by the *Elizabeth*. While waiting for the rest of his fleet, Grenville managed to capture a couple of small Spanish ships and build a new boat. Having no sign of the rest of his missing ships, he sailed on for Roanoke Island with his new fleet.

Near Roanoke Island, the Outer Banks mark the edge of a shallow area of water along the mid-Atlantic coast. Large ships could sail up to the eastern side of the banks, but could get caught trying to cross to the western side and the shallow waterway separating the banks from the mainland. Vessels with shallow drafts could easily sail the sounds between the banks and the mainland. Later, when charted by the English, English pirates and privateers would find the area useful for avoiding their pursuers. At the time Grenville arrived, the channels were still largely uncharted, except for what Raleigh's earlier expedition had learned. After a good voyage from Puerto Rico, the *Tiger* ran aground trying to cross over to the western side. Some provisions were lost, damaged by incoming seawater. They managed to save the *Tiger*. Better news awaited Grenville: both the *Roebuck* and the *Dorothy* had made the crossing successfully.

Figure 4.1 Secotan Ceremony | John White was famous for his paintings of scenes of life in the colonies; this one depicts a Secotan ceremony.

Author: John White
Source: Library of Congress

Grenville took time to explore further inland, traveling to different towns of the Secotan. The Indian reception of the English was generally good. It was during this time of exploration that John White made his famous illustrations of the Indians. The English wanted to learn more about the lands further inland and, in particular, if they held gold, silver, and other riches. One unpleasant incident occurred: a silver cup belonging to the English was apparently stolen.

They accused the Indians of one village of taking it, and, when it was not returned, they burned the village and its fields. This act foreshadowed the troubled relations ahead. Meanwhile, a site on the north end of Roanoke Island, not accessible by large ships, was chosen for the colony. The supplies had to be off-loaded from the ships onto the smaller boats, then taken to the settlement site and there again unloaded. The area was cleared of trees and underbrush, and fortifications were constructed, as well as a dock for the small boats, housing, storerooms, workshops, and enclosures for the livestock.

Grenville returned to England knowing that he had not been able to fully provision the colonists he left behind under the command of Ralph Lane. He did, however, believe that another fleet would arrive soon with more provisions and colonists. On his way home, he tried his luck again at attacking Spanish shipping and claimed a great prize: a Spanish ship carrying a fortune in gold and other items, more than most people of the day could even imagine. Grenville returned home to England with his Spanish prize to find the mood in England was very negative towards Spain. The conflict had been brewing for some time and had worsened while Grenville was away, so his arrival with a Spanish fortune made him a hero.

The Spanish issue caused the next fleet scheduled to arrive at Roanoke to be diverted, though Grenville had no way of knowing this when he left the little colony. Without the anticipated supplies, Lane and his men had to rely on trade with the local Secotan for food. For their part, the Secotan had welcomed the English but had not expected them to be such a burden. As with any hunter-gatherers and farmers, the Secotan food supply depended greatly on the seasons of the year. In the fall and winter, they relied on what they had harvested and had to keep the supply safe to feed all of their people throughout the winter until spring, when hunting, fishing, and gathering would improve. In addition to the burden the English were placing on the Secotan food supplies, the English had also unwittingly brought disease. Where the English visited, death often followed for the Indians, who had no immunity against such European diseases as smallpox and influenza. Neither the Secotan nor the English understood the cause of illness, but there was no doubt that a connection existed between the English presence and the sickness and death of the natives.

The Secotan chief, Wingina, also known as Pemisapan, moved to protect his people. He had all their stores hidden so there would be nothing available when the English came to trade. Relations between the two groups continued to deteriorate. Pemisapan plotted against the English, and Lane learned of it. He decided on a bold plan to attack Pemisapan before Pemisapan could attack the English. The final result was several murdered Secotan. Pemisapan himself was beheaded.

The English had won, but at what cost? Their strategy of reacting strongly against any opposition caused the Indians to fear them, which was the English goal. However, they also caused the Indians to fear their continued presence. Some tribes remained friendly to the English, yet their list of enemies was growing. The colony site on Roanoke was no longer viable. Lane planned to relocate when, quite unexpectedly, an English fleet arrived.

Sir Francis Drake, another of Raleigh's famous seafaring relations, had the largest English fleet to date to reach North America. He arrived off shore in June, 1586. Lane asked Drake for aide, and Drake obliged with supplies, boats, and a small ship capable of sailing the shallows—in short, everything Lane needed to keep his small group going until Raleigh could reinforce the settlement. Lane was prepared to remain when suddenly a massive hurricane hit. The storm battered the fleet of over twenty ships anchored offshore. The little ship that Drake gave to Lane was lost along with some of Lane's men. Huge hailstones rained down, endangering the sailors and damaging their ships. For three days, the fleet and Lane's group were battered by what may have been one of the worst hurricanes to hit the Carolinas. When it ended, so too did Lane's resolve to stay. He and his men sailed back to England with Drake.

Lane had no way of knowing that supplies from Raleigh and more colonists with Grenville were finally on their way; otherwise, he would not have left. Similarly, the supply ship and Grenville had no way of knowing Lane had abandoned Roanoke, much less why. Both arrived to find Roanoke deserted. Grenville had brought 200 men but chose to leave only fifteen at Roanoke and took the rest back to England. Lane's departure from Roanoke was a setback for Raleigh, but valuable lessons had been learned. The men left with Lane at Roanoke had been soldiers, not farmers, and certainly not diplomats. They were ill-suited for the type of work needed to help the colony succeed. They could not farm, and they were easily offended and prone to violence. Their attitude did not help create good relations with the Indians. The lack of dependably scheduled support ships also had hurt the colony. The location, while protected from attack by large ships, was not suited to serve as a port of call for the English fleet, as visiting ships had to anchor two miles offshore. There, they were unprotected from storms and clearly visible to any other passing ships, including those of the Spanish who would find them easy targets in such an exposed anchorage.

Lane believed from his explorations that a better option lay to the north, the Chesapeake Bay. He had traveled there while exploring the region and found that it had harbors that would accommodate the largest English ships. The Indians there were Algonquian and friendly, and the area was quite attractive. Also, from the stories the Indians told him, he thought it might be an even better place to use as a base for a search for gold in the interior. Unfortunately, Lane, having abandoned Roanoke, was out of favor and would not be allowed to go on the next expedition.

The honor of leading Raleigh's next voyage fell to John White, an artist, map maker, explorer, and friend of Raleigh's. White had sailed with Grenville on the first attempt to settle Roanoke in 1585. White's famous watercolors of the Indians, their villages, and the flora and fauna of the region were the first images the English public was able to see of North America. The plan was for White to lead this new group, first to Roanoke to check on the garrison left by Drake and to return the two Indians from that area. Then, White was to move onto Chesapeake to establish his colony away from the troubles of Roanoke. White's fleet, led by the *Lion*, left Plymouth, England on May 8, 1587. It sailed towards the Canary Islands for the first leg of the journey. Because of ocean currents and winds, ships did not simply sail off in a straight line from point A to point B; rather, they followed a route. From England to the Canaries, across to the West Indies, and then up along the Atlantic seaboard was the favored passage of the time. The route took advantage of the currents off the coast of West Africa at the Canaries that drove ships and hurricanes westward to the Caribbean. As predictable as any crossing of the Atlantic could be, it provided points where the ships could resupply and, if they became separated in the crossing, regroup.

The trip had been well planned, but even the best of plans can fail. Before leaving England, some of the colonists abandoned the project. White and Raleigh had recruited families for this attempt, not just soldiers and sailors as in the past. The colonists had skills that would help a colony survive on its own and not be dependent on its Indian neighbors. As the time for departure had approached, some of these colonists backed out, leaving White with fewer people than expected to make the crossing. Then, before even reaching the Canaries, storms separated one of the ships carrying supplies and colonists, further reducing their numbers. Even so, White pressed on.

By June, White had reached the Indies where more problems befell the little group. Several became ill from fruit and water consumed on the first island they reached. While no fatalities occurred, the incident added to the unpleasant conditions aboard the ships. White was in charge of the colonists; a pilot named Fernandes was in charge of the ship. Fernandes, a trusted sailor for Raleigh, had been the pilot for each expedition to the Outer Banks. He had clashed with Grenville in the past, and now he and White found themselves at odds. Throughout the voyage, Fernandes made decisions that were not in the best interests of the colony, including a critical error when he did not take the time to acquire more provisions while in the Indies. White could only object and argue; he was powerless to force Fernandes to follow his orders. When they reached Roanoke late in July, again Fernandes acted on his own. He decided to leave White there and not go on to the Chesapeake Bay. He did not simply abandon White; he unloaded the colonists and their baggage and provisions and gave White a ship small enough to sail around the shallow sounds and large enough to sail up to the Chesapeake Bay.

Only one of the fifteen men of Drake's garrison was found, and he was long dead, leaving nothing but bleached bones. The settlement area for Lane's colonists was still there and usable, although in need of repair. The colonists set to work, clearing the settlement area again and expanding it for new houses suitable for families to use. White's luck seemed to be improving when the ship that had been lost before they reached the Canaries arrived undamaged with all hands, colonists, and provisions intact. White now had a colony of one hundred and eighteen men, women, and children.

White also had a coastline inhabited by angry Indians. He had left Roanoke before the relations between the Secotan and Lane's men had fallen apart. He wasn't there when Lane's men attacked and murdered the Secotan chief, Wingina Pemisapan. How much White knew of the enmity that Lane and his men had created with the Secotan is unknown. White's first real indication of the anger of the Secotan was the brutal murder of one of the colonists, George Howe. He was shot repeatedly with arrows, and his skull was caved in.

Manteo, one of the Croatoan Indians who had first traveled to England with Grenville and returned home with White, learned from his people that Drake's garrison and the attack on Howe was the work of the Secotan. White, when at Roanoke, previously had had good relations with thc Secotan; among those who stood for his portraits was their chief Wingina, later murdered by Lane. White had hoped to be able to reestablish those happy relations even after the murder of Howe. However, when the Secotan did not respond to his offer of peace, White chose to follow the English pattern and launched an attack against a Secotan village in the dark. The attack was a dismal failure, as the Secotan of that village, realizing that the English would almost certainly attack them in retaliation for the murder of Howe, had left. The Algonquian, such as the Secotan, used a multi-village system, moving from one to another as need arose due to the seasons, farming, or threats. If there was a problem at one village, the inhabitants would simply leave. When White and his men arrived at the village at night, they did not realize that the Indians they found there were Croatoan, his allies, not Secotan, his enemies; both were Algonquian and had the same language and dress. As soon as they realized their mistake, the English halted their attack, but they had already injured and killed some of the Croatoan. The Croatoan had realized the Secotan would leave and not be able to take all of their food stores with them. The Croatoan, short on corn, had therefore sent a foraging party to the abandoned village. This incident was the second time the English has accidentally attacked their greatest allies.

Among the families at the colony was that of John White. His daughter and her husband, Eleanor and Ananias Dare, came as part of the colony, even though Eleanor was pregnant. On August 18, she gave birth to the first English child born in the New World, a daughter, Virginia Dare. The colonists were adapting well, but the threat posed by the Secotan, in addition to all the other problems of settling at Roanoke, reaffirmed for White the need to move the colony. At the same time, someone needed to return to England to convince Raleigh to send support as soon as possible. White had tried to find someone willing to sail for England amongst his colonists; they, in turn, were quite determined that White himself should go. With great misgivings, he agreed. Before his departure, White and the colonists agreed on a sign that they would leave behind in the event the colonists left Roanoke before White returned. The colonists would carve the name of their intended destination on a tree. White then sailed for England in the small ship. His trip was very difficult, and White nearly perished. After several weeks, he arrived in London at the worst possible time to ask for aide. The situation with the Spanish had reached the point of war, and all forces, including Sir Walter Raleigh, were committed to the protection of England. Still, Raleigh did try to send a support fleet. The situation with the Spanish interfered with the plans, as Raleigh's ships were ordered to support Drake in defending England from invasion and not sail for Roanoke. A couple of smaller ships were found and prepared, and White was able to sail on them in April, 1588, but the captain of one chose to play the pirate, endangering his ship and crew, resulting in White and many others being injured; the chance to reach Roanoke was lost.

Unbeknownst to the English, the Spanish had been searching for the settlement at Roanoke, whose precise location was a mystery. So determined were they to find the English that they sailed all the way up the Atlantic coast. In June, 1588 as they were passing the Outer Banks on the voyage back south, they found evidence of the English settlement but recorded no sign of any Englishmen. White had been absent from his colony for ten months, during which time the colony had no contact with England.

Meanwhile, White continued tirelessly to look for ships for his return voyage to Roanoke. At every turn, his efforts were thwarted, and he was unable to sail for Roanoke until 1590; in August, three years after leaving, White finally reached Roanoke. He found the settlement abandoned and overgrown. The ship and boats that had been left were gone. He found his own belongings packed in chests which had clearly been there for a good length of time and had been ransacked. Evidence showed signs of Indians but not of an attack. The letters CRO were carved in one place, the word "Croatoan" in another. If the colonists had left under duress, they were to carve a cross as a sign, along with the name of their intended destination. No crosses were to be seen. White and company returned to their ship with the intent to sail for Croatoan but were forced off by storms. Rather than waiting them out, the ship sailed away, eventually returning to England without ever making it back to Croatoan.

John White was never again able to return to the Outer Banks to search for his family and colony, the Lost Colony of history. Sir Walter Raleigh allowed his personal life to nearly destroy him, marrying a lady of the queen without obtaining the queen's permission. He lost the favor of Queen Elizabeth I and was arrested and imprisoned in the Tower of London. Because of his imprisonment, his loss of favor, and other distractions, Raleigh did not send anyone to the Outer Banks until 1603. With the death of Queen Elizabeth I and the accession of King James I, Raleigh's fortunes took a permanent turn for the worse, and he lost his hold on colonization in North America.

No other English ships of the time made any effort to look for the colony, as the goal of English ships sailing along the North American coast was to hunt Spanish ships further south, rather than to search for missing Englishmen in the mid-Atlantic. Not until a new colony was established in the Chesapeake at Jamestown would any English take up a serious search for their lost countrymen. None would ever be found, although stories of blond haired, light-eyed Indians would persist.

4.3.1 Before You Move On...

Key Concepts

The attempts to colonize Roanoke Island provided painful lessons for the English which contributed to the success of later colonies. Diplomacy and consistency were needed to build goodwill with the natives. Too often individual English jeopardized relations with the natives through rash and violent acts. The Indians also learned painful lessons, discovering that the English were at best a mixed blessing. Disease brought by the English devastated the native population, contributing to the downward spiral in relations. In the end, the colony at Roanoke failed due to English mistakes. The fate of the Lost Colony remains unknown to this day. We can surmise that they did at first go to the Croatoan village, but what happened beyond that and why they left is unknown.

Test Yourself

1. Sir Walter Raleigh was the man behind the attempt to colonize Roanoke.

    a. True

    b. False

2. The Secotan were an Algonquian people.

   a. True

   b. False

3. The Indians did not have any problems with English illnesses.

   a. True

   b. False

4. The first English person born in North America was a girl, Virginia Dare, on Roanoke Island.

   a. True

   b. False

See page 157 for answers

4.4 JAMESTOWN

In 1606, new groups, the Virginia Company of London and the Plymouth Company, were given the rights to colonize North America. The Virginia Company would focus on the mid-Atlantic region, the Plymouth further north. Captain Christopher Newport was given command of a fleet of three ships, the *Susan Constant,* the *Godspeed,* and the *Discovery*, all carrying just over a hundred colonists. Their goal was to reach the Chesapeake Bay in order to find a suitable location far enough inland to be reasonably secure from discovery by the Spanish. The ships set sail from England before Christmas and arrived in the Chesapeake region in April, 1607, after the usual stopover in the Indies. The colonists searched for a suitable place for settlement and on May 15 chose a rather unhealthy, marshy area along the James River on which to land. The reason for the choice is not clear, as the James had many suitable building sites with better environments. Perhaps the colonists thought that, being in a marsh, they would be less likely to attract unwanted attention from the natives or Spanish. Whatever the reason, the location would prove to be a difficult one.

4.4.1 The Powhatan

The Indians of the region, the Powhatan, whose dialect was Algonquian, knew of Englishmen from their neighbors to the south. Unlike the Indians at Roanoke, the Powhatan were a large and powerful confederation of many tribes under one chief, Wahunsonacock, also known as Powhatan. The territory he commanded stretched from the Potomac in the north to the Carolinas in the south, from the Chesapeake Bay inland to the west of what is now Richmond. Essentially, he controlled Tidewater Virginia in what has been described as the largest Indian confederation in North American history.

The Powhatan dressed much like their neighbors to the south, wearing skins for clothes, copper and pearls for jewelry. After settling the colonists at Jamestown, named in honor of James I, Newport set about exploring the rivers. He discovered the Fall Line at the site of modern Richmond, Virginia, a natural boundary making the transition from the Tidewater to the Piedmont regions of the territory. Boulders and rapids mark the end of the English portion of the river. The colonists met both friendly and hostile Indians and survived an early attack on their settlement that served to convince them of the need to invest time and effort in strong defenses. The colonists finished the construction of a three-sided fort in just a month. A trench was dug, into which logs were stood upright and packed tight to form a wall. At each corner, the walls were formed into a circular area, with extra earth packed in to create a mount for watchmen and a cannon.

When Captain Newport sailed back to London in June, he left what he thought was a colony sufficiently established to survive until further support arrived. By August, however, the colony was beginning to struggle. The location of the settlement was within the tidal area of the James River where salt water from the Chesapeake Bay mixed with fresh water from the James, creating a brackish brew not fit to drink. While the marsh waters were not good for humans, they proved a breeding ground for mosquitoes. The colony had been well provisioned, but the food stores spoiled due to the heat, leaving the colonists short on supplies and desperately in need of new sources of food. The final misery was the local Indians who continually harassed the colonists whenever the opportunity arose to inflict injury and death. While Newport was in London spreading the news of the success and great potential future success of the Jamestown settlement, over half the colonists died.

The sweltering summer heat had caused the colonists to suffer terribly. Fall provided a moment of relief before winter came, bringing to those down on the river a peculiar type of cold, a damp chill that went right through the body of anyone not properly attired, leaving them feeling as if they would never be warm again. Such was the miserable state of the last forty-some members of the colony in the winter of 1607.

4.4.2 Captain John Smith

The one bright spot of these members, Captain John Smith, was also one of the most troublesome. Of all the colonists, John Smith became the most famous in no small measure due to his own self-promotion: he wrote one of the first celebrity autobiographies. It helped the English learn of the New World and its inhabitants and of the fabulously adventurous life of John Smith. Smith's stories seemed too fantastic to be true, yet apparently they were. As much as he may have been a braggart, Smith truly was a most resourceful man of action. Unfortunately his bravado drove most people, including the colonists and the colony leaders, to distraction. Part of the problem was that Smith was a commoner while the leaders were gentlemen, that is, his social betters. Such details meant little to the gruff Smith, who had been a soldier of fortune and valued mettle over social status. He had been arrested and kept locked below decks for much of the crossing, as he argued with and angered the leaders. Once the ship landed, he was released and continued to annoy those around him. With the colonists facing the real possibility of starvation and Smith eager for action, the colony leaders chose to set Smith on the Indians.

The Famous Rescue of Smith by Pocahontas

Smith was charged with exploring the surrounding area, seeking a passage to the Pacific and, as always, gold. He traded with the Indians for provisions and, because of this, was successful in learning the area and the ways of the natives, including their language. He did hear stories of a western sea and of mountains and gold. He also heard about the Roanoke colony and was given reason to believe there had been survivors who were still alive. Most important to the Jamestown colonists, he also brought back enough food to help keep the colony alive. At the same time, Smith was careful to nurture the image of the English as being strong and interested in trade for trade's sake, rather than out of any need. Smith did not want to give an impression of weakness that might tempt the Indians to an all-out attack. He was cautious as well with what he revealed about the English plans, taking care not to provoke violence. Those who traveled with Smith were not always so cautious.

While exploring the Chickahominy River, Smith left some men in a boat and went on shore. While he was gone, the men spotted women along the banks. The colony had no women. The Indian women appeared friendly, so the men left the boat against Smith's instructions and walked into a trap. Men from the Chickahominy tribe had been waiting under cover to ambush Smith's men, who ran to escape. One, George Cassen, did not make it. He was not killed outright; instead, he was tied between stakes, stripped naked, and tortured to death. Excoriated by seashells, head first, his skin was then burned before his eyes; his fingers were cut off piece by piece, and his entrails taken out and burned. Still alive, Cassen was then burned to death. This death demonstrated sheer brutality on par with the English form of execution of being drawn and quartered. Smith and the men he had brought to shore heard sounds of alarm, but too late to rescue Cassen. They ran, trying to save themselves, and were cut down by the Indians. Smith alone of the English on shore survived; he slipped and fell and was captured. Not wanting to meet the same fate as Cassen, Smith resolved to convince the Indians that he was an important man, a useful man to know. He showed them a compass, made a grand speech, and somehow was spared for the moment and taken on a long journey to meet the great chief, Powhatan.

Figure 4.2 Rebecca Rolfe | Formerly known as Matoaka and Pocahontas, Rebecca Rolfe is shown in this portrait as she appeared in London in 1616, based on an engraving by Simon van de Passe.

Author: Flickr User "cliff1066"
Source: Flickr
License: CC-BY 2.0

What happened next became the most famous story of Jamestown and perhaps all of Colonial American history. The account of the story comes from Smith himself who wrote of it in his autobiography. Some historians doubt any of it is true; others believe Smith embellished the details, and others that, while Smith gave the facts correctly, he did not understand the significance of the event. This seems doubtful as Smith, of all the English, was the most widely traveled, had the most experience in meeting different cultures, and seems to have been the most successful in dealing with Powhatan. How could he have done so well if he was unable to grasp the meaning of his encounter with Powhatan and his daughter? According to Smith, although he was held captive, he was treated well. Various important men questioned him, but he was not abused. He was brought before Powhatan, who was seated as a king with attendants surrounding him. Among the crowd was a little girl, roughly ten years old and quite pretty: Matoaka, more commonly known as Pocahontas. Large stones were brought out and placed before Powhatan, then Smith was brought forward and made to place his head on one of them. He expected to be executed by having his skull crushed between the stones. Suddenly, Pocahontas flew forward and threw herself protectively over Smith, wrapping her arms about him and putting her own head over his. Was this a spontaneous act on the part of Pocahontas? Probably not. Smith was spared, given a new name, Nantaquoud, and adopted by Powhatan. Before setting him free, Powhatan even offered him lands. Such adoptions of foreigners were not uncommon among Indians. Adoptions could strengthen tribes and cement diplomatic relations. Powhatan knew Smith was a man of some importance among the English, and Smith had put on a good show. Even when faced with having his skull crushed, he acted with bravery, a trait admired by the Indians. Smith was returned to Jamestown with an escort. He had promised cannons to Powhatan but had no intention of delivering them. He showed his escort the largest cannons there, which were far too heavy for the Indians to move, so they agreed to accept other gifts for Powhatan instead.

With his troubles with the Indians over for the present, Smith was immediately faced with a crisis at Jamestown. The colony had been reduced to just forty cold, sick, and miserable men, who wanted to go home. Newport was overdue on his promised return; he had left one ship, the *Discovery,* to be used as needed, but had not intended it to be used to sail home to England. Smith forced the men to stay by threatening to fire on them and the ship. They, in turn, voted to have Smith arrested on charges of being responsible for the deaths of his men and then executed. For the second time in days, Smith's life was endangered, this time by his own people. At the eleventh hour, Captain Newport returned to take charge on New Year's Day, 1608. Newport had sailed accompanied by another ship, as was typical of the English, but the ships had become separated, and the other was not seen again. Still, Newport's arrival meant Smith was saved and so too was the colony, thanks to Newport's supplies and fresh colonists.

The fortunes of the colony turned again when a fire consumed the fort, destroying all the buildings and supplies. All the new colonists had were the materials they had brought with them that had not yet been unloaded from the ship; all the old colonists had was whatever they were wearing when the fire broke out. This devastating turn of events made the colonists even more dependent on trade with the natives. Powhatan sent food for Smith and Newport, as Smith had told Powhatan that Newport was his important "father." The corn and venison eased the hunger of the colonists. At the same time, Smith noted a rate of inflation in trade with the Indians; they were still being generous, but were expecting more in return. Jamestown did not have an unlimited supply of trade goods, as they all had to be brought from England. The Indians were experienced in barter and quickly learned the value of their own goods to the English.

4.4.3 All That Glitters

Captain Newport was faced with multiple problems; the first was that the colony leadership fell into petty squabbles when he was not around to lead them; the second was that he had told the Virginia Company in London and others that he had found gold in Virginia. In some areas of Virginia, the creeks appeared to be running in golden channels, but it was only pyrite or Fool's Gold. Newport had been misled by the golden glitter and now was more pressed than ever to find real gold as quickly as possible.

To this end, the colonists spent the early part of 1608 in the hunt for gold. They packed the pyrite-laden dirt onto Newport's ship in the vain hope that it would prove to be gold laced. Meanwhile, nothing necessary for the survival of the colony was being done: the fort's defenses were not being strengthened, the region was not being fully explored, the colonists were not producing enough of their own food to be self-sustaining, and the sailors, waiting to return to England, had to survive on the colony's food and water supplies, further straining the colony's resources.

Smith blamed Newport for the colony's focus on gold, not appreciating the position Newport was in with the financial backers of the colony who would not be impressed by anything other than gold, no matter how many other valuable resources Virginia was found to have. Newport further created problems for Smith by trading most generously with Powhatan on terms that could not, and, in Smith's view should not, be sustained. Newport had even given swords to Powhatan, and Smith was utterly opposed to giving weapons to the Indians. To Newport, it was good business, as he wanted Powhatan to see the English as useful neighbors and allies. He and Powhatan had even exchanged boys as a gesture of goodwill and so that each boy could learn the other people's ways and then be of service to their own people in understanding the other, an ancient practice of diplomacy.

Newport finally sailed for England on a ship loaded with worthless, sparkling dirt and the two leaders of the group who had tried to take the *Discovery*. Smith was left to deal with the rest of the gentlemen who resented his manner and with Indians who had been given elevated expectations of what the English would deliver. Powhatan appreciated the usefulness of the English metal weapons and tools. Smith was not as willing as Newport to give them up, so the Indians resorted to stealing what they wanted. Smith was not foolish or murderous enough to react to the thievery with the type of violence that Lane had used at Roanoke. Instead, the colonists tried to stay alert and drive away potential thieves without offending Powhatan.

The ship that had accompanied Newport and was thought lost suddenly appeared in April, a few days after Newport sailed for England. The commander, Thomas Nelson, had sailed south to winter after losing contact with Newport. He brought more supplies and colonists, and things seemed to be looking up for the colony, although the conflicts amongst the leaders continued to cause problems within, and the Indian's continued harassment from without. Nelson did not linger. After off-loading the supplies and colonists, he stayed long enough to take on a shipment of cedar before setting sail for England. For the Virginia Company, Jamestown was becoming something of a disappointment.

4.4.4 John Ratcliffe's Bad Decisions

In Jamestown, John Ratcliffe, president of the colony, behaved in ways which had a negative impact on the colony. Early in the venture, Smith had supported Ratcliffe for leadership, but he had since been disappointed by Ratcliffe's actions and interests. In Smith's absence, Ratcliffe had ordered the colonists to build him a home outside the fort. The idea was foolhardy, since a house outside the fort would be a natural target for the Indians. While working on Ratcliffe's home, the colonists were unable to do the work needed for the colony's maintenance. With the summer months, the weather had again turned unpleasantly hot and muggy, and many of the colonists were ill. Worst of all, Ratcliffe was consuming much-needed provisions. When Smith returned, Ratcliffe was removed from office. Smith, although recovering from a severe stingray attack and still unwell, was voted in as president. Whatever the state of Ratcliffe's mind, he made his situation all the worse by attempting mutiny.

Smith allowed the colonists much-needed time to recover before setting them to the task of preparing the colony for winter. Newport returned in September to find Smith in charge and the colonists hard at work. Newport brought another load of supplies as well as colonists, including the first married couple, and the first single Englishwoman in North America, Anne Burras. Anne was a maid to Mistress Forest, the first married Englishwoman in North America. Anne became the first Englishwoman to marry in North America, accepting the proposal of John Layton, one of the first colonists.

As 1608 drew to a close, Jamestown continued to survive but was not making a profit. As a business, it was operating at a loss. The Virginia Company of London was formed to invest in the colonization of Virginia with the goal of making a profit for its investors. By 1608, the investors had paid money to send ship after ship of colonists and supplies to Jamestown and had received back only two shiploads of dirt and one shipload of cedar. Rather than making a return on their investments, they were losing money. The company renewed Newport's instructions: to find gold, the lost colony, or the west passage to the Pacific was to be the colony's priority. Also, Newport was to crown Powhatan. Smith considered everything the company wanted as a general waste of valuable time that the colonists needed to spend on producing food. Over Smith's objections, Newport followed directions. He presented a crown to Powhatan, along with many other gifts. He sailed up the James to the Fall Line and then led an expedition overland from there and found neither gold nor a passage west. Smith had been right; Newport had wasted time, and, worse, he had managed to offend Powhatan. Suddenly, their unstable relations now reached a new low. The colony still could not produce its own food, and none was to be had from Powhatan's people. Smith blamed Newport, who had disregarded Smith's warnings and placed the colony in jeopardy.

Smith made finding food a priority. He sailed to various villages only to find that Powhatan had forbidden them to give the English food. Smith, desperate, would set fire to one of the village buildings and threaten to burn the rest if food was not brought. The tough tactics worked to an extent; the Indians did give him food, but not very much. They said, and it may well have been true, that they were also low on food. Powhatan had become convinced that the English intended to settle permanently in his lands, which he did not want. Smith's concern was the survival of Jamestown, which needed food and security. The situation remained uneasy as Smith tried to acquire more food and Powhatan tried to find a way to murder Smith. Powhatan's daughter, Pocahontas, saved Smith with a warning, at great personal risk. Smith did not realize that Powhatan too had his informants: Germans who had arrived with Newport's last visit. Smith had sent them to the Powhatan to build them an English-style house at Powhatan's request. When the Germans saw how much better life was in an Indian village than in the English fort of Jamestown, they asked to stay and serve Powhatan, who accepted at once.

Smith returned to Jamestown with the provisions he had managed to gather only to find that what food stores had been at the fort had been ruined by rats during his absence. Now the official leader of the colony, Smith set about making the changes he thought necessary for its survival. He ordered everyone, including the gentlemen, to work. Those who did not work would not eat. He secured a good supply of fresh water by having a well dug. He had new housing built. He increased security and put men to work farming. Some Indians who remained captives at the fort taught the English how to plant, and things were finally moving in the right direction. Smith was dealing well with both Indians and English, but he had not conquered the rats. Once again, they destroyed the colony's stores. Smith managed the crisis well and kept everyone alive but noted that there was a group that still would do little except feed themselves, a fact which clearly tried his patience.

When he lost all patience with Newport and the unreasonable monetary expectations of the Virginia Company, Smith wrote a strong and clear complaint to which the Virginia Company listened. They re-wrote the colony charter: no longer would a council and president control Jamestown; instead, a governor would be selected. Rather than sending ships with a hundred or fewer colonists at a time, several hundred would be sent together. Instead of the useless gentlemen that Smith considered to be a plague, the company would send working class men, skilled laborers and artisans well supplied. The new ideas were good; however, the execution of the new plan was poor. No official notice of the plan was sent to Smith. He did hear some general information from an English captain who sailed to the area. The company, though, told him nothing. On August 11, four large ships sailed up the James River. They carried a new shipment of colonists, hundreds of them, not just men but families with children, at the worst time of year. They brought the news that even more were on their way following close behind; they had been a fleet of eight and were separated in a storm. Several of the people Smith loathed the most, including Ratcliffe, were amongst the colonists. The ensuing conflict was immediate; Smith's old rivals wanted to enforce the new charter; however, the new charter was on a ship that had not arrived, leaving Smith to insist that the original charter was still in force.

4.4.5 Farewell John Smith

Smith won because the charter was lost with the ship that carried it. The new governor had also not arrived, so Smith remained in charge. He divided the colonists and sent them out to new settlements, as he had done previously to deal with the food shortage. The uneasy peace between the English and the Indians depended on both sides demonstrating restraint. The new gentlemen did not seem to understand this need and soon came into conflict with different tribes, attacking them with little or no provocation, destroying their homes and the very crops that the English had depended on as an object of trade; they robbed and killed them yet did not understand how these actions constituted a problem. They were worse than Lane's men at Roanoke. One group even managed to take a grandson of Powhatan, and, while he was restrained, shot him, claiming it was an accident. The young man's father, Parahunt, launched a constant attack against the men. Smith tried to negotiate a peace and was successful in dealing with the Indians, but he could do nothing with the English who would not listen to him. As Smith sailed back down river to Jamestown, something ignited the black powder he carried in a bag for his gun. It exploded, causing terrible burns to his body and leaving Smith in agony. His injury was so severe as to be life-threatening. Also, his office as president was coming to an end one way or another, as his term was expiring even without the new charter. Moreover, ships were on hand preparing to return to England. These combined factors convinced Smith to return home. The English told the Indians, including Pocahontas, that Smith was dead.

4.4.6 The Starving Time

Powhatan had respected Smith, even though he had tried to have the Englishman killed. But the Indian chief had no such respect for the new leaders at Jamestown. The Indians attacked almost anywhere they encountered the English, sometimes with direct attacks, sometimes in ambush, sometimes by luring the English into traps. The troublesome and self-serving Ratcliffe had thought to trade for corn with the Indians. He was captured, tied between stakes before a fire, and, like George Casson, excoriated then burned alive. Order broke down among the leaders of Jamestown as desperation set in. One group that had sailed up to the Potomac to find corn took their corn and sailed for England. For those who were left alive, the winter of 1609-1610 would be one of the cruelest experiences in American History, known as the "Starving Time."

With food supplies low and the leadership inept, the colony faced its most desperate situation yet. John Smith, who understood just how tenuous the colony's hold on survival had always been, focused on water, food, shelter, and security: the things the colony needed to survive. Now without Smith's leadership, the colony fell apart. Their official leader was a well-educated aristocrat, George Percy, who had no experience in dealing with any of the problems of the colony. Powhatan's men continued to harass the colony, killing colonists who wandered away from the protection of the fort and destroying English resources outside the fort. Inside the fort, hunger drove men to rash acts; some tried to rob the almost empty stores and were executed by Percy. To relieve the pressures on the dwindling food supply, Percy sent some colonists out to Point Comfort where they would remain for the winter, out of touch with the main group at Jamestown and unaware of the horrors that would happen there.

Soon the starving colonists resorted to eating cats, dogs, rats, and mice that were living in the fort. Nothing was left alive except the colonists themselves, so next they turned to leather items such as belts and shoes. They even boiled and ate their neck ruffs to obtain starch. Eventually they began to eat thc human dead, including an Indian who had been killed and buried. Finally, one colonist was driven to commit a terrible crime: Henry Collins killed then cannibalized his pregnant wife. He tossed the body of the baby into the river.

When his crime was discovered, he was tortured until he confessed, then executed.[10] Many colonists were so demoralized that some, fearing they would not be given a burial, dug their own graves and waited in them to die. As the winter came to an end in the spring of 1610, only sixty colonists were left alive at Jamestown and those were in pitiable condition. They had numbered five hundred when Smith left. Other English still remained alive at Point Comfort; they had, in fact, wintered quite well but dared not venture out to see how things were at Jamestown. Percy criticized the Point Comfort leaders, but the truth was they had succeeded where he had miserably failed.

4.4.7 Bermuda and the Lost Ship, the Sea Venture

The lost ship that had been carrying the new charter and new governor was the *Sea Venture*, and its colonists and crew had ended up on Bermuda, a paradisiacal island at that time. Here they had food, both meat and fruits, plenty of fresh water, and a wonderful, gentle climate. Many did not want to leave this pleasant island. Their ship, the *Sea Venture,* had been damaged in the storm that had separated the fleet. When the storm cleared, the captain, Admiral Sir George Somers, looked for land. He spotted Bermuda, which would be a safe place away from the Spanish, and ran the *Sea Venture* aground on a reef off the island's coast. Under the circumstances, it was probably the best that Somers could do, as his ship was in need of repairs, so they could not stay out to sea; Bermuda was surrounded by shallows and reefs and rocks, giving the ship no good approach. Somers managed to ground *Sea Venture* in such a way that all passengers and crew were safely transported to the island and the ship itself could be salvaged, to a certain extent. She could not be saved, but from her and the islands forests, new, smaller ships, the *Deliverance* and the *Patience,* were crafted. Shipbuilding was time-consuming under ideal circumstances. For Somers and company to craft two sea-worthy ships on a desert island was a remarkable achievement. As the work progressed, the members of the little company became attached to their island home. Remaining was not an option because of their duty to the Jamestown colony, so they set sail for Jamestown on May 10, 1610.

4.4.8 Governors Gates and West

They arrived less than two weeks later at Point Comfort, where they found Percy, who told them things were bad at Jamestown. Somers sailed on, reaching the fort on May 24. The fort appeared abandoned. The buildings and fortifications were damaged, the gates were down, and there were no people or even sounds of them. A bell was sounded to see if that would draw anyone out. Somers and the new governor Sir Thomas Gates might well wished it had not worked. The people who emerged from the buildings were emaciated beyond belief, appearing more dead than alive. Their bodies starved, their minds unwell, they came out and approached the new arrivals. Governor Gates faced his first crisis as the new governor of Jamestown. He had had no way of knowing what was happening at the colony while he was on Bermuda. Even if he had known, he could not have imagined the utter misery he found at Jamestown. While he took time to assess the situation, he could find no solution other than to remove all of the residents, load them on the four ships that had been left there, and find ways to return them to England.

Gates, Somers, and the *Sea Venture* had been believed lost by the other captains in their fleet, and that loss had been reported back to the company in England. They had therefore selected a new governor, Thomas West, Lord De La Warr, and gave him a small fleet with new colonists, and good provisions before sending him off to Jamestown. He arrived at Point Comfort just as Gates was sailing down the James to leave Virginia. West stopped Gates and turned the little fleet around. He had no intention of abandoning Jamestown. Gates and West, with their combined ships, sailed back to the fort. West was disgusted, believing and declaring that much of the problem had been the fault of the lazy colonists. Taking a page from John Smith, West ordered the fort to be cleaned and made it clear that the colonists would work. In addition to dealing with the foul conditions at Jamestown, he also focused on food, even though he had brought plentiful supplies. West had no intention of falling into the trap of his predecessors by waiting for a crisis to come along.

In dealing with Jamestown and the colonists, West had been clear-headed and decisive, if a bit stern. Dealing with the Indians was another matter. The careful balance John Smith had managed to maintain would be forever destroyed by the actions of the colony's new leadership which repeated the mistakes made by the Roanoke Colony of escalating violence instead of using diplomacy.

West, having been informed of the Indians' equipment thefts, sent a message to Powhatan demanding the return of the items and any prisoners Powhatan might be holding. Powhatan did not agree, so West chose Percy, who had been responsible for the Starving Time, to lead a punitive raid. The two men then for no particular reason chose to target the Paspahegh tribe, but Percy set out with a group of men. They came to the village at night and killed several men, burned the village to the ground and captured the queen, as the Europeans referred to her, and her children. In apparent bloodlust, Percy and his men took the queen and her children back to their ship where they tied the children up and threw them overboard, using them for target practice as they drowned. The queen watched as her children died. Percy took the queen back to West. What exactly happened next is a matter of debate. According to Percy, West wanted nothing to do with the queen and was angered that she was alive and ordered Percy to burn her at the stake. Others doubt West ordered this; still, she was taken ashore and executed.

The new leadership of the colony did not last. Somers had sailed off to Bermuda to attempt to capture hogs for the colony. He died of unknown causes, possibly a heart attack, on the island. West, who was to have been the governor for life, left after a few months with failing health in 1611. Sir Thomas Dale came to Jamestown in 1611 and soon earned a reputation for tough leadership. Dale, a soldier by trade and nature, instituted a rigid discipline on the fort. The effect on morale was not good, but the colonists worked hard, behaved themselves, and kept their homes and fort clean. To do otherwise could mean a whipping or even execution under Dale's command. Dale established new settlements to expand the colony and had no more qualms about killing the Indians than he did about killing his fellow English.

In 1613, Sir Samuel Argall, a ship's captain who had assisted the colony, discovered the location of Pocahontas, still the favorite daughter of Powhatan. He persuaded a local chief to help him capture her and lured her onto his ship. Argall took Pocahontas to Jamestown where Dale received her in a fair and friendly manner; the English thought they would now have bargaining power over Powhatan. In order to recover Pocahontas, Powhatan would have to release his captives and return the stolen tools and weapons. They were wrong. They kept Pocahontas at the settlement at Henricus where she was instructed by a minister in Christianity and where she also met John Rolfe, one of the colonists from the *Sea Venture*. Rolfe had lost his newborn daughter on Bermuda and his wife either on Bermuda, in Virginia, or on the journey between the two. At some point, a romance developed between Rolfe and Pocahontas. When Dale took Pocahontas to a village where he expected to find Powhatan in hopes of exchanging her for his stolen goods, Powhatan was not there, and Pocahontas declared to the Indians present that she wanted to stay with the English. Everyone, especially the English, was shocked. Whatever her motives, Pocahontas had freed her father from any obligation to agree to the demands of the English. She returned to Rolfe and her Christian lessons. She eventually was baptized as Rebecca, and she and Rolfe married in 1614 with the approval of Powhatan. Some of Pocahontas's family attended the service. The wedding achieved peace. Once more the English and Powhatan traded goods instead of lead shot and arrows.

John Rolfe was also important to the colony, and indeed to American History, for something else entirely: he pioneered tobacco cultivation in Virginia. The Virginia Indians had a variety of tobacco they used which was hardy but rough to smoke. Rolfe knew of a smoother, sweeter variety from the Caribbean. He had managed to secure some seeds and began growing his Orinoco tobacco at Jamestown. By 1612, he was planting it at Varina, up the river from Jamestown. The peace with Powhatan made it possible to create plantations where tobacco could be grown in large quantities. Tobacco production became the golden resource the Virginia Company had so long desired as tobacco use became phenomenally popular in England and Europe.

In the summer of 1616, Pocahontas sailed with her husband, son, and some Powhatan warriors to England where she was admired by many. They stayed in England until 1617. John Smith came to visit her, and she was very moved by seeing him again, especially as she had thought him dead. As the Rolfes prepared to sail for Virginia, she became suddenly ill and died within a few hours. Rolfe buried her in England, left his son Thomas there to be raised, and returned to Virginia and tobacco. Powhatan outlived his beloved daughter by roughly a year and died in 1618. He had given up trying to push the English out, which was why there was such a period of peace. His brother, however, still did not accept the English presence.

4.4.9 House of Burgesses

During this period of peace, the tobacco boom led to a rapid expansion of the colony. New settlements had to be established. At the same time, the colonists' drive to produce tobacco to the exclusion of most everything else, even such necessary things as growing food, was a cause of concern. Colonists were given grants of land and plantations were established. With the growth of the colony came a need for a new form of government, one that would allow the colonists a place to voice their concerns and to work for the common good. On July 30, 1619, the House of Burgesses met for the first time at Jamestown. This was the first group of elected representatives to meet in the New World. The timing of the first meeting was unfortunate as an outbreak of malaria forced the session to be cut short, but it is still significant for establishing the model that would be followed for the next 24 years.

In 1618, a leadership change at the Virginia Company brought important changes for the colony. The Virginia Company still wanted a profitable colony and one attractive to colonists. To this end they sent a new governor, Sir George Yeardley, with a document that is known as the "Instructions to George Yeardley" and also as the "Great Charter" which instructed him to make significant changes to the colony's government. These changes included an end to martial law and the establishment of English Common Law, an administrative reorganization, and new rules concerning colonists' transportation and owning of land in what would become known as the Headright System, as well as the establishment of a General Assembly that would include members elected to represent the citizens from the various areas of the colony. All free men could vote. Each settlement area was allowed to elect two representatives, called Burgesses. A burgess is simply someone elected to represent a town, borough, or university in a parliament or other assembly. They were the only elected members of the government for the colony, as all others were appointed. The colony had 11 such areas in 1619:

- James City
- Charles City
- Henricus
- Kicoughtan,
- Captain Martin's Plantation
- Smythe's Hundred
- Martin's Hundred
- Flowerdew Hundred
- Argall's Gift Plantation
- Captain Lawne's Plantation
- Captain Ward's Plantation

The Governor and the Governor's Council, originally six men selected by the governor and the burgesses, met in a unicameral session as the General Assembly. The first meeting was held in the church at Jamestown and began with a prayer and an oath to King James I. This first meeting dealt with issues such as tobacco prices, indentured servants, mulberry trees (in hopes of developing silk production), Indian relations (restricting what could be traded with the Indians and insisting that the Indians be fairly treated), marriages, and observation of the Sabbath; everyone was required to attend church twice on Sunday and to bring their weapons or pay a fine. Jamestown, unlike some of the later New England colonies, had not been established with a religious purpose, yet the colonists there as in other places took their religion seriously. These colonists were all officially Protestants, all members of the Church of England, or Anglicans. As England still wrestled with issues of religious identity that would ultimately lead to the founding of other colonies, the Virginia Company stockholders and the Jamestown colonists were all Anglican, and whether truly devout or not, the colonists were all active in the church thanks to mandatory church attendance. The Bishops of London provided the ministers to the colony. For the Jamestown colonists, their religious identity as Anglicans was tied to their cultural identity as English. By swearing their oaths to their king, they also were swearing oaths to the head of their church. Catholics were easily seen as enemies; non-Anglican Protestants were also not trusted. Other faiths would eventually gain a foothold in Virginia, but Anglicanism remains even to this day.[11]

Another important issue decided in this first session of the Assembly was the question of who was rightfully in the colony and who had the right to be represented in the Assembly. This last issue was raised because one of the plantation holders, Captain Ward, had not followed the standard procedures and had not received the appropriate permission from the Virginia company to be a part of the colony, but he and his men had proved valuable in their support of the colony, especially in catching fish, so he was encouraged to apply to the Virginia Company to have his status made legal. The other problem was Captain Martin who did have all the proper patents and more; he had a special arrangement that meant he and his people could actually ignore the rulings of the colonial government. The burgesses agreed that it would not be appropriate to have members who were not bound by the decisions of the Assembly, and Captain Martin was advised to contact the Virginia Company to renegotiate his patents to bring him and his plantation under the same rule as the rest of the colony. In this way the first meeting of the General Assembly established its authority over the entire colony. The governor still had the power to veto any ruling of the Assembly, to call it into session, and to end the sessions as he saw fit.[12]

As the colony expanded, so did the House of Burgesses, evolving from having two representatives elected for each settlement to having two elected for each county, plus single representatives for towns and one for the College of William and Mary. In 1643 the House of Burgesses became the lower house of the Virginia General Assembly, and the Governor's Council formed the upper house. The Governor's Council had also evolved from six members, with the Crown rather than the Governor appointing its members for life. They would continue to meet at Jamestown until the capitol of the colony was moved to Middle Plantation, which became Williamsburg in 1699.[13]

4.4.10 Servitude in Virginia

After it became clear that the colony would need a strong labor force, but before slavery was developed, the solution to the labor problem was indentured servants. The early colonists were free men and women who either paid their own passage or had someone else fund the voyage, such as a husband paying for his wife's passage. After the changes brought by Governor Yeardley in 1619, anyone paying for their own or another's passage was given 50 acres of land as a headright, or 50 acres per person or head transported. The intention was to encourage more people to come to the colony to help it develop a stable population. Wealthy members of the colony who traveled back and forth to England could abuse the system by claiming a headright for each passage back to the colony, so the system was not perfect.[14] Soon though, another group of colonists developed: indentured servants. These were people who were free-born English and other Europeans who either choose to become indentured or who, in the case of children, were indentured by their families. They were not slaves and their indenture was not a lifetime commitment. This system had benefits for both the person paying for the indentured servant as well as for the indenture servants themselves. For the sponsor, they had a guaranteed worker, provided the indentured servant did not die, and after 1619 they received a headright for transporting the indentured person. For the indentured servant, they offered several years of their labor in exchange for passage to the colony, being provided for while indentured: food, clothes, shelter, and then once the term of their indenture was ended, they were given land, supplies, tools, livestock, and possibly some money depending on the terms of their contract, to begin their lives as free colonists. They also had the skills they developed while serving their indenture. So, rather than being a new colonist, just off the boat without any knowledge of the hazards of Virginia, the former indentured servants were well-seasoned and better prepared for success.[15] Many became small farmers, while others became wealthy landowners.

One such man was John Chandler. Chandler was a child of nine and apparently the youngest immigrant to the colony at the time when he sailed on board the Hercules. He landed at Jamestown June 10, 1610. It seems young John sailed alone without any family and was almost certainly an indentured servant. Why his family would indenture him at such a young age is not known, as it was a risky business for anyone to undertake, especially a child. Chandler survived the lean years and dangers, and by 1623, he was listed as living in Elizabeth City, now Hampton, Virginia, a survivor of the massive attack of 1622. By 1624, he was in the service of Ensign Thomas Willoughby and may have been giving military service. Still, he had a small piece of land and wealthy neighbors, the Lupos. Lieutenant Albiano Lupo was an investor in the Virginia Company who had transported himself and others to the colony. His young wife Elizabeth held in her own right as she had paid for her own transport. Together they had over 400 acres of land when Albiano Lupo died in 1626. Elizabeth inherited her husband's property, which made her a very wealthy widow. Shortly after the death of her husband, she married her neighbor, John Chandler. This arrangement was not unusual; due to the circumstances of life in the colony, women generally did not stay single for long. As for John Chandler, he suddenly became a man of wealth and property and his prosperity grew in the following years, due in part to the headright system as he paid the transportation of nineteen others. His holdings grew to thousands of acres and included parts of Hampton and Newport News. His new social status led him to become a judge and also serve as a member of the House of Burgesses.[16]

The headright system was successful in putting land in the hands of the planters and small farmers. The push to be successful in growing tobacco placed a high demand not only on labor but also on land. Land that could be cultivated for tobacco in a relatively safe location was not limitless. The wealthier landowners invested their fortunes in purchasing more land in the best locations, leaving small farmers and those who hoped to be farmers with fewer and fewer options. As they settled on land in the less secure areas closer to Indian settlements, conflicts arose. By 1674, there was great dissatisfaction among these poorer members of the colony who felt their governor, William Berkeley, was not doing enough to protect them. What they wanted was for Berkeley to kill all the Indians. A collection of dissatisfied poor land holders, landless men, indentured servants, and slaves found a leader in Nathaniel Bacon, a wealthy aristocratic landowner who also felt Berkeley was not doing enough to protect the colonists from the Indians. Bacon would go on to lead his motley group in Bacon's Rebellion in 1676.[17]

The practice of indenture did have its drawbacks. A heavy investment was required of someone getting an indentured servant, and the indentured servants were just as likely to die as anyone else in that time. If the indentured servant survived, they would leave service eventually, taking all their job skills with them, leaving their former employer in need of new workers. For those thinking of being indentured, it was not an easy choice. Conditions were often harsh. Although a contract might specify that the indentured servant was to be fed and sheltered, if his employer had no food, the indentured servant had no food either. The final problem with indentured service for the colony was that it did not produce enough people to join the labor force needed to produce the tobacco, the colony's only successful cash crop.

In 1619, a Dutch ship carrying slaves arrived at Jamestown. These slaves were almost certainly from Ndongo Angola in Africa, captured and sold into slavery by the Portuguese. Although these Africans were considered slaves, when they arrived and were purchased by the governor of the colony, slavery as such did not exist in Jamestown. There was only indentured servitude, so these first Africans became indentured servants, not slaves in Jamestown. The colony needed labor to produce tobacco, but slavery developed slowly, not overnight. For those early Africans who survived, some expectation of freedom existed. Records show that some not only were free, but also became tobacco farmers with their own land and slaves. However, records indicate that they were not seen as equal to the colonists or the Indians.

Slavery was already established in Massachusetts when the first law passed concerning slaves in Virginia in 1640. The law does not refer to slaves but to blacks. Free citizens of the time were required to have and maintain weapons so that they could be used if need be for the defense of the colony, but the law from 1640 excused blacks from this duty. Another law passed allowed black women to be taxed. Then, in 1662, the first law directly concerning slavery in Virginia declared that it was possible for blacks to be servants for life. Indians also could be enslaved. In 1667, it was declared that baptism would not result in freedom; for some colonists, owning a Christian was, if not a sin, at least considered wrong. So, if slaves were baptized, the owner might set them free rather than own Christians. From that point on, laws concerning slaves were passed more frequently and became harsher; it was not, for example, a crime to accidentally kill a slave through punishment. It became natural for blacks to be slaves for life. A child of a female slave was automatically born a slave. Other laws included the following: thirty lashes to punish a slave who threatened a Christian in 1680, harsh punishments for slaves who ran away, separate slave laws, a white who married a slave would be banished, and, by 1705, slaves were to be considered real estate and, if unruly, could be dismembered. In 1625, twenty-three blacks appeared in Virginia. Seventy-five years later, their number increased to over 16,000, a change spurred by the need for cheap labor to grow tobacco.

4.4.11 Opechancanough

Sometime after the death of Powhatan, his brother Opechancanough became the chief, or *werowance*, of the Powhatan. He had never stopped wanting to rid Virginia of the English. He had been the first chief to hold John Smith captive. He had seen how the English grew in numbers and knew that if they were not eliminated while they were still relatively few, they would continue to spread out into Indian territories. Therefore, on March 22, 1622, Opechancanough launched the largest coordinated attack against the English. Nearly 400 English were killed all across the colony. If Opechancanough's security had been better, so that his plans had not leaked, the death toll would have been much higher.

For the English, who had had peace for so long, the event was a terrible shock. The newer colonists probably could not understand why the attack happened; only the oldest colonists would know of all the events that had happened over the years that fueled Opechancanough's anger, but they did not care about Opechancanough's motives. Opechancanough had expected the English to leave after the devastating attack. They did not. Instead, they wrought revenge, poisoning a couple hundred Indians in an attempt to kill Opechancanough, who escaped.

For King James I, the massacre was an adequate excuse to rid the Crown of the annoyance the Virginia Company had become. On May 24, 1624, he declared the company to be dissolved, and Virginia became a royal colony. The war continued fitfully between the Powhatan and the English until a treaty was signed in 1632. Opechancanough's feelings had not changed; he still wanted to eliminate the English, but with their superior weapons, they were able to inflict great damage, despite Opechancanough's superior numbers.

In 1642, the longest serving governor of Virginia arrived at Jamestown, Sir William Berkeley. Berkeley was a man of many talents. He proved to be an able colonial governor as well as a planter of diverse crops. He believed and so practiced that a colony could and should diversify its economic base by growing more than just tobacco. Tobacco's value as a cash crop was so great that few followed his lead, but his efforts and personal success are still noteworthy.

Early in his time as governor, Berkeley had to deal with the long-time enemy of the colony, Opechancanough. On April 18, 1644 Opechancanough attacked again as he had done in 1622, killing between 400 and 500 colonists. Again the English did not leave, and their colony had grown so large it was not possible for the Powhatan to drive them out. In 1646, Opechancanough was finally captured. He was quite old, perhaps over ninety. A common soldier who was to guard him shot him in the back instead. The callous act spared Opechancanough from the humiliation of being taken to England and put on public display. Opechancanough ultimately was captured because the Powhatan, who were powerful in 1607, had dwindled away to almost nothing in the span of forty years. Berkeley signed a treaty with Necotowance, Opechancanough's successor, which ended the two year conflict. The Powhatan tribes were given reservations in exchange for a tribute to be paid to the governor annually, a tradition that still exists today although much of the reservation lands have long been lost to the Indians.

Berkeley had external troubles as well. Berkeley, a Royal Governor, and Virginia, a Royal Colony packed with Anglicans, remained loyal to the Stuarts during the Civil War, leading Virginia to earn the nicknames the Cavalier State and the Old Dominion. Unfortunately for Berkeley and Virginia, the Stuarts lost, and King Charles I was beheaded. With the Puritans taking control in England, Puritan settlements had already been spreading in the colonies, including Virginia, which did not sit well with the Anglican colonists, who were loyal to the Stuarts. Puritans had been settling in Virginia since the 1620s on the south side of the James River and grew steadily in both population and influence, even though they were not particularly welcomed by their Anglican neighbors. Berkeley, a man who encouraged good relations and trade with Indians, was not so welcoming towards Puritans as politics and religion were tied all too closely. Berkeley did not want to have a religious conflict divide his colony as it did England, but at the same time, his tactics against the Puritans were increasingly oppressive. By 1648, ministers were ordered to conform to the Anglican Book of Common prayer or else be punished. To disobey was to disobey the government of the colony. By the early 1650's most of the Puritans had moved onto colonies friendlier to their religious beliefs, such as neighboring Maryland.[18] [19]

Berkeley would be ousted as governor by the Puritan regime in England, only to be recalled for one more term in office (1660-1677). The major crisis of his second term would be the last he would handle, Bacon's Rebellion. Berkeley's native-friendly and planter-friendly policies created an atmosphere of unrest among the poorer members of the colony even as the colony as a whole continued to prosper and grow.

In 1699, the capital was moved from Jamestown to the Middle Plantation, or Williamsburg, a place more centrally located in the colony, as the English had moved steadily west. The Jamestown fort itself would fall into ruin and eventually be lost, only to be rediscovered in modern times thanks to archeologists. Williamsburg would become a jewel of a colonial capitol, with the College of William and Mary and many fine shops reflecting the change in the colony brought on by the prosperity based on tobacco. With the struggle for survival over, the wealthier colonists could concentrate on finer things, such as fashion, food, and leisure activities. For the slaves, physical conditions improved, but their slavery remained. For the Indian tribes on tribal lands, they would see a steady encroachment of colonists and their land holdings would be largely lost along with their language and much of their culture.

4.4.12 Before You Move On...

Key Concepts

The English arrived at Jamestown with the goals of finding gold, a passage west to the Pacific, and the Lost Colony. They found none of these things. Their colony did well when well led and barely survived when its leadership was lacking. John Smith was best able to deal with the Powhatan Indians; most of the other English leaders of Jamestown repeated the mistakes of the Roanoke Colony in their Indian relations by acting with violence rather than diplomacy. A headright system was established to encourage immigration to the colony. The colony was established to make money for the investors of the Virginia Company but failed to do so until John Rolfe cultivated tobacco. Tobacco became the major cash crop of the colony and required land and labor to produce. Tobacco was so profitable a crop that vast amounts of land were cultivated for it, requiring an enormous labor force, more than could be provided by indentured servants. This need resulted in the development of a plantation system and the encouragement of the slave trade. Jamestown was the first successful English colony in North America, but its success resulted in the devastation of the native population. The natives were destroyed over the decades of contact with the English through disease and violent conflict. The once-powerful Powhatan Confederacy was reduced to almost nothing after forty years of contact with the English. The first legislature in the New World was established at Jamestown.

Test Yourself

1. John Smith told the colonists that if they did not work, they would not ________.

2. The Starving Time was not the fault of the colonists.
   a. True
   b. False

3. Newport discovered gold.
   a. True
   b. False

4. John Rolfe's tobacco completely transformed the colony.
   a. True
   b. False

See page 157 for answers

4.5 THE CHESAPEAKE COLONIES: MARYLAND

The bay region of the Potomac River and Maryland was first encountered by Captain John Smith, who, while he resided at Jamestown, had sailed to the region as part of his explorations. In 1632, George Calvert, the first Lord Baltimore, applied to King Charles I for a royal charter to establish a new colony in the Chesapeake region of North America, where he had already created a colony in Newfoundland. However, when he observed Newfoundland firsthand, he did not like the land, which was not as described to him. A devout convert to Catholicism, he wanted to establish a colony where Catholics could practice their religion freely, something not always possible in England, and he wanted the colony to be created further south where the climate was kinder and the popular cash crop, tobacco, could be grown. Calvert, who died in April, 1632, did not live to see his charter materialize. His eldest son and heir, Cecilius Calvert, the second Lord Baltimore, was granted the charter his father had long worked to gain. The new colony was called Maryland, named for Henrietta Marie, wife of Charles I. The Maryland charter was interesting in that it did not simply grant the Calverts the right to establish a colony; it granted the Calverts actual ownership of all the land of the colony, with the colonists swearing oaths to the Baron. The Baron in turn had the right to sell land to aristocrats as he saw fit, thus creating a landed aristocracy class for the colony. Maryland became the first proprietary English colony in North America.

Leonard Calvert, the younger brother of Cecilius, was appointed the governor of the new colony and set sail with three hundred colonists on two ships, the *Ark* and the *Dove*. They arrived at St. Mary's, Maryland on March 27, 1634. The first group of colonists was composed of both Catholics, including Jesuit priests, and Protestants. Of the thirteen original colonies, Maryland had one of the most progressive governments in terms of religious freedom and its treatment of Indians. It guaranteed religious freedom to all Christians and treated Indians as persons, including paying for their land. In 1642, the first Africans arrived. Lord Baltimore intended Maryland to be a tobacco growing state, so a labor force was needed, and indentured servants were the norm at that time. The Africans arrived as slaves, but the Marylanders balked at enslaving Christians, so, if Africans were willing to be baptized, they could well be set free, an outcome which would create a financial loss to their owners. Laws were eventually enacted to protect the rights of slave owners, just as there were laws to protect the rights of those who had indentured servants.

The site of St. Mary's had been a village belonging to the Yaocomico Indians, one of the many Algonquian language tribes found in the Chesapeake region. Calvert purchased the village area to found his capital city and made great efforts to remain on good terms with the Indians of the colony. Like other Algonquian speakers of the region, the Yaocomico wore deerskin robes with shells and feather decorations. They painted and tattooed themselves, perhaps in a style like that depicted in White's portraits of the Secotan from the Outer Banks further south. The Yaocomico were good friends to the new colony. They stayed nearby as their village was transformed to an English settlement and helped the colonists adjust to agriculture in their new home. Odds are the Yaocomico suffered the same fate as many of the Secotan of Roanoke; although they stayed near the English, they did not develop immunities to the English diseases. They vanished without further mention before 1700.

Conflicts, of course, occurred; the first was with Virginia, Maryland's neighbor to the south. The colonies share a border marked, for the most part, by the Potomac River. Virginia, a royal colony by the time of the founding of Maryland, had been interested in having the territory added to its own, or, at the very least, not having it given to another colony and potential competitor in the lucrative tobacco market. A Virginia planter, statesman and Puritan, William Clayborne, had set up a trading post and settlement on Kent Island in 1631. The island was included in the charter granted to the Calverts for Maryland. Clayborne and Virginia protested but lost. The conflict, which sometimes included military action and fatalities, continued into the 1650s. For Virginia and Maryland, the issue was territorial and financial, and Virginia would eventually side with Maryland against Clayborne. For Clayborne, the issue was financial, religious, and personal, so he did not drop the matter willingly. During the

Figure 4.3 St. Mary's City, Maryland | Reconstruction of an early house at St. Mary's.

Author: Sarah Stierch
Source: Flickr
License: CC BY 2.0

same time period, Maryland was at war with the Susquehannock, an Iroquoian tribe who earlier had threatened the Yaocomico.

4.5.1 Maryland and the Civil War in England, 1642-1660

Maryland was also affected by the English Civil War. The Catholic Calverts supported King Charles I, while many Protestants in the colony and in Virginia, including Clayborne, supported Parliament. A Captain Richard Ingle joined with Clayborne, seized St. Mary's in 1644, and began the Plundering Time, in which he rode up and down Maryland, seizing whatever he wished, terrorizing the citizens and capturing Jesuits for shipment back to England. Only the return of Governor Calvert in 1646 from his exile in Virginia ended Ingle's reign of terror. Calvert died the next summer, in 1647, passing the governorship to Thomas Greene, one of the earliest colonists and a Catholic.

Tensions were growing between the dominant, minority Catholics and the majority Protestants. In 1648, Lord Baltimore appointed William Stone as the first Protestant governor. Stone had earlier founded the city of Providence on the Severn River as a new home for Puritans leaving Virginia, which had become more firmly Anglican under Governor William Berkeley.

The conflict between Protestants and Catholics led to the Maryland Toleration Act of 1649 which guaranteed religious freedom to all Christians. This move was a bold one on the part of Maryland and established a very liberal religious policy that was not common in the English colonies at the time. Maryland, therefore, became an attractive location for those Christians who sought freedom from religious persecution. The law was clear, however, that it applied only to Christians; anyone who denied the divine nature of Christ could be put to death. Although the Toleration Act made Maryland an attractive haven for non-Anglican Protestants, it did nothing to assure these groups that the Catholic minority controlling the colony were fair to all parties. The impression of favoritism to Catholics continued in the minds of many Protestant Marylanders and would continue to break out in rebellion until the Calverts' control of the colony in 1689.

The Toleration Act became a victim of the English republican period. The Calverts' dream of a haven for Catholics where Protestants and Catholics could live together in peace was not shared by the Protestant supporters of the Parliament during the war. After the execution of Charles I in 1642, Oliver Cromwell, the head of the English republic, gave William Clayborne, his loyal supporter, control of Maryland. Clayborne was able to get the Maryland Assembly to repeal the Act. Then Clayborne went further and succeeded in passing a ban which made it illegal to publicly practice Catholicism in a colony founded for Catholics.

Stone, who had been driven from Maryland by Cromwell's supporters, returned with an army and fought the Battle of the Severn but was defeated and captured. One of Stone's officers, Josiah Fendall, became the next governor of Maryland appointed by Lord Baltimore. Lord Baltimore had reached an agreement with Cromwell's government to have his own governor once again in charge of his colony. Fendall managed to restore order and improve conditions in the colony. Still, the Protestants displayed unrest and expressed dissatisfaction with having a Catholic Lord Proprietor. Fendall and the Assembly attempted to break away from the Calverts and create a new government. The timing was not in Fendall's favor. Cromwell died in 1658, and England reverted to a monarchy with the arrival of King Charles II, who fully supported Lord Baltimore. Baltimore appointed another of his brothers, Philip Calvert, to be the new governor temporarily, and then his son and heir, Charles Calvert, arrived to serve as governor in 1661.

4.5.2 Slavery in Maryland

Maryland had been chartered with the intention of being an agriculturally based colony, with tobacco as its primary crop. The conflicts Marylanders experienced had been a distraction from that goal. With the political horizon finally clearing, the colonists turned their attention once again to tobacco and an important issue facing tobacco planters: sources of labor. As in Virginia, the need for labor to plant and harvest tobacco had encouraged the slave trade and, because the demand for tobacco grew exponentially, so too did the need for permanent, inexpensive labor. In 1664, Maryland passed the first law to create a permanent slave class. Those who were slaves would remain slaves for life, as would those born to slaves; the law applied to all slaves, regardless of race. The earliest slaves in Maryland had been able to gain their freedom by becoming Christians, but that path to freedom was closed in 1671 with another law that allowed slaves to be baptized but expressly denied them freedom based on baptism.

4.5.3 Maryland in the late Seventeenth Century

Charles Calvert, who took his position as governor of Maryland in 1661, just one year after the Restoration of monarchy in England, was a Catholic, as were his father and grandfather; not surprisingly, he gravitated toward Catholics in both his private and public life. His first wife was from a Catholic family, and the majority of his advisors were Catholic aristocrats. His colony's population, however, was largely Protestant. Because Maryland was a proprietary colony, Charles Calvert and the Catholic minority controlled the Protestant majority. The Protestants were neither happy nor comfortable with this situation. An influx of Protestants, who were largely Puritans from Virginia and New England, migrated to the colony. Because they were unused to the proprietary form of government, they expected to have a greater voice in it than the Calverts were willing to give.

Maryland did have an Assembly which represented the people, but ultimately power was in the hands of the proprietors, who could support or deny any decision the Assembly made. To make matters worse, in the 1670s, the Calvert family attempted to control the colony by enacting a series of laws restricting access to political power. According to these laws, only those colonists who owned a significant amount of property, either land or personal property, could vote; similarly, only those with large land holdings could serve in the Assembly. No average farmer would be able to gain the required amount of land to do either. In addition, because the proprietors owned the land and had the right to choose to whom it would be sold, many of the largest land owners were Catholics. Charles Calvert reduced the size of the Assembly by reducing the number of delegates from each part of the colony. In this way, the colonists still had representation and the proprietors would have fewer elected voices with which to contend and consequently fewer opinions opposed to their own. The common people, particularly the Protestants, were displeased with these measures.

In 1675, Cecilius Calvert, the second Lord Baltimore, died; his son and heir Charles immediately became the third Lord Baltimore and left Maryland for England to deal with his father's estate and his own inheritance. While Lord Baltimore was away in England, rebellion arose again in Maryland, as Lord Baltimore was accused of a variety of things that alarmed the British Crown, including that of creating religious conflicts with his insistence on religious toleration. Lord Baltimore responded, quite accurately, that Maryland did not recognize an official church. His own faith was Catholic, but Catholics were a minority. Some in Maryland were Anglicans, but the Church of England was also in the minority in Maryland. The existence of religious tolerance had drawn people of many different Christian denominations to settle in Maryland; it would be imprudent, if not impossible, to declare one to be the colony's official church and have it be accepted by all the people. The rebellion was quickly put down, but the issues that led to it continued to simmer.

The year 1681 brought yet another rebellion, this one led by a former governor and rebel, Josias Fendall. As with his first rebellion, this one, too, was a failure. Fendall's life was spared once again, though he paid a heavy monetary penalty. The people continued to be frustrated by the gap between those with power over the colony and the rest of the colonists. Making matters worse, the price of tobacco had been dropping and continued to drop. Lord Baltimore had considered working with Virginia to raise the prices by holding back the crop one year, but refused as it would have been too difficult for the small farmers who needed their income to survive. The drop in prices of Maryland's main cash crop created hardship for many of the colonists. Lord Baltimore's failure to find a solution, or to at least find a way to help the people through the hard times, added to the resentment against him, especially since Calvert and his closest friends and advisors were a privileged class who did nothing to hide it.

William Penn added to Lord Baltimore's growing list of problems. Penn had been granted a charter by King Charles II to found his own colony, Pennsylvania, to the north of Maryland. The charter did not define Pennsylvania's borders as well as was needed, and soon there was a conflict between Pennsylvania and Maryland. Penn and Lord Baltimore were unable to resolve the issue on their own, even though it was simple: Maryland's northern boundary was the 40th parallel; Penn was building his capitol, Philadelphia, below the line in Maryland territory and advising farmers in the area that they were not in Maryland but Pennsylvania. Lord Baltimore once again sailed for England in 1684 in an effort to resolve the issue there. Penn was wrong and Lord Baltimore right, but Penn was allowed to keep Philadelphia and other lands as well; the issue was not resolved until the Mason-Dixon Line was surveyed in the 1760s.

Charles, Lord Baltimore, never returned to Maryland, where conflict seemed to be a constant condition. He had left his nephew, George Talbot, in charge in his absence, but before Lord Baltimore had reached England, his nephew murdered a royal official. When hearing of the incident, Lord Baltimore replaced Talbot with William Joseph, an Irishman and Catholic who also did not manage to avoid controversy. Joseph became governor of the volatile colony just as the Glorious Revolution was happening in England.

King Charles II had died and was succeeded by his brother, King James II, who had been raised in France and was Catholic. James II was deposed in 1688 in what was called the Glorious Revolution, a bloodless coup by Protestants who wanted no more Catholic kings. The Protestants, in particular the Puritans back in Maryland, felt the same way, and once again, rebellion erupted in 1689. James Coode, who had been involved in the rebellion of 1681, was the leader and succeeded in taking over the colony. With the rebellion and all the other problems of the colony, Calvert lost control of his colony to the Protestants who governed until 1692 when Maryland became a royal colony under the direct authority and management of the Crown. Maryland remained a Royal Colony until 1715 when it was again given to the Calverts as a proprietary colony as it remained until the American Revolution.

4.5.4 Before You Move On...

Key Concepts

The first Lord Baltimore envisioned Maryland as a proprietary colony providing a safe haven for Catholics with an economy based on the cash crop, tobacco. This reasoning was in reaction to the discrimination and harassment faced by Catholics in England in the decades after the Protestant Reformation. His eldest son inherited the charter, and his grandson, Leonard Calvert, founded the colony and became its first governor in 1634. Although the Calverts had encouraged Protestants as well as Catholics to settle in the colony, many Protestants were not happy with the Catholic Calvert's leadership. There was a view that the Catholic minority was ruling the Protestant majority which created resentment. The Calvert family maintained an active involvement with the colony until 1689, when their charter was lost due to Protestant rebellion. They continued to have an interest in the colony, leading to a restoration as the proprietors in 1715. The Calverts tried to practice religious toleration for all Christians and had one of the most tolerant policies concerning religion of any of the colonies, and they worked to deal fairly with the Indians. However, slavery became firmly entrenched in 1664 in response to the need for a permanent labor force to raise tobacco.

Test Yourself

1. Who is Maryland named for?

   a. The Virgin Mary

   b. Henrietta Marie, wife and queen of Charles I

   c. Queen Mary of England

   d. Queen Mary of Scotland

2. Where was George Calvert's first colony? ___________

3. George Calvert was born a Catholic.
   a. True
   b. False

4. Religious tolerance created a happy and unified Maryland Colony
   a. True
   b. False

See page 157 for answers

4.6 THE ESTABLISHMENT OF THE NEW ENGLAND COLONIES

New England is the area of the Atlantic seaboard north and east of New York. During the seventeenth century, it consisted of the colonies of Plymouth, Massachusetts Bay, Connecticut, Rhode Island, and New Hampshire. Several of these colonies are usually referred to as "Puritan" (Plymouth, Massachusetts Bay, Connecticut) because they were settled by Puritans (Massachusetts Bay and Connecticut) or Pilgrims (Plymouth), all of whom were Calvinists who had been persecuted in England and who sought freedom to practice their religion without interference in the Americas. Connecticut and Rhode Island were actually offshoots of Massachusetts Bay, settled either by Puritans or by those, in the case of Rhode Island, who had conflicts with the Puritan establishment in Massachusetts Bay. The New England colonies were settled before 1640.

4.6.1 Puritans and Puritanism

Puritanism was a major factor in the creation and the social, religious, and economic life of the New England colonies. Plymouth and Massachusetts Bay were founded by those who wished to practice their Calvinist-based Protestantism without persecution by the English Church or Parliament. Both the Pilgrims who settled Plymouth and the Puritans who settled Massachusetts Bay were Calvinists who wanted to carry John Calvin's theories to their logical conclusions. Though the theology of the Church of England created a compromise between Catholicism and Calvinism, neither the Puritans nor the Pilgrims thought the Church had gone far enough to rid itself of Catholic theology and practice. New England Calvinists, like their counterparts in England, wanted to do away with stained glass in churches, robes for ministers, the use of incense during services, genuflecting at the sign of the cross, marriage as a sacrament, and the imposition of last rites. The Puritans and Pilgrims believed that idleness was a sin, and, hence, that monasteries were a waste of time. They equally disliked mysticism, meditation, and prescribed prayers. Those Calvinists who settled Massachusetts Bay insisted that the Church of England could be "purified" of its Catholicism; the Pilgrims of Plymouth were "Separatists" who were sure that the Church of England could not be reformed so that their only choice was to separate from it entirely. In 1609, as the result of intense persecution, the Pilgrims immigrated to Holland, where they created a Congregational Church in Leiden.

4.6.2 Plymouth Plantation

The Scrooby Congregation that followed their minister John Robinson to Leiden was, according to historian Nathan Philbrick, the "radical fringe of the Puritan movement."[20] Although the Dutch welcomed them and Leiden and its surroundings were reminiscent of their countryside of East Anglia (along England's eastern coast), after a decade of living among the Dutch and fearing that their children were becoming unfamiliar with their English heritage, the Scrooby Congregation decided to practice their beliefs in the Americas. William Bradford, whose *Of Plymouth Plantation* tells the story of the Pilgrims in Holland and the new world, lamented that the children of the congregation were overworked to the extent that their "bodies became decreped [sic] in their early youth." But worse than this and

> ...of all the sorrows most heavie to be borne,--many of their children, by the great licentiousness in that countrie [Holland], and the manifold temptations of the place...were drawn away...into extravagant and dangerous courses, tending to dissoluteness and the danger of their souls.[21]

So, in 1620, the Separatists sought permission from the Virginia Company to move to its territory in North America. William Bradford reasoned that the trip to the Americas would be "well tolerated" as the immigrants were already "weaned from the delicate milke of our mother countrie, and enured to the dificulties of a strange and hard land [a reference to Holland]."[22] After a good bit of negotiation, the Separatists received a charter from the Virginia Company and permission from the English Crown, and in spring 1620, set sail in the *Mayflower*. According to Bradford's narrative, these "Pilgrims," as they called themselves, went to the Americas with hopes of practicing their religion without interference and with "inward zeall...of laying some good foundation, or at least to make some way thereunto, for the propagating and advancing the gospell of the kingdom of Christ in those parts of the world."[23] Their goals were not unlike those stated by Columbus, Richard Hakluyt, in the Charters of Roanoke Island and the Chesapeake colonies and the settlers of Massachusetts Bay.[24]

The Voyage of the Mayflower

In July, 1620, 101 passengers left Delfshaven, Holland aboard the *Mayflower* for the sixty-five day journey to the New World. Fewer than one-third of the passengers were Pilgrims; the remainder Bradford referred to as "strangers," or those not among the "elect" who were predestined for salvation. Among the "saints," or Pilgrims, were William Bradford, William Brewster, and John Carver. The "strangers" included Captain Miles Standish, a soldier, and John Alden, an adventurer. After a long and stormy voyage, the *Mayflower* anchored at Provincetown, Cape Cod, on November 21, 1620. It was not the best time of

Figure 4.4 Mayflower in Plymouth Harbor | An 1882 painting of the ship that brought the Pilgrims to the new world.

Artist: William Halsall
Source: Library of Congress

year to attempt to establish a new settlement in a strange land.

Because they landed north of the land granted by the Virginia Company with no charter and no title to the land, and in an area named "New England" by John Smith[25] rather than Virginia, they drafted the *Mayflower Compact,* which created a government by social contract and bound them together in a common purpose.

Figure 4.5 Mayflower Compact | The pilgrims signing the compact, on board the May Flower, Nov. 11th, 1620.

Artist: Engraving by Gauthier after painting by T.H. Matteson
Source: Library of Congress

The Pilgrims signed the *Mayflower Compact* on November 21, 1620. After signing the *Compact* there was one more task to be completed: the election of a governor. For this role, they chose John Carver. When Carver died several months later, William Bradford was elected to replace him. Bradford served as governor for more than three decades.

The Pilgrims landed initially at Cape Cod but soon discovered a more suitable site at the harbor named Plymouth, also by John Smith; they settled here on December 23, 1620. The first winter was as harsh as that at Jamestown. The Pilgrims, not unlike the Jamestown residents, spent a month exploring the surrounding area which left them with few provisions for the winter. One half of the company, including Governor Carver, died before spring; however, when the *Mayflower* sailed for England in April, 1621, not one of the original colonists was aboard.[26] They had all decided to stay.

The Mayflower Compact

Text	Transcription
In the Name of God, Amen. (1) We whose names are underwritten, **the loyal subjects of our dread sovereign Lord, King James,**	1. The Puritans opened the document with a form of prayer, expressing the religious beliefs which would later dictate the structure of their society
(2) by the grace of God, of Great Britain, France and Ireland, King, Defender of the Faith, etc. Having undertaken, for the glory of God, and advancement of the Christian faith and honor of our King and Country, a voyage to plant the first colony in the northern parts of Virginia, do by these presents solemnly and mutually in the presence of God, and one of another, **covenant and combine ourselves together into a civil body politic,**	2. The Pilgrims had left England ten years before, as they were persecuted as dissenters from the Anglican Church. They had been in Leiden for a decade, yet they still claimed to be loyal subjects of the English king. And even during the American Revolution, many colonists remained Loyalists.

Text	Transcription
(3) for **our better ordering and preservation and furtherance of the ends aforesaid**; (4) and by virtue here of to **enact, constitute and frame such just and equal laws, ordinances, acts, constitutions and offices from time to time**,	3. The covenant was a Puritan concept that referred to the covenant between the elect and God. Here, the Puritans linked their social, civil bonds to God, foreshadowing John Winthrop's utopian vision of a Puritan "city on a hill." 4. It would become a common idea in the eighteenth century that law and reason were actually embedded in nature, and that the function of government was to protect and improve the lives of its people. In the next line it is also made clear that laws are enacted only to promote the welfare of the people; the suggestion is that any other legislation was not needed. This is an early statement of an ideal later expressed by John Locke.
(5) as shall be thought most meet and convenient for the general good of the Colony: **unto which we promise all due submission and obedience**. (6) In witness whereof we have hereunder subscribed our names at Cape Cod the 11 of November, in the year of the reign of our sovereign Lord, King James of England, France and Ireland the eighteenth, and of Scotland the fifty-fourth. Ano. Dom. 1620.	5. This phrase refers to "equal laws," implying that all were treated equally under the law. In the Puritan colonies, however, only members of the "elect" were treated equally; others had no rights to cast ballots or hold public office. 6. The Pilgrims vowed obedience to this compact, pledging to uphold social order. The *Mayflower* Compact was followed until Plymouth merged with the Massachusetts Bay Colony in 1692.

The Pilgrims, the Indians, and the First Thanksgiving

William Bradford's narrative recounts the impact of the Pilgrims having arrived in an unknown land "with no friends to welcome them nor inns to entertain or refresh their weather beaten bodies and...no houses or much less towns to repair to." In fact, the only inhabitants they encountered were Indians who "were readier to fill their sides full of arrows than otherwise." And as if these problems were not serious enough, it was winter, "and they [knew] the winters of that country to be sharp and violent, and subject to cruel and fierce storms, dangerous to travel to known places, much more to search an unknown coast."[27] Edward Winslow, a fellow traveler, echoed Bradford's concerns when he wrote in *Good News from New England* (1624): "How few, weak, and raw were we at our first beginning, and there settling, and in the midst of barbarous enemies."[28] He would remark later, however, that the Indians and especially Squanto (whom Winslow called

Tisquantum) were much like the Englishmen in that they were "worthy" of trust, "quick of apprehension, [and] ripe witted."[29]

By early spring, 1621, conditions in Plymouth had improved, including relations with the local Indians. In March, the Pilgrims were surprised when the Abenaki sachem, Samoset, who had picked up some words of English from fishermen in the waters off the coast of Maine, appeared in the settlement and greeted the settlers with the words: "Welcome, Englishmen." Samoset and Squanto, a member of the Pawtuxet tribe of the Wampanoag Confederacy, helped orient the English to life in the wilderness. Squanto, who had spent time in England after being kidnapped by Thomas Hunt, one of John Smith's lieutenants, taught the Pilgrims how to use local herring to fertilize the soil; soon thereafter crops, including maize, began to flourish. Bradford wrote in March,

> ...it pleased God the mortalities began to cease amongst them [the Pilgrims] and the sick and lame recovered apace which put as [it] were new life into them: though they had borne their sad affliction with much patience and contentedness."[30]

In addition to giving the new arrivals horticultural advice, Squanto acted as an interpreter in their dealings with the Wampanoag sachem, Massasoit, who came with Squanto to visit the English settlement. Due to the efforts of Squanto, an agreement was reached between Governor Carver and Massasoit in 1621, the contents of which were recorded by William

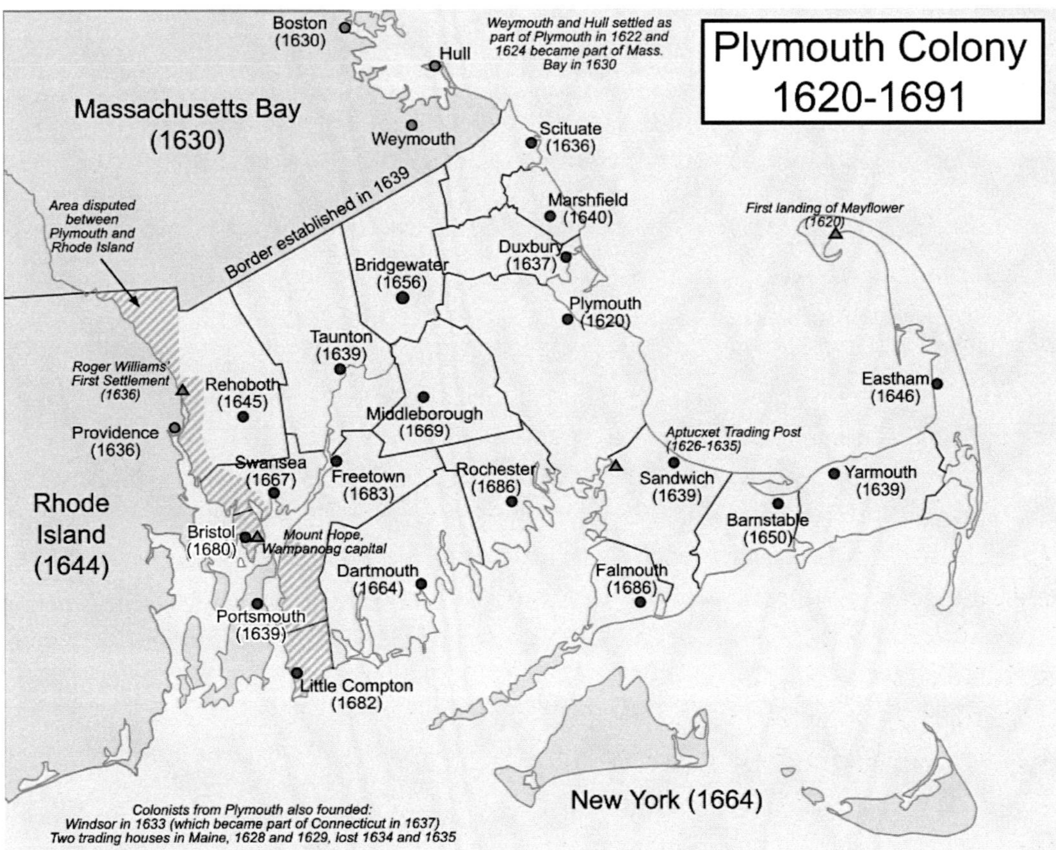

Figure 4.6 Plymouth Colony | Map of the Plymouth Colony to 1691.

Author: Wikipedia User "Hoodinski"
Source: Wikimedia Commons

Bradford. According to the treaty, the Indians would not injure the English or steal their tools, and if either party were engaged in warfare, the other would come to the aid of the first; the treaty lasted for twenty-four years. [31]

The famous "first" Thanksgiving took place in September or October, 1621 on a day when the Pilgrims had killed a large number of ducks and geese and Massasoit arrived with about one hundred Indians who later killed five deer to add to the feast. The deer were roasted on spits, and those assembled feasted on venison, fish, fowl, and beer. Historian Nathaniel Philbrick points out that there was no pumpkin pie or cranberry sauce, and no eating utensils except knives. Instead, the participants ate with their fingers and sprawled on the ground as they consumed the feast. Edward Winslow, in *Mourt's Relation*, described the occasion:

> Our harvest being gotten in, our governor sent four men on fowling, that so we might after a special manner rejoice together, after we had gathered the fruits of our labors....Many of the Indians coming amongst us, and amongst the rest their greatest king Massasoit, with some ninety men, whom for three days we entertained and feasted, and they went out and killed five Deer, which they brought to the [Plymouth] Plantation and bestowed on our Governor, and upon the Captain and others. And although it not always be so plentiful, as it was at this time with us, yet by the goodness of God, we are so far from want. [32]

Government in Plymouth

Because the settlers at Plymouth had established a town outside of the area of the charter they held from the Virginia Company, they had bound themselves together with the *Mayflower Compact*. But this agreement was not recognized by the Crown, so they later requested and received a charter from the Council for New England in which no specific boundaries were mentioned. Thus, to clarify their position, they created a formal structure of government. The executive body consisted of a governor and seven councilors who were chosen annually by popular vote. A legislative body, the "General Court," was to be a meeting of the forty-one men who had signed the *Mayflower Compact*. As the colony grew in population and area, the towns began to send representatives to the meeting of the Court. In 1639, the Pilgrims adopted the *Fundamentals of Plymouth*, which recognized the structure that existed and guaranteed habeas corpus (the right to be charged upon arrest) and the right to a jury trial. Up until 1660, all adult males could vote; after this time, a property qualification was imposed. Plymouth, always small in population, was overshadowed by the larger Puritan colony of Massachusetts Bay, which absorbed Plymouth in 1691.

4.6.3 Massachusetts Bay

Ten years later, a second group of Puritans applied for a charter from the Council for New England. Led by a prominent Member of Parliament and lawyer, John Winthrop, these Puritans fled persecution in England, which had intensified in the 1620s under the increasingly pro-Catholic Charles I. Charles began his eleven-year rule without Parliament in 1629. Once Parliament was dismissed, Charles and the Archbishop of

Canterbury, William Laud, began the arbitrary arrest and imprisonment of those who did not conform to Anglicanism. The Puritans who followed John Winthrop to North America were non-separating Calvinists. Instead of breaking entirely with the Church of England, as had been the case with the Pilgrims, they intended to "purify" the Church, hence their name of "Puritan."

The Massachusetts Bay Charter, which was issued in March, 1629, created "the Governor and Company of the Massachusetts-bay in New England." The recipients of the charter were referred to as "freemen;" they were the only ones who had a voice in the government. There was a governor, an assistant governor, and a legislative body, the General Court, which would make laws for the colony. For his part, Charles appears to have been only too happy to approve the Puritans' application to emigrate, as it was easier to send them to the New World than to deal with them in England.

If the motives of the King were somewhat unclear to those at the time, no doubt existed about the motives of John Winthrop and his Puritan compatriots, who in 1630 sailed for New England. Seventeen ships and 1,000 settlers comprised the Winthrop armada, the lead ship of which was the *Arbella*. While on board the *Arbella*, Winthrop delivered a sermon, "A Modell of Christian Charity," that has since become famous as a statement of the purpose for those leaving England. Winthrop insisted,

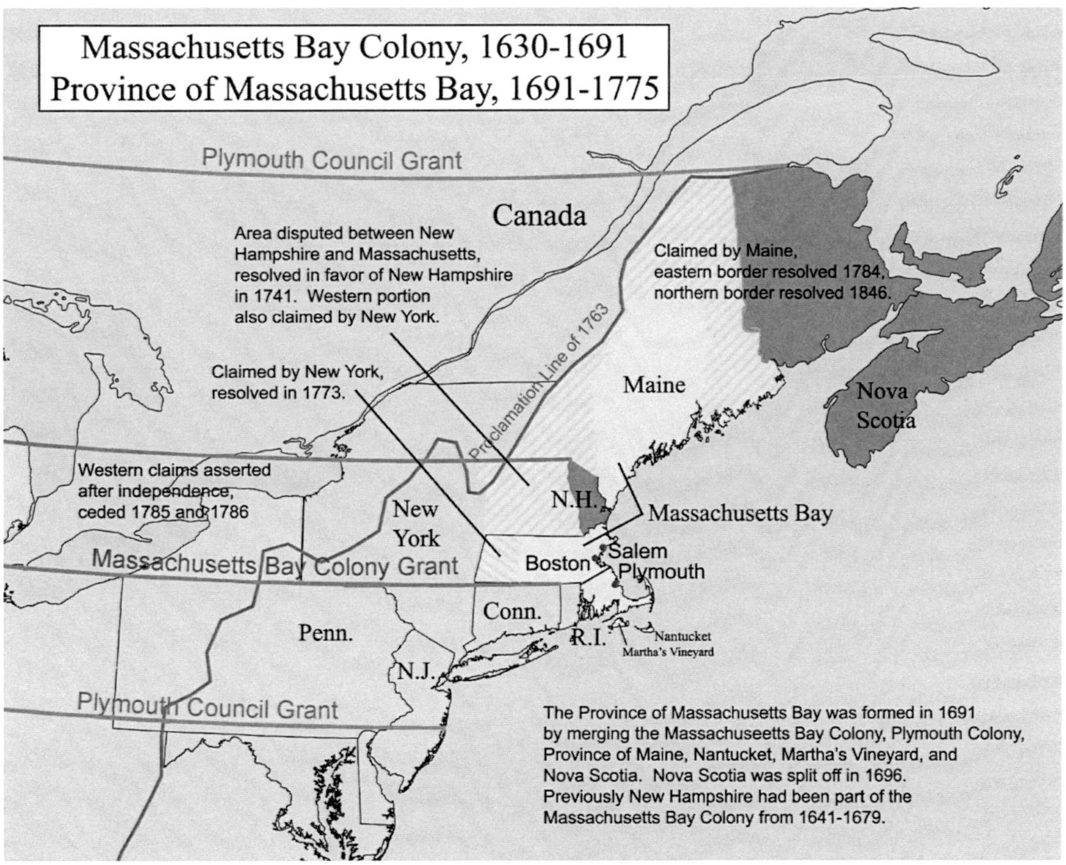

Figure 4.7 Massachusetts Bay Colony | Map of Massachusetts Bay Colony.

Author: Karl Musser
Source: Wikimedia Commons

> We must consider that wee shall be as a citty upon a hill. The eies of all people are upon us. Soe that if wee shall deale falsely with our God in this worke wee haue undertaken...wee shall be made a story and a by-word through the world.[33]

The settlers would, in other words, create a political and religious example in the new world that would be used as a model for reforming England and Europe.

Boston became the capital of the colony, and soon a "Great Migration" of some 80,000 English headed for Massachusetts Bay. Only official church members, referred to as "visible saints," could be freemen in the Massachusetts Bay Company, which became the temporary governing body of the colony. It is interesting that the basis for service in the legislative assembly was church membership rather than land ownership as was true of colonies like Virginia.

Governing the Colony

As was pointed out earlier, the outline of government was provided in the Massachusetts Bay Charter, which was moved to the colony in 1631. When working out the details of government, however, the General Court moved far from the specifications of the Charter. In its meeting of May, 1631, the Court confirmed that only freemen could participate in the government by voting or holding public office, but went further than the charter in insisting that only church members could be freemen. The office of Assistant, whose membership came from the membership of the General Court, would be held for life, rather than by annual election. The governor was elected from among the Assistants; the governor and the Assistants made law. They planned a government of the "elect," or those predestined to be saved. This system, through which the Puritan leadership exercised firm control over the colony, was modified over the next few years. Before the end of 1632, Puritan leadership decided that the freemen, and not the Assistants, would elect the governor, though the governor still must come from the membership of the Assistants and a man still had to be a church member in order to vote. Additional changes were made in 1634, when the membership of the General Court was expanded to include freemen who represented the towns that had sprung up around Boston. Additional changes were made through the 1630s and 1640s, and, taken together, formed the *Book of Laws and Liberties Concerning the Inhabitants of Massachusetts*.

Because only church members could vote and only the elect could be full members of the Church, Massachusetts Bay was not a democracy if one defines "democracy" as a system in which all persons over a certain age are allowed to vote. However, the New England town meeting to which all inhabitants were invited was definitely a democratic feature. Dorchester was the first town to adopt monthly meetings, but soon other communities followed suit, and, before long, most towns in Massachusetts Bay held regular town meetings. The system could be complicated and differed from one community to the next. In most towns, however, lived two classes of residents. On the one hand were "inhabitants" who had been granted land by the town, and admitted to church membership by the congregation; these exercised full political rights. The other category was that of "squatters," or those who held no land, and while they could attend town meetings and voice opinions, they could not vote.[34]

Puritan Orthodoxy: The Bible Commonwealth

The Puritans, or Calvinists, who immigrated to Massachusetts Bay followed a well-defined theology, differing from the belief system of the Pilgrims mainly in their conviction that the Anglican Church could be reformed; they intended to encourage this reformation by setting an example for the Anglican Church to follow. They were not, like the Pilgrims, Separatists. But here the differences ended; they all adopted the teachings of John Calvin.

One of the most important bases of Calvin's theology, and a key issue for the Puritans, was the doctrine of predestination, which affected how they conducted themselves in their daily lives. According to this doctrine, humans were sinful and could not be saved by their own actions. Rather, salvation came from the unmerited grace of God. A person, at the time of birth, was predestined to be either saved or damned, and nothing done in life could change this. Nor was there a way for anyone to know for sure whether they were saved, that is, among the "elect"; only God knew this. However, Puritans did believe that actions *might* reflect the state of the soul. It was thus common for Puritans to look for signs that they themselves, or their neighbors and friends, were among the elect. Most Puritans kept diaries in which they laboriously listed their activities, looking for any indication that pointed to their "election." And when individuals applied for church membership, they must prove to the church council that they had experienced a true conversion and thus were one of the elect.

Congregational Churches of Visible Saints

The churches that were organized in Massachusetts Bay and Connecticut were created by visible saints who covenanted together to form a church body. The founders then examined any persons who wanted to join the church, taking care that anyone admitted to full membership was most likely among the elect. Once the church was established, a pastor was selected and other church officers elected. The New England churches were called "congregational" because they had no hierarchical structure of bishops and archbishops, as in the Anglican Church; rather, each congregation was independent of every other congregation. Leading ministers of the Puritan establishment in Massachusetts were John Cotton, Richard Mather, Increase Mather, and Cotton Mather, all of whom oversaw the social and religious activities of the colonists, both saints and strangers.

4.6.4 Life in Puritan New England

Puritan belief permeated every aspect of life in New England. Because of their emphasis on election and calling, the Puritans believed that the Bible and Calvinist theology provided "complete blueprints for a smooth, honest, civil life in family, church and state."[35] Not only did Puritans think that they themselves should be socially virtuous, they believed that their neighbors should be socially virtuous as well.[36] And though they did not believe that one could earn salvation by doing good works, they did believe that such good works were a reflection of salvation. Thus, all of the elect would live orderly, hardworking lives, see to it that their children were educated and well behaved, attended church regularly, obeyed both secular and religious laws, and took care that they not slip from the prescribed way into moral decline.

Education

One of the most important necessities of life, in the opinion of the Puritans, was education, as it was crucial that all who wanted to qualify for church membership be able to read the Bible and understand and explain the tenets of their religion. Without education, salvation would not be possible. To this end, Harvard University was established in 1636 and the Old Deluder Satan Law passed in 1647. Acknowledging that the "one chief project of that old deluder, Satan, [is] to keep men from the knowledge of the Scriptures," the latter required that towns with a population of fifty families provide an elementary school in which students would be taught to read and write and required to study the Bible. Towns with over a hundred families must provide a grammar school. The families in the town were to pay the wages of a school master and see to it that their children attended school and progressed in their studies.[37]

Cotton Mather and Richard Mather, leading Puritan ministers, warned of the consequences that would befall parents who neglected their duty to educate their children. If a child "should want Knowledge, and saving wisdom thro' any gross Negligence of thine," Cotton Mather roared, "thy punishment shall be terrible in the Day of the Lords." And Richard Mather reminded parents that in the Day of Judgment, uneducated children would cry, "Woe unto us that we had such Carnall and careless parents." [38]

Doing God's Work: The Importance of the "Calling"

All Puritans, whether the Pilgrims of Plymouth or those living in other New England colonies, emphasized the importance of having a "calling." Two facets shaped the concept of the calling. On the one hand, individuals were called on by God to live a chaste life, go to church, pray, and adhere to the dictates of their religion. On the other hand, each had a personal calling by which they earned their living. Those who were faithful to God were expected to practice both callings with reverence and dedication. So, it was the duty of pious Puritans to work hard, help their neighbors, and contribute to the needs of the society. The callings were also gender specific. Most women might be called to be wives; they would never be called to be ministers. Children also had a place in an ordered society. Their callings involved obedience to the laws of the family and colony.

The Puritan leadership often elaborated on the necessity of practicing one's calling, even to the deprivation of sleep. Increase Mather, a leading minister and son of Richard Mather, wrote in his diary that he was not willing "to allow myself above Seven Hours and Four and Twenty, for Sleep: but would spend the rest of my Time in Attending to the Duties of my personal or general calling." Similarly, John Cotton wrote in *Parentator* that a calling should "not only aim at our own, but at the publike good" for no occupation "is lawful but what is useful unto humane society."[39] It was, therefore, the responsibility of all Puritans to work hard, pray, care for one another, and be ever watchful for evidence of the work of the devil in society. The work of the devil, for example, brought the witchcraft scare to Massachusetts Bay.

4.6.5 Offshoots of the Bay Colony: Connecticut, New Haven, and Rhode Island

Three additional colonies appeared in New England before the outbreak of the English Civil War in 1642. In 1636, the Reverend Thomas Hooker, pastor of the church in Cambridge and a proponent of expanded suffrage in electing colonial officers, received permission from the General Court of Massachusetts Bay to move with his congregation south into what became Connecticut. Two years later, the Reverend John Davenport and Theophilus Eaton, a wealthy London merchant and farmer, both of whom were strict Puritans, established New Haven, which maintained a separate existence from Hooker's river towns until 1664. In New Haven, as in Massachusetts, participation in any part of the government was limited to church members.

In 1639, the Connecticut freemen adopted the *Fundamental Orders of Connecticut*, which created, by compact, a government for the colony. The executive branch, consisting of the governor and the assistants, was to be elected annually; the members of this branch could not succeed themselves. All freemen, or church members, voted for the executive. The legislative branch was to be elected by all inhabitants; in other words, a man did not have to be a church member to vote for the legislature. This practice departed from the restricted suffrage of Massachusetts Bay and New Haven.

Rhode Island was founded by Roger Williams, a graduate of Cambridge University and Puritan theologian. He arrived in Boston in 1631 and quickly became a popular teacher and pastor. However, Williams, who was a Separatist, quickly became a thorn in the side of the Puritan establishment, regularly denouncing the teachings of the ministers in Boston as misinterpretations of Scripture. He condemned religious persecution by political authorities, believed in complete freedom of religion (for all except Quakers), and insisted that all laws requiring compulsory attendance at church and religious orthodoxy for voting should be done away with. He also insisted that the land belonged to the Indians and that the king had had no right to grant it to the Massachusetts Bay Company.

It did not take long for the General Court to act, and in 1635, it instructed the church at Salem to dismiss Williams. Williams left Salem with five supporters. After spending a long winter in the woods of Massachusetts, he finally found friends within the Narragansett tribe. He purchased land from them and established Providence in spring, 1636.

Williams was soon joined by another "heretic" who had been banished from the Bay colony: Mrs. Anne Hutchinson. Hutchinson, who had been interested in theology and theological debate before coming to Massachusetts, was the wife of a wealthy Bostonian and a neighbor of John Winthrop. She had been influenced by the sermons of John Cotton, to adopt Antinomianism, or the idea that once the doctrine of grace had been bestowed upon a person, it could not be removed. Thus the sermons of leading Massachusetts divines, including those of her own minister, Reverend John Wilson, were theologically unsound because they put too much emphasis on the strict moral code which was the basis of law in Massachusetts and too little on the what she called the "inner light." She made the mistake of holding "theological salons" in her home in which she and other members of Wilson's congregation commented on the content of the his sermons and their theological validity. Though initially Hutchinson had the support of the Reverend John Cotton, her claims to

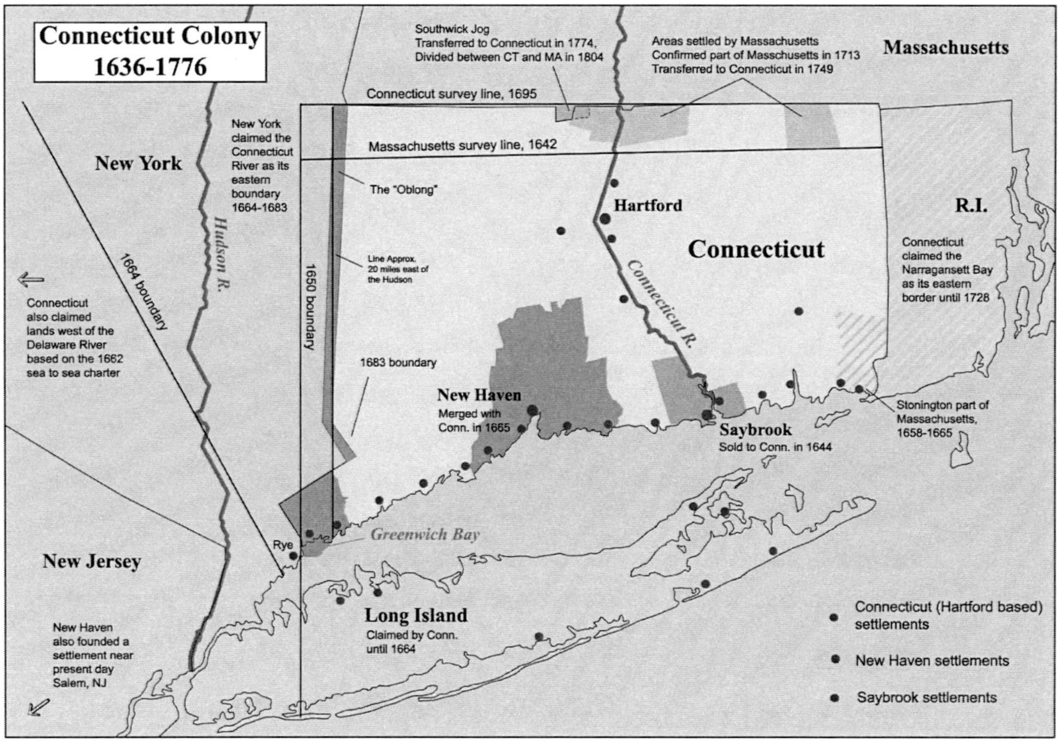

Figure 4.8 Colony of Connecticut | Map of The Colony of Connecticut, 1636-1776.

Author: Karl Musser
Source: Wikimedia Commons
License: CC BY SA 2.5

divine inspiration made the Puritan community nervous, and when an "Antinomian Controversy" threatened to upset the "holy experiment" in 1636, the leaders of the Bay Colony suspected "a plot of the old serpent [Satan] against Massachusetts."[40]

The Puritan oligarchy could not have a dissenter such as Hutchinson in their otherwise holy commonwealth. In November, 1637, she was brought before the General Court, condemned for her activities, and banished from the colony. In 1638, she was excommunicated and immediately left for Rhode Island, where she and her followers established the town of Portsmouth. When her husband died four years later, she moved with her children to Long Island, where she and her family were murdered in an Indian raid.

By the time the English Civil War broke out, Rhode Island had no charter. The land had been bought from the Indians, an action that no one in England, or most of the colonies for that matter, thought produced a legitimate claim. Therefore, Williams petitioned Parliament for title to the land, which Parliament granted in 1644. Thus, the "Providence Plantations, in the Narragansett Bay in New England" was created. The government structure was much like that of Connecticut, with expanded suffrage and limited terms of office. The Puritan oligarchy was under siege as Rhode Island and other colonies surrounding Massachusetts Bay moved toward democracy and toleration.

4.6.6 New Hampshire

The remaining colony of New England, consisting of the territories of New Hampshire and Maine, saw sporadic settlement during the decades of the 1630s and 1640s. Most of the area had been given to the Englishmen Sir Ferdinando Gorges and Captain John Mason in 1622 by the Council for New England. They divided the tract into northern and southern portions. The first permanent settlements in New Hampshire were established at Exeter and Hampton in 1638 by two diverse groups: the Reverend John Wheelwright, the brother of Anne Hutchinson and like her an exile from Boston, and a group of orthodox Puritans from another part of the Bay colony. Most of the towns of New Hampshire were created between 1623 and 1640; all were annexed by Massachusetts in 1641-1643, partly because of the death of Gorges and partly because the Civil War in England gave elevated importance to Puritans in England and the American colonies. New Hampshire remained part of Massachusetts Bay until 1677 when it became independent; in 1679 it became a royal colony.

Maine was mostly an outpost for fishers, though recent discoveries have revealed an early settlement in Maine at Popham. It appears that in 1607, when James I granted land for the creation of what became Jamestown, he supported the establishment of a second colony in Maine. The colonists arrived at Popham in August, 1607 and began building what they called Fort St. George. As winter approached and supplies ran low, however, half of the colonists decided to return to England. At the end of winter, the remainder headed home, as well.[41] The settlement there had lasted for less than a year. The sparse settlements in Maine were annexed by Massachusetts between 1652 and 1656; in 1691 Plymouth and Maine were formally joined with Massachusetts by the English Privy Council.

4.6.7 Slavery in New England

The "institution of slavery" is usually most closely associated with agriculture in the antebellum South, where slaves numbered in the millions. But, despite the common assumption that slavery was a southern phenomenon, "slaves were brought into New England throughout the entire colonial period" and were common in these colonies until the America Civil War. The first slaves arrived in Massachusetts Bay in 1638, having been exchanged for Pequot War captives, and though the number remained "quite small" for the first forty years, slave population doubled between 1677 and 1710.[42] Even John Winthrop, well-known governor of Massachusetts Bay, not only owned slaves at his home, Ten Hills Farm, but helped pass one of the first laws making chattel slavery legal in North America in 1641. The Massachusetts Body of Liberties of 1641 states, "There shall never be any bond slaverie, villinage or Captivitie amongst us *unles* it be lawfull Captives taken in just warres, and such strangers as willingly selle themselves or are sold to us. And these shall have all the liberties...which the law of god established in Israell concerning such persons." [*sic*][43]

Two decades later, John Winthrop's grandson, Wait Winthrop, gave his older brother advice on handling a slave recently arrived from Africa: "Have an eye to him...and [if] you think it not worthwhile to keep him, sell him or send him to Virginia or the Barbadoes."[44] A visitor to Boston in the late 1600s wrote, "you may...own Negroes and Negresses...There is not a House in Boston, however small be its Means that has not one or two. There are those that have five or six."[45]

In 1715, the first "general census of New England" reported that there was approximately one "negro" for every six families in those colonies. However, the slave population was not found throughout the colonies; rather, it was "clustered along the seacoast, in major cities and in agricultural areas in Rhode Island and Connecticut."[46] By the 1770s, slaves were present in significant numbers in Connecticut, Massachusetts, and Rhode Island, where they made up 30 percent of the population of South Kingston. There was also a notable presence of slaves in Boston (10 percent) and New London (9 percent). Most prominent New England merchants had ties to the slave trade and made vast fortunes from it. [47]

Because of sectional differences in economic development, slave occupations in New England were more diverse than in the South. Rather than working primarily on large agricultural units, northern slaves more often performed household duties and provided skilled labor in any number of industries: ship building, carpentry, printing, tailoring, shoe making, blacksmithing, baking, and weaving. In fact, "many became so talented in the crafts that the free white workers lost jobs to them."[48]

4.6.8 The New England Confederation, 1643

The New England colonies, especially Massachusetts Bay, posed a problem for the English monarchs during most of the pre-Revolutionary period. The settlers' "independent spirit" first appeared with the foundation of the New England Confederation in 1643. The union of Massachusetts Bay, Plymouth, Connecticut, and New Haven, all Puritan colonies, was created without consulting Parliament or the Crown. The purpose of the Confederation was to pool the resources of the colonies and solve their mutual problems, primarily their struggles with the native populations. England was engaged in a civil war and therefore unable to give adequate protection to her colonies. This reason along with the Pequot War spurred the New England colonies into action. The preamble of the Confederation of "the United Colonies of New England" explained the motivation and purpose behind its establishment: "Whereas we all came into these parts of America, with one and the same end...and whereas we live encompassed with people of severall Nations...we enter into a present Consotiation...for mutuall help and strength."[49]

It made no reference to the king or Parliament, and the wording was not unlike that of the Articles of Confederation, America's first constitution, created 130 years later. The colonies entered into a "firm and Perpetuall league of friendship...for offence and defence, mutuall advice...both for preserving and propagating...the liberties of the Gospel and for their own mutuall safety and welfare."[50] The union lasted from 1643 to 1691, though it was not effective after the first decade. When Charles II was restored to the throne of England in 1660, he turned his ire on Puritanism and Puritans, holding them responsible for the execution of his father in 1642. In 1684, he revoked the charter of Massachusetts Bay, making it a royal colony, and his brother James II later established the Dominion of New England, which was placed under the control of a colonial administrator, Sir Edmund Andros, who had, among other things, served as the fourth royal governor of New York and was one of the original proprietors of the territory of New Hampshire and Maine.

4.6.9 Before You Move On...

Key Concepts

The New England colonies were founded between 1620 and 1642, when the English Civil War broke out. With the exception of Rhode Island, these colonies (Plymouth, Massachusetts Bay, New Haven, and Connecticut) were Puritan, and Puritanism influenced their social morés, economics, and politics. Believing in a strict adherence to Calvinist doctrine and in the value of a society composed solely of "visible saints," most New England colonists, with the exception of those in Rhode Island, did not welcome what they called "strangers," nor did they practice toleration in any form. The colony of Rhode Island was different, as it was created by refugees from Massachusetts who disagreed with Puritan orthodoxy and the chokehold it had on Massachusetts society. The laws of this colony reflected religious and social toleration. Anne Hutchinson, who had been embroiled in the Antinomian Controversy in Massachusetts Bay, and Roger Williams, who purchased the land that became Rhode Island from the Indians, reflect the independence that could evolve from various ways of interpreting Calvinist doctrines.

Because Puritans believed that anyone seeking membership in the church had to have a working knowledge of Scripture, education became an important aspect of life in their colonies, as did industry, because to be idle was a sign of the devil at work. Unlike the colonies in the South, where education was the responsibility of the family, New England was seen as the province of the state. While Plymouth remained small in population, Massachusetts Bay grew throughout the seventeenth century and became large and prosperous; in 1691 Massachusetts became a royal colony, absorbing the territories of Maine and Plymouth. In the same year, New Hampshire became a royal colony, independent of Massachusetts.

Test Yourself

1. Who among the following were banished from the Massachusetts Bay Colony?

    a. John Cotton and Richard Mather

    b. John Winthrop and Roger Williams

    c. Roger Williams and Anne Hutchinson

    d. Anne Hutchinson and John Winthrop

2. Which of the following founders and colonies is incorrect?

    a. John Winthrop/Massachusetts Bay

    b. William Bradford/Plymouth

    c. William Brewster/New Haven

    d. Thomas Hooker/Connecticut

3. The General Court in Puritan colonies was the ______ of the government.

   a. executive branch

   b. legislative branch

   c. judicial branch

   d. religious branch

4. One important difference between the Puritans of Massachusetts Bay and those of Plymouth was that:

   a. the Pilgrims wanted to reform the Church of England rather than separate from it.

   b. the Puritans of Massachusetts Bay wanted to reform the church of England rather than separate from it.

   c. the Pilgrims did not believe in the doctrine of election.

   d. the Puritans were not Calvinists.

5. According to the doctrine of predestination, a person was either saved or damned from the time of his birth.

   a. True

   b. False

See page 157 for answers

4.7 THE PURITANS AND THE INDIANS

The leading New England Indian tribes were the Mohegan and Pequot in Connecticut, the Narragansett in Rhode Island, the Patuxet and Wampanoag in Plymouth, and the Nipmuckin Massachusetts, and Pennacook in Massachusetts Bay. No political unity existed among the tribes, though they were able to communicate through the spoken word. The Indians were hunters but also horticulturalists, who believed that the land should be shared and contain no boundaries and no fences. Indian villages shared the proceeds from the land; no one went hungry in a village unless everyone did. Sachems led the tribes and were assisted by a council of lesser sachems and important warriors.

Puritan ideas about the land were quite different. Their approach was best expressed by John Winthrop, who said, "As for the Natives in New England, they enclose no Land, neither have any settled habitation, nor any tame Cattle to improve the Land, and so have no other but a Naturall Right to those countries, so as if we leave them sufficient for their use, we may lawfully take the rest."[51] Or as the records of the Milford, Connecticut town records state, "the earth is the Lord's...the earth is given to the Saints...[and] we are the Saints." Many of the settlers agreed with William Bradford who maintained that the Indians were "savage people who are cruel, barbarous and most treacherous."[52]

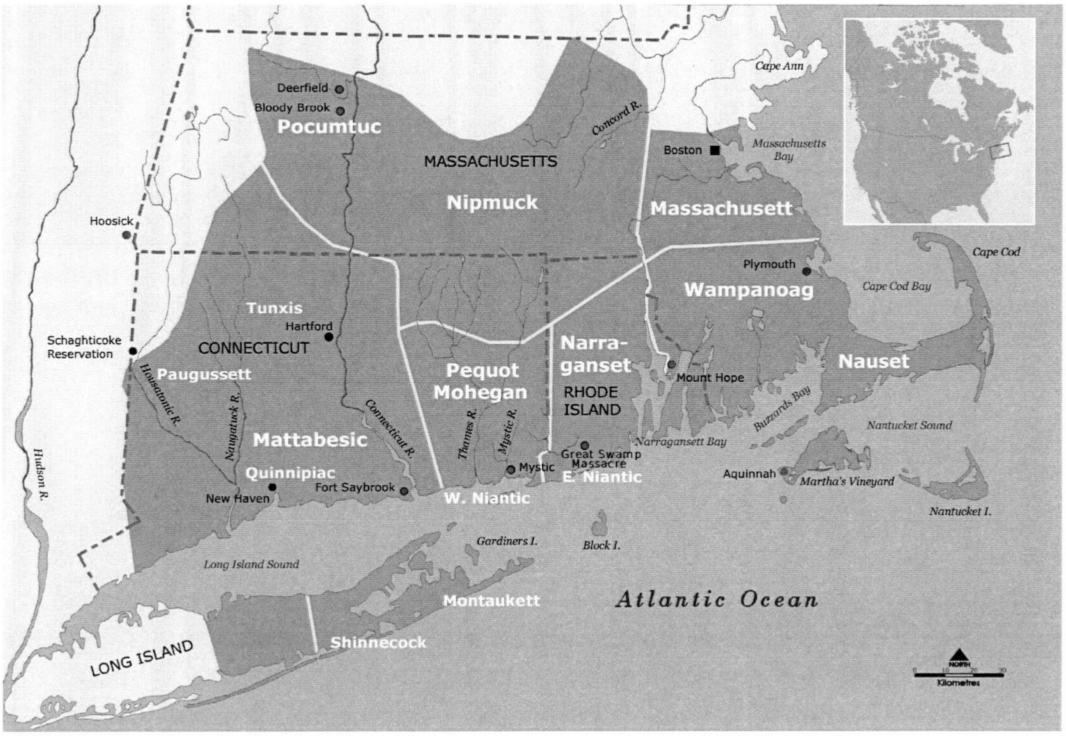

Figure 4.9 Tribal Territories | Map of the Tribal Territories of Southern New England.

Author: Wikipedia Users "Nikater" & "Hydrargyrum"
Source: Wikimedia Commons

4.7.1 Puritan Mission and the Indians

The charter of the Massachusetts Bay Company proclaimed that the purpose of those who traveled to the Americas was "to win and incite the natives of this country, to the knowledge and obedience of the only true God and Saviour of mankind." This mission was not unique to Massachusetts or even to those who sailed from England, as Columbus mentions in his journal that, as soon as he encountered the Taino people of the Caribbean islands, he saw that "they were very friendly...and perceived that they could be much more easily converted to our holy faith by gentle means than by force."[53] Similarly, Hernan Cortes, sent to conquer the Aztec Empire of Mexico, mentioned in his letter to Charles V, king of Spain and Holy Roman Emperor, that the Aztecs acknowledged that the Spanish explorers "having more recently arrived must know better than themselves what they ought to believe; and that if I [Cortes] would instruct them in these matters, and make them understand the true faith, they would follow my directions, as being for the best."[54] Those living in Massachusetts Bay were continually reminded of their duty because the seal of the colony of Massachusetts Bay contained the image of a native crying, "Come over and help us!"

Years passed, however, before the Puritans actually began the work of conversion. One of the greatest obstacles was language. Puritans believed that conversion could come only when the converts could read and discuss the Bible. Through much of the 1630s, the Puritans dealt with the natives only through sign language, which worked well when bartering but was not sufficient for purposes of conversion. In order to have a true conversion experience, the natives needed a written language and a Bible written in that language. The conversion efforts did not begin seriously until after the Pequot War.

4.7.2 The Pequot War, 1636-1638

The first major conflict between the Puritans and Indians began in 1636. The Pequots, the most powerful of those living in the Connecticut Valley, looked with suspicion and alarm as the number of English settlers beginning to inhabit their land increased. The English had a hard time understanding why the Indians needed as much land as they apparently thought they did and refused to recognize these claims because the lands were not under cultivation. Cultivation to the Puritan way of thinking bestowed the right of ownership. Problems invariably arose with the result that the Indians murdered several settlers at Saybrook and Wethersfield in 1635-1636 at the height of the Antinomian controversy. Even before these incidents, the government of Massachusetts Bay had sent an expedition under John Endicott into Pequot territory to avenge the murder of an English trader, John Oldham. In May, 1637, settlers in Connecticut raised a force of ninety men under the command of John Mason and John Underhill, both of whom had experience fighting Indians. One of the most notorious battles was the English attack on the Pequot fort at Mystic, Connecticut. The settlement, the greatest of the Pequot strongholds, had about four hundred inhabitants and seventy wigwams; many of the residents were women, children, and the elderly. The English and their Indian allies, the Narragansett, approached the fort at night and set it on fire. Those inhabitants who did not die in the fire were slaughtered as they attempted to flee the inferno. Of the hundreds living in the fort, only seven survived. The Treaty of Hartford, signed September 21, 1638, ended the war; the remaining Pequot were enslaved by the Mohegan or Narragansett or sold into slavery in Bermuda and the West Indies and their lands seized.[55] Historians Curtis Nettels and Samuel Eliot Morison comment that the Pequot were "virtually exterminated" by the war and the subsequent enslavement.[56]

John Eliot, Disciple to the Indians

Up until the defeat of the Pequot in 1638, New England Indians had been reluctant to accept the God of the Puritans. With the success of the English against the Pequot, however, "the Indians of Southern New England were impressed by the power of the white man and became more interested in the God responsible for his success."[57] John Eliot, later given the title "Apostle to the Indians," received a Pequot servant at the end of the war from whom he began to learn the Algonquin language spoken by the Massachusett, Nauset, Narrangansett, Pequot, and Wampanoag. In 1644, the General Court instructed the county courts to see to it that the Indians residing in their villages should be civilized and "instructed in the knowledge and worship of God."[58]

In 1646, Eliot preached his first sermon in the Algonquin tongue to the inhabitants of the village of Nonantum. The same year, the General Court appointed Eliot to a committee whose purpose was to buy land from the Indians that should be set aside "for the encouragement of the Indians to live in a more orderly way among us."[59] Five years later, in 1651, the first "Praying Town," Natick, was created. Although Natick remained the most famous of the Praying Indian towns, thirteen additional towns were created in the Bay colony by 1675. In 1663, Eliot translated the Bible into the Algonquin language, and, in 1666 he published a grammar for the Massachusetts called "The Indian Grammar Begun." The towns had been located so as to serve as buffers for the defense of the colony; this function ended with the outbreak of King Philip's War. By this time, however, 20 percent of the Indians of Massachusetts Bay lived in the Praying Towns that appeared throughout the colony.

4.8 NEW ENGLAND IN THE LATE SEVENTEENTH CENTURY: DECLENSION, WITCHCRAFT, AND THE DOMINION OF NEW ENGLAND

By 1660, New England had grown in population and wealth. Despite this fact, or perhaps because of it, many among the Puritan leadership lamented that their mission was in danger of failing; this falling away from their original purpose is known as "declension." There were several indicators that declension had indeed set in. The most obvious sign was that the children and grandchildren of the first generation appeared to be losing the piety characteristic of their elders, and, as a consequence, the proportion of church members to non-members was declining alarmingly. Puritan ministers pointed out that should this trend continue it would affect not just the current church population but also that to come, as only children of full church members could be baptized. Those who were not baptized could not become church members themselves. In 1662, in a desperate move to avoid this eventuality, Massachusetts clergy adopted the *Half-Way Covenant*. According to this doctrine, children of partial members could be baptized and thus would be eligible for full church membership upon a conversion experience. The more orthodox Puritans denigrated this approach, and many left the Congregational Churches to join what they saw as the more strictly separatist sect, the Baptists. Fears of declension and the adoption of the Half-Way Covenant were only the beginning of troubles for the New England colonies, however. More serious problems came just before and after the Glorious Revolution of 1688.

4.8.1 The Dominion of New England

Charles II died in 1685. Before his death, he had begun to curtail the activities of the Bay Colony, especially in light of the fact that in the 1660s and 1670s, the colony refused to obey the Navigation Acts, would not allow appeals from the courts in the Bay Colony to England, and purchased Maine from the Gorges proprietors without permission. To make matters worse, in 1678 the General Court of Massachusetts announced to Parliament that "The laws of England are grounded within the four seas, and do...not reach America."[60]

Thus, in 1684, the Crown revoked the Charter of Massachusetts Bay and combined all of the New England colonies, in addition to New York and East and West Jersey, into the Dominion of New England. Local assemblies, including the revered New England town meetings, were abolished, and the Dominion was placed under the direct control of a governor-general appointed by the Crown, a lieutenant governor, and an appointed council. Male suffrage was expanded, taxes were raised, and no longer did one have to belong to the Congregational church to be able to vote. Sir Edmund Andros was appointed the first royal governor of the Dominion. A further slap in the faces of the Puritan leaders came when an Anglican Church was established in Boston, bringing the Puritan monopoly to an end.

When Charles's brother, James II, came to the throne in 1685, he immediately alarmed English Protestants. His open support of English Catholics and Catholicism in general led to the Glorious Revolution of 1688 and the succession of his Protestant daughter Mary and her husband William of Orange. In the colonies, a series of uprisings broke out that threw royal governors out of office and replaced them with colonial leaders. In Massachusetts, a rebellion led to the overthrow of Andros and the dissolution of the Dominion of New England. William and Mary, however, refused the request of Massachusetts for a new charter; instead, Massachusetts Bay was combined with Plymouth and became a royal colony. Though the General Court was re-established, a person no longer had to be a church member to be elected to the Court; it appeared that the holy experiment had come to an end.

4.8.2 Witchcraft in Salem

Three years later, in spring 1692, when a new royal charter had just been issued and tension spread throughout Massachusetts, several girls in Salem Village, what is now Danvers, became ill. Among those afflicted were the daughter and niece of the local minister Samuel Parris. After the girls began to have fits, which a minister described as "beyond the power of natural disease to effect," and were closely questioned, they admitted that they had been experimenting with the occult under the tutelage of Tituba, a West Indian servant and possibly a slave, in the Parris household. The fact that the devil was at work in society was part and parcel of the Puritan belief system, and they tended to blame the works of the devil for all the misdoings in society. Indeed, Cotton Mather, a leading Puritan minister in Boston, was famous for his pronouncements on witches. In his book,

Figure 4.10 Salem Witch Trials | A witness writhes on the floor of the courthouse at the proximity of an accused.

Author: William A. Crafts
Source: *Pioneers in the Settlement of America: From Florida in 1510 to California in 1849*

Memorable Providences Relating to Witchcrafts and Possessions (1689 and reprinted in 1691), he examined the case of a mason in Boston, whose children had been possessed by the devil and encouraged to steal from neighbors; the woman accused of witchcraft was executed. Mather was determined "after this, never to use but just one grain of patience with any man that shall go to impose upon me a Denial of Devils, or of Witches. I shall count that man Ignorant who shall suspect, but I shall count him down-right Impudent if he Assert the Non-Existence of things which we have had such palpable Convictions of."[61]

When the girls of Salem Village confessed that they had been studying the occult and were perhaps the victims of witchcraft, they were ordered to reveal their afflicters. They pointed to Tituba who, upon being whipped, named her two accomplices: Sarah Good and Sarah Osborne. These two women made perfect victims for what is considered by most historians to have been mass adolescent hysteria, as Sarah Good was a homeless beggar and Sarah Osborne had long been suspect because of her refusal to attend church services. Non-conformity was not a value in Puritan society, and anyone who was outside the mold was viewed suspiciously. A special court was established to hear the cases, in which the girls were the main witnesses. During the cross examination of the "witches," the girls threw themselves on the floor and writhed and groaned. The initial accusations were only the beginning, and as the girls received more and more attention, they pointed their fingers at additional residents of Salem Village and nearby Ipswich, whom they claimed to have seen riding broomsticks, sitting in trees, floating through the air, appearing as wolves, and anything else they imagined that witches would be able to do. If rational residents accused the girls of nonsense, they, too, became victims of the accusers. Before the hysteria ended in the summer of 1693, more than one hundred persons had been cited and nineteen put to death. Of those executed, eighteen were hanged, and one, Giles Corey, an eighty-year-old farmer, was pressed to death. One of the victims, George Burroughs, was a Congregational minister; fourteen of the nineteen executed were women.[62]

Robert Calef, an eyewitness to the execution of Reverend Burroughs, whose accusers claimed that the ghost of a deceased woman told them that Burroughs had killed her, described the scene:

> Mr. Burroughs was carried in a Cart with others, through the streets of Salem, to Execution. When he was upon the Ladder, he made a speech for the clearing of his Innocency, with such Solemn and Serious Expressions as were to the Admiration of all present; his Prayer (which he concluded by repeating the Lord's Prayer) was so well worded, and uttered with such composedness as such fervency of spirit, as was very Affecting, and drew Tears from many, so that it seemed to some that the spectators would hinder the execution. The accusers said the black Man [Devil] stood and dictated to him. As soon as he was...[hung], Mr. Cotton Mather, being mounted upon a Horse, addressed himself to the People, partly to declare that [Mr. Burroughs] was no ordained Minister, partly to possess the People of his guilt, saying that the devil often had been transformed into the Angel of Light. And this did somewhat appease the People, and the Executions went on; when he [Mr. Burroughs] was cut down, he was dragged by a Halter to a Hole, or Grave, between the Rocks, about two feet deep...[63]

Before he was hung, Reverend Burroughs recited the Lord's Prayer perfectly, an act that witches were not supposed to be able to perform.

The mass hysteria that was the witchcraft "scare" ended in the fall of 1693, when well-connected people, including the wife of Governor Phipps, were accused and the educated elite of Boston began to pressure the Governor to set aside spectral evidence. Even Increase Mather wrote in 1693 that the devil could take the shape of an innocent person and that it was better that ten witches go free than one innocent person be condemned. But while many of the ministers of Massachusetts Bay eschewed the proceedings after the fact, none spoke up until the hysteria had consumed the colony for eighteen months. Influenced by the writings of ministers such as Cotton and Increase Mather, they could in fact see the workings of the devil in Massachusetts; it was far easier to blame the Devil than to look too closely at the society Puritan orthodoxy had created. When the mass hysteria ended in 1693, it coincided with the end of the Holy Commonwealth and the decline of the "city on a hill."

Compared to the witch hunts that occurred in Europe at about the same time, the one in Salem Village was mild and had at least some humane features, if the word humane can be applied to a witch hunt. In the first place, the Salem witches were hung and not burned to death, and, in the second, most of those involved in the furor later confessed their mistakes. Twenty years later, the Massachusetts courts annulled the convictions and granted indemnity to the victims and their families.

Sidebar 4.1: Puritans In Historical Literature

The following points of view illustrate the historical controversies that have arisen about the Puritans over the last one hundred years. The Puritans, those of Massachusetts Bay as well as the Pilgrims of Plymouth, were in fact the earliest American historians and thought of their own history as the manifestation of God's will. They considered themselves to be the chosen people who, like the Jews, were given a place set apart for them to build a new Canaan. According to John Winthrop, Massachusetts was "a city on a hill," a model for a new Christian utopia. Although Thomas Jefferson and numerous other important figures would later reject the Puritan interpretation of history, historian Perry Miller's claim in The American Puritans, 1956, that "without some understanding of Puritanism, there is no understanding of America" is not without merit and can be seen in later reevaluaWtions of the significance of the Puritans in American thought

The Anti-Puritan Perspective

Historians have been of two minds about the Puritans. According to one group, represented by Harvard graduates Charles Francis Adams and Brooks Adams at the turn of the twentieth century, the Puritans founded undemocratic colonies dominated by a Puritan elite. These colonies repressed dissenters, resisted change, and were narrow-minded in their outlook. According to this historiographical school, the Puritans created a "glacial period" of frozen, stifled intellectual life that lasted until the American Revolution. In the Progressive era of the early twentieth century through the 1920s, negative appraisals of the Puritans were even more common. H. L. Mencken wrote in 1924 that Puritanism was "the haunting fear that someone, somewhere, may be happy." Mencken saw parallels between the Puritans and those of his own day who wanted to censor books and continue prohibition. James Truslow Adams agreed that the Puritans repressed not only the individual's public life but regulated private life as well with restrictive religious precepts. Further, he argued that Puritanism was an economic ideology promoted by the middle class to justify its domination of the lower classes. The Puritan leaders "looked with fear, as well as jealousy, upon any possibility of allowing control of policy of law and order, and of legislation concerning person and property, to pass to others."[64] Other historians like Vernon Parrington, writing in *Main Currents in American Thought,* argued that the Puritans contributed little to important American ideals.

Intellectual Contributions

On the other hand, a second group of historians has tended to appreciate the contributions of the Puritans to intellectual life. These historians point out that the Puritans established the first public school system in the Americas and the first college. They also see the Puritans as the torchbearers of liberty, who came to America in search of religious freedom. Their austerities and other seemingly repressive measures were dictated by the harsh conditions of the land and times in which they lived. This school of thought, represented by John Gorham Palfrey (1858-1890), credits the Puritans with the development of such American virtues as hard work, thriftiness, and social responsibility. In a reaction to the anti-Puritanism of the 1920s, historians of the 1930s, such as the Harvard professor Samuel Elliot Morison, attempted to portray the Puritans as "real" people who were not averse to the simple pleasures of life and who contributed much to the intellectual life of early America. Daniel Boorstin argued that the Puritans were successful because of their practicality, another American virtue.

4.8.3 Before You Move On...

Key Concepts

When charters were issued to the Puritans who settled Plymouth and Massachusetts, a key component was the statement of purpose for the removal of these Calvinists to the Americas; both charters mentioned the need to spread the Christian gospel to the Indians. And, though the Puritans were ever mindful of their purpose, early relations with the natives were uneven at best; not until after the Pequot War did the work of John Eliot, Apostle to the Indians, begin. Eventually, Praying Towns appeared in Massachusetts Bay, and "praying Indians" were educated in the teachings of the Bible. Many went on to attend Harvard, which its president hoped would become the "Indian Oxford." But apart from success with Christianization, the late seventeenth century was not a positive period for the New England Puritans. Declension became a problem as more and more of the second and third generations failed to join the church. Massachusetts Bay lost its charter and was incorporated with the other New England colonies into the Dominion of New England, and even when the Dominion was Massachusetts Bay and Plymouth failed to obtain new charters from the Crown. Rather, these two Puritan settlements were combined under one royal governor. These problems, in addition to the witchcraft, led ministers to lament in one jeremiad after another that their mission had failed and the holy experiment was at an end.

Test Yourself

1. Who among the following was banished from the Massachusetts Bay Colony?

   a. John Cotton and Richard Mather

   b. John Winthrop and Roger Williams

   c. Roger Williams and Anne Hutchinson

   d. Anne Hutchinson and John Winthrop

2. The "Apostle to the Indians" was the Puritan minister:

   a. John Eliot

   b. John Cotton

   c. John Winthrop

   d. Cotton Mather

3. The West Indian servant whose tales of witchcraft initiated the witchcraft scare in the Salem Village was:

   a. Sarah Good

   b. Sara Parris

   c. Tituba

   d. Massasoit

4. King Philip's war broke out when a praying Indian and graduate of Harvard was assassinated by a Wampanoag.

   a. True

   b. False

5. The Dominion of New England was created in part to punish Massachusetts Bay for its failure to convert the local Indian tribes.

   a. True

   b. False

See page 158 for answers

4.9 Conclusion

The year 1660 marks a break between two waves of English colonization. Prior to 1640, colonies were created in New England, Virginia, and Maryland. For the most part, the colonies established during this period were created by charters held indirectly from the Crown. Those that appeared after 1660 were mainly proprietary, given as grants to the friends of Charles II, who was "restored" to the throne in 1660. The late seventeenth century witnessed an attempt by the English monarchy to tighten the reins over their American colonies, as new Acts of Trade and Navigation were passed by Parliament and the Dominion of New England created. When James II was overthrown in 1688, a series of revolts in the colonies brought an end to such institutions as the Dominion of New England. By the end of the century, however, many colonies had lost their charters and became royal colonies under the direct control of the Crown. In 1735, the last English colony, Georgia, was established as a buffer colony between the American colonies and Spanish Florida.

4.10 CRITICAL THINKING EXERCISES

- John White was put in a terrible position when his colonists asked him to leave them and return to England for aide. If you were John White, what would you do?
- The Secotan attacked White's colony because of what had happened with Lane's earlier group. Was there any way for White to have prevented the troubles? Was the Secotan's anger justified?
- Ralph Lane's legacy at Roanoke was a failed attempt at a colony and the lasting enmity of the Secotan towards the English. How do you think Lane should have handled the problems with the Secotan?
- If you were Powhatan or a Pequot, how would you have reacted to the arrival of the English?
- If you were an English citizen in 1606 and had the opportunity to be a part of founding Jamestown, would you have done it?
- Why do you think the Narragansett and Mohegan tribes fought with the Puritans against fellow Indians, the Pequot?
- Do you think that witchcraft was practiced in Salem Village in 1692?

4.11 KEY TERMS

- Algonquian
- William Bradford
- Calvert
- Calvinism
- Canary Islands
- Charles I
- Charles II
- Chesapeake Bay
- Chickahominy
- Croatoan
- Oliver Cromwell
- Virginia Dare
- Doctrine of Election
- Sir Francis Drake Elizabeth I
- Elizabethan Settlement
- Fall Line
- Sir Richard Grenville
- Sir Gilbert Humphrey
- Anne Hutchinson
- Iroquoan
- James I
- James II
- James River
- Jamestown
- Long Parliament
- Lord Baltimore
- Manteo
- Marian Exiles
- Massachusetts Bay
- Massasoit
- Mid-Atlantic
- Narragansett
- Captain Christopher Newport
- Opechancanough
- Orinoco
- Outer Banks
- Parahunt
- Pemisapan
- Pequot War
- Pilgrims
- Plymouth
- Pocahontas
- Point Comfort
- Powhatan
- Praying towns
- Predestination
- Puritans
- Pyrite (Fool's Gold)
- Qaocomicos
- Sir Walter Raleigh
- Ralph Lane
- Ratcliffe
- Rhode Island
- Roanoke Island
- John Rolfe
- Roger Williams
- Samoset
- Secotan
- Captain John Smith
- Squanto
- Susquehannocks
- The Mayflower
- The Mayflower Compact
- The Starving Time
- Tituba
- Tobacco
- Varina
- Virginia Company of London
- West Indies
- John White
- John Winthrop

4.12 CHRONOLOGY

The following chronology is a list of important dates and events associated with this chapter.

Date	Event
1158-1603	Reign of Elizabeth I of England
1578	Sir Humphrey Gilbert granted the right to colonize North America
1583	Sir Humphrey lost at sea
1584	Walter Raleigh's expedition discovered the Outer Banks and Roanoke Island
1585	Raleigh's second expedition under Sir Richard Grenville sailed for Roanoke and left a small colony of soldiers under Ralph Lane
1586	Lane abandoned Roanoke and returned to England with Sir Francis Drake, leaving behind a small garrison. Grenville arrived, and finding no one, returned to England
1587	Raleigh's third expedition under John White with a colony of families landed on Roanoke Island. White returned to England for supplies.
1588	England defeated the Spanish Armada; Grenville barred from sailing to Roanoke; White sailed with a privateer.
1590	White reached Roanoke, found sign suggesting that the colony moved to Croatan.
1602	Raleigh sent an expedition to Outer banks, found no sign of "lost" colony.
1603	Elizabeth I died; James VI of Scotland (James I of England) assumed the throne
1606	Virginia Company of London created; Colonizers sent to Virginia
1607	Colonists landed at Jamestown
1609	Starving Time begans in Jamestown
1610	Starving Time ended with more than 80 percent of the Jamestown colonists dead.
1616	Tobacco production began in earnest in Virginia

Date	Event
1620	*Mayflower* landed in Plymouth, Massachusetts
1621	First Thanksgiving celebrated in Plymouth
1623	John Mason and John Wheelwright founded Hover, New Hampshire
1625	Charles I assumed English throne
1629-1640	The Eleven-Year Tyranny
1630	*Arbella* landed in Massachusetts Bay
1631	William Clayborne of Virginia set up a trading post on Kent Island in what would become Maryland territory
1632	George Calvert, Baron Baltimore applied for a charter for a royal colony at Maryland
1634	Leonard Calvert, son of George, arrived in Maryland
1636	Harvard University Founded; Providence, Portsmouth, and Hartford, Connecticut founded.
1637-1638	Pequot War
1638	New Haven Colony founded
1639	Fundamental Orders of Connecticut adopted
1640	"Long" Parliament convened in London
1641	New Hampshire became part of Massachusetts Bay
1642	Old Deluder Satan Law established schools in Massachusetts Bay; English Civil War begins
1643	New England Confederation created
1660	The Half Way Covenant adopted by the Massachusetts General Court; Charles II restored to English throne
1663	Albonquin language Bible published in Massachusetts Bay
1675	King Philip's War; Death of Cecilius, 2nd Baron Baltimore; Rebellion in Maryland
1679	New Hampshire became royal colony, independent of Massachusetts Bay
1681	Rebellion in Maryland
1684	Dominion of New England created

Date	Event
1685	Death of Charles II; James II ascended to the English throne
1688	James II of England overthrown in the "Glorious Revolution"; the Glorious Revolution in the Colonies; Dominion of New England dissolved; Coode's Rebellion in Maryland; Calvert family lost charter of Maryland
1689	Maryland became a royal colony
1691	Massachusetts Bay and Plymouth united into one royal colony
1692-1693	Witchcraft scare in Salem Village

4.13 BIBLIOGRAPHY

Adams, James Truslow. *The Founding of New England*, New York: Dodo Press, 2009.

Barck, Oscar Theodore and Hugh Talmage Lefler. *Colonial America*. New York: Macmillan Company, 1958.

Beckenstein, Myron. "Maine's Lost Colony." *Smithsonian Magazine*, February 2004. *http://www.smithsonianmag.com/history-archaeology/Maines_Lost_Colony.html?c=y&page=2.*

Boorstin, Daniel. *The Americans: the Colonial Experience*. New York: Random House, 1958.

Bremer, Francis J. *The Puritan Experiment: New England Society from Bradford to Edwards*. New York: St. Martin's Press, 1976.

Calef, Robert. More Wonders of the Invisible World. *Salem Witch Trials: Documentary Archive and Transcription Project. http://etext.virginia.edu/salem/witchcraft/speccol/calef/calef.html.*

Catton, Bruce and William B. Catton. *The Bold And Magnificent Dream: America's Founding Years, 1492-1815*. New York: Doubleday, 1978.

Colonial Williamsburg. *http://www.history.org/history/teaching/slavelaw.cfm.*

Colonial Ancestors. *http://colonialancestors.com/md/proprietary.htm.*

Columbus, Christopher. *Journal*. Modern History Sourcebooks. *http://www.Fordham.edu/Halsall.*

Cortes, Hernan. *Second Letter to Charles V, 1520*. Modern History Sourcebooks. *http://www.Fordham.edu/Halsall.*

Famous American Trials: The Salem Witchcraft Trials. University of Missouri, Kansas City School of Law. *http://law2.umkc.edu/faculty/projects/ftrials/salem/salem.htm.*

Foster, Stephen. *Their Solitary Way: the Puritan Social Ethic in the First century of Settlement in New England*. New Haven: Yale University Press, 1971.

Horn, James. *A Kingdom Strange, The Brief and Tragic History of the Lost Colony of Roanoke*. New York: Basic Books. 2010.

Jamestown Rediscovery. *http://www.apva.org/history/.*

Karlsen, Carol F. *The Devil in the Shape of a Woman*. New York: W.W. Norton, 1988.

Kenyon, J. P. *The Stuarts, a Study in English Kingship*. New York: Bow Historical Books, 1977.

Manegold, C.S. Ten Hills Farm: The Forgotten History of Slavery. Princeton, N.J. Princeton University Press, 2010.

Maryland State Archives. *http://www.msa.md.gov/msa/homepage/html/mdhistory.html.*

Mather, Cotton. *Memorable Providences Relating to Witchcrafts and Possessions*. 1689. *http://law2.umkc.edu/faculty/projects/ftrials/salem/asa_math.htm.*

Melish, Joann Pope. Disowning Slavery: Gradual Emancipation of Race in New England, Ithaca, New York: Cornell Univ. Press, 1998.

4.14 END NOTES

1 Daniel J. Boorstin, The Americans: The Colonial Experience. New York: Random House, 1958, 105.

2 Charter to Sir Walter Raleigh: 1584. Yale University Avalon Project: http://avalon.law.yale.edu/16th_century/raleigh.asp.

3 Richard Hakluyt, *Divers Voyages Touching on the Discovery of America and the Islands Adjacent,"*1582, Google Books, http://books.google.com/books?id=imcMAAAAIAAJ&pg=PA1&hl=en#v=onepage&q&f=false, 14.

4 J.P. Kenyon, *The Stuarts, a Study in English Kingship(* New York: Bow Historical Books, 1977), 57.

5 Kenyon, *Stuarts,* 57.

6 Kenyon, *Stuarts*, 70-71.

7 *First Virginia Charter*, Modern History Sourcebooks, http://www.fordham.edu/halsall.

8 See for example, Christopher Hill*, God's Englishman* (New York: Dial Press, 1970); Lacey Bald win Smith, *This Realm of England (*New York: Cengage Learning, 2000).

9 Smith, *This Realm,* 115.

10 Dennis Montgomery.*Such a dish as powdered wife I never heard of* CW Journal. The Colo nial Williamsburg Foundation, Winter 2007 http://www.history.org/foundation/journal/winter07/jamestownSide.cfm.

11 Jamestown-Yorktown Foundation. *Religion at Jamestown* http://www.historyisfun.org/pdf/Background-Essays/ReligionatJamestown.pdf.

12 The Project Gutenberg. *Colonial Records of Virginia* http://www.gutenberg.org/files/22594/22594-h/22594-h.htm#Footnote_111_125.

13 Matt Gottlieb. *House of Burgesses.*Encyclopedia Virginia, Virginia Foundation for the Humanities. http://encyclopediavirginia.org/House_of_Burgesses#start_entry.

14 Library of Virginia. *Headrights*, VA-NOTES. http://www.lva.virginia.gov/public/guides/va4_headrights.htm.

15 PBS. Oregon Public Broadcasting. *Indentured Servants in the US*History Dectives 0 PBS.org. http://www.pbs.org/opb/historydetectives/feature/indentured-servants-in-the-us/.

16 The Chandler Family Association. *John Chandler*. http://chandlerfamilyassociation.org/dna_group_7a.html.

17 National Park Service. *Bacon's Rebellion*. Historic Jamestowne, http://www.nps.gov/jame/historyculture/bacons-rebellion.htm.

18 Warren M. Billings, *Sir William Berkeley.* Jamestown Interpretive Essays, Virtual Jamestown http://www.virtualjamestown.org/essays/billings_essay.html.

19 Kevin Butterfield, *Puritans in Virginia* Encyclopedia of Virginia. Virginia Foundation for the Humanities http://www.encyclopediavirginia.org/Puritans_in_Colonial_Virginia#start_entry.

20 Nathan Philbrick, *Mayflower: A Story of Courage, Community and War (* New York: Viking, 2006), 4.

21 Oscar Barck and Hugh Talmage Lefler. *Colonial America (*New York: Macmillan Company, 1958), 73.

22 Bradford, *Of Plymouth Plantation*, Modern History Sourcebooks, *http://fordham.edu/halsall,* 33.

23 William Bradford, *Of Plymouth Plantation*, 28.

24 See the "Charter of Maryland: 1632," Avalon Project, Yale Law School, http://avalon.law.yale.edu/17th_century/ma01.asp and "The First Charter of Virginia: 1060, ibid.

25 See John Smith, *Description of New England*, 1616. At University of Nebraska, Lincoln. Digital Commons: Electronic Texts in American Studies. http://digitalcommons.unl.edu/cgi/viewcontent.cgi?article=1003&context=etas.

26 Samuel Eliot Morison, Henry Steele Commager and William E. Lauchenberg, *A Concise History of the American Republic*, vol. 1 to 1877 (New York: Oxford University Press,1977), 25.

27 Bradford, *Of Plymouth Plantation*, 35.

28 Edward Winslow, Good News From New England (London: *William Bladen* and *John Bellamie, 1624),* http://www.mayflowerhistory.com/PrimarySources/GoodNews.pdf.

29 Philbrick, *Mayflower*, 119.

30 Barck and Lefler, *Colonial America*, 77.

31 Bradford, *Of Plymouth Plantation*, 33-34.

32 Edward Winslow, *Mourt's Relation*, Pilgrim Hall Museum, http://www.pilgrimhall.org/1stthnks.htm.

33 "A Modell of Christian Charity," delivered aboard the *Arbella*," University of Virginia, Religious Freedom Library, http://religiousfreedom.lib.virginia.edu/sacred/charity.html.

34 Bremer, *Puritan Experiment*, 93-96; Oscar Theodore Barck, Jr. and Hugh Talmage Lefler, *Colonial America* (New York: MacMillan, 1958), 93-95.

35 Edmund Morgan, *The Puritan Family (* New York: Harper and Row, 1966), 2.

36 Morison, *Concise History,* 37.

37 Old Deluder Satan Law, http://americareclaimed.org/elements/docs/documents.

38 Quoted in Morison, *Puritan Family*, 92.

39 Increase Mather and John Cotton, quoted, ibid., 71.

40 Quoted in John C. Miller, This New Man, The American: the Beginnings of the American People, New York: McGraw-Hill, 1964, 143.

41 Beckenstein, Myron. "Maine's Lost Colony," 2. *Smithsonian Magazine*, February 2004. http://www.smithsonian-mag.com/history-archaeology/Maines_Lost_Colony.html.

42 Joann Pope Melish, Disowning Slavery: Gradual Emancipation of Race in New England, Ithaca, New York: Cornell Univ. Press, 1998), 19-20.

43 The Massachusetts Body of Liberties, 1641, #91, Hanover Historical Texts Project, http://history.hanover.edu/texts/masslib.html.

44 Winthrop quoted, C.S. Manegold, *Ten Hills Farm: The Forgotten History of Slavery*, Princeton, N.J. Princeton University Press, 2012), 116.

45 Ibid., 118.

46 Joan Pope Melish, Disowning Slavery, 16.

47 "Slaves in New England," Medford Historical Society, Medford, Massachusetts, http://www.medfordhistorical.org/newenglandslavery.php.

48 Slaves in New England, Medford Historical Society.

49 The Confederation preamble quoted in Barck and Lefler, *Colonial America*, 113.

50 Ibid., 113-114.

51 Alan Taylor, *American Colonies (* New York: Viking, 2001), 192.

52 Ibid., 194.

53 Christopher Columbus, *Journal*, History Sourcebooks, ed. Paul Halsall, http://www.Fordham.edu/halsall.

54 Hernan Cortes to Charles V, Modern History Sourcebooks, ed. Halsall, http://www.Fordham.edu/halsall.

55 Samuel Eliot Morison, *Builders of the Bay Colony* (Boston: Northeastern University Press, 1981), 294.

56 Ibid., and Curtis Nettels, The Roots of American Civilization: A History of American Colonial Life, 2nd edition. New York: Appleton-Century-Crofts, 1963, 212-213.

57 Morison, *Builders*, 294.

58 General Court records quoted in Morison, *Builders*, 290-91.

59 Quoted in Morison, *Builders*, 296.

60 Quoted in Taylor, *American Colonies,* 276.

61 Cotton Mather, *Memorable Providences Relating to Witchcrafts and Possessions*. 1689. http://law2.umkc.edu/faculty/projects/ftrials/salem/asa_math.htm, 22.

62 Carol F. Karlsen, The Devil in the Shape of a Woman, New York: W.W. Norton, 1988/1998, 267-271.

63 Robert Calef *More Wonders of the Invisible World.* Documentary Archive and Transcription Project. http://etext.virginia.edu/salem/witchcraft/speccol/calef/calef.html.

64 James Truslow Adams, *The Founding of New England (* New York: Dodo Press, 2009), 143.

ANSWER KEY FOR CHAPTER FOUR: THE ESTABLISHMENT OF ENGLISH COLONIES

Check your answers to the questions in the Before You Move On Sections for this chapter.

Correct answers are **BOLDED**

Section 4.3.1 - p101

1. Sir Walter Raleigh was the man behind the attempt to colonize Roanoke.
   A. TRUE
   b. False

2. The Secotan were an Algonquian people.
   A. TRUE
   b. False

3. The Indians did not have any problems with English illnesses.
   a. True
   B. FALSE

4. The first English person born in North America was a girl, Virginia Dare, on Roanoke Island.
   A. TRUE
   b. False

Section 4.4.12 - p119

1. John Smith told the colonists that if they did not work, they would not **EAT.**

2. The Starving Time was not the fault of the colonists.
   a. True
   B. FALSE

3. Newport discovered gold.
   a. True
   B. FALSE

4. John Rolfe's tobacco completely transformed the colony.
   A. TRUE
   b. False

Section 4.5.4 - p124

1. Who is Maryland named for?
   a. The Virgin Mary
   B. HENRIETTA MARIE, WIFE AND QUEEN OF CHARLES I
   c. Queen Mary of England
   d. Queen Mary of Scotland

2. Where was George Calvert's first colony? **NEWFOUNDLAND**

3. George Calvert was born a Catholic.
   a. True
   B. FALSE

4. Religious tolerance created a happy and unified Maryland Colony
   a. True
   B. FALSE

Section 4.6.9 - p139

1. Who among the following were banished from the Massachusetts Bay Colony?
   a. John Cotton and Richard Mather
   b. John Winthrop and Roger Williams
   C. ROGER WILLIAMS AND ANNE HUTCHINSON
   d. Anne Hutchinson and John Winthrop

2. Which of the following founders and colonies is incorrect?
   a. John Winthrop/Massachusetts Bay
   b. William Bradford/Plymouth
   C. WILLIAM BREWSTER/NEW HAVEN
   d. Thomas Hooker/Connecticut

3. The General Court in Puritan colonies was the ______ of the government.
   a. executive branch
   B. LEGISLATIVE BRANCH
   c. judicial branch
   d. religious branch

4. One important difference between the Puritans of Massachusetts Bay and those of Plymouth was that:
   a. the Pilgrims wanted to reform the Church of England rather than separate from it.
   B. THE PURITANS OF MASSACHUSETTS BAY WANTED TO REFORM THE CHURCH OF ENGLAND RATHER THAN SEPARATE FROM IT.
   c. the Pilgrims did not believe in the doctrine of election.
   d. the Puritans were not Calvinists.

5. According to the doctrine of predestination, a person was either saved or damned from the time of his birth.
   A. TRUE
   b. False

Section 4.8.3 - p148

1. Who among the following was banished from the Massachusetts Bay Colony?
   a. John Cotton and Richard Mather
   b. John Winthrop and Roger Williams
   C. ROGER WILLIAMS AND ANNE HUTCHINSON
   d. Anne Hutchinson and John Winthrop

2. The "Apostle to the Indians" was the Puritan minister:
   A. JOHN ELIOT
   b. John Cotton
   c. John Winthrop
   d. Cotton Mather

3. The West Indian servant whose tales of witchcraft initiated the witchcraft scare in the Salem Village was:
   a. Sarah Good
   b. Sara Parris
   C. TITUBA
   d. Massasoit

4. King Philip's war broke out when a praying Indian and graduate of Harvard was assassinated by a Wampanoag.
   A. TRUE
   b. False

5. The Dominion of New England was created in part to punish Massachusetts Bay for its failure to convert the local Indian tribes.
   a. True
   B. FALSE

Chapter Five: English Colonization After 1660

Contents

Chapter Five: English Colonization After 1660

5.1 INTRODUCTION

The years between 1640 and 1660 were ones of chaos in England. It was in this period that a king, Charles I, was beheaded, and England converted into a republic under the leadership of the Puritan Oliver Cromwell. No new colonies were founded during this time, though immigrants continued to move to already-established colonies. When the son of Charles I, Charles II, was "restored" to the throne, he brought with him an interest in colonization as well as an elaborate court life and fiscal excesses. Between his succession to the throne in 1660 and his death in 1685, Charles rewarded those who had been loyal to him and to his father by bestowing upon them grants of land in the Americas. During his reign, New Jersey, Pennsylvania, Delaware, and Carolina were founded as proprietary colonies. Most of the North American colonies, including Virginia, Georgia, North and South Carolina, Pennsylvania, Maine, Maryland, New York, New Jersey, and Delaware were proprietary for at least part of their existence.

Proprietary colonies were not unlike the fiefdoms of the Middle Ages in that the proprietors were the ultimate sources of authority in their respective colonies, controlling all actions and institutions of government. In the early eighteenth century, Georgia, the last colony to be established, was under the control of a Board of Trustees; the trustees envisioned the colony both as a buffer between Spanish Florida and the Carolinas and a refuge for English debtors. By the early eighteenth century, many of the colonies, including those granted to the proprietors, had become Royal Colonies, under the direct control of the English Crown.

5.1.1 Learning Outcomes

After completing this chapter, you should be able to:

- Analyze the developments in England between the Restoration of Charles II in 1660 and the overthrow of James II in the Glorious Revolution of 1688 and explain why anti-Catholic sentiment played a role seventeenth century England
- Explain and analyze the founding and development of the middle colonies, including the motives for settlement and the experience of the colonists.
- Examine the foundation of the colony of Georgia and explain the ways in which its founding and purpose differed from that of most other colonies.
- Analyze the motives of those who founded the Carolina colony and explain the positions of the Lords Proprietors.

5.2 THE ENGLISH BACKGROUND, 1660-1715

In 1660, following the English Civil War, the decapitation of Charles I, and the period when England was a republic under Oliver Cromwell, Charles II was restored to the throne at the invitation of Parliament; both houses of Parliament were also restored (Lords had been abolished during the period of the English Republic), as was an established Anglican Church. Far removed from the austere person of Oliver Cromwell, who "had been converted to a strong Puritan faith," the style of Charles II was "extravagant, irresponsible and un-businesslike."[1] Charles II's reign would witness a continued distrust on the part of Parliament and the English people generally of any move toward introducing Catholic practices into the liturgy of the Anglican Church, or Catholics themselves into the inner circle of the King.

5.2.1 The Reign of Charles II

Several issues arose almost immediately after Charles's coronation in 1660. One was the question as to the position Charles should take regarding the large number of religious sects that had appeared during the 1650s, a period when religious toleration by the Puritan leadership was the norm. Another question was about the future relationship between the king and Parliament, especially whether Parliament would vote adequate funds to support the monarchy; this problem was faced by both Charles II's father, Charles I, and grandfather, James I. Lastly, and perhaps most importantly, there was the question as to who would follow Charles to the throne. He had no children, which meant that the throne would pass to his brother, James, who was an avowed Catholic, and Catholics had been hated and distrusted by Parliament and the Anglican leadership since the death of "Bloody" Mary Tudor, oldest daughter of Henry VIII.

The first question was answered by the Test Act, passed by Parliament in 1673 and reluctantly accepted by Charles. This act defined religious orthodoxy and specified that those outside of the Church of England, including Catholics, could not vote, hold public office, preach, teach, or attend universities. The issue of funding developed almost immediately because Parliament was unwilling to accept Charles's assertion that Parliamentary funds were not adequate, especially in light of the blatant, very visible extravagance of his personal lifestyle. In the opinion of the Members of Parliament, public money was being wasted rather than falling short.[2]

Unfortunately, in an attempt to increase the revenues of the Crown, in 1671 Charles signed the secret *Treaty of Dover* with his cousin, the Catholic Louis XIV of France. The treaty specified that England would join France in war against Holland, Charles would publicly convert to Catholicism, and the laws against Catholics in England would be relaxed; if this occurred, 100 years of anti-Catholic legislation would be reversed. In return, Charles would receive an annual allowance of £200,000 from France and the prospect of victory spoils; both sources of income would solve his fiscal problems. Details of the agreement with Louis XIV inevitably leaked out and anti-Catholic, anti-Charles fervor swept the nation. As if these problems were not enough, Charles had no legitimate heir, having married a Portuguese princess who was unable to have children. Though Charles had many illegitimate children, they could not assume the throne, so it was obvious from early in his reign that his successor would be his younger brother, James, who had openly converted to Catholicism in 1673.

If Charles had been capable of adopting policies that reassured the English people of his determination to defend their traditional religion and civil liberties, and of his basic soundness and responsibility as a leader, none of these difficulties would have caused as much trouble as they did. Instead Charles made these problems worse, and by the end of his reign, England was failing as a leader in European affairs, nonconformists were rebelling and being savagely persecuted, and, because Charles could not work with Parliaments, he called none. Fiscal chaos was the result. Charles had created a country that was weak abroad and severely divided at home.[3] It was this situation that Charles's brother, James, an avowed Catholic, would inherit when Charles died in 1685.

5.2.2 James II and the Glorious Revolution

If Charles II was unsuccessful as a monarch, James II was a disaster. As a Catholic, James moved quickly to put aside the limitations placed on Catholics by the Test Act of 1673 by appointing Roman Catholics to positions in the army, the church, the universities, and local governments. When his actions were taken before the courts of law, he began suspending laws, and by 1687 his opponents feared that he would suspend the Test Act altogether. It appeared that James was about to impose absolutism on England when in the summer of 1687 he dissolved Parliament. Historian John Miller remarks that "James's actions seemed to threaten to destroy the laws and the independence of Parliament, the very foundations of the traditional constitution."[4]

The final blow came when James's second wife (his first wife, a Protestant, had died after giving birth to two daughters), the Catholic Italian princess Mary of Modena, became pregnant; a healthy boy was born in June 1688. It was now inevitable that James's Protestant daughter, Mary, would not succeed her father to the throne, but rather the new son—called James III by some—would do so; this new son was a Catholic. Rumors abounded in England that the child had actually been a girl who was switched at birth for a baby boy, although this was never proven. Contemporary pamphlets circulated with images of what would happen if a "Papist" came to the throne of England. The troops would ravish "your wives and daughters, dashing your little children's brains out against the walls, plundering your houses and cutting your own throats."[5]

In April 1688, even before the birth of the baby, William of Orange, a Dutch prince from the noble family of Orange and husband of Mary, James's oldest daughter, had made it known that "if he was invited by some men of the best interest to...come and rescue the nation and religion" he was agreeable to invading England.[6] There is much controversy about William's true motives, but the prevailing theory is that "he wished to bring England into his war against Louis XIV's France and a free Parliament was seen as more likely to support this."[7]

For this invasion, the prince of Orange amassed an armada "four times the size of that launched by the Spanish in 1588."[8] A "Protestant wind," as the English had called it in 1588, prevailed once again; William's invasion began in early November. By late December, James had fled the country, and the family of Orange had come to the throne of England.

In his 1690 defence of William's accession to the throne of England, John Locke emphasized that "when such a single person or prince sets up his own arbitrary will in place of the laws which are the will of the society...who shall be judge whether the prince or the legislative act contrary to their trust[?]...To this I reply the people shall be the judge."[9]

Historians refer to the events of 1688 and 1689 as the Glorious Revolution, mainly because the change in monarchs was accomplished with little bloodshed. With the Revolution also came a series of reforms forced on William and Mary by Parliament; these reforms created a permanent definition of the relationship between the monarchy and Parliament.

According to the Settlement, William and Mary were to rule as joint monarchs, the first time this had occurred in English history. William insisted on this action, as he had a claim in his own right to the English throne. In exchange for Parliament's recognition of the dual reign, he and Mary agreed to the following: Parliament was to be called every three years whether or not called by a monarch (the Triennial Act); Parliamentary laws, once passed, could not be suspended by a monarch; funds could not be created by royal prerogative; and a standing army in peacetime must be approved by Parliament. In other words, the source of law was to be in the hands of Parliament.

In addition, the Revolutionary Settlement included a series of penalties levied at English Catholics, who would not be allowed to bear arms or worship freely. It also specified that the kings of England would forever be Protestants as "none of the royal family [will] marry Catholics."[10] An Act of Toleration guaranteed freedom of worship to all sects except Catholics. As William assured Parliament, "I had no other intention in coming hither than to preserve your religion, law and liberties, so you may be sure that I shall endeavor to support them."[11]

The Glorious Revolution was by no means a democratic one, but it created a Bill of Rights that recognized equality under the law. However, voting was limited to the nobility and gentry, and Parliament continued to represent these two classes alone. There was no universal male suffrage, and women were not given the right to vote until 1928.

William and Mary ruled jointly until her death in 1694. William remained as the sole monarch until his own death in 1702. William was followed on the throne by Mary's younger sister Anne, the last Stuart ruler, under whom the Act of Union was created, unifying the Parliaments of Scotland and England. From this point in time on, England is referred to as Great Britain. Because Anne's heir had predeceased her, upon her death the English Crown passed to the nearest Protestant relatives of the Stuarts, the Electors of Hanover. George I was the first Hanoverian to take the throne of England. His grandson George III was the king at the time of the American Revolution.

5.2.3 Before You Move On...

Key Concepts

Events in seventeenth century England were important to the establishment and progress of the colonies in America. During the Puritan Revolution, when there was freedom of religion in the mother country, and when no grants of land in the Americas were forthcoming from the government (for there was no "Crown"), no colonies were founded. With the Restoration of Charles II, however, who was excessively extravagant and a great believer in rewarding his friends and nobility for their service to the Crown, colonization began again. The period 1660-1688 was one of struggle for political ascendency in England between Parliament and the king. The Glorious Revolution, like the Civil War and Restoration, was played out in the colonies, as the latter chaffed against controls by the royal governors and the Crown. The ideals of the English Bill of Rights adopted in 1689 were reflected in the literature that came out of the colonies in the mid-eighteenth century as colonial leaders increasingly insisted on their rights as English and into the state constitutions adopted during the American Revolution.

Test Yourself

1.The term "Restoration" refers to:

a. the restoring of power to Parliament in 1689.

b. Charles II's being brought to the throne of England in 1660.

c. the Bill of Rights.

d. William and Mary's accession to the throne in 1688.

2. According to the Triennial Act,

a. no Catholic could become an English monarch.

b. Parliament must raise the salary of the monarchy at least once in every three years.

c. Parliament must meet every three years even if not called by the Crown.

d. England would have not one, but three Parliaments.

3. According to John Locke, the Glorious Revolution was a legitimate one.

a. True

b. False

4. Which of the following was NOT one of the restrictions placed on Catholics after the Glorious Revolution?

a. Catholics could not sit in Parliament.

b. Catholics could not worship freely.

c. Catholics could not marry.

d. Catholics could not bear arms.

5. Although William of Orange was married to James II's daughter, Mary, he also was in line for the throne of England.

a. True

b. False

See page 201 for answers

5.3 THE CAROLINAS

Geography played a major role in the development pattern of the Carolinas. The area once known as Albemarle, which today is North Carolina, was not attractive to English colonists. It had a difficult coastal region featuring large swamps and marshlands and lacking natural harbors and rivers providing access to the interior, such as were found in Virginia and further south. Some Virginians did move south into the area, but more to escape society in Virginia where they were viewed as landless misfits than to make a colony in Carolina.

5.3.1 Carolina: The Proprietary Colony of the South

The earliest English attempt at a colony in Carolina was Roanoke, the lost colony which vanished between 1587 and 1590. In 1629, Charles I granted a charter for colonization but with little result. Then in 1663 King Charles II granted a new charter to eight Lords Proprietors, the Earl of Clarendon, the Duke of Albemarle, Lord Craven, Lord Berkeley, the Earl of Shaftesbury, Sir George Carteret, Sir William Berkeley, and Sir John Colleton, which opened the door for a new attempt. These eight men were given near absolute authority in their new colonial territory. As the Lords Proprietors, they would be responsible for the colony's organization and promotion, recruitment of colonists, government, and any funding, transportation, and supply needs the new colony would have; further, they would receive any profits the colony made. They would each be able to pass on their role to their heirs.

5.3.2 The Lords Proprietors

The proprietors, or owners of the colony of Carolina, were mostly Royalists, men who had supported the Stuarts before and during the English Civil War. They were rewarded for their devotion when Charles II was restored in 1660. William Berkeley was the Governor of Virginia; he and Sir George Carteret had been Lords Proprietors previously of

New Jersey. Sir John Colleton had holdings in Barbados and was a member of the Royal African Company which was involved in bringing African slaves to the colonies. He died in 1666 before seeing a permanent colony established in Carolina. Lord Craven was a soldier, patron of the arts, and member of the Royal Society. The Earl of Clarendon had been Lord High Chancellor to Charles I and was the father-in-law of James, Duke of York, the future James II. The Duke of Albemarle had actually been a supporter of Cromwell but threw his support behind Charles II once Cromwell was gone. Lord Berkeley, brother of Sir William, was a more traditional Royalist, loyal to the Stuarts, and who served as the president of the Council for Foreign Plantations, making him quite influential in the colonies. Anthony Ashley-Cooper, the Earl of Shaftesbury, like the Earl of Clarendon, had been a supporter of the Puritan Oliver Cromwell but came to feel it best to have Charles II on the throne. He was very active in the colonization of the Americas, having investments in Barbados and Hudson Bay as well as Carolina. Although he supported Charles II early on, he ended up dying in exile in Holland because he did not agree with some later policies of the king. Like many Protestants, he feared the eventual succession of Charles's brother, James, a devout Catholic.

The Earl of Shaftesbury's importance to the colony is indicated by the names of the two rivers that meet at Charleston, the Ashley and the Cooper, both named after him. He, along with his secretary, philosopher, and sometime physician, John Locke, created the "Fundamental Constitutions of Carolina," a document which defined the colony's government and social structure even to the point of creating a perpetual landed aristocracy. The Constitutions provided for an unwieldy, multi-layered administrative structure that was impractical at best, dysfunctional at worst, and not designed to deal with the day to day needs of the colony. It may well be the single most ill-advised piece of work ever created by Locke, yet it did have one redeeming feature, a provision for religious tolerance uncommon in the majority of the colonies. While the Constitutions recognized the Anglican Church as the official church of the colony, it specifically called for tolerance of other religions, even non-Christian native ones. This religious tolerance made Carolina attractive to those outside the mainstream Anglican faith, such as other Protestants and Jews.

5.3.3 The First Colonists at Charles Town

The first colonists under the new charter set out from England in 1669 for Barbados, an island in the Lesser Antilles east of the Caribbean. Barbados had been an English colony since 1624. By 1669, opportunities for those seeking land were becoming fewer, so several men from Barbados decided to try their luck in the new Carolina colony. They brought with them their experience in colony building and a belief in slavery as a solution to labor problems such as those found on plantations.

In Carolina, as in other colonies, a man with the proper social status and money could acquire a large grant of land, while a man with less money and social status but who paid his own way to the colony would receive a holding of many acres of land. After a brief stop in Bermuda, the three ships transporting the colonists and the men from Barbados made their way to the point at which the Ashley and Cooper Rivers join, what is today the South Carolina coast. The ships sailed up the Ashley River and established Charles Town in 1670, naming their new home after Charles II. In the first few years, the colonists set about building their town, cementing relations and trade with the Indians, and working towards making the colony self-sufficient, a key to survival. For their part, the Lords Proprietors had to keep the colony supplied with provisions and new colonists, a job that at first was made difficult due to the rumors about Carolina. Attracting and recruiting potential colonists could be a competitive business. Someone therefore started a rumor which soon spread that Carolina was an unhealthy place to live, with the implication that a smart colonist would go elsewhere, say to New England. Part of the Proprietors' job was to squelch such rumors and to promote all the benefits of settling in Carolina.

In 1680, Charles Town, Charleston, was moved to its current location with its large natural harbor. In 1686 when the Spanish captured Port Royal, a colony further south along the coast, Charleston became an especially important seaport as it thence became the southernmost seaport in English hands on the continent. Although the new location proved great as a port, it was vulnerable to attack from the sea. The Spanish, the French, and even pirates all threatened Charleston. The most famous of the pirates to plague Charleston's waters was Edward Teach, also known as Blackbeard. These threats led to Charleston's development as a fortified city.

5.3.4 Cash Crops

The earliest exports of Carolina included furs, deerskins, cattle, lumber, and the naval stores of turpentine, resin, and pitch, which come from pine trees and were needed for the repair and maintenance of the wooden sailing ships of the day. These important goods helped to give Carolina a firm foundation before the development of its first true cash crop, rice.

Rice was first planted in the area in the early 1680s. The exact origins of rice as a Carolina cash crop are disputable, with one story of its introduction being that Dr. Henry Woodward planted seeds he received from a captain of a ship who brought them from Madagascar. The uncomfortably humid Carolina low country, with its tidal waters, proved to be an excellent place to grow rice, and later another cash crop, indigo. What is not disputed is that the slave trade in Carolina expanded rapidly as a result of the introduction of rice. Rice production was labor intensive. Slaves were needed to transform the coastal wetlands into rice fields by clearing out the native vegetation, building irrigation systems, forming the fields which must be banked to hold in the water, and tending to the crop throughout the long, hot summer. The importance of rice therefore increased the demand for slaves from rice growing regions of West Africa. The more rice was grown, the more slaves were needed; consequently, Charleston became a major center of the slave trade, importing Africans and exporting Indians. By 1708 African slaves were in the majority in the colony, by 1720 they made up 65% of the colony's population.[12] Carolina colonists would use friendly Indians to capture Indians from other tribes who were not allied to the colony. They then would be exported to the British colonies in the islands, such as Barbados and Bermuda, and in return African slaves from those islands would be imported in Carolina.

One source of Indian slaves for the slave trade was war with and among the native Indians. Indians captured by tribes that traded with the colonists sometimes found themselves sold as slaves. The Tuscarora were natives of what would be North Carolina, dwelling along the coast of the region. They were divided into upper and lower town groups. They had initially accepted the colonists and traded peacefully with them. Over time the relationship soured as the Tuscarora, like other native peoples, fell victim to European diseases, in addition to being swindled out of their land, being victims of unfair trade, and even being enslaved. The groups of Tuscarora most affected by these conditions were the ones who lived in the southern or lower town in the area of Pamlico Sound. They were led by Chief Hancock. In 1711, a land dispute led Chief Hancock to attack the colonists. Over a hundred colonists were killed, leading Governor Hyde to call on Indian allies and South Carolina to come to North Carolina's aide. The war would last until 1715. Ultimately, Chief Hancock was killed, many of his people were taken as slaves to South Carolina, and Governor Hyde died of yellow fever which ravished the area in 1712. Although the war ended, the problems which caused it did not. Colonists continued to encroach on native land and generally mistreated the natives. Many Tuscarora fled north, going as far as New York in hopes of finding a life free from the expanding grasp of the European colonists. Others settled on a tract of land specified in the treaty that ended the war, only to see that land lost as well, piece by piece to the expanding colony.

Among the native allies of the colonists during the Tuscarora War were the Yamasee Indians of South Carolina. In 1715, as the war with the Tuscarora ended, the Yamasee war began. This war involved not only the Yamasee and other smaller tribes, but also two of the largest in the South Carolina-Georgia region—the Creek and the Cherokee. The Creek sided with the Yamasee against the colonists, so the Cherokee, enemies of the Creek, supported the colonists. North Carolina supported its sister colony, South Carolina. The war ended with a victory for the colonies and made new territory available for them.

In 1691, Peter Guerard patented a machine to hull the rice; the machine removed the grains of rice from their casings, or hulls. This process helped to boost rice production, as the rice could be prepared for shipping much faster. By 1695, the Proprietors were accepting rice as rent payments. Production continued to increase, reaching 20 million pounds by 1720.

Along with rice came indigo, a plant that produces a blue dye used in fabrics. Indigo and rice work well together because they can be raised in the same area and have different growing seasons. Slaves would raise the indigo in the spring, harvesting it in time to plant rice for the summer, which would be harvested in the fall. Indigo production began in Carolina with Eliza Lucas, a rather remarkable young lady who in 1738 at the age of sixteen was managing her family's plantation. Her father sent her some indigo seeds from the West Indies. Within three years she had her first success in raising the indigo and extracting the blue dye, which was then formed into cakes. By 1748 South Carolina was exporting over 130,000 pounds of indigo to England.

5.3.5 The Arrival of the Huguenots

French Huguenots, or Protestants from France, began arriving in 1685, driven from their home country by religious persecution and drawn to Charleston by the promise of religious toleration. The Huguenots were born during the Protestant Reformation, persecuted early on, and then involved in a long religious war in France. The Huguenots rejected Catholicism, the mainstream religion of France, in favor of a Calvinist variety of

Protestantism. John Calvin, himself a Frenchman living in Switzerland, had developed his own protestant theology separate from Luther and from the Anglican Church of England. Their religious war in France ended in 1598 when the French King Henry IV signed the Edict of Nantes, granting the Huguenots the right to practice their religion within certain guidelines and only in specified areas. In 1685, Louis XIV revoked the Edict and persecution of the Huguenots began again. Some stayed hoping for a change in France while others fled to more Protestant-friendly countries and colonies such as Carolina. Many of the Huguenots were artisans, not aristocrats, and so brought much-needed skills to the young colony. By 1704, the French Huguenots established the town of Bath, the first town in what would become North Carolina.

5.3.6 Carolina Splits into Two Royal Colonies

The southern part of Carolina continued to develop more rapidly as a center of agriculture and trade with the colony centered on Charleston, despite its vulnerability to sea attacks and threats by Indians and the Spanish. In 1718, the pirate Blackbeard blockaded Charleston's harbor, demanding medical supplies. Unhappy with the continuing dangers and generally dissatisfied with the Lords Proprietors, the citizens of the colony moved in 1719 to become a Royal Colony with a government and protection provided by the Crown. Carolina subsequently was divided into North and South, with South Carolina becoming a Royal Colony. In 1729 North Carolina would follow by becoming a Royal Colony as well. Both North and South Carolina would remain Royal Colonies until the American Revolution.

5.3.7 Before You Move On...

Key Concepts

The Carolinas began as one colony with two distinct areas: the north, Albemarle, which was not easy to colonize due to its geography, and the south, which centered on Charleston, a city founded in 1670. The first attempts to colonize Carolina failed. The later attempt in 1663 to establish Carolina as a proprietary colony with eight Lords Proprietors was successful. Carolina's policy of religious toleration made it attractive to non-Anglicans. Charleston's location as the southern-most English seaport in North America helped it to grow yet also made it vulnerable to attack. The development of labor-intensive rice and indigo as cash crops encouraged the slave trade. The vigorous slave trade in Charleston involved importing Africans and exporting Indians. Dissatisfaction with the Lords Proprietors led the colonists in South Carolina to petition, successfully, to become a Royal Colony in 1719. In 1729 North Carolina also became a Royal Colony. Both remained Royal Colonies until the American Revolution.

Test Yourself

1. North and South Carolina began as one colony, Carolina.

   a. True

   b. False

2. In a proprietary colony, the Proprietors have no responsibilities except to collect the profits.

a. True

b. False

3. John Locke wrote the original constitution for Carolina, but it was not what the colony needed.

a. True

b. False

4. Carolina's policy of religious toleration helped to attract new colonists.

a. True

b. False

See page 201 for answers

5.4 THE MIDDLE COLONIES

During the early part of the seventeenth century, the English focused on developing their colonies in New England and the Chesapeake, thereby largely neglecting the land between the two settlements. So, the Dutch and the Swedes began to settle the mid-Atlantic region along the Hudson and Delaware Rivers. After the Restoration, Charles II and James II hoped to build the power of the English monarchy by expanding their overseas empire at the expense of the Dutch. By the early 1680s, the English had turned New Netherland into several proprietary colonies, including New York, New Jersey, Pennsylvania, and Delaware. In the years after the English takeover, the middle colonies became the most diverse and fastest-growing region in North America.

5.4.1 The Dutch in the New World

After the Dutch asserted their independence from Spain in the late sixteenth century, the Netherlands set up a republican government. Unlike other European nations at the time, the Dutch allowed both intellectual and religious freedom. Soon, dissidents from other countries flocked to the tiny nation along the North Sea. The liberal government, coupled with the immigration, made the country a powerful force in Europe as well as in the race for overseas empire. The Dutch also expanded their navy in an attempt to attack Spanish and Portuguese trade. After the founding of the Dutch East India Company (DEIC), the Dutch became the primary shippers of spices from Asia, slaves from Africa, and sugar from the Americas.

Initially, the Netherlands focused on establishing its control over the carrying trade. Like the other sea powers, it hoped to find an alternate route to Far Eastern markets. In 1609, the DEIC sent Henry Hudson to the New World to find the Northwest Passage. Hudson sailed into the Delaware Bay and the North River, known later as the Hudson River. He realized, of course, that neither inlet was the Northwest Passage, but he recorded the possibilities for fur trading and farming. Hudson also established a friendly relationship with the Iroquois Nations. Following these discoveries, the DEIC sent several expeditions to explore the land and trade with the Iroquois. Dutch merchants also persuaded the government to charter the New Netherland Company to handle the fur trade.

By 1614, the company established a trading post, Fort Nassau, near present-day Albany. From there, traders travelled by canoe westward toward the Great Lakes and northward toward the St. Lawrence River. The New Netherland Company possessed a monopoly over the trade; however, the government opted not to renew the charter in 1618. Soon, merchants formed the Dutch West India Company (DWIC). In 1621, the Dutch government granted it a broad charter. Subsequently, the company had the authority to trade and settle anywhere in America as well as to govern new territories as it saw fit. Thus, the company could appoint officials, make laws, administer justice, make war, and negotiate treaties.[13]

At the outset, the DWIC did not plan to colonize in the New World. Rather, it hoped to continue the lucrative fur trade. Company officials believed they could keep costs down and discourage illegal trade if they did not establish permanent settlements. For several years, their plan worked. The DWIC then decided permanent settlements would help protect the fur trade from English and French piracy. It sent the first settlers in late 1624. The company recruited Protestants from the Spanish Netherlands to populate their colony because it thought these Protestants, or Walloons, had the stamina and work ethic to survive pioneer life.

Under the direction of Cornelius May, the migrants built Fort Orange on the Hudson River to replace Fort Nassau, which had been destroyed by constant flooding. They also established a new Fort Nassau on the Delaware River. Under the direction of Peter Minuet, they settled New Amsterdam at the mouth of the Hudson River. The DWIC told Minuet not to expel the Indians with violence; it did not want the fur trade interrupted. In 1626, Minuet purchased Manhattan Island for sixty guilders from the local Indians. New Amsterdam subsequently served as a major seaport and seat of government for New Netherland. The colony shared the mother country's religious toleration, but not its liberal republican government.[14]

The upper portion of New Netherland continued to focus on the fur trade. To preserve that trade, the DWIC worked to sustain a healthy relationship with the five tribes of the Iroquois Nations, especially the Mohawk. The friendship proved beneficial for both sides. The Dutch did not need to worry about French or Algonquian attacks on their settlements. The Iroquois gained access to new goods to trade with interior tribes, which helped to expand their power. While the fur trade expanded significantly in the coming years, the DWIC struggled to make money because many traders

Figure 5.1 Fort Amsterdam | In the 1620s, the Dutch began to settle the New World. This depiction of their settlement on Manhattan Island appeared in Charles Hemstreet's The Story of Manhattan published in 1901, with the caption "Earliest Picture of Manhattan."

Author: Charles Hemstreet
Source: *The Story of Manhattan*

defied its monopoly. In 1639, the company opened the fur trade to any colonist and taxed fur exports. However, the colonists simply evaded the tax by smuggling their goods out through New Sweden or New France.[15]

The lower portion of New Netherland focused on farming in order to supply the colony and ship its excess to other Dutch settlements. The DWIC wanted to avoid spending money on supporting its settlements, so it established the patroon system in 1629. Under the system, the company awarded generous plots of land with riverfronts to proprietors willing to take financial responsibility for settling the plot. However, the system did little to encourage settlement because most settlers preferred to own their land rather than become tenants. To meet demands for labor, the company relied on free and bound labor in the lower settlements. The initial plans for colonization divided colonists into free and indentured status, depending on whether they could pay for their passage.

Unlike in the fur trading areas, the farming communities had a poor relationship with the Indians. According to historian Alan Taylor, "the downriver Dutch...regarded the Algonquians as a nuisance best removed as quickly as possible." Tensions boiled over in the early 1640s when William Kieft, the Dutch governor, demanded the Algonquian tribes pay an annual tribute and live under Dutch law. After they refused, Kieft launched a surprise attack on an unsuspecting tribe in 1643. The other Algonquian tribes fought back by burning and looting rural settlements in what became known as Kieft's War. Using the same tactics the English used in the Pequot War, including the butchering of women and children during night raids, the Dutch wore the Algonquians down. They sued for peace in 1645. In subsequent wars, the Algonquians lost much of their territory to the Dutch.[16]

Seeing that the Dutch confined their settlement to the eastern banks of the Delaware River, the Swedes established a settlement on the western bank in the 1630s. The Swedish monarchy created the New Sweden Company at the urging of several Dutch traders seeking to defy the Dutch West India Company's monopoly on the fur trade. The Swedish company recruited Peter Minuet, who the DWIC removed from his position as governor of New Netherland for unspecified reasons, to lead an exhibition in 1638. Minuet and his fifty settlers built Fort Christiana near present-day Wilmington, Delaware, purchased land from the Indians, and began actively trading furs with the Algonquian Lenape and the Iroquois Susquehannock. The New Sweden Company did not earn much money, nor did the colony attract many settlers. It did, however, attract the attention of the Dutch, who resented the competition. In 1655, the Dutch readied for an attack. The Swedish commander, apparently bribed by the Dutch, surrendered without a fight, and New Sweden became part of New Netherland.[17]

Over the years, New Netherland drew a diverse group of settlers because of its religious toleration. Free artisans and farmers from Belgium, France, Scandinavia, and Germany settled in the Hudson and Delaware River Valleys. Moreover, dissident Puritans from New England migrated to Long Island. Finally, the company imported African slaves to work on its wharves and ships. Still, the colony grew slowly; its population lagged behind the surrounding English colonies. The slow growth stemmed partly from the fact that people in the Netherlands had few reasons to emigrate. The liberal government, strong economy, and religious toleration at home eliminated the major factors for migration in the seventeenth century. It also stemmed from the fact that the benefits of migrating could not make up for the arbitrary government set up by the DWIC. The worst of the DWIC's appointments was Peter Stuyvesant, who ruled the colony from 1647 to 1664. He was a less than tactful leader, and his tyranny antagonized the settlers. In 1649, he threatened to burn down residents' houses in Fort Orange in order to build up a better defense against the Indians. In 1653, he disbanded a convention of residents calling for government reform. Throughout his reign, he persecuted religious dissenters who did not belong to the Dutch Reformed Church. When the English threatened the colony, few cared to resist.[18]

5.4.2 The English Take Over

While the English had resented the Dutch settlement in the New World, for much of the early seventeenth century European politics prevented them from attacking New Netherland. During the Thirty Years' War (1618-1648) in Europe, the Protestant powers fought the Catholic powers. As such, England and the Netherlands became allies and kept their rivalry in check. When the conflict ended, so did their détente. The English Parliament sought to undermine the power of the Dutch carrying trade by passing the Navigation Acts in the 1650s and 1660s. These acts forced New England, Chesapeake, and Caribbean colonists to ship on English vessels. Moreover, they mandated that certain goods must pass through English ports so the government could collect customs duties. Parliament, and later the king, saw the acts as a means to increase government revenue, stimulate shipbuilding, and increase the number of trained English sailors, benefits that allowed the English to supplant the Dutch as the leading commercial empire.

The Navigation Acts led to three wars between the Dutch and the English. In the First Anglo-Dutch War (1652-1654), the English prepared to attack New Netherland. However, forces in New England received word of a peace settlement before they could mount their raid. The Second Anglo-Dutch War (1664-1667) came after the Restoration. When Charles II ascended to the English throne, he wanted to consolidate his power at home and abroad. The first step in the process was to remove the Dutch threat in the New World. Given that John Cabot had explored the mid-Atlantic for England before Henry Hudson explored it for the Netherlands, Charles II planned to take the Dutch colony by force if necessary. He named his brother James, the Duke of York, proprietor of a large swath of territory in the New World, including the Dutch colony. James then appointed Captain Richard Nicolls to command an assault against New Netherland.

Four English ships arrived on the shores of New Amsterdam in August 1664; Nicolls offered the Dutch a chance to surrender. At first, Peter Stuyvesant refused, but eventually he gave up. First, the Dutch had not properly provisioned their fort, meaning they could not defend New Amsterdam for long. Second, the colonists refused to fight; they feared the destruction of their property more than English rule. Under the terms of the surrender, the Dutch settlers retained the right to their property, the right to religious freedom, and the right to maintain Dutch legal customs. The formal peace treaty in 1667 confirmed the transfer of power, and New Netherland officially became New York. However, the region passed briefly back into the hands of the Dutch during the Third Anglo-Dutch War (1672-1674). This time, the English settlers surrendered without much of a fight. However, when the two nations made peace, England retained the territory.[19]

English Rule in New York

After the English took control, the Duke of York appointed Captain Nicolls as the colony's first governor. As an absolutist, James preferred to run New York with as little input from his subjects as possible, so he opted not to set up a colonial assembly. Given the ethnic and religious diversity of the population, such heavy-handedness surely would produce resentment among the people living in New York. According to historian Oliver Chitwood, Nicolls was ideally suited for the task of managing the transition from Dutch to English rule because he understood the need to work with the local population. First, Nicolls practiced a policy of religious toleration. He did not force the colonists to accept the Anglican Church as the official church of New York. But, he did require each community to support a church of its choosing.

Then, Nicolls gradually established English institutions. In the areas heavily populated by Dutch settlers, he slowly replaced their customs. He renamed New Amsterdam as New York and Fort Orange as Albany. Later, he shifted toward an English-style of local government. After some Dutch settlers assisted in the re-conquest in the 1670s, another governor eliminated most of the remaining Dutch customs and ruled more arbitrarily. Nevertheless, Dutch influence could be felt for years after the takeover. In the areas heavily populated by English settlers, Nicolls successfully encouraged the settlers to accept the Duke's Laws, which set up the conditions of local government for Staten Island, Long Island, and Westchester. The Duke's Laws granted the people the right to elect for their town a board of overseers who worked in conjunction with a constable to maintain order. They also provided for justices of the peace, appointed by the governor, who had the authority to make laws with the consent of the governor. Within a few years, Nicolls applied the Duke's Laws to the entire colony.[20]

While New York's colonists accepted the Duke's Laws, they also struggled with the lack of a representative assembly. After Nicolls departed in 1668, the Duke of York's appointments as governor failed to work successfully with the local population. The colonists bristled at the governors' arbitrary rule; they longed for a more direct say in matters of taxation. While Edmund Andros served as governor (1674-1683), the colonists refused to pay for their own defense or the required customs duties, leading to political unrest and economic problems in New York. When the duke appointed Thomas Dongan as governor (1683-1688), he made an important concession to the colonists regarding a representative assembly. Knowing they would be wary of the Irish Catholic Dongan, James instructed him to establish a colonial assembly.

In 1683, New York's assembly met for the first time; it drew up the "Charter of Liberties and Privileges" to outline the rights of the colonists with respect to representation, taxation, and religion. In 1684, the duke approved the provisions. After Charles II died and James ascended to the throne, the new king wanted to make significant changes to the administration of all the northern colonies. He overturned his previous ruling about the charter and revoked the right to a representative assembly in New York. His decision paved the way for New York's inclusion in the Dominion of New England under the direction of Edmund Andros in Massachusetts and his deputy Francis Nicholson in New York. Nicholson appointed many Catholics to important positions in his administration, which aroused suspicion among the predominantly Protestant residents and paved the way for a revolt against his rule.[21]

After William and Mary deposed James II, unrest in New York led to Leisler's Rebellion. When word of the Glorious Revolution reached New York, Nicholson hesitated to recognize the new monarch's authority until he received official word from England. However, rumors began to circulate that he planned to burn down New York City and sell the people into slavery. Jacob Leisler, a successful merchant of German descent, then led a revolt against Nicholson's rule. Leisler captured Fort James in the name of William and Mary. Nicholson then fled to England, leaving control in the hands of a three-man council. At the same time, a convention of colonists appointed Leisler the commander of the province. In late 1689, William and Mary sent a broadly addressed letter to New York with instructions for governing the colony. Leisler claimed he was the intended recipient, so the messenger gave him the dispatch. After reading it, Leisler took on the role of lieutenant governor.

Under his leadership, the government restored order and collected taxes. Leisler also convened a representative assembly, which he dismissed when several members raised questions about his policy of imprisoning his political opponents. In the end, Leisler's government polarized the residents along cultural and religious lines. The average Dutch residents supported him, whereas the average English and very wealthy Dutch opposed him. Alan Taylor suggested Leisler "lacked the political experience and the sophistication" to cope with the diversity in New York. When William and Mary learned of the deteriorating situation, they appointed Henry Sloughter as the new governor. Sloughter sent Major Robert Ingoldsby ahead of him to New York.

When Ingoldsby arrived, he demanded Leisler relinquish his control of the colony. Leisler refused because he had no official documentation regarding the transfer of power. Leisler only gave up his control after most of his supporters defected. His hesitation allowed his opponents to convince Sloughter that Leisler had committed an act of treason. Shortly after taking office, the governor tried and convicted Leisler and several of his supporters. Sloughter then arranged for Leisler's execution before he could appeal to England. For years after the rebellion, New York remained divided between two political factions those that supported Leisler and those that did not. At the same time, William and Mary believed the lack of a representative government caused the unrest in New York. So, they instructed Sloughter to set up a new elected assembly, which met for the first time in 1691.[22]

Indian Relations in New York

The English also took control of the fur trade in the region and became the primary trading partner of the Iroquois Nations. At the same time Fort Orange grew as trading center, so too did Montreal in New France. The Iroquois's friendship with the Dutch had allowed them to blunt the influence of French expansion into the Great Lakes. When the English came to power, the Iroquois hoped for the same level of commitment from the English. Alan Taylor suggested, "the English bitterly disappointed" them.[23] In the 1660s and 1670s, the English preferred to continue fighting with the Dutch, rather than beginning a new fight with the French. Moreover, the Anglo-Dutch Wars limited the supplies going into Albany for trade with the Indians. Prices of goods went up at a time when the Iroquois needed those goods to trade with interior tribes in order to keep the peace. Finally, the English colonists did little to help the Iroquois fend off an attack by the French and the Huron in 1666. As part of their peace agreement with the French, the Iroquois had to allow French Jesuits into their communities.

Not until 1674 did the situation for the Iroquois Nations improve. With the end of the Third Anglo-Dutch War, supplies began to flow back into Albany. Moreover, Edmond Andros worked diligently to repair the English relationship with the Iroquois as the English looked toward eliminating French presence in the New World. The English and the Iroquois agreed to the Covenant Chain, whereby the English helped the Iroquois dominate other tribes in the Northeast. Under the Covenant Chain, the English and Iroquois met annually to renew their friendship and discuss land and trade. Both sides benefitted from the arrangement. The agreement gave the English a strong ally in their fight against the Algonquian in other parts of the empire. In the future, when the English wanted to take more land in the interior, they provided gifts to Iroquois leaders who in turn sent their warriors to attack the Algonquians. The agreement allowed the Iroquois to banish the French Jesuits from their territory and to resume their efforts of expanding their control in the interior in the 1680s. To underscore their relationship, Thomas Dongan and Francis Howard (Lord Effingham), the governors of New York and Virginia respectively, negotiated the 1684 Treaty of Albany with the Iroquois. According to the treaty, the Iroquois agreed to become subjects of the English monarch.[24]

The Founding of New Jersey

Charles II and his brother James hoped to use the colonies in the New World to enrich the monarchy through taxes on commerce. However, they also used the colonies to award the loyalty of their longtime political supporters, granting their friends tracts of land from what England had taken from the Netherlands. In 1664, James, then Duke of York, ceded some of the territory south of Manhattan Island, from the Atlantic coast to the Delaware River, to Sir George Carteret and Lord John Berkeley. The duke called the new proprietary colony New Jersey to honor Carteret's defense of Jersey Island during the English Civil War. Under the terms of the patent, Carteret and Berkeley had the right to dispose of the land under their control and to earn money from the land. The patent did not give them the right to govern the colony; however, they claimed that right anyway.

In 1665, Carteret and Berkeley adopted the "Concessions and Agreement" to outline the colony's governing structure and land grant policy. The proprietors retained the right to appoint the governor, but they also provided for an annually elected representative assembly to make laws subject to proprietary approval. Moreover, the document allowed for liberty of conscience, or freedom of religion. The proprietors then began to recruit settlers for their sparsely-populated territory. Philip Carteret, a relative of the proprietor, brought approximately thirty families to the colony when he took up his position as the first governor. However, most of the colonists came from New England and Long Island. Puritans found the provisions for a representative assembly particularly appealing. Later, New Jersey began to attract a large number of Quakers from England because of this religious toleration.

While the population increased, New Jersey experienced a fair amount of unrest in its early years. First, the predominantly Puritan settlers elected to the assembly passed laws that favored the Puritans over other religious groups. Philip Carteret objected to these laws, as they created a sense of hostility. Moreover, Richard Nicolls, at the behest of the Duke of York, gave some settlers land in the region before it passed to Carteret and Berkeley. Those settlers refused to pay the annual taxes on their land, known as quitrents, and they refused to take an oath of allegiance to New Jersey. Finally, the colonial assembly refused to recognize Philip Carteret as their governor; they chose instead to support his brother. In 1674, the unrest prompted Berkeley to sell his interest in New Jersey to Edward Byllynge, who hoped to create a Quaker colony in America. In 1676, George Carteret agreed with his new partner to divide the colony into two parts. He retained East Jersey, while Byllynge took West Jersey.

Meanwhile, a dispute with New York over who had the right to govern New Jersey emerged. Carteret and Berkeley's decision to form a government had always rested on dubious grounds. Thus, the Duke of York, through his proxies in New York, fought for the right to rule the Jerseys. When the Duke appointed Edmund Andros as governor of New York in 1674, he granted him jurisdiction over New Jersey as well. Andros then attempted to collect duties on goods going in and out of New Jersey. Andros went so far as to arrest Philip Carteret. After years of dispute, James agreed to submit his claim on the land to arbitration in England. When the court found in favor of Carteret, the duke accepted the decision and, in 1680, gave up all attempts to govern the Jerseys. In spite of the decision in his favor, Carteret decided in 1682 to sell his interest in East Jersey to several Quaker investors. Both East and West Jersey suffered from mismanagement in the following years, passing into royal hands in 1702.[25]

5.4.3 The Quakers in America

During the 1640s, a new, radical Protestant sect emerged in England. Led by George Fox, the Society of Friends saw religion as a personal matter since the Holy Spirit instructed every person in matters of faith. As did the Puritans, the Friends distrusted the hierarchy and authority of the Church of England. However, they took their criticism even farther than the Puritans. The Friends rejected all sacraments, liturgies, and paid ministers. Instead, they met twice a week and sat in quiet contemplation until the Holy Spirit moved a member to share his or her spiritual experience. The Friends also refused to pay tithes, bear arms, take oaths, or subscribe to the markers of social hierarchy. One sign of their attempt to achieve social harmony and to eliminate hierarchy was that men and women possessed the same rights in the church. By the mid-1660s, the Friends numbered about eighty thousand. Most of the members worked as small farmers, traders, and shopkeepers.

The Friends faced significant persecution from their opponents, who called them the Quakers for their propensity to tremble at God's word. The English government, both during the Commonwealth and the Restoration periods, objected to the Friends' tendency to shun church and secular authority. It also disapproved of the Friends' tendency to interrupt Anglican and Puritan services. Quakers faced stiff penalties for their unwillingness to conform to such conventional social and political norms, with penalties including fines, public whippings, and imprisonment. Some Friends sought refuge in the New World, but there too Puritan and Anglican communities were less than welcoming. Massachusetts strictly forbade Quakers from living in their colony and fined Puritans for even entertaining them. Thus, George Fox concluded that the Friends needed their own colony. Quaker investment in West Jersey, and later East Jersey, was the first step in their attempt to create a safe haven in the New World. William Penn, who invested in West and East Jersey, then approached the Stuarts for help in forming a larger and more successful Quaker colony.[26]

The Founding of Pennsylvania

William Penn joined the Society of Friends in 1667. According to historians Oscar Theodore Barck and Hugh Talmadge Lefler, Penn served as "one of the foremost exponents of Quakerism," but he was also "a paradoxical figure." The son of a successful naval officer who owned an estate in Ireland and played a role in the restoration of Charles II, William Penn lived a privileged life. At the same time, he became very interested in religion especially after he met Thomas Loe, a Quaker missionary. His father tried to curb him of his Quaker ways by sending him to France to live among the nobility of Louis XIV's court. Unimpressed by the French displays of wealth, when he returned to England Penn began attending Quaker meetings on a regular basis. Penn spent most of his adult life balancing between his Quaker values and his elitist tendencies. After his conversion, Penn preached on behalf of his faith, held meetings on his estate, and published several religious tracts. For his efforts, he spent a better part of the years between 1667 and 1671 in prison. However, Penn could never quite abandon the legacy of someone born to wealth. Although the Friends viewed all members as equals, Penn still expected some deference from his social inferiors. So, Penn never became as radical in defending his faith as some of the early Quakers. In fact, after Penn joined the Society, other wealthy merchants and gentry joined as well. These so-called "weighty Friends" hoped to make their faith more respectable, so they sought to secure legal protection from the government, either in England or in the colonies.[27]

Figure 5.2 William Penn | This image, from an engraving by J. Posselwhite, depicts the proprietor of Pennsylvania as he looked toward the end of his life.

Artist: J. Posselwhite
Source: Library of Congress

After Penn's father died in 1670, he possessed the necessary financial resources to help establish a Quaker colony in America. In 1676, Penn assisted in trying to right the problems in West Jersey after the Quakers took over. To attract settlers, the West Jersey proprietors promised religious tolerance, which attracted a large number of non-Quakers to the region. However, Fox, Penn, and others struggled to govern the religiously and ethnically diverse colony. Therefore, Penn decided to take advantage of his father's close relationship with the Stuarts. When his father died, Penn inherited a claim against the crown of approximately £16,000. In 1680, Penn petitioned the king for territory between New York and Maryland. For Charles II, it was a convenient way to settle his debt. While short on cash, he had plenty of land in America. Nevertheless, the king seemed reluctant to follow through with the plan. Granting a large tract of land to a Quaker would counter his policy of persecution at home; furthermore, it might undermine his plans to consolidate royal power in the colonies. In the end, Charles II, at the urging of his brother James, granted Penn a charter in 1681. Although he disapproved of Quakerism, the Duke of York personally liked Penn and thought granting Quakers more religious toleration might benefit English Catholics as well.

Under the terms of the charter, Penn took control of approximately 45,000 acres of land. However, the vagueness of the charter regarding the new colony's northern and southern borders led to disputes with New York and Maryland, disputes which lasted until the end of the colonial period. The charter also gave Penn the ability to govern his land as he saw fit so long as he upheld the Navigations Acts, allowed colonial court decisions to be appealed in England, and maintained an agent in London. Charles II called the new colony Pennsylvania in honor of Penn's late father for his loyal service to the crown, much to the new proprietor's dismay, as such vanity went against Quaker beliefs.[28]

Settling and Governing the Quaker Colony

William Penn looked at his new colony as a holy experiment, which would serve as an example to other nations. At the same time, he viewed the colony as a commercial venture, recognizing the value of the land on which he settled. Therefore, his choices about governing the colony and settling the colony reflected both desires. According to Alan Taylor, Penn put a "Quaker twist on the Puritan concept of a colony as a 'City upon a Hill.'" He made religious toleration a priority, and not just for the Friends; he welcomed all persecuted people. The colony never supported a church, but only Christians were permitted to participate in its government.[29]

To ensure the rapid development of the colony, Penn sought out fellow Quakers as investors to help spread his financial burden. He sold them plots of land, which they in turn could distribute to settlers in exchange for rent or duties. He also supported the development of a port city, Philadelphia, to encourage industrious merchants to migrate. Then Penn recruited settlers from all over Europe, promising residents equal rights and financial opportunities. In 1681, the first new colonists arrived. In the coming years, the English, Welsh, Germans, and Ulster Scots (Scotch-Irish) poured into the colony. In 1686, the population reached 8,000, and it continued to climb. Most of the migrants came from the middling ranks of European society, though a significant minority came as indentured servants, especially in the eighteenth century.[30]

In 1682, Penn journeyed to his colony and brought with him an outline of the proposed government known as the first "Frame of Government." The document expressed Penn's belief in the divine right of government, the ability of good men to make good laws, and the need to avoid absolutism. It noted, "Any government is free to the people under it (whatever be the frame) where the laws rule, and the people are a party to those laws, and more than this is tyranny, oligarchy, or confusion." The first frame also set up a complex government, which had an appointed rotating advisory council of seventy-two members to make laws and an elected assembly of two hundred members to approve those laws. Finally, it guaranteed freedom of religion and the preservation of the rights of the English.[31] When the first assembly met, it adopted the "Great Law" for Pennsylvania. Members revised the initial government structure by shrinking the size of the council and assembly to seventy-two members, eighteen of whom would serve on the council and fifty-four of whom would serve in the assembly. In 1683, the assembly proposed additional changes. The second "Frame of Government" specified that a certain number of delegates would come from every county as the colony grew.[32]

After Penn returned to England, there arose problems in the colony between Quaker and Anglican settlers as well as concerns about providing for the colony's security in the event of war. In 1692, William and Mary deprived Penn of his governing powers in the colony, making Pennsylvania a royal colony. However, in 1694, they reinstated his powers. To help smooth out lingering problems with the assembly, Governor William Markham, Penn's representative in the colony, proposed the third "Frame of Government" in 1696. It gave the assembly greater power at the expense of the governor and the advisory council. In 1701, Penn approved a final modification to his colony's government in the "Charter of Privileges." It eliminated the advisory council and underscored the religion freedom of the colonists. This structure, which lasted until the American Revolution, gave the residents far more control over the government than in any other English colony.[33]

Indian Relations in Pennsylvania

As part of his holy experiment, William Penn sought to develop a better relationship with the Indians than the other English colonies had managed. Not long after Charles II issued the charter, the new proprietor sent a letter to the Indians suggesting his "great love and regard" for them and his desire to have a "kind, just, and peaceable" relationship.[34] Two factors aided Penn in his effort to build a positive relationship. One, the Algonquian Lenape living in Pennsylvania numbered only about 5,000, making it hard for them to fend off attacks from the Iroquois Nations. Two, the Swedish and Dutch settlers treated the Lenape around Philadelphia kindly. Thus, tribal leaders saw the new colonists as potential allies as opposed to enemies. Penn capitalized on these sentiments by respecting Indian culture and land rights. He insisted on buying land from the Lenape and other tribes for a fair price. Meanwhile, the Indians willingly sold their land for needed trade goods.

Colonial and tribal leaders also encouraged their people to respect the treaty agreements; for over fifty years, the two communities lived in harmony. During the late seventeenth and early eighteenth centuries, numerous displaced tribes settled in Pennsylvania because of the fair treatment they received. Peace with the Indians helped Penn create a commercially successful colony. Moreover, the refuges helped provide a much-needed defense line on the colony's western frontier. Pennsylvania's leaders encouraged the refugee Indians to settle along the Susquehanna River because they chose not to tax for defense purposes. Those tribes stood as a buffer between the English and the French colonists as the war for empire in North America continued to heat up in the eighteenth century. Unfortunately, rapid expansion in Pennsylvania threatened the peace between the Europeans and the

Indians. As more settlers arrived, the need for land trumped the willingness to respect the rights of the Indians. After Penn's death, his sons and others defrauded the Indians out of their land, leading many tribes to turn away from the English and towards the French.[35]

The Founding of Delaware

When the English took over New Netherland, the Swedish and Dutch settlements west of the Delaware Bay passed to the Duke of York, who paid little attention to the region. Settlers for the most part governed themselves until the early 1680s, although technically the governor of New York ruled the region. Given the diversity of the population, the settlers supported religious toleration and a liberal government. In 1682, the Duke of York ceded

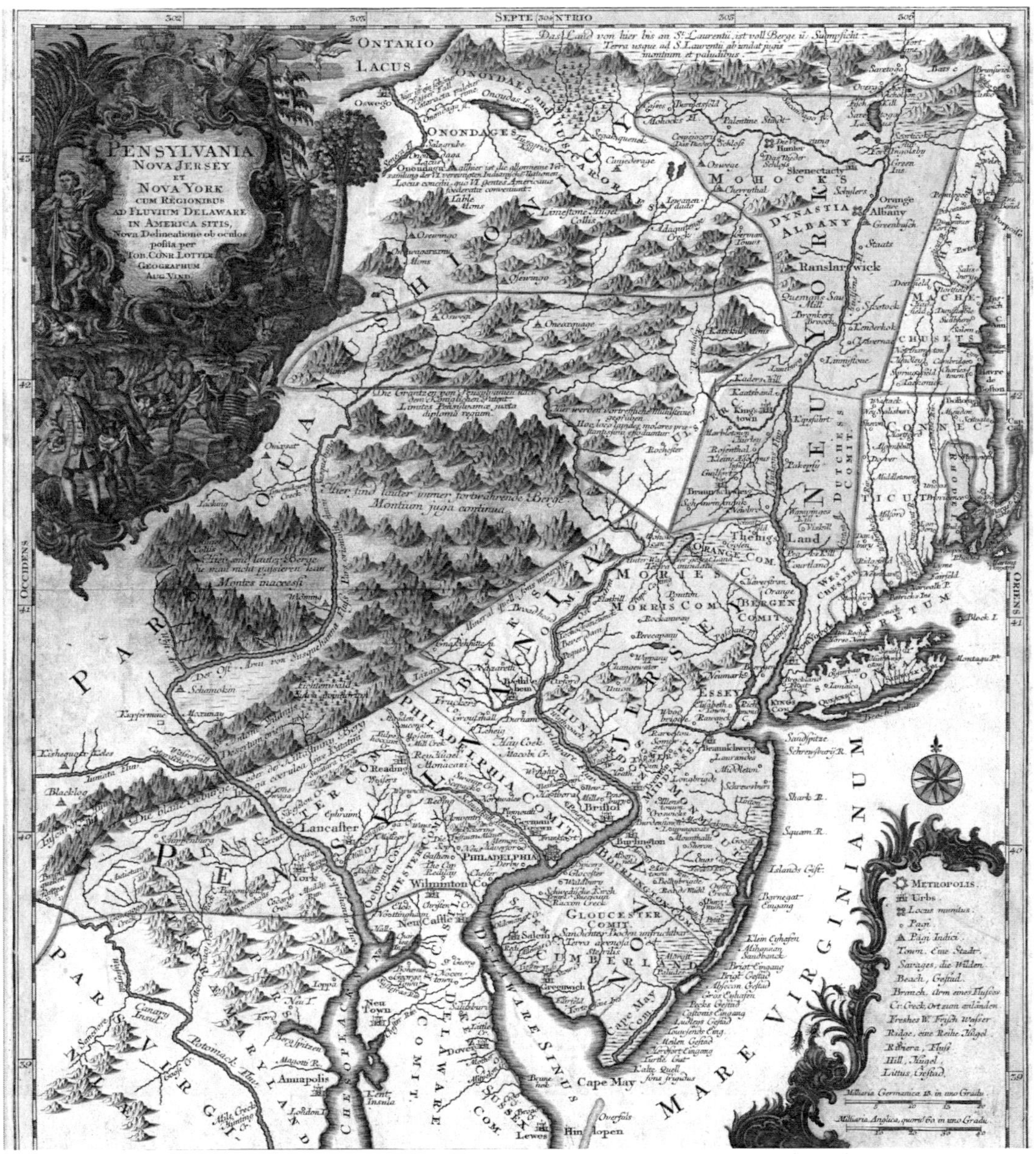

Figure 5.3 Historical Map of the Middle Colonies | This map dating from 1756 depicts the middle colonies of Pennsylvania, Delaware, New Jersey, and New York.

Author: Tobias Conrad Lotter
Source: Wikimedia Commons

the "Territories" to William Penn. Although the land patent said nothing about Penn's right to govern the territory, he incorporated the so-called "Lower Counties" (Delaware) with the so-called "Upper Counties" (Pennsylvania). Under an act of the legislature, the Lower Counties had seats on the council and in assembly on equal terms as the original Upper Counties, and the two regions shared a governor.

Over time, the predominantly non-Quaker settlers in the Lower Counties chafed at Quaker control. As the Anglo-French rivalry grew in the late seventeenth century, the Lower Counties looked to the assembly to appropriate more money to ward off French and pirate attacks. The pacifist-Quakers refused to tax for the purposes of defense. By the turn of the century, it became apparent to Penn that the Lower and Upper Counties could not or would not resolve their differences. In the "Charter of Privileges," Penn authorized the creation of a separate assembly for the Lower Counties if the residents so desired the change. In 1704, the Delaware assembly convened for the first time, but until 1776, the two colonies shared a governor.[36]

5.4.4 Life in the Middle Colonies

During the late seventeenth century and into the eighteenth century, the middle colonies outpaced their northern and southern neighbors in population and economic growth. Moreover, the region had higher levels of ethnic and religious diversity. New York, New Jersey, and Pennsylvania were the most heterogeneous of the North American colonies. This diversity stemmed partly from the patterns of settlement under Dutch rule, partly from the patterns of immigration to these colonies after the English took control, and partly from the rapid economic development in the region. The middle colonies, according to historian Jack P. Greene, "were characterized by little civic consciousness, slight concern for achieving social cohesion, high levels of individual competitiveness and public contention." However, the diversity helped the colonists develop "a pragmatic, accommodative, and tolerant approach to one another."[37]

Population and Economic Growth

When the English took over New Netherland, the population of the region was around 9,000 people. Although the DWIC encouraged migration, few people chose to migrate in the early seventeenth century. The colonists who did settle on Long Island and Manhattan Island, as well as the Hudson River Valley and the Delaware River Valley, came mostly from Northern Europe and Africa. When the English took over, they made up about a fifth of the population. The non-English population included Dutch, Swedes, Finns, Walloons, Flemings, French Huguenots, Germans, Norwegians, and Africans. For the most part, the settlers chose to stay and live under English rule. In the remainder of the colonial period, the region became more, rather than less, diverse.[38]

Natural increase and immigration contributed to the population growth. The middle colonies, by the 1660s, had passed their starving time. Disease took less of a toll on settlers. So, the average settler could expect to live into their sixties, which, by the late seventeenth century, was similar to settlers in northern colonies and higher than settlers in the southern colonies. Moreover, most new settlers to the region came as family units. So, the new English colonies became self-sustaining much quicker than did the New England and Chesapeake colonies. Finally, the proprietors recruited settlers from all over Europe, a tactic which increased both the population and its cultural diversity. More free and indentured German Mennonites, Welsh Quakers, and Ulster Scot Presbyterians settled in the region, as did newly imported African slaves. The combination of natural increase and immigration meant the population in the middle colonies was around 63,000 in 1710, 200,000 in 1740, and 520,000 in 1770. Pennsylvania and Delaware saw greater growth than New York and New Jersey. Combined, however, they outpaced the northern and the southern colonies.[39]

Beginning in the late seventeenth century, the middle colonies also experienced rapid economic growth. The former Dutch settlements of New York and New Jersey had always had a commercial focus. When the English proprietors took over, they wanted to use the colonies to build their financial future. The Duke of York believed his colonies would increase his wealth. William Penn and the other "weighty Friends" who invested in the Quaker colonies had economic goals in addition to religious goals. Their commercial interests made the Quakers less socially cohesive than the Puritans, but more financially sound. Settlers in middle colonies benefited from the expansion of the fur trade as well as the sale of lumber products, grain products, and livestock. In time, grain, especially wheat and flaxseed, became the most important commodity in the middle colonies because of the long growing season and fertile land. More importantly, farmers could sell grain to both internal and external markets. In order to coordinate the export trade, the size of the merchant class in the middle colonies grew in the colonial period as well. To lower shipping times, the merchants introduced technological innovations, which stimulated shipbuilding and its associated industries.[40]

Labor Patterns

In the colonial period, economic growth kept the demand for agricultural and manufacturing output and labor in the middle colonies high. Most of the agricultural output in the region came from family farms, worked predominantly by free labor. Most farmers grew a variety of crops and raised livestock, but there was some specialized agriculture to meet market demand. The size of farms in the middle colonies declined in the eighteenth century, but those farms remained profitable because they required fewer workers. In Pennsylvania, most farmers owned their land. In New York, rates of tenancy rose in the eighteenth century. However, Jack P. Greene suggested that "leaseholds...were nearly as profitable...as were the freehold properties" because they tended to be comparable in size.[41]

In Philadelphia, New York, and smaller towns in the mid-Atlantic, the demand for skilled and unskilled labor increased in the colonial period, especially as the region began to enlarge its internal and external trade. Men took positions in the shipping industry, the extractive industries, and in trades. Women worked as domestic servants. Much of the early understanding of urban workers comes from Benjamin Franklin's *Autobiography*, which chronicles his rise from apprentice to gentleman. Written long after he retired from the printing trade, it paints a rosy picture of the possibility of social mobility for urban workers. More recently, historians suggested Franklin's interpretation held until about the

1740s. As the nation drew closer to the revolution, the status of urban workers declined, and concerns about urban poverty grew. However, skilled and unskilled workers tended to earn more than their counterparts in Europe.[42]

To meet the colonies' labor demands, farmers and merchants turned to the use of bound labor, either indentured servants or slaves. Historian Richard S. Dunn maintained that the labor pattern in the middle colonies differed in three ways from the southern colonies and the Caribbean. First, employers preferred white indentured servants over black slaves, especially in urban centers where white servants filled the lower ranks of the trades as apprentices and journeymen. Second, they tended to use non-English labor, especially from Germany and Northern Ireland. Third, the patterns of employment for workers resembled that of England rather than the plantation colonies. Servants and slaves worked on small farms, in the craft shops, or as domestics. The patterns of bound labor tended to vary between rural farms and urban centers. In Pennsylvania, Delaware, and West Jersey, indentured servants were more common; in New York and East Jersey, slaves were more common. In the middle colonies, slaves made up about 8 percent of the population. The number of indentured servants has been much harder to estimate because of the lack of records.[43]

Indentured servitude in the middle colonies took two forms before the revolution. Ulster Scots, who adopted the name Scotch-Irish after they migrated, and Irish migrants followed seventeenth-century patterns of indenture. These Presbyterians and Catholics tended to be young, single, and looking for better economic opportunities in the colonies. They sold their labor for four to seven years in exchange for the cost of transportation and maintenance, usually because they could not afford their passage. Scotch-Irish and Irish indentured servants made their contract before they embarked to the colonies. Once their term of service ended, they tended to blend into free society. Thus, records of the total numbers of indentured servants from Northern and Southern Ireland have remained vague.[44]

German migrants adopted a new pattern of indenture more suited to their tendency to come as families and sometimes even with whole neighborhoods. Redemptioners were primarily Germans who sold their labor or the labor of their children once they arrived in the colonies, also because they usually did not have enough money to cover their passage. Most contracts gave redemptioners two weeks upon arrival to find someone to purchase their contract. After that, anyone who needed labor could bid on the contract; most redemptioners' contracts went to other Germans. About a third of the German migrants to Pennsylvania ended up as redemptioners for four to five years before they sought out their own farms on the frontier where they could acquire cheap land.[45]

As with indentured servitude, slavery in the middle colonies differed from slavery in the other English colonies. The system resembled that of the New England colonies, but a larger percentage of the population owned slaves in the middle colonies. Slave owning appeared common for gentlemen, merchants, small farmers, and artisans. Masters tended to own two to three slaves, and records showed a higher rate of turnover, suggesting northerners saw slavery as only one possible labor arrangement. However, slavery remained an important part of the middle colonies' economy. Demand for new slaves continued throughout the colonial period. Most northern slaves lived in or near coastal urban regions. They labored as domestic servants, laundresses, and dockworkers. They also served as field hands or iron workers. More often than not, slaves worked together with their masters and lived in their homes.[46]

Slavery in the middle colonies did not possess the harsh nature of slavery in the southern colonies or on the Caribbean Islands. However, slaves still suffered from the same loss of freedom and degradation. Slaves in the middle colonies found it difficult to form families. Small holdings and high turnover made it hard to find a partner, especially since there tended to be more men than women in the slave population. The desire to raise a family led some slaves to run away or attempt to do so. Moreover, living in such close proximity could lead to greater understanding between master and servant, but it could also lead to greater hostility. Slaves attacked their masters' property and, in rare cases, their master.[47]

Another sign of the slaves' discontent came when they revolted in New York City in 1712 and again in 1741. In the 1712 incident, African and Indian slaves hatched a plot to kill all of the whites in the city. They set fire to a building and then attacked the whites who came to fight the blaze. The governor followed their capture with new restrictions on free and enslaved blacks. In the 1741 conspiracy, the city was dealing with a major theft problem when a series of mysterious fires broke out in the city. City officials believed the incidents were connected especially after they found a witness, a 16-year-old Irish servant who was awarded her freedom for her testimony, who supported their theories. They began to round up suspects, hold trials, convict, and execute blacks and whites thought to be part of the plot. [48]

Because they lived among their masters, northern slaves tended to blend their African culture with Euro-American culture at a faster rate than did southern slaves. However, they also created a distinctive slave culture that adapted their traditional African beliefs with their experience in the New World. In the eighteenth century, slaves in New York and New Jersey participated in a uniquely African-American festival known as Pinkster during the month of May or June. This festival could last up to a week; participants crowned an African-born slave king and gathered to eat, drink, gamble, and dance. Slaves came in their best clothes, sometimes borrowing attire and other supplies from their masters. According to historian Shane White, northern slavery was "hard, unforgiving, and often soul-destroying." However, the Pinkster "displayed the creative response of black people those to situations." It allowed slaves for a brief period to control their own lives and interact with other slaves without white supervision.[49]

The Best Poor Man's Country

Throughout the colonial period, population and economic growth led to social stratification in the middle colonies. In the cities and towns, growth led to occupational diversification and more economic opportunity. In turn, neighborhoods were increasingly defined by economic resources. In rural areas, some elites acquired large property holdings. However, property and wealth remained more evenly distributed among the population. For a majority of the population, urban or rural, the standard of living was higher than in other English colonies because of this relatively even distribution of wealth. Moreover, as people learned to live with one another and adjust to their environment, according to Jack

P. Greene they developed a "common cultural core" in spite of their diversity. They lived in the same type of houses, ate the same type of foods, wore the same type of clothing, and followed the same type of agricultural practices. Geographer James Lemon maintained that Pennsylvania became the "best poor man's country" in the eighteenth century, which in many ways applies to New York, New Jersey, and Delaware as well.[50]

5.4.5 Before You Move On...

Key Concepts

In the late seventeenth century, England focused its attention on settling the region between the New England and the Chesapeake colonies. Charles II hoped to consolidate his power and increase the commercial prospect of his empire by taking the Dutch holdings there. In 1664, under the threat of an English attack, the Dutch turned control over their New World territory to the English. To spread the financial burden of colonization, Charles II issued proprietary grants for the land to loyal supporters. He gave some of it to his brother, James. Under the Duke of York's leadership, two new colonies took shape, New York and New Jersey. In order to repay a debt to him, the king in 1681 granted land to Quaker William Penn, land which became Pennsylvania and Delaware. After their founding, the middle colonies were marked by high levels of population and economic growth as well as by ethnic and religious diversity.

Test Yourself

1. The Dutch founded New Netherland with the intention of building a large agricultural settlement to grow export crops in the New World.

    a. True

    b. False

2. Which of the following colonies was not considered a middle colony?

    a. New Jersey

    b. Maryland

    c. New York

    d. Pennsylvania

3. Pennsylvania differed from the other English colonies in North America because

    a. it had friendly relations with neighboring Indians.

    b. it had no representative assembly.

    c. it allowed women to vote.

    d. it required all residents to join the Society of Friends.

4. Which of the following statements best describes the middle colonies in the colonial period?

a. The middle colonies tended to grow only one crop.

b. The middle colonies had a short growing season keeping their export trade low.

c. The middle colonies had few cities or towns.

d. The middle colonies were marked by ethnic, religious, and economic diversity.

See page 201 for answers

5.5 GEORGIA: THE FINAL COLONY

Georgia was the last of the original thirteen colonies to be established. As British settlement spread to the south and west, it came into increasing contact with the Spanish in Florida and the French in the Mississippi River valley. From an imperial viewpoint, Georgia functioned as buffer zone between British settlements and their imperial rivals; the new colony was to be a garrison province that would defend the British, especially from Spanish Florida. James Oglethorpe, English politician, social reformer, and the founder of the colony, envisioned an additional purpose for the Georgia: a haven for the "worthy poor" and an alternative to debtor's prison for some English.

In the years before the founding of the Georgia colony, both the English and the Spanish sought to control the border area at the limits of Carolina and Florida through trade and alliances with Indians, as well as through warfare. Throughout the southeast, a large and lucrative Indian slave trade developed alongside European, and especially British, colonization. The growing need for labor in the Americas, especially in the Caribbean sugar islands, meant that there was a new market for people taken as captives in intertribal warfare and raids. The British used this Indian slave trade to establish greater power and presence in the southern colonies and in the borderlands between British and Spanish settlements as they negotiated and formed alliances with many groups selling captives into slavery through ports such as Charles Town. To the south, the Spanish laid claim to the area through a different means of interacting with native peoples, by establishing a chain of religious mission villages among the Guale, Timucua, and Apalachee Indians. The two most important centers of the mission system were located in St. Augustine in the east and Tallahassee, Florida in the west, but mission outposts pushed north as far as the present cities of Valdosta and Folkston, as well as St. Catherine's Island on the coast. These missions not only served to Christianize and acculturate southeastern Indians, but also as a source of labor and food and a buffer between British Charles Town and Spanish St. Augustine.[51]

Eventually, hostilities broke out as the colonial areas of control grew, and the two European powers came into contact. Throughout the 1680s, Indian slave catchers, many allied with the British, raided the missions of Guale. In 1686, these raids forced the Spanish to withdraw south of the St. Mary's River into modern day Florida. The outbreak of Queen Anne's War (also known as the War of Spanish Succession) further weakened Spain's hold. From 1700-1703, Carolina governor James Moore and a force made up of colonists and Indian allies conducted a series of raids on the missions, devastating the Guale and Mocama provinces and razing St. Augustine, laying siege but ultimately failing to take the fortress of Castillo San Marcos. In 1704, Moore again raided the missions of Spanish Florida, this time attacking the Apalachee province to the west, killing and enslaving much of the population in the "Apalachee massacre." Ultimately, the destruction of the Apalachee missions (and the labor and food derived from it) was the biggest blow to St. Augustine and Spanish Florida, considerably weakening their Indian alliance system and the Spanish hold on the southeast. Conversely, the success of the raids reaffirmed many of the British alliances with tribes such as the Creek and Cherokee, strengthening British power and presence in the southeast and paving the way for the founding of the Georgia colony.[52]

The British were not entirely successful in their Indian relations. The growing Indian slave trade contributed to the outbreak of the invasion of the Carolinas known as the Yamasee War in 1715. The Spanish and French used the war as an opportunity to push further into the frontier. Spain reestablished some of the Guale missions to the north; the French built Fort Toulouse near the present city of Montgomery, Alabama. Georgia and the southern frontier remained contested ground, and the British emerged from the Yamasee War in 1717 with the realization that they were losing ground in the region. In 1721, they began construction of Fort King George, a permanent outpost at the mouth of the Altamaha River. The fort established a British presence, albeit a tenuous one, deep within the frontier. Soldiers stationed at Fort King George lived on the edge of starvation, and may have deliberately set fire to the fort in hopes that it would be abandoned. Ultimately, the British recalled most of the force and left a skeleton crew at the fort to act as lookouts to warn of Spanish activities in the contested area of the frontier.

5.5.1 Trustee Georgia

In London, Parliamentary representative James Oglethorpe chaired a Parliamentary committee on prison reform in England. His experiences and the findings revealed by this committee convinced him that poverty in London and Great Britain as a whole was linked to urbanization: as people came in from the countryside, they became members of the working poor and fell into debt, sometimes resorting to criminal activity. In 1730, Oglethorpe and like-minded politicians formed the Trustees for the Establishment of the Colony of Georgia in America. The plan called for the formation of a colony that would serve as a place for the insolvent to go to escape poverty, setting themselves up as smallholding farmers. Land would be parceled into fifty acre bundles, made up of a town plot, a small garden area near town, and a 45 acre farm in the country. Thus, the family farm would be the centerpiece of the colonial system. Wealthy colonists would be able to buy more than one fifty acre parcel, but the amount of land they were able to buy was directly related to the number of indentured servants they brought to the colony. Finally, the indentured servants themselves would receive a land grant after they had completed their term of service.

Oglethorpe and the Trustees gained support for the Georgia colony by promoting it as a military buffer between the Carolinas and the Spanish holdings in Florida. The colonists, including small farmers, merchants, and artisans, would serve as a militia force against

Spanish and Indians alike. Parliament would have to provide an initial investment in the colony, but Oglethorpe and the Trustees argued that Georgia would quickly become self-sufficient. Their plans called for the colony to become a source of luxury items such as wine and silk. Both colonial industries failed; the silk industry failed to produce even one profitable crop. In 1732, the Trustee's plans were approved, and the first group of colonists departed for Georgia aboard the ship *Anne*, founding the city of Savannah in 1733 after negotiation with the Yamasee, and later the Creek. Families were assigned lots within the town for their houses, a five acre garden at the edge of town, and a 45 acre farm in the countryside.[53]

Over the next decade, Oglethorpe and the Georgia colonists worked to ensure that Georgia could defend itself against the encroachment of the Spanish, realizing Georgia's role as military buffer zone. They began construction of a chain of forts on the Georgia's coast. The most important of these fortified outposts was by far Fort Frederica, located on St. Simon's Island. Built in 1736, the fort housed several hundred regular British troops, sent by the Crown on advice of Oglethorpe, and a growing settlement of colonists. The forts and the garrison soon after saw action when the War of Jenkins' Ear (part of the larger conflicts of King George's War or the War of Austrian Succession) broke out in 1739. Oglethorpe and a force of about 1,500 sailed for St. Augustine, laying siege to the city in conjunction with a blockade by the Royal Navy. The expedition was initially successful, capturing several Spanish outposts, including the settlement of Gracia Real de Santa Teresa de Mosé (renamed Fort Mose by Oglethorpe), populated by runaway slaves from the British colonies. These men and women were granted freedom by the Spanish in an attempt to undermine the plantation economy of the British colonies. Oglethorpe's force was eventually expelled from Georgia because of the failure of the blockade to prevent the resupplying of St. Augustine and the defeat of Oglethorpe's forces at Fort Mose, known as "Bloody Moosa." Black militiamen from the settlement of Mosé were among the Spanish forces that expelled the Georgians from Florida. Border warfare between Georgia and Florida continued through 1743, with an invasion of Georgia and another of St. Augustine, to little overall effect and the imperial outpost colonies resumed their stalemate for the duration of the war.

From 1732-1752, Georgia was governed by a Board of Trustees based in London. Unlike the other British colonies, there was no governor in the colony, nor was there a governing legislative body. The Trustees in London were barred from holding office or owning land in Georgia. In many ways, the Trustees conducted a social experiment in the new colony through its population and through the Georgia charter. Although few colonists were the debtors envisioned by Oglethorpe, many were indeed among the "deserving poor." However, rather than finding relief from debt in the colony, most colonists found themselves further indebted for their passage to the colony. In most cases, the colonists were indebted to the Georgia Trust itself, Adults typically served terms of five years of indentured servitude to the Trust, but children were often bonded for much longer terms; some were bound to service for terms of seventeen or even twenty-one years. Some of the indebted servants fled the colony to escape their debts. This was especially true in the north, where perhaps as much as three-fourths of the indentured servants had fled.[54]

The social provisions of the Georgia Charter also ensured religious liberty for "all" (while specifically excluding Catholics); the population reflected this as religious refugees from Switzerland, Scotland, and Germany arrived in the colony. When a group of Jews arrived in Georgia in 1733, Oglethorpe allowed them to stay in the colony in spite of the Trustees' objections, making Savannah home to one of the oldest Jewish congregations in the modern-day United States. During 1732-1752, the Trustees also banned hard alcohol in the colony and tried to prevent the Carolina colony from shipping rum through Georgia, bringing the colonies into conflict. Despite the Trustees' opposition, many of the Georgia colonists participated in the Indian trade, including the rum trade. The town of Augusta was established as an Indian trading town, and quickly grew to become one of the largest Indian trading centers in the south.

Finally, the trustees also banned slavery in the colony during this period. Numerous reasons have been cited for this decision. Oglethorpe's vision of smallholding farmers would be undermined by slave labor. To the south, Spanish Florida tried to undermine the British settlements by granting freedom to any runaway slave who made it to Florida and embraced Catholicism. Moreover, a large slave population would undermine Georgia's value as a military buffer with the Spanish, as slaves could not serve in the militia. Bringing slavery to Georgia, the Trustees reasoned, would undermine the colony in a variety of ways. Nothing indicates, however, that the Trustees banned slavery because of any abolitionist sentiments.

From the foundation of Georgia, Oglethorpe had been the only Trustee resident in the colony, and had served as a *de facto* ruling figure. In London, the Trustees were often frustrated by Oglethorpe's poor correspondence habits as well as his habit of making decisions without consulting the Trustee board. In 1741, the Trustees divided Georgia into two counties: Savannah in the north and Frederica in the south. They appointed William Stephens president of Savannah and asked Oglethorpe to make a recommendation for a president in Frederica. Oglethorpe failed to respond, and soon after left Georgia in 1743, prompting the Trustees to appoint Stephens president of the entire colony.

Under the leadership of Stephens, Georgia moved away from the model of charity colony for the deserving poor. The Trustees gave Stephens the power to grant land in the colony. Very quickly, immigration patterns into the colony shifted as wealthier immigrants established large plantations through land grants. In the years after 1741, the number of land grants to charity colonists declined sharply. Larger land grants, the growth of a solvent population, and pressure from South Carolina plantation owners eager to expand into Georgia increased pressure on the Trustees to lift their prohibition of slavery in the colony. In particular, a group within Georgia called the "Malcontents" worked to force the Trustees to lift their ban. However, many of Georgia's free laborers feared that legalizing slavery would devalue their labor, forcing wages down and people out of jobs. Other groups, most notably Protestant immigrants from Salzburg, opposed lifting the ban on slavery for religious reasons. Although the Trustees kept the ban on slavery in place for the next decade, Stephens and his council made little effort to enforce it. In 1750, slavery was legalized in Georgia by legal decree, a grave blow to the already waning Trustee system. After the ban was lifted, Stephens tied land grants to slave ownership, effectively meaning that the more slaves someone held, the more land they could get in the colony.[55]

By early 1750s, the group of Trustees in London had largely abandoned the meetings governing the colony. The colony also had deep economic problems. From the beginning of the charter, Georgia had received economic subsidies from the British Parliament, a circumstance tied to the colony's founding intent of being for the "deserving poor." The British government paid for much of the colony's expenses. In 1733, Parliament devoted £10,000 to Georgia; in other years, the government gave lesser sums, making Georgia the only one of the original thirteen colonies dependent on yearly stipends from the government. Finally, in 1751, Parliament refused to fund the colony. For all of these reasons, the Georgia Trustee system collapsed in 1752 and was replaced by a system of government much more like that of its sister colonies. From 1752 until the American Revolution, Georgia was a royal colony, ruled by a series of royal governors on behalf of the king.

5.5.2 Life in the Colony

Georgia's colonial experience was very different from the other North American British colonies. Founded fifty years after Pennsylvania, the twelfth colony, and almost seventy-five years after Carolina, it had by far the shortest colonial experience. Perhaps in part for the same reason, Georgia also had the smallest population and the least economic development of the thirteen colonies.

Immigrants came to the colony from all over Europe. Many came as religious refugees under the Georgia Charter. A significant example of this was a group that came to be known as the Salzburgers. The Salzburgers were a group of about 300 German-speaking Lutherans who had been expelled from the principality of Salzburg in modern Austria. The Salzburgers proved to be an important group in Georgia's colonial period. First, unlike many individual immigrants to Georgia, the Salzburgers were not in debt for their passage to the colony; their passage had been sponsored by the Augsburg-based organization the Society for Promoting Christian Knowledge. Their settlement New Ebenezer proved to be one of the most successful in the colony, with the first gristmills in the colony, and some of the earliest sawmills. Moreover, despite the Trustees' visions of Georgia as a producer of luxury goods such as silk, the Salzburgers were one of the only Georgians able to make an effort to raise silkworms and produce silk. The Trustees had mandated that colonists plant one hundred mulberry trees for every ten acres of land granted to a colonist; however, few of the debt-ridden Georgia colonists could afford to do so. The Salzburgers were a significant exception.[56]

The Trustees' early ideas for Georgia to be a producer of luxury goods quickly came to an end. Food was scarce in the colony in the early period, and for many, it was hard enough to produce food, let alone plant mulberry trees for silkworms. Moreover, the coastal soil proved unsuitable for wine production. Instead, colonists turned to cattle, timber, and Indian trade as sources of income and subsistence. Colonists grazed cattle on their own land grants as well as inland on ungranted land to supplement the food they grew. Salted beef soon became a dietary staple in the colony. Colonists also turned to timber for firewood as well as manufactured wood products such as pitch, tar, shingles, and planks to supplement their income. Most colonists could not afford the equipment to produce manufactured products for sale, and so produced only firewood. However, timber quickly became one of the main industries in Georgia and presently remains so. Finally, many colonists engaged in Indian trade for supplementary income. For many, it quickly became a main source of income as Augusta emerged as a major center of Indian trade in the southeast. [57]

5.5.3 Before You Move On...

Key Concepts

The colony of Georgia was the last of the thirteen original colonies to be founded. It was a strategically important area because it was a buffer zone between the two most powerful empires in North America: the British and the Spanish. For many years, the two empires struggled over control of the area through forging alliances with Indians and through warfare. The colony was founded in part because the British sought to control the area through a greater population and political presence. Weakening Spanish influence in the aftermath of Moore's 1700-1704 raids on Spanish Florida during the War of Jenkins' Ear also provided an opening for the British to move into the territory.

Colonial Georgia was founded as a Trustee colony. The colony was governed by a group of trustees based in London, who drew up the Georgia Charter, which provided for religious freedom for all Protestants. The Trustees outlawed alcohol and slavery, two unpopular provisions that did not outlive the Trustee system itself. By the end of the 1740s, the Trustee system was not functioning well, and in 1752 the Crown assumed control of the colony.

Georgia's colonial experience was very different from the other North American British colonies. Founded fifty years after Pennsylvania, the twelfth colony, and almost seventy-five years after Carolina, it had by far the shortest colonial experience. Perhaps in part for the same reason, Georgia also had the smallest population and the least economic development of the thirteen colonies.

Test Yourself

1. The Georgia Charter did all of the following EXCEPT

   a. grant religious freedom for all.

   b. outlaw slavery.

   c. outlaw alcohol.

   d. provide for religious freedom for all Protestants.

2. The Trustee system was advised by a royal governor who lived in Savannah.

   a. True

   b. False

3. Indian alliances were an important means of establishing power in the southeast for the European empires.

   a. True

   b. False

See page 202 for answers

5.6 Conclusion

During the last decades of the seventeenth century, a series of colonies were created in North America; most of these colonies were proprietary, growing out of grants of land to friends and supporters of the English monarchy. As with the New England colonies founded in the early part of the century, religion played an important role in these colonies; in Pennsylvania and the Jerseys, Quakers found a haven from persecution, and in Carolina nonconforming Protestant sects, as well as Jews, could enjoy the freedom to practice their beliefs as their religions dictated. Georgia, the last colony, established in 1732, also offered a haven for the "deserving poor." With the creation of Georgia, the thirteen colonies were in place. The remainder of the eighteenth century witnessed a struggle between the colonies and the mother country as the colonies became more and more "independent minded" and the British Crown more determined to tighten its control. In the end, of course, the colonies and the mother country would go their separate ways.

5.7 CRITICAL THINKING EXERCISES

- As you look back over England's history from 1660 to 1688, why do you think that Parliament was so opposed to a Catholic taking the throne of England?
- Why is it said that Charles II was "restored" to the throne when he had never been in power before 1660?
- If you were in charge of finding a site for a new colony, what would you look for in terms of climate and geography? What features of the landscape would you try to find and which would you try to avoid?
- If you were in charge of recruiting colonists for a new colony, how would you do it? What would you do to convince people to leave all that they know and try to build a new life for themselves in a possibly dangerous new land?

5.8 KEY TERMS

- Act of Union, 1707
- Albemarle
- Apalachee Massacre
- Anthony Ashley-Cooper
- Barbados
- Bill of Rights, 1689
- Blackbeard
- Carolina
- Cash Crop
- Charles II
- Charter of Liberties and Privileges (New York)
- Charter of Privileges (Pennsylvania)
- Concessions and Agreement
- Covenant Chain
- Oliver Cromwell
- Duke's Laws
- Dutch West India Company
- East Jersey
- Frame of Government
- Fundamental Constitutions of Carolina
- Georgia Trustees
- Glorious Revolution of 1688
- Hanoverians
- Iroquois Nations
- James II
- Kieft's War
- Leisler's Rebellion
- Lords Proprietors
- James Moore
- New Netherland
- New Sweden
- New York
- James Oglethorpe
- Patroon System
- William Penn
- Pennsylvania
- Pinkster
- Pirates
- Proprietary Colonies
- Queen Anne
- Redemptioners
- Restoration of 1660
- Society of Friends (Quakers)
- Test Act, 1673
- Theory of Revolution
- Toleration Act, 1689
- Treaty of Dover, 1973
- Triennial Act, 1689
- West Jersey
- William and Mary

5.9 CHRONOLOGY

The following chronology is a list of important dates and events associated with this chapter.

Date	Event
1609	Henry Hudson explored the Delaware and Hudson Rivers
1614	Dutch merchants established Fort Nassau (near present-day Albany)
1621	Dutch government granted a charter to the Dutch West India Company (DWIC)
1624	DWIC sent its first settlers to the Hudson River Valley and Manhattan Island
1626	Peter Minuet purchased Manhattan Island from the local Indians
1638	New Sweden Company began to colonize the Delaware River Valley
1643	Kieft's War between the Dutch and the Algonquians begins
1655	New Netherland took over New Sweden
1663	Carolina granted to the Lords Proprietors
1664	Peter Stuyvesant surrendered New Netherland to English forces; Richard Nicholls implemented the Duke's Laws for Staten Island, Long Island, and Westchester; Duke of York ceded portions of New York to Sir George Carteret and Lord John Berkeley
1665	Bubonic Plague hit England; New Jersey's proprietors issued the "Concessions and Agreement"
1666	Great Fire of London destroyed much of the city
1667	William Penn joined the Society of Friends (the Quakers)
1670	Charles Town founded in the Carolinas; Secret Treaty of Dover between Charles II and Louis XIV of France
1673	The Test Act placed restrictions on Catholics and Non-Conformists
1674	English and Iroquois leaders entered into the Covenant Chain; Lord Berkeley sold his interest in New Jersey to a Quaker investor

Date	Event
1676	New Jersey divided into East Jersey and West Jersey
1680	Charles Town moves to its present location
1681	Charles II makes William Penn the proprietor of Pennsylvania
1682	Sir Carteret sells his interest in East Jersey to Quaker investors
1683	New York's colonial assembly met for the first time and drew up the "Charter of Liberties and Privileges"; Pennsylvania assembly adopted the "Great Lawn" and the second "Frame of Government"
1684	English and Iroquois leaders signed the Treaty of Albany in which the Iroquois became subjects of the English Monarch
1685	James II ascended to the throne and canceled the "Charter of Liberties and Privileges" for New York; Huguenots began arriving in Carlina
1688	Glorious Revolution; William and Mary succeed to the throne as joint rules
1689	Act of Religious Toleration passed; English Bill of Rights created by Parliament; Leisler's Rebellion occurred in New York in response to the Glorious Revolution; The Triennial Act passed
1692	Pennsylvania briefly became a royal colony
1694	Death of Mary II; Pennsylvania reverted to a proprietary colony.
1696	Pennsylvania assembly adopted the third "Frame of Government"
1700-1704	James Moore and Indian allies raided Spanish Florida
1701	William Penn approved the "Charter of Privileges" for Pennsylvania and Delaware
1702	New Jersey became royal colony; Death of William and accession of Anne I
1704	Apalachee massacre
1707	Act of Union unified the Parliaments of England and Scotland, created the Kingdom of Great Britain

Date	Event
1719	Carolina split into two colonies; South Carolina became a royal colony
1729	North Carolina became royal colony
1732-1752	Georgia governed by the Georgia Trustees
1733	Savannah, Georgia founded
1751	Slavery made legal in Georgia

5.10 BIBLIOGRAPHY

"An Appeal from the Country to the City (1689)," in John Miller. *Glorious Revolution.*

Barck, Oscar Theodore and Hugh Talmage Lefler. *Colonial America*, second edition. New York: Macmillan, 1968.

Chitwood, Oliver Perry. *A History of Colonial America*, third edition. New York: Harper & Row, 1961.

Dunn, Richard S. "The Recruitment and Employment of Labor." In *Colonial British America: Essays in the New History of the Modern Era*, eds. Jack P. Greene and J.R. Pole. Baltimore: Johns Hopkins University Press, 1984.

Gallay, Alan. *The Indian Slave Trade: The Rise of the English Empire in the American South, 1670-1717.* New Haven: Yale University Press, 2002.

Greene, Jack P. *Pursuits of Happiness: The Social Development of Early Modern British Colonies and the Formation of American Culture.* Chapel Hill: University of North Carolina Press, 1988.

Hann, John H. *A History of the Timucua Indians and Missions.* Gainesville: University of Florida Press, 1996.

Hutton, Ronald. *Charles II.* London: Blackwell, 1989.

Hutton, Ronald. *Charles II: The Masquerading Monarch.* BBC History, April 14, 2012. http://www.bbc.co.uk/history.

Hutton, Ronald. *The Rise and Fall of Merry England.* New York: Oxford University Press, 1994.

Hutton, Ronald. *The Royalist War Effort.* London: Taylor and Francis, 1981.

Kenyon, J. P. *Stuart England.* 2nd Edition. London: The Pelican Group, 1985.

Lemon, James T. *The Best Poor Man's Country: Early Southeastern Pennsylvania.* Baltimore: Johns Hopkins University Press, 1972.

Miller, John. *The Glorious Revolution.* 2nd Edition. Harlow, England: Pearson Education Limited, 1997.

Murrin, John M. "Beneficiaries of Catastrophe: The English Colonies in North America." In *The New American History*, revised and expanded edition, ed. Eric Foner. Philadelphia: Temple University Press, 1997.

Potter, Jim. "Demographic Development and Family Structure." In *Colonial British America: Essays in the New History of the Modern Era*, eds. Jack P. Greene and J.R. Pole. Baltimore: Johns Hopkins University Press, 1984.

Sheridan, Richard B. "The Domestic Economy." In *Colonial British America: Essays in the New History of the Modern Era*, eds. Jack P. Greene and J.R. Pole. Baltimore: Johns Hopkins University Press, 1984.

Taylor, Alan. *American Colonies: The Settling of North America.* New York: Penguin Books, 2001.

Trent, William P. and Benjamin W. Wells, eds. *Colonial Prose and Poetry.* New York: Thomas Y. Crowell & Co., 1901. Bartleby.com, April 12, 2012. http://www.bartleby.com/br/163.html.

Vallance, Edward. *The Glorious Revolution.* BBC History, April 14, 2012. http://www.bbc.co.uk/history.

White, Shane. "Slavery in the North." *OAH Magazine of History* 17: (April 2003): 17-21.

5.11 END NOTES

1 Ronald Hutton, *Charles II: The Masquerading Monarch,* BBC History, April 14, 2012, http://www.bbc.co.uk/history, 1.

2 Hutton, *Charles II,* 5.

3 Hutton, *Charles II,* 6.

4 John Miller, *The Glorious Revolution*, 2nd edition (Harlow, England: Pearson Education Limited, 1997), 8.

5 "Appeal from the Country to the City," 1689, in Miller, *Glorious Revolution*, 11.

6 Quoted in Miller, *The Glorious Revolution*, 11.

7 Hutton, *Charles II,* 11.

8 Hutton, *Charles II,* 12.

9 Excerpt of Locke, *Two Treatises on Government,* in Miller, *Glorious Revolution*, 108.

10 Quoted in Miller, *The Glorious Revolution*, 34.

11 Quoted in Miller, *The Glorious Revolution*, 34.

12 Michael Trinkley, SCIWAY, South Carolina's Information Highway, http://www.sciway.net/afam/slavery/population.html.

13 Alan Taylor, *American Colonies: The Settling of North America* (New York: Penguin Books, 2001), 248-250; Oliver Perry Chitwood, *A History of Colonial America*, third edition (New York: Harper & Row, 1961), 159; Oscar Theodore Barck and Hugh Talmage Lefler, *Colonial America*, second edition (New York: Macmillan, 1968), 164-165.

14 Barck and Lefler, *Colonial America*, 166-167; Taylor, *American Colonies*, 252, 255; Chitwood, *A History of Colonial America*, 161.

15 Taylor, *American Colonies*, 253; Chitwood, *A History of Colonial America*, 163.

16 Barck and Lefler, *Colonial America*, 166, 171-172; Chitwood, *A History of Colonial America*, 161, 163-164; Taylor, *American Colonies*, 253.

17 Taylor, *American Colonies*, 254-255.

18 Taylor, *American Colonies*, 255-256; Chitwood, *A History of Colonial America*, 168.

19 Taylor, *American Colonies*, 257-259; Chitwood, *A History of Colonial America*, 171-172, 175.

20 Chitwood, *A History of Colonial America*, 171-175; Taylor, *American Colonies*, 259-261.

21 Barck and Lefler, *Colonial America*, 178-179, 212; Chitwood, *A History of Colonial America*, 175-176, 225.

22 Barck and Lefler, *Colonial America*, 213-215; Taylor, *American Colonies*, 281-281, 284-285; Chitwood, *A History of Colonial America*, 243-245.

23 Taylor, *American Colonies*, 261.

24 Taylor, *American Colonies*, 261-262; Barck and Lefler, *Colonial America*, 179-180: "Covenant Chain," *The Encyclopedia of New York State* (Syracuse: Syracuse University Press, 2005), August 16, 2012, http://www.syracuseuniversitypress.syr.edu/encyclopedia/entries/convenant-chain.html.

25 Barck and Lefler, *Colonial America*, 183-187; Chitwood, *A History of Colonial America*, 176-181; Taylor, *American Colonies*, 262-263.

26 Barck and Lefler, *Colonial America*, 181-182; Chitwood, *A History of Colonial America*, 201-202; Taylor, *American Colonies*, 264-265.

27 Barck and Lefler, *Colonial America*, 183; Taylor, *American Colonies*, 265-266.

28 Barck and Lefler, *Colonial America*, 187-188; Chitwood, *A History of Colonial America*, 204; Taylor, *American Colonies*, 264; Charter for the Province of Pennsylvania–1681, *The Avalon Project*, Yale Law School, April 12, 2012, http://avalon.law.yale.edu/17th_century/pa01.asp.

29 Taylor, *American Colonies*, 266.

30 Taylor, *American Colonies*, 266-267; Barck and Lefler, *Colonial America*, 191-192.

31 Frame of Government of Pennsylvania–May 5, 1682, *The Avalon Project*, Yale Law School, April 12, 2012, http://avalon.law.yale.edu/17th_century/pa04.asp.

32 Frame of Government of Pennsylvania–February 2, 1683, *The Avalon Project*, Yale Law School, April 12, 2012, http://avalon.law.yale.edu/17th_century/pa05.asp.

33 Chitwood, *A History of Colonial America*, 212-213; Frame of Government of Pennsylvania–1696, *The Avalon Project*, Yale Law School, April 12, 2012, http://avalon.law.yale.edu/17th_century/pa06.asp; Charter of Privileges Granted by William Penn, esq. to the Inhabitants of Pennsylvania and Territories–October 28, 1701, *The Avalon Project*, Yale Law School, April 12, 2012, http://avalon.law.yale.edu/18th_century/pa07.asp.

34 William Penn to the Indians, 18 August, 1681 in *Colonial Prose and Poetry*, eds. William P. Trent and Benjamin W. Wells (New York: Thomas Y. Crowell & Co., 1901), Bartleby.com, April 1, 2102 www.bartleby.com/163/.

35 Taylor, *American Colonies*, 268-269; Chitwood, *A History of Colonial America*, 207-208.

36 Barck and Lefler, *Colonial America*, 1945-195; Chitwood, *A History of Colonial America*, 213-214; Taylor, *American Colonies*, 270.

37 Jack P. Greene, *Pursuits of Happiness: The Social Development of Early Modern British Colonies and the Formation of American Culture* (Chapel Hill: University of North Carolina Press, 1988), 50.

38 Taylor, *American Colonies*, 268, 271; Greene, *Pursuits of Happiness*, 48; Jim Potter, "Demographic Development and Family Structure," in *Colonial British America: Essays in the New History of the Modern Era*, eds. Jack P. Greene and J.R. Pole (Baltimore: Johns Hopkins University Press, 1984), 143-144; John M. Murrin, "Beneficiaries of Catastrophe: The English Colonies in North America," in *The New American History*, revised and expanded edition, ed. Eric Foner (Philadelphia: Temple University Press, 1997), 16.

39 Greene, *Pursuits of Happiness*, 125, 132; Richard B. Sheridan, "The Domestic Economy," in *Colonial British America*, 60; Barck and Lefler, *Colonial America*. 252-254; Chitwood, *A History of Colonial America*, 210-211.

40 Sheridan, "The Domestic Economy," 59-60; Greene, *Pursuits of Happiness*, 49-50, 126, 129-131.

41 Greene, *Pursuits of Happiness*, 128-129.

42 Richard S. Dunn, "The Recruitment and Employment of Labor," in *Colonial British America*, 181-182; Barck and Lefler, *Colonial America*, 310-311; Taylor, *American Colonies*, 298-299.

43 Dunn, "The Recruitment and Employment of Labor," 180; Greene, *Pursuits of Happiness*, 131-133; Taylor, *American Colonies*, 333.

44 Chitwood, *A History of Colonial America*, 341-342; Dunn, "The Recruitment and Employment of Labor," 169-170.

45 Barck and Lefler, *Colonial America*, 313-316; Dunn, "The Recruitment and Employment of Labor," 171-172; Taylor, *American Colonies*, 319-320.

46 Shave White, "Slavery in the North," *OAH Magazine of History* 17 (April 2003): 18; Taylor. *American Colonies*, 333; Greene, *Pursuits of Happiness*, 133.

47 White, "Slavery in the North," 18; Taylor, *American Colonies*, 333-334.

48 Howard Zinn, *A People's History of the United States* (New York: HarperCollins, 2012), 35-37.

49 White, "Slavery in the North," 20-21.

50 Greene, *Pursuits of Happiness*, 136-138; James T. Lemon, *The Best Poor Man's Country: Early Southeastern Pennsylvania* (Baltimore: Johns Hopkins University Press, 1972).

51 Alan Gallay, *The Indian Slave Trade: The Rise of the English Empire in the American South, 1670-1717* (New Haven: Yale University Press, 2002), 40-69; John H. Hann, *A History of the Timucua Indians and Missions* (Gainesville: University of Florida Press, 1996).

52 Gallay, *Indian Slave Trade*, 127-154.

53 Christopher C. Meyers and David Williams, *Georgia: A Brief History* (Macon, Georgia: Mercer University Press, 2012) 14-15.

54 Meyers and Williams, *Georgia*, 22-23.

55 Meyers and Williams, *Georgia*, 26-29.

56 Meyers and Williams, *Georgia*, 23.

57 Meyers and Williams, Georgia, 23-25.

ANSWER KEY FOR CHAPTER FIVE: ENGLISH COLONIZATION AFTER 1660

Check your answers to the questions in the Before You Move On Sections for this chapter.

Correct answers are **BOLDED**

Section 5.2.3 - p164

1.The term "Restoration" refers to:

a. the restoring of power to Parliament in 1689.
B. CHARLES II'S BEING BROUGHT TO THE THRONE OF ENGLAND IN 1660.
c. the Bill of Rights.
d. William and Mary's accession to the throne in 1688.

2. According to the Triennial Act,

a. no Catholic could become an English monarch.
b. Parliament must raise the salary of the monarchy at least once in every three years.
C. PARLIAMENT MUST MEET EVERY THREE YEARS EVEN IF NOT CALLED BY THE CROWN.
d. England would have not one, but three Parliaments.

3. According to John Locke, the Glorious Revolution was a legitimate one.

A. TRUE
b. False

4. Which of the following was NOT one of the restrictions placed on Catholics after the Glorious Revolution?

a. Catholics could not sit in Parliament.
b. Catholics could not worship freely.
C. CATHOLICS COULD NOT MARRY.
d. Catholics could not bear arms.

5. Although William of Orange was married to James II's daughter, Mary, he also was in line for the throne of England.

A. TRUE
b. False

Section 5.3.7 - p169

1. North and South Carolina began as one colony, Carolina.

A. TRUE
b. False

2. In a proprietary colony, the Proprietors have no responsibilities except to collect the profits.

a. True
B. FALSE

3. John Locke wrote the original constitution for Carolina, but it was not what the colony needed.

A. TRUE
b. False

4. Carolina's policy of religious toleration helped to attract new colonists.

A. TRUE
b. False

Section 5.4.5 - p186

1. The Dutch founded New Netherland with the intention of building a large agricultural settlement to grow export crops in the New World.

a. True
B. FALSE

2. Which of the following colonies was not considered a middle colony?
    a. New Jersey
    B. MARYLAND
    c. New York
    d. Pennsylvania

3. Pennsylvania differed from the other English colonies in North America because
    A. IT HAD FRIENDLY RELATIONS WITH NEIGHBORING INDIANS.
    b. it had no representative assembly.
    c. it allowed women to vote.
    d. it required all residents to join the Society of Friends.

4. Which of the following statements best describes the middle colonies in the colonial period?
    a. The middle colonies tended to grow only one crop.
    b. The middle colonies had a short growing season keeping their export trade low.
    c. The middle colonies had few cities or towns.
    D. THE MIDDLE COLONIES WERE MARKED BY ETHNIC, RELIGIOUS, AND ECONOMIC DIVERSITY.

Section 5.5.3 - p192

1. The Georgia Charter did all of the following EXCEPT
    A. GRANT RELIGIOUS FREEDOM FOR ALL.
    b. outlaw slavery.
    c. outlaw alcohol.
    d. provide for religious freedom for all Protestants.

2. The Trustee system was advised by a royal governor who lived in Savannah.
    a. True
    B. FALSE

3. Indian alliances were an important means of establishing power in the southeast for the European empires.
    A. TRUE
    b. False

Chapter Six: Growing Pains in the Colonies

Contents

Chapter Six: Growing Pains in the Colonies

6.1 INTRODUCTION

By the beginning of the eighteenth century, the fortunes of many colonists in British North America had changed for the better. Although they still faced somewhat trying conditions, migrants could earn their own keep without being beholden to anyone, own land, and practice their faith openly. The colonists became somewhat self-sufficient because of their economic ties to the mother country through the mercantilist system. Moreover, the colonists defined their rights by the British political system they lived under, which they considered truly enlightened. Likewise, intellectual trends and religious developments helped to increase ties between the colonists that did not exist in the seventeenth century. Finally, the imperial wars between Britain, France, and Spain brought the colonists' similarities sharply into focus because the wars exacerbated the tensions between the colonies and the mother country. In the end, the road to the revolution originated in the early eighteenth century as the British colonies began to mature economically, politically, and socially.

6.1.1 Learning Outcomes

After completing this chapter, you should be able to:

- Describe and analyze the evolution of British colonial policy towards the North American colonies from the mid-seventeenth century to the Revolution.
- Describe the structure of colonial governments in British North America and explain how the colonial political system differed from that of the mother country.
- Analyze the impact of the Enlightenment and the Great Awakening on British colonial society in North America.
- Explain how the Colonial Wars reflected both European and colonial political struggles.

6.2 COLONIAL ADMINISTRATION

By the mid-seventeenth century, the British actively sought ways to expand their overseas empire. To achieve this goal, they needed a strong navy and a healthy commercial network. The navy helped protect British merchants at home and in the colonies; meanwhile, duties on commerce funded much of the navy's rapid growth. As these military and commercial interests melded together, the government developed policies based on the theory of mercantilism to meet the needs of the empire.[1] By the early eighteenth century, the British worked out a system that enlarged the prestige and power of the empire as well as provided benefits to many people in the mother country and the colonies. The system also helped set the foundations for the American Revolution.

6.2.1 Developing a Commercial Empire

During the 1650s, Parliament thought more about the commercial interests of England. Merchants in and out of the government sought ways to extend English control over the carrying trade, or shipping, to the New World while also improving their own financial situation. To undercut the Dutch monopoly, Parliament passed the Navigation Act of 1651. The measure required all goods going to and from the colonies to be transported on English or colonial ships. In theory, it closed colonial ports to foreign ships, but Parliament neglected to include a strong enforcement provision in the act. Therefore, the colonists routinely smuggled in goods from the Dutch and the French.[2] After the Restoration of 1660, Charles II examined the commercial potential of the empire. Merchants and manufactures continued to support the expansion of trade, but so too did many of the king's loyal supporters. Oliver Cromwell's rule left many royalists, including the king, in dire financial situations. Thus, economic motives pushed Charles II to implement policies based on the theory of mercantilism.

The Mercantilist System

Generally, mercantilism sought to strengthen a nation at the expense of its competitors by increasing its wealth, population, and shipping capabilities. In some ways, mercantilism was the ultimate expression of national greed. A country could increase its wealth by accumulating gold and silver. Short of resorting to piracy to steal such precious metals, a country needed a favorable trade balance. In England, this effort led the government to encourage domestic manufacturing. To enlarge the merchant marine, the government sought to monopolize the carrying trade between the mother country

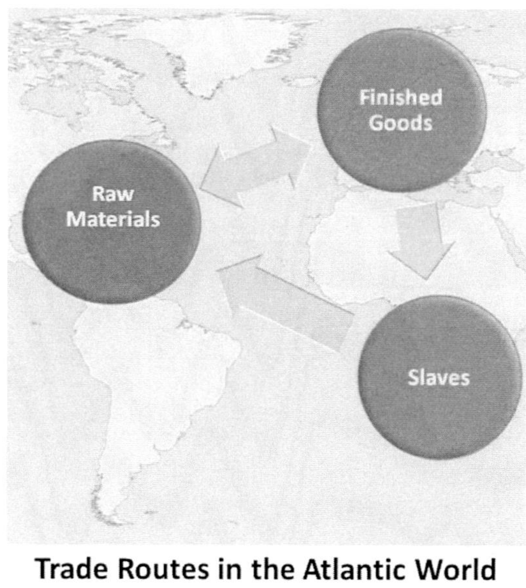

Figure 6.1 Trade Routes in the Atlantic World | Using the mercantilist system, the British government sought to obtain a favorable balance of trade. Africa provided the slaves necessary to grow large amounts of raw materials in the American colonies, which then went to England to support domestic manufacturing. In addition to the international trade depicted in this map, the colonies also trade goods with one another.

Author: Sarah Mergel
License: CC BY SA 3.0

and the colonies. With a monopoly, British shippers would need more ships and trained sailors, both of which the navy could use in times of war. Finally, population increases at home and in the colonies helped to provide more consumers for manufactured goods; some of the growth came from natural increase while some came from immigration.[3]

In the mercantilist system, colonies played an important role in developing a successful empire; consequently, most European nations sought New World colonies in the seventeenth century. Colonies provided the raw materials to fuel industrial growth. In the British North America, most settlers chose to farm because of the availability of fertile land. Initially, they did so out of necessity. The distance to England, coupled with the smaller size of ships in the seventeenth century, meant the colonists needed to provide for themselves. For much of the colonial period, however, they continued to farm because, under mercantilism, it could be quite profitable. At the same time, they engaged in some manufacturing for local markets; they did not compete directly with the industries developing in England. Most of their finished goods such as flour or iron required only slight changes from their raw state and aided colonists in growing more raw materials. Over time, regional differences developed in the colonial economies that stemmed from the availability of land and labor.[4]

In the New England colonies, most farmers grew for self-sufficiency rather than for the market because of the long winters and the rocky soil. However, the region engaged in whaling and fishing for the export market. It also became a leader in shipbuilding. In the middle colonies, most farmers grew grains such as wheat, rye, oats, barley, buckwheat, and corn. They also grew a wide variety of vegetables, flax, and hemp. Additionally, they raised livestock. By the mid-eighteenth century, the region also led the colonies in iron manufacturing. In the Chesapeake colonies, most colonists remained committed to tobacco production. However, they also raised wheat, corn, flax, hemp, and apples to help offset bad tobacco harvests. In the southern colonies, North Carolina turned to its forests for export goods, which yielded the tar, pitch, and timber necessary for shipbuilding. Besides these naval stores, interior settlers ran pottery shops and tanneries. The shorter winters in South Carolina and Georgia allowed colonists to export rice, indigo, and salt pork often to the Caribbean colonies, goods which they exchanged for slaves. The southern colonies also actively participated in the deerskin trade.[5]

Figure 6.2 New England Ship-building | Regional differences developed in the colonial economies that stemmed from the availability of land and labor. In this picture, New England colonists work on constructing a ship.

Artist: Ray Brown
Source: *American Merchant Ships and Sailors*

Extending Imperial Control

Knowing colonies served a vital role in the success of any empire, the British set out to expand their presence in the New World during the Restoration period. Through proprietary arrangements, Charles II closed the gap between the New England and Chesapeake colonies as well as extended the crown's control south of Virginia by the early 1680s. By eliminating the Dutch from North America, the British paved the way for increasing their volume of trade with their North American and

Caribbean colonies. To further that goal, the government proposed a series of trade laws to improve the British position vis-à-vis their imperial rivals.

First, Parliament passed the Navigation Act of 1660. The measure reiterated the provisions of the 1651 act, which restricted all shipping in the empire to English and colonial vessels. It also added a provision listing several "enumerated articles" that could only be traded within the empire. These goods included sugar, tobacco, cotton, wool, and indigo. Theoretically, the restrictions helped make England more self-sufficient and increased the crown's tax revenue. Second, Parliament approved the Staple Act of 1663. It placed restrictions on foreign goods imported into the colonies by requiring merchants to ship through an English port. The act made the colonies more dependent on the mother country because England became their staple, or market, for all foreign goods. Finally, Parliament voted in favor of the Plantation Duty Act of 1673. Designed to cut down on smuggling, the act established provisions to collect customs duties in colonial ports before the goods shipped to other colonial ports. Under the measure, the British government stationed customs collectors in the colonies for the first time. These agents reported to their superiors in England, not to the colonial governor or assembly.[6]

The Glorious Revolution, when William and Mary came to power, brought about new mercantilist policies for three reasons. First, the government wanted to quell the unrest in the colonies caused by James II's efforts to consolidate royal control. William and Mary hoped to find a solution that would meet both the economic and political needs of English merchants and colonial planters. Second, lax enforcement of the Navigation Acts during King William's War (1689-1697) increased smuggling and privateering, which put the economic health of the empire at risk. Third, after the adoption of the English Constitution, Parliament determined the empire's fiscal policy. Dominated by wealthy landowners and merchants, the House of Commons wanted to assure political and economic strength. Thus, Parliament, with the crown's approval, took measures to strengthen the trade restrictions on the colonies.[7]

Parliament passed the Navigation Act of 1696 and the Trade Act of 1696. The Navigation Act sought to shore up previous acts by closing the loopholes that contributed to lax enforcement. In order to improve the collection of duties in the colonies, the law granted royal officials in the colonies the right to seek writs of assistance to search for and to seize illegal goods. The Trade Act created the Board of Trade, an administrative agency, to replace the more informal Lords of Trade created under Charles II. British merchants wanted a stronger body to develop and supervise commerce, since the Lords of Trade failed to devote enough attention to the colonies. William and Mary approved the change largely because, like many merchants, they believed stronger control over colonial development would have a positive effect on the British economy.

In 1697, the Board of Trade recommended the creation of Vice Admiralty Courts in the colonies. By using these courts, the Board denied colonists accused of violating the Navigation Acts the right to a jury trial because most colonial juries would not convict people accused of smuggling. The Board also recommended several other measures to restrict colonial industry and trade. For example, the Woolens Act of 1699 prevented colonists from producing wool goods for export; the Hat Act of 1732 did the same for hats.

Figure 6.3 The Board of Trade | Created by the Trade Act of 1696, the Board of Trade advised the British government on all matters relating to colonial trade and politics. This picture from Ackermann's *Microcosm of London* (1808-1811) depicts the members hard at work in London.

Authors: Rudolph Ackermann, William Henry Pyne, and William Combe
Source: *Microcosm of London*

The most controversial of these measures was the Molasses Act of 1733, which raised the duties on rum, molasses, and sugar imported into the colonies from foreign countries. In time, most merchants realized that the duties on molasses did more to harm than help trade. Seeing as the act largely defied the logic of mercantilism, Robert Walpole, the king's chief minister from 1720 to 1742, chose not to enforce the measure. His decision led to a period of "salutary neglect," where government officials largely ignored economic development in the colonies.[8] In instances where the British government chose to enforce its economic policies, many colonists simply evaded the law by smuggling. In the years leading up to the American Revolution, some merchants—especially those in Boston—found the Dutch, French, and Spanish more than willing to help them evade British trade laws. While certainly not the only reason for tensions between the colonists and the crown in the mid-eighteenth century, the decision to enforce the Navigation Acts and add additional regulations caused problems.[9]

Trade and the Consumer Culture

While many colonists objected in principle to trade restrictions imposed by Parliament in the seventeenth and eighteenth century, few had reason to complain about the positive economic benefits of being part of the British Empire. Policymakers designed the Navigation Acts to increase trade relationships between the mother country and her colonies. If the policies significantly harmed colonial economies, they became pointless because colonists would not buy British goods. Imbedded into the trade acts were benefits for the colonists. First, the colonies had a monopoly over the enumerated articles. No one in England, for instance, could grow tobacco or indigo. Second, the colonists received rebates on goods imported from England, so they tended to pay lower prices for finished products. Third, the colonists did not need to worry about piracy because they fell under the protection of the Royal Navy.[10]

Greed and self-interest underscored the theory of mercantilism at the national and the personal level. British merchants clearly had a stake in seeing imperial commerce thrive, but so too did the colonial farmers and shippers. With the exception of the Puritans, most people migrating to North America wanted to improve their economic position. American colonists, according to historian T.H. Breen, "obeyed the Navigation Acts because it was convenient and profitable for them to do so, not because they were coerced." In the eighteenth century, economic growth, coupled with lower tax rates in British North America, provided the colonists with not only a decent standard of living but also more disposable income. Most colonists wanted very much to participate in the consumer revolution happening in Europe. In other words, they wanted to purchase consumer goods considered luxuries in the seventeenth century such as table and bed linens, ceramic cups and saucers, pewter cutlery, and manufactured cloth and clothing.[11]

Figure 6.4 The Consumer Culture | Economic growth in the eighteenth century allowed American colonists to participate in a consumer revolution. Colonists routinely imported necessities and luxury items from Britain. With the rise of a tea culture, tea sets were a much sought after item. This Wedgewood tea set, on display at the Victorian and Albert Museum in London, typifies the style of tea set found in homes of the colonial elite.

Author: Valerie McGlinchey
Source: Wikimedia Commons
License: CC BY SA 2.0 England and Wales

Throughout the eighteenth century, the demand for imported consumer items grew in the North American colonies. The more raw materials the colonists exported, the more necessities and luxury items they could purchase on credit. British and colonial merchants also worked to fuel demand for goods by advertising in the growing number of colonial newspapers. Likewise, hundreds of peddlers spread trade goods from colonial seaports to the interior. Despite the self-sufficient farmer's image carrying a great deal of weight in popular memory of colonial America, the colonists never achieved the means to take care of all of their own needs. So, they imported basic necessities and niceties.[12]

The fluid nature of colonial society meant that the elite wanted to set the standards for polite society, marked especially by the rise of a tea culture, as a means to distance themselves from the lower classes. They used their ability to purchase luxury items as a way to display their status. At the same time, the lowering sorts used their disposable income to erase the line between the elites and the commoners. Colonial women took a leading role in the consumer revolution. They had a good deal to gain from importing household items because they would no longer have to produce them in the home and could use those goods to mark their families' place in American society.[13]

Over time, the large number of imports helped to deepen the connection between the mother country and the colonies, and in some respect, helped to build a common identity among the colonies because everywhere people purchased the same goods. The consumer culture effectively created material uniformity. Moreover, the expanding coastal and overland trade brought colonists of different backgrounds into greater contact with one another. It gave them added opportunities to exchange ideas and experiences, even though they remained largely unaware of the importance of such connections as they continued to see themselves as New Yorkers, Virginians, and Carolinians, not Americans. T.H. Breen concluded that "the road to Americanization ran through Anglicization." In other words, the colonists had to become more integrated in the British Empire before they could develop a common cultural identity as Americans.[14]

6.2.2 Developing a Political System

Throughout the colonial period, the British struggled to determine how much authority to exert over the colonies. As England settled the New World, expedience usually determined the political system of each colony. As such, three models of government emerged: the royal colony, the proprietary colony, and the corporate colony. In each system, a governor shared power with a legislature usually composed of an upper house appointed by the governor and a lower house elected by the property-holding men. The chief difference between the models came in the selection of the governor. In the royal colonies, the crown appointed the governor. In the proprietary colonies, the proprietor chose the governor with the crown's approval. In the corporate colonies, the voters selected the governor and did not need the crown's approval. By the late seventeenth century, to further the goals of mercantilism, the crown and Parliament looked for ways to achieve greater control while also balancing the expectations of the colonies.[15]

Colonial Administration

Initially the British administration of the colonies was somewhat haphazard, which explained why the different models of government emerged. However, the monarchy needed to find an arrangement to administer the colonies that would benefit all interested parties so as to successfully use the colonies to promote the economic development of the mother country. In the 1650s, Parliament began to tinker with the administrative system when they passed the Navigation Act of 1651 but largely left the colonies to govern themselves. During the Restoration period, Charles II and James II attempted to assert greater control over the colonies. They reorganized the existing colonies as royal colonies and created new proprietary colonies subject to greater royal authority.[16]

The unrest caused by the creation of the Dominion of New England, whereby James II eliminated the vestiges of self-government by creating one administrative unit to oversee the northern colonies, suggested the mother country needed a new governmental policy. During the reign of William and Mary, the British finally found a working arrangement to manage its colonies that pleased merchants and colonists; the government retained some of the previous policies when it came to trade issues in an effort to bind the colonies more closely with the mother country. Thus, Parliament passed a revised Navigation Act and created the Board of Trade. At the same time, William and Mary restored the colonial assemblies, which their predecessor had disbanded. This compromise met the needs of both the colonies and the empire. Under the system, says historian Oliver Chitwood, "neither liberty nor security would be sacrificed" because "each province was to rotate on its own axis, but all of them were to revolve around England as the center of the imperial system." The compromise would only work so long as the mother country could keep the colonies in line. Sentimental attachment to England helped in this effort, but so too did economic self-interest on the part of the colonies and the threat of force on the part of the mother country.[17]

After the Glorious Revolution, Parliament held more power over matters of taxation and expenditures. However, the monarchy still largely supervised the colonies. Over the course of the eighteenth century, several different administrative bodies had their hand in colonial affairs. The Privy Council, the king's official advisers, took the lead in colonial matters such as making royal appointments, issuing orders to governors, disallowing colonial laws in violation of English law, and hearing appeals from the colonial courts. Through a variety of secretaries, subcommittees, and boards, the Privy Council handled these tasks. The Treasury Board, which oversaw the empire's money, was responsible for enforcing all trade restrictions and collecting all customs duties. The Admiralty supervised the Royal Navy that protected trade to and from the colonies. Further, the High Court of Admiralty, or its subsidiary Vice Admiralty Courts, tried cases relating to violations of the Navigations Acts. Finally, the Board of Trade advised the monarchy and Parliament on most colonial matters relating to commerce, industry, and government. Although the Board of Trade could not make any laws or official policies, the Privy Council frequently accepted its recommendations about appointments, laws passed by the colonial assemblies, and complaints made by the assemblies.[18]

Colonial Governments

The system of colonial administration set up in the late seventeenth century provided for British oversight and local autonomy regardless of whether the colonies were royal, proprietary, or corporate. By the mid-eighteenth century, the royal colonies included New Hampshire, Massachusetts, New York, New Jersey, Virginia, North Carolina, South Carolina, and Georgia. The proprietary colonies included Pennsylvania, Delaware, and Maryland. The corporate colonies included Connecticut and Rhode Island.[19] Each colony developed governmental structures that resembled the structure of the British government with the king, his council, and Parliament in the form of the governor, the upper house, and the lower house. A colonial agent, who represented the colonies' interests in London, also aided the governor and the assembly. Moreover, each colony had a judiciary modeled on the British system with justices of the peace, county courts, and circuit courts. Finally, in each colony the county or the township dominated local politics. The county system prevailed in the southern and middle colonies, while the township system prevailed in the northern colonies. Both took responsibility for issues such as local taxation, defense, public health, and probate.[20]

Governors, who served at the pleasure of the king or the proprietor, functioned as the chief royal officials in the colonies. They had the power to do what the king did at home without seeking prior approval from Parliament. In the eighteenth century, the Board of Trade drafted the governors' orders for most of the colonies. These instructions underscored the mercantilist system in that they guided the governor to promote legislation to benefit the mother country while also seeking to improve the general welfare of the colony. Once in office, the governor became the commander of the colonial militia. He also held the power to decide when the assembly would meet and when it would disband and to approve or to veto all legislation passed by the assembly. Furthermore, the governor sent all official communication to London, which included sending colonial laws for approval by the crown. Finally, he appointed all judges, magistrates, and other officials, and he made recommendations to the crown or the proprietor regarding the composition of his advisory council. The governor's council had three functions: it advised the governor on all executive decisions, it acted as the upper house of the legislature, and in conjunction with the governor, it served as the highest appeals court in the colony.[21]

The colonial assemblies had the power to initiate legislation. More importantly, they controlled the budget because they voted on all taxes and expenditures, including colonial officials' salaries and defense appropriations. Members were immune from arrest during assembly sessions and could speak freely and openly in those meetings. Finally, the assemblies had the right to petition the monarchy for the redress of grievances. By modern standards, the colonial assemblies were far from democratic. Nevertheless, more men could vote in America than in England because of the wider distribution of land ownership. At the local level, the county or township administrators supervised the election of the assembly. Those chosen increasingly believed they had the obligation to represent the local entity that elected them. This idea of direct representation differed from the British system, where Parliament supported the concept of indirect or virtual representation. Members believed they represented the whole empire, not just the region they hailed from.[22]

Colonial Politics

As in England, during the eighteenth century the power of the assembly in the colonies grew in relation to the governor, meaning the colonists expected lax enforcement of royal dictates as well as control over most colonial matters. At the same time that Parliament adopted a policy of salutary neglect when it came to trade, the crown allowed the colonies greater political control over their affairs. This habit of self-government stemmed from two factors. First, the distance between the mother country and her colonies mitigated the ability to keep tight control over colonial affairs. Colonial assemblies often made decisions because the time lag in communication between the two continents simply made waiting on answers from London infeasible. Moreover, in the eighteenth century the crown often found itself distracted by other problems such as the wars with France and Spain. Second, more men met the property qualifications to vote in the colonies, therefore felt a more direct connection to their government. As such, the well-to-do who served in the assemblies needed to be more responsive to the needs of their constituents to stay in office. Like their counterparts in Britain, colonial leaders engaged in patronage where they awarded commissions, judgeships, and land grants to their supporters. In turn, most colonists put greater faith in their assemblies than in their governors because the colonists helped elect or appoint members to serve in those assemblies. As historian Jack P. Greene points out, "coherent, effective, acknowledged, and authoritative political elites" dominated local politics. They possessed "considerable social and economic power, extensive political experience, confidence in their capacity to govern, and...broad public support."[23]

To maximize the interests of their fellow colonists, the assemblies frequently used the power granted by their colonial charters to put pressure on the governor. On several occasions, the assemblies made official complaints about their governors' power to determine when and for how long they could meet. When the monarchy refused to address the problem, the assemblies used their power to control the budget. Should a governor veto legislation the assembly favored, it slowed and sometimes stopped the appropriation of funds for the governor's salary or defense measures. In the 1720s and 1730s, the governors in New York, Massachusetts, and New Hampshire went without pay for several years. According to historian Alan Taylor, the colonists also "could effectively play...dirty politics." They sometimes resorted to rumors and gossip to undermine the authority of their governor and force his recall by officials in London. In the 1700s, New Yorkers exposed the then governor, Lord Cornbury, as a cross-dresser, so soon British officials removed him from office. Many governors tried to use their powers to grant land or bestow patronage to counter the power of the assembly, but their efforts rarely worked.[24]

Figure 6.5 The Colonial Assemblies | During the eighteenth century, representative assemblies in the colonies looked to expand their power and responsibility over colonial affairs. Whenever possible, they used financial pressure to bend the colonial governor to their will. This photograph, taken by Frances Benjamin Johnston, shows the chamber where the House of Burgesses, Virginia's representative assembly, met in Williamsburg.

Author: Frances Benjamin Johnston
Source: Wikimedia Commons

In the colonies, political tension was common because the assemblies constantly looked for ways to expand their power and responsibility over colonial affairs. Meanwhile when new governors arrived from England, they looked to shuffle the local power structure to win colonists over to their policies. In the end, most governors accepted the assemblies' demands in order to retain their position, thus perpetuating the idea of self-government in the colonies.[25] Many colonists believed they lived under the most enlightened form of government in Europe. Like their counterparts in England, the colonists believed the Bill of Rights protected their liberties. In the eighteenth century, the colonists concluded that they were free to protest against objectionable policies and laws emanating from Parliament because they were British citizens. Moreover, they expected the balance of power to remain in their favor since the governors often came around to their position.

6.2.3 Before You Move On...

Key Concepts

During the seventeenth and eighteenth centuries, the British sought to expand their empire. Using the theory of mercantilism, they set up an economic and political system designed to benefit the mother country and her colonies. Through the passage of the Navigation Acts and the creation of the Board of Trade, the government sought to increase the nation's wealth through commercial ties with the New World. The colonies provided raw materials for British industry and, in turn, purchased finished goods produced in the mother country. To further their economic goals, the monarchy also sought to extend greater political control over the colonies. Colonial resistance to James II's policies prompted William and Mary, as well as their successors, to blend royal control with representative assemblies. The large volume of trade brought benefits to most people involved in the system and thereby increased Britain's power over its European rivals. However, lax enforcement of many of the regulations, plus the growing power of the colonial assemblies, planted seeds of discontent that boiled over in the 1760s.

Test Yourself

1. The Navigation Acts specified enumerated goods that

   a. colonists could not export.

   b. colonists could manufacture the same goods as produced in Britain.

   c. colonists could only ship within the British Empire.

   d. colonists could only trade to other colonists.

2. Most colonists in eighteenth century North America were largely self-sufficient, so they did not need to import consumer goods from Britain.

   a. True

   b. False

3. Colonial governors possessed the right to veto legislation passed by the colonial assemblies.

   a. True

   b. False

4. During the eighteenth century, colonial assemblies

   a. lost their power to appropriate taxes.

   b. were appointed by the king.

   c. included both men and women.

   d. expanded their power and influence.

See page 235 for answers

6.3 THE ENLIGHTENMENT AND THE GREAT AWAKENING

To understand the Enlightenment and fully appreciate its significance, we must review the state of the western world before the Scientific Revolution. Today most people believe the earth is a round planet orbiting in a solar system around a star known as the sun. We tend to accept this view without question. In the 1400s, people's view of the world differed from ours. For most of that century, many Europeans believed the earth might be flat and that all the planets and stars and even the sun revolved around it. The centrality of the earth to the universe was a religious as much as a scientific concept for many, while the flat earth concept had existed since ancient times.

The ancient astronomer Ptolemy's geocentric theory, that Earth was the center of the universe, remained accepted as fact over 1,200 years after his death. Nicolaus Copernicus, whose varied interests in theology, medicine, law, language, mathematics, and especially astronomy marked him as a true Renaissance man, observed the heavens and studied

Ptolemy's theories. Believing Ptolemy wrong, Copernicus took what he knew to be fact and developed a heliocentric theory where the sun and not the earth was at the center of the universe. Copernicus appears to have conceived his basic model before 1514 and spent the rest of his life developing his theory, which was published shortly before his death in 1543. His work, *On the Revolutions,* touched off the Scientific Revolution which continued well into the seventeenth century.

Among all the great figures of the Scientific Revolution, Sir Isaac Newton most importantly distilled the theories and discoveries of the Scientific Revolution from Copernicus to himself. His greatest work, *Philosphia Naturalis Principia Mathematica,* published in 1687, presented a reasonable, understandable, and demonstrable model for the workings of the universe, which was based on science and excluded theology. Newton's concepts, such as his Law of Gravity, gave a predictable and comprehensible framework from which to view the world and beyond.

6.3.1 The Enlightenment

The ideas of the Scientific Revolution inspired people in many fields besides science. With Newton demonstrating rational explanations for the functions of the universe, philosophers were inspired to re-think humanity and its place in the universe. The Scientific Revolution, then, was at the root of the Enlightenment.

With the Enlightenment came a new spirit of thought and intellectual investigation. Old ideas and theories could be questioned and new ones proposed on virtually any subject. Acceptance of what had always been was no longer sufficient support for belief; instead, understanding with reasoned explanations and arguments were needed. Of the many great thinkers of the Enlightenment, including Rousseau, Voltaire, and Hume, the one whose works on politics and philosophy had the greatest direct impact on the revolutionary spirit in the Colonies was an Englishman, John Locke.

In 1690, two of Locke's greatest works were published. In the first, *An Essay Concerning Human Understanding*, Locke explained that humans learn only from experience. We experience things through sensation, with our senses giving us information, and through reflection, with our pondering what we have learned through sensation. Experience then leads to simple ideas which lead to complex ones. Locke discounted the commonly-held idea that humans are born with innate knowledge. His revolutionary view was that we are born instead knowing nothing at all. For Locke, humans possessed no innate concepts, ideas, or morals. At birth, our minds are complete blanks, a tabula rasa, which by being completely empty can be filled with what we know to be true through experience.

His other great work of that year was *Two Treatises of Government.* In the first treatise, Locke rejected the theory of the divine right of kings; in the second, he explained his beliefs concerning government, democracy, and the rights of men. Locke believed that government should be for the benefit of the people, and if the government or the leader of the government failed in their duty to the people, then the people had the right to remove or overthrow that government. He believed that to safeguard against corruption and failure to serve the people, a government should have multiple branches with each serving to check the others. His ideas would continue to resonate long after his death in 1704 and would profoundly influence our Founding Fathers who used Locke's ideas to frame their reasons for the American Revolution and thereby justify their cause. Locke's ideas later formed the basis of the U. S. Constitution. From Locke came the concept that all people have the right to Life, Liberty, and Estate or Property.

6.3.2 The Enlightenment in America

The Enlightenment, with its ideas and ideals of human rights and the relationship of citizens and governments as expressed by such writers as Locke, formed the basis of thought of the American Revolution. Thomas Paine, Benjamin Franklin, John Adams, Thomas Jefferson, and other Founding Fathers were influenced by the Enlightenment and took those ideals, that a government has a duty to the people, and used that as a lens through which to view the relationship between the American colonies and the British government of King George III. With the concept of a duty to the people firmly in mind, the failings of the British government to respond to the needs of the colony became more than mere points of contention and instead because causes for revolution. Thomas Paine, in his critical work *Common Sense,* made the case in clear language that spoke to the average colonist that equality was a natural condition for humans and having a king was not. Paine put forth the idea that while a king could be useful, there was no justification for a hereditary monarchy and ultimately, if the king did not see to the interest of his subjects, the subjects had no reason to have a king. The British government, according to Paine, had put its own interests ahead of the interests of the colonies, thereby failing in its duty to the colonists. Further, whereas the colonies in their infancy had needed the guidance and protection of the British, now they were able to stand on their own. Indeed, the British government had evolved from promoting the growth of the colonies to prohibiting that growth and becoming an obstacle to their economic development by inhibiting trade between the colonies and other nations around the globe. By covering the economic realities as well as the higher principles of natural rights, Paine's pamphlet appealed to both the practical-minded merchant and the principled philosopher. His writing was a hit and helped the colonists restless under British rule to understand exactly why continuing as colonies was not the solution to the situation.[26]

The Enlightenment provided a moral justification for revolution and the end of British rule in the colonies—at least in the view of the revolutionary thinkers such as Franklin and Jefferson. Humanity's natural rights could not be denied to any well-reasoned mind. The colonists had the right to determine for themselves where their loyalties lay and what form their government would take. They had the right to be heard, to have their concerns addressed in a way not possible for the British over the seas. Yet, the break was not easy. Many in the colonies, even if they felt their rights had been violated, remained loyal to England and hoped for a reconciliation. The relationship was often described in terms of a parent and child. To the leaders of the revolution, the child had grown up and was ready to have its independence, with a new government, one not seen before that would be guided by the principles of the Enlightenment.[27]

6.3.3 The Great Awakening

The Great Awakening was a religious revival in the American colonies triggered by a belief among Calvinists that the spiritual life of the colonists was endangered. With a focus on the material rather than the spiritual, the pursuit of wealth rather than the pursuit of a good Christian life, the lifestyle choices of the colonists alarmed and then invigorated evangelical ministers, launching the Great Awakening. Ultimately, ministers from both sides of the Atlantic would inspire each other and be involved in this spiritual revival.

The Church of England—The Anglican Church

Like much of Europe, England had been a Catholic country until the Protestant Reformation. Henry VIII had at first defended the Catholic Church from the criticisms of Martin Luther, but later broke with the Catholic Church in order to divorce Ann Boleyn and, in 1534, declared himself the head of the Church of England. Unlike other Protestant movements, in which churches were formed based on the ideas of their founders such as Luther or Calvin, the Anglican Church alternated in concept from Catholicism to Protestantism, depending on what religious views were held by the current monarch and his or her advisors, since the Church and State were then tied together. The result was a church caught in the middle, blending Catholicism and Protestantism. The Anglican Church remained Catholic in its administrative structure and in the ritualized nature of its services, with Protestantism influencing its architecture, theology, and conduct of services. Because the Anglicans retained a detailed liturgical structure, any Anglican, whether in England or in the colonies, would know what Scriptures would be read and what prayers would be said on any given Sunday, as all Anglican churches followed a common guide. For many, this formal, predictable style of worship did not meet their spiritual needs. Indeed, some felt England to be almost a spiritual desert.

The Wesley Brothers and Their Conversion

The Wesleys attended Oxford and, in 1729, Charles founded the Holy Club, a group of students who were devout in their religious practices. In fact, they were absolutely methodical in the way they carried on their religious devotions and other activities, a practice which led to their nickname, Methodist. The name eventually served to identify the Protestant denomination they founded. The Wesleys, who practiced what they preached, believed in public service and missionary work, even going to the colonies in the 1730s as missionaries. On their return to England, John and Charles encountered Moravian passengers, Moravians being a Protestant group with German roots extending back to Jan Huss. This encounter led the brothers to associate

Figure 6.6 John Wesley | This portrait is of John Wesley, the founder of Methodism

Artist: Unknown
Source: Library of Congress

with Moravians in England and to read the writings of Martin Luther, in particular his *Justification by Faith*. In 1738, within just a few days of each other, both brothers experienced a deep religious conversion which led them to preach of a personal, emotional relationship with God; this preaching would carry over to the colonies.

George Whitefield, a Powerful Voice in New England and the Colonies

George Whitefield, who attended Oxford, also joined the Holy Club and was influenced by the Wesleys. Still, for Whitefield, not Luther but Calvin was the key to his conversion. Another great influence on Whitefield was Jonathan Edwards. Whitefield read Edwards's *A Faithful Narrative,* and found it inspirational.[28] For the Wesleys and Whitefield, the old Anglican Sunday services no longer sufficed, so they began preaching revivals and in the open air. They preached to people who did not normally attend church and to anyone who listened. They believed the Holy Spirit could be felt at work in their hearts; this very personal, emotional religious experience was also felt by those whom they converted. As one might expect, these services were not the calm, quiet services of the traditional Anglican Church but emotional services during which the congregation openly wept, especially when listening to Whitefield. Whitefield became famous on both sides of the Atlantic for his sermons, which he preferred to deliver in the open air. Whitefield's preaching was considered remarkable for several reasons: his voice carried for a tremendous distance, enabling him to be clearly heard by thousands; his style was such as to impress even those who, like Benjamin Franklin, did not agree with his theology; and he was able to stir up a storm of emotions in his audience so that they were often left weeping.

He preached daily, usually multiple times a day, for the rest of his life, inspiring many to a religious awakening, and inspired many who, if they did not become Methodists, at least experienced the Great Awakening. Unfortunately, while many welcomed this new evangelical form of worship, others did not. In the Colonies, those who preferred to stay with their old religious practices were called the Old Lights, while those who favored the new were called New Lights. The division between Old and New Lights crossed denominational boundaries, for while the Methodists were in the forefront of the Awakening, this was a spiritual matter rather than a doctrinal one. People could stay with their own church and still have the same deeply personal, internal conversion as the Wesleys. Even so, new denominations, including Methodists, Presbyterians, and Baptists, did take hold in the Colonies even where they were prohibited by law. All these denominations originated in the Old World and flowered in the Colonies powered by the zeal of the Awakening, thus changing the face of Colonial religion.

6.3.4 The Great Awakening Begins in the Middle Colonies

In the 1730s the Great Awakening began with the Tennents, a Presbyterian family of preachers who reached out to Presbyterians in their home of Pennsylvania and on into New Jersey. The Tennents and others were so successful in their revivals that they led to the founding of Princeton and to the inspiration of Jonathan Edwards. Their revivals spread from Pennsylvania northwards into New England, striking a cord with the Congregationalists or Puritans and Baptists there, leading ministers in New England to have their own revivals by the 1740s.[29]

Jonathan Edwards

Jonathan Edwards, a Connecticut preacher well educated in theology and philosophy, and who read Locke and Newton, came to be one of the most important theologians of his day. Inspired by Gilbert Tennent, Edwards was preaching successful revivals by 1735, when, tragically, his uncle committed suicide due to his despair concerning salvation. This proved a temporary setback to Edwards's revivals.[30] As Edwards was temporarily quieted, George Whitefield arrived from England in 1739, full of revival spirit. Just as Edwards writing had inspired Whitefield, Whitefield's emotional preaching inspired Edwards. Edwards greatly admired Whitefield who, as we might expect, touched him emotionally and made him weep. Edwards's own style was far more restrained than Whitefield's. Edwards reached his listeners through reason rather than through sermons infused with overt emotion, though the effect of his sermons on his audience could be very emotional. Edwards is most famous for his sermon entitled *Sinners in the Hands of an Angry God.* When he delivered this sermon at a meeting in Enfield, Connecticut in 1741, the reaction was overwhelming, with people crying out for salvation. Weeping, shouting, and fainting all occurred at these meetings in a tide of passion never before seen in Colonial churches. The Great Awakening in the Colonies was felt everywhere, yet New England stands out, due in no small part to Edwards. Conversions increased as church attendance exploded, with very few, if any, who did not know someone who had recently converted in this time of religious fever.

6.3.5 Before You Move On...

Key Concepts

The Scientific Revolution led to the Enlightenment. In both, an emphasis on reason was key. Ideas from the Enlightenment concerning human nature and that of government put forth by philosophers such as John Locke helped to inspire the American Revolution and shape the United States. The Great Awakening, a spiritual revival felt both in Britain and the colonies, focused on an individual's personal relationship with God. The Tennents, Jonathan Edwards, and George Whitefield all were key figures in the Great Awakening in the colonies, which resulted in the spread of new evangelical Protestant denominations.

Test Yourself

1. What are the three rights of every person as listed by Locke?

2. Early Methodists were called that because they were so methodical.

   a. True

   b. False

3. The Wesleys began as Anglicans but were inspired to conversion by the writing of whom?

4. Unlike with the Wesleys, who was key to Whitefield's conversion?

See page 235 for answers

6.4 COLONIAL CONFLICTS AND WARS

From 1675 to 1748, violence and warfare plagued the British colonies. Several conflicts were fought in North America during this period. The first of these was Metacom's War, also known as King Philip's War (1675-1676), a brutal engagement between the New Englanders and the Wampanoag Indians. Shortly thereafter, Bacon's Rebellion (1676) broke out in Virginia, which also involved disputes with the Indians and the colonial government. Following these conflicts were King William's War (1689-1697), Queen Anne's War (1702-1713), and King George's War (1744-1748). These wars were the North American theater of European wars between the British, French, and Spanish. Escalating imperial tensions at the end of the seventeenth century contributed to each of these wars. In the case of Metacom's War and Bacon's Rebellion, the expanding colonial population increased tensions over land between the British colonies and the Indians. In the case of the remaining three wars, tensions between European powers translated into conflict between their colonial possessions.

6.4.1 Metacom's War

In the early years of British settlement in New England, the colonists and the Indians had a fairly stable relationship because of trade. However, a dramatic increase in migration to the British colonies in the 1630s changed the relationship. When new colonists arrived en masse, hungry for land, it could lead to armed conflict. In 1636, settlers viciously attacked the Pequot in southeastern Connecticut when they refused to pay a tribute to colonial leaders. When the Pequot War ended, the Pequot lost the bulk of their land. Similar problems led to Metacom's War approximately thirty years later. Ill feelings were compounded by British religious proselytizing amongst the Indians. In 1646, the General Court of Massachusetts passed "An Act for the Propagation of the Gospel Among the Indians."[31] Over the next decades, a small population of "praying Indians" grew in the New England colonies, primarily in Massachusetts. These Christian Indians were a part of both Indian and colonial society; nevertheless, they were not seen by others as completely belonging to either group. Religious tensions between colonists and Indians, and Indians and praying Indians, also contributed to the outbreak of the war.

Tensions came to a boiling point in 1662 when Wamsutta, the sachem, or political leader, of the Wampanoag, was taken into Plymouth at gunpoint, only to die shortly thereafter of a sudden illness. Many of the Wampanoag suspected that their sachem had been poisoned. Wamsutta's successor, his brother Metacom, who was called King Philip by the colonists, took advantage of the situation by beginning to build an alliance against English expansionism. Colonists were informed of the alliance by a group of praying Indians. When a group of Indians was found with firearms, the government of Massachusetts forced Metacom to sign a new treaty which bound the Wampanoag to consult with the colonists in the disposal of Indian land and in the affairs of war, and to abide by their decisions. The treaty also named the Wampanoag as subjects of the royal government, bound by the laws of the colony. This 1671 treaty deepened the hostilities.

In 1675, war broke out in the aftermath of the trial and execution of three Wampanoag Indians convicted of the murder of John Sassamon, a praying Indian. Sassamon, a graduate of Harvard, had been an adviser to Metacom and often acted as a mediator for the Wampanoag and the colonial government. In early 1675, Sassamon informed the colonial government that Metacom was gathering alliances for an attack on expanding colonial towns; days after this, he was found dead. Many speculated that Metacom was behind the assassination. The Pilgrims responded by trying and hanging the three Wampanoag responsible for the death of Sassamon. In retaliation, Wampanoag warriors began to loot and burn colonial villages. Better armed than in the Pequot War, the Indians attacked during the summer and fall of 1675 and burned fifty-two of the region's ninety towns.

The war was short, lasting little more than a year, and brutal for both sides. The Indian alliance grew to include many New England tribes, such as the Narragansett, Nipmuck, Podunk, and Pocanoket. Colonies banded together to form the New England Confederation, which consisted of the Plymouth Colony, Massachusetts Bay Colony, New Haven Colony, and Connecticut Colony. Although the New England Confederacy won the war, their victory was extremely costly. By the end of the war, twelve colonial towns lay in ruins, and many more were heavily damaged. At least 600 colonists died in the conflict, which comprised about 10 percent of the colonies' men. The war also crippled the colonial economy, costing about £100,000, an incredible sum for the time. For the Indians, about 3,000 died, and more were tried in colonial court and executed or sold as slaves to Bermuda. Some were forced into servitude to local families. Metacom himself was one of the war's casualties. After he was shot in battle, Metacom's body was beheaded, then drawn and quartered. Colonists displayed his head in Plymouth for the next decade as a warning against further uprisings. Most significantly, many historians see Metacom's War as a tipping point in Indian relations; after this conflict, wars against Indians were fought with the purpose of extinction.

6.4.2 Bacon's Rebellion

As the New England colonists wrapped up their conflict with the Wampanoag, trouble began between Indians, from various tribes, and the Virginia colonists, which eventually produced a civil war in Virginia. The leading protagonists in the conflict were Governor William Berkeley and Nathaniel Bacon, Jr., his cousin by marriage. The war stemmed from their difference on the colony's Indian policy, but also from larger political and economic tensions in Virginia. Berkeley had been the governor of Virginia since 1641, and so he wielded a great deal of power. For years, he used that power to build support among the wealthiest colonists. He granted them the best public office, the best public land, and a near monopoly over the lucrative Indian trade. When Bacon arrived in the colony in 1675, Berkeley gave him a large land grant and appointed him to the governor's council (after all, he was family). Bacon, who was a bit of a troublemaker, wanted more power. He sensed weakness in his aging cousin and sought to exploit it. Bacon's social pedigree rivaled Berkeley's; thus, he thought he could win support among the smaller planters who Berkeley had overlooked.[32]

As Bacon schemed, tensions mounted between frontier colonists and the Indians. The trouble began in the northern part of the colony. Thomas Mathew, a Potomac River land owner, found himself in a dispute with nearby Algonquian Doeg, and violence ensued. The Virginia militia tracked the Doeg into Maryland where they killed not only their supposed enemy, but also innocent Iroquoian Susquehannock. The resulting Susquehannock War led to a dispute over Indian policy between the governor and his cousin. Berkeley wanted to fight a defensive war by building nine new forts on the frontier; the frontier residents, however, preferred an offensive war. Not only did it give them an opportunity to attack the Indians, whom many blamed for all of their problems, but it was a far less expensive prospect. The frontier residents found a leader in Nathaniel Bacon, who subsequently sought a commission from his cousin to lead forces against the Indians, but Berkeley refused. Bacon proceeded to lead attacks against the Doeg anyway, as well as the Susquehannock and the other tribes in the area, without the commission.[33]

Bacon's actions prompted the governor to label him a traitor and to expel him from the governor's council in May 1676. The following month, Bacon's supporters elected him to the colony's House of Burgesses which prompted a showdown between Bacon and Berkeley on June 23 in Jamestown. Bacon and his supporters surrounded the statehouse and raised their weapons against the governor. Berkeley then dared Bacon to shoot him on the spot. Bacon chose not to do so, but the burgesses, clearly fearing for their lives, awarded Bacon the commission he wanted and pushed Berkeley to pardon him for his treasonous activities. Berkeley agreed, and then fled the capital. Having won the first round, Bacon turned his attention back to the Indians. He launched an attack on the Powhatan, who had been allies of the English since the 1640s, that forced most of them off their land. Meanwhile, in September, Berkeley briefly took the capital back; however, he lost it almost immediately. At that point, Bacon decided rather than to hold the city he would burn it and go off to attack more Indians. During his hunt, Bacon died of natural causes on October 26, 1676. The rebellion, however, continued until January 22, 1677 when Berkeley finally managed to reestablish his control. English officials then recalled Berkeley to explain the situation; before he had a chance to defend his actions he died on June 16, 1677.[34]

Figure 6.7 Bacon's Rebellion | In 1676, Nathaniel Bacon led a rebellion against Governor William Berkeley. This illustration, from the *Makers of Virginia History* (1904), captured the showdown between the two men outside the statehouse on June 23, 1676.

Author: J.A.C. Chandler after painting by unidentified "Kelley"
Source: *Makers of Virginia History*

While Bacon's Rebellion stemmed from a small dispute between a Virginia land owner and the Doeg, its causes ran much deeper. Resentment against Governor Berkeley's rule had been growing long before Bacon arrived in the colony. Berkeley had curried favor from the wealthiest residents at the expense of the smaller planters and landless tenants. Not only did these "commoners" receive the worst land, they paid high taxes to support the inflated salaries of the governor and the burgesses. Most of the colonists could afford those taxes, just barely, when the price of tobacco was high. However, the price began a steady decline in the 1660s because of the implementation of the Navigation Acts as well as the crown's trade war with the Dutch.

Since the governor refused to address their grievances, many former indentured servants moved to the frontier. There they faced the sometimes hostile Indians, and, frustrated with their situation, they blamed those Indians for all their troubles. When the Susquehannock War began, Berkeley's defensive posture proved more than most residents could take because it would invariably mean an increase in their taxes. They turned to Bacon to lead a rebellion. He willingly accepted leadership, because he needed troops to help in his effort to unseat Berkeley and gain more power for the colony's smaller planters. Not long after the rebellion ended, Lieutenant Governor Alexander Spotswood noted that Berkeley's refusal "to let the people go out against the Indians" caused the conflict.[35]

For years, contemporaries and historians viewed Bacon's Rebellion as the first phase of the American Revolution. But in reality, Bacon's intent and even the intent of his followers was not to end English rule in Virginia. On several occasions Bacon suggested his effort would eliminate a corrupt governor and benefit the crown. Bacon's Rebellion did little to shift the center of power in Virginia; smaller planters still found themselves marginalized. In fact, it consolidated power in the hands of fewer powerful families such as the Washingtons, the Lees, and the Randolphs. They quickly moved to lower taxes, to implement Bacon's Indian policy, and to encourage a shift from indentured servitude to slavery. While both forms of labor existed in the colony before 1676, Virginia's leaders reasoned after the rebellion that if they relied more on slavery than servitude they would have fewer men competing for the available land. The slave population increased rapidly and much of the very poor white population left Virginia for North Carolina.[36] Bacon's Rebellion in no way marked the end of the colonists' confrontations with the Indians. In the eighteenth century various tribes became involved in the brewing tensions between Britain and the other European powers in the New World.

6.4.3 The Colonial Wars

Towards the end of the seventeenth century, North America became a front of expansion for European wars as military engagements between imperial powers spilled over into their colonial holdings. Each of the wars began in Europe and spread to the colonial holdings, involving not only the British, French, and Spanish colonists, but also their Indian allies. With each conflict, the European powers hoped to eliminate their competition from the New World. None of the conflicts did much to redraw the map of the Americas; however, they did create tensions between the colonies and their respective mother countries.

King William's War (1688-1697)

King William's War began when the Protestant monarch William of England joined the League of Augsburg in a war against Catholic France, which under Louis XIV sought to expand into German territories. After ascending to the throne in the Glorious Revolution, William felt the need to defend Protestantism and his Dutch Allies. In North America, the war centered on control of the Great Lakes region, the focal point of the fur trade. From the perspective of the English colonists, this war provided the perfect opportunity to take Canada from the French.

The war also saw the establishment of lasting alliances between colonists and native confederacies. The Iroquois Confederacy chose to ally with the British; the Wabanaki Confederacy with the French. In large part, these native confederacies reflected often longstanding regional divisions; each confederacy was made up largely of culturally and linguistically related groups that shared a loose political affiliation. The Iroquois Confederacy and the Algonquin-speaking Wabanaki groups had been fighting a series of wars for regional control and economic and political dominance for many years; the presence of European colonies and the development of the fur trade merely served to intensify their conflict. The economic focus of the war also stretched north to include struggles over control of the Hudson Bay and the lucrative trading posts of the Hudson's Bay Company.

Finally, the war also resulted from land hunger and border disputes between the British colonists of the Massachusetts Bay colony, who were expanding into modern-day

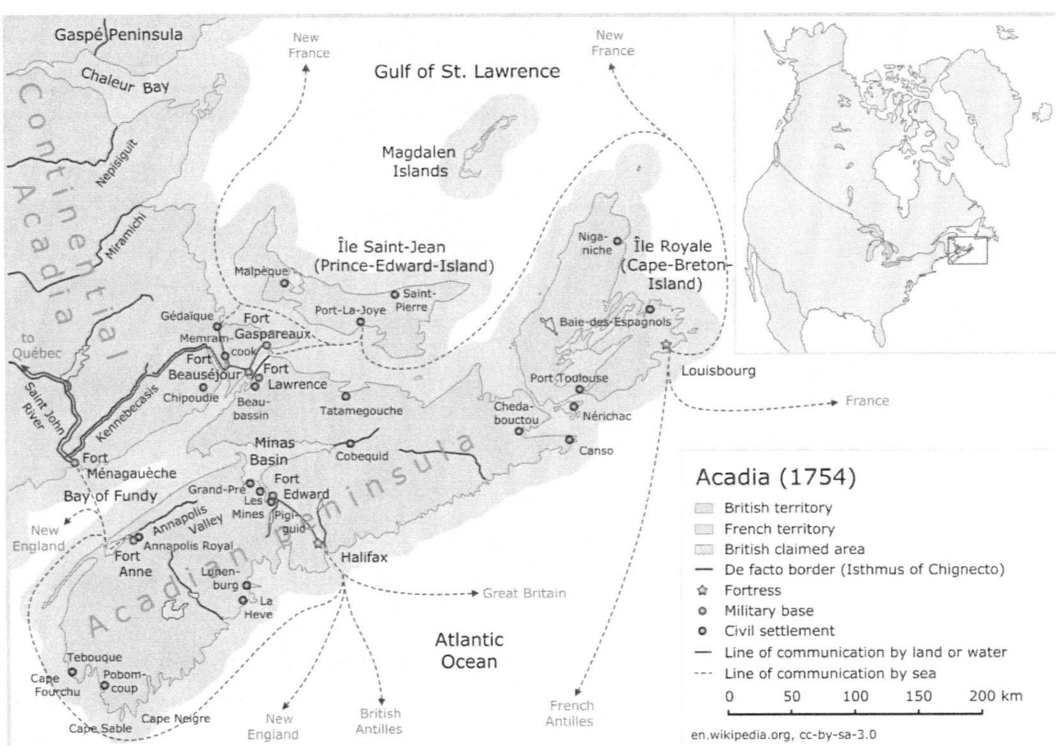

Figure 6.8 Acadia | The region of Acadia in Canada was the focus of hostilities throughout the intercontinental colonial wars.

Author: Wikimedia User "Mikmaq"
Source: Wikimedia Commons
License: CC BY SA 3.0

Maine, and the colonists of Acadia in New France, who laid claim to much of the same area. The most contested area was the region around the Kennebec River; British and colonial forces led several raids into the Acadian territory. In each instance, they suffered an embarrassing defeat in part because each colony had their own agenda. The war ended with the Treaty of Ryswick of 1697, which returned the colonial borders to what they had been before the war. The treaty failed to establish a lasting peace in North America, and tensions remained; within five years, war had broken out once again in the colonies. More importantly, the British colonists felt disappointed that the crown did not do more to help them assault Acadia. William was more concerned with maintaining an English presence in Ireland than with expanding his holdings in North America. Therefore, his military leaders could not send soldiers or ships to the American colonies.[37]

Queen Anne's War (1702-1713)

Like King William's War, Queen Anne's War emerged in North America when the War of Spanish Succession spilled over into the colonies. In this case, the war was being waged over the possible merging of France and Spain under the Bourbon monarchs. Anne, who succeeded William and Mary to the English throne, sought to prevent a Catholic dominated Europe. While the English won numerous victories in Europe, they struggled to do the same in North America. The war there once again focused on control of the continent. France, Spain, and their Indian allies fought the British and their Indian allies. The war was fought on two fronts throughout the North American colonies. In the south, the English, French, and Spanish fought over control of *la Florida*; in the north, border disputes once again emerged in Acadia, with the war stretching as far north as Newfoundland.[38]

In 1702, James Moore, governor of the Carolinas, led an attack on Spanish Florida. Although the British forces managed to sack and burn the town of St. Augustine, they were unable to take the city stronghold, the Castillo San Marcos. British and Indian forces were forced to withdraw when a fleet from Havana arrived to reinforce the town. The greatest blow to Spanish Florida came not from the attack on St. Augustine, but with the destruction of dozens of Indian missions. The Spanish population relied on these missions and their populations for labor and for corn; their destruction was quite a blow to the already weakened St. Augustine. Spanish Florida never really recovered from the war either economically or populationally.

In the north, the main combatants were the British and French colonists, along with their Indian allies. From the perspective of the American colonists, one of the more noteworthy events of the conflict came in 1704 when French commanders leading mostly Indian soldiers attacked Deerfield, in western Massachusetts. In the early hours on March 1, the enemy crept into the snowy village. Before they could defend themselves, the attackers set about destroying the village. Within a matter of hours, what historian John Demos calls "a village size holocaust" had ended. The French and Indians took those that survived the onslaught, including the village's minister John Williams, prisoner and forced them on a long march back to Canada. For those who managed to escape the attack, they returned to find their homes destroyed. More significantly, they found loved ones slaughtered in most gruesome ways or missing entirely. After burying the dead in a mass grave, the villagers worked to secure the release of their family and friends. One of the last to return home was John Williams; however, his daughter Eunice, also a captive, decided to remain with the Indians and she married into their community.[39]

The Deerfield Massacre, though exceedingly brutal, was not exceptional. As Demos notes, “Much of the actual fighting was small-scale, hit-and run, more a matter of improvisation than of formal strategy and tactics.”[40] However, on occasion other towns in New Hampshire and Massachusetts became targets of the French. On a larger-scale in the region, like King William’s War, most of the hostilities in the north focused on control of the area of Acadia. The British campaign to take Acadia culminated in the 1710 Siege of Port Royal, the capital of Acadia. After a successful campaign, the British gained control of Acadia, renaming it Nova Scotia. They also tried to take Quebec, but failed when the English admiral in charge of the operation deemed the St. Lawrence River too hazardous. In the Carolinas, Queen Anne’s War and its aftermath coincided with growing trouble regarding trade, land, and slavery between the British settlers and the Indians. In the Tuscarora War (1711) and the Yamasee War (1715-1716), both tribes lost their battle with the settlers and had to give much of their land away. The Tuscarora moved north to join the Iroquois Confederacy after their defeat; meanwhile, the Yamasee moved south and aligned themselves with the Spanish in Florida.

Queen Anne’s War ended with the negotiation of the Treaty of Utrecht in 1713. Anne accepted French control of the Spanish monarchy; however, she also secured more territory in North America, including Acadia and Newfoundland, and of the Atlantic slave trade for thirty years. Overall, this war confirmed the shifting balance of power in North America, with Britain on the rise and France and Spain on the wane. British conquest of Acadia and the weakening of Spanish Florida set the stage for both King George’s War and the more important French and Indian War (1754-1763) because after the Treaty of Utrecht the British focused more of their attention on maritime commerce than territorial acquisition in Europe. And so, securing the strength of their American colonies became of more interest.[41]

King George’s War (1744-1748)

After Queen Anne’s War came to an end, the European powers managed to check their rivalry for a number of years largely because their conflicts proved physically and economically exhausting. However, tensions between Britain, France, and Spain remained high, especially in their colonies. Ultimately, events in British Georgia and Spanish Florida sparked another imperial conflict. In the early 1730s, to undercut French power, the British decided to loot Spanish possessions in the Caribbean. When Spanish authorities caught British captains in acts of piracy, they meted out tough justice. For example, in 1731 the Spanish severed the ear of Robert Jenkins, who then presented his ear to Parliament to demonstrate Spanish treachery. In the coming years, the Spanish and the British worked to avoid an open conflict, but they could not contain their hostility. The War of Jenkins’s Ear—the first imperial struggle tied directly to a colonial issue—broke out in 1739. The ongoing Anglo-Spanish rivalry over land in the South as well as the Anglo-French rivalry over the Caribbean sugar trade became interlaced with local concerns in the southern colonies.

Just before the war broke out, the governor of Florida announced that he would grant freedom to any slave who made their way to Spanish territory, which prompted the Stono Rebellion, where slaves took up arms and attempted to march to Spanish Florida. Residents in both British colonies recognized South Carolina's weakness in the British conflict with Spain. South Carolinians looked the recently founded Georgia to provide a buffer between slavery and freedom. In an effort to protect South Carolina, General James Oglethorpe, a leading trustee in Georgia, led several raids into Florida and managed to capture two forts. However, his efforts to capture St. Augustine failed in 1740. In 1742, the Spanish launched an attack on Georgia, resulting in two skirmishes which the British won. The last major battle in the war came in 1743 when Oglethorpe once again tried and failed to take St. Augustine. After that effort, the focus of the colonial conflict shifted to the northern colonies when the French finally decided to back their Spanish allies. The War of Jenkins's Ear morphed into King George's War or the War of Austrian Succession.[42]

As in King William's War and Queen Anne's War, the British, French, and their Indian allies launched small-scale operations. The French tended to attack frontier towns in order to divert the British colonists' attention away from Canada. However, New England residents desperately wanted Canada. In 1745, William Shirley, the governor of Massachusetts, led a small continent in an attack on Fort Louisburg and much to everyone's surprise managed to take the fort. The victory gave the British the advantage in the North American contest because it made it far more difficult for the French to supply their settlers and Indian allies living down the St. Lawrence River. In 1746, the colonists sought to capitalize on their victory and move against Quebec. However, much-needed British reinforcements failed to arrive. Even more galling news came in 1748, when word reached the colonies that the war had ended. In the Treaty of Aix-la-Chapelle, the British traded control of Louisburg, the one thing the colonists were truly proud of, back to the French in exchange for French withdrawal from Indian and Flanders. Essentially when the war came to an end, nothing had changed in North America, which meant the colonists had another war to look forward to.[43]

6.4.4 Before You Move On...

Key Concepts

The era of the colonial wars was a period of shifting political influence in the colonies. During the course of these wars, colonists and Indian confederacies forged alliances and chose sides. Metacom's War was a significant engagement between British colonists and local New England native groups. The war was one of the most costly in American history, both in terms of its consequences for the colonial economy and population. It also proved devastating for natives. Bacon's Rebellion highlighted the ongoing tensions between the colony's residents and their government over the availability of land, which in turn caused problems with the native population. The remaining colonial wars were intercontinental engagements that saw military action both in Europe and in North America. Each of the three wars saw European political tensions and military action spill over into their colonial holdings. Although each of the wars was fought for different political reasons in Europe, in North America, the wars focused on the balance of political power and control of the continent. The North American war fronts emerged at the periphery where colonial boundaries met, such as Acadia and Florida. Overall, the results of King William's, Queen Anne's, and King George's Wars showed the balance of power in North America shifting to England, weakening the French and Spanish North American holdings.

Test Yourself

1. One of the most contentious areas of struggle in Queen Anne's War and King George's War was

   a. Florida.

   b. the Carolinas.

   c. Acadia.

   d. the Mississippi.

2. Metacom's War was significant because

   a. it marked the shift in policy in Indian warfare to a policy of extinction.

   b. it allowed the Wampanoag to retake much of Massachusetts.

   c. although the British won, it devastated many towns and the colonial economy.

   d. A and B

   e. all of the above

3. Queen Anne's War was significant because the _________helped shift the control of the continent to England.

   a. conquest of Florida

   b. conquest of the Carolinas

   c. conquest of New England

   d. conquest of Acadia

See page 235 for answers

6.5 Conclusion

During the eighteenth century, British North American colonists experienced many economic, social, and political changes. In an attempt to expand the empire, the British adopted mercantilist policies to tie the colonies to the mother country. Through a series of Navigation Acts, the British pushed the colonies into a trade network that proved beneficial to most participants. The colonies produced raw materials and exchanged them for goods manufactured in the mother country. Such economic growth caused an increase in the colonists' standard of living. To underscore mercantilism, the British attempted to extend their political control over the colonies. Under the political system that gave power to the colonial governor and the colonial assembly, the colonists concluded they had certain political rights, including the right to protest policies they did not like.

The American colonists also experienced social changes stemming from the Great Awakening, a wave of religious revivalism, and the Enlightenment, a period of intellectual development promoting personal improvement and social betterment. Both led to positive developments in American society during the eighteenth century. They caused the American colonists to be distrustful of institutionalized authority, yet favorably disposed to education and the instruction of educators. Moreover, the Enlightenment caused America's educated elite to be suspicious of any attempt to shackle their minds or erode the rights of English citizens. Although different in their goals, the Great Awakening and the Enlightenment had similar motivations, largely in the way they revealed the fundamental pragmatism and practicality of the American people.

The attempt to expand the empire did not just affect internal colonial policy. The British wanted to eliminate France and Spain from the New World. Metacom's War centered on tensions between New England settlers and the Wampanoags as the number of settlers increased. Bacon's Rebellion focused on concerns about the availability of land in Virginia as more indentured servants survived their terms of service and looked to obtain their own plots. However, the remaining wars, King William's War (1689-1697), Queen Anne's War (1702-1713), and King George's War (1744-1748), stemmed from the tensions between the European powers. Many colonists paid a high price for their participation in these wars. Their losses certainly lent themselves to a feeling that the colonists had made significant sacrifices for England, and therefore deserved equal and fair treatment as citizens of the British crown. British attempts to expand their power in North America ultimately paved the way for the revolution.

6.6 CRITICAL THINKING EXERCISES

- By following mercantilism, the British government thought their policies would strengthen the empire. What factors helped to blunt the impact of mercantilism and cause unrest in the colonies? How might the problems contribute to the American desire for independence?
- John Locke believed we are born with our minds being a blank slate and learn only through experience. What do you think?
- How did the wars in seventeenth and eighteenth century America reflect the broader tensions between Great Britain and its rivals, the Netherlands, France, and Spain?

6.7 KEY TERMS

- Acadia
- Anglicans
- Bacon's Rebellion
- Board of Trade
- Colonial Government
- Deerfield Massacre
- Jonathan Edwards
- The Enlightenment
- The Great Awakening
- King George's War
- King William's War
- John Locke
- Mercantilism
- Metacom's War
- Methodists
- Moravians
- Navigation Acts
- Isaac Newton
- Protestants
- Queen Anne's War
- Salutary Neglect
- John Sassaman
- The Scientific Revolution
- Theology
- Vice Admiralty Courts
- War of Jenkins's Ear
- John and Charles Wesley
- George Whitefield
- Writs of Assistance

6.8 CHRONOLOGY

The following chronology is a list of important dates and events associated with this chapter.

Date	Event
1632	John Locke born
1642	Isaac Newton born
1651	Navigation Act of 1651 passed
1660	Navigation Act of 1660 passed
1663	Staple Act of 1663 passed
1673	Plantation Duty Act of 1673 passed
1675-1676	Metacom's War
1676	Bacon's Rebellion
1687	Newton's Principia
1689-1697	King William's War
1690	Locke's Essay and Two Treaties written
1696	Navigation Act of 1696 and Trade Act of 1696 passed
1702-1713	Queen Anne's War
1703	Jonathan Edwards and John Wesley born
1704	John Locke died
1707	Charles Wesley born
1714	George Whitefield born
1727	Isaac Newton died
1729	Holy Club founded
1733	Molasses Act of 1733 passed
1738	Conversion of the Wesleys
1739-1744	War of Jenkin's Ear
1741	Edwards delivered "In the Hands of an Angry God"
1744-1748	King George's War
1758	Jonathan Edwards died
1770	George Whitefield died

Date	Event
1788	Charles Wesley died
1791	John Wesley died

6.9 BIBLIOGRAPHY

Barck, Oscar Theodore and Hugh Talmage Lefler. *Colonial America*, second edition. New York: Macmillan, 1968.

Breen, T.H. "An Empire of Goods: The Anglicization of Colonial America, 1690-1776." *The Journal of British Studies* 25, no. 4 (1986): 467-469.

Chitwood, Oliver Perry. *A History of Colonial America*, third edition. New York: Harper & Row, 1961.

Edwards, Jonathan. "Sinners in the Hands of an Angry God (1741)." Christian Classics Ethereal Library, May 11, 2012. http://www.ccel.org/ccel/edwards/sermons.sinners.html.

Farley, William P. "Jonathan Edwards and the Great Awakening." Enrichment Journal, May 11, 2012. http://enrichmentjournal.ag.org/200201/200201_104_johnathan.cfm.

Greene, Jack P. *Pursuits of Happiness: The Social Development of Early Modern British Colonies and the Formation of American Culture*. Chapel Hill: University of North Carolina Press, 1988.

Hallsell, Paul., ed. "Enlightenment." Internet History Sourcebook, Fordham University, May 11, 2012. http://www.fordham.edu/Halsall/mod/modsbook10.asp.

Hibben, John Grier. *The Philosophy of the Enlightenment*. New York. Charles Scribner's Sons. 1910.

Huntington, The Reverend William Reed, D.D., D.C.L. A Short History Of The Book Of Common Prayer (New York: Thomas W. Whittaker, 1893). The Anglican Church, May 11, 2012. http://justus.anglican.org/resources/bcp/short_history_BCP.htm.

Locke, John. An Essay Concerning Human Understanding. Institute for Learning Technologies, Columbia University, May 11, 2012. http://www.ilt.columbia.edu/publications/Projects/digitexts/locke/understanding/letter.html.

Piper, John. "I Will Not Be a Velvet-Mouthed Preacher!" The Life and Ministry of George Whitefield: Living and Preaching as Though God Were Real (Because He Is). Desiring God 2009 Conference for Pastors, May 11, 2012. http://www.desiringgod.org/resource-library/biographies/i-will-not-be-a-velvet-mouthed-preacher.

Rice, James Douglas. "Bacon's Rebellion (1676–1677)." *Encyclopedia Virginia*. Ed. Brendan Wolfe. Virginia Foundation for the Humanities. September 26, 2012, http://www.encyclopediavirginia.org/Bacon_s_Rebellion_1676-1677.

Sawers, Larry. "The Navigation Acts Revisited." *The Economic History Review* 45, no. 2 (May 1992): 262-284.

Taylor, Alan. *American Colonies: The Settling of North America*. New York: Penguin Books, 2001.

The Society for Propagating the Gospel among the Indians and Others of North America. University Press: 1887.

The United Methodist Church. General Commission on Archives and History, Mary 11, 2012. http://www.gcah.org.

Tyler, John W. *Smugglers and Patriots: Boston Merchants and the Advent of the American Revolution*. Boston: Northeastern University Press, 1986.

Wesley, John. "The Character of a Methodist." The Works of John Wesley (Thomas Jackson, 1872). Global Ministries of the United Methodist Church, May 11, 2012). http://new.gbgm-umc.org/umhistory/wesley/character/.

Wood, Gordon S. *The Radicalism of the American Revolution*. New York: Vintage Books, 1991.

6.10 END NOTES

1 Alan Taylor, American Colonies: The Settling of North America (New York: Penguin Books, 2001), 298.

2 Oscar Theodore Barck and Hugh Talmage Lefler, Colonial America, second edition (New York: Macmillan, 1968), 134-135; Oliver Perry Chitwood, A History of Colonial America, third edition (New York: Harper & Row, 1961), 414-415.

3 Barck and Lefler, Colonial America, 139-141; Taylor, American Colonies, 299.

4 Chitwood, A History of Colonial America, 356, 371.

5 Chitwood, A History of Colonial America, 363, 377-380; Barck and Lefler, Colonial America, 139-141; Taylor, American Colonies, 194; T.H. Breen, "An Empire of Goods: The Anglicization of Colonial America, 1690-1776," The Journal of British Studies 25, no. 4 (1986): 474.

6 Barck and Lefler, Colonial America, 141-145; Chitwood, A History of Colonial America, 417-419.

7 Barck and Lefler, Colonial America, 217, 229.

8 Barck and Lefler, Colonial America, 145, 230-235; Chitwood, A History of Colonial America, 421-424.

9 Larry Sawers, "The Navigation Acts Revisited," The Economic History Review 45, no. 2 (May 1992): 271, 273, 278; see also, John W. Tyler, Smugglers and Patriots: Boston Merchants and the Advent of the American Revolution (Boston: Northeastern University Press, 1986).

10 Barck and Lefler, Colonial America, 245.

11 Breen, "An Empire of Goods," 470, 474, 476; Taylor, American Colonies, 310-311.

12 Taylor, American Colonies, 304, 307, 310-311.

13 Breen, "An Empire of Goods," 479-481, 495-496; Taylor, American Colonies, 312-313.

14 Breen, "An Empire of Goods," 496-497.

15 Barck and Lefler, Colonial America, 238; Chitwood, A History of Colonial America, 406-407.

16 Chitwood, A History of Colonial America, 407-408.

17 Chitwood, A History of Colonial America, 408-409.

18 Barck and Lefler, Colonial America, 236-237; Chitwood, A History of Colonial America, 410-411.

19 Barck and Lefler, Colonial America, 238.

20 Barck and Lefler, Colonial America, 238; 246-248.

21 Barck and Lefler, Colonial America, 238-240.

22 Barck and Lefler, Colonial America, 241-242, 247.

23 Barck and Lefler, Colonial America, 244-245; Gordon S. Wood, The Radicalism of the American Revolution (New York: Vintage Books, 1991), 77-80; Jack P. Greene, Pursuits of Happiness: The Social Development of Early Modern British Colonies and the Formation of American Culture (Chapel Hill: University of North Carolina Press, 1988), 199.

24 Barck and Lefler, Colonial America, 243-244; Taylor, American Colonies, 286-288.

25 Taylor, American Colonies, 287-288.

26 Thomas Paine, Common Sense, US History.org, October 15, 2012, http://www.ushistory.org/paine/commonsense/singlehtml.htm.

27 Henry J. Sage. The Enlightenment, Academic American History, October 15, 2012, http://www.academicamerican.com/colonial/topics/enlighten.htm; Dr. Richard Beeman, Benjamin Franklin and the American Enlightenment. October 15, 2012, http://www.benfranklin300.org/_etc_pdf/Enlightenment_Richard_Beeman.pdf.

28 Taylor, American Colonies, 347.

29 Christine Leigh Heyrman, "The First Great Awakening," Divining America, TeacherServe, National Humanities Center, October 10, 2012, http://nationalhumanitiescenter.org/tserve/eighteen/ekeyinfo/grawaken.htm.

30 Taylor, American Colonies, 346.

31 The Society for Propagating the Gospel among the Indians and Others of North America (University Press: 1887), 6.

32 Taylor, American Colonies, 149.

33 James Douglas Rice, "Bacon's Rebellion (1676-1677)," Encyclopedia Virginia, ed. Brendan Wolfe, Virginia Foundation for the Humanities, September 26, 2012, http://www.encyclopediavirginia.org/Bacon_s_Rebellion_1676-1677.

34 Rice, "Bacon's Rebellion (1677-1677)."

35 Taylor, American Colonies, 147-148; Spotswood quoted in Rice, "Bacon's Rebellion (1676-1677)."

36 Taylor, American Colonies, 149-151; Rice, "Bacon's Rebellion (1676-1677)."

37 Taylor, American Colonies, 288-290.

38 Taylor, American Colonies, 292-293.

39 John Demos, "The Deerfield Massacre," American Heritage 44, no. 1 (February/March 1993), September 23, 2012, http://www.americanheritage.com/content/deerfield-massacre?page=show.

40 Demos, "The Deerfield Massacre."

41 Taylor, American Colonies, 293.

42 Taylor, American Colonies, 422; Julie Ann Sweet, "War of Jenkin's Ear," New Georgia Encyclopedia, Georgia Humanities Council, September 23, 2012, http://www.georgiaencyclopedia.org/nge/Article.jsp?id=h-807.

43 Taylor, American Colonies, 423-424.

ANSWER KEY FOR CHAPTER SIX: GROWING PAINS IN THE COLONIES

Check your answers to the questions in the Before You Move On Sections for this chapter.

Correct answers are **BOLDED**

Section 6.2.3 - p21

1. The Navigation Acts specified enumerated goods that
    a. colonists could not export.
    b. colonists could manufacture the same goods as produced in Britain.
    C. COLONISTS COULD ONLY SHIP WITHIN THE BRITISH EMPIRE.
    d. colonists could only trade to other colonists.

2. Most colonists in eighteenth century North America were largely self-sufficient, so they did not need to import consumer goods from Britain.
    a. True
    B. FALSE

3. Colonial governors possessed the right to veto legislation passed by the colonial assemblies.
    A. TRUE
    b. False

4. During the eighteenth century, colonial assemblies
    a. lost their power to appropriate taxes.
    b. were appointed by the king.
    c. included both men and women.
    D. EXPANDED THEIR POWER AND INFLUENCE.

Section 6.3.5 - p219

1. What are the three rights of every person as listed by Locke? **LIFE, LIBERTY, AND ESTATE**

2. Early Methodists were called that because they were so methodical.
    A. TRUE
    b. False

3. The Wesleys began as Anglicans but were inspired to conversion by the writing of whom? **MARTIN LUTHER**

4. Unlike with the Wesleys, who was key to Whitefield's conversion? **JOHN CALVIN**

Section 6.4.4 - p228

1. One of the most contentious areas of struggle in Queen Anne's War and King George's War was
    a. Florida.
    b. the Carolinas.
    C. ACADIA.
    d. the Mississippi.

2. Metacom's War was significant because
    a. it marked the shift in policy in Indian warfare to a policy of extinction.
    b. it allowed the Wampanoag to retake much of Massachusetts.
    c. although the British won, it devastated many towns and the colonial economy.
    D. A AND C
    e. all of the above

3. Queen Anne's War was significant because the ________helped shift the control of the continent to England.
    a. conquest of Florida
    b. conquest of the Carolinas
    c. conquest of New England
    D. CONQUEST OF ACADIA

Chapter Seven: The Road To Revolution, 1754-1775

Contents

Chapter Seven: The Road To Revolution

7.1 INTRODUCTION

During the seventeenth and eighteenth centuries, the Americans became embroiled in a series of wars that were also fought on the European continent. King William's War, Queen Anne's War, and King George's War originated in Europe; the French and Indian War, on the other hand, began in the colonies two years before it "spread" to Europe and became known as the Seven Years' War. During most of the eighteenth century before 1763, the British had followed a policy that William Pitt nicknamed "salutary neglect." This theory was based on the notion that if the colonies were left alone to pursue their own economic interests, they would prosper and thereby ultimately benefit the mother country. This approach to colonial management ended in 1763 with the conclusion of the French and Indian War. Determined to make the colonies defray part of the expenses of the war and of their own domestic needs following the war, the Parliament enacted a series of measures designed, in the words of the colonists, to "raise a revenue." Colonial opposition to these policies became strident between 1763 and 1775, and the rallying cry "no taxation without representation" underscored the differences in the way the colonies and the mother country looked at taxation, regulation, and control.

The climax of the protests came in 1773 as tea from the East India Tea Company was dumped into the harbors of ports along the eastern seaboard. The British reacted with the "Intolerable" Acts, to which the colonies responded in spring, 1774, by sending a list of grievances to the king and Parliament. Matters were made worse when George III came to the conclusion late in the year that "blows must be exchanged to determine whether [the American colonies] are to be subject to this country or independent."

In May, 1775, a month after the firings at Lexington and Concord, the Second Continental Congress convened to consider the response of George III to the petition submitted in spring, 1774, and ultimately to oversee the war. It would be in session until replaced by the Confederation Congress, which assembled in 1781.

7.1.1 Learning Outcomes

After completing this chapter, you should be able to:

- Analyze the evolution of British colonial policy towards the North American colonies from the end of the French and Indian War, 1763, to the firing at Lexington and Concord.
- Define salutary neglect and explain why the British abandoned this policy following the French and Indian War.
- Evaluate the impact of the French and Indian War on the British colonies and the Indians.
- Identify the important people and groups involved in the colonial protests leading up to the Revolution.

- Identify the significant Parliamentary acts passed in the years following the French and Indian War.
- Explain the various instances of inter-colonial cooperation in the years between 1763 and 1776, including the Committees of Correspondence, the Stamp Act Congress, the Continental Congresses, and the boycotts of British goods.
- Recognize that people living in Great Britain and in Colonial America saw the conflicts of the times very differently.

7.2 THE FRENCH AND INDIAN WAR (1754-63)

The late seventeenth and early eighteenth centuries was a time of warfare in the colonies and in Europe. Over the period, the British, French, and Spanish empires in North America clashed and vied for control of the continent. Each of the colonial powers engaged in a series of shifting alliances with native peoples, who participated in the colonial wars in order to ensure or bolster their own regional economic or political power. Much of the fighting in King William's, Queen Anne's, and King George's Wars had taken place at the periphery of the colonial borders, in Acadia and Spanish Florida. The next and greatest of these wars, the French and Indian War, emerged along the colonial boundaries in modern-day Pennsylvania. Unlike the previous colonial wars, which began in Europe and spread to the colonies, this war began in the colonies and spread to Europe and beyond. The name French and Indian War refers only to the engagement in North America; the greater global war is referred to as the Seven Years' War.

The French and Indian War arose from border tensions when Virginians crossed the Allegheny Mountains into the Ohio River Valley, an area claimed by both the British and the French. The French responded to this incursion by building a series of forts in western Pennsylvania. Tensions intensified as both sides tried to strengthen their hold on the region through increased presence and thwarted attempts to force the other power to leave the region. Militia leader George Washington was one of the prominent British officers in these actions.

In 1753, Washington was sent by Virginia lieutenant governor Robert Dinwiddie to negotiate a French removal from the area. Not surprisingly, the French refused to leave and asserted that the French claim to the region was stronger than England's. In the aftermath of the failed negotiations, both sides decided to focus their efforts on the convergence of the Monongahela, Allegheny, and Ohio Rivers, the site of modern-day Pittsburgh. In 1754, Washington, his regiment of Virginians, and a small group of Mingo warriors, were charged to build a fort at the site. They arrived at the convergence of the rivers to find that the French had already constructed their own fort at this location. Washington and his men fell back and made camp; the next morning, they ambushed a small party of Frenchmen, killing many of them. The Battle of Jumonville Glen, named for French commander Joseph Coulon de Villers de Jumonville, was the first engagement of the French and Indian War. Although a British victory, overall, it was a completely botched mission that embarrassed Washington and damaged his reputation. To this day, historians do not know with any certainty what exactly happened at the Battle of Jumonville Glen. There is documentary evidence for two different accounts of the pivotal event of the day: the death of French

Figure 7.1 George Washington | Washington wearing his French and Indian War colonel's uniform of the Virginia Regiment. This is the earliest authenticated portrait of Washington and appears in Woodrow Wilson's book *George Washington*.

Artist: Charles Willson Peale
Source: *George Washington*

commander Jumonville. Some sources assert that Washington effectively lost control of his Indian allies. After a ceasefire had been called, the leader of the Mingos split open Jumonville's skull, scalping him in what some historians have called a ritual slaying. Several sources assert that after this, the Mingo set about killing and scalping many of the wounded Frenchmen, to the horror of Washington. Other accounts suggest that Jumonville was shot and killed in the skirmish.[1] In the aftermath of the battle, Washington and his men retreated and hastily constructed Fort Necessity, where Washington was forced to surrender to attacking French forces a month later. The French and Indian War emerged from this series of blunders. British politician Horace Walpole remarked on the situation, "the volley fired by a young Virginian in the backwoods of America set the world on fire."[2] In effect, Washington's actions triggered a world war.

While Washington was fighting the French at Fort Necessity, colonial representatives from seven of the thirteen British colonies were meeting to discuss defensive measures against the French and improving foreign relations with the Indians. This meeting, called the Albany Congress, was the first time in the series of colonial wars when the colonies considered some kind of formal union. Great Britain's Board of Trade had called for the meeting in order to discuss Indian relations and to meet with the Iroquois, hoping for an alliance. They were disappointed; the Iroquois refused to commit themselves to the British. Much of the meeting instead was spent debating Benjamin Franklin's Plan of Union, which sought to create a formal colonial union. The plan called for a colonial union comprising a "grand council," which would pass legislation, and a president appointed by the Crown. Although the plan was approved by the delegates at the Albany Congress, the colonies rejected the plan and the Colonial Office, as they were all feared their powers being eroded by the proposed colonial union. Although the Plan of Union failed, it later became a tremendous influence on the 1777 Articles of Confederation and, eventually, the Constitution.

One measure of the Plan of Union that was enacted was the appointment of a supreme commander of British and colonial military forces. In 1775, General Edward Braddock arrived in the colonies and assumed command of the forces. His first action was to return to western Pennsylvania and Fort Duquesne, the fort at the convergence of the rivers. Braddock led his force 125 miles from Fort Cumberland, Maryland, to within six miles of Fort Duquesne. They traveled slowly, laden down with their cannons. Along the way, they constructed a road to ensure easy transport between Cumberland and the Ohio Valley, an area which Braddock fully expected easily to take from the French. The French, realizing that the fort could not withstand Braddock's heavy artillery, decided to attack the British before the British could lay siege to the fort.

The French and Indian forces planned to ambush Braddock's men; however, they were too late and were surprised to meet the British forces just after the British had crossed the Monongahela River. The resulting Battle of the Wilderness was fought on July 9, 1755. In the course of the battle, both the French commander and Braddock were shot; the French commander died on the field while Braddock lingered and died days later.

Figure 7.2 Join or Die | Franklin's cartoon encouraging membership in the Albany Congress has since been viewed by many as predictive of the formation of the United States, as many parts make up the whole.

Artist: Benjamin Franklin
Source: Library of Congress

The Battle of the Wilderness is significant because it illustrates the dramatic differences between European warfare and an emerging "American way of war."[3] Braddock tried in vain to make his troops hold formations and to maintain his own position on horseback in the manner of European warfare, only to have the French and Indian troops, concealed in the woods, make easy targets of his men and his horses: Braddock had several horses shot out from under him before he himself was shot. After Braddock was shot, George Washington managed to maintain order and disengage his forces. Washington was acclaimed for his actions at the Battle of the Wilderness, actions that led in part to his later appointment as commander in chief of the American forces in the Revolution.

From this unexpected beginning, the French and Indian war by 1756 had spread to Europe, becoming the Seven Years' War. This war involved nine European powers. In the midst of the growing European involvement, William Pitt assumed the leadership of the British government. Pitt's strategy named North America as the primary field of engagement against France, where he mobilized an enormous force of 45,000 troops composed of both British regulars and colonial militiamen. Pitt was able to amass such a huge army because he offered the colonies subsidies for their wartime participation. His strategy also called for the British navy to blockade ports and cut off French reinforcements as well as French trade. This hurt the French army both directly and indirectly, as not only were they denied French troops, but also the lack of trade goods hurt their relationship with their Indian allies.

The turning point of the war came in 1759 in the so-called *Annus Mirabilis*, or Year of Miracles. Over the course of the year, the war turned in favor of the British. In North America, they conquered Quebec, drove the French out of the Ohio Valley, and captured the rich island of Guadeloupe. Victories in India, in Europe, and at sea further empowered the British. Although the British gained the upper hand globally, in North America, the war limped weakly on until 1763. The newly-ascended British monarch, King George III, desired to bring the war to an end; however, Spain's late entry into the Seven Years' War prevented his doing so. A second "year of miracles" in 1762 saw the capture of the Spanish ports of Havana, Cuba, and Manila, Philippines, and, by 1763, the French and Spanish both were defeated.

The Treaty of Paris of 1763 brought the Seven Years' War, and related French and Indian War in America, to an end. The treaty wrought enormous changes on the North American map, as the British were awarded everything east of the Mississippi River, including Spanish Florida and only excepting New Orleans and Louisiana. Great Britain was now the uncontested European power in eastern North America. The treaty was vociferously protested by France's Indian allies, who had been given no voice in the negotiations. Most groups asserted that France had no right to cede Indian lands to the British. From a European point of view, though, the lands of France's Indian allies now rightfully belonged to the British as these lands were ceded as spoils of war upon France's, and, by extension, its Indian allies', defeat. Though the European war had ended, many tribes consequently remained hostile to the British, and violence simmered beneath the surface.

7.2.1 Pontiac's War (1763-64)

After the end of the war, many tribes of the Ohio Valley expected that British colonists would pour over the Appalachian Mountains into their lands. The British quickly moved into French forts in the valley and did not trade with the tribes. Pontiac of the Ottawa nation responded to the growth of British power in the area by calling for tribes to join forces against the British. Pontiac used the message of a prophet named Neolin to encourage others to join his confederacy against the British. Neolin said that he had experienced a mystical vision in which he visited the realm of the Creator, that is, heaven, and seen the punishments of hell. In his vision, the route to heaven was obstructed by the British, because Indians had been neglecting their traditional ways, being corrupted instead by white ways. He attributed the misfortunes of the Indians to this corruption and so advocated restoring aboriginal rituals, beliefs, and practices. He concomitantly called upon Indians to exorcise white influences, such as alcohol and other European trade goods. The Indians, he said, must purify themselves through reforming their ways and driving the British from their lands.

Pontiac took advantage of Neolin's message, incorporating it into his own speeches and campaigns in order to win tribes into the confederacy. Ultimately, the group included the Shawnee, Munsee, Wyandot, Seneca, Delaware, Huron, Potawatomi, Ojibwa, and Ottawa. In May of 1763, the Ottawa attacked Fort Detroit; other groups led raids on British settlements in Ohio and western Pennsylvania. Over the course of the year, more than 600 Pennsylvanians were killed and more than a dozen soldiers were massacred in the destruction of Fort Sandusky. By the fall of 1764, the British military led invasions of the Ohio Valley to subdue the confederacy. The British were able to force the tribes to surrender because, cut off from trade, they were quickly running out of ammunition. Pontiac's War illuminated several things. First, it showed how reliant the Ohio Valley tribes had become on French trade. Second, it showed what a weak grasp Britain had over the Ohio Valley. In response to this war, Great Britain would enact the Proclamation of 1763, drawing a line east of the Appalachian Mountains where British colonists would be forced to live and setting aside the land west of the mountains for the Indians.

7.2.2 Before You Move On...

Key Concepts

The French and Indian War was the most significant event of the century prior to the Revolutionary War. The war and the rejection of the Albany Plan of Union highlighted the fact that the British North American colonies had developed a fairly strong sense of individual autonomy that would take extraordinary efforts to overcome. Indeed, this colonial political structure would carry over into the early years of the United States in the context of the debate over states' rights and federal power. The war drastically changed the balance of power in North America, with the elimination of the French presence from the continent. This outcome not only had an impact on international affairs; it also profoundly impacted the dynamics within the colonial situation. The ever-present enemy on the western border now disappeared. In the absence of such a threat, the colonists would be able to shift their focus to other problems, such as changing British colonial policies. Of course, the war was a major factor in changing British policy. The expenditures of war had driven up the imperial debt, and the removal of the French immediately precipitated a violent response from the Indians of the Ohio Valley region in what became known as Pontiac's War. The British government's responses to these problems would ultimately lead to conflict with the colonies.

Test Yourself

1. An increasing sense of common identity among the colonists was one of the legacies of the French and Indian War.

   a. True

   b. False

2. The Proclamation of 1763 was enacted in part as a response to Pontiac's War.

   a. True

   b. False

3. The Ohio Valley was one of the major points of contention between the French and British in the French and Indian War as well as the British and Indians in Pontiac's War.

   a. True

   b. False

See page 269 for answers

7.3 THE END OF THE SEVEN YEARS WAR AND WORSENING RELATIONS, 1763-1772

Prior to the Seven Years' and ensuing Pontiac Wars, the British had practiced in America their unwritten policy of salutary neglect. This policy, maintained throughout much of the seventeenth and eighteenth centuries, was based on the ideas of Robert Walpole, the first Prime Minister of Great Britain. Walpole believed that the colonies would flourish if left alone; thus, he did not believe in enforcing Parliamentary restrictions like the Acts of Trade and Navigation. The term "salutary neglect" was actually coined by Edmund Burke who, in an address to Parliament in 1775, reminded its members that the colonies had flourished not by being "squeezed" by a "watchful and suspicious government," but rather through a "wise and salutary neglect." However, this policy, which had worked so well in the past, ended as the French and Indian War concluded with the Peace of Paris.

7.3.1 The French and Indian War and the End of Salutary Neglect

The French and Indian War was a great success, at least the colonists and the English so believed. Though the two allies shared this opinion, they saw their individual contributions to the war effort in very different ways. The British believed that they had fought an expensive war in order to protect the colonists from enemies on the western frontier and were convinced that they had done more than their share to finance the war costs: fully two-fifths of the monies the colonists spent in recruitment, clothing, and paying the troops came from the mother country. The colonists, on the other hand, believed that they had performed splendidly in the war and that their reward would be opening the western territories to settlement. They did not anticipate that the British would tighten their control of the colonies in an attempt to gain additional revenues to offset war costs.

For their part, the British disliked the self-satisfied post-war colonial attitude that gave too little credit or assistance to the mother country. Indeed, the Commander-in-Chief in the Americas complained: "It is the constant study of every province here to throw every expense on the Crown and bear no part of the expense of this war themselves."[4] Colonial America historian Curtis Nettles points out that there were three sources of colonial opposition to assuming the responsibility for war expenses as the British expected. On the one hand, some colonial leaders argued that their respective colony was simply too poor to contribute to the war effort. Other colonies, like the Quaker colonies of Pennsylvania and New Jersey, were opposed to warfare generally by virtue of their pacifist leanings and had no intention of funding a military action. And then there were those colonies, such as Rhode Island, Delaware, and New Jersey, that did not have frontier borders and were therefore uninterested in contributing to a war that so little concerned their own experiences.[5] Another problem to surface frequently in inter-colonial relations was that each colony waited to see how much the others would contribute before making any sort of commitment of its own. Thus the British and the colonists could only see the issue of military monies from their own particular standpoint; the British thought the colonies should be grateful, while the colonists thought the British were lucky to have had any of their support at all. As they saw it, the French and Indian War was just another extension of a war that began in Europe. Of course, this view was mistaken, a fact that the British underscored in dozens of communications with America.

Adding to the growing disharmony in American-British relations came the question of the western lands. The colonies with frontiers abutting the Appalachian and Allegheny Mountains fully expected that, upon the signing of the Peace of Paris, these lands to be opened to settlement. Their characteristic thirst for land would thereby be quenched. The colonists had fought and won the "European" War and were now headed west. Not surprisingly, the British viewed the question of the western lands very differently. First, the mother country no longer needed colonists to settle along the frontiers as a defense against the French and Indians. Second, their allowing colonists to settle beyond the Appalachians would put an increasing number out of Parliament's reach; consequently, taxes would be more difficult to collect and imperial laws harder to enforce. Finally, once remote from the control of royal officials in America, the colonists would become increasingly independent-minded.

7.3.2 The Proclamation of 1763

Ignoring the obstructionist messages coming from the colonies, the British government in 1763 threw caution to the winds and issued the Proclamation of 1763. Established in large part "to pacify the Indians," the British saw what came to be known as the "proclamation line" as a temporary measure that would give them time to define a more permanent policy. They worded the Proclamation so as to make it appear advantageous to the colonies:

> WHEREAS, we have taken into Our Royal Consideration the extensive and valuable Acquisitions in America, secured to our Crown by the late Definitive Treaty of Peace concluded at Paris the 10th Day of February last; and being desirous that all Our loving Subjects, as well as our Kingdom as of our Colonies in America, may avail themselves with all convenient Speed, of the great Benefits and Advantages which must accrue therefrom to their Commerce, Manufactures, and Navigation. We have thought fit, with the Advice of our Privy Council to issue this Royal Proclamation. [6]

Members of Parliament believed this settlement to be extremely generous, especially in light of what they saw as the potential benefits to the colonies from the war.

Expecting to assuage American fears and mistrust with the Proclamation, the British used it to outline their new policy, one that left no doubt as to the motivation of Parliament and the Crown. Most importantly, the Proclamation specified that colonists could not settle beyond the Allegheny-Appalachian Mountain chain. The British reserved this territory for the Indian tribes. The only exception was that white traders could apply for licenses to trade with the Indians. The British militia would enforce the Proclamation.[7] The colonists, long used to salutary neglect, ignored this law: "scores of wagons headed westward." [8]

7.3.3 The Implications of the New British Approach: The Parliamentary Acts of 1764

The British followed the Proclamation of 1763 with two equally contentious acts of Parliament: the Sugar Act and the Currency Act. The Sugar Act, drafted by George Grenville, First Lord of the Treasury, replaced and lowered the taxes on imported sugar created by the Molasses Act of 1733; this act had long been ignored by the colonists for whom smuggling was acceptable. The difference between the Sugar Act and the Molasses Act, however, was that Parliament intended to collect the tax created by the former; in addition, the tax was intended, as the colonists saw it, not to regulate trade but to "raise a revenue." It would do so by cutting British taxes on molasses in half, a decrease that would reduce the need to smuggle in tax-free molasses from the French West Indies.

According to Grenville, the tax money would be used to defend the colonies. But James Otis, Chair of the Massachusetts Bay House of Representatives, insisted that measures like the Sugar Act "have a tendency to deprive the Colonies of some of their most essential Rights as British Subjects, and...particularly the Right of assessing their own Taxes."[9] While the Sugar Act lowered the tariff on sugar, it increased the powers of the Admiralty Courts as well as ending the lucrative sugar and slave trade with the West Indies. It is interesting to note that although Otis claimed that citizens of the British Empire had the right to assess taxes on themselves, nowhere in the Empire was this "right" recognized. The House of Commons was elected by the wealthy and landholders, not by the citizens as a whole, and it legislated accordingly.

The Currency Act, passed the same year, gave Parliament control of the colonial currency system. The act specified that from 1765 onward, "no act, order, resolution, or vote of assembly, in any of his Majesty's colonies or plantations in America, shall be made, for creating or issuing any paper bills, or bills of credit of any kind or denomination whatsoever, declaring such paper bills, or bills of credit, to be legal tender in payment of any bargains, contracts, debts dues or demands."[10] Thus the Act abolished the use of paper money altogether and put the colonists at a further economic disadvantage in their trade relations with British merchants. This move in turn caused a severe shock to the colonial economy already depressed due to war expenses.

7.3.4 The Stamp Act of 1765

If the Sugar Act was the first act intended to raise a revenue, then the second was the Stamp Act, which levied the first internal tax. The Stamp Act specified that stamps were to be placed on newspapers, pamphlets, almanacs, wills, deeds, licenses, insurance policies, bills of lading, college diplomas, and even playing cards. While the colonists did not necessarily object to the principle of taxation as such, they did draw lines as to how and why taxes should be applied. Indeed, ample precedent already existed for British taxation to regulate colonial trade, even if tax revenues went directly to the British government. However, the colonial legislatures had for some time assumed the role of levying taxes for what they deemed as "internal" applications; these internal applications included paying colonial officials, supporting the militia, internal improvements, and the mail service. Therefore, the colonists drew a fine if definite line between such "internal" taxes and taxes of an external nature, which were for the purpose of regulating trade. In *Reasons Why the British Colonies in America Should Not Be Charged with Internal Taxes*, Governor Thomas Fitch of Connecticut argued that "If these internal taxations take place and the principles upon which they must be founded are adopted and carried into execution, the colonies will have no more than a shadow of legislation left."[11]

Moreover, colonial political systems and ideologies had largely developed within the context of direct representation, which assumed that taxes of an internal nature could only be levied by those who directly represented the electorate. Therefore, when Parliament attempted to levy taxes that would be used to pay for defense of the colonial frontier and the housing and supply of British soldiers in the colonies, some colonists began to raise the cry of "no taxation without representation," claiming that such taxes could be imposed only by the colonial legislatures; if imposed on them by Parliament, then the colonies must be directly represented in that body.

The response from England to the argument regarding "actual" representation was that the colonies were in fact represented in Parliament, only virtually. Members of Parliament had long assumed that they re-presented the interests of all groups in England and her colonial possessions, rather than only narrow, local interests. Thus, according to the theory of virtual representation, Parliament legislated for the well-being of the Irish, the Scots, and the American colonists, in addition to those who lived in England proper. Moreover, the British government was quick to point out that the French and Indian War had been very costly, that Americans paid fewer taxes than the remainder of those in the British possessions, and that the monies raised by the stamp tax would pay for the defense of the colonies.

These arguments fell on deaf ears, as virtual representation had no meaning for the Americans. Colonial leaders responded to the new tax laws by counter-arguing that, because they had not voted for them, these taxes could not be imposed on their colonies. Later writers also pointed out that the Vice-Admiralty courts that enforced the revenue laws excluded juries and put the burden of proof on the defendants. All of these practices infringed on their rights as British citizens. James Otis for one insisted:

> ...the colonists, black and white, born here are freeborn British subjects, and entitled to all the essential civil rights of such is a truth not only manifest from the provincial charters, from the principles of the common law, and acts of Parliament, but from the British constitution, which was re-established at the [English] Revolution with a professed design to secure the liberties of all the subjects to all generations.[12]

The colonial response to the notion of "virtual" representation was much like their reaction to internal taxation. Governor of Rhode Island, one of the only two colonies that elected its governor, Stephen Hopkins, insisted that England and her empire was "an imperial state, which consists of many separate governments each of which hath peculiar privileges...all laws and taxations which bind the whole must be made by the whole."[13] The impasse over these different views of representation and taxation would ultimately lead to armed conflict.

The Stamp Act Riots and Congress

In 1765, the Stamp Act was soon followed by the Quartering Act which delineated where and how British soldiers found room and board in the colonies. Immediately after these acts' enactment, the colonists sprang into action. Patrick Henry stirred the Virginia House of Burgesses with a speech opposing the Stamp Act. He proclaimed that if his condemnation of this Act "be treason...make the most of it!"[14] The Sons of Liberty in Boston burned a mock figure of Andrew Oliver, the Stamp Master in Boston, destroyed one of his buildings at the docks, and smashed the windows, furniture, and paneling in his home. A week or so after these events, another mob stormed the home of Lt. Governor Thomas Hutchinson, destroying a collection of books and old documents that Hutchinson was planning to use to write a history of Massachusetts. Hutchinson described the action thus:

> Not contented with tearing off all the wainscot and hangings and splitting the doors to pieces they beat down the Partition walls and although that alone cost them near two hours they cut down the cupola and they began to take the plate and boards from the roof...The garden fence was laid flat and all my trees &c broke down to the ground. Such ruins were never seen in America.[15]

Intimidated, most of the tax collectors resigned from their posts.

These "Sons of Liberty," as the rebels became known, led similar riots in Newport, Rhode Island, New York City, Pennsylvania, Maryland, and South Carolina. In each case, mobs took to the streets and Stamp Masters were burned in effigy, or worse. As the recently-arrived Governor of New York commented in November, 1765:

> The Tumults which have been raised in different parts of the Continent and which have been artfully fomented by ill designing people, have spread so much terror, that the Officers appointed for the execution of the Act, have resigned their posts and I am sorry to observe that the Power of Govern[men]t was too weak to protect them from the insults they were threatened with.[16]

Figure 7.3 Thomas Hutchinson | At different times Lt. Governor and Acting Governor of Massachusetts, 1758-1774 Thomas Hutchinson, was a thorn in the side of the Massachusetts patriots throughout the pre-Revolutionary War years and vice versa. Hutchinson had an ardent interest in the history of the colonies, and before his death began work on a three volume History of the Province of Massachusetts Bay; the third volume was published posthumously. He was replaced as Governor by General Thomas Gage in 1774. This image is taken from *The Life of Thomas Hutchinson, Royal Governor of the Province of Massachusetts Bay* by James K. Hosmer

Artist: Copley
Source: *The Life of Thomas Hutchinson, Royal Governor of the Province of Massachusetts Bay*

Meanwhile, in August, 1765, the Massachusetts House of Representatives had issued a circular letter calling on all of the colonies to send representatives to a Congress that would consider the nature and implications of the Stamp Act. Nine colonies sent 27 representatives to the meeting, which convened in New York on October 7, 1765. The Congress issued the following: a *Declaration of the Rights and Grievances of the Colonies*, a petition to the king for economic relief, and a petition to Parliament for repeal of the Stamp Act. It was, the drafters insisted,

> ...the indispensable duty of these colonies, to the best of sovereigns, to the mother country, and to themselves, to

> endeavour by a loyal and dutiful address to his Majesty, and humble applications to both Houses of Parliament, to procure the repeal of the Act for granting and applying certain stamp duties, of all clauses of any other Acts of Parliament, whereby the jurisdiction of the Admiralty is extended as aforesaid, and of the other late Acts for the restriction of American commerce.[17]

Although only nine colonies sent representatives to the Congress, with the important colony of Virginia being absent, the legislatures of all of the colonies except one voted to accept the Resolves. The Congress was an important first step toward united colonial action.

The Colonies Apply Economic Pressure

Perhaps more important than the actions of the Stamp Act Congress, and even the "Stamp Act Riots" that rocked almost every colony, were the boycotts the colonists imposed on British goods. New York merchants first boycotted British goods; those in other colonial cities soon followed. Colonial women agreed not to buy or drink tea or buy British cloth for their dresses. "Sage and sassafras" took the place of tea, and homespun garments became the fashion. British merchants reacted by pressing Parliament to realize the extent to which the welfare of the mother country was tied to the economic well-being of the American colonies. When the Marquis of Rockingham followed George Grenville as Prime Minister, the temperament of Parliament changed. This new attitude was reflected by the aging William Pitt who insisted that, while he was "no courtier of America[,]...the Stamp Act [must] be *repealed absolutely, totally*, and *immediately.*" At the same time, he also recommended that "the sovereign authority of this country over the colonies, [should] be asserted in as strong terms as can be devised."[18]

Thus pressured by British merchants and its own members, Parliament repealed the Stamp Act in February, 1766, with the following comment read into Parliamentary record:

> Whereas an Act was passed in the last session of Parliament entitled, An Act for granting and applying certain stamp duties...and whereas the continuance of the said Act would be attended with many inconveniencies, and may be productive of consequences greatly detrimental to the commercial interests of these kingdoms; may it therefore please your most excellent Majesty that it may be enacted...in this present Parliament assembled...that from and after the first day of May, one thousand seven hundred and sixty-six, the above-mentioned Act...shall be, and is and are hereby repealed and made void to all intents and purposes whatsoever.[19]

When news of the repeal of the Stamp Act reached America, general rejoicing ensued, so much so that the colonists paid little attention to the accompanying Declaratory Act. This act echoed William Pitt's sentiments by delineating clearly the relationship between the colonies and the mother country. In all future endeavors, the colonies were

> ...to be subordinate unto, and dependent upon the imperial crown and parliament of Great Britain; and that parliament...assembled, hath, and of right ought to have, full power and authority to make laws and statutes of sufficient force and validity to bind the colonies and people of America, subjects of the crown of Great Britain, in all cases whatsoever.[20]

7.3.5 The Townshend Duties: External Taxes to Regulate Trade

The following year, the colonists learned the implications of the Declaratory Act when Parliament created the Townshend Duties. Charles Townshend, Chancellor of the Exchequer, proposed a new set of taxes for the colonies, one based on the colonists' distinctions between internal and external taxation. The Americans did not like internal taxes, so he planned to give them external ones. There were three primary Townshend Acts. The first, the Restraining Act, was aimed at New York for its refusal to provide for British troops. It nullified all legislation of the New York colonial assembly. The second act tightened British control of colonial trade. The most onerous was the third act, which placed duties on colonial imports of glass, lead, paint, paper, and tea. It also set up a Board of Customs Commissioners in Boston to oversee collection of these duties. The Townshend Acts also established four Vice-Admiralty courts in the colonies that would try those who attempted to evade the taxes by smuggling.

The colonialists had reacted to earlier acts by intimidating stamp tax collectors. They were not constrained by the British Navy that would be anchored off the harbors of major ports in order to collect the duties. An added aggravation was the fact that the new taxes were intended to pay British government officials residing in the colonies. Up to this time, the colonial assemblies had paid the salaries of royal government officials and therefore were able to influence officials by using what has been called "the power of the purse." Threats of withholding payment of salaries or other benefits often influenced a stubborn governor or tax collector in the colonies' favor. Once imposed, these new taxes clearly would release British officials from financial dependence on the colonial assemblies.

Again, as with their reactions to the Sugar and Stamp Acts, the colonials were galvanized into action. They put boycotts into effect, and colonists like John Dickinson argued that Parliament did not have the power to levy either internal or external taxes on the colonies. Dickinson declared in his *Letters from a Pennsylvania Farmer*: "We *are taxed* without our own consent, expressed by ourselves or our representatives. We are therefore ---------- SLAVES!"[21] These essays were printed in nearly every colonial newspaper and became as popular and influential as *Common Sense,* published in 1776.

Similarly, Sam Adams and James Otis wrote a circular letter in which they agreed that all parliamentary taxation was illegal, warned that the new duties would be used to pay colonial officers, and invited the other colonies to join in the boycott taking place in Massachusetts. Colonial women also formed groups called the Daughters of Liberty, which agreed not to drink tea or buy any English products, just as they had done in an earlier boycott. The women got down spinning wheels from their attics and began to make their clothes rather than buy the English products. When Townshend died in 1768, all duties except that on tea were repealed.

7.3.6 Trouble Continues to Brew: The Boston Massacre

Because the Sons of Liberty continued to intimidate merchants and enforce the boycott, Thomas Hutchinson, now acting governor of Massachusetts, requested that British soldiers be relocated to Boston. Not surprisingly, the arrival of the troops created great consternation among the Bostonians. Benjamin Franklin mused on the presence of troops in Boston from his perspective in England:

> I am glad to hear that Matters were yet quiet at Boston, but fear that they will not continue long so. Some Indiscretion on the part of their warmer People, or of the Soldiery, I am extreamly [sic] apprehensive may occasion a tumult; and if Blood is once drawn, there is no foreseeing how far the Mischief may spread."[22]

Franklin was correct in his fear that blood might be shed. On one wintry day in March, 1770, a crowd of boys threw rocks and snowballs at the British soldiers standing guard outside the Boston Customs House. There were some men in the crowd who worked in the local shipyards, one of them being Crispus Attucks, a black man of Wampanoag and African descent. According to bystanders, one soldier was knocked down by the rock-laced snowballs, and someone, perhaps even an onlooker wishing to stir up trouble, yelled "fire." Regardless of who cried out, the soldiers fired on the crowd, and, when the smoke cleared, five people lay dead or dying, and eight more were wounded. Crispus Attucks was among the first to die.

Boston went into an uproar. A mass meeting was held at Faneuil Hall where those in attendance issued a statement calling for the removal of troops from the city. Thomas Hutchinson moved the troops to an island in the harbor and promised to put to trial the soldiers involved in the massacre. But no lawyer wanted to take the case; even those who were loyal to the crown refused. Finally John Adams, a well-known patriot and cousin of Sam Adams, agreed to defend the soldiers. He made this unpopular move because Adams believed that the men had a right to be represented in court. He may also have wanted to avoid any embarrassing questions about who first yelled "fire." When the trials ended, all but two of the soldiers were acquitted. The two who were found guilty of manslaughter were sentenced only to branding on their thumbs.

Figure 7.4 Crispus Attucks | Crispus Attucks was among the first colonials killed in the skirmish between the Bostonians and British soldiers in what was called the "Boston Massacre."

Author: Unknown
Source: Library of Congress

The two years following the Boston Massacre were ones in which colonial tempers simmered without coming to a full boil. The Townshend duties were repealed, except for that on tea (which the colonies continued to smuggle in from Holland). Although, the Stamp Act was gone, the Sugar, Currency, and Quartering Acts remained as reminders of America's colonial status. And though British soldiers had been withdrawn from Boston, they remained in the colony while the British navy still patrolled the Massachusetts coastline.

7.3.7 The Evolution of a Formal Theory of Revolt

During this period, a philosophy of revolt crystallized in American thinking. The elements, logically laid out, were these:

- the American colonists were citizens of the British Empire;
- their aim was not independence from Britain but only to be given the "natural rights" to which they were entitled;
- one of these rights was the right to be taxed only by elected bodies in which they were actually represented;
- the colonies were not represented in Parliament, did not recognize virtual representation, and therefore could not be taxed by Parliament.

Throughout this theory ran the issues on which the colonies and the mother country could not agree as well as reflections of the impact of the colonial experience on their thinking. Colonists insisted that they had a right to be represented in Parliament by representatives they elected and that they could not be taxed by councils in which they were not represented. As an inevitable conclusion of Locke's natural rights theory also came just the suggestion of an idea that the colonists were only beginning to consider: if the natural rights of British colonists were not protected, then the only option was to separate from the mother country.

7.3.8 Before You Move On...

Key Concepts

In the nine years following the end of the French and Indian War, the colonies and the mother country clashed on issues involving taxation, regulation of trade, and the rights of English under the British constitution. These rights, defined most recently in the English Bill of Rights of 1689, were cited repeatedly as the colonists argued that, because they were not represented in Parliament, they were not subject to the laws, and especially to the taxes, created by that body. While the British adhered to the idea of "virtual" representation, the colonists decried the notion as inappropriate to their peculiar circumstances.

During these years, the British government made several attempts to tighten its control on the colonies. The Proclamation Line was designed to keep the colonists on the eastern seaboard, while the Sugar Act and the Townshend duties attempted to regulate trade and the Sugar and Stamp Acts to raise revenues to defray the costs of maintaining the colonies. For the colonists, the "internal" taxes of the latter were anathema and beyond the accepted authority of a mother country. Although a two-year lull followed the violence of the Boston Massacre, problems were far from being resolved, and the first shots of the Revolutionary War were only a few short years away.

Test Yourself

1. The purpose of the Proclamation Line of 1763 was to

   a. keep the colonists on the eastern seaboard.

   b. raise a revenue to defray the costs of war.

   c. encourage colonial movement past the Appalachian Mountains.

   d. reward the colonists for their participation in the French and Indian War.

2. Which of the following Parliamentary acts were designed to "raise a revenue"?

   a. Proclamation Line of 1763

   b. Currency Act

   c. Sugar Act

   d. Declaratory Act

3. The act that claimed Parliament's right to legislate for the colonies in "all cases whatsoever" was the

   a. Declaratory Act.

   b. Currency Act.

   c. Proclamation Line of 1763.

   d. Townshend Act.

4. The most effective tools used by the colonists in getting the Stamp Act repealed was

   a. the Boston Massacre.

   b. rioting against the Stamp Masters.

   c. the boycott of English goods.

   d. the arguments of the colonists against internal taxation.

5. The colonies made a very clear distinction between

   a. internal and external taxation by Parliament.

   b. taxes to regulate trade v. those designed to raise a revenue.

   c. actual v. virtual representation in Parliament.

   d. All of the above

   e. None of the above

See page 269 for answers

7.4 THE DOWNWARD SLIDE TO REVOLUTION, 1772-1775

Two incidents in June 1772 marked the beginning of the end of the calm that followed the Boston Massacre. The first involved a British schooner, the *Gaspee*, which had been patrolling for smugglers when it ran aground near Providence, Rhode Island. The townspeople boarded the vessel, removed the crew, and destroyed the ship. Though a commission of inquiry looked into the incident, no one could be found to testify. The second occurrence centered in Boston, a city that had long been a thorn to the Empire and the royal governor, Thomas Hutchinson. Concerned about a recent announcement from Hutchinson that salaries of royal officials would come from customs revenues rather than the colonial assembly, Sam Adams persuaded the Boston town meeting to create a Committee of Correspondence. This committee would facilitate the exchange of ideas between those in Boston and other towns of Massachusetts. Other colonies soon followed the example of Massachusetts with their own Committees of Correspondence that became one more example of inter-colony cooperation. These Committees were effective in stirring up and coordinating colonial expressions of resentment about British rule.

7.4.1 The Tea Act and Party of 1773

The lull before the storm ended permanently in 1773. At that time, in a move designed to help the nearly bankrupt British East India Company, the British passed the Tea Act. This Act made it easier for the British East India Company to sell tea in the colonies by eliminating the duties on the tea coming into England. The Act also permitted the company to sell its tea directly to customers in the colonies, instead of going through colonial merchants. Tea was thus cheaper than previously and, in fact, the colonists could now buy tea more cheaply than could those living in England.

If members of Parliament and the ministers of George III thought that the Americans would be pleased with the act and the ability of colonials to buy cheap tea, they were sadly mistaken. American leaders and the Committees of Correspondence railed against the act, declaring it to be an underhanded means for getting the colonists to pay a tax on tea. They argued that not only would the act deprive American merchants of profits but also the tax money would be used to pay public officials in the colonies, thus depriving the colonial assemblies of the "power of the purse." A member of the Sons of Liberty in the state of New York put it bluntly: "Whoever shall aid or abet, or in any manner assist, in the introduction of tea from any place whatsoever, into this colony...shall be deemed an enemy to the liberties of America."[23]

The colonial reaction to the Tea Act was strong and swift. The Sons of Liberty in many of the major towns forced company agents to resign and many ships loaded with tea to return to England. In Boston, however, when Governor Hutchison refused to let the ships depart, meetings were held to protest this unconscionable action. One meeting was held on December 16, 1773 at the Old South Church in Boston, during which the delegates drafted one last plea to Hutchinson to address their grievances. When the town meeting reconvened the following day to receive the governor's response, the members were greeted by the sheriff of Suffolk who held a command from Hutchinson for them to disband.

Several people at the meeting knew that, if Hutchinson still refused to let the tea ships sail, they had an alternative plan. When news of the Hutchinson's final refusal reached Sam Adams, he ended a speech with words some had been anticipating: "This meeting can do no more to save the country."[24] Thus, disguised as Indians, fifty young men left the church and headed for the docks. A crowd watched as the "Indians" threw 342 chests of tea overboard. When their job was completed, the crowd broke up and awaited the reaction of the British government. John Adams, who was not nearly the revolutionary that his cousin Sam was, wrote in his diary: "3 Cargoes of Bohea Tea were emptied into the Sea. This is the most magnificent moment of all. There is a Dignity, a Majesty, a Sublimity, in this last Effort of the patriots that I greatly admire."[25]

Figure 7.5 Boston Tea Party | On December 16, 1773, a group of "Indians" stormed a British tea ship anchored in the Boston harbor and dumped 342 chests of tea overboard. The reaction of the British would eventually lead the colonies to revolution and independence.

Author: Lithograph by Sarony & Major
Source: Library of Congress

In early 1774, just months after the Tea Party, the British Crown and Parliament decided that the time had come to punish Boston and all of Massachusetts Bay for its continuing recalcitrant activities. A furious Parliament quickly enacted four Coercive Acts:

1. The *Boston Port Bill* closed the port of Boston until the town paid for the tea.
2. The *Massachusetts Government Act* revoked the Massachusetts charter and changed the legislative assembly so that no longer would the upper house be elected. Rather it would now be appointed by the crown. A final insult was the provision that in no town in Massachusetts could there be more than one town meeting a year.
3. The *Administration of Justice Act* specified that any person charged with committing murder while enforcing royal authority in Massachusetts was to be tried in England or in another colony. The Act was modestly entitled: *An act for the impartial administration of justice in the cases of persons questioned for any acts done by them in the execution of the law, or for the suppression of riots and tumults, in the province of the Massachusetts Bay, in New England.*[26]
4. The *Quartering Act* directed the royal governor of Massachusetts to requisition houses for quartering British troops.

These acts were followed the same year by the *Quebec Act* which confirmed the following: Roman Catholicism was the official religion in Quebec; there would be no elected legislature in Canada; and that the new boundaries of Quebec included the western lands north of the Ohio River, lands that had long been claimed by Pennsylvania, Virginia, and Connecticut. All of these provisions were anathema to the colonists, who had come to prize religious toleration and representative government, and who still looked to the land west of the mountains as theirs to settle.

The four *Coercive Acts* and the *Quebec Act* quickly became known in America as the "Intolerable Acts." The message spread throughout the colonies that, while Boston may be the target at the moment, none of the colonies were safe from the long arm of the British Crown. While Parliament had issued the *Coercive Acts* to punish Massachusetts, the acts had the effect of uniting the colonies. In Virginia, Thomas Jefferson called on the Virginia Assembly to set aside June 1, the date when the *Boston Port Act* went into effect, as a day of prayer and fasting. When dissolved by the royal governor of Virginia, the assembly met in a nearby tavern and drew up a resolution calling for a Continental Congress.

7.4.2 The First Continental Congress, 1774

Several previous instances displayed inter-colonial cooperation; none was as significant as the Continental Congress that met in Philadelphia in September, 1774. Its proceedings explained that, "justly alarmed at the arbitrary proceedings of Parliament," the colonies had elected representatives to consider a response to Parliament.[27] An impressive array of colonial leaders were in attendance, including Samuel Adams and John Adams of Massachusetts, John Jay of New York, Joseph Galloway and John Dickinson of Pennsylvania, and Patrick Henry, Richard Henry Lee, Thomas Jefferson, and George Washington of Virginia. Participation in the Congress was better than in the Stamp Act Congress, with only Georgia withholding a delegation.

The Congress set to work and moved quickly to make American displeasure with the *Intolerable Acts* known to the British Crown. First, the delegates approved the *Suffolk Resolves*, which declared the Intolerable Acts null and void. Second, they drafted a *Declaration of American Rights* specifying that Parliament had no right to pass legislation that interfered with the internal workings of the colonies and including a list of grievances leveled at the Crown and Parliament. According to the statement of rights, each colonist was entitled to protection under the law of the realm, including the 1689 Bill of Rights and Act of Religious Toleration; any person could petition the king; and all colonists were entitled to "life, liberty and property." It further reminded the British government that the Americans had "never ceded to any foreign power whatever a right to dispose of [these privileges] without their consent."[28] Most probably, few Americans expected this tactic to bring the relief they wanted, however. Indeed, John Adams wrote to Patrick Henry, "I expect no redress, but, on the contrary, increased resentment and double vengeance."

The list of grievances against George III and Parliament included in the *Declaration of American Rights* was not unlike those that would appear in the *Declaration of Independence*. The delegates railed against the Admiralty Courts, which had always been intended to deprive the colonists of the right to a fair trial, against the establishment of the Catholic Church in the Canadian provinces, against the forcible quartering of British troops in American homes, and against the maintenance of a standing army in times of peace. Before concluding the meeting, the Congress created the Continental Association of 1774, whose purpose was to oversee a boycott of all British goods. The representatives vowed:

1. That from and after the first day of December next, we will not import into British America, from Great-Britain or Ireland, any goods, wares or merchandize whatsoever...
2. That we will neither import, nor purchase any slave imported, after the first day of December next; after which time, we will wholly discontinue the slave trade...
3. As a non-consumption agreement, strictly adhered to, will be an effectual security for the observation of the non-importation, we, as above, solemnly agree and associate, that, from this day, we will not purchase or use any tea imported on account of the East-India Company, or any on which a duty hath been or shall be paid.[29]

The boycott was to be put into effect by September 5, 1774. The Congress gave power to the Committees of Correspondence, along with the Continental Association, to oversee the boycott of British goods and to make sure that violators be "universally condemned as the enemies of American liberty."[30]

During the meeting, discussion inevitably arose about the relationship of the colonies to the mother country. In the course of these conversations, Joseph Galloway of Pennsylvania proposed an imperial union with Britain, in which Parliament could legislate for the colonies, but the legislation would not take effect until approved by an American Assembly. The proposal was defeated by one vote only; the "independent thinking" of the colonists, as George III called it, was fully evident. Before disbanding, the Congress agreed to meet one year later to consider the response of the Crown to its enactments. By the time the Second Continental Congress convened in May, 1775, however, the firing at Lexington and Concord had occurred and the first Americans lay dead.

It soon became evident that the colonists would not get their hoped for response from the King and Parliament. Shortly after the arrival of the petitions from the colonies, George III complained that "blows must be exchanged to determine whether [the American colonies] are to be subject to this country or independent."[31] And in early 1775, Parliament declared that Massachusetts was in rebellion and specified that New England could not trade with any country outside of the British Empire. In May, 1775, Lord North, the Prime Minister, presented a *Conciliatory Proposition*, which was as far as Parliament would go to meet the demands of the Americans. The *Proposition* affirmed that Parliament would continue to legislate for the colonies, but that any taxes imposed would be to regulate trade. In addition, the monies collected would go to the individual colonies, as long as they agreed to assume partial responsibility for their own defense. These provisions, while perfectly reasonable in the eyes of the British, far from met colonial expectations, and when the Second Continental Congress convened in May, 1775, they were faced with both an unsatisfactory response and with British "aggression" at Lexington and Concord.

7.4.3 Lexington and Concord, April 19, 1775

In 1775, the situation in Massachusetts Bay was delicate and deteriorating. The citizens of the colony chafed at the continuing British occupation of Boston. The British, too, were on edge, expecting a colonial uprising at any time. Colonial militia existed throughout the colonies, composed of volunteer forces of local men who provided emergency defense against enemies, such as hostile Indians. They were originally formed to provide protection in the absence of available British forces. By 1775, the British were the enemy that concerned the militia. To prepare for their defense, the militia maintained stores of weapons, shot, and powder at various locations. General Gage, the British military commander in Massachusetts, learned that the militia had such a store in Concord. He had received orders to disarm the rebels and arrest their leaders. By all accounts, Gage was sympathetic to the Americans; he had personal ties to the colonies, as his wife was from New Jersey. He therefore tried not to provoke the people of Massachusetts, even as he did his duty for the British Crown.

Sidebar 7.1: Battles At Lexington and Concord

- **Location**: Middlesex County, Massachusetts Bay, the road from Boston to Concord
- **American Commanders:** Colonel James Barrett, Colonel John Buttrick, Dr. Joseph Warren, Captain John Parker, Brigadier General William Heath
- **British Commanders:** Lieutenant-General Hugh Percy, Major John Pitcairn, Major-General Francis Smith
- **American Force:** 3,800 total: 77 at Lexington, 400 at Concord and fewer numbers at other points
- **British Force**: 1,500 total: 400 at Lexington, 100 at Concord; number varies at other points
- **American Losses:** 49
- **British Losses:** 73
- **Who won?** The Americans

At the same time, by early spring, George III had lost all patience with the American colonies, believing it time to teach them a lesson. He and his ministers were well aware that each of the colonies had formed colonial militia, the Minutemen, so called by their vow to be ready for military action at a moment's notice. The British were also under the impression, as Major John Pitcairn commented, "that one active campaign, a smart action, and burning two or three of their towns, will set everything to rights."[32] As it turned out, Pitcairn was overly optimistic. On April 14, Thomas Gage, commander of the British garrison in Boston, sent 1,000 troops to move against the colonials at Lexington and then Concord, where, he had heard, the Americans were stockpiling weapons and gunpowder.

Despite Pitcairn's best efforts to keep the colonists in the dark about his plans, by mid-April, the Americans were receiving alarming information concerning British intentions. They knew through sources that Gage was ordered to seize the munitions and leaders of the rebellion, such as Samuel Adams and John Hancock. When Gage took action to prevent news of the British movements from leaving Boston and to locate the leaders, his actions confirmed the colonists' fears. Worse for Gage, he was too late. As the British made preparations to march, both Samuel Adams and John Hancock had already slipped away from Boston and were staying with Hancock's relatives in Lexington. The militia stores in Concord had been moved out to other towns for safekeeping, and Paul Revere and William Dawes were riding towards Lexington, spreading the word that the British were on their way.

By the time the British left Boston in the early hours of April 19, Adams and Hancock were safely out of Lexington. The riders, Revere, Dawes, and others, continued to pass the news. A system of alarm was engaged using bonfires, bells, and other means to alert the people

Sidebar 7.2: Colonial Fighting Forces

The colonial militia had been created in most of the colonies in the seventeenth century. This militia was composed of able-bodied men in every colony (except Pennsylvania where Quakers eschewed violence) who were responsible for furnishing and caring for their own weapons. The Minutemen grew out of the tension following the Tea Party of December, 1773. In most colonies they were an elite arm of the colonial militia, ready to assemble at a moment's notice, hence the name. The Continental Army was created by the second Continental Congress and charged with fighting the war against Britain. The colonial militia continued to participate in the fighting until the war's end.

of Massachusetts to the approach of the possibly hostile British forces. The Lexington militia assembled, and more volunteers in the surrounding countryside answered the call as well. As for the British, their morning was a miserable affair. Boston in 1775 was almost an island, with only one narrow passage connecting it to the mainland. Rather than march on foot out of Boston, the British troops were packed onto barges and transported across the bay, where they were then forced to disembark in deep water. The 700 wet and muddy troops formed up and began to make the seventeen-mile journey to Concord, passing through difficult, swampy terrain. The British had hoped to catch the militia unaware. Instead, they were surprised and alarmed to see that everyone on the road to Concord already knew they were coming. Colonel Smith sent Major Pitcairn and his troops ahead, hoping that the speed of a quick march might still be somewhat of a surprise to the militia. He also sent word back to Boston for reinforcements.

On April 19, the first "battle" of the Revolutionary war then took place. Pitcairn arrived in Lexington to find the militia of seventy-seven awaiting the British on the green; the seventy-seven included the Minutemen, who had been quickly assembled after the warnings of Revere and Dawes. There was also a crowd of abou 130 bystanders. Evidently these colonials had planned a protest only; rather than ignoring the militia and continuing

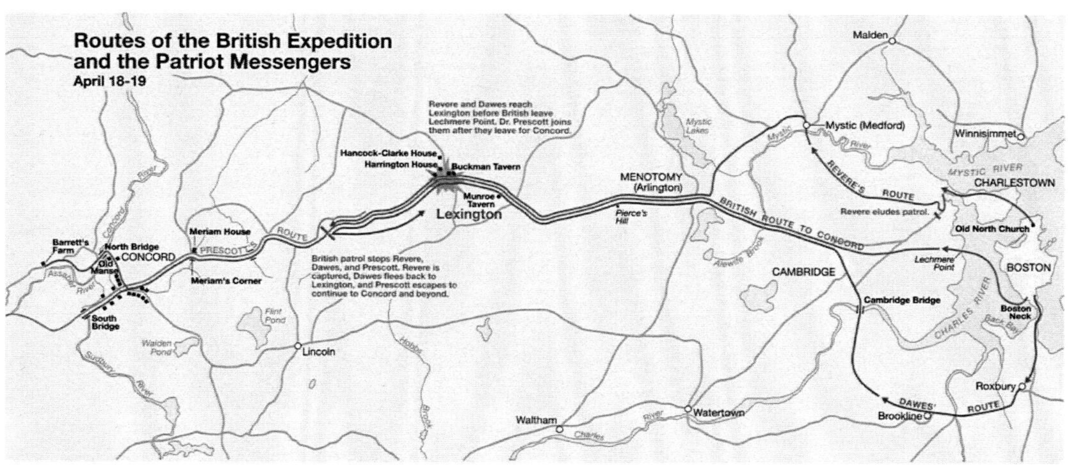

Figure 7.6 Routes of the British Expedition and the Patriot Messengers | This maps is a depiction of the outbound routes taken by Patriot riders and British troops in the Battles of Lexington and Concord on April 19, 1775.

Author: United States National Park Service
Source: Wikimedia Commons

to march down the road adjacent to the green, however, the officer leading the march, Marine Lieutenant Jesse Adair, decided to form up on the green itself in order to disperse the militia. But the militia stood their ground, facing the hundreds of British troops, even as Major Pitcairn arrived and ordered the colonists to leave, shouting "Disperse, you damned rebels! You dogs, run!" Some records say the militia did begin to do just that when suddenly a shot rang out. It seems clear that whoever fired the shot was not actually on the green. Other than that, nothing is known about the person who, in the words of Ralph Waldo Emerson, fired the "shot heard round the world," so called because it marked the beginning not only of the American Revolution, but the inspiration for the French Revolution as well.[33]

In the moments before the shot was fired, both the militia and the British were in disarray; the sound of the shot was all that was needed to set off tragedy. The British troops, tired from lack of sleep and the wet march and nervous at being in hostile territory, opened a volley on the militia. While some of the Minutemen ran, others did not. After firing their volleys, the British troops charged the remaining militia with bayonets. Eight militiamen were killed, including Captain Parker's cousin, Jonas Parker, who was bayoneted. Ten were wounded, including a slave, Prince Estabrook. The British troops then turned their attention to the village, firing at will. Colonel Smith, who was still travelling with the slower troops, heard the sounds of the gunfire and hurried to Lexington. He brought the British back in line and then moved them off towards Concord, leaving the people of Lexington to tend to their own dead and wounded.

Colonel Smith later sent the following account to General Gage, governor of Massachusetts:

> [When Pitcairn approached Lexington] a body of country people drawn up in military order, with arms and accoutrements, and, as appeared after, loaded; and that they had posted some men in a dwelling and Meeting-house. Our troops advanced towards them, without any intention of injuring them, further than to inquire the reason of their being thus assembled...[when] one of them fired...and three or four more jumped over a wall and fired from behind it among the soldiers; on which the troops returned it, and killed several of them."[34]

Meanwhile, the militia in Concord did not know what had happened in Lexington, other than that shots had been fired. They had intended to confront the British but retreated when they saw Colonel Smith's full force on the road, a force which outnumbered theirs by almost three to one. Their commander, Colonel James Barrett, decided to surrender the town and moved his men out of Concord to a nearby hillside where they could watch the British. They were joined by militia from surrounding towns, which increased their number to several hundred.

The British combed the town for supplies as the militia looked on; most of the provisions had been removed, but the troops under Smith were able to seize and destroy some food and munitions. The British, now outnumbered, fell back across a bridge where command fell to Captain Laurie, a less experienced officer. Laurie, with fewer than one hundred soldiers, was facing possibly as many as 400 colonials. The Americans killed fourteen British troops at the North Bridge, and, within an hour of fighting, Colonel Smith turned his troops back on the road to Boston. By this time, the militia and Minutemen numbered over a thousand.

Colonel Smith well understood the position he and his troops were in. The road from Concord to Boston meanders in a general west to east direction. In 1775, it was narrow by today's standards and had in many places walls along its sides, confining the troops marching along it and forcing them to form columns. The militia and minutemen were able to leave their towns and villages and come near the road and wait for the long red line of British soldiers. Then they could take their shots, retreat into the shelter of the woods, and move down the road to find a new position from which to attack. The British, marching on foot and having to follow the road, could neither outrun nor hide from the colonists. They were exposed and had no cover from enemy fire for the full seventeen miles back through Lexington to Boston with the militia firing on them. A British soldier explained the situation thus:

> ...upon on our leaving Concord to return to Boston, they began to fire on us from behind the walls, ditches, trees, etc., which, as we marched, increased to a very great degree, and continued without the intermission of five minutes altogether, for, I believe, upwards of eighteen miles; so that I can't think but it must have been a pre-concerted scheme in them, to attack the King's troops the first favourable opportunity that [was] offered.[35]

By the time the redcoats reached Boston, they had lost three times more men than had the colonists. In commenting on the shots exchanged at Lexington, Benjamin Franklin expressed outrage to a member of Parliament: "[You] have doomed my country to destruction. You have begun to burn our towns and murder our people"[36] As if the situation at Lexington and Concord were not bad enough, news reached the southern colonies that a member of Parliament had suggested several months earlier, in January 1775, that a general emancipation of American slaves would "humble the high aristocratic spirit of Virginia and the southern colonies."[37] The measure did not pass, but that did nothing to reassure the Americans.

The actions at Lexington and Concord were accidents, but given the high tension of the times, they were all that was needed to spark a war. General Gage, in his attempt to prevent a war, helped to cause one. His miscalculations concerning the people of Massachusetts Bay and the poor security and mishandling of his internal communications led to his failure to preserve the peace. Afterwards, he would be blamed by the colonists throughout New England, members of the British government, and even his own soldiers for the events of April 19, 1775.

7.4.4 Before You Move On...

Key Concepts

The lull in action that followed the Boston Massacre ended in 1773 with the passage of the Tea Act. Although this act actually lowered the price of the tea in the colonies, making it cheaper than in the mother country, the colonists were enraged, and insisted that the tea ships return to England. When this did not happen, and after petitioning Governor Thomas Hutchinson with unsatisfactory results, a group of "Indians" boarded the tea ship in the Boston Harbor and threw its content overboard. At this point, there was no turning back, and in the next year and a half relations between mother country and colonies deteriorated. Britain responded to the action of Massachusetts with a series of acts designed not only to punish, but also to bring sweeping changes to the government and economic endeavors of the Bay colony. The Boston port was closed to traffic and even the long-revered New England town meetings were disbanded.

In a spirit of cooperation reflective of the Committees of Correspondence, the colonists, with the exception of Georgia, sent representatives to the First Continental Congress, whose purpose it was to respond formally to the Intolerable Acts by drafting a list of grievances and a statement of the rights of the colonists. The delegates agreed to meet in one year's time to consider the Crown's response, but before this Second Continental Congress could assemble, the first shots of the Revolutionary War had been fired at Lexington and Concord, and this Congress would become involved in leading the war effort and providing a government for the new American states.

Test Yourself

1. The colonists did not necessarily object to the principle of taxation, but rather how the tax money would be applied.

   a. True

   b. False

2. Which of the following Parliamentary Acts was not one of the Intolerable Acts?

   a. Boston Port Bill

   b. Massachusetts Government Act

   c. Quebec Act

   d. Tea Act

3. The purpose of the First Continental Congress was to

   a. raise an army.

   b. draft a declaration of war against Great Britain.

   c. compile a list of grievances against the British government.

   d. draft a Declaration of American Rights.

4. Which of the following as a provision of the Quebec Act?
   a. Quebec was to be annexed to Massachusetts Bay.
   b. The boundaries of Quebec were extended into the Ohio Valley.
   c. A state of war existed between England and France.
   d. Tea ships forced to leave the colonies would be redirected to the St. Lawrence Seaway.

See page 269 for answers

7.5 Conclusion

The twenty years beginning with the onset of war in 1754 were ones of turmoil between Great Britain and her American colonies. British-American success in the French and Indian War had given the American colonists the expectation that they would be rewarded for their participation in the war and, among other things, allowed to enter into the area west of the Allegheny and Appalachian Mountains. But the Crown had other ideas, and, rather than giving the colonists access to the land they had so recently fought for, the British government decided to tighten its reins on its American subjects. Salutary neglect, long the policy toward the colonies, was discarded as Parliament passed a series of acts designed to raise monies to defray the costs of protecting and maintaining the colonies. American leaders quickly created and publicized arguments in which they defined their rights under the British constitution. They argued vehemently against virtual representation, maintaining that they could only be taxed by a legislature that they themselves elected. Nor would they accept taxes that were designed to raise revenues rather than regulating trade, and internal taxes were equally unacceptable.

In many ways, even in 1763, the year the French and Indian War ended, it was almost too late to achieve any type of consensus between the colonies and the mother country; the American experience of the former had led the colonists to take for granted ideas that were foreign to the British. Measures like the Sugar and Stamp Acts, which raised revenues and taxed the colonies internally, the Declaratory Act, which proclaimed the right of Parliament to legislate for the colonies in "all cases whatsoever," and the Intolerable Acts, which punished Massachusetts for the Tea Party, only heightened the tension that was building. And while conditions worsened between mother country and colonies, there was developing in America a spirit of inter-colony cooperation reflected in the Committees of Correspondence and the First and Second Continental Congresses. The First Continental Congress, representing all of the colonies except Georgia, drafted a statement of American rights, and the Second Continental Congress would conduct a war against Britain and draft a *Declaration of Independence*. In the words of Thomas Paine, whose influential work *Common Sense* was published in 1776, the "cause of America" was becoming "in great measure the cause of all mankind."[38]

7.6 CRITICAL THINKING EXERCISES

- Read the following accounts of the skirmish at the Lexington Common on April 19, 1775 and answer the following questions:

  1. Do you detect differences in the events recounted?

  2. Why do you think these differences do or do not exist?

  3. Which account do you believe is most accurately describes what actually occurred on April 19, 1775?

  - *From the Annals of the Second Continental Congress:* "In April of 1775, general Gage, who in the course of the last year had taken possession of the town of Boston, in the province of Massachusetts-Bay, and still occupied it a garrison, on the 19th day of April, sent out from that place a large detachment of his army, who made an unprovoked assault on the inhabitants of the said province, at the town of Lexington, as appears by the affidavits of a great number of persons, some of whom were officers and soldiers of that detachment, murdered eight of the inhabitants, and wounded many others. From thence the troops proceeded in warlike array to the town of Concord, where they set upon another party of the inhabitants of the same province, killing several and wounding more, until compelled to retreat by the country people suddenly assembled to repel this cruel aggression."

  - *From Colonel Smith, a British soldier to General Gage, governor of Massachusetts Bay:* "[As we approached the Lexington Green] a body of country people drawn up in military order, with arms and accoutrements, and, as appeared after, loaded; and that they had posted some men in a dwelling and Meeting-house. Our troops advanced towards them, without any intention of injuring them, further than to inquire the reason of their being thus assembled...[when] one of them fired...and three or four more jumped over a wall and fired from behind it among the soldiers; on which the troops returned it, and killed several of them."[39]

- What did the Americans mean by "no taxation without representation"? On what experiences did they base this idea? Why did the British Parliament have a hard time understanding this concept?

- Why did the colonists believe that it was all right for Parliament to impose taxes to regulate trade, but not to raise revenues?

7.7 KEY TERMS

- Albany Congress
- John Adams
- Samuel Adams
- Battle of the Wilderness
- Boston Massacre
- Boston Tea Party
- Edward Braddock
- Coercive Acts and Quebec Act (Intolerable Acts)
- Colonial Militia
- Committees of Correspondence
- *Conciliatory Proposition*
- Currency Act, 1764
- John Dickinson: *Letters from a Pennsylvania Farmer*
- First Continental Congress: *Statement of Rights of the American People*
- French and Indian War
- The *Gaspee*
- George III
- George Grenville
- John Hancock
- Patrick Henry
- Internal v. external taxation
- Thomas Jefferson
- Lexington and Concord
- Mercantilism
- Minutemen
- "No taxation without representation"
- Thomas Paine: *Common Sense*
- Plan of Union
- Pontiac's War
- Proclamation Line of 1763
- Redcoats
- Paul Revere
- Salutary Neglect
- Second Continental Congress: *Declaration of Independence*
- Seven Years' War
- Sons of Liberty
- Stamp Act, 1765
- Sugar Act, 1764
- Taxation to regulate trade v. taxation to raise a revenue
- Tea Act of 1773
- Townshend Duties
- Treaty of Paris, 1763
- Vice Admiralty Courts
- Virtual v. actual representation
- Robert Walpole
- George Washington

7.8 CHRONOLOGY

The following chronology is a list of important dates and events associated with this chapter.

Date	Event
1754-1763	French and Indian War
1754	Albany Congress; Plan of Union
1755	Battle of Wilderness
1759	Annus Mirabilis (Year of Miracles)
1763	End of the Seven Years' War; Peace of Paris; Proclamation Line of 1763
1763-1764	Pontiac's War
1764	Sugar Act and Currency Act passed by Parliament
1765	The Stamp Act and Quartering Act (both create internal taxes) enacted by Parliament; Stamp Act Congress met in New York City
1766	Declaratory Acts; Riots in New York City over enforcement of the Quarting Act
1767	Townshend Acts passed; Colonial Resistance built
1769	Virginia Resolves introduced into the House of Burgesses; Royal Governor closed the House
1770	Boston Massacre; Townshend Acts repealed
1772	Gaspee Incident; Committees of Correspondence created in many colonies
1773	Tea Act went into effect; Boston Tea Party
1774	Coercive Acts and Quebec Act (Intolerable Acts) passed by Parliament; First Continental Congress assembled in September and approved Declaration of Rights and Grievances; Continental Association formed to enforce boycotts
1775	Lexington and Concord; Second Continental Congress convened; drafted the Olive Branch Petition; Patrick Henry's "Give me Liberty or give me Death"; Minutemen and Redcoats clash at Lexington and Concord
1776	Paine's Common Sense Published; Second Continental Congress accepted the Declaration of Independence

7.9 BIBLIOGRAPHY

Alberts, Robert C. *A Charming Field for an Encounter: The Story of George Washington's Fort Necessity* Washington: Office of Publications, National Park Service, U.S. Department of the Interior, 1975.

Ammerman, David. *In the Common Cause: American Response to the Coercive Acts of 1774.* Charlottesville: University of Virginia Press, 1974.

Anderson, Fred. *Crucible of War: The Seven Years' War and the Fate of the Empire in British North America, 1754-1766.* New York: Alfred A. Knopf.

Bailyn, Bernard, ed. *The Ideological Origins of the American Revolution.* 1992.

Bailyn, Bernard, ed. *Pamphlets of the American Revolution.* Harvard University Press, 1965.

Berkin, Carol. *Revolutionary Mothers: Women in the Struggle for America's Independence.* 2005.

Butler, Jon. *Becoming America: the Revolution before 1776.* 2000.

Declaration and Resolves of the First Continental Congress, History.org: http://www.history.org/Almanack/life/politics/polhis.cfm.

Draper, Theodore. *A Struggle for Power: The American Revolution.* New York: Random House, 1996.

Gipson, Lawrence Henry. *The Coming of the Revolution.* NY: Harper Torchbooks, 1853.

Journals of the First Continental Congress. Library of Congress.org.

McCullough, David. *1776.* New York: Simon and Schuster, 2005.

McCullough, David. *John Adams.* New York: Simon and Schuster Paperbacks, 2001.

Morgan, Edmund S. and Helen M. Morgan. *The Stamp Act Crisis: Prologue to Revolution.* 1962.

Nettels, Curtis P. *The Roots of American Civilization: A History of American Colonial Life.* New York: Appleton-Century-Crofts, 1963.

Paine, Thomas. *Common Sense.* American History Sourcebook, ed. Paul Halsall. Fordham.edu/halsall.

Quarles, Benjamin. The Negro in the American Revolution, 1961.

Resolutions of [the Second Continental] Congress on Lord North's Conciliatory Proposal. http://www.avalon.law.yale.edu.

A Royal Proclamation, October 1763. ushistory.org: http://www.ushistory.org/declaration/related/proc63.htm.

Smith, Page. *A New Age Now Begins*, vol. I, New York: McGraw-Hill Book Company, 1976.

The American Revolution.org: http://www.theamericanrevolution.org/documents.aspx.

The Events Leading to Independence. http://www.ushistory.org.

Tuchman, Barbara W. *The First Salute: A View of the American Revolution* .New York: Alfred A. Knopf, 1988.

Weigley, Russell F. *The American Way of War: A History of United States Military Strategy and Policy.* Bloomington: Indiana University Press, 1973.

Yale Law School. *The Avalon Project: Documents in Law, History and Diplomacy.* http://avalon.law.yale.edu/subject_menus/18th.asp.

7.10 END NOTES

1 Fred Anderson, *Crucible of War: The Seven Years' War and the Fate of the Empire in British North America, 1754-1766* (New York: Alfred A. Knopf), 745-747.

2 Robert C. Alberts, *A Charming Field for an Encounter: The Story of George Washington's Fort Necessity* (Washington: Office of Publications, National Park Service, U.S. Department of the Interior, 1975), 20.

3 Russell F. Weigley, *The American Way of War: A History of United States Military Strategy and Policy* (Bloomington: Indiana University Press, 1973) 3-18.

4 Lord Loudon quoted in Curtis P. Nettels. *The Roots of American Civilization: A History of American Colonial Life* (New York: Appleton-Century-Crofts, 1963), 595.

5 Nettels, *Roots of American Civilization,* 596.

6 Royal Proclamation of 1763, U.S. History.org: www.ushistory.org.

7 Theodore Draper. *A Struggle for Power: The American Revolution*. (New York: Random House, 1996), 196-99.

8 Royal Proclamation of 1763, U.S. History.org.

9 James Otis quoted in Lawrence Henry Gipson, *The Coming of the Revolution*. (NY: Harper Torchbooks, 1853), 68.

10 The Currency Act, US History.org.

11 Thomas Fitch, "Reasons Why the British Colonies in America Should Not Be Charged with Internal Taxes," in Bernard Bailyn, ed., *Pamphlets of the American Revolution.* (Harvard University Press, 1965), 393.

12 *The Rights of British Colonists,* USHistory.org.

13 Stephen Hopkins quoted in Theodore Draper, *A Struggle for Power: The American Revolution*. (New York: Random House, 1996), 229.

14 Patrick Henry, March 23,1775, Colonial Williamsburg, http://www.history.org/almanack/life/politics/giveme.cfm.

15 Thomas Hutchinson quoted in Draper, *Struggle for Power,* 245.

16 Quoted in Draper, *Struggle for Power*, 249.

17 *Resolutions of the Stamp Act Congress, 1765*, UShistory.org.

18 Pitt quoted in Draper, *Struggle for Power*, 279.

19 *An Act Repealing the Stamp Act*, *The Avalon Project: Documents in Law, History and Diplomacy,* Avalon Project*,* avalon.law.yale.edu.

20 The *Declaratory Act*, Avalon Project, avalon.law.yale.edu.

21 Dickinson quoted in Draper, *Struggle for Power,* 306.

22 Franklin quoted in Draper, *Struggle for Power,* 35.

23 Association of the Sons of Liberty in New York, December 15,1773, Avalon Project.

24 Boston Tea Party Official Site: http://www.boston-tea-party.org/in-depth.html.

25 John Adams quoted in Page Smith, *A New Age Now Begins*, vol. I (New York: McGraw-Hill Book Company, 1976), 381-82.

26 See David Ammerman, *In the Common Cause: American Response to the Coercive Acts of 1774, Charlottesville: University of Viriginia Press, 1974*.
27 *Declaration and Resolves, Avalon Project, Avalon.law.yale.edu.*

28 *Declaration and Resolves, Avalon Project,Avalon.law.yale.edu.*

29 *Declaration and Resolves*, U.S. History.org.

30 *Declaration and Resolves*, U.S. History.org.

31 The *Events Leading to Independence:* U.S. History.org.

32 The American Revolution.org/documents.

33 Ralph Waldo Emerson, "Concord Hymn," Poetry Foundation, http://www.poetryfoundation.org/poem/175140.

34 Lieutenant Colonel Smith to Gage, April 20, 1775, at U.S. History.org.

35 Smith Letter, U.S. History.org.

36 Benjamin Franklin to William Stratham, July 5, 1775.

37 Quoted in Gary B. Nash, The Unknown American Revolution: The Unruly Birth of Democracy and the Struggle to Create America. New York: Viking, 159.

38 Thomas Paine, *Introduction to Common Sense*, 1776, American History Sourcebook., ed. Paul Halsall, Fordham.edu/halsall.

39 "Battle at Lexington Green, 1775: The British Perspective," EyeWitness to History, www.eyewitnesstohistory.com (2010).

ANSWER KEY FOR CHAPTER SEVEN: THE ROAD TO REVOLUTION, 1754-1775

Check your answers to the questions in the Before You Move On Sections for this chapter.

Correct answers are **BOLDED**

Section 7.2.2 - p242
1. An increasing sense of common identity among the colonists was one of the legacies of the French and Indian War.
    A. TRUE
    b. False

2. The Proclamation of 1763 was enacted in part as a response to Pontiac's War.
    A. TRUE
    b. False

3. The Ohio Valley was one of the major points of contention between the French and British in the French and Indian War as well as the British and Indians in Pontiac's War.
    A. TRUE
    b. False

Section 7.3.8 - p252
1. The purpose of the Proclamation Line of 1763 was to
    A. KEEP THE COLONISTS ON THE EASTERN SEABOARD.
    b. raise a revenue to defray the costs of war.
    c. encourage colonial movement past the Appalachian Mountains.
    d. reward the colonists for their participation in the French and Indian War.

2. Which of the following Parliamentary acts were designed to "raise a revenue"?
    a. Proclamation Line of 1763
    b. Currency Act
    C. SUGAR ACT
    d. Declaratory Act

3. The act that claimed Parliament's right to legislate for the colonies in "all cases whatsoever" was the
    A. DECLARATORY ACT.
    b. Currency Act.
    c. Proclamation Line of 1763.
    d. Townshend Act.

4. The most effective tools used by the colonists in getting the Stamp Act repealed was
    a. the Boston Massacre.
    b. rioting against the Stamp Masters.
    C. THE BOYCOTT OF ENGLISH GOODS.
    d. the arguments of the colonists against internal taxation.

5. The colonies made a very clear distinction between
    a. internal and external taxation by Parliament.
    b. taxes to regulate trade v. those designed to raise a revenue.
    c. actual v. virtual representation in Parliament.
    D. ALL OF THE ABOVE
    e. None of the above

Section 7.4.4 - p261
1. The colonists did not necessarily object to the principle of taxation, but rather how the tax money would be applied.
    A. TRUE
    b. False

2. Which of the following Parliamentary Acts was not one of the Intolerable Acts?
    a. Boston Port Bill
    b. Massachusetts Government Act
    c. Quebec Act
    D. TEA ACT

3. The purpose of the First Continental Congress was to
    a. raise an army.
    b. draft a declaration of war against Great Britain.
    c. compile a list of grievances against the British government.
    D. DRAFT A DECLARATION OF AMERICAN RIGHTS.

4. Which of the following as a provision of the Quebec Act?
    a. Quebec was to be annexed to Massachusetts Bay.
    B. THE BOUNDARIES OF QUEBEC WERE EXTENDED INTO THE OHIO VALLEY.
    c. A state of war existed between England and France.
    d. Tea ships forced to leave the colonies would be re-directed to the St. Lawrence Seaway.

Chapter Eight: The American Revolution

Contents

Chapter Eight: The American Revolution

8.1 INTRODUCTION

The American Revolution is generally considered one of the most important revolutions in human history due not only to the founding of the United States but also to its influence on other countries who later fought for the right to Life, Liberty, and the pursuit of Happiness. The American Revolution, grown out of the colonies' frustration with British rule, has been seen by historians as an encouragement to others to throw off the burdens of colonialism or an oppressive government. Yet, the American Revolution proved difficult. Not all Americans wanted to be independent of Great Britain. The war brought suffering to many, both to soldiers on the front lines and to their families back home. Our Founding Fathers could agree, after much debate, on the need to break from Britain, but then found themselves in disagreement as to what the new nation should be. Their struggles over conflicting ideas shaped our nation.

8.1.1 Learning Outcomes

After completing this chapter, you should be able to:

- Explain the reasons that by 1775 war between the mother country and the colonies was inevitable.
- Analyze the motives of both the mother country and colonial leaders as the year 1775 progressed.
- Analyze the motives of those who argued for and against independence.
- Explain the activities of the Second Continental Congress and analyze the need for a central government once the war began.
- Analyze the relative military strengths and weaknesses of England and the colonies during the war.
- Explain why the Americans won their independence.
- Analyze the content of the Treaty of Paris and its impact on future diplomacy for the new United States.
- Explain the impact of the war for independence on loyalists, women, and blacks.
- Explain the impact of Indian participation in the war on both colonial and British strategies.

8.2 THE SECOND CONTINENTAL CONGRESS, 1775-1781

When the Second Continental Congress convened on May 10, 1775, the first job of the delegates was to address the *Conciliatory Proposition* sent to the colonies from Lord North earlier in May. Thomas Jefferson wrote the response to this *Proposition* that was entered into the records of the Congress in July 1775. Britain's *Conciliatory Proposition* had suggested that taxes would be used only for the purposes of regulating trade, an idea that had once been acceptable to the colonies, and that any taxes collected internally would be given to the colony itself, provided that the colony in question would help defray expenses for its protection. But the petition was too little, too late. The recent conflict at Lexington and Concord was on everyone's mind, and those who assembled in Philadelphia in May were well aware of Patrick Henry's outburst at a meeting of Virginia leaders in March. The colonies, he insisted, "have done everything that could be done to avert the storm which is now coming on. It is vain...to cry 'peace, peace'...The war is actually begun!"[1] Even John Dickinson, author of the *Letters from a Pennsylvania Farmer* and a supporter of reconciliation, was pessimistic, musing "what topics of reconciliation are now left for men who think as I do? To recommend reverence for the monarch, or affection for the mother country?...No. While we revere and love our mother country, her sword is opening our veins."[2]

As was the case with the First Continental Congress, the delegates to the Second Congress were a distinguished group of colonial leaders. John Hancock, a wealthy Bostonian, was chosen president of the Congress. Thomas Jefferson was present, as was Benjamin Franklin, who had come to the opinion, after months of trying to achieve conciliation in London, that independence was the only solution to the impasse between colonies and mother country. Georgia was represented at the Congress, though marginally at first, as only one delegate, Lyman Hall, attended. Despite the convictions of Patrick Henry, Thomas Jefferson, John Adams, and Benjamin Franklin, winning the majority to the cause of independence was an uphill battle, and in June the Congress decided to make one last effort at reconciliation. The *Olive Branch Petition* drafted that same month suggested that the colonists either be given free trade and taxes equal to those levied on citizens living in the mother country, or no taxes at all and strict trade regulations. The petition was approved on July 5, and taken to London by William Penn later that month. The king was less than gracious, especially in light of the battle of Bunker's Hill. He refused to see Penn and, on August 23, issued a proclamation that declared the colonies to be in "open and avowed

Figure 8.1 Patrick Henry | Patrick Henry, first and sixth governor of Virginia after Independence, is perhaps most well-known for his remarks in March 1775: "Almighty God! I know not what course others may take; but as for me: Give me Liberty, or give me Death!"

Authors: George Bagby Matthews, Thomas Sully
Source: U. S. Senate Collection

rebellion."[3] This did not persuade the colonials of the good intentions of the mother country, nor did a rumor circulating as early as January 1775 that a member of Parliament had derived a method of "humbling the aristocratic" Virginia planters by calling for general emancipation. Then in November, Virginia's royal governor, John Murray, fourth earl of Dunmore, released a proclamation from on board the British warship *Fowey* on which he had taken refuge, declaring martial law in Virginia and promising that any "indentured Servants [or] Negroes free...that are able and willing to bear Arms, they joining His MAJESTY'S troops."[4]

Even before the *Olive Branch Petition* was drafted, Congress set about preparing for war. Proclaiming that "the colonies are reduced to a dangerous and critical situation" by "hostilities that have already commenced in Massachusetts Bay," the delegates warned the colonies that they should begin arming themselves, and the first week in June voted to borrow £6,000 for the purchase of gunpowder. On June 14 and 15, Congress created a continental army "to defend the Lives, Liberties and Immunities of the Colonists" and adopted a comprehensive set of military regulations designed to govern the troops.[5] George Washington was appointed commander-in-chief. A week later, on June 22, the delegates approved the release of $1 million in bills of credit (paper currency). Proclaiming that it was doing so in "defense of American liberty," Congress authorized another $1 million in July. By the end of 1775, Congress had authorized a total of $6 million in bills of credit.[6]

The body adjourned in early August, and when it reconvened in September, it continued mobilizing for war and began to look for help from European countries. Meanwhile, Parliament had been at work, passing early in 1776 the *Prohibitory Act*, which warned all American vessels that they were subject to confiscation by the British Royal Navy. In March, the Congress responded with a warning of its own. In light of the fact that the British had encouraged "Savages to invade the Country" and "Negroes to murder their Masters," not to mention the most recent act for the confiscation of American ships, Congress specified that any British ship sailing in American waters could be seized and its merchandise considered "lawful prize."[7]

8.2.1 Movement toward Independence, 1775-1776

While John Dickinson was drafting the *Olive Branch Petition*, he was also on a committee with Thomas Jefferson that was drafting *The Causes and Necessities of Taking Up Arms*. Adopted by Congress just two days before the *Olive Branch Petition*, *The Causes of Taking up Arms* admonished Parliament for attempting "to effect their cruel and impolitic purpose of enslaving these Colonies by Violence, and have thereby rendered it necessary for us to close with their last Appeal from Reason to Arms."[8] The proclamation insisted: "Our cause is just. Our union is perfect. Our internal resources are great, and, if necessary, foreign assistance is undoubtably [sic] attainable."[9] Although the document was approved in July, 1775, it would be a year before independence was declared.

By spring 1776, however, opposition to independence had disappeared from the records of Congress. In part, this change of sentiment was influenced by the publication of Thomas Paine's *Common Sense*. Paine, a native of Britain, wrote about what had already been said in the preceding months in Congress, provincial assemblies, and colonial newspapers.

What Paine did was to offer "simple facts, plain arguments, and common sense" about the condition of the American colonies.[10] Also, members of Congress were exploring the possibility of securing aid from foreign countries, and beginning in early May, the body took an important step: on May 10 it recommended to the colonies that they adopt state governments to replace the colonial structures. Later that month, it appointed a committee consisting of John Adams, Benjamin Franklin, Roger Sherman, Robert Livingston, and Thomas Jefferson to prepare a declaration of independence for possible use; on July 4, this *Declaration of Independence* was released to the Congress and approved. Only New York withheld approval until July 15.

The Second Continental Congress was the only governing body in the American states other than the state legislatures until the approval of the *Articles of Confederation* in 1781. During the course of most of the war, the Congress attempted to maintain the colonial army, create coherent diplomatic policies, and direct military strategy. A committee, meanwhile, was working to draft a document uniting the states into one government; the Congress approved the Articles of Confederation in 1777 and released it to the states for ratification.

8.2.2 The Declaration of Independence

The Declaration of Independence is the most important document to emerge from the Second Continental Congress. It consists of five parts: the introduction, the preamble or a statement of principles, the body of the document which consists of two parts, and the conclusion.

The Sections	Annotation
The Introduction *When in the Course of human events it becomes necessary for one people to dissolve the political bands which have connected them with another and to assume among the powers of the earth, the separate and equal station to which the Laws of Nature... entitle them...a decent respect to the opinions of mankind requires that they should declare the causes that impel them to the separation...*	The introduction explains that at various times in history it has been necessary for one body to separate itself from another. When this occurs, it is "decent" that the reasons for the separation be stated.

The Sections	Annotation
The Preamble *We hold these truths to be self-evident-that all men are created equal, that they are endowed by their Creator with certain unalienable Rights, that among these are Life, Liberty and the pursuit of Happiness. That to secure these rights, Governments are instituted among Men... That whenever any Form of Government becomes destructive of these ends, it is the Right of the People to alter or to abolish it and to institute new Government...*	The preamble includes a list of principles based on the theories of English political philosopher, John Locke, who wrote 100 years earlier. According to Locke, humans living in what he called a "state of nature," in other words, before the existence of governments, held certain "natural" rights, which he specified as life, liberty, and property. In order to better protect these rights, humans had created contracts between themselves and a ruler, which implied that, in exchange for protecting their natural rights, a ruler would receive the obedience and support of the people. If, however, their natural rights were not protected, they had the right to rebel, replacing one government with another. Notice two things about the preamble. One is that Jefferson, a slave holder himself, included the statement that "all men are created equal." Some controversy arose at the time over whether this statement should be put in the document, as it might be construed as hypocritical in a society in which slavery was widespread. Historian Robert Middlekauff, however, points out that there is no evidence that the inclusion of the equality of humankind created immediate public outcry or even discussion.[11] Second, Jefferson does not include property as one of the natural rights; rather, he substitutes "pursuit of happiness." Although Locke did not include the latter in his list of natural rights, he did write in the *Essay Concerning Human Understanding* (1693) that "the highest perfection of intellectual nature lies in a careful and constant pursuit of true and solid happiness."

The Sections	Annotation
The Body of the Document *Obstructed the Administration of Justice by refusing his Assent to Laws for establishing Judiciary powers;* *Made Judges dependent on his Will alone;* *Kept among us, in times of peace, Standing Armies without the Consent of our legislatures;* *Quartered large bodies of armed troops among us;* *Protected [British officials] from Punishment for any Murders which they should commit on the inhabitants of these States;* *Imposed taxes upon us without our consent...*	The body of the Declaration consists of two parts. The first part contains a lengthy list of the misdeeds of king and Parliament. Included in this list are grievances that had been stated before in the Resolves of the Stamp Act Congress and the various colonial petitions to George III. The king, the document insisted, had performed the deeds listed in the body. In all, there are around thirty grievances enumerated; in this list can be seen many of the themes that were obvious during the colonial protests of the 1760s and 1770s: taxation must come only from bodies in which the taxed were represented, armies should not be maintained in times of peace and no troops should be arbitrarily quartered in the homes of colonials, and Royal officials should not be allowed to return to England for trial, especially when the charge was murder against colonists. The second section of the body explains the endeavors the colonists had taken in the past, short of outright rebellion, to right these wrongs: "In every stage of these Oppressions We have Petitioned for Redress in the most humble terms: Our repeated Petitions have been answered only by repeated injury."
The Conclusion *WE THEREFORE, the Representatives of the UNITED STATES OF AMERICA, in General Congress, Assembled, appealing to the Supreme Judge of the world...do, in the Name and by Authority of the good People of these Colonies, solemnly publish and declare that these United Colonies are, and of Right ought to be FREE AND INDEPENDENT STATES...*	And so, the document concludes, only one action remains open to the American colonists: they must declare their independence from Great Britain and become "free and independent states."

The *Declaration* was released from committee and read into the records of the Continental Congress on July 4, 1776. After accepting its text and signing the manuscript, Congress released the document first as a broadside that was distributed *en masse* to the public; unfortunately, this first manuscript copy of the *Declaration* has been lost. The document that is usually thought to be the actual *Declaration of Independence* is the copy that was signed on August 2, 1776 and is currently housed in the National Archives in Washington, D.C.

8.2.3 Before You Move On...

Key Concepts

The Second Continental Congress gathered in May, 1775 to consider the response of George III to the petition drafted by the First Continental Congress in 1774. A month before they assembled, the skirmishes at Lexington and Concord had taken place, and Congress decided to try one last time at reconciliation with the mother country. It soon became obvious, however, that it was too late to patch up the differences that had been building for over 100 years. Slowly, Congress came to the conclusion that independence was the only option for the American colonies; therefore a committee was created to draft a statement for independence. The committee released the *Declaration of Independence* to Congress on July 4, 1776, and it was soon released to the new states. No longer would the Americans fight for a "redress of grievances," but rather for their independence from the mother country.

Test Yourself

1. The rationale that Jefferson used in the Declaration of Independence came primarily from the theories of John Locke.

   a. True

   b. False

2. Which of the following documents was NOT one drafted by the Second Continental Congress?

   a. The Prohibitory Act

   b. The Declaration of Independence

   c. The Olive Branch Petition

   d. The Causes and Necessity of Taking Up Arms

3. In the Conciliatory Proposition, the mother country gave in to most of the demands of the American colonists.

   a. True

   b. False

4. The Declaration of Independence consists of ______ sections:
   a. One
   b. Two
   c. Three
   d. Four
   e. Five

See page 313 for answers

8.3 REVOLUTIONARY WAR BATTLES

Most engagements, large and small, during the American Revolution took place in the Thirteen Colonies in revolt, a few in Canada, and some notable encounters at sea. The first engagement of the war, at Lexington and Concord, occurred before the Americans even had an official army or commander-in-chief. The colonials, who had hoped to avoid war, found themselves pushed into it. A shot rang out at Lexington, fired by an unknown person, and the war began almost as an accident. The war ended six years later at Yorktown, not with a great battle, but rather with the ultimate surrender of the British who found themselves in a natural trap. Between Lexington in 1775 and Yorktown in 1781, hundreds of engagements occurred. Early in the war, the area around Boston and New York were the focus of the military efforts. But after three years of fighting, the British had made no great progress against George Washington and his Continental Army. Indeed, Washington's army had grown into a stronger, more cohesive force as they gained experience with each battle. The British turned their attention to the South in what is known as the "Southern Strategy," where they hoped that a combination of British and Loyalist forces together would be able to make headway in the war effort that had not been possible in the North. In 1778 the British captured Savannah, Georgia and began moving slowly northwards from there. Charleston fell to the British in 1780, giving the British control of the two major southern ports. The American forces were not idle in the South and had success against the British further inland, preventing the British from achieving the victories they needed to win the war. The following is a selection of some of the more notable engagements of the war, beginning just after Lexington and Concord and ending with Yorktown.

8.3.1 Bunker Hill

- **Date:** June 16, 1775
- **Location**: Charlestown, Massachusetts Bay
- **American Commanders**: Dr. Joseph Warren, General Israel Putnam, General William Prescott
- **British Commander**: Major General Sir William Howe
- **American Force**: 2,400

- **British Force**: 3,000
- **American Losses**: 115
- **British Losses**: 226
- A British Victory

Following Lexington and Concord, Gage found himself trapped in Boston. His troops that had retreated to Charlestown with Percy had been brought back to Boston and more reinforcements had arrived from Britain, leaving Gage with an army stuck in the middle of a harbor while the mainland was in the control of the colonists in revolt. Gage needed to get out of Boston.

Gage and his generals devised a plan to break out in June, 1775. To succeed, they would need to gain control of Charlestown, which they had essentially abandoned after bringing their troops back to Boston following Lexington and Concord. Charlestown was important because of its hills, Breed's Hill and Bunker's Hill. These hills offered a view of Boston and the harbor, making them strategically important and excellent locations for artillery batteries and observation posts.

In a replay of the preparations for Concord, once again Gage's plans became known to the colonists before Gage could carry them out. On the night of June 16, General Prescott set out with 1,500 American troops to take Bunker's Hill. Instead, for unknown reasons, Prescott took and fortified Breed's Hill, creating an impressive earthwork overnight. The British were taken by surprise but determined to go ahead with their plan to take Charlestown.

Major General Sir William Howe was given command of the British force. The Americans continued to work on their fortifications as the British prepared for their main attack. Americans were on both Breed's Hill and Bunker's, with the main concentration of troops and fortifications on Breed's. The British Navy in the harbor began a bombardment of Breed's Hill that was not particularly effective but did discourage more Americans from moving into positions there. The Americans were still working out the details of being an army, and so their force suffered from chain-of-command issues and organizational problems, resulting in units not being where they were most needed.

As the Americans watched, Howe landed with 1,500 troops. He had believed that taking the hill would be a simple matter, so he planned a direct attack. After landing and seeing Americans on both hills, he asked for more reinforcements, bringing his total of men up to 3,000. The British began their attack in mid-afternoon. Just as at Lexington and Concord, the Americans had some troops firing independently from cover. They could not match the large numbers of British, but they could harass the British troops and unsettle them. Many of the colonists seemed to be around the town of Charlestown, so the British Navy set the little town on fire to drive the Americans out.

The first two British assaults on Breed's Hill were repulsed. The Americans, despite their difficulties, proved they could stand and fight. As the British approached in formation, the Americans opened fire, causing heavy casualties among the British, who retreated. The British had also fired, but the Americans had the advantage of fortified positions that gave them some cover. Howe had intended to use artillery on the American positions, but the British also suffered their share of organizational problems: they had brought the wrong ammunition for the cannon. Howe called up reinforcements and launched his third attack directly at the center of the Americans. Among the officers involved in the charge was Major Pitcairn, who had been wounded in the retreat from Concord. He was killed in the third assault on Breed's Hill as the British again took casualties. The Americans began the day short on ammunition and paid for it with the third assault. Unable to fire, they could not prevent the British from overrunning their position. The British fixed bayonets and attacked the Americans, who had their guns but no shot and few swords or bayonets of their own. The Americans were forced to abandon Breed's Hill. As they fell back, Joseph Warren, an important member of the revolutionary committee, was killed. The British pressed their advantage and drove the Americans from Bunker's Hill and the Charlestown peninsula. The Americans retreated back to the mainland and Cambridge. About thirty Americans were captured by the British, and of these, twenty died in captivity, but not due to mistreatment. All those captured had been terribly wounded and so were left behind by the retreating Americans.

This battle, which has long held the misnomer of Bunker's Hill when it should be called Breed's Hill, proved to the Americans that they could stand and face what was considered one of the best armies in the world. For the British, the cost of victory was terribly high. While they lost only 226 soldiers, they had over 800 wounded, including many officers. Technically the British won because they achieved their objective of driving the Americans out of Charlestown. However, the battle was a boost to American confidence while devastating to the British forces. As a result of this battle, the British government's confidence in General Gage was lost, and he was removed from command. Somewhat ironically, the officer who would eventually be given Gage's command was General Howe, who was responsible for the high casualty rate among the British by ordering frontal assaults against fortified positions.

8.3.2 Quebec

- **Date:** December 31, 1775
- **Location**: Quebec, Quebec, Canada
- **American Commanders**: Colonel Benedict Arnold, Lieutenant Colonel Daniel Morgan, Brigadier General Richard Montgomery
- **British Commanders**: Captain William DeLaPlace, General Sir Guy Carleton
- **American Force**: 1,200
- **British Force**: 1,800
- **American Losses**: 48
- **British Losses**: 5
- A British Victory

As the war progressed, the Americans sought to find new allies and reduce British options in North America. To this end, they invaded Canada and attempted to capture Quebec (the city, capital of Quebec the province). The British and the French had both sought to colonize Canada, with the British eventually succeeding. Still, many French remained and formed the Province of Quebec. Although under British control, the French Canadians of Quebec remained resoundingly French. To the Americans, these French Canadians appeared to be the perfect allies, as they had no love for the British. With that in mind, Colonel Benedict Arnold planned to capture Quebec and form an alliance with the French Canadians against the British.

General George Washington supported the plan and assigned over 1,000 men for the campaign. Brigadier General Richard Montgomery and Colonel Arnold were in charge. They took two different routes to Quebec, with Montgomery traveling by Lake Champlain and Arnold coming through Maine. Each had to fight against British forces at points along the way as well as suffer from the journey through the wilderness before joining up at Quebec and preparing for the December attack.

By December, the British forces at Quebec were isolated due to the weather; the St. Lawrence River was frozen. General Sir Guy Carleton knew of the impending attack, but with the frozen river could not expect reinforcements. Instead, he had to fortify Quebec and organize a defense with the few soldiers he had on hand. Montgomery had arrived in early December but did not have the resources to lay a proper siege. Still, he did what he could and sent demands for the surrender of the city, demands which were rejected. Even if the Americans had had enough supplies, time was against them. Arnold's men were enlisted only to the end of December; then they would be free to leave. Even if they were convinced to stay, once spring came, reinforcements for the British would surely arrive as well. Montgomery felt he had to take Quebec in December if he was to take it at all.

Montgomery and Arnold planned to attack Quebec from two different directions at the same time so as to force the defenders to divide and thereby weaken themselves. Montgomery attacked from the north while Arnold attacked the lower parts of the city. They hoped for a snowstorm to provide cover; instead, they got a blizzard that made advancing difficult. Montgomery led his men against the defensive works and managed to enter the city. As he led his men through Quebec, the defenders opened fire. Montgomery was killed with a shot to the head. Several of his men were also shot, so his troops quickly retreated back out of the city.

Arnold had no way of knowing what happened to Montgomery while he was attacking a different area of the town. Arnold also was able to penetrate the defenses and enter Quebec. As he led his men through the town, Arnold was shot in the ankle when the defenders opened fire. His wound was so serious that he was unable to continue, a failure which turned out to be lucky for him. Command of Arnold's men fell to Lieutenant Colonel Daniel Morgan, who led the men further into town. They found shelter where they were able to regroup but were soon trapped. Morgan was forced to surrender himself and his men. Arnold escaped, having been sent back due to his injury and was able to continue the siege of Quebec until March, despite the loss of men who were either captured or had deserted. The siege had little impact on Quebec, which was well supplied. Arnold was sent back to Montreal.

The attempt to take Quebec was a failure. Not only did the Americans fail to take the city, they also failed to convince the French Canadians to join their cause. Arnold was promoted and given other commands before his personal conflicts would lead him to become the most famous traitor in American history.

8.3.3 Long Island, also known as Brooklyn Heights

- **Date:** August 27, 1776
- **Location**: Brooklyn, New York
- **American Commander**: General George Washington, Israel Putnam, William Alexander
- **British Commanders**: Lord Charles Cornwallis, Sir Henry Clinton, Sir William Howe
- **American Force**: 10,000
- **British Force**: 20,000
- **American Losses**: 300
- **British Losses**: 64
- A British Victory

New York City's location, large harbor, access to the Hudson River, infrastructure, and other resources made it a point of strategic importance in the Revolution. Holding New York City would give either side greater flexibility in troop and supply movements. Because of the city's strategic importance, General George Washington had begun to prepare New York City's defenses as soon as the British were driven from Boston in 1775.

The American effort was hampered by lack of manpower and continued organizational difficulties. The Continental Army, as the American forces were called, drew units from all colonies, each bringing their own ideas on how to run an army. In addition, there were discipline problems with this army of unprofessional soldiers. Equipment shortages made it impossible to uniformly equip the soldiers. Only some had bayonets; others even lacked muskets. The uniforms varied from unit to unit and even within units. A Continental soldier might be found wearing a coat of some shade of blue, green, black, brown, even red or, instead of a coat, a hunting shirt of brown, buff, or purple. Bringing unity and discipline to the Continental Army and finding supplies and equipment were ongoing challenges at this point in the war.

Realizing that the British would target New York City sooner or later, the Continentals set about constructing forts, entrenchments, and other fortifications at strategic points, particularly on Long Island. They also created obstacles in the water to reduce the threat from the formidable British Navy. But all the preparations were for naught. First the British fleet arrived with over 100 ships under the command of Admiral Richard Howe, the brother of the British commanding general, Sir William Howe. The sight of so many British naval vessels naturally caused concern, even panic, in the city. Then the British troops began arriving, landing first on Staten Island where they met little opposition. On August 22 the British moved to Long Island, which was well fortified and guarded, with the exception of the Jamaica Pass, which inexplicably was practically abandoned with only a token guard. To make matters worse, the information Washington received of the nature and number of the British force was completely inaccurate. Based on this poor intelligence, Washington did not grasp the true intentions of the British and did not prepare adequately for their attack.

By August 26, the British had landed their full force of British and German mercenaries, known as Hessians, and prepared to attack the Americans. While about 4,000 British and Hessian troops maneuvered around the front of the American lines, convincing the Americans that they were the main British force, General Howe led the majority of the British troops through the Jamaica Pass by night with the intent to flank the Americans. Howe's plan worked. The fighting on every front was brutal, but for most of the day the Americans had no idea where the main British force was attacking. By using his forces in separate but coordinated attacks, Howe was able to catch the Americans between his forces, pinching them and cutting them off from the rest of the Continentals and possible aid. The Continentals were forced to retreat towards the Brooklyn Heights. Howe's army had essentially herded the Continentals. The advantage of Brooklyn Heights was its height, making it an excellent place for fortifications. Properly prepared and staffed, it would be a costly place to take by force. The disadvantage, however, was that getting off Brooklyn Heights could be just as difficult. Howe's troops extended their lines to cut off Brooklyn Heights by land, laying siege to the Continental position. On the opposite side was the water of the East River—where the British Navy under Admiral Howe waited. Washington and most of his army had fallen into a trap.

Both Washington and Howe realized Washington was trapped. Howe was content to settle down and have his men work steadily on trenches that would allow them to move closer to the American lines without taking unnecessary risks. Howe had every reason to believe time was on his side. Washington was still able to communicate with his forces over on Manhattan Island and requested reinforcements. Troops from Pennsylvania were sent in response. After a consultation with his officers, Washington's bold plan involved having the new troops essentially pretend to be his entire army. In the dark and rain of the evening, Washington's army prepared to leave in utter silence. The men were not allowed to speak; anything that might make a noise, including wagon wheels, was wrapped to muffle the sound. Stealth was of the utmost importance, and everyone in Washington's army maintained unusual cooperation. The campfires were kept lit so the British would think the Americans were right where they should be; the British had used the same trick when they began their march to Jamaica Pass. The Pennsylvanians manned the battlements, making it appear that Washington's troops were staying alert and in place. By morning, the rain turned to fog, making it difficult for the British to see the American positions. As the sun rose and burned away the fog, the British began to notice a lack of Americans watching them from the fortifications. By the time the British realized Washington was gone, he and his entire army of 9,000 soldiers were in Manhattan.

As remarkable as Washington's retreat was, it was still a retreat. The British had driven the Americans from Long Island and captured their fortified positions. The British celebrated their victory; nevertheless, their best chance of capturing Washington and ending the war had slipped away in the night after General Howe failed to press the attack when he had the chance. Still, Howe was hailed a hero and British confidence in a successful war rose.

8.3.4 Battle of Trenton

- **Date:** December 26,1776
- **Location**: Trenton, New Jersey
- **American Commander**: General George Washington

- **British Commander**: Colonel Johann Rall of Hesse-Cassel
- **American Force**: 2,400
- **British Force**: 1,500 Hessians
- **American Losses**: 2
- **British Losses**: 22
- An American Victory

In a bold move, General George Washington crossed the Delaware, a miserably icy river, and landed near Trenton. The weather was so terrible that not all the American troops managed the crossing. Washington and his troops then marched approximately nine miles to Trenton. The Hessians had thought themselves safe from attack due to the bad weather. They were caught by surprise when Washington personally led his troops into Trenton. The Hessians fell back, but Washington had stationed troops to cut off their retreat before he advanced into Trenton. The Hessians fought with great discipline but were let down by their weapons when in several instances their guns would not fire. Washington's troops kept up the pressure, following the Hessians through the street in house-to-house fighting. Colonel Rall, the commander of the Hessians, was mortally wounded, and all of the other Hessian colonels were killed during the battle. With the end of the battle, Washington captured not only the Hessian forces, but also much-needed supplies, weapons, and ammunition.

The news of Washington's victory at Trenton spread quickly throughout the colonies, boosting American morale at a time when it was most needed. The war had been going very badly for the Americans; victory was a welcome relief.

Figure 8.2 George Washington Crossing the Delaware | Emanuel Leutze's famous painting of George Washington Crossing the Delaware prior to his attack on the Hessians at Trenton on December 25, 1776, was a great success in America.

Artist: Emanuel Leutze
Source: Library of Congress

8.3.5 Battle of Saratoga, NY

- **Date:** September 19-October 17, 1777
- **Location:** Saratoga County, New York
- **American Commander**: Major General Horatio Gates and Brigadier General Benedict Arnold
- **British Commander**: Major General John Burgoyne
- **American Force**: 12,000
- **British Force**: 6,600
- **American Losses**: 90
- **British Losses**: 440
- An American Victory

Major General John Burgoyne developed a plan to invade New England from his base in Canada. The purpose was to cut off New England from the rest of the colonies and subdue the region. After taking New England, the British would then be in a better position to take control of the rest of the rebellious colonies. Burgoyne intended to take Albany, New York, and with it control of the upper Hudson River, the lower Hudson already being under the control of the British at New York City.

Nothing went as Burgoyne had planned. The success of his campaign depended on two British columns coming in from Canada, one of which he would command. The other column became engaged in facing American forces and so was unable to move down the Hudson. He had expected to have support from Indians; they abandoned Burgoyne. Men who were supposed to bring in supplies from Vermont encountered American forces and lost. Burgoyne's own column was delayed in the wilderness, as he had not considered the difficulty of the terrain.

The Americans under Major General Gates knew Burgoyne was coming down the Hudson River Valley, and Burgoyne's troubles, which delayed his progress, gave Gates time to bring his own army to meet him. On September 19, the two armies collided unexpectedly. Americans had seen British troops moving across a nearby farm and attacked, thinking they were attacking skirmishers, not the main British force. Fighting continued throughout the day as more units became engaged in the battle. In the end, the Americans retreated, leaving Burgoyne the victor, but due to the heavy British losses and the Americans still holding control of the Hudson, it proved a hollow victory.

Burgoyne decided to dig in. Instead of retreating or advancing, he pulled his army together and fortified his position. He was facing a larger American force, but he anticipated relief coming from General Henry Clinton at New York City. The relief never came; Clinton did move out, but he became occupied with other targets and never reached Saratoga. On October 3, Burgoyne cut the rations for his troops, as his supplies were now desperately short. On October 7, Burgoyne, having given up hope of Clinton's arrival, tried to break away from the Americans with a flanking maneuver but failed and suffered great losses from the American counter-attack. Burgoyne pulled back to his fortified position.

The American army continued to grow and moved to surround Burgoyne. With no relief coming, many wounded in need of care, his rations almost gone, and outnumbered by more than two-to-one, Burgoyne surrendered.

The defeat of Burgoyne raised American morale across the colonies. Further, this American victory convinced the French to support the Americans both financially and militarily. For these reasons, Saratoga is often considered a turning point in the war. With French involvement in the war, the British were forced to turn their attention to both to the West Indies and Europe, distracting them from their previous focus on the now-independent American states.

Saratoga has one other point of significance in American history. Benedict Arnold's personal morale took a blow at Saratoga. Arnold had been passed over for command and felt that he was not being given credit for his achievements, his glory instead stolen by others. At Saratoga, Gates had planned to sit and wait for Burgoyne to come to him. Arnold had insisted on sending out men, including the ones that first encountered Burgoyne's troops, yet Arnold was not mentioned in Gates's report to Congress about the actions of September 19. Arnold reacted poorly, shouting at Gates, and was relieved of command. He then sat in his tent until he joined the action on October 7 without authorization from Gates. Arnold was wounded in the leg and spent months recovering from his injury, during which time he became increasingly embittered. After he recovered, Washington made Arnold the military governor of Philadelphia. Again Arnold fell into controversy, but he also fell in love and married a woman from a Loyalist family. Feeling continually slighted by Americans and associating increasingly with Loyalists, Arnold crossed the line and committed treason.

8.3.6 Siege of Charleston

- **Date:** March 29-May 12, 1780
- **Location**: Charleston, South Carolina
- **American Commander**: Major General Benjamin Lincoln
- **British Commander**: General Sir Henry Clinton
- **American Force:** 5,466
- **British Force**: 13,500
- **American Losses**: 76
- **British Losses**: 92
- A British Victory

General Clinton sailed from New York, determined to take Charleston, an important American harbor in the Southern colonies. Clinton knew Charleston's harbor was well fortified; the defensive works there had been decades in the making. So, instead of a direct assault, Clinton planned to take Charleston by going overland rather than by sailing directly into the harbor.

His forces landed a few days' march south of Charleston on February 11 and began the trek to their target. The fleet sailed back up the coast, coming in to provide supplies to the forces on land. Once Clinton's force reached the Charleston area, they set about attacking and occupying strategic locations around the harbor and the rivers that flow into it.

The British fleet began moving into the harbor on March 20 in coordination with the movements of the army units on land. The American naval commander, seeing the size of the British fleet, sank his own ships near the entrance of the Cooper River. This action created a water hazard and prevented the British from taking the American ships.

By April 14, the British successfully cut Charleston off from the rest of the state. No relief for the Americans was expected, yet still the Americans held out a few days longer. Then on April 21, the American commander, Major General Benjamin Lincoln, offered to surrender with honor. Clinton refused. His forces had Charleston under control and time was on his side. Over the next several days, the Americans would try again to surrender with honor and again be refused. Finally, on May 11, Clinton ordered an artillery barrage using "hot shot"—cannon balls that have been heated so that they can cause fires when they hit flammable material, such as a wooden building. Lincoln surrendered without condition only hours after the barrage began.

The Siege of Charleston may well be the best designed and executed plan by the British during the war. The victory was complete, marking the worst defeat for the Americans of any engagement in the war. Charleston would prove to be a high tide mark for the British in the South. After this, while they would still win some battles, the campaign would be long and difficult, eventually ending at Yorktown.

8.3.7 Cowpens

- **Date:** January 17, 1781
- **Location:** Cowpens, Spartanburg County, SC
- **American Commander:** Brigadier General Daniel Morgan
- **British Commander:** Lieutenant Colonel Banastre Tarleton
- **American Force:** 1,912
- **British Force:** 1,150
- **American Losses:** 25
- **British Losses:** 110
- An American Victory

Cowpens, as the name suggests, was a large cow pasture of approximately 500 square yards in size. This wide open pasture was kept clear of brush, weeds, and grass by cattle, making it a good site for a battle. Brigadier General Morgan and his men were being pursued by Lieutenant Colonel Tarleton. Morgan reached Cowpens and set up camp. The nearby Broad River was running high due to recent rains, making it difficult to cross. Morgan's army had its flank to the Broad River and turned to face Tarleton's oncoming forces. On paper, Morgan would appear neatly trapped. In fact, Morgan had worked out a careful plan to use the terrain to his advantage. In some battles, inexperienced troops panicked and fled. His had nowhere to run, thanks to the river. He knew that Tarleton was an experienced and very aggressive officer, and he knew that, while his own army had a chance to rest while waiting for Tarleton, Tarleton was pushing his troops hard. By the time Tarleton reached Cowpens, his army was hungry and exhausted. Tarleton, hearing of Morgan's position against the river, did exactly as Morgan expected and formed up, focused on Morgan's center. Morgan deployed his least experienced troops first and then had them fall back, letting his more experienced soldiers deal with the British when they approached close to his position. Morgan's riflemen intentionally targeted the British officers, creating confusion in the British lines. As the Americans maneuvered, pulling units back, the British pressed forward only to encounter other Americans they had not expected and were forced to fall back themselves. Once the British had been pulled out of position, Morgan went on the offensive. The colonists charged with bayonets, catching the British by surprise. More American units engaged, and the British lines broke. By this point, Tarleton was widely hated by the Americans because it was believed that he intentionally killed Americans who had already surrendered. Some at Cowpens sought revenge, bayoneting British soldiers who surrendered, in a move called "Tarleton's Quarter." The American officers stepped in and stopped it as best they could. Tarleton and the remains of his army retreated back to the main British force under Cornwallis.

8.3.8 Yorktown

- **Date:** September 28-October 19, 1781
- **Location**: Yorktown, Virginia
- **American Commander**: General George Washington
- **British Commander**: Lieutenant General Lord William Cornwallis
- **American Force**: 11,133 and 7,800 French
- **British Force**: 8,885
- **American Losses**: 23 and 65 French
- **British Losses**: 156
- An American Victory

Following the brutal battle of Guilford Courthouse, Lord Cornwallis moved his army to Yorktown and Gloucester Point, Virginia with the intention of securing a port and having his troops removed by the British Navy. His army needed relief after their long campaign in the South, so, after reaching Yorktown, they settled in, built defensive works, and waited for the British Navy. To reach Cornwallis, the British Navy needed to sail into the Chesapeake Bay, then up the York River to Yorktown, located on a peninsula formed by the York River on the north, the Chesapeake Bay on the east, and the James River on the south. Gloucester is on the opposite side of the York River.

Cornwallis believed that General Washington was occupied at New York and that the other American and French forces were not a significant threat. He did not know until too late that a French fleet was sailing to the Chesapeake Bay, nor did he know that Washington, having been informed of Cornwallis's location at Yorktown, was bringing his army with all speed to meet him. For these reasons, Cornwallis maintained his position at Yorktown, allowing his army to be trapped instead of moving to a position further west, which would have allowed him to maneuver away from an advancing enemy force.

Figure 8.3 Surrender of Cornwallis | The siege of Yorktown was the last major action of the Revolutionary War. The British defeat led to surrender and the end of the War.

Artist: John Trumbull
Source: Architect of the Capitol

The French and British fleets met and the British were defeated, leaving the French in control of the bay and able to blockade the York River.

The American and French armies combined at Williamsburg, Virginia. On September 28, they marched down the peninsula to Yorktown and laid siege to Cornwallis's army, effectively blocking Cornwallis from moving west. His army was trapped on the peninsula. His small force at Gloucester was also surrounded. Relief from Lieutenant General Henry Clinton had been promised, but in Cornwallis's view would not arrive in time. On October 16, Cornwallis planned a breakout that would move his army across the York River to Gloucester Point, but the plan, his last hope, failed. Washington offered terms of surrender, and Cornwallis accepted, officially surrendering his army on October 19, 1781. This battle was the last major action of the American Revolution.

8.3.9 Before You Move On...

Key Concepts

The Americans began the war without a professional army and ended it by defeating one of the finest militaries of the age. Mistakes and acts of cruelty were committed by both sides. The conditions for the soldiers were often brutal, particularly when fighting in winter. One factor of paramount importance to the American victory was the diplomatic alliance between the American states and the French. Coming into the war on the side of the Americans after the Battle of Saratoga, the French forces offered much-needed relief to the American troops and turned the American War into one with a global scope. This participation would have a crucial impact on France as the war debt and resulting fiscal depression would lead in less than ten years to the French Revolution and the end of the old regime in Europe.

Test Yourself

1. One of the most important results of the American victory at Saratoga was
   a. the Hessian removal from the British force.
   b. the French participation in the war on the side of the British.
   c. the French participation in the war on the side of the Americans.
   d. the end of the war.

2. The siege of Charleston was well conducted.
   a. True
   b. False

3. Famous for leading his troops against the Hessians at Trenton, New Jersey was
   a. General George Washington.
   b. Brigadier General Daniel Morgan.
   c. Major Benedict Arnold.
   d. Major General Benjamin Lincoln.

4. Benedict Arnold is America's most famous traitor.
   a. True
   b. False

See page 313 for answers

8.4 THE IMPACT OF WAR

The Revolution changed the lives of Americans in ways that were both expected and unforeseen. The emotional and physical toll of the war affected everyone living in the colonies no matter which side they supported. The movement of troops proved detrimental to those civilians in their path because it led to the flight of refugees, epidemic disease, confiscation of supplies, plundering of property, and the possibility of physical assault. The Revolution disrupted normal patterns of life as the economy faltered, men went off to fight, women stayed home to tend farms and business, and slaves attempted to pursue their freedom.[12] While American battlefield victories helped secure independence, the challenges on the home front called into question the meaning of that independence.

Prior to the war, and one of the issues leading to it, was the feeling of many Americans that they were in fact British citizens living in the colonies, whereas to those in England, the Americans were something other than truly English. They were subjects of His Majesty and living in British colonies, but they were not English, not in the way that those born, raised, and living in London were English citizens. Worse, in not being truly English, the Americans were somehow less than equal. The idea of some English that Americans did not merit the same considerations as proper English would persist into the early nineteenth century and the War of 1812. For the Americans, however, the need to be accepted and treated as English ended with the Revolution. They were now Americans, more specifically Virginians, Georgians, Pennsylvanians, and so on. Whether Americans were indeed primarily Americans, or identified first with their states and then with their country, would continue as an issue until the Civil War.

After the Revolution, just as before, American society was multi-layered with the wealthy landed gentry at the top, the landless citizens below, and slaves at the bottom. Merchants, farmers, traders, and artisans of all types formed the middle class. Government and politics before the war had been the business of the upper class. With the Revolution, people in the middle were drawn into playing a larger part in the running of their colonies, political activities, and service in the military; they were no longer willing to leave the decisions in the hands of the gentry. More than ever before, they became active participants in the political process. These changes also led to new questions about the rights of loyalists, slaves, free blacks, women, and Indians.

8.4.1 The Cost of Supporting the Patriot Cause

Wars also have definite impact on the economy of a country, with soldiers needing to be fed and equipped. As military technology improved over time, the cost of equipping soldiers only increased. The Continental Congress resisted taxing the citizens to pay for the war effort especially because questions about the right to tax contributed to the desire for independence. While Congress relied on the states for some assistance, lack of funds forced it to print $200 million during the war. That amount did not factor in how much the states printed and how much counterfeit money the British spread in an effort to destabilize the American financing effort. Therefore, the value of the "continental" as the currency was depreciated rather quickly. Congress also borrowed money from other nations and from wealthy patriots through interest-bearing loan certificates. In dire times, both the British and the American armies simply took what they needed from the civilian population. They entered homes to confiscate food and clothing, and even furniture they could burn to keep warm. Military leaders on both sides tried to stop such looting, but they did not always succeed.[13]

The cost of supporting the patriot cause did not just come in the form of public debt. Economically speaking, the war impacted the combatants and their families. The government's decision to print money caused inflation, especially as goods became scarce in British-occupied cities. According to historian Harry M. Ward, goods imported from the West Indies like rum and sugar increased over 500 percent. Even worse, beef cost $.04 a pound in 1777 and $1.69 a pound in 1780, which amounted to about a 4,000 percent increase in the price. Because so many men left home to serve in the army, wages also went up for farm hands and laborers. However, they did not keep pace with the prices. Moreover, those serving in the military often did not receive their pay on time and sometimes not at all. Thus, all people on the home front struggled to get by, but the poor suffered most. Congress as well as the individual states experimented with wage and price controls, but that did little to improve the situation for most Americans. Frustration led to at least forty food and price riots during the conflict, led mostly by women. For example, in 1777, Boston's women assaulted wealthy merchant Thomas Boylston for refusing to sell coffee at a fair price. To deal with the worst of the war's economic consequences, private organizations and sometimes local governments coordinated relief efforts because the Continental Congress seemed unwilling to help.[14]

In 1783, when the war finally ended, the public debt was approximately $43 million and the new government had difficulty in paying all of its obligations, including those to the very men who had fought in the war. Many veterans were not fully compensated for their service. Some were promised grants of land in lieu of payment during the conflict, only to lose their grants due to mishandling, unwieldy government regulations, and speculator's schemes. Many veterans applied for pensions in the years following the wars, tracking down former comrades to certify that they had indeed served, only to be denied their pension on a technicality, such as not proving six month's continuous service, or for no clear reason at all. For many veterans who had suffered economically by neglecting their farms and businesses to serve, and then who were never properly paid for their trouble, being denied their rightful pensions was a painful loss—one that would cause problems for the new American government by the end of the 1780s.

8.4.2 The Struggle of the Loyalists

Not all people living in colonies at the time of the Declaration of Independence chose to support the patriot cause. Loyalists, or Tories as the patriots called them, accounted for about one-third of the American population (though estimates vary). Neutralists, who remained ambiguous about their allegiance, accounted for another one-third of the population. Loyalists and neutralists came from a variety of backgrounds. Some were American-born and some were European-born. They tended to live in urban centers, especially the port cities, although some people in the frontier regions supported the British. Overall, loyalists tended to be slightly older than their patriot counterparts and were often members of the Anglican Church. Loyalists in many cases saw the revolution as a threat to their personal political, social, and economic rights. Historian Robert Middlekauf suggests the loyalists were often a minority in their communities and as such were dependent on the royal government. Therefore, they opted to support that government during the war. For example, Highland Scots and Germans feared they might lose land granted by the crown if they sided with the revolutionaries. Merchants and shippers feared the economic consequences of terminating their relationship with Britain. Frontier farmers relied on the British army to protect them from the Indians.[15]

Generally speaking, loyalists and neutralists shared many of the same concerns about a break with Britain. Loyalists feared the consequences of break with Britain more than they disliked living under Parliament's rules. In the years before independence, some loyalists joined in the calls for greater representation. Colonial governors, like William Franklin of New Jersey, sympathized with the residents. However, he thought an armed rebellion would not produce the desired result, and when it came he tried to keep New Jersey out of the conflict. The colonists' concerns seemed legitimate, but to some loyalists constitutional ties and mutual interests bound them to the British Empire. Others took a more negative view of the situation; they feared the mob rule and lack of respect for the public good that would come from independence. Some neutralists shared these concerns, but for fear of their safety they did not vocalize them, or they professed to support the patriot cause even if they did not. At the same time, many pacifists objected to war on principle and chose not to fight for either side. Other neutralists simply hoped to avoid the consequences of the war and declared loyalty to one side or the other when it suited their needs.[16]

Loyalists helped the British cause in a variety of ways. They served in the British army and loyalist militia units to help fight the war. They engaged in crowd action such as when tenants on Livingston Manor led an uprising against their patriot landlords to distract the American forces and possibly gain titles to the land they farmed. While most of the uprisings did not accomplish their goals, they did demonstrate that not all Americans supported the patriot cause. The loyalists also helped the British procure much-needed supplies during their occupations of Boston, New York, Philadelphia, and Charleston. And finally, they helped gather intelligence on American activities. For example, Ann Bates, a schoolteacher from Philadelphia, used passes from Benedict Arnold to travel into Washington's encampments around New York City and pass information on the weapons his army possessed onto the British in 1778.[17]

The patriots deemed the Tories enemies of the cause, so loyalists faced potentially severe consequences for their choice. As Harry Ward observes, "war and independence... tolerated no dissent." The Continental Congress left it up to the states to find and punish those loyalists suspected of malfeasance. Most states took quick action to expel European-born loyalists from their states. However, they found it much more difficult to deal with American-born loyalists.[18] They created committees to maintain public safety to expose loyalists. They also required all citizens to pledge an oath of loyalty; those who refused faced disarmament, heavy bonds in exchange for their freedom, or imprisonment. Loyalists often lost their right to vote or to travel freely. Loyalists who seemed determined to promote the British cause faced even more severe consequences. States defined most overt loyalist activities, such as enlisting in or providing supplies to the British army, as treason. Punishment could be the death penalty, but states realized executing loyalists would not necessarily build support for the cause. So, more often than not, the government confiscated the property of the guilty, which also provided a source of revenue for the government. Government action tended to keep individual attacks in check, but some loyalists found themselves the victims of angry patriot attacks.[19]

When the war finally ended, some 80,000 loyalists opted to evacuate with the British largely because Parliament agreed to fund their relocation. Most exiles stayed in British North America, but some went to England. The terms of the Treaty of Paris suggested that the American government should treat loyalists who chose to stay fairly. The Confederation Congress resolved to return confiscated property in 1784, but many states chose not to comply. Loyalists living in the United States spent several years trying to regain their property. Only in the late 1780s did they successfully manage to do so.[20]

8.4.3 The Role of Women

For American women, religious customs and social conventions made them second class citizens in their own homes. They could not vote and had little access to education, and yet, when their husbands went off to serve the Revolution, the women were left to raise their children and run their homes, farms, and in some cases their husbands' businesses by themselves. The war led to anxiety and opportunity. For women, personal and political factors motivated their response to the conflict. On the personal level, they wanted to aid their husbands, sons, fathers, and brothers who joined in the military effort. On the political level, they hoped the war might just remedy some of the inequality they faced. Patriot women had the opportunity to make more of a conscious decision to support their cause than did loyalist women. Therefore, they tended to cope better with the emotional and physical costs of war. While both groups suffered because of the war, once a loyalist husband vocalized his feelings, his wife faced isolation, confiscation, and evacuation.[21]

Whether they became patriots or loyalists, women worried about the fate of their husbands, sons, fathers, and brothers who fought in the war. For most women, the departure of their loved ones left them quite lonely. Ipswich, Massachusetts resident Sarah Hodgkins wrote to her husband Joseph regularly during the war about how much she longed to see him and how she prayed he would survive the war. She could barely hide her opposition when he decided to reenlist, noting "I have got a Sweet Babe almost six months old but have got no father for it."[22] On the other hand, a few women saw the departure of their husbands as a blessing. Grace Growden Galloway, whose loyalist husband was in London, wrote in her journal that "Liberty of doing as I please Makes even poverty more agreeable than any time I ever spent since I married." For several years she resisted his calls to come to London.[23] Still other women wrote to their husbands about their behavior while away from home. Preston, Connecticut resident Lois Crary Peters heard reports of the loose morals of many Continental Army soldiers. She wrote then to her husband, Nathan, about the rumors that he "Did not Care for your wife and family at home." He denied the accusation and she in return said the accounts had not really troubled her.[24]

Women also went to great lengths to support the war effort. Mary Fish Silliman was a reluctant patriot until the night she witnessed loyalists kidnap her husband and son from their home in Fairfield, Connecticut in 1779. Gold Selleck Silliman served as a brigadier general in the Connecticut militia and the loyalists took him to have a prisoner to exchange of equal rank to someone the patriots held. Mary Silliman then worked diligently to secure the release of her husband. Frustrated by the pace of negotiations, she enlisted several friends to kidnap Thomas Jones, a noted loyalist living on Long Island. After five months, the British and the Americans finally worked out terms of exchange and the men returned to their respective families.[25]

Not all women went to the lengths that Mary Silliman did, but women avidly supported the war effort in a variety of ways. They formed spinning societies to make homespun cloth for their families; moreover, they sewed shirts and knitted socks for members of the army. They also collected scrap metal and pewter to be turned into ammunition and they donated spare household liners to be turned into bandages. Women also supported fund drives. The patriot women of Philadelphia, for instance, canvassed door-to-door to raise money to make the lives of the soldiers better. All told, they turned over about $7,500 in specie (coin money) to General Washington. The coordinator of the drive, Esther DeBerdt Reed, requested that the funds be used supplement the soldiers' pay. Worried that the supplement would make soldiers aware of how woefully underpaid they were, Washington put the money toward purchasing new shirts. Women in other cities quickly followed suit in an attempt to show support for the patriot cause.[26]

In spite of their trepidation about being left to fend for themselves, many women found they were more than capable in running their husbands' farms and businesses while also carrying for their children. The effort of course was never easy, but not only did they persevere, many prospered. Meanwhile, their husbands continued to direct their efforts; in time, however, most women found the advice more of a hindrance than a help. When her husband Ralph became trapped in Boston, Elizabeth Murray Smith Inman of Cambridge set about managing the farm, and she made a tidy profit when the crop of hay came in. When the patriots interred her pacifist husband Thomas in Virginia, Sally Logan Fisher of Philadelphia at first despaired about how she would manage without him. Increasingly though, her diary entries suggested a renewed spirit in her ability to support her family. When her husband Josiah went to Philadelphia to serve in the Continental Congress, Mary Bartlett worried she would not be up to the task of maintaining the family business. However, within a couple of years she began to write him of "our business," not "his business," showing how the war blurred the line between the public and private spheres.[27]

After the war was over and the men returned home, they expected their wives to resume their subservient past. Women attempted to resist such efforts, but found little support for their rights inside or outside of the home. For many political leaders, women's contributions to the war actually reinforced the idea that a women's place was in the private sphere caring for the family. Still, in the 1780s, women gained some additional social and legal rights. As the Church of England lost control in many of the states, divorce proceedings fell into the realm of civil authorities instead of religious authorities. While it was by no means simple to obtain a divorce, it became easier. Most states retained the practice of coverture, whereby the husband retained legal control over the person, property, and choices of his wife. Single women and widows gained greater property rights, but that did not in most cases lead to the political rights that property conferred (such as the right to vote). Discussion of the role of women during and after the war led to small improvements in the status of women. In the postwar years, many men and women subscribed to the concept of "Republican motherhood." Women had a public duty to educate their children to become virtuous citizens and as such they needed to have more education to successfully mold good Americans.[28]

8.4.4 The Future of Slavery

The ideas of liberty and equality which helped to ignite the Revolution also brought to mind questions of liberty and equality for blacks—both slave and free. For slaves, the fight for independence raised questions about their future because in a republic based on the premise "all men are created equal," many people wondered whether slavery should continue to exist. Many slaves looked to use the war to secure their own freedom. For free blacks, questions about slavery also played a role in their wartime experience. Most recognized that if states maintained the institution of slavery even though they had their freedom, they would not be able to achieve equality. In 1775, Benjamin Franklin had founded the first abolitionist society in America, the Society for the Relief of Free Negroes Unlawfully Held in Bondage. After that, the abolitionist ideas spread to other states. During and after the war, many northern states embraced gradual emancipation; however, most southern states renewed their commitment to the use of race-based slavery.

Slavery had been part of American life since the seventeenth century when the first Africans arrive in Jamestown in 1619. For years it existed alongside indentured servitude as the primary mode of labor on tobacco and rice plantations in the South. However, in the North people also purchased slaves to work in their fields and homes. In 1760, somewhere around 350,000 blacks were enslaved. Around 145,000 lived in Virginia and Maryland, 40,000 lived in South Carolina and Georgia, and the rest lived in the northern colonies, especially New York and New Jersey. Thus, slavery at the time of the American Revolution was a national institution, not a southern institution. While only one-quarter of the population owned slaves, slavery became a key component of the successful American economy. Slaveholders found it to be the most cost effective form of labor. At the same time, many non-slaveholders, including merchants, ship builders, and their employees, benefited from the side effects of the international slave trade.[29]

Many slaves grudgingly accepted their life of servitude while also looking for ways to gain their freedom. Some liberated themselves by running away, but others were emancipated by their owners. The free black community grew slowly in the prewar years; however, by virtue of their freedom they became speakers of their race and increasingly called for widespread emancipation. As the American colonists increasingly vocalized a desire to be free from their imperial masters, many slaves used similar rhetoric to call for emancipation. In 1773, Felix, a Boston slave, sent Lieutenant Governor Thomas Hutchinson a petition on behalf of his fellow slaves asking for help to redress "their unhappy state" and trusting in the governor's "wisdom, justice, and goodness" to help them. Other such petitions followed and became increasingly forceful in their requests for an end to slavery.[30]

Some white colonists also began to speak out against slavery before the Revolution, most notably among the Quaker communities in Pennsylvania and New Jersey. Quakers John Woolman and Anthony Benezet argued that the sin of slavery was a sign that the Friends had become negligent of their faith. They called on the Quakers to condemn the slave trade and free their slaves. In time, their sentiments spread beyond the Quaker community. While ministers from other faiths continued to condemn slavery as a sin, James Otis linked the cause of independence with the cause of emancipation, noting the irony of pursing one and not the other. As his argument spread, several Massachusetts towns instructed their delegates to the colonial legislature to pass a law banning the importation of slaves. Elsewhere in the colonies, talk of ending slavery ensued; Arthur Lee, son of a prominent Virginia slaveholder, noted "freedom is unquestionably the birth-right of all mankind, of Africans as well as Europeans." Of course, not all colonists supported such a move; fellow southerners widely denounced Lee's essay.[31]

When the revolution began, blacks—slave and free—looked for opportunities to use the conflict to gain their freedom. After Lord Dunmore's Proclamation in 1775, southern slaves sought to take advantage of the offer to fight for the British and receive their freedom. Only about 300 slaves managed to respond because Virginia slaveholders made it quite difficult for slaves to escape. Later, General Clinton made a similar request, calling blacks to defend the crown in exchange for their freedom. Over the course of the war, blacks served in British units and provided needed support services; however, exact numbers have been hard to come by. Colonel Tye, a runaway, led a band of black loyalists in terrorizing the New York and New Jersey patriots in 1778 and 1779. Boston Kin managed to escape twice, first from his master and then from a band of loyalists who tried to sell him back into slavery, in order to serve the British. Other slaves, especially women, took advantage of the chaos brought on by the war to flee to the British in hopes of gaining their freedom.[32]

Northern slaves and free blacks more often than not enlisted in the Continental Army; throughout the course of the war, over 5,000 served the patriot cause. More might have served, but the Continental Congress succumbed to pressure from southern representatives to bar slaves from service so the government would not have to compensate their owners. In spite of the obstacles, free blacks and some slaves continued to enlist. The promise of the Declaration of Independence inspired them to join in the battle for American freedom, which they hoped would translate into personal freedom. Moreover, they provided much-needed manpower. Rhode Island, so desperate for soldiers, recruited an all-black regiment, as did Massachusetts and Connecticut; the other states integrated blacks into regular units. During the course of the war, black soldiers served with distinction: Peter Salem, Salem Poor, and Prince Whipple all won praise for their contribution to the campaign in Massachusetts in 1775.[33]

During and after the war, many Americans, especially in the North, embraced emancipation and worked to end slavery within their borders. As Robert Middlekauf suggests, “the irony of white Americans claiming liberty while they held slaves did not escape the revolutionary generation.” Pennsylvania and Vermont banned slavery in their state constitutions in the 1770s. Massachusetts and New Hampshire significantly curtailed slavery through court action. Connecticut and Rhode Island passed laws providing for gradual emancipation in the early 1780s; New York and New Jersey also adopted policies of gradual emancipation but not until the late 1790s. Southerners, for a variety of reasons, resisted the shift toward statewide emancipation, though some slaveholders did free their slaves on an individual basis. However, by the early 1800s the practice of manumission fell out of use. The failure to end slavery on the national level caused slavery to become a southern phenomenon sometimes called the “peculiar institution” and the number of slaves there increased dramatically after the invention of the cotton gin in the 1790s. Meanwhile, the free black population continued to grow, but they faced continued prejudice and discrimination. For blacks—slave or free—the revolution failed to live up to their expectations.[34]

Figure 8.4 Salem Poor Stamp | Commemorating Black Patriots–Salem Poor was one of the more than 5,000 blacks who joined in the patriot cause during the American Revolution. In 1975, the United States Postal Service honored his service as part of their Gallant Soldier series.

Author: U.S. Postal Service
Source: Wikimedia Commons

8.4.5 Indians and the American Revolution

Throughout the colonies and the American frontier, Indians debated foreign policy, weighed their options, and chose sides in the American Revolution. Indian participation in colonial wars was certainly not a new development. Many of the native peoples of North America had participated in colonial wars, such as Queen Anne's and King William's Wars; the French and Indian War was the most important example of native interests in European colonial conflicts.

At the outset of the American Revolution, many tribes chose to remain neutral in the conflict. Unlike the French and Indian War and other wars of the previous hundred years, this war did not concern many nations. The nascent American government fully supported this neutrality. The Second Continental Congress wrote to the Iroquois Confederacy on the matter, stating,

> We desire that you will hear and receive what we have now told you, and that you will open a good ear and listen to what we are now going to say. This is a family quarrel between us and old England. You Indians are not concerned in it. We don't wish you to take up the hatchet against the King's Troops. We desire you to remain at home, and not join either side, but keep the hatchet buried deep.[35]

Although the Second Continental Congress claimed that the war did not concern native people, as the conflict escalated, many tribes quickly concluded that there was much at stake for the Indian population. From a native point of view, the Revolution was a contest for Indian lands. Protecting and securing lands against encroaching American settlement inspired many, both as individuals and as tribes, to abandon neutrality and choose a side in the fight. For the majority of Indians, fighting for the British cause made the most sense. The British supported the Proclamation Line of 1763. Although not meant to be a permanent measure, it provided some degree of security against expansion. Although most groups supported the British, some native peoples did side with the Americans. Indian support for the American cause was strongest in New England, where the populations had lived closely with their colonial neighbors for the longest period of time.

Although both the Americans and the British initially desired for Indians to remain neutral, once the war broke out, each side abandoned this policy and cultivated native allies. The powerful Iroquois Confederacy was one of the most important potential native alliances. For more than one hundred years, the Iroquois had been a major political force in the Northeast. In 1775, the Iroquois Confederacy declared itself to be neutral in the war. However, the decision was not unanimous. Each of the six nations had freedom in determining its individual war policy. In a series of meetings from 1776 to 1777, the Iroquois nations debated their involvement in the American Revolution. Mohawk Joseph Brandt (Thayenadanega) was a key figure who argued for forming an alliance with the British. Brandt had been educated at a Christian Indian school and worked as a translator for the British. He helped to bring four of the six Iroquois nations into an alliance with the British, these four being the Mohawk, Cayuga, Seneca, and Onondoga. The remaining two nations, the Oneida and Tuscarora, allied with the Americans in the war. Ultimately, the Iroquois Confederacy underwent a major political split over the issue of the American Revolution.

Brandt and the British-allied Iroquois nations conducted a series of successful campaigns against American frontier settlements in the Mohawk Valley, devastating many villages. In retaliation, Washington ordered General John Sullivan to lead an expedition into Iroquois lands with the objective of ending frontier warfare in the region and capturing Fort Niagara. In the summer of 1779, Sullivan's forces entered the Mohawk Valley. The campaign saw only one major battle, which the American forces decisively won; however, they ultimately failed to capture Fort Niagara. The major effect of the campaign was Sullivan's scorched earth policy, which resulted in the total destruction of dozens of Iroquois villages. Moreover, rather than quelling frontier war and Iroquois involvement, Sullivan's expedition against Iroquois lands inspired many Oneida and Tuscarora to reconsider their American alliance and switch to fighting for the British.

In the South, the Creek, Chickasaw, and Choctaw fought with the British; the Catawba fought on the American side. Cherokee elders favored neutrality in the war, but the younger generations, having seen tremendous land loss over the course of their lives, tended to favor allying with the British in an attempt to prevent further encroachment. The most important leader of the faction of younger Cherokee was Dragging Canoe (ᏥᏳ ᎦᏅᏏᏂ), son of famed warrior Attakullakulla. In the summer of 1776, Dragging Canoe led a series of successful raids in Eastern Tennessee and soon broadened the scope of the frontier battles to Kentucky, Virginia, Georgia, and North Carolina. The colonial forces retaliated by taking the war into Cherokee lands, destroying more than fifty towns, killing hundreds and selling hundreds more Cherokee into slavery. The conflict continued throughout the American Revolution and for ten more years after the war's end; for this reason, the Cherokee war within and beyond the American Revolution is referred to as the Chickamauga Wars (1776-1794).

8.4.6 Before You Move On...

Key Concepts

The American Revolution impacted the lives of Americans in more ways than simply a political independence from Great Britain. Americans had come to think of themselves in new ways and suffered new and unexpected economic hardships. While the Continental Congress struggled to meet their financial obligations, the soldiers and their families faced rampant inflation and constant shortages of goods; the end of the war brought little relief from their economic suffering. Americans who did not support the patriot cause, the loyalists or Tories, chose to aid the British war effort in a variety of ways. They often suffered physical and economic consequences at the hands of the patriot governments in their communities.

The lofty rhetoric of the Declaration of Independence also inspired many women to fight for greater political and economic rights and blacks to fight for an end to slavery and real equality. Women found themselves more than capable of managing their families' farms and businesses in the absence of their husbands and fathers. When the war came to an end, they hoped to retain some of that economic freedom and expand their political rights. However, most men refused to listen to their calls.

Meanwhile, blacks—slave and free—sought to use the revolution to end bondage and inequality. Southern slaves flocked to the loyalist cause in hopes of securing freedom; northern slaves and free blacks, on the other hand, tended to support the patriot cause. While the war led to the end of slavery, on a gradual basis, in the northern states, the same was not true in the southern states, where it continued to grow.

The presence of Indians in North America complicated alliances during the American Revolutionary War. Although both the colonists and the British would have preferred that the tribes remain neutral, many did not. Neutrality was declared by the Iroquois Confederacy, but the decision was not unanimous and individual tribes proceeded to create alliances, mostly with the British. In the South, the majority of the tribes that became involved sided with the British; only the Catawba of North Carolina fought on the side of the Americans. And while most Cherokee elders favored neutrality, younger tribal members rallied against the colonials and wreaked havoc on Tennessee, Kentucky, North Carolina, and Georgia.

Test Yourself

1. Revolutionary war soldiers were well rewarded for their service.

   a. True

   b. False

2. Many women found themselves incapable of handling the burdens of war when their husbands and fathers went off to fight.

   a. True

   b. False

3. Benjamin Franklin established the first abolitionist society in America.

   a. True

   b. False

4. Most Indian tribes and nations supported the British because they feared that an American victory would mean a greater loss of land through expansion.

   a. True

   b. False

5. All of the tribes in the Iroquois Confederacy maintained neutrality during the Revolutionary War.

   a. True

   b. False

See page 313 for answers

8.5 THE TREATY OF PARIS, 1783

For the British, the American Revolution was but one of several conflicts taxing the resources of the British military in 1783. Not only were the American colonists in revolt, aided by Britain's long-standing enemy, France, but there were conflicts with the Spanish and Dutch and a separate issue with the French as well. Diplomatic negotiations known as the Peace of Paris saw the signing of several treaties that put these conflicts to rest, at least for the moment.

The Treaty of Paris, 1783, was the treaty that dealt specifically with the American Revolution. For the Americans, John Adams, Benjamin Franklin, and John Jay led the negotiations and signed the treaty for the United States. David Hartley, British MP signed as the representative of King George III. The treaty laid out the terms for peace between the United States and Great Britain in ten straightforward articles. The French had hoped to keep the Americans from signing a separate treaty with the British. Keeping the British occupied with a war against their own colonies was to the French advantage, as it tied up resources, both financial and military, that the British might use in a conflict with France. The American negotiators realized though that prolonging the war was not in the best interests of their fledgling nation: it drained them financially and of human life. With this in mind, the Americans made their separate peace.

Article I

In Article I, Britain promised to recognize sovereignty of the United States, listing each of the former colonies by name: New Hampshire, Massachusetts Bay, Rhode Island and Providence Plantations, Connecticut, New York, New Jersey, Pennsylvania, Delaware, Maryland, Virginia, North Carolina, South Carolina, and Georgia. All British claims to the United States were relinquished.

Article II

The borders of the United States as recognized by Great Britain were established. The intention was particularly to define the borders between the United States and those North American colonies still loyal to Britain in Canada. This treaty did not deal with the issue of Florida, which was settled between Great Britain and Spain in a separate treaty.

Article III

Article III covered fishing rights, particularly the rights to fish the Grand Banks off of Newfoundland and the Gulf of St. Lawrence. In 1783, they were important to the economy of Canada and New England as well as Europe.

Article IV

Before the Revolution, colonial merchants and planters were heavily involved with British banking houses and merchants. This article guaranteed the rights of people in both countries to collect their debts. Although the right to collect debts was recognized, collecting international debts in 1783 was not always easy or even possible.

Article V

Article V was concerned with the rights of British subjects and Loyalists. With Article V, the United States promised that Congress would make an effort to encourage the various state legislatures to protect the property rights of British subjects and Loyalists who had their property seized during the war. It is worth noting that while this article promised that Congress would encourage the legislatures to respect the property rights of Loyalists, nowhere in the article does it actually guarantee that those property rights would be respected. In other words, Congress was bound by this treaty to bring the matter to the attention of the various legislatures, but the legislatures, in turn, were free to do as they pleased.

Article VI

This article continues with the issue of Loyalists who remained in the United States. With this article, the United States essentially promised to protect Loyalists from further harassment, either by having property seized or being charged with crimes. Further, any Loyalist who was imprisoned at the time of the ratification of the treaty would be immediately released.

Article VII

Article VII promised a tidy end to the war. The British were to remove their troops and property from the United States as soon as they could without any theft, including of slaves that belonged to the Americans. All prisoners on both sides were to be released, and any documents or records of importance to Americans that were in British hands were to be returned.

Article VIII

Article VIII promised that both Americans and British subjects would always be allowed to travel the full length of the Mississippi River, "...from its source to the ocean..." In 1783, the end of the Mississippi where it pours into the Gulf of Mexico was well-known. However, the actual source was not, to Americans and Europeans alike. Not until 1806 would it be known that there definitely was no Northwest Passage, and not until 1832 would the area of the headwaters of the Mississippi River be discovered and explored by non-Indians.

Article IX

Article IX promised that if any American territory fell into British hands, or British territory fell into American hands during the Revolution, the territory would be returned to its proper owner without any difficulties.

Article X

A ratification deadline of six months from the date of signing was specified with this article.

8.5.1 Before You Move On...

Key Concepts

Although the Treaty of Paris promised the best intentions of both sides, in the end, it was just a piece of paper. It signaled the end of the war and the beginning of a new period of peace between the United States and Great Britain, but the articles of the Treaty, particularly those that required the obedience of the states, were not always followed. In addition, the British were slow in some cases to actually move out of the areas they were to vacate and the emotions that led to the persecution of Loyalists during the war did not instantly subside. While the treaty addressed several issues, it failed to mention Indian tribes which had fought on both sides and so had a stake in the outcome of the war. Even the most important provision of the treaty, that Britain would recognize the sovereignty of the United States, would be imperfectly applied, leading to increasing abuse by the British of American shipping. The perhaps inevitable conflict less than thirty years later was known as the War of 1812.

Test Yourself

1. For all practical purposes, the Treaty of Paris ignored the American Indians.

   a. True

   b. False

2. Both the Americans and the British gave up claims to the Mississippi for the sake of peace.

   a. True

   b. False

3. Loyalists were protected by the treaty and well treated after it was signed.

   a. True

   b. False

See page 314 for answers

Sidebar 8.1: How Revolutionary Was the Revolution?

Just how "revolutionary" was the American Revolution? Certainly the English colonials won their independence, and the system of government they would eventually adopt would not be a monarchy; neither was it a full-fledged democracy, a reality later reflected in the Constitution of 1789.

Historians are generally divided into two camps in their interpretation of the American Revolution. Some historians argue that the Revolution was primarily a colonial rebellion whose aim was simply independence from Britain. According to these historians, colonial society was essentially a democratic society, and the Revolution sought to maintain the status quo. Other historians take a more radical view of the Revolution, seeing it as a violent social upheaval that was the result of a class conflict in which the lower classes of colonial society attempted to implement a greater degree of democracy and attain greater equality.

Historians who wrote in eras when nationalism was an important ideal or issue tend to view the Revolution as a radical event which helped to forge greater unity among the colonists and a greater degree of liberty. George Bancroft's *History of the United States*, written in the period between the Jacksonian era and the Civil war, is an example of a work which tended to emphasize the unity of the colonists in their quest for liberty against the tyrannical policies of the British.

The Imperial School of Historians

In the twentieth century, historians began to look more critically at nationalistic views, such as those of Bancroft. The so-called "imperial" school of historians, represented by the work of George Beer, Charles Andrews, and Lawrence Gipson, argued that the American Revolution should be understood within the context of the British Empire as a whole. Gipson's multi-volume *The British Empire before the American Revolution*, published between the 1930s and the 1960s, argued forcefully that British taxation of the colonies was justified, as the mother country had defended the colonies with soldiers and money during the French and Indian War (1754-1763). The imperial school of historians argued that conflicts over constitutional issues were at the heart of the Revolution; while the mother country sought greater control over her empire, the colonies were moving toward self-government. Essentially, the Revolution, for the imperialist historians, represented a conflict between two incompatible societies.

The Progressive School of Historians

On the other hand, the school of progressive historians, who wrote in an age dominated by concern about concentration of power in the hands of a few elite, argued that social and economic issues were the root cause of the Revolution. Carl Becker argued that the American Revolution was not one revolution but two: an external revolution against Britain caused by a conflict of economic interests, and an internal revolution of one class in American society against another to determine "who should rule at home" (*The History of Political Parties in the Province of New York,* 1760-1776, 22). In *The American Revolution Considered as a Social Movement*, J. Franklin Jameson spelled out in great detail the radical social and economic reforms achieved in the Revolution. Loyalist estates were confiscated and sold in smaller plots to farmers. Land ownership was more widespread than it was in England, there were no titles of nobility or any of the other trappings of monarchy, and religious freedom was guaranteed in most state constitutions and in the Constitution of 1789. Property qualifications for voting were lowered, slavery was abolished in some of the states, some slaves received their freedom in return for service in the war, and the Anglican Church was disestablished. The progressive historians, then, saw the Revolution as a radical turning point in American history, in which the dispossessed lower classes advanced their cause and attained greater rights and equality.

The Neoconservative School of Historians

Since World War II, however, the "neoconservative" historians have challenged the radical view of the Progressives. Historians such as Robert E. Brown have challenged the Progressive view that colonial America was undemocratic. Brown and others argue that very few colonists, for example, were disenfranchised as voters based on property qualifications; his study of *Middle-Class Democracy and the Revolution in Massachusetts* suggested that the vast majority of adult males in colonial America owned enough property to vote. Similarly, Daniel Boorstin argued in *The Genius of American Politics* that the American revolutionaries fought not to achieve a radical new social order, but only to defend the traditional order against British intrusions. According to this school of thought, the Revolution was an ideological movement concerned with preserving rights, as opposed to a radical movement that sought sweeping social, economic, and political changes. Sometimes referred to as the "consensus school" of historians, these critics downplayed class conflict within colonial society and instead depicted the "patriot" element of society as having essentially the same goals and aspirations, regardless of social class.

Ideology and the Revolution

Beginning in the 1960s, a new focus fell on the intellectual underpinnings of the American Revolution, taking the discussion of the event in a new direction. Beginning with Bernard Bailyn's *Ideological Origins of the American Revolution*, historians stressed ideas as the cause of the Revolution, rather than social and economic factors. They asserted that the colonists, impacted by Whig politics in England and the earlier tradition of anti-authoritarian thought promulgated in the Glorious Revolution, truly came to believe their liberties were in danger.

New Left Historians

During the 1960s, another group of historians, referred to as the "New Left," criticized earlier historians' focus on colonial elites and began to assert that the revolution was influenced by the desires of the "lower sort" in colonial society. Referred to as "bottom up" history, the work of scholars such as Alfred E. Young and Edward Countryman has redirected a great deal of research to non-elite groups such as militia members and artisans.

The Debate Continues

Few topics in American history have elicited such a wide range of interpretations from historians. The Revolution is still a very active area of research today. More recent works, such as Gordon Wood's *The Radicalism of the American Revolution*, have returned to older themes of colonial class dynamics, while incorporating New Left perspectives of examining changing attitudes and lifestyles among everyday Americans. Wood's focus turns to the social changes wrought by the revolution, and in the end, as the title implies, asserts that the political changes brought on by the Revolution in creating a republic radically altered American society. The Revolution, according to Wood, shifted colonial society from a people tied to an old world culture of deference and tradition to a modern, liberal, and democratic people. Wood's work immediately resulted in a new debate over the merits of this perspective. Undoubtedly, further examinations of this momentous event will continue to emerge in the years to come.

8.6 Conclusion

The social unease which led to the American Revolution did not automatically ignite a violent conflict between Great Britain and her American colonies. Many on both sides hoped for a peaceful solution, reconciliation, or amicable agreement that would have addressed the grievances of the colonists while preserving the colonial relationship. This was not to be. Instead, tensions mounted and the quiet plans made by General Gage in Boston to diffuse the situation unintentionally ignited the war at Lexington. The Second Continental Congress met in Philadelphia at first to consider reconciliation and then to move on to form the government of colonies in revolt. They created and sent the Declaration of Independence to Britain, announcing to all the fateful decision to seek true independence and the reasons for it. On the home front, the Congress attempted to create a government that would be able to support an army to fight for independence. George Washington of Virginia became the Commander of the American forces. He faced the challenge of taking men from all over the colonies with diverse backgrounds, few with military experience, and molding them into a fighting army, often without proper weapons, uniforms, or other equipment and supplies. From 1775 to 1781, the two main armies and other smaller forces clashed from Canada to South Carolina, finally ending in Yorktown, Virginia where the main British force under Lord Cornwallis was cornered and forced to surrender to Washington. Although the military conflict was over, the revolution did not officially end until the ratification of the Treaty of Paris. The American Revolution was a time not just of military battles, but also of social upheaval for the civilians, men and women, whites and blacks, both free and slave, and Indians as all together they faced an uncertain future. No colony, no level of society, was left untouched. In the end, the American Revolution led to the founding not just of a new nation, but of a new national model of democracy that would have influence around the world in the centuries to follow.

8.7 CRITICAL THINKING EXERCISES

- Why do you think that the Continental Congress created an army and began preparing for war before George III had given a response to the *Olive Branch Petition?*
- Why would delegates to the Second Continental Congress hope that the colonies and the mother country could be reconciled? Why did they ultimately change their minds?
- Why do you think that Thomas Jefferson and those on the committee that drafted the Declaration of Independence decided to use the "pursuit of happiness" instead of John Locke's "property" as a natural right?
- Why would simple farmers and shopkeepers train as soldiers and risk their lives fighting a professional army as at Lexington and Concord?
- What could the British have done to prevent violence at Lexington and Concord?
- How did the ideas of the revolution inspire abolitionists such as Benjamin Franklin?

8.8 KEY TERMS

- John Adams
- Samuel Adams
- Benedict Arnold
- Artillery
- Articles of Confederation
- Joseph Brandt
- John Burgoyne
- Chickamauga Wars
- Henry Clinton
- *Common Sense*
- Charles Cornwallis
- *Conciliatory Proposition*
- Dragging Canoe
- *Declaration of Independence*
- *Declaration of the Causes of Taking up Arms*
- John Dickinson
- "Firm League of Friendship"
- Fortifications
- Benjamin Franklin
- Thomas Gage
- Horatio Gates
- Hessians
- House of Commons
- William Howe
- Hudson River Valley
- Thomas Jefferson
- Benjamin Lincoln
- John Locke
- Locke's theory of revolution
- Militia
- Daniel Morgan
- Natural Rights
- *Olive Branch Petition*
- Thomas Paine
- Preamble
- *Prohibitory Act*
- Paul Revere
- Second Continental Congress
- Spy
- Sullivan Expedition
- Banastre Tarleton
- Tarleton's Quarter
- George Washington

8.9 CHRONOLOGY

The following chronology is a list of important dates and events associated with this chapter.

Date	Event
1775	Fort Ticonderoga captured by Ethan Allen and the Green Mountain Boys; Battle of Bunker/Breeds Hill; Second Continental Congress convened; Olive Branch Petition Presented to George III
1776	*Common Sense* published;Declaration of Independence adopted by Second Continental Congress;Battle of Long Island/Brooklyn Heights; Battle of Trenton
1777	Second Battle of Trenton; Battle of Princeton; British occupy Philadelphia; Battles of Saratoga; Surrender of British army under General Burgoyne; Articles of Confederation adopted by Second Continental Congress; Continental Army wintered at Valley Forge
1778	Treaty of Alliance signed with France; British occupation of Philadelphia ended
1780	Battle of Charleston; American General Benjamin Lincoln surrendered to the British
1781	Articles of Confederation ratified; Battle of Cowpens; Battle of Guilford Court House; British surrendered at Yorktown
1782	British government officially recognized American independence
1783	Treaty of Paris brought an end to the American Revolutionary War

8.10 BIBLIOGRAPHY

Baack, Ben. "The Economics of the American Revolutionary War." *EH.Net Encyclopedia*. Ed. Robert Whaples, October 1, 2012. http://eh.net/encyclopedia/article/baack.war.revolutionary.us.

Deloria, Jr., Vine, and Raymond J. DeMaille, Documents of American Indian Diplomacy: Treaties, Agreements, and Conventions, 1775-1979. Norman, Oklahoma: University of Oklahoma Press, 1999.

Henry, Patrick. "Give Me Liberty or Give Me Death." University of Oklahoma Law School, Historical Documents. http://www.law.ou.edu/ushistory/henry.shtml.

"In Defense of American Liberty," Massachusetts Historical Society, The Coming of the American Revolution, http://www.masshist.org/revolution/congress2.php.

Battle of Saratoga. http://battle1777.saratoga.org/.

British Battles.com. http://www.britishbattles.com/.

Bureau of the Public Debt. http://www.publicdebt.treas.gov/.

Digital History. http://www.digitalhistory.uh.edu/.

Jordan, Louis. "Colonial Fiscal Documents." *Colonial Currency*. University of Notre Dame, Department of Special Collections, October 1, 2012. http://www.coins.nd.edu/ColCurrency/CurrencyText/FiscalDocsUS.html.

Middlekauff, Robert. *The Glorious Cause: The American Revolution.* New York: Oxford University Press, 1982.

Morison, Samuel Eliot, Henry Steele Commager and William E. Lauchenberg, *A Concise History of the American Republic*, vol. 1 to 1877. New York: Oxford University Press,1977).

Nash, Gary B. *The Unknown American Revolution: The Unruly Birth of American Democracy and the Struggle to Create America.* New York: Viking, 2005.

Nelson, William H. *The American Tory.* Boston: Beacon Press, 1964.

Norton, Mary Beth. *Liberty's Daughters: The Revolutionary Experience of American Women, 1750-1800.* Ithaca: Cornell University Press, 1996.

Paine, Thomas. *Common Sense.* Modern History Sourcebook, ed. Paul Halsall. www.fordham.edu/halsall.

"Proclamation of King George III For suppressing Rebellion and Sedition," Massachusetts Historical Society, The Coming of the American Revolution, http://www.masshist.org/revolution/congress2.php.

Resolutions of [the Second Continental] Congress on Lord North's Conciliatory Proposal. Yale University, Avalon Project, http://www.avalon.law.yale.edu.

"Revolution, 1750-1805 (Narrative)." *Africans in America.* PBS, October 3, 2012. http://www.pbs.org/wgbh/aia/part2/narrative.html.

"Rules and Arguments for the Better Government of the Troops," Massachusetts Historical Society, The Coming of the American Revolution, http://www.masshist.org/revolution/congress2.php.

Second Continental Congress. *Causes and Necessity of Taking Up Arms.* Modern History Sourcebook, ed. Paul Halsall. www.fordham.edu/halsall.

National Archives. http://www.archives.gov/.

National Park Service. http://www.nps.gov/.

US History.org. http://www.ushistory.org/.

Ward, Harry M. *The War for Independence and the Transformation of American Society.* London: UCL Press, 1999.

8.11 END NOTES

1 Patrick Henry quoted in Morison, Commager and Leuchtenburg, *A Concise History of the American Republic*, vol. 1 to 1877. (New York: Oxford University Press,1977), 78.

2 Quoted in Robert Middlekauff, *The Glorious Cause: The American Revolution* (New York: Oxford University Press, 1984), 378-379.

3 *Proclamation of King George III For suppressing Rebellion and Sedition*, Massachusetts Historical Society, The Coming of the American Revolution, http://www.masshist.org/revolution/congress2.php.

4 "Lord Dunmore's Proclamation, November 7, 1775," Portland State College of Urban and Public Affairs, http://www.upa.pdx.edu/IMS/currentprojects/TAHv3/Content/PDFs/Dunmore_Proclamation_1775.pdf.

5 "Rules and Arguments for the Better Government of the Troops, Massachusetts Historical Society," The Coming of the American Revolution, http://www.masshist.org/revolution/congress2.php.

6 "In Defense of American Liberty," Massachusetts Historical Society, The Coming of the American Revolution, http://www.masshist.org/revolution/congress2.php, 2.

7 "Whereas the Petitions of these United Colonies to the King, for the Redress of great and manifest Grievances," Massachusetts Historical Society, The Coming of the American Revolution, http://www.masshist.org/revolution/congress2.php.

8 *The Causes and Necessities of Taking Up Arms*, in History Sourcebooks, ed. Paul Halsall, www.fordham.edu.

9 *Causes and Necessities.*

10 Paine quoted in Robert Middlekauff, *Glorious Cause*, 318-19.

11 Middlekauff, Glorio*us Cause*, 328.

12 Robert Middlekauff, *The Glorious Cause: The American Revolution, 1763-1789* (New York: Oxford University Press), 544-545; Mary Beth Norton, *Liberty's Daughters: The Revolutionary Experience of American Women, 1750-1800* (Ithaca: Cornell University Press, 1996), 195.

13 Middlekauff, *The Glorious Cause*, 552-553, 614-616; Ben Baack, "The Economics of the American Revolutionary War," *EH.Net Encyclopedia*, ed. Robert Whaples, October 1, 2012, http://eh.net/encyclopedia/article/baack.war.revolutionary.us; Louis Jordan, "Colonial Fiscal Documents," *Colonial Currency*, University of Notre Dame, Department of Special Collections, October 1, 2012, http://www.coins.nd.edu/ColCurrency/CurrencyText/FiscalDocsUS.html.

14 Harry M. Ward, *The War for Independence and the Transformation of American Society* (London: UCL Press, 1999), 149-157.

15 Ward, *The War for Independence and the Transformation of American Society*, 35; Middlekauff, *The Glorious Cause*, 564-565.

16 Ward, *The War for Independence and the Transformation of American Society*, 37-38; William H. Nelson, *The American Tory* (Boston: Beacon Press, 1964), 7, 105.

17 Ward, *The War for Independence and the Transformation of American Society*, 40-44.

18 Ward, *The War for Independence and the Transformation of American Society*, 38.

19 Middlekauff, *The Glorious Cause*, 566-567.

20 Ward, *The War for Independence and the Transformation of American Society*, 45, 48.

21 Norton, *Liberty's Daughters*, 212-213.

22 Sarah Hodgkins quoted in Middlekauff, *The Glorious Cause*, 546.

23 Grace Growden Galloway quoted in Norton, *Liberty's Daughters*, 217-218.

24 Lois Crary Peters quoted in Middlekauff, *The Glorious Cause*, 549.

25 Middlekauff, *The Glorious Cause*, 547-548.

26 Ward, *The War for Independence and the Transformation of American Society*, 148; Norton, *Liberty's Daughters*, 179-181.

27 Norton, *Liberty's Daughters*, 217-221.

28 Ward, *The War for Independence and the Transformation of American Society*, 164-166, 169.

29 "Revolution, 1750-1805 (Narrative)," *Africans in America*, PBS, October 3, 2012, http://www.pbs.org/wgbh/aia/part2/narrative.html; Gary B. Nash, *The Unknown American Revolution: The Unruly Birth of American Democracy and the Struggle to Create America* (New York: Viking, 2005), 33.
30 "Revolution, 1750-1805 (Narrative)," *Africans in America*; Felix's Petition, 6 January 1773, *Africans in America*, PBS, October 3, 2012, http://www.pbs.org/wgbh/aia/part2/2h22t.html; Nash, *The Unknown American Revolution*, 126-127. Historians are not entirely sure "Felix" wrote the petition since literacy rates were low among the enslaved population; some speculate that Boston slave and poet Phillis Wheatley drafted the statement. See, Nash, *The Unknown American Revolution*, 127.

31 Nash, *The Unknown American Revolution*, 41-42; 62-63; Arthur Lee quoted in Nash, *The Unknown American Revolution*, 115.

32 Ward, *The War for Independence and the Transformation of American Society*, 180-182; Nash, *The Unknown American Revolution*, 230-231; "Revolution, 1750-1805 (Narrative)," *Africans in America*.

33 Ward, *The War for Independence and the Transformation of American Society*, 178-180; Nash, *The Unknown American Revolution*, 223-229; Middlekauf, *The Glorious Cause*, 570-571.

34 Middlekauf, *The Glorious Cause*, 571-572; Ward, *The War for Independence and the Transformation of American Society*, 186-187.

35 Vine Deloria, Jr., and Raymond J. DeMaille, *Documents of American Indian Diplomacy: Treaties, Agreements, and Conventions, 1775-1979* (Norman, Oklahoma: University of Oklahoma Press, 1999), 38.

ANSWER KEY FOR CHAPTER EIGHT: THE AMERICAN REVOLUTION

Check your answers to the questions in the Before You Move On Sections for this chapter.

Correct answers are **BOLDED**

Section 8.2.3 - p278

1. The rationale that Jefferson used in the Declaration of Independence came primarily from the theories of John Locke.
   A. TRUE
   b. False

2. Which of the following documents was NOT one drafted by the Second Continental Congress?
   A. THE PROHIBITORY ACT
   b. The Declaration of Independence
   c. The Olive Branch Petition
   d. The Causes and Necessity of Taking Up Arms

3. In the Conciliatory Proposition, the mother country gave in to most of the demands of the American colonists.
   a. True
   B. FALSE

4. The Declaration of Independence consists of _______ sections:
   a. One
   b. Two
   c. Three
   d. Four
   E. FIVE

Section 8.3.9 - p291

1. One of the most important results of the American victory at Saratoga was
   a. the Hessian removal from the British force.
   b. the French participation in the war on the side of the British.
   C. THE FRENCH PARTICIPATION IN THE WAR ON THE SIDE OF THE AMERICANS.
   d. the end of the war.

2. The siege of Charleston was well conducted.
   A. TRUE
   b. False

3. Famous for leading his troops against the Hessians at Trenton, New Jersey was
   A. GENERAL GEORGE WASHINGTON.
   b. Brigadier General Daniel Morgan.
   c. Major Benedict Arnold.
   d. Major General Benjamin Lincoln.

4. Benedict Arnold is America's most famous traitor.
   A. TRUE
   b. False

Section 8.4.6 - p301

1. Revolutionary war soldiers were well rewarded for their service.
   a. True
   B. FALSE

2. Many women found themselves incapable of handling the burdens of war when their husbands and fathers went off to fight.
   a. True
   B. FALSE

3. Benjamin Franklin established the first abolitionist society in America.
    A. TRUE
    b. False

4. Most Indian tribes and nations supported the British because they feared that an American victory would mean a greater loss of land through expansion.
    A. TRUE
    b. False

5. All of the tribes in the Iroquois Confederacy maintained neutrality during the Revolutionary War.
    a. True
    B. FALSE

Section 8.5.10 - p304

1. For all practical purposes, the Treaty of Paris ignored the American Indians.
    A. TRUE
    b. False

2. Both the Americans and the British gave up claims to the Mississippi for the sake of peace.
    a. True
    B. FALSE

3. Loyalists were protected by the treaty and well treated after it was signed.
    a. True
    B. FALSE

Chapter Nine: Articles of Confederation and the Constitution

Contents

Chapter Nine: Articles of Confederation and the Constitution

9.1 INTRODUCTION

During the Revolutionary War, American colonists papered over many of their regional differences in order to fight the British. However, much still separated the Revolution's participants. Nationalism grew during the war, but the states still saw themselves as separate entities. Moreover, many residents initially did not see much need for a central government. American leaders thus relied on virtue or patriotism to help form bonds between the people. According to historian John Murrin, patriotism "would inspire the settlers to sacrifice their private interests, even their lives, for the general welfare."[1] To win the war and maintain the peace, however, American leaders recognized the need for a political framework; patriotism alone would not suffice. So from 1776 to 1789, they worked to lay out government structures for the states and the nation. The war gave Americans an opportunity to put the ideas of the *Declaration of Independence* into practice. Furthermore, it allowed them to address many of the political and economic problems that had emerged under the British system.

Americans debated how to structure their state and national governments. Most colonists agreed that the consent of the governed was necessary, but they did not always agree on how this consent was to be given. Ultimately in both the state and national systems, they settled on a republican framework in which elected representatives mediated the will of the people. When it came to this national system, though, Americans debated how much power should be given to the central government. Most framers initially favored a weak central government that would defer to the rights of the states, an approach they adopted in the *Articles of Confederation*. Political, social, and economic problems during the 1780s, however, prompted them to reconsider their initial ideas. At the Constitutional Convention of 1787, delegates met to revise the *Articles of Confederation;* this document was quickly set aside as they developed a new framework, which became the United States Constitution. Enough states ratified the document for the new government to be put in place in 1789.

9.1.1 Learning Outcomes

After completing this chapter, you should be able to:

- Explain the formation of the individual state governments and assess how ideas about republicanism and democracy influenced the deliberations over state constitutions.
- Explain the need for an overarching political framework for the newly-independent American states and analyze the first attempts to provide structure for the American states, including the Second Continental Congress and the Articles of Confederation.
- Identify the accomplishments and weaknesses of the central government under the Articles of Confederation and explain the need for a central government stronger than that created by the Articles.

- Analyze the provisions and nature of the United States Constitution, including such concepts as nationalism, federalism, constitutionalism, and democracy.
- Explain the differences between the Virginia Plan, the New Jersey Plan, and the Connecticut Compromise, and analyze why the smaller states did not like the Virginia Plan.
- Understand the conflict between the rights of the individual states and the rights of the national government and assess the importance in this conflict of such clauses as the "necessary and proper" clause and the Tenth Amendment.
- Discuss the issues that arose at the time of the ratification of the U.S. Constitution and differentiate between the two factions that debated the Constitution in the states: Federalists and Antifederalists.
- Explain the powers given to each branch of government by the Constitution.

9.2 THE STATE GOVERNMENTS

The American colonies began to transition to independent republics or states in the months after Lexington-Concord in 1775. First, the residents overthrew royal authority by closing courts and chasing royal officials out of office. Then, to meet the demands of war, they set up provincial congresses to fill the void left by the departing British governments. Finally, they worked to create lasting governments that would promote order and independence. Most states found it easier to depose their governments than to construct new ones. However, the people avidly took to the cause. "The building of this permanent founding of freedom," says historian Gordon S. Wood, "became the essence of the Revolution."[2] As John Adams noted in 1776:

> "How few of the human race have ever enjoyed an opportunity of making...[a] government, more than of air, soil, or climate, for themselves or their children! When, before the present epoch, had three millions of people full power and a fair opportunity to form and establish the wisest and happiest government that human wisdom can contrive?"[3]

9.2.1 The Need for New Constitutions

Even before the Declaration of Independence, the Continental Congress addressed the need to write new state constitutions. Many revolutionaries saw the formation of new republics as an instrumental part of the move toward independence. More importantly, the necessities of war prompted Massachusetts to ask Congress for guidance on replacing colonial authority. It needed an established body to help maintain order, tax the citizens, staff the militia, and ensure public safety. In June 1775, the Continental Congress instructed Massachusetts to resume its Charter of 1691, which Parliament annulled in the Massachusetts Government Act of 1774, as a temporary solution to the lack of government. New Hampshire and South Carolina then requested advice on whether or not to form new governments.[4]

Into 1776, members of the Continental Congress discussed whether to issue a resolution on the formation of state governments and how specific their instructions should be if they made a recommendation. It seemed most delegates wanted to say something, but the precedent they might set troubled them. For example, John Adams worried about making any resolution on government because "if such a Plan was adopted it would be if not permanent, yet of long duration: and it would be extremely difficult to get rid of it." However, as the nation ebbed closer to declaring independence, calls for action by the Continental Congress increased, leading to two separate resolutions in May.[5]

On May 10, 1776, Congress recommended to the "United Colonies" that "where no government sufficient to the exigencies of their affairs have been hitherto established, to adopt such government as shall, in the opinion of the representatives of the people, best conduce to the happiness and safety of their constituents in particular, and America in general." On May 15, 1776, Congress resolved that it was "necessary that the exercise of every kind of authority under the said crown should be totally suppressed, and all the powers of government exerted, under the authority of the people of the colonies."[6] By that point, New Hampshire and South Carolina had temporary constitutions in place, and the rest of the states began the process of forming governments almost immediately. In June, Virginia adopted the first permanent constitution.

Historian Gary B. Nash sees these two resolutions as a "virtual declaration of independence." Over the course of five years as the war continued, the former colonies worked diligently to fulfill the promise of independence by creating new governments. While their new constitutions varied by state, the people seemed to agree "that the consent of the governed was the only true source of political authority." Some states applied this idea more radically than others, meaning some states implemented quite experimental constitutions while others followed the British model more closely. The internal debates over constitution-making led to divisions among Americans that the Founding Fathers obscured in their attempt to promote a vision of unity at the time of the nation's creation.[7]

9.2.2 Political Thought Shaping the State Constitutions

Most of the states followed an orderly process in forming their new governments. New Hampshire, Massachusetts, New York, New Jersey, Pennsylvania, Delaware, Maryland, North Carolina, Georgia, and Vermont, then in the process of declaring independence from New York, held special conventions to draft their constitutions. According to historian Marc W. Kruman, the conventions "located sovereignty in the people, who in turn, would instruct a political body to act on their behalf to form governments." Given that the electorate chose the representatives for these conventions, they effectively consented to the government formed by the conventions. In South Carolina and Virginia, the state legislature wrote the constitutions. In Connecticut and Rhode Island, the legislature simply deleted all references to royal authority, and both governed themselves much as before, since they were essentially self-governing under their colonial charters. Most of the states completed their work in 1776 and 1777, although it took Massachusetts until 1780 to finalize its constitution.[8]

Based on their colonial experiences, most Americans agreed the people should be the source of political authority. They did not support the maintenance of a monarchy or the adoption of pure democracy; rather, they sought to implement republicanism. In the late 1780s, James

Madison said a republican government "derives all its powers directly or indirectly from the great body of the people; and is administered by persons holding their offices during pleasure, for a limited period, or during good behavior." The people, broadly construed in Madison's interpretation of republicanism, exercised their power by electing representatives to the governing body.[9] In addition to their belief in republicanism, Americans shared similar assumptions about the structure of government, the role of the governor, and the nature of representation, though, they certainly did not agree on every detail.

The Structure of Government

Many states believed in the need to define the people's liberties before creating a government. Virginia took the lead on this issue when George Mason drafted the Declaration of Rights in 1776 and Thomas Jefferson drafted the Statute of Religious Freedom in 1777. The Declaration of Rights stated that "all men are by nature equally free and independent and have certain inherent rights" which the state could not violate. Furthermore, it suggested a government "ought to be, [sic] instituted for the common benefit, protection, and security of the people, nation, or community." Finally, it protected the people's common law rights, such as the right to a free press, the right bear arms, and the right to a speedy jury trial. Several states, including Delaware and North Carolina, followed Virginia's lead in issuing a specific declaration on the rights of the people; other states, including New York and Georgia, embedded the ideas of the declaration directly into their constitutions.[10]

The Statute of Religious Freedom, which the Virginia legislature finally approved in 1786 at the urging of James Madison, ended state support for the Anglican Church and separated one's religious belief from one's civil liberties. As Jefferson said, "no man shall be compelled to frequent or support any religious worship, place, or ministry whatsoever...nor shall otherwise suffer on account of his religious opinions or belief, but that all men shall be free to profess, and by argument to maintain, their opinions in matters of Religion, and that the same shall in no wise diminish, enlarge or affect their civil capacities." Most states adopted the principle of religious toleration for Christians in their constitutions, though some were more tolerant than others. Georgia Constitution suggested that people had "the free exercise of religion" so long as it was "not repugnant to the state." However, it also indicated those eligible for public office "shall be of the Protestent [sic] religion." The South Carolina Constitution,

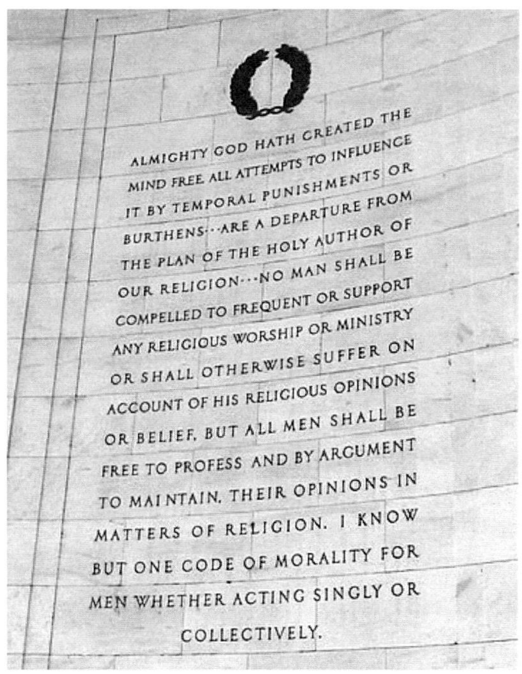

Figure 9.1 Virginia Statute of Religious Freedom | In 1777, Thomas Jefferson drafted the Statute of Religious Freedom. Jefferson was very proud of his effort to separate church from state and he wanted the statute to be included in his epitaph. And so, the U.S. government chose it as one of the inscriptions for the interior walls of the Jefferson Memorial.

Author: Jim McKeeth
Source: Wikimedia Commons
License: CC BY SA 3.0

however, provided religious toleration only to those "who acknowledge there is one God... and that God is to be publicly worshipped."[11]

With these liberties in mind, the states sought to establish balanced governments that would allow the people to participate in their government but would have checks on the people's will. During the revolution, most Americans continued to see the British system as the most enlightened form of government in the world because it contained elements of monarchy, aristocracy, and democracy in the Crown, the House of Lords, and the House of Commons respectively. When the system functioned properly, it would prevent the monarch from becoming despotic and the people from becoming disorderly. Therefore, the best way to prevent tyranny or anarchy was to create a system in which several bodies shared political power.[12]

To many Americans, the British perversion of its mixed government, especially Parliament's attempts to undermine colonial charters, justified the move toward independence. As they approached constitution-making, the Americans envisioned an end to monarchy, but not an end to mixed government. The bigger question for most revolutionary leaders centered on which branch of the government should have the most influence. When Virginian Carter Braxton wrote a pamphlet calling on the representative assembly to elect members of the state's upper house for life, Richard Henry Lee called the ideas "contemptible." Lee did not object to having a bicameral legislature; rather, he objected that Braxton's proposal seemed too aristocratic. Therefore, the Americans worked diligently to define the role of the governor and determine representation in the legislature so as to achieve a mixed government.[13]

The Role of the Governor

Americans in the Revolutionary Era held traditional views about power, especially when it came to the governor. Based on their reading of history and their own colonial experience, many believed that an appointed or an elected governor could become drunk with power and tyranny would ensue. Yet, they still saw the need for an executive of some kind to help manage the state. Consequently, most states modified the traditional role of the governor when drafting their constitutions. Fearing the restrictions of their rights, most states made the governor strictly an administrator. In his draft of the Virginia Constitution, Thomas Jefferson indicated the governor could not, among other things, veto legislation, call into or dismiss the assembly, declare war, raise an army, make peace, coin money, or pardon criminals. While not every state specifically spelled out governors' powers, they clearly limited the role the executive would play in making laws.[14]

To further limit the governor's power, most state constitutions had the legislature, not the people, choose the governor on an annual basis so that the governor would not become beholden to the voters. They also placed limits on the number of consecutive terms a governor could serve to prevent the emergence of an elected monarchy. Most states also curbed the governor's power of patronage to prevent him from using his right to appoint officials to develop an independent source of power. Finally, the states supported the separation of powers. As the residents of Boston noted in instructions to their constitutional convention delegates, "It is essential to liberty, [sic] that the legislative, judicial, and executive powers of government be, as nearly as possible, independent of, and separate from each other" in order to avoid "a wanton exercise of power." In insisting on the separation of powers and clearly demarcating the responsibilities of each branch, the states hoped to prevent the executive from influencing the other branches of government. Pennsylvania was the only state without a chief executive; instead, it opted to have an elected governing council appointed by the legislature. Meanwhile, New York vested considerably more power in the hands of its governor than did the other states.[15]

The Nature of Representation in the Legislatures

Americans saw the legislature as the most important branch of their state governments because they possessed most of the powers formerly held by the governor and they made the laws; this respect for the legislature later appeared in the U.S. Constitution. The legislature no longer served simply to check the power of the governor. Rather, they governed the state, which marked a clear shift in political power. As such, representation became the cornerstone of free government in the American states because it provided the best security of the people's liberties. As the states drafted their constitutions, they focused on providing equal representation for the people so as to preserve or undermine elite control of the government depending on the radical or conservative nature of the state conventions. Given their respect for the British system of a mixed and balanced government, most states opted for bicameralism, or a two-house legislature. However, Pennsylvania, Vermont, and Georgia implemented unicameralism, or a single-house legislature.[16]

Debates about the merits of virtual representation versus actual representation had played a large role in the road to the revolution and continued to play a part in determining the nature of representation. In the 1760s, the colonists increasingly protested that the members of Parliament could never represent their interests; in other words, they challenged the theory of virtual representation. Most colonists did not want to send representatives to Parliament; they wanted local assemblies to make the decisions affecting them. The Americans translated their concerns about virtual representation to their constitution-making in the late 1770s. In his *Thoughts on Government*, John Adams noted the assembly "should be in miniature, an exact portrait of the people at large. It should think, feel, reason, and act like them." Drafters took his ideas to heart as they planned for representation; however, they also believed the ablest men, the natural aristocracy, would serve in the assemblies. Moreover, these men, according to a contemporary newspaper, "would employ their whole time for the public good."[17]

Many revolutionaries believed a direct connection existed between the length of service in an assembly and the propensity for corruption or manipulation by the governor. Thus all the states, except South Carolina, held annual elections for their lower house. While delegates to the upper house served longer terms, they too faced regular election. Maryland's constitution provided for the election of delegates to the lower house every year and the upper house every five years. To ward off against the possibility that legislatures would act for special interests, most states required legislators to live within the community they represented. Georgia's constitution required that a person live in the state for at least one year and the county for at least three months before representing a county in the legislature.[18]

Some states also made an effort to ensure the equality of representation in the legislature. Pennsylvania's constitution based representation on the number of taxable residents in an electoral district and provided for reapportionment based on a census every seven years. North Carolina's constitution continued the colonial practice of having a set number of representatives from each county in the state and had provisions for including new counties in the legislature. Finally, most states set property qualifications for members of their assemblies, with the lower house set at one level and the upper house set at a higher level. Some delegates did argue they could only live up to John Adams's call to make legislatures an "exact portrait" if they chose members from the middling sorts. However, the majority thought those with more property could better serve the public good.[19]

9.2.3 Divisions on the Road to Republican Government

As the people thought about creating their state governments, questions about the structure of the legislative branch and the extension of voting rights tended to divide them more than did other issues. Historian Francis D. Cogliano suggested that the American people split into two camps, democrats and elitists, on the political questions raised by the revolution. The democrats were men whose involvement in the war made them more politically aware. Most hailed from humble origins and distrusted the elites' ideas about the structure of the government and the electorate. They wanted to give the common people more power in drafting state constitutions because the common people would bring honesty, common sense, and plain understanding to the process. The elitists, the leading figures in colonial politics, on the other hand, favored a government closely modeled on the British system and an electorate composed primarily of property-holding men. They feared excesses of democracy, especially a decentralized government, would lead to anarchy.[20] Pennsylvania and Massachusetts, which wrote the most radical and most conservative constitutions respectively, struggled to balance the interests of the democrats and the elitists. Meanwhile, New Jersey temporarily expanded the electorate in a way that no other state seriously considered when it allowed single women to vote.

Pennsylvania

Given that the democrats controlled the constitutional convention, Pennsylvania adopted the most radical state constitution of the Revolutionary Era. When it came time to select the members of the convention, Pennsylvania's lawmakers allowed all taxpaying men who would swear an allegiance to the revolutionary cause to vote for delegates. Since most elites remained loyal to Britain, they could not participate in the process of making the constitution. A majority of the voters in 1776, and the delegates they selected to frame the government, came from the middling ranks of society. The small farmers, merchants, lawyers, and artisans who served as drafters firmly believed in the democratization of politics; they thought all people, not just property owners, should have a say in the government.[21]

During their deliberations, as Gary B. Nash notes, the delegates "considered and then rejected three of the most honored elements of English republican thought." They chose not to implement bicameral legislature; they felt a unicameral legislature would better serve the common good. They decided not to have a governor; instead, they implemented a weak elected governing council to manage the state, not to make laws. Finally, they abandoned traditional notions about voting rights; they expanded suffrage to all taxpayers instead of all property holders, meaning most adult males could vote—a policy known as taxpayer suffrage. Beyond these changes, the delegates proposed to have annual elections for the assembly by secret ballot instead of by voice, to open all legislative sessions to the public, to make all proposed laws subject to public debate for one year, to impose term limits for government service, to create a Council of Censors to meet every seven years to review the legislature's performance, and to provide for reapportionment every seven years based on a census.[22]

Through these measures, the framers hoped to create the most democratic form of republican government possible. Skeptical of wealthy property holders, who governed Pennsylvania in colonial times, many democrats saw their constitution as a means to check the growth of absolute power. Inside and outside of Pennsylvania, however, the elitists reacted negatively to the work of the convention. The criticisms began as soon as the convention released the proposed constitution for public comment. Pennsylvanian Benjamin Rush described the constitution as "rascally." Meanwhile, North Carolinian William Hooper called it "a Beast without a head."[23] Many elitists hoped to cripple the constitution after its adoption in 1776. They called for the legislature to amend the constitution; they withdrew from the legislature to deny the majority a quorum, blocking any new measures necessary to fight the war; and they refused to serve as justices of the peace, sheriffs, and militia officers even when elected to do so.

The debate caused a major divide in Pennsylvania, which continued into the post-revolutionary years. In 1790, the elitists ultimately won the battle over the constitution when the state adopted a new constitution that included a bicameral legislature, a governor with veto power, and an independent judiciary. However, the new constitution retained taxpayer suffrage. Moreover, with the exception of Virginia and Delaware, the states followed Pennsylvania's lead in expanding the electorate. Some implemented taxpayer suffrage, while others lowered the property qualifications for voting.[24]

Massachusetts

For all of its revolutionary ferment in the 1760s and 1770s, Massachusetts adopted the most conservative constitution of the Revolutionary Era. While the elitists controlled the process, the democrats repeatedly called for measures to disperse power among the people. Initially, the General Court, the legislature, moved slowly because it seemed unsure whether they even had the right to author a constitution. By the time it secured permission from the electorate to frame the government, elitists in the legislature wanted to draw out the constitution making in hopes of curbing the most radical ideas of the democrats in the state.[25]

In 1777, the General Court asked the towns to authorize the two houses to work as one body to write a constitution, which it would submit to the voters for inspection. Essentially, the united legislature would serve as the constitutional convention. To garner as much support as possible for the drafting process, the legislature temporarily expanded the electorate to all free adult males. A majority of towns approved the proposal, though some dissenting towns thought a special constitutional convention should be called and others wanted more than just inspection of the new constitution. To address the concerns of the towns, the legislature agreed to hold new elections for the General Court before work on the draft began, allowing the voters to choose the people from their town to work on the constitution. Finally, in the summer the newly elected Generally Court selected a drafting committee.[26]

The structure of the legislature, unicameral or bicameral, and the composition of the electorate proved the most contentious issues for the drafting committee during the six months of debate on the constitution. The elitists won a bicameral legislature with strict property qualifications on who could serve; the democrats won taxpayer suffrage for the lower house but not for the upper house and the governor. In 1778, the drafting committee completed its work, and the legislature submitted the constitution to the voters for approval. Four out of five towns rejected the proposed constitution, with many towns voting unanimously against it. Many people objected, said Gary B. Nash, to what they "saw as an attempt to deny political rights to ordinary men."[27]

The concerns of the ordinary people over the proposed constitution suggested the impact the fight for independence had on ideas of democratization. Frustrated elitists, after eight months of stalling, concluded they had no choice but to propose a separate constitutional convention because the state's economic problems continued to grow worse and the sitting government had lost much of its legitimacy. The people overwhelmingly approved voting for a special convention in 1779. At that point, John Adams returned to Massachusetts from Paris where he had been working on securing an alliance with France. Braintree chose him as one of their delegates to the convention. The drafting committee, which he was not chosen to serve on, asked him to draw up the first draft of the new constitution.[28]

Adams wrote a very conservative constitution that drew largely on his *Thoughts on Government*. He began with a declaration of rights but proceeded to create a government strikingly similar to the colonial system in terms of providing for a bicameral legislature and a powerful governor. Adams also eliminated the provision for taxpayer suffrage for the lower house; all voters had to own property. Moreover, he increased the property qualification for running for the upper house and for governor. Since the constitution clearly tilted toward the elitists, Adams suggested that all free adult males vote in a referendum on the constitution. In so doing, if the document passed, then the democrats could not legitimately complain about any perceived disenfranchisement. In 1779, the convention sent Adams's constitution to the voters. In 1780, the delegates declared that two-thirds of the voters approved the constitution; shortly thereafter, it took effect. Massachusetts still uses Adams's constitution with a few modifications. Nevertheless, social divisions caused by objections to representation in the legislature plagued Massachusetts throughout the 1780s.[29]

New Jersey

State constitutions generally extended suffrage to more American men by providing for taxpayer suffrage or reducing the property qualifications for men. Georgia, South Carolina,

North Carolina, and Virginia continued the colonial practice of denying free blacks the right to vote, but, in the other states, the constitutions did not distinguish between free blacks and free whites. No state considered letting slaves, servants, felons, or the mentally disabled vote. Revolutionary fervor, however, did cause some Americans to question whether women should have the right to vote. Although political leaders around the country discussed the issue, only New Jersey went so far as to allow single women suffrage.[30]

Opponents of women's suffrage pointed to women's dependent state to justify disenfranchisement. The *Essex Result*, likely written by Theophilus Parsons of Massachusetts, suggested women did not possess the discretion to vote because of the "natural tenderness and delicacy of their minds, their retired mode of life, and various domestic duties." Furthermore, most states still practiced the doctrine of coverture. Married women could not own property nor did they pay taxes; therefore, in many states they did not meet the qualifications for voting.[31] Proponents of women's suffrage noted the inequity in barring single, property-holding women from voting. Virginian Hannah Corbin suggested to her brother Richard Henry Lee, a member of the Continental Congress, that single women should either possess the right to vote or should be exempt from paying taxes on their property; he privately agreed with her. While delegates to the constitutional convention mulled over voting rights, an anonymous New Jersey politician made the same point.[32]

Beginning in 1775, New Jersey's Provincial Congress received petitions from residents asking for taxpayer suffrage; the state legislature responded by reducing the property qualifications for voting. When the Continental Congress instructed the colonies to write constitutions, the expanded electorate in New Jersey selected delegates to the constitutional convention. The drafting committee initially suggested language granting all "freeholders and householders...worth fifty pounds" the right to vote. For over a year, delegates to the constitutional convention discussed voting rights, as evidenced by the changes in the suffrage clause from the initial to the final draft. According to the New Jersey Constitution, adopted in 1776, "All inhabitants of this Colony...who are worth fifty pounds...clear estate...and have resided within the county in which they claim a vote for twelve months immediately preceding the election, shall be entitled to vote for Representatives in Council and Assembly; and also for all other public officers, that shall be elected by the people of the county at large." Therefore, women who met the property requirements could cast ballots. Suffrage for single women in New Jersey ended in 1807 when the state revised its constitution. However, the fact women could and did vote under the original constitution set a precedent for ending the gendered division of the political community.[33]

Sidebar 9.1: The Political Role of Women in the Early Republic

On March 31, 1776, Abigail Adams wrote to her husband John that she longed to hear the Continental Congress declared independence. More importantly, she suggested that when the delegates, including her husband, came together to write a new code of laws that they "would Remember the Ladies, and be more generous and favourable to them than your ancestors. Do not put such unlimited power into the hands of the Husbands." She also implied that American women would engage in their own rebellion should they have no voice in the new government. In his response, John noted "As to your extraordinary Code of Laws, I cannot but laugh."[67] John Adams recognized the importance of the women in his life. He would not have been able to serve in the Continental Congress if Abigail did not run the family farm, and all through his years of public service he relied on her for advice on a variety of political issues. However, in 1776 he could not conceive of a shift in the public role of women in American society and his attitude did not seem to bode well for the short-term future of women's rights. And yet, later that same year, New Jersey saw fit to allow at least some women the right to vote. [68] Given the public debate during and after Revolution about women's rights, historians have disagreed on why New Jersey gave women the right to vote.

Mary Beth Norton maintains "the constitution's phraseology probably represented a simple oversight on the part of its framers" because the inclusion of women did not spark much debate in New Jersey. In other words, if the public had known about this "novel extension of the suffrage," then they most surely would have discussed the issue more than they did. On the other hand, Judith Apter Klinghoffer and Lois Elkis argue that the inclusion of women was no oversight, given that delegates debated the issue of suffrage for over a year. Klinghoffer and Elkis suggest "the revolutionary-era political strife responsible...for the politicization of new population segments, including women, was so strong in New Jersey that it led to the extension of the suffrage to single women." Along the same lines, Marc W. Kruman and Gary B. Nash suggest the discussion of women's suffrage alone showed how much the revolution transformed American life. In the end, the effort to end women's suffrage in New Jersey, says Linda Kerber, was "one of a series of conservative choices that Americans made in the postwar years as they avoided the full implication of their own revolutionary radicalism."[69]

9.2.4 Before You Move On...

Key Concepts

While fighting a war with Great Britain, the rebellious colonies also framed their individual governments because revolutionary leaders saw constitution-making as an important part of the move toward independence. So in 1776, the Continental Congress instructed the states to set up new governments. For the next five years, the states worked on their constitutions. While the governments they created varied by state, the framers agreed on the need to form republican governments based on the consent of the governed. They also worked diligently to secure the people's liberties from abuse by the state. To ensure that outcome, most states opted for mixed governments composed of a legislature, a chief executive, and a judiciary. Moreover, a majority of states granted extensive power to the representative assembly, whether they adopted a bicameral or a unicameral system, and they made the governor an administrator rather than a legislator. To prevent corruption, they worked to ensure equal representation in the assemblies and a regular rotation of officeholders. At the same time, most states retained property qualifications for government service. While most states agreed on the structure of government, questions about the structure of the legislative branch and the composition of the electorate divided the population. In Pennsylvania, elitists opposed the decision to adopt a unicameral legislature. In Massachusetts, democrats opposed retaining high property qualifications for voting. In New Jersey, the delegates took the unprecedented step of allowing single women the right to vote. The debates over the provisions of the state constitutions showed how much the political thought in the Revolutionary Era affected the American people; they also influenced the drafting of a national constitution.

Test Yourself

1. As the states began to adopt constitutions during the Revolutionary War, they chose to create republics over monarchies or democracies.

   a. True

   b. False

2. Which of the following men drafted the Virginia Statute of Religious Freedom?

   a. George Mason

   b. George Washington

   c. James Madison

   d. Thomas Jefferson

3. Pennsylvania adopted one of the most conservative constitutions of the Revolutionary Era.

   a. True

   b. False

4. No state constitution in the Revolutionary Era allowed women the right to vote.

   a. True

   b. False

See page 353 for answers

9.3 THE ARTICLES OF CONFEDERATION GOVERNMENT

By 1777 it had become obvious that if the new American states were to succeed diplomatically in gaining allies in their rebellion against Britain, then a more inclusive national government than the Second Continental Congress, which had been conducting the war until that point, would have to exist. A government that spoke and legislated for the states as a whole was needed. And so in 1777, the Second Continental Congress appointed a committee to draft a constitution for the states, which, when ratified, would bind them into a "firm league of friendship" for their common defense, the security of their liberties, and their mutual and general welfare. There was to be a common treasury that would "defray the charges of war."[34]

In terms of a national structure, this constitution, or the Articles of Confederation, created a one-house congress composed of two delegates from each state who served one-year terms. The "President of the United States" was the chair of the Confederation Congress, elected by its members; there was no separate executive branch, no national judiciary, and no national headquarters. While Congress could pass laws for the states as long as three-quarters of its members approved, borrow and coin money, and conduct diplomatic relations, it could not regulate trade, tax the states, or, without a national judiciary, enforce its laws. Congress also lacked the power to keep the states from issuing their own currency and imposing their own tariffs. The Articles of Confederation was released to the states for ratification, and by 1781, the states had approved it. It would be in effect for eight years until it was replaced by the U.S. Constitution.[35]

9.3.1 The "Critical Period"

The period during which the Articles were in effect, 1781-1789, was first called a "critical" one for the new United States, by John Quincy Adams in 1787 as he addressed the graduating class of Harvard University. It was, he insisted, a time when the new U.S. was "groaning under the intolerable burden of...accumulated evils."[36] It was, in other words, a period of diplomatic and financial challenge and internal confusion. While trade flourished and new markets were opened with the Dutch, Swedes, Prussians, Moroccans, and Chinese, the need for a national bank, with the power to issue government bonds and tax, was acute. The weak national government, the result of a reaction to the restrictions placed on the colonies after the French and Indian War, faced continuing crises with which it had a hard time coping, especially when it came to dealing with foreign governments and the nation's war-related debt. Many Americans assumed the transition from their status as British colonies to an independent nation would go smoothly. However, such attitudes were misplaced because foreign governments saw the United States as weak and treated the new government accordingly. Furthermore, many Americans believed prosperity would come quickly after the war; trade did resume, but efforts to fund the debt at the national and state levels caused problems.

Establishing sovereignty over territory ceded to the United States in the Treaty of Paris proved difficult. First, the British excluded American ships from their ports, which impacted the trade of timber, wheat, and other goods. They also did not evacuate all of their trading posts in the Northwest. Merchants found other markets and they also engaged in smuggling, but the Confederation Congress lacked the power to do more to secure a commercial treaty or to force the British to evacuate American land. Second, the Spanish disputed the border between New Spain and the United States. They also closed the Mississippi River to American traffic, which significantly affected the ability of southerners to conduct their international trade through New Orleans. Congress sent John Jay, the secretary of foreign affairs, to negotiate with Spain and instructed him to stand up for American rights in the Southwest. When it became clear his Spanish counterpart would not budge, Jay deviated from his instructions. He sacrificed navigation on the Mississippi for a commercial treaty. However, southerners in Congress blocked the measure. Many states did not want Congress to negotiate on their behalf; they wanted to make their own commercial arrangements. Thus, issues with Great Britain and Spain continued to fester.[37]

During the war, the Confederation Congress struggled to meet its financial obligations, and this pattern continued in the postwar years because the central government lacked a dedicated source of revenue. Early in the conflict, Congress issued paper currency to finance the war; the currency lost value almost immediately and so the government printed more money. Large amounts of paper currency in circulation, which could not be exchanged for specie or coin, did not bode well for the financial health of the new country. In 1781, Robert Morris became the Confederation's minister of finance, and he proposed two measures to remedy the nation's financial problems. He suggested imposing a five percent tax on all foreign imports. However, Rhode Island and Virginia opposed the measure, and since the vote needed to be unanimous, that effort to raise revenue failed. Morris also proposed the creation of a national bank but could not convince enough members of Congress of the importance of a bank. After Morris left the government, some members of Congress tried again to win support for the import tax in 1784. They again failed, after which they simply let the states choose how to pay their portion of the debt.[38]

Figure 9.2 Dealing with the Nation's Debt | Robert Morris, a Pennsylvania merchant, served as the first minister of finance for the Confederation Congress from 1781 to 1784. During that time he struggled in vain to devise an acceptable plan to fund the nation's debt.

Artist: Charles Willson Peale
Source: Library of Congress

Just as the Confederation Congress struggled to meet its financial obligations, so too did many states. They resorted to high taxes to fund their debt. In doing so, they angered the people who could not afford to pay those taxes. Many citizens resented the personal economic problems they faced in the 1780s, and they had little desire to contribute to their states' efforts to fund the public debt. As frustration mounted, nationally-minded leaders looked for ways to address the weakness of the central government. In December 1786, leaders from New York, New Jersey, Pennsylvania,

Delaware, and Virginia met in Annapolis, Maryland to discuss the possibility that the states would grant Congress the right to regulate commerce. The New Jersey delegation, along with delegates from other states like Alexander Hamilton and James Madison, hoped for greater change. However, those present could do little to enact change because so few states participated in the Annapolis Convention. The fear of the republican experiment failing had not yet reached crisis proportions. Added to the financial woes was the fact that American artisans were demanding new supplies of paper money and creditors to be paid in gold or silver. By 1785 the demand for paper money had become so insistent that seven states began issuing what would become worthless paper.

Despite the overwhelming problems the Confederation Congress faced, it did in fact create two long-lasting pieces of legislation that addressed the Northwest Territory, ceded by Britain to the United States at the end of the Revolutionary War. The Land Ordinance of 1785 divided the area north of the Ohio River Valley and west of the Appalachians into townships, six miles squared. The townships were in turn divided into thirty-six sections: thirty-five were to be sold, and one was to be set aside for schools. Each section consisted of 640 acres, which were sold for no less than $1.00 per acre. Settlers and speculators began to pour into the region, paving the way for a series of conflicts as the Americans insisted on taking land from the Indians, who had not acquiesced to the Treaty of Paris and considered the land rightfully theirs.[39]

The Northwest Ordinance, which followed in 1787, set out the process by which a territory could become a state. It specified that if a territory had fewer than 5,000 white adult males, it would be governed by a governor and a three-judge panel, all of whom were to be appointed by the Confederation Congress. When a territory held 5,000 to 60,000 white male inhabitants, a legislature could be elected by all white males, but the governor was still appointed by Congress. When the population of a territory exceeded 60,000, it could adopt a constitution—which must forbid slavery and protect religious freedom—and apply for statehood, which would be granted by Congress. The measure gave Congress greater control over the settlement of the western territories; self-government came only with statehood. And finally, the Northwest Ordinance barred slavery, except as punishment for a crime in the territory, though it did provide for the return of fugitive or runaway slaves.[40]

For the most part, however, the period during which the Articles of Confederation was in effect was indeed "critical" for the fledgling country; the final straw came in 1786 with the rebellion of a group of Massachusetts farmers led by Daniel Shays.[41]

9.3.2 Shays's Rebellion

One of the most serious challenges to the Confederation government, and an important impetus to calling for a constitutional convention, came in the form of a "rebellion," or what Alexander Hamilton called a Massachusetts "civil war" led by a "desperate debtor,"[42] Daniel Shays. Like farmers in many states, those of western Massachusetts suffered from high taxes, crushing debt, and widespread foreclosures. These farmers, in an effort to influence the legislature and governor in Boston and forestall foreclosures on their lands, drafted a list of grievances, among which were the following:

1. The present system of taxation operated "unfairly between the poor and the wealthy classes"
2. There existed "a shortage of cash money"
3. "Farm goods [were] not accepted as payment for debts and taxes"
4. Taxes and the fees charged by lawyers and the courts were too high
5. "State government officials are being paid fattened salaries"[43]

By fall, 1786, resistance to the policies of the Massachusetts state government had escalated to the point of an insurrection led by Daniel Shays, a Revolutionary War veteran. Marching through the countryside of Massachusetts, Shays and his men succeeded in taking over the Court of Common Pleas in Northampton, Massachusetts in an effort to prevent the trials of indebted farmers. The Governor of Massachusetts, with help from bankers and merchants in the eastern part of the state, raised troops and quickly crushed the rebellion.

Despite the fact that Shays's "rebels" numbered only 1,200, many of America's most distinguished and reasoned leaders evidently believed that anarchy was about to consume all of the states and that Shays's Rebellion might just be the spark that set it off. According to many, mob rule was at hand. James Madison, reading reports that set the number of farmers at 12,000, came to the conclusion that the whole affair had been instigated by the British.[44] Even George Washington cried out, "What, gracious God, is man that there should be such inconsistency and perfidiousness in his conduct?"

Some leaders, however, took a view different from that of Washington and Madison, regarding Shays's Rebellion as an almost legitimate form of popular protest, a sign of the vigor and political alertness of the populace and of their determination to guard their liberties. "What signify a few lives lost in a century or two," Jefferson wrote. "The tree of liberty must be refreshed from time to time with the blood of patriots and tyrants. It is its natural manure." In a letter, Jefferson explained himself further to James Madison, who shared Washington's attitude about Shays's rebels:

> I am anxious to learn your sentiments on the late troubles in the eastern states. So far as I have yet seen, they do not appear to threaten serious consequences...Those states have suffered by the stoppage of the channels of their commerce, which have not yet found other issues. This must render money scarce and make the people uneasy. This uneasiness has produced acts absolutely unjustifiable; but I hope they will provoke no severities from their governments...
>
> The mass of mankind under...a government wherein the will of everyone

Figure 9.3 Trouble in Western Massachusetts | In 1787, Daniel Shays, pictured here with Job Shattuck, led farmers in Western Massachusetts in an uprising against the state government to protest the treatment of indebted farmers.

Artist: Unknown
Source: National Portrait Gallery, Smithsonian Institution

> has a just influence enjoys a precious degree of liberty and happiness. [There will be occasional turbulence]...but I hold it that even a little rebellion now and then is a good thing.[45]

The unhappiness of the farmers spread to other areas of the northeast where similar rebellions broke out. Although the unrest was put down in several months, the fact that the Confederation Congress did not take a stand on the rebellions and could not send troops into the states underscored the problem, long voiced by leaders like George Washington, James Madison, and Alexander Hamilton, that a stronger national government was needed, one with power to create and maintain peace and harmony within the states, between the states, and between the states and the national government. Thomas Jefferson looked at the situation from the standpoint of diplomatic weakness mused in 1786: "The politics of Europe render it indispensably necessary that with respect to everything external, we must be one nation only, firmly held together."[46]

The *Articles of Confederation* thus assumed the role of chief culprit in causing the need for a stronger government. Traditional accounts assail the Articles for being too democratic, as evidenced by the fact that the national government lacked the independent power to tax, pay down the national debt, raise an army, turn back the threat posed by such mobs as the participants of Shays's Rebellion, and guarantee prosperity. An economic downturn following the revolution has frequently been attributed to the Articles. Therefore, in the development of the Constitution, the Founding Fathers have usually been praised for recognizing the need for a federal government that could force the states in the interests of order and liberty.

9.3.3 Before You Move On...

Key Concepts

The United States had been established and functioned under the notion that a constitution was necessary in the creation and definition of a government. It was desirable in order to define and perhaps limit the scope of a central government and to protect the rights of the people and the states. England's adoption of a Bill of Rights in 1689 and the ideas publicized during the Enlightenment, like those of the Baron Montesquieu and Jean Jacques Rousseau, led the Continental Congress to create a committee in 1777 to draft a constitution; this first constitution was called the *Articles of Confederation*. Described as a "firm league of friendship," the Articles reflected the distrust of its members and of the states generally of a central government that wielded too much power. Reeling from their recent experience with Britain and her attempt to tighten her hold on the colonies, the delegates who drafted the Articles created a government that was powerless in most areas. Although the Confederation Congress could pass laws, it had no authority to enforce them, as there was no separate executive or judicial branch. The Confederation Congress could request funds from the states but could not tax; it could request troops but could not draft citizens.

Sometimes called a "critical" period, the seven years that the Articles were in effect were ones of little significant progress for the new United States. Two land ordinances were passed, but, for the most part, the government under the Articles was ineffective and powerless. It could not do much to solve border issues with Spain and Great Britain, nor could it do anything to secure better commercial relations with those countries. To make matters worse, the Articles made it almost impossible for the Confederation Congress to resolve issues of public finance caused by the war. By 1787 it was obvious that a stronger central government was called for if European countries were to take the United States seriously.

Test Yourself

1. Under the Articles of Confederation, the national government consisted of

   a. Congress and a court system.

   b. Congress and an executive.

   c. Congress, a court system, and an executive.

   d. Congress.

2. Which of the following was a power given to the national government in the Articles of Confederation?

   a. The right to collect taxes from the states.

   b. The right to enforce laws passed by the Confederation Congress.

   c. The right to pass legislation.

   d. The right to draft troops.

   e. All of the above were powers possessed by the national government.

3. The Land Ordinance of 1787

   a. specified the process by which a territory could become a state.

   b. divided the northwest territory into townships.

   c. basically left the course of the territories to the territories themselves with little oversight from the central government.

   d. addressed the parish system in Louisiana.

See page 353 for answers

9.4 THE NEED FOR A STRONGER GOVERNMENT: CREATING THE U.S. CONSTITUTION: ANNAPOLIS AND PHILADELPHIA

By 1785 a conviction had developed among several influential leaders in the various states that greater inter-state cooperation was needed if the United States was to reach its true economic potential. In that year, leaders from Virginia and Maryland met at Mount Vernon at the invitation of George Washington to discuss, among other things, navigation of the Potomac River. As those assembled came to agreements, they increasingly acknowledged the efficacy of an expanded meeting, which would include at the least Pennsylvania and Delaware, states struggling over transportation between the Chesapeake Bay and the Ohio River. The result was a convention held at Annapolis in 1786 to which nine states named representatives, though representatives of only five attended (absent were the New England states, the Carolinas, and Georgia). Despite the disappointing showing at Annapolis, Alexander Hamilton was determined to follow up on the idea of a states-wide meeting and presented a resolution to the Confederation Congress for a convention "to render the constitution of the Federal Government adequate to the exigencies of the Union."[47] When the resolution calling for such a meeting passed through Congress, the wording was a bit different: those who met in Philadelphia would have as their "sole and express purpose... revising the Articles of Confederation."[48] Some states were slower than others to respond, but by May, 1787, eleven states had elected representatives. The meeting convened on May 14, though it was not until May 25 that a quorum was reached and George Washington elected president of the proceedings. The delegates worked through the summer, releasing the document on September 17, 1787.

During the weeks before the meeting was to convene, it became apparent that there were two schools of thought as to the ultimate goals of those who would attend. One group, centered on Edmund Randolph of Virginia and including Thomas Jefferson, currently Ambassador to France, held onto the idea that the Articles need only to be revised, patched like a fabric, as Jefferson commented. On the other hand, leaders like George Washington, John Jay, Alexander Hamilton, and James Madison believed that the Articles should be thrown out and an entirely new outline of government drawn up. Madison had become convinced before his arrival in Philadelphia that there should be a bi-cameral legislature, a separate judicial branch, and an executive, separate from either of the other branches. The central government should have the right of taxation and the power of the veto over state laws "in all cases whatsoever." In this phrase he echoed the wording of the Declaratory Act of 1766, passed upon the repeal of the Sugar Act by Parliament.[49] In 1787, Madison prepared a tract entitled *Vices of the Political System of the United States* in which he made clear his leanings. Historian Joseph J. Ellis comments that the document "reads like an indictment of the Confederation Congress prepared by a relentless special prosecutor" as in the tract, Madison decries the encroachment of the states on the federal government and on the laws of each other, their failure to "comply with Constitutional requisitions," and their unconcern for the "common interest" of the citizens of the United States.[50]

And so on May 25, a quorum of twenty-nine delegates from nine states empowered by their state governments to revise the Articles of Confederation met at Independence

Hall in Philadelphia, the site of the drafting of the Declaration of Independence. Rhode Island was the only state that did not participate at all in the proceedings. The delegates met for four months, and when the convention ended, they emerged with a document that laid out a completely new plan of government. Those who gathered in Philadelphia were an impressive array of American leaders: Benjamin Franklin from Pennsylvania; James Madison, George Washington, George Mason, and Edmund Randolph from Virginia; William Paterson from New Jersey; James McHenry from Maryland; Charles Pinckney and John Rutledge from South Carolina; and Elbridge Gerry from Massachusetts. Several notable Americans were not present at the convention: Thomas Jefferson, who, along with Benjamin Franklin, Robert Livingston, and John Adams had drafted the *Declaration of Independence*, was in France, John Adams was in Europe trying to raise money to pay off war debts, and Patrick Henry, who distrusted all centralized governments, refused to participate, claiming he "smell[ed] a rat." Both Jefferson and Adams, however, kept a close eye on developments in Philadelphia.

Despite the fact that the states had empowered delegates to "revise" the *Articles of Confederation,* within days, those in attendance reached two important decisions: their deliberations must be held in secrecy, and the Articles should be scrapped in favor of a completely new document. Edmund Randolph, who later introduced the Virginia Plan, explained the reasoning behind the latter decision, pointing out that the Articles did not "protect the United States from attacks from foreign powers," it did not "secure harmony and blessings to the states," nor was it "superior to State constitutions."[51] Similarly, Alexander Hamilton wrote to George Washington in July: "the people begin to be convinced that their 'excellent form of government' [the Articles] as they have been used to call it, will not answer their purpose; and that they must substitute something not very remote from that which they have lately quitted."[52] The latter, an allusion to the British monarchy, probably overstated the leanings of the convention as a whole and may have been more the preference of Washington and Hamilton, both of whom were ardent proponents of a strong national government.

Figure 9.4 Jefferson and the Constitution | Thomas Jefferson, one of the authors of the Declaration of Independence, was not present at the Constitutional Convention, but closely monitored its proceedings from France.

Artist: Charles Willson Peale
Source: Diplomatic Reception Rooms, U.S. Department of State

The Founding Fathers held many principles in common. They believed in John Locke's natural rights theory that all people were entitled to life, liberty, and property—what Jefferson called "the pursuit of happiness" in the *Declaration of Independence*—and were proponents of the idea of the Baron Montesquieu, an Enlightenment writer of France, that the best political system was one in which power was shared by more than one branch of a national government. Most of the delegates did not want a monarchy, and they wanted the states to be recognized as separate entities, holding some independent power of their own. Many of the delegates distrusted true democracy, in which all men over a certain age would have the right to vote, holding firm to the belief that freeholders, those owning land, were the best guarantors of liberty; in other words, many delegates thought landholders were the only ones who should be allowed to vote. With rare exception, American historians have seen the creation of the Constitution as the triumph of an effort to create a government of ordered liberty, an achievement seldom duplicated elsewhere. Because this effort represented a reversal of the American Revolution's trend toward greater democratization and decentralization of power, historians have usually taken pains to describe the Confederation era (1781-1787) as a time of dangerous economic and political instability requiring the strongest countermeasures to overcome it.

However, divisive issues became apparent almost from the first week of deliberations. One had to do with the relative power of the national and state governments and the manner in which representatives to the central government should be apportioned. Those who were proponents of the rights of the states were predominantly from the smaller states of Delaware, New Jersey, Connecticut, and Maryland, and were satisfied with the traditional structure, true of every congress since independence, of equal representation for all states, regardless of population. They were also convinced that the states should exercise some power independently of the national government. Nationalists like George Washington, Alexander Hamilton, and James Madison, on the other hand, who favored a strong central government with legislative representation based on population, tended to be from the larger states. Their verbiage pointed to the powerlessness of the Confederation government, which was clearly too weak to enjoy diplomatic or domestic success, and touted the need for representation to be based on population. Those states with the greater population should be granted the largest number of seats in the national legislature, for after all, why should the residents in large states receive less representation than those living in small states? A stronger central government, with representation based on population, was called for. Of course, there were also reasons why the small states might want a stronger central government, as they, like the large states, wanted a government that could regulate commerce, maintain order against disturbances like Shays's revolt, create and maintain a healthy economy, and protect the republic against the diplomatic encroachments. As Oliver Ellsworth commented, "We were partly national; partly federal. I trusted that on this middle ground a compromise would take place."[53] Benjamin Rush of Pennsylvania echoed this sentiment when he wrote to John Adams that "with such excellent principles among us...there is little doubt of our adopting a vigorous and compound federal structure," in other words, a system of government in which power is divided between a central governing authority and constituent political units, like states.[54]

Similarly, sectional divisions became apparent as the delegates debated the institution of slavery. Should slavery be recognized at all in the document being framed? How were slaves to be counted for purposes of representation and taxation, or should they be counted at all? Should the document provide for the abolition of slavery altogether, and, if it were not abolished, should its existence be limited in some way?

9.4.1 Debating the Plans for Government

On May 29, a plan for a central government was introduced by Edmund Randolph of Virginia. Called the "large state" or "Virginia" Plan, it called for a two house "National Legislature," an independent executive, and a national judiciary. In terms of Congressional delegates, voters would elect the lower house, the lower house would select the upper house from a list of nominees from the state legislatures, and both houses would choose the President and the judiciary. Although the Plan was praised by the larger states, representatives of the small states were quick to point out that under this plan the less populous states might very likely have no representatives in the upper house and very little input into who was elected president. Consequently, in mid-June, William Paterson presented a "small state" or "New Jersey" Plan. This plan envisioned a national government consisting of a one house legislature with equal representatives from all states, a plural executive, and an independent judiciary.[55]

As the Convention debated the features of each plan, a committee, headed by Roger Sherman of Connecticut, drafted what has been called the Great Compromise (also called the Connecticut Compromise in honor of its architects)[56] which dealt with representation in the House and Senate and became a prominent feature of the U.S. Constitution. Sherman and Oliver Ellsworth, both of Connecticut, suggested a two house national legislature, with the lower house elected by the freeholders, the upper house by the state legislatures, and the President by electors, to be chosen by the state legislatures. In the lower house, the House of Representatives, representation was apportioned according to the population of the individual states; each state would have two representatives in the upper house or Senate. [57]

A second compromise, known as the Three-Fifths Compromise, addressed the issue of slavery. Some of the delegates wanted the institution abolished completely, though these were in the minority. Most Southern representatives wanted slaves counted by head for purposes of determining numbers of legislators, but did not want them counted when determining the imposition of national taxes on the states. The Northern states wanted just the opposite. The Three-Fifths Compromise settled this controversy: a slave would be counted as three-fifths of a person for the purpose both of determining representation and taxation. Another issue dealt with the slave trade. Many wanted the slave trade with Africa stopped completely, as had already occurred in some Northern states, while Southern slave holders strongly objected to its cessation. The compromise reached was that the slave trade would not be stopped before 1808. A last agreement was reached over the use of the word "slave" in the Constitution; the term was not used. Instead, the document refers to "free persons" and "all other persons," in other words, the enslaved.

9.4.2 The Nature of the Government

In the end, what was created was a government that was neither strictly national nor strictly federal, but rather contained elements of each. On the one hand, there was a separate executive branch, consisting of a president and connected executive departments. The president would be elected by electors, who themselves were elected by the state legislatures. Thus the executive would be indirectly elected, as would be the Senate, which was the upper house of the two-house Congress. The Senate, like the electors, was to be elected by the state legislatures. Only the House of Representatives was popularly elected. There was a national judiciary consisting of a Supreme Court, whose justices would be appointed by the president and would serve life terms. The number of justices that would sit on the high court was not established, nor was a lower court system created. The power to create "Tribunals inferior to the supreme Court" was given to Congress in Article I, section 8.

The final draft of the Constitution obviously adheres to the Baron Montesquieu's idea of checks and balances, as the president would appoint judges, who in turn had to be approved by the Senate. All bills would have to pass both the House and Senate to become laws, and, while the president could make treaties, these also had to be approved by the Senate. The president could veto Congressional laws, but vetoes could be overridden by a two-thirds vote of both houses of Congress. A provision for the removal of a sitting president placed a further check on the executive. The House of Representatives could impeach, or indict, the president. Once indicted, the president would be tried by the Senate, with the Chief Justice of the Supreme Court presiding. Nor was the Supreme Court exempt from checks, as Congress could impeach judges, and the approval of the Senate was required to confirm presidential appointments to the judiciary. The un-amended Constitution had no provision for judicial review, the right of the Supreme Court to review Congressional laws to determine their constitutionality.

In the two centuries since the adoption of the Constitution, power has been classified according to type: those powers that are enumerated, or actually listed in the Constitution as belonging to one of the branches of the national government; those that are implied, using such devices as the "necessary and proper clause" of Article I, section 8 (see Annotated Constitution below); those that are shared between the states and the national government; and those which are reserved to the states by the Tenth Amendment.

The 1787 Constitution also had both national and federal features. In terms of nationalism, Congress was given broad powers that could be expanded by Article I, section 8, known as the "necessary and proper" clause; by the Supremacy Article, which proclaimed that the Constitution and all laws made under it were the "supreme law of the land;" and by the fact that the un-amended Constitution had no Bill of Rights. On the other hand, the states were recognized as individual entities in Article IV and were given jurisdiction over their own internal affairs through the reserved powers of the Tenth Amendment.

James Madison proclaimed in Number 39 of the *Federalist Papers*, which were written mainly by Madison and Alexander Hamilton, that: "The constitutional reallocation of powers created a new form of government, unprecedented under the sun. Every previous national authority either had been centralized or else had been a confederation of sovereign states. The new American system was neither one nor the other; it was a mixture of both."[58]

9.4.3 The U.S. Constitution Explained: An Annotation of Key Clauses

The Key Clauses	Annotation of the Clauses
Article I, Section 2 Representatives and direct taxes shall be apportioned among the several states which may be included within this union, according to their respective numbers, which shall be determined by adding to the whole number of free persons, including those bound to service for a term of years, and excluding Indians not taxed, three fifths of all other Persons.	This is known as the three-fifths clause, precipitated by the debate over how to count slaves in determining the number of representatives a state would be entitled to in the House of Representatives. It was one of three clauses in the original Constitution that provided legal protection for slavery. Note that the authors of the Constitution consciously avoided the term "slave," while the clause is clearly referring to the slave population. This reflects the ambiguity felt by the Founding Fathers over the "peculiar institution," particularly in the wake of the Revolution, with its cries of liberty and equality.
Article I, Section 3 The Senate of the United States shall be composed of two Senators from each state, chosen by the legislature thereof, for six years; and each Senator shall have one vote.	This clause is reflective of the "Great Compromise" which provided equal representation for smaller states in the federal government. It also reflects the Founding Fathers' fear of "democracy out of control," by placing the election of Senators beyond the direct influence of the general electorate.
Article I, Section 8: The "Necessary and Proper Clause" To make all laws which shall be necessary and proper for carrying into execution the foregoing powers, and all other powers vested by this Constitution in the government of the United States, or in any department or officer thereof.	This phrase comes at the end of Section 8, which enumerates the various duties and powers of Congress. It also represented one of the first great Constitutional controversies after its ratification, when Alexander Hamilton referred to it in his defense of the creation of the Bank of the United States. This clause became the basis for the doctrine of "implied powers," which allowed Congress to act in a manner not explicitly stated in the Constitution, as long as it acted in a manner "necessary and proper" to execute the powers delegated to it.
Article I, Section 9: *The Slave Importation Clause* The migration or importation of such persons as any of the states now existing shall think proper to admit, shall not be prohibited by the Congress prior to the year one thousand eight hundred and eight, but a tax or duty may be imposed on such importation, not exceeding ten dollars for each person.	Here is another clause relating to slavery while avoiding the use of the term. Only two states chose to continue importing slaves during this period: South Carolina and Georgia. While the clause did not exactly mandate the end of the slave trade, Congress dutifully drafted and passed a law in 1807 that made the importation of slaves into the United States illegal. This law went into effect on January 1, 1808. It highlights an interesting paradox about slavery that existed until the Civil War, where individuals in the South could speak of the "evils" of the slave trade, and yet somehow separate that from the institution of slavery, which they held to be a positive good.

Article II, Section 1 Each state shall appoint, in such manner as the Legislature thereof may direct, a number of electors, equal to the whole number of Senators and Representatives to which the State may be entitled in the Congress: but no Senator or Representative, or person holding an office of trust or profit under the United States, shall be appointed an elector. The electors shall meet in their respective states, and vote by ballot for two persons, of whom one at least shall not be an inhabitant of the same state with themselves. And they shall make a list of all the persons voted for, and of the number of votes for each; which list they shall sign and certify, and transmit sealed to the seat of the government of the United States, directed to the President of the Senate. The President of the Senate shall, in the presence of the Senate and House of Representatives, open all the certificates, and the votes shall then be counted. The person having the greatest number of votes shall be the President, if such number be a majority of the whole number of electors appointed; and if there be more than one who have such majority, and have an equal number of votes, then the House of Representatives shall immediately choose by ballot one of them for President; and if no person have a majority, then from the five highest on the list the said House shall in like manner choose the President. But in choosing the President, the votes shall be taken by States, the representation from each state having one vote; A quorum for this purpose shall consist of a member or members from two thirds of the states, and a majority of all the states shall be necessary to a choice. In every case, after the choice of the President, the person having the greatest number of votes of the electors shall be the Vice President. But if there should remain two or more who have equal votes, the Senate shall choose from them by ballot the Vice President.	Here, again, is a clause that limits the influence of the general electorate on the federal government, by placing the buffer of "electors" between the electorate and the candidate. The original wording of this clause also caused problems in the election of 1800, when Thomas Jefferson and Aaron Burr received the same number of votes, although it was clearly intended for Burr to be the Vice President. The existence of the Electoral College has created two other incidents where the president ultimately was chosen by the House of Representatives, in the elections of 1824 and 1876.
Article III The judicial Power of the United States shall be vested in one Supreme Court, and in such inferior Courts as the Congress may from time to time ordain and establish.	The Articles of Confederation did not make provision for a national court system and consequently the enforcement of the laws of the Confederation Congress was left up to state courts, which might, or might not, enforce them. Most delegates to the Constitutional convention believed that an independent judiciary was necessary to the well-being of a national government. Notice that only the Supreme Court was established; the lower courts, if there were to be some, would be created by Congress, and the judges appointed by the president with the approval of the Senate. The first lower courts were created in the Judiciary Act of 1789.
Article IV, Section 1 Full Faith and Credit shall be given in each State to the public Acts, Records and judicial Proceedings of every other State. And the Congress may by general Laws prescribe the Manner in which such Acts, Records and Proceedings shall be proved and the Effect the effect thereof.	The "full faith and credit" clause specifies that every state will recognize and respect the laws and judicial decisions of every other state. This is one statement that confirmed the future existence of independent state governments.

Article IV, Section 2 No person held to service or labor in one state, under the laws thereof, escaping into another, shall, in consequence of any law or regulation therein, be discharged from such service or labor, but shall be delivered up on claim of the party to whom such service or labor may be due.	This is the last of the three clauses in the Constitution that deal with slavery. Again, the word slave is avoided in the writing of the clause. This is perhaps the most powerful of the clauses in terms of providing a Constitutional protection for slavery, because it mandates federal support for the return of runaway slaves.
Article VI The Constitution, and the Laws of the United States which shall be made in Pursuance thereof; and all Treaties made, or which shall be made under the Authority of the United States, shall be the supreme Law of the Land.	Article VI is called the "Supremacy Article" and is an example of the nationalist sentiments of the Constitutional Convention. The intention of this Article is to make clear that in a conflict between the laws of the state and the laws of the nation, in other words laws passed the U.S. Congress, Congressional law would be supreme. The first Supreme Court case in which the Supremacy Article was cited was that of *McCulloch v. Maryland* in 1819, in which the high Court used both the necessary and proper clause to affirm the right of Congress to establish a bank and the Supremacy Article to maintain that state law could not tax a national institution. The majority opinion of the Supreme Court stated clearly "that we are unanimously of opinion that the law passed by the Legislature of Maryland, imposing a tax on the Bank of the United States is unconstitutional and void." Moreover, "the people have, in express terms, decided it by saying, 'this Constitution, and the laws of the United States, which shall be made in pursuance thereof,' 'shall be the supreme law of the land.'"[59]
Article VII The ratification of the conventions of nine states, shall be sufficient for the establishment of this Constitution between the states so ratifying the same.	Here one can see how the Founding Fathers attempted to separate the process of adopting the new Constitution from the influence of the general electorate. The rarely-used conventional method required each state to choose delegates who would debate its merits and then vote for or against the Constitution. Interesting also was the choice of nine as the number of states necessary to ratify the Constitution. What if four states had rejected it? Fortunately, that was never an issue.

9.4.4 Ratification: The Constitution Debated in the States

Article VII of the Constitution states that the document would go into effect when "the Conventions of nine states," not quite three-quarters, had approved it. The document was released to the states in September 1787, and soon debates began over its merits, the structure of the government it created, and the powers given to the central government and the states (a few state powers were listed). The debates intensified in the fall of 1787. Those who spoke in favor of the Constitution had several advantages. Calling themselves Federalists, they were well-organized, literate, and provided a positive message. The irony was that, in terms of political orientation, they were in fact nationalists, favoring a strong central government. They deliberately chose the name "Federalist" in order to stress the federal nature of the government defined by the Constitution and direct the attention of those they were trying to persuade away from the fact that the central government was imbued with remarkable powers. It was, in fact, more national than federal. Their opponents made the mistake of calling themselves "Antifederalists," thus giving two impressions: their message was basically negative, and they were opposed to federalism. In terms of political theory, many of these men, like Patrick Henry, George Mason, and Richard Henry Lee, felt that the Constitution created a central government at the expense of the states, were in fact federalists.

Federalists and Antifederalists

Antifederalists, like perhaps a majority of Americans in 1787, opposed the founders' decision to replace rather than revise the Articles of Confederation. Patrick Henry, in newspapers, the Antifederalist Papers, and debates in the Virginia state legislature, pointed out that the drastic changes to the Articles of Confederation had been unwarranted and unnecessary. "Unless there be great and awful dangers," he warned in Antifederalist Paper No. 4, "[this] change is dangerous, and the experiment ought not to be made." Richard Henry Lee agreed that "important changes in the forms of government [should]...be carefully attended to in all their consequences." And George Mason, also from Virginia, warned that a single executive was a lightning rod for disaster: "If strong and extensive Powers are vested in the Executive, and that Executive consists only of one Person, the Government will of course degenerate."

In addition, Antifederalists disliked the fact that the Constitutional Convention was held in secrecy during the drafting itself and that the ratification process was replete with extra-legal irregularities. Requiring not unanimity as the Articles of Confederation had done, but only nine states for ratification, the Founding Fathers changed the rules to guarantee success, but they did so at some cost to traditional parliamentary procedure. Equally worrisome was the fact that the founders wisely refused to submit the document to the state legislatures, reasoning that the states would not voluntarily agree to surrender their existing powers. So, they required that special conventions elected for the purpose of considering ratification be given the task of considering the issue. When many Antifederalists, objecting to this change in rules, refused to vote for delegates to the ratification conventions, those elected turned out to be overwhelmingly, and not surprisingly, Federalist in opinion.

Another point of contention was that the document did not contain a bill of rights, adding to a general feeling that the document was hostile to popular participation in government.[60] Antifederalists took this position, but so did many who would otherwise be in favor of approving the document. Historian Robert Middlekauff comments that the Constitution faced an uphill battle, and "the absence of a bill of rights was the reason."[61] A last point made by many Antifederalists was that representation as defined by the Constitution, that is, two Senators from each state and a maximum of 435 members of the House of Representatives, would be inadequate to appropriately represent the population of a large nation, which the United States would invariably become.[62]

The Federalists, on the other hand, were primarily well-to-do bankers and wealthy planters like Alexander Hamilton, George Washington, James Madison, and Benjamin

Franklin. In addition to being well-organized and literate, they published an impressive tome of well-constructed arguments, the *Federalist Papers*. The *Papers,* written largely by Madison, Hamilton, and John Jay, explained the advantages of a strong national government, though at the same time emphasizing in the minds of their readers that the government's structure was also federal. In *Federalist No. 2*, Jay defined the issue at hand: "whether it would conduce more to the interest of the people of American that they should...be one nation, under one federal government, or that they should divide themselves into separate confederacies."[63] Alexander Hamilton warned his readers of an "alarming danger---those which will in all probability flow from dissensions between the States themselves." Weak nations allowed themselves to be forced into a confederation[64] while a "FIRM Union" provided a barrier against domestic faction and insurrection."[65] Now regarded as a classic collection of rigorous thinking on matters of political science, these documents did sway opinion that was wavering or in doubt. The authors explained the diplomatic and domestic advantages that would come from a strong central government. Not only would "the dangers to which we should be exposed, in a state of disunion, from the arms and arts of foreign nations" be avoided by a strong central authority, but also would be "those which will in all probability flow from dissensions between the States themselves, and from domestic factions and convulsions."[66]

Historian Charles Beard argued in 1913 that conflict over the Constitution could be seen in economic class terms with wealthy property holders in favor of the Constitution and poorer elements of the community opposed. While economic concerns were important in determining an American's opinion on the Constitution, it nevertheless appears not to have been a struggle between haves and have-nots. Rather, it appears that urban Americans, rich and poor alike, were in favor of ratification, believing that the Constitution would encourage commerce and business activity. Both rich and poor rural Americans, however, opposed it. Their opposition was not good news for the Federalists because the vast majority of Americans were the people whom Jefferson called "the chosen people of God," in other words, the farmers.

The final decision that led to the ratification of the Constitution was the promise that a bill of rights would be included in any Constitution ratified by the states. The necessary nine states were obtained when New Hampshire ratified the document in 1788. New York and Virginia only narrowly approved the document, New York by three votes and Virginia by five. Without the approval of these large states, the Constitution and perhaps the American national experiment would have been doomed. The victory of the Federalists became complete when Rhode Island ratified the document in 1790. The prospects for its success were unclear, but one factor helped. Most of the Antifederalists, including Patrick Henry, who were bitter in their defeat, retired from national politics. Consequently, nearly all those elected to the first Congress under the Constitution were Federalists, that is, friends of the government created by of the Constitution. For all practical purposes, the Antifederalists disappeared, but, in the future, other American groups would revive their cautionary warnings about the dangers of concentrated American power.

9.4.5 Before You Move On...

Key Concepts

By 1785, it had become obvious that a stronger central government was needed, one that would be able to speak for the new American states as a whole. In 1787, delegates therefore met in Philadelphia; these delegates were elected and empowered by the state legislatures to revise the Articles of Confederation. The document that emerged from what came to be called the Constitutional Convention was very different from the Articles of Confederation, which had been scrapped shortly after the convention reached a quorum. The U.S. Constitution created a government that was both national and federal. As national, it gave expanded powers to the central government; as federal, it recognized the individual states as enduring entities. The lack of a bill of rights created a problem during ratification, as the Federalists and Antifederalists took their messages to the states. By 1789, however, despite the objections raised by those who opposed adoption, nine states had approved the document, and it was put into effect.

Test Yourself

The Constitutional Convention

1. The Constitutional Convention met in 1787 for the purpose of revising the Articles of Confederation.

   a. True

   b. False

2. The Virginia Plan is also known as

   a. the "small state plan."

   b. the "large state plan."

   c. the New Jersey Plan.

   d. the Connecticut Compromise.

3. During ratification debates, the Antifederalists were really Federalists.

   a. True

   b. False

4. Who among the following was NOT a Federalist?

   a. George Washington

   b. Patrick Henry

   c. James Madison

   d. Alexander Hamilton

5. The Three-Fifths Compromise dealt with the issue of representation and taxation.

a. True

b. False

The Constitution

1. The necessary and proper clause has had the effect of limiting the power of the national government.

a. True

b. False

2. The source of powers "reserved" to the states is the

a. Supremacy Article.

b. full faith and credit clause.

c. Tenth Amendment.

d. necessary and proper clause.

3. The "full faith and credit" clause applies to

a. the national judiciary.

b. interstate relations.

c. Congressional power.

d. the Supremacy Article.

4. Which of the following is NOT a Congressional power enumerated in the U.S. Constitution?

a. The right to create a lower national court system

b. The right to enforce its laws

c. The right to declare war

d. The right to negotiate treaties

e. Neither b or d were Congressional power

5. According to the Constitution, _____ appoints judges; these appointments must be approved by _____.

a. The Senate; the Presidency

b. The President; the Supreme Court

c. The President; the House of Representatives

d. The President; the Senate

See page 353 for answers

9.5 Conclusion

While fighting their war for independence, Americans quickly realized the importance of framing new state governments. Leaders of the revolution thought that creating state governments would help underscore the fight for independence by implementing structures based on the consent of the governed. However, they seemed a little more reluctant to form a national government. They worried that forming a national government might undermine the very rights for which the people fought. Therefore, in the late 1770s and 1780s, the American people debated the framework of their new governments because no one was quite sure how much power to place in the hands of either the people or the national government.

In the end, most states adopted constitutions modeled on the British system. At the same time, they expanded the electorate to give the people a greater say in their government. At the national level, leaders initially created a weak central government in the Articles of Confederation so as to preserve the rights of the state. However, the ineffectiveness of the Confederation Congress pushed nationally-minded leaders to propose revisions to the overarching political framework. In 1787, delegates met in Philadelphia. Rather than revise the Articles, as the state legislatures instructed them, they devised an entirely new system that gave the central government greater authority but also tried to balance that power with the rights of the states. In 1788, although the people greatly debated the proposed framework, enough states ratified the document for the United States Constitution to take effect the following year. At that time, Americans looked to create the "more perfect union" the framers outlined in the preamble.

9.6 CRITICAL THINKING EXERCISES

- How did the state constitutions show the promise and the limits of American revolutionary thought?
- During the ratification period, supporters of the Constitution referred to themselves as "Federalists," even though they supported a government that could be called national due to its structure and the central government's amount of accrued power. Why did they choose this name? What did they hope to achieve among the American populace? And why was Antifederalists, the name taken by the opponents of the Constitution, an unfortunate choice?
- In what ways did the "necessary and proper clause" and the Tenth Amendment create the basis for conflict between the states and the national government?
- Why is the Tenth Amendment a natural inclusion in a statement of rights that belong to U.S. citizens?

9.7 KEY TERMS

- *Articles of Confederation*
- Bicameralism
- Bill of Rights
- Checks and Balances
- Congressional Resolutions of May 1776
- Constitutional Convention
- Electoral College
- Oliver Ellsworth
- Enumerated Powers
- Federalists v. Antifederalists
- Full faith and credit clause
- Great/ Connecticut Compromise
- Alexander Hamilton
- House of Representatives
- Impeachment
- Thomas Jefferson
- Land Ordinance, 1785
- John Locke
- James Madison
- Mixed and Balanced Governments
- National Judiciary
- Natural rights
- Necessary and Proper clause
- New Jersey Plan
- Northwest Ordinance, 1787
- Presidential veto
- Property Qualifications
- Republicanism
- Reserved powers
- Second Continental Congress
- Shays's Rebellion
- States' rights v. the rights of the State
- Supremacy Article
- Taxpayer Suffrage
- Tenth Amendment: Reserved powers
- *The Federalist Papers*
- Three-Fifths Compromise
- Townships; sections
- U.S. Senate
- Unicameralism
- Virginia Declaration of Rights
- Virginia Plan
- Virginia Statute of Religious Freedom
- George Washington
- Women's Suffrage

9.8 CHRONOLOGY

The following chronology is a list of important dates and events associated with this chapter.

Date	Event
1776	Continental Congress instructed the states to devise state governments; George Mason drafted Virginia's Declaration of Rights; New Hampshire, South Carolina, Virginia, New Jersey, Delaware, Pennsylvania, Maryland, and North Carolina adopted new state constitutions; Connecticut and Rhode Island revised their colonial charters
1777	Thomas Jefferson drafted the Virginia Statute of Religious Freedom; Georgia and New York adopted new state constitutions
1778	South Carolina revised its constitution
1781	Massachusetts adopted a constitution; The *Articles of Confederation* took effect
1784	New Hampshire revised its constitution
1785	Land Ordinance outlined a plan for surveying and selling government lands
1786	Virginia legislature approved the *Statute of Religious Freedom*
1786-1787	Shays's Rebellion
1787	Constitutional Convention held in Philadelphia
1787-1788	*The Federalist Papers* were published
1788	Confederation government was phased out
1790	Pennsylvania revised its constitution; Rhode Island became the last state to ratify the Constitution

9.9 BIBLIOGRAPHY

"Account of William Jonas of Worcester County," Massachusetts, September 5, 1786, in Constitutional Rights Foundation, May 30, 2012. http://www.crf-usa.org/bill-of-rights-in-action/bria-4-1-b-shays-rebellion-a-massachusetts-farmers-account.html.

Antifederalist Papers. At *Antifederalists,:*, http://www.u-s-history.com/pages/h374.html.

Cogliano, Francis D. *Revolutionary America, 1763-1815: A Political History*, Second Edition. New York: Routledge, 2009.

Documents from the Continental Congress and the Constitutional Convention. Library of Congress, May 30, 2012. http://memory.loc.gov/ammem/collections/continental/index.html.

Ellis, Joseph J. *American Sphinx: The Character of Thomas Jefferson*. New York: Vintage Books, 1996.

Federalist Papers. Library of Congress. http://thomas.loc.gov/home/histdox/fed_09.html.

Hamilton, Alexander, John Jay, and James Madison. *The Federalist Papers*. Library of Congress, May 30, 2012. http://thomas.loc.gov/home/histdox/fedpapers.html.

Kerber, Linda. *Women of the Republic: Intellect and Ideology in Revolutionary America*. Chapel Hill: UNC Press, 1980.

Klinghoffer, Judith Apter and Lois Elkis. "'The Petticoat Electors': Women's Suffrage in New Jersey, 1776-1807." *Journal of the Early Republic* 12, no. 2 (1992): 159-193.

Kruman, Marc W. *Between Authority and Liberty: State Constitution Making in Revolutionary America*. Chapel Hill: University of North Carolina Press, 1997.

Kurland, Philip B. and Ralph Lerner, eds. *The Founders' Constitution*, Volume 1. Chicago: University of Chicago Press, 1986. University of Chicago Press and the Liberty Fund, May 14, 2012. http://press-pubs.uchicago.edu/founders/.

Lloyd, Gordon, comp. *The Constitutional Convention: Selected Correspondence from the Summer 1787*. Teaching American History, May 30, 2012. http://teachingamericanhistory.org/convention/correspondence.html.

McCulloch v. Maryland. Legal Information Institute, Cornell University School of Law, May 30, 2012. http://www.law.cornell.edu/supct/html/historics/USSC_CR_0017_0316_ZO.html.

McCullough, David. *John Adams*. New York: Simon and Schuster Paperbacks, 2001.

Murrin, John M. "A Roof without Walls: The Dilemma of American National Identity." In *Beyond Confederation: Origins of the Constitution and American National Identity*, eds. Richard Beeman, Stephen Botein, and Edward C. Carter. Chapel Hill: University of North Carolina Press, 1987.

Middlekauff, Robert. *The Glorious Cause: The American Revolution, 1763-1789*. New York: Oxford University Press, 1982.

Nash, Gary B. *The Unknown American Revolution: The Unruly Birth of Democracy and the Struggle to Create America*. New York: Viking, 2005.

Norton, Mary Beth. *Liberty's Daughters: The Revolutionary Experience of American Women, 1750-1800*. Ithaca: Cornell University Press, 1996.

Wood, Gordon S. *The Creation of the American Republic, 1776-1787*. Chapel Hill: University of North Carolina Press, 1969.

9.10 END NOTES

1 John M. Murrin, "A Roof without Walls: The Dilemma of American National Identity," in *Beyond Confederation: Origins of the Constitution and American National Identity*, eds. Richard Beeman, Stephen Botein, and Edward C. Carter. (Chapel Hill: University of North Carolina Press, 1987), Part III, City College of New York, May 31, 2012, http://academic.brooklyn.cuny.edu/history/dfg/amrv/murrin.htm.

2 Gary B. Nash, *The Unknown American Revolution: The Unruly Birth of Democracy and the Struggle to Create America* (New York: Viking, 2005), 264; Marc W. Thurman, *Between Authority and Liberty: State Constitution Making in Revolutionary America* (Chapel Hill: University of North Carolina Press, 1997), 1; Gordon S. Wood, *The Creation of the American Republic, 1776-1787* (Chapel Hill: University of North Carolina Press, 1969), 127, 129.

3 John Adams, *Thoughts on Government* (1776), *The Founders' Constitution*, Volume 1, Chapter 4, Document 5, The University of Chicago Press, May 12, 2012, http://press-pubs.uchicago.edu/founders/documents/v1ch4s5.html.

4 Wood, *The Creation of the American Republic*, 130.

5 John Adams, *Diary of John Adams*, November 4, 1775, Adams Papers Digital Editions, Massachusetts Historical Society, May 11, 2012, http://www.masshist.org/publications/apde/portia.php?id=DJA03d320; Nash, *The American Unknown Revolution*, 265-266.

6 Continental Congress, Resolution and Preface of May 10-15, 1776, *How to Stage a Revolution*, MIT Open Courseware, May 11, 2012, http://ocw.mit.edu/courses/history/21h-001-how-to-stage-a-revolution-fall-2007/readings/cc_resolution.pdf.

7 Nash, *The Unknown American Revolution*, 266-267.

8 Nash, *The Unknown American Revolution*, 268; Wood, *The Creation of the American Republic*, 133; Kruman, *Between Liberty and Authority*, 5-6, 20-21.

9 James Madison, "Federalist No. 39," in *The Founders' Constitution*, Volume 1, Chapter 4, Document 24, The University of Chicago Press, May 12, 2012, http://press-pubs.uchicago.edu/founders/documents/v1ch4s24.html; Francis D. Cogliano, *Revolutionary America, 1763-1815: A Political History*, Second Edition (New York: Routledge, 2009), 138.

10 The Virginia Declaration of Rights, *Virginia Memory*, Library of Virginia, May 12, 2012, http://www.virginiamemory.com/docs/VADeclaration.pdf; Kruman, *Between Authority and Liberty*, 37.

11 An Act for Establishing Religious Freedom, *Virginia Memory*, Library of Virginia, May 12, 2012, http://www.virginiamemory.com/docs/ReligiousFree.pdf; Constitution of Georgia, 1777, *The Avalon Project,* Yale Law School, September 21, 2012, http://avalon.law.yale.edu/18th_century/ga02.asp; Constitution of South Carolina, 1778, *The Avalon Project*, Yale Law School, September 21, 2012, http://avalon.law.yale.edu/18th_century/sc02.asp.

12 Wood, *The Creation of the American Republic*, 197-200.

13 Wood, *The Creation of the American Republic*, 201-206.

14 Wood, *Creation of the American Republic*, 134-137; Thomas Jefferson, Draft Constitution for Virginia [1776], *The Avalon Project*, Yale Law School, May 12, 2012, http://avalon.law.yale.edu/18th_century/jeffcons.asp.

15 Wood, *The Creation of the American Republic*, 150-158; Instructions of the Inhabitants of the Town of Boston to Their Representatives in Congress (1776), *The Founders' Constitution*, Volume 1, Chapter 10, Document 8, The University of Chicago Press, May 12, 2012, http://press-pubs.uchicago.edu/founders/documents/v1ch10s8.html; Nash, *The Unknown American Revolution*, 274, 282-283.

16 Wood, *The Creation of the American Republic*, 162-164.

17 Wood, *The Creation of the American Republic*, 178-180; Adams, *Thoughts on Government*.

18 Wood, *The Creation of the American Republic*, 165-167; Kruman, *Between Authority and Liberty*, 81-86.

19 Wood, *The Creation of the American Republic*, 170-172, 180-181; Nash, *The Unknown American Revolution*, 275, 287-288; Kruman, *Between Authority and Liberty*, 66-67.

20 Cogliano, *Revolutionary America*, 138-140; Nash, *The Unknown American Revolution*, 270.

21 Nash, *The Unknown American Revolution*, 268-271.

22 Nash, *The Unknown American Revolution*, 273-276.

23 Wood, *The Creation of the American Republic*, 229; Benjamin Rush quoted in Nash, *The Unknown American Revolution*, 277; William Hooper quoted in Nash, *The Unknown American Revolution*, 279.

24 Nash, *The Unknown American Revolution*, 279-280; "Pennsylvania's Constitution: A Brief History," Pennsylvania Bar Association, Constitutional Review Commission, May 14, 2012, http://www.pabarcrc.org/history.asp.

25 Nash, *The Unknown American Revolution*, 290-292; Kruman, *Between Authority and Liberty*, 30.

26 Kruman, *Between Authority and Liberty*, 31-32; Nash, *The Unknown American Revolution*, 293-294.

27 Nash, *The Unknown American Revolution*, 296-297.

28 Cogliano, *Revolutionary America*, 143; Nash, *The Unknown American Revolution*, 300.

29 Cogliano, *Revolutionary America*, 143-144; Nash, *The Unknown American Revolution*, 301-304.

30 Kruman, *Between Authority and Liberty*, 103-104.

31 "The Essex Result," *The Founders' Constitution*, Volume 1, Chapter 13, Document 12, The University of Chicago Press, May 15, 2012, http://press-pubs.uchicago.edu/founders/documents/v1ch13s12.html; Kruman, *Between Authority and Liberty*, 104.

32 Kruman, *Between Authority and Liberty*, 104-105; Nash, *The Unknown American Revolution*, 289.
33 Judith Apter Klinghoffer and Lois Elkis, "'The Petticoat Electors': Women's Suffrage in New Jersey, 1776-1807," *Journal of the Early Republic* 12, no. 2 (1992): 165-168; Constitution of New Jersey [1776], *The Avalon Project*, Yale Law School, May 15, 2012, http://avalon.law.yale.edu/18th_century/nj15.asp.

34 Committee Report, Nature of the [Articles of Confederation] Government, June 12, 1786, Documents of the Continental Congress and Constitutional Convention, Broadside Collection, Library of Congress, May 30, 2012, http://memory.loc.gov/ammem/collections/continental/index.html.

35 Articles of Confederation and Perpetual Union, Documents of the Continental Congress, Broadside Collection, Library of Congress.

36 John Quincy Adams, Harvard Commencement Address 1787, quoted in George Brown Tindall and David Emory Shi, *America: A Narrative History* (New York: W.W. Norton Company, 2010), 270.

37 Robert Middlekauff, *The Glorious Cause: The American Revolution, 1763-1789* (New York: Oxford University Press), 607-609.

38 Middlekauff, *The Glorious Cause*, 605-606, 615-617.

39 "An ordinance for ascertaining the mode of disposing of lands in the Western Territory," Documents of the Continental Congress, Broadside Collection, Library of Congress; Middlekauff, *The Glorious Cause*, 611.

40 Northwest Ordinance (1787), The National Archives and Records Administration, January 30, 2012, http://www.ourdocuments.gov/doc.php?flash=true&doc=8; Middlekauff, *The Glorious Cause*, 611.

41 Middlekauff, *The Glorious Cause*, 620-621.

42 Alexander Hamilton, "Federalist No. 6: Concerning Dangers from Dissensions Between the States," Avalon Project. Yale University: http://avalon.law.yale.edu/18th_century/fed06.asp.

43 The Account of William Jonas of Worcester County, Massachusetts, September 5, 1786, Constitutional Rights Foundation, May 30, 2012, http://crf-usa.org/bill-of-rights-in-action/bria-4-1-b-shays-rebellion-a-massachusetts-farmers-account.html.

44 Joseph J. Eilis, *American Creation: Triumphs and Tragedies at the Founding of the Republic* (New York: Alfred A. Knopf, 2007), 96.

45 Thomas Jefferson to James Madison, 30 January 1787, Archiving Early America, May 30, 2012, http://www.earlyamerica.com/review/summer/letter.html.

46 Jefferson quoted in Joseph J. Ellis, *American Sphinx: the Character of Thomas Jefferson* (New York: Vintage Books, 1996), 116.

47 Quoted in Shi and Tindal, *America,* 283.

48 Quoted, Ibid., 283.

49 Ellis, *American Creation*, 102-103.

50 Ellis, *American Creation*, 104; James Madison, *Vices of the Political System of the United States*, Document Library, Teaching American History.org, *www. teachingamericanhistory.org.*

51 Edmund Randolph to David Shepard, 25 July 1787, Document Library, Teaching American History, May 30, 2012, http://www.TeachingAmericanHistory.org/library/index.asp?documentprint=1800.

52 Alexander Hamilton to George Washington, 3 July 1787, Document Library, Teaching American History, May 30 2012, http://teachingamericanhistory.org/library/index.asp?documentprint=1851.

53 Oliver Ellsworth quoted in "Themes of the Constitutional Convention: The Connecticut Compromise." Teaching American History, May 30, 2012, http://teachingamericanhistory.org/convention/themes/5.html.

54 Benjamin Rush to John Adams quoted in David McCullough, *John Adams* (New York: Simon and Schuster Paperbacks), 378.

55 The New Jersey Plan, *The Avalon Project*, Yale Law School, May 30, 2012, http://avalon.law.yale.edu/18th_century/debates_615.asp.

56 "July 16, 1787: A Great Compromise." U.S. Senate: Art and History, http://www.senate.gov/artandhistory/history/minute/A_Great_Compromise.htm.

57 Madison Debates, June 15-16, 1787: The Great Compromise, *The Avalon Project*, Yale Law School, May 30, 2012, http://avalon.law.yale.edu/18th_century/debates_615.asp.

58 Madison, "Federalist Paper No. 39," Library of Congress. http://thomas.loc.gov/home/histdox/fed.

59 *McCulloch v. Maryland*, Legal Information Institute, Cornell School of Law, May 30, 2012, http://www.law.cornell.edu/supct/html/historics/USSC_CR_0017_0316_ZO.html.

60 Middlekauff, *The Glorious Cause*, 656-657.

61 Middlekauff, *The Glorious Cause*, 657.

62 See, for example, George Clinton, "Extent of Consolidated Territory Too Large to Preserve Liberty," *Antifederalist Paper, No. 14*, Antifederalist Papers, ThisNation.com: http://www.thisnation.com/library/antifederalist/14.html.

63 John Jay, "Federalist No. 2 , Concerning Dangers from Foreign Force and Influence," Federalist Papers, http://thomas.loc.gov/home/histdox/fed_02.html.

64 Alexander Hamilton, "Federalist No. 6: Concerning Dangers from Dissensions between the States," Federalist Papers, The Library of Congress: http://thomas.loc.gov/home/histdox/fed_06.html.

65 Alexander Hamilton, "Federalist No. 9: The Union as a Safeguard Against Domestic Faction and Insurrection," Federalist Papers, The Library of Congress: http://thomas.loc.gov/home/histdox/fed_09.html.
66 Alexander Hamilton, Federalist No. 6," *The Founders' Constitution,* Volume 1, Chapter 7, Document 10, The University of Chicago Press, May 30, 2012, http://press-pubs.uchicago.edu/founders/documents/v1ch7s10.html.

67 Letters from Abigail Adams to John Adams, 31 March - 5 April 1776 [electronic edition], *Adams Family Papers: An Electronic Archive*, Massachusetts Historical Society, September 21, 2012, http://www.masshist.org/digitaladams/; Letter from John Adams to Abigail Adams, 14 April 1776 [electronic edition], *Adams Family Papers: An Electronic Archive,* Massachusetts Historical Society, September 21, 2012, http://www.masshist.org/digitaladams/.

68 Mary Beth Norton, *Liberty's Daughters: The Revolutionary Experience of American Women, 1750-1800* (Ithaca: Cornell University Press, 1996), 189-190.

69 Norton, *Liberty's Daughters*, 191; Klinghoffer and Lois Elkis, "'The Petticoat Electors,'" 162-163; Kruman, *Between Authority and Liberty*, 103; Nash, *The Unknown Revolution*, 288; Linda K. Kerber, *Women of the Republic: Intellect and Ideology in Revolutionary America* (Chapel Hill: UNC Press, 1980), 287.

ANSWER KEY FOR CHAPTER NINE: ARTICLES OF CONFEDERATION AND THE CONSTITUTION

Check your answers to the questions in the Before You Move On Sections for this chapter.

Correct answers are **BOLDED**

Section 9.2.4 - p327
1. As the states began to adopt constitutions during the Revolutionary War, they chose to create republics over monarchies or democracies.
    A. TRUE
    b. False

2. Which of the following men drafted the Virginia Statute of Religious Freedom?
    a. George Mason
    b. George Washington
    c. James Madison
    D. THOMAS JEFFERSON

3. Pennsylvania adopted one of the most conservative constitutions of the Revolutionary Era.
    a. True
    B. FALSE

4. No state constitution in the Revolutionary Era allowed women the right to vote.
    a. True
    B. FALSE

Section 9.3.3 - p333
1. Under the Articles of Confederation, the national government consisted of
    a. Congress and a court system.
    b. Congress and an executive.
    c. Congress, a court system, and an executive.
    D. CONGRESS.

2. Which of the following was a power given to the national government in the Articles of Confederation?
    a. The right to collect taxes from the states.
    b. The right to enforce laws passed by the Confederation Congress.
    C. THE RIGHT TO PASS LEGISLATION.
    d. The right to draft troops.
    e. All of the above were powers possessed by the national government.

3. The Land Ordinance of 1787
    A. SPECIFIED THE PROCESS BY WHICH A TERRITORY COULD BECOME A STATE.
    b. divided the northwest territory into townships.
    c. basically left the course of the territories to the territories themselves with little oversight from the central government.
    d. addressed the parish system in Louisiana.

Section 9.4.5 - p344
The Constitutional Convention
1. The Constitutional Convention met in 1787 for the purpose of revising the Articles of Confederation.
    A. TRUE
    b. False

2. The Virginia Plan is also known as
    a. the "small state plan."
    B. THE "LARGE STATE PLAN."
    c. the New Jersey Plan.
    d. the Connecticut Compromise.

3. During ratification debates, the Antifederalists were really Federalists.

A. TRUE
b. False

4. Who among the following was NOT a Federalist?
   a. George Washington
   B. PATRICK HENRY
   c. James Madison
   d. Alexander Hamilton

5. The Three-Fifths Compromise dealt with the issue of representation and taxation.
   A. TRUE
   b. False

The Constitution

1. The necessary and proper clause has had the effect of limiting the power of the national government.
   a. True
   B. FALSE

2. The source of powers "reserved" to the states is the
   a. Supremacy Article.
   b. full faith and credit clause.
   C. TENTH AMENDMENT.
   d. necessary and proper clause.

3. The "full faith and credit" clause applies to
   a. the national judiciary.
   B. INTERSTATE RELATIONS.
   c. Congressional power.
   d. the Supremacy Article.

4. Which of the following is NOT a Congressional power enumerated in the U.S. Constitution?
   a. The right to create a lower national court system
   b. The right to enforce its laws
   c. The right to declare war
   d. The right to negotiate treaties
   E. NEITHER B OR D WERE CONGRESSIONAL POWER

5. According to the Constitution, _______ appoints judges; these appointments must be approved by _____.
   a. The Senate; the Presidency
   b. The Presidents; the Supreme Court
   c. The Presidents; the House of Representatives
   D. THE PRESIDENTS; THE SENATE

Chapter Ten: The Federalist Era

Contents

Chapter Ten: The Federalist Era

10.1 INTRODUCTION

After the ratification of the Constitution, a new American government began to take shape in what historians refer to as the Federalist Era. From 1789 to 1801, national leaders grappled with questions relating to implementing the Constitution. The framers had sought to create a more centralized national government to handle domestic and foreign policy issues. They had also wanted to curb what they saw as the excesses of democracy at the state level. Finally, they had hoped to create a "more perfect union" led by disinterested leaders. However, few members of the new government realized how difficult it would be to achieve these goals. The democratic ideals of the Revolutionary Era continued to grow in the 1790s. The American people became quite vocal about their opinions on the issues of the day, and they rarely agreed on the appropriate course of action. Nor, for that matter, did their leaders. Disagreements that had surfaced in Philadelphia about the real purpose of the central government remained.

During the presidencies of George Washington and John Adams, two political parties emerged to represent the broad views of the people on how to interpret the Constitution. The Federalists, the party in power, preferred a strong central government. They saw the federal government as a positive agent for change, which would bring prosperity to all Americans. The Republicans, the opposition party sometimes labeled Democratic-Republicans to distinguish them from the modern Republican Party, preferred a limited central government. They feared a strong government would trample the rights of the people, believing too much power corrupted even the most well-intentioned politicians. Divisions between the two parties marked the Federalist period. Debates arose, primarily over Alexander Hamilton's economic plans and the nation's foreign policy in the wake of the French Revolution. The Federalist Era proved to be a turbulent period because the future of the republic appeared uncertain.

10.1.1 Learning Outcomes

After completing this chapter, you should be able to:

- Explain Alexander Hamilton's vision for the republic and the reasons why his vision garnered such opposition.
- Evaluate the reasons for the emergence of the two-party system and the ideas about political parties held by Americans of this era.
- Compare and contrast the philosophical positions of Federalists and Republicans on the issues of public credit, the bank, tariffs, internal improvements, new lands, and foreign policy.
- Analyze the significance of the French Revolution, the Whiskey Rebellion, the Quasi-War, the Alien and Sedition Acts, and the Virginia and the Kentucky Resolutions on the development of political parties in the 1790s.
- Explain the reasons for the peaceful transfer of power in the election of 1800.

10.2 THE WASHINGTON YEARS: IMPLEMENTING A "MORE PERFECT UNION"

The Federalist Era began during George Washington's presidency as national leaders sought to implement the "more perfect union" they envisioned when drafting the Constitution. The new president hoped to create a strong central government respected both by the American people and by foreign governments. He also looked to outline the strongest possible role for the president given what the Constitution said about the executive branch. During his time in office, Washington and his advisers pursued economic and diplomatic policies that became associated with the Federalist Party. To deal with the country's economic problems, the administration introduced initiatives to promote growth suggested by Alexander Hamilton. To help secure the nation's borders, they sought to remove the threats posed by the Indians as well as the British and the Spanish in the borderlands (the western territories). Although these policies did have positive effects, they also paved the way for the development of an opposition party, the Republicans, before the end of Washington's first term.

10.2.1 Beginning the New Government

On April 23, 1789, George Washington arrived triumphantly in the nation's capital, New York City. A week later, he made his way to Federal Hall through streets filled with well-wishers to take the oath of office. On a portico facing Broad and Wall Streets, Washington swore to uphold the laws of the nation. Afterwards New Yorker Robert Livingston, who administered the oath, bellowed, "Long live George Washington, President of the United States." The crowd roared, and church bells tolled throughout the city. The president then retreated into the Hall to deliver his inaugural address to the members of the First Congress. Historians James McGregor Burns and Susan Dunn suggest Washington "sounded a note of profound elegance" when he mentioned how the preservation of liberty had been placed in the hands of the people.[1]

At the same time, the new president seemed almost apprehensive; he and the assembled members of Congress realized the awesome task they had before them—to put the principles of the Constitution into practice and demonstrate that the republican form of government could be successful. Washington knew he had to serve both as a political and a symbolic leader because the Constitution provided only a sketch of the president's responsibilities. Congress recognized it had to determine the structure of the executive and legislative branches. Initially, members of the national government recognized the necessity of gaining the respect of the American people and foreign governments.[2] In the coming years, their task would become more complicated because they disagreed on how to implement the Constitution.

The Naming Controversy

Though Congress had serious work to attend to in its opening session, the Senate's first major debate focused on how to address the president. John Adams, the vice president, felt it was extremely important to establish a title of respect for the nation's leader. Adams worried that without the proper title, foreign leaders would ridicule the American president. Moreover, he believed that a proper title would help focus the people's attention away from their state governments and toward the federal government.[3] The vice president suggested "His Highness" or "His Most Benign Highness." Other members of the Senate favored an even more honorific title. Eventually, a Senate committee settled on "His Highness, the President of the United States and Protector of their Liberties." However, the House of Representatives leaned against such a lofty title. James Madison and other republican-minded members pushed for a title that did not appear so king-like.[4] Eventually, Congress settled on "Mr. President" in order to show respect without too much deference.

Such a debate might seem trivial, but the choice of terms was important. It signified what type of government the opposing groups favored. The soon-to-be-labeled Federalists, like Adams, saw nothing wrong with aristocratic leadership because it would curb the excesses of democracy and bring stability to the nation. Titles and ceremony would convey strength and bring dignity to the new republic. Moreover, it would show the power of the central government over the states. The upcoming Republicans, like Madison, believed that in a republican society, there should be no sign of monarchy because it would undermine the people's sovereignty. During the debate, Madison argued that simplicity would bring dignity.[5] Congress quickly moved onto other issues, but the ideological issues raised during the naming controversy continued to divide national leaders.

The Bill of Rights

Most of the delegates at the Constitutional Convention of 1787 never thought of including a bill of rights in the new Constitution; however, as the states debated ratification, Anti-Federalists demanded some protection for the people against the excesses of government. Some Federalists agreed to consider amendments designed to protect the people in exchange for the ratification of the Constitution. Thus, the new Congress discussed possible amendments even though many Federalists saw outlining the people's specific rights as unnecessary, and many Anti-Federalists wanted more than cosmetic changes.[6]

James Madison took the lead in drafting the amendments. His decision did not stem from a strong belief in the advisability of amendments; he had promised his fellow Virginians he would support amendments if they elected him to Congress. Madison carefully drafted the amendments so they would not dilute the power of the central government; his proposals focused solely on personal rights. He also managed to convince the House and the Senate to move forward on the proposals. In the end, Congress sent twelve amendments to the states for ratification. According to historian Gordon Wood, two amendments, on congressional appropriation and congressional salaries, "were lost in the initial ratification process." The remaining ten became the Bill of Rights.[7]

The First Amendment protected the freedoms of speech, press, and religion. The Second and Third Amendments—relating to the people's fear of standing armies—granted the right to form citizen militias and to bear arms as well as to protect and limit the government's ability to house soldiers in private homes. The Fourth, Fifth, Sixth, Seventh, and Eighth Amendments defined a citizen's rights when under arrest or in court, including protecting against unreasonable search and seizure as well as cruel and unusual punishment. The

Ninth Amendment stated the government could not limit the citizens' rights to only those listed in the Bill of Rights. Finally, the Tenth Amendment indicated that powers not listed in the Constitution remained with the states and the people.

After the ratification of the amendments, Federalists could claim they considered the opposition's request to protect the people's liberties. On the other hand, Anti-Federalists worried that the amendments did not do enough to alter the Constitution on issues of the judiciary and direct taxation. Nevertheless, their addition prompted North Carolina and Rhode Island to ratify the Constitution. Moreover, they allowed Congress to move onto questions relating to the framework of the executive and judicial branches. Congress approved the creation of three executive departments—state, treasury, and war—whose heads would be appointed with the consent of the Senate. It also passed the Judiciary Act of 1789, which set the number of Supreme Court justices at six and created a system of district and circuit courts as well as the position of attorney general.

Defining the Role of the President

In debates at the Constitutional Convention, delegates struggled to define the executive branch. Some preferred the creation of an elected monarchy, whereas others preferred some form of governing council. The expectation that George Washington would become the first president convinced many delegates opposed to a strong executive to agree to a single elected executive. Those delegates trusted in the former general's public virtue and rationality.[8] When Washington took office, he thought about how to shape the role of the president in order to calm suspicions about the chief executive's power. He looked for ways to strike the proper balance between developing respectability and deflecting concerns that he desired to be a monarch, while also looking for ways to develop a strong sense of nationhood. Washington never fully enjoyed being the center of attention, but he willingly sat for numerous portraits in the hopes of cultivating patriotism. Moreover, he promoted internal improvements, the post office, and a national university to bind the fledgling nation together.[9]

Early on, Washington sought advice from John Adams, Alexander Hamilton, John Jay, and James Madison on everything from the style of his residence to the structure of his social calendar. The president integrated some aspects of ceremony into his routine, such as riding in an elaborate coach drawn by four to six white horses and holding weekly receptions for people who wished to meet the president. His administration also carefully prepared his visits to the Northeast in 1789 and to the South in 1791. The president tried to balance the more ceremonial aspects with daily afternoon walks around New York City, and later Philadelphia, and by adopting what he considered plain dress. Although some criticism of the ceremonial aspects of Washington's administration emerged in the press, Thomas Jefferson (recently returned from France) believed the president's moderation worked to preserve the liberty the revolution established.[10]

On a political level, Washington sought to become an energetic leader. He wanted to lay the foundation for a strong chief executive for his successors; moreover, he thought a "steady hand" should guide the nation.[11] According to James McGregor Burns and Susan Burns, the president believed "accountability, diligence, and speed" were the marks of a good government. Washington was a hands-on leader who used the strengths of his cabinet officers to his advantage. He chose Thomas Jefferson as the secretary of state, Alexander Hamilton as the secretary of treasury, Henry Knox as the secretary of war, and Edmund Randolph as the attorney general. Washington also instructed his cabinet secretaries "to deliberate maturely, but to execute promptly."[12]

Washington deferred to Congress only on small matters because he wanted to create a strong presidency. When it came to an issue of executive authority, he rarely gave in to Congress. For example, when Congress debated the creation of executive departments in 1789, Washington, with the help of James Madison, fought hard to protect the president's right to remove cabinet officers. Some congressmen maintained that because the Constitution granted the Senate the right to consent to presidential appointments, it also granted members the right to consent to removal. Madison, however, successfully convinced the House that no president could effectively control his own administration if he could not remove poorly performing officials. The Senate was not so easily convinced; they wanted to protect their rights when it came to appointments. Vice President Adams cast the tie-breaking vote that preserved the president's right of removal and his independence of action. In the end, as Gordon Wood points out, Washington "created an independent role for the president and made it the dominant figure in the government."[13]

10.2.2 The Road to Economic Recovery and Growth

Throughout the 1780s, economic issues—namely the war-related debts incurred by the state and the national governments—plagued the country. The total debt hovered at just under $78 million. Political leaders realized the necessity of dealing with public credit in order to develop greater respect for the new government. If the nation did not at a minimum make interest payments, then it would be hard for Americans to obtain credit at home or abroad. Not long after George Washington chose Alexander Hamilton as the secretary of treasury, the House of Representatives requested the secretary of treasury draw up plans to address the nation's financial problems. Hamilton's reports on public credit, a national bank, and manufacturing became a blueprint for the country's future economic growth and for a strong central government. At the same time, the debates surrounding Hamilton's vision further divided Washington, Hamilton, Adams, Jefferson, Madison, and others. Questions about the government's role in the economy clearly divided those who supported strong central authority and those who supported states' rights.

Dealing with the Debt

Alexander Hamilton first set out to deal with the debt, most of which stemmed from the effort to win independence. The Confederation Congress borrowed approximately $12 million from foreign governments and banks and approximately $42 million from the American people through a variety of bills, notes, and certificates. During the 1780s, the Confederation government found it difficult to make payments to creditors because it did not have an independent revenue source, so it borrowed more money just to make the interest payments. Meanwhile, the states also borrowed another $25 million from the people. Some of the states managed to pay their debt; others struggled because their residents balked at the high tax rates needed to fund the debt.

When the Washington administration began, no one seriously doubted the need to pay the foreign debt, but the question of the domestic debt was more complicated. Cash-poor farmers and merchants had sold their government certificates to speculators for much less than their face value in the 1780s. Some American leaders thought the government should pay the debt in full regardless of who held the certificates. Others thought the government should consider scaling it down or at least distinguishing between the original holders and the speculators. Furthermore, some leaders argued the federal government should assume the state debts, meaning it would take responsibility for paying those debts. Others argued such a move would discriminate against the states that had already met their financial obligations.

On January 14, 1790, Hamilton sent the Public Report on Credit to Congress. He outlined a proposal to pay the debt and to provide a base of capital for industrial projects. The secretary of treasury argued the government should pay the face value or full amount to the current holders of government certificates. Full payment would send a message to future creditors that the government could meet its obligations; paying anything less would be a breach of contract. Hamilton also proposed to assume the state debts in order to build loyalty to the national government. If the federal government took responsibility for paying all the debt, then the states could eliminate most of their taxes and thereby avoid the domestic turmoil of the 1780s. He further proposed the government should fund or refinance the debt by issuing new securities to certificate holders on which it would make annual interest payments. In theory, the government would also work to pay off the entire debt. For Hamilton, however, retiring the debt was not a priority.[14]

Hamilton based his approach to public credit on the British model where the wealthiest citizens held most of the securities. When the government made annual interest payments from tax revenues, those citizens continued to invest in the government. In turn, they could use their securities as a form of capital (currency) to fund internal improvements and business ventures. To Hamilton, the plan was economically sound and politically wise. He believed the key way to develop the people's loyalty to the United States was to focus on the self-interest of the elite, which in turn would bring economic benefits to all citizens. The president, who supported development to promote nationalism, approved of the secretary of treasury's plan as did most other nationally-minded Congress representatives.[15]

However, some in Congress seemed less convinced about the merits of Hamilton's plan. James Madison saw numerous problems with the proposal, which surprised Hamilton since the two men had collaborated on the *Federalist Papers* supporting a strong central government. In 1790, Madison still had nationalist tendencies in that he supported paying the debt. However, he pushed for greater equity in handling the domestic debt. He hated to see speculators benefit more than the nation's veterans. He also did not want to see states that funded their debts pay more than their share. Though Madison made an impassioned plea to protect the interests of the soldiers who fought for independence, the House ultimately sided with Hamilton on the question of paying the current holders of the securities the full value.[16]

The question of assumption took longer to decide. Madison maintained that the proposal did an injustice to states like Virginia, Maryland, and Georgia. They had paid their debts, but now the government would tax their citizens to fund the debts of states like Massachusetts, Connecticut, and South Carolina. If Madison could not stop assumption altogether, then he wanted "settlement" before assumption to prorate the amount the states would have to contribute to the refinanced national debt. In assessing Hamilton's proposals, Madison began to have reservations about the central government he helped create in the Constitution. He still believed in the importance of a national government, but he also worried the states might have to give up too much of their independence. Others who disagreed with assumption went so far as to suggest Hamilton wanted to do away with the states altogether. By June, the House and the Senate had deadlocked; most northerners were for assumption and most southerners were against it.[17]

Thomas Jefferson sided with Madison, but he also realized reaching a compromise was important for the future of the republic. Jefferson had a somewhat disturbing conversation with Hamilton, who believed the failure of his financial plan would lead to the disintegration of the union. So, Jefferson invited Hamilton and Madison to his home one night to discuss a solution. The compromise stemmed from a suggestion earlier made by Virginian Richard Bland Lee, who had linked resolution of the assumption bill with the future location of the nation's capital. Many southern legislators wanted to move the capital away from New York City so it would be closer to the South. It would also separate the nation's political and financial interests, which they believed would curb the power of northern elites.[18]

The meeting led to the Compromise of 1790—where Madison agreed not to fight assumption, and Hamilton agreed to support moving the capital to a site on the Potomac River. In July, Congress passed the Residence Bill and the Assumption Bill. The first stated the capital would move to Philadelphia for ten years while the government constructed the Potomac site carved out of Virginia and Maryland. The second made provisions for the federal government to assume the state debts.[19] While the two sides reached an agreement, the debate over public credit further divided the nation's leaders into factions. Jefferson and Madison saw the government more as an umpire who meditated the tensions between the states; Washington and Hamilton viewed the government as a player deeply involved in the fiscal affairs of the states. Hamilton's other reports only further exacerbated those tensions.[20]

Promoting Economic Development

For Alexander Hamilton, dealing with public credit was only the first step in securing the economic future of the United States. His Report on the Bank (1790) and Report on Manufactures (1791) promoted a greater connection between the federal government and the country's manufacturing interests. Hamilton believed his plans would strengthen the relationship between the country's agricultural and manufacturing sectors. He thought neither could prosper without the other; moreover, all Americans would prosper from the expansion of commerce. Trade brought revenue to the people and to the government, which in turn would make the United States a powerful nation. Economic development would also help secure liberty because revenue from tariffs would lessen the need to tax private property directly. The secretary of treasury, however, recognized his proposals likely would meet resistance because much of the population feared commerce.[21]

The Report on the Bank detailed the importance of creating a national bank. Hamilton proposed Congress charter the Bank of the United States for a period of twenty years and capitalize it at $10 million. Once chartered, the government would own 20 percent of the bank's stock. The bank would sell the remaining 80 percent to private individuals. Investors had to pay 25 percent of the value in specie, but the remaining 75 percent could be in government securities. The bank would also facilitate the payment of federal taxes and tariffs, serve as the government depository and government creditor, help regulate the state banks, and work to create paper money by issuing bank notes in the form short-term loans to merchants. Hamilton felt the creation of paper money served as the bank's most important function. Since the bank would exchange its notes for specie, the notes could change hands without losing value, making them an acceptable substitute for coin.[22]

Since most Americans had very little experience with banks, Hamilton's proposal was a novel solution to the nation's economic issues for its time. Southerners especially doubted the need for any financial institution that might concentrate the nation's economic power in the hands of only a few people. When Congress began to debate the bank bill in 1791, James Madison once again led the opposition. He argued against the concentration of power, which reminded him of the British monarchy. Instead, he suggested chartering several regional banks. Furthermore, he doubted the constitutionality of the measure. Madison promoted a limited interpretation of the Constitution, often referred to as strict construction. The bank charter did not propose to collect taxes or borrow money for the general welfare of the people. Therefore, it was not a necessary function of the government. Madison concluded that the measure "was condemned by the silence of the Constitution."[23]

Hamilton's supporters in Congress such as Fisher Ames, Elbridge Gerry, and Theodore Sedgwick effectively negated Madison's arguments in the House and Senate debates. Ames, for example, suggested that not only was the bank a proper function of the government, but that much of what Congress and the president had done in the previous two years relied on a broad interpretation of powers granted to the government. To him, the "necessary and proper" clause (Article I, Section 8) established the "doctrine of implied powers."[24] The bank bill passed through both chambers in February, leaving the president to decide whether to sign or veto the measure.

Washington very much respected Madison's judgment and thus, according to Gordon Wood, "was deeply perplexed by the issue of constitutionality." So, he asked Secretary of State Thomas Jefferson, who recently returned from Paris where he had served as the minister of France, and Attorney General Edmond Randolph for advice. Both men opposed the bank and in their written responses relied on the provisions of the Tenth Amendment. Impressed by their arguments, the president asked Madison to draft his veto message. However, he also invited Hamilton to respond to the criticism leveled by his fellow cabinet members. The secretary of treasury laid out a case for broad construction, arguing the bank was vital to the country's economic interests. In the end, Hamilton successfully convinced Washington the bank was both necessary and proper; the president signed the bill. Once the Bank of the United States—headquartered in Philadelphia—began selling its securities, Washington expressed pleasure at how quickly the value of those securities had risen. It suggested the people had confidence in the government and had economic resources.[25]

The Report on Manufactures proposed four different measures to support domestic industry: (1) Congress should protect the nation's infant industries through a protective tariff; (2) Congress should pay bounties to individuals who started businesses vital to the national interest; (3) Congress should fund a national transportation system of roads and canals, which would link industry and agriculture together; and (4) Congress should support industry through the encouragement of the labor of women and children. In the early 1790s, American farmers produced a surplus of goods. Thus, Hamilton wanted to create a domestic market for their surplus. If the nation started to industrialize, its laborers could be the market for much of what the farmers produced. In turn, those farmers could buy American-made manufactured goods. Such steps would make the nation less dependent on Europe. At the same time, Hamilton believed in the importance of maintaining some foreign trade since he planned to use a protective tariff or import tax to fund economic development.[26]

Hamilton had much less success convincing the president or Congress on the necessity of his proposal supporting domestic manufacturing. Although Washington adopted an increasingly urban focus, as James McGregor Burns and Susan Dunn maintain, he still had "land in his blood." He envisioned a balance between agriculture and industry in the United States, and yet he seemed incapable of giving up his belief that self-sufficient yeoman farmers would make the nation great. Consequently, he deemed the proposals unnecessary in 1792. Before he left office, Washington did recommend Congress consider support for domestic manufacturing to better prepare for times of war.[27]

Meanwhile, Congress began to debate enacting bounties or rewards for the fishing industry and revising the tariff. Although the fishing measure passed, Madison managed to substitute "allowance" for "bounty," thereby undermining Hamilton's plan to promote industry. To Madison, Congress could grant an allowance under the Constitution because it dealt with a deficiency. A bounty, on the other hand, could expand the role of the government beyond the vision of the framers.[28] As for the tariff, Congress had twice approved an import tax in 1789 and 1790. The measures raised revenue for the federal government, but they did not promote industry. While Congress raised the tariff rates in 1792, it did not adopt the principle of protectionism as Hamilton had hoped. In the short run, the federal government refrained from supporting domestic manufacturing. Hamilton's vision simply was ahead of its time. In the long run, Hamilton's proposals provided a guide for industrialization in the nineteenth century.

10.2.3 Foreign Policy Challenges

Beyond the efforts to define the role of the president and to promote economic recovery, George Washington had to deal with several foreign policy challenges relating to the settlement of the borderlands. The Indians living on that land, as well as the British and the Spanish governments, threatened the territorial integrity of the United States. The Washington administration sought to remove these threats. Washington saw the failure to resolve the issues on the frontier as problematic for the nation's security and economic development. Both relied on the peaceful settlement of western land and the ability to navigate the Mississippi River. The president relied on the military and the diplomatic corps to achieve his goals.[29]

At the same time, Washington had to define the role the legislative branch would play in foreign policy. The Constitution indicated the Senate would advise and consent on all treaties with foreign governments while the House would vote on the necessary appropriations for treaties. In 1789, Washington sought the Senate's input on a treaty with the Southern Indian tribes. John Adams read the treaty more than once to the assembled members and then the debate over each provision began. Meanwhile, Washington waited impatiently in the chamber, apparently making some of the senators uncomfortable. When one senator suggested submitting the treaty to a subcommittee for study, the president became visibly upset. He expected their approval would come quickly, not that he would have to submit the treaty to serious study. Based on the experience, the president opted to drop the advisement role of the Senate. Thenceforward, the Senate only consented when it voted to ratify completed treaties. In 1796, the House sought to weigh in on the provisions of Jay's Treaty with Great Britain. However, Washington refused Madison's attempt to expand the role the House played in treaty making.[30]

Disputes with the Indians

The Treaty of Paris ended the Revolutionary War and ceded western lands, and the frontier problems that went along with them, to the United States. In 1787, the Northwest Ordinance had laid out a blueprint for the expansion of the nation and set the tone for how the government would deal with Indians in the expansion process, proclaiming that "the utmost good faith shall always be observed towards the Indians; their lands and property shall never be taken from them without their consent...unless in just and lawful wars authorized by Congress; but laws founded in justice and humanity, shall from time to time be made for preventing wrongs being done to them."[31] Many saw this as an indication that the United States recognized the inevitability of expansion, but desired "expansion with honor." However, these lofty ideas and language of "expansion with honor" were negated when the document called for towns and cities to be laid out in the places where Indian lands had been "extinguished."

The new government sought to control frontier violence, settle the western lands peacefully, and promote the territorial integrity of the United States. One way of accomplishing these goals was the adoption of legislation that clearly defined the role of the federal government in foreign policy with Indians. From 1790 to 1834, Congress passed a series of acts, known as the Indian Intercourse Acts, which prohibited unregulated trade between Indians and Americans. The Acts established that only the federal government could license traders to buy Indian lands. This was confirmed by the Supreme Court in the 1823 *Johnson v. M'Intosh* case, which established that private individuals were not authorized to purchase land from Indians.[32] The Act further regulated trade by setting up a series of authorized trading posts, or "factories," where all trade between Indians and Americans was to take place. Ostensibly, the factories were to protect Indians from being defrauded by private individuals; in actuality, the United States often secured substantial tracts of Indian lands by trading access to the factories for land.

Over the course of the 1780s, the United States government strived to end frontier tensions by negotiating a series of treaties with some of the nations of the Ohio Valley.

However, hostilities between settlers and Indians continued to grow as more Americans pushed westward. Matters came to a head in 1785-1786, when representatives of many of the nations of the Ohio Valley met to establish a group that would present a united front to the United States. This became known as the Miami Confederacy or the Northwest Confederacy. Participating groups included the Miami, Shawnee, Wyandot, Ojibwe, Lenape, and Kickapoo, among others. In a series of meetings, the Confederacy declared that the United States would have to deal with them as a group, not as individual tribes. They declared the Ohio River to be the boundary between the lands of the settlers and the lands of the Indians. Furthermore, the group declared that it would not honor treaties signed by only one individual or one group, which they referred to as "partial treaties." The Confederacy was supported by a number of British agents still present in the region. These agents sold weapons and ammunition to the Indians, encouraged attacks on American settlers, and did much to increase tensions between the Indians of the Ohio Valley and the United States. The mid-1780s were marked by a series of disputes, including raids on American settlements and Indian towns alike. Hundreds died and mistrust grew, continuing the pattern of frontier violence that sparked the Northwest Indian War (1785-1795).

In 1790, war began in earnest when Washington and Secretary of War Henry Knox authorized a major campaign into the Ohio Valley, specifically calling for campaigns into the Miami and Shawnee lands. Some 1,500 troops, under the command of General Josiah Harmar, assembled to march into the Valley. Harmar planned to attack Kekionga, one of the largest villages in the region. His plans were thwarted by Miami leader Little Turtle, who evacuated the village before Harmar could attack, then ambushed and defeated Harmar's troops, killing almost 200 soldiers. The following year, General Arthur St. Clair led the army back into the Valley. St. Clair's troops, untrained and ill-equipped for war, were quickly overrun by Little Turtle's Confederacy forces. The defeat was devastating, resulting in tremendously high casualties for the young American army and nation; some 630 officers and soldiers were killed, the highest casualties ever in an Indian war in American history.

The defeat was a triumph for the Confederacy. Many of the regional and Confederacy leaders, including leaders of the powerful Iroquois nation, wanted to take advantage of this strong position and negotiate with the Americans while the Confederacy had the upper hand. This idea was met with resistance by the majority of the Confederacy, who maintained that the Ohio River remained the absolute boundary between Indian and American lands. They would accept nothing less.

In the meantime, Congress laid plans to fund a large army. They appropriated one million dollars to create the Legion of the United States, a well-trained group created expressly to fight Indian wars. Under the command of General "Mad" Anthony Wayne, the Legion arrived in the Ohio Valley in late 1793 to find the Northwest Confederacy greatly weakened by fighting between the factions. Wayne and his troops built Fort Recovery on the site of St. Clair's defeat. Little Turtle led an investigation of the newly arrived army and an unsuccessful attack against the fort; afterwards, he argued to the Confederacy that the Legion could not be defeated and advised a truce. The Confederacy responded by replacing Little Turtle with Shawnee leader Blue Jacket. The war culminated with the

Battle of Fallen Timbers. Although both sides only suffered light casualties, the battle was significant. Blue Jacket had chosen to station his forces at a fortified area marked by trees that had blown over in a storm. The spot was close to Fort Miami, held by the British who traded with local groups and had supplied and supported the Confederacy. After losing the battle and abandoning the battlefield, Blue Jacket and his men fell back to Fort Miami, anticipating that they would find refuge there. The British commander refused to open the gates to the Confederacy troops, unwilling to start a war with the Americans. For many of the Northwest Confederacy, this lack of support by the British was even more discouraging than the loss of the battle.

The Northwest Indian War was concluded with the 1795 Treaty of Greenville. Little Turtle, one of the representatives of the Northwest Confederacy, delivered a speech defending the sovereignty of Native Americans and called for peace with the United States. The treaty ceded about two-thirds of the Ohio Valley to the United States and parts of modern-day Indiana, including the sites of the future cities of Detroit, Chicago, and Toledo. In return, the Confederacy was guaranteed lands beyond the "Greenville Treaty Line," which more or less followed the Cuyahoga River. Although the Treaty of Greenville promised a "lasting boundary," settlers pushed into Indian lands a few years later.

The Northwest Indian War left a lasting legacy in several ways. As the first significant post-revolutionary military engagement, the decisive defeat of St. Clair and the army proved a real test of the young nation. Moreover, Congress was forced to raise a great deal of money in the midst of the debt crisis to fund the war and the newly created Legion of the United States. Washington's administration and Congress were also delving into uncharted waters as they sought to establish the primacy of the federal government in Indian affairs. Finally, the Treaty of Greenville established the practice of paying yearly annuities of money and goods to nations that granted the United States some role in tribal affairs, a practice which continued and grew in the later Indian Wars.

Disputes with Great Britain and Spain

Both Great Britain and Spain complicated the Washington administration's dealings with the Indians. The major European powers saw the fledgling United States as a weak nation in the 1780s and continued to do so in the 1790s. In 1783, Britain had lost the thirteen colonies and the land between the Appalachians and the Mississippi. Although it still controlled Canada, the boundary with Canada and the United States was unclear in places. At the same time, Britain returned Florida to Spain, and Spain claimed the Tennessee River as the border between the United States and New Spain. As a result, the United States faced threats on all of its borders. The British government encouraged the Indians to unite and resist American settlement. Moreover, the British severely discriminated against American merchants who wanted to sell to the British West Indies. To make matters worse, the Spanish government closed the Mississippi to American traffic. Spanish agents then encouraged settlers in Kentucky and Tennessee to break away from the United States so they could use the Mississippi to ship their produce to market.[33] While Washington opted to rely on the army to resolve issues with the Indians, he turned to his diplomats to handle relations with Britain and Spain.

Tensions mounted between the Americans and the British in 1793, when France (during its revolution) declared war on all monarchies, including Britain. The United States hoped to remain neutral in the conflict, but the need to trade in Europe complicated matters since Britain blockaded the continent. The Washington administration prepared for war but hoped to avoid such an outcome. The chance for settlement came when Washington received word the British intended to ease their seizures of American ships in the West Indies. He sent John Jay, the chief justice, to London in 1794 as a special envoy. He instructed Jay to secure the evacuation of the northwestern forts on U.S. territory in the Great Lakes region still occupied by the British, to win reparations for seized American ships, to secure compensation as for slaves seized by the British during the war, and to negotiate a commercial treaty granting Americans trade with the British West Indies.[34]

Jay's Treaty (formally known as the Treaty of Amity, Commerce, and Navigation) did not live up to Washington's expectations, because the chief justice only managed to secure the evacuation of the forts and damages for the seized ships. Nevertheless, the president sent the treaty to the Senate for ratification. When the public learned of the contents of the treaty, hostility to settlement mounted because so many Americans distrusted the British and favored the French in their ongoing conflict. In spite of the public reaction, the Senate approved the treaty by the barest margin in 1795. Washington signed for two reasons: he thought it would calm the political tensions, and he thought the agreement might pave the way for future improvements in the Anglo-American relationship.[35] The president turned out to be wrong on both accounts.

The possibility of a treaty with Great Britain did, however, encourage Spain to negotiate an agreement with the United States. Washington sent William Short to Madrid in 1792, but Spanish negotiators seemed more interested in expanding their New World Empire than in making concessions to the Americans. Meanwhile, western settlers in Kentucky and Pennsylvania criticized Washington for doing nothing to assist them. Just as in the 1780s, it appeared as though the states might break from the American republic if the situation was not resolved. So, Washington sent Thomas Pinckney to Madrid in 1795. Spanish negotiators decided to conclude an agreement before the British and Americans could collaborate to erode their possessions in the Americas. In Pinckney's Treaty (formally known as the Treaty of San Lorenzo), the Spanish accepted the 31st parallel (much farther south than the Tennessee River) as the border and agreed to the free navigation of the Mississippi River. The Senate ratified, and the president signed the treaty in 1796.[36] Jay's Treaty and Pinckney's Treaty secured the American borders in the West, but they hardly ended the political factionalism throughout the nation.

10.2.4 Before You Move On...

Key Concepts

In 1789, the Washington administration and Congress hoped to put the principles of the Constitution into practice and demonstrate that the republican form of government could be successful—to truly create a "more perfect union." Congressional leaders followed through with promises made in 1787 and 1788 to add a Bill of Rights to the Constitution.

The executive and legislative branches also made strides in promoting the economy. Hamilton's suggestions on public credit and the bank helped resolve the financial problems of the Confederation period. Madison eventually agreed to support a measure to fund the war debt in full as well as to assume the state debts in exchange for moving the nation's capital to a site on the Potomac River. Hamilton's supporters in Congress also convinced enough members to support a measure to create the Bank of the United States, to hold government deposits and issue currency.

The administration also sought to control frontier violence, settle the western lands peacefully, and promote the territorial integrity of the United States. Greenville's Treaty, ending the Northwest Indian War, ceded Indian land in the Ohio Valley to the United States and reserved the land beyond the treaty line for the Indians. Jay's Treaty and Pinckney's Treaty proved that the newly-constituted central government had the strength to deal effectively with foreign governments to resolve its trade and border issues.

In spite of Washington's efforts to curtail political differences, domestic and foreign policy issues began to divide political leaders into two factions by the end of Washington's first term in office. Increasingly, Federalists (who favored a strong central government) and Republicans (who favored a limited central government) disagreed on how to interpret the Constitution.

Test Yourself

1. The Bill of Rights did all of the following except
   a. constitute the first ten amendments to the Constitution.
   b. appease some initial critics of the Constitution.
   c. safeguard freedoms such as press, speech, and assembly.
   d. settle all questions about federal versus state authority.

2. Madison and Jefferson objected to the national bank in the 1790s primarily because
   a. they believed in strict construction when interpreting the Constitution.
   b. they felt it was not powerful enough to meet the nation's financial needs.
   c. it would cost the government too much money.
   d. it would be located in New York rather than Virginia.

3. The Treaty of Greenville was an agreement between the United States and
   a. Great Britain.
   b. Indians on the northwest frontier.
   c. Spain.
   d. Canada.

4. Jay's Treaty, ratified by the Senate in 1795,
   a. guaranteed the right of Americans to trade in the West Indies.
   b. forced Hamilton's resignation from the cabinet.
   c. infuriated American people for its concessions to the British.
   d. was most strongly opposed in New England.

See page 398 for answers

10.3 THE EMERGENCE OF PARTISAN POLITICS

When the framers wrote the Constitution, they very much hoped they could avoid the emergence of permanent political parties. However, two distinct factions appeared by the mid-1790s. The Federalists coalesced in support of Alexander Hamilton's vision for the nation early in the Washington administration. The Republicans, or Democratic-Republicans, formed in opposition to Hamilton's vision. The opposition, led by Thomas Jefferson and James Madison, took longer to develop, largely because no national leader could really conceive of a legitimate counter-party to the group in power. Most agreed any conflict would not strengthen the nation, but lead to disunion. In the 1790s, partisan politics was unsettling because people on both sides thought the future of the republic was at stake. The French Revolution and the Whiskey Rebellion helped contribute to the creation of the first party system in the United States, which in turn set the stage for the nation's first partisan presidential election in 1796.

10.3.1 The Federalists and the Republicans

The nationally-minded leaders who went to the Constitutional Convention in 1787 all agreed about the need to curb the excesses of democracy at the state level and create a stronger central government. Once the Washington administration began to outline its domestic and foreign policies, ideological divisions resurfaced among the president's advisers and among members of Congress. Soon those divisions spread to the wider public through the partisan newspapers. During the debates over Hamilton's plans for economic growth, two rival Philadelphia papers, John Fenno's *Gazette of the United States* and Philip Freneau's *National Gazette*, published essays by Hamilton, Madison, and others under pen names discussing the proposals. Both editors took the opportunity not just to address the political issues, but to sharpen the divide between those who supported Hamilton and those who did not. Soon more partisan newspapers appeared to help provide a political identity to voters during the infancy of the two-party system in the United States.[37]

While still hostile to the idea of political parties, people around the country began speaking of the Federalists and the Republicans by 1792. The emergence of the Democratic-Republican clubs in 1793 further exacerbated the political divisions. The clubs, modeled on the radical Jacobin clubs in France, pledged to monitor the government and support opposition candidates. They communicated with one another much as the Committees of Correspondence had in the pre-revolution years, frightening many national leaders—Federalist and Republican alike. No elite could yet envision a truly democratic future for the nation where all citizens had an equal say in the government.[38]

At heart, Federalists and Republicans disagreed about how much power to vest in the central government or, conversely, about how capable the people were in governing themselves. Federalists Alexander Hamilton and John Adams believed promoting social stability would best preserve the people's liberty. Furthermore, the nation could only achieve stability if the government promoted the self-interest of the wealthiest farmers, merchants, and manufacturers. Federalists believed the government should serve the interests of the few; doing so would provide benefits for all and would create a strong national union. Federalists never opposed popular elections, but they felt once the people voted, they should leave the important decisions to those they elected. As evidenced by their position on the creation of a national bank, Federalists supported broad construction when it came to interpreting the Constitution. They took a wide view of the necessary and proper clause, seeing things like federally funded internal improvements as a legitimate government function.[39]

Republicans Thomas Jefferson and James Madison believed any attempt to cater to minority interests would undermine the people's liberty; government should work to support the interests of ordinary citizens—the majority. Any other course of action would put the nation back on the road to monarchy. Republicans spoke primarily for agricultural interests and values. They distrusted bankers, cared little for commerce or manufacturing, and believed that freedom and democracy flourished best in a rural society composed of yeoman farmers. They felt little need for a strong central government; it would only become a source of oppression. They wanted the central government to handle foreign policy and foreign trade. However, everything else should be left to the states. Moreover, Republicans supported strict construction when it came to interpreting the Constitution. Reading the Constitution literally would limit the opportunities the government had to undermine citizen's rights.[40]

As the two parties formed, they attracted a diverse group of voters. Federalists attracted wealthy citizens with commercial and manufacturing interests; people who worked in the Atlantic seaports also found their agenda more appealing. Dependent on foreign trade for their livelihood, many artisans wanted to see the government pursue economic development. The Federalists were strongest in the North, but they also had a presence in Virginia, North Carolina, and South Carolina. Republicans tended to attract wealthy landowners tied to plantation-based slavery. At the same time, ordinary farmers who wanted to see the economy remain tied to agriculture and less prosperous merchants who wanted to challenge the control of entrenched leaders supported the Republicans. Finally, the Republicans attracted many new immigrants with radical political ideas who fled England, Ireland, and other places in Europe. The Republicans were strongest in the South, as well as the western areas of Pennsylvania and New York.[41] Since both parties developed support based on economic outlook and sectional interest, the coalitions remained fluid in the 1790s as they tried to broaden their constituencies. Therefore, partisan politics played a role in how the government responded to the French Revolution and the Whiskey Rebellion.

10.3.2 The French Revolution

The French Revolution began just as the new American government took shape in 1789. Most Americans celebrated the French people's attempt to overthrow their aristocratic leaders and create a republic. They believed that their own effort to oust the British inspired the French cause for liberty. French actions, such as declaring three days of official mourning when Benjamin Franklin died in 1790 and extending honorary citizenship to George Washington, James Madison, and Alexander Hamilton, encouraged the American people to express sympathy for the Revolution. As Federalist John Marshall later noted, "We are all strongly attached to France...I sincerely believed human liberty to depend...on the success of the French Revolution."[42] However, two events in 1793 began to divide the American people as well as members of their government.

When the Reign of Terror began with the execution of King Louis XVI, many Federalists questioned the liberty and equality of the French effort. These leaders thought the people had gone too far; legitimate revolution descended into popular anarchy. Federalists concluded that any attempt to encourage the French would destroy the American experiment. Alexander Hamilton suggested the Americans had fought for liberty, while the French fought for "licentiousness." Republicans seemed undisturbed by the turn of events in France. They saw the violence as evidence of the people casting off the evils of monarchism. Thomas Jefferson and James Madison maintained the fate of France's nobility served a "greater cause." Citizens across the country expressed their sympathy for the French cause by wearing tricolored ribbons and singing revolutionary songs.[43]

More importantly, France began a war against Great Britain in February. To underscore their revolutionary effort, the French hoped to destroy all monarchies. Based on the Treaty of Alliance, the Americans had an obligation to assist the French. Under the terms of the treaty, each country pledged to defend the other in the event of a war with Great Britain. George Washington had to decide whether to live up to the commitments made in 1778.[44] Regardless of their opinions about the French Revolution, his advisers thought the United States should be neutral in the war. Secretary of State Jefferson, although he did not want to take any action to harm the French, did not want to jeopardize American security. Secretary of Treasury Hamilton did not want to aid the French because it might interrupt his economic vision, which relied on good trade relations with the British.[45]

On April 22, 1793, Washington issued a proclamation stating the United States "should with sincerity and good faith adopt and pursue a conduct friendly and impartial toward the belligerent Powers." Moreover, the government would punish Americans citizens for "abetting hostilities" or carrying contraband. Although the proclamation did not include the word neutrality, the president hoped the message would convey the Americans' desire to stay out of the European conflict.[46] Federalists tended to support Washington's position, whereas Republicans widely lambasted the neutrality policy. Immediately after it went into effect, Jefferson distanced himself from the policy, and Madison called it an "unfortunate error."[47]

The neutrality proclamation also sparked a constitutional debate on the president's authority to make foreign policy. Writing anonymously, Hamilton and Madison debated the issue in the partisan papers. Hamilton maintained the president had the authority to declare neutrality since the Constitution gave the executive department the responsibility to conduct business with foreign nations. Furthermore, he argued the provisions of the 1778 treaty only covered defensive wars, and France had launched an offensive war against Britain. In response, Madison opted to speak only about the larger constitutional issues raised by the proclamation, as opposed to addressing the policy itself. Since Congress had the power to declare war and ratify treaties, he argued it also had the power to declare neutrality. Furthermore, Madison suggested the opposition defined executive authority by looking to "*royal prerogatives* in the *British government*."[48]

As Washington and his advisers mulled over neutrality, they also had to decide whether the government should receive the new minister, Edmond Charles Genet, when he arrived from France. Hamilton opposed receiving Genet unless the administration also indicated that the United States had suspended all treaties made with the former French government. He feared recognizing France would be the same as saying the United States backed their war. Jefferson, who had more affection for the French people and their cause because of his time in Paris, supported receiving Genet, which amounted to recognizing the French government. He argued against suspending the alliance because doing so would undermine the decision to recognize the government. On this issue, the president sided with Jefferson.[49] However, no one in the Washington administration could have foreseen the problems Citizen Genet would cause.

The French government sent Genet to the United States with three goals: encourage the Americans to live up to the provisions of the 1778 treaty; secure the right to outfit privateers (privately owned warships commissioned to prey on enemy ships) in American ports; and gain American assistance in undermining British and Spanish rule in the New World. When Genet arrived in Charleston, South Carolina, well-wishers met his ship and those good feelings continued. As he made the journey to Philadelphia, everywhere he went people showered him with praise and collected money for the Revolution. Across the country, he met with Democratic-Republican clubs. Moreover, he recruited soldiers to launch an attack on New Spain and sailors to work as privateers. Genet also turned the *Little Sarah* (a captured British ship held by the French in Philadelphia) into the *Little Democrat* and sent it out to attack British ships, something he told the Washington administration he would not do. To make matters worse, Genet threatened to take his cause to the American people if their government complained.[50]

At first, Thomas Jefferson had encouraged Genet's efforts to drum up support for the war. But no matter how much Jefferson wanted to help the French, the *Little Democrat* incident forced him to approach Washington about Genet's threats to appeal directly to the American people. When the president found out, he was furious. At heart, he worried how other European governments would view the United States if it allowed Genet to dictate policy. Washington's cabinet agreed the Americans had to request Genet's recall. Jefferson sent a letter to the French government detailing Genet's activities, taking care to separate those actions from the intentions of the government. The letter also underscored the American desire to continue its friendly relationship with the French.[51] France recalled their ambassador, but Genet sought asylum in the United States. Washington granted the request because he recognized Genet would likely become another victim of the Reign of Terror if he returned.

The Citizen Genet Affair further exacerbated the growing tensions between the Federalists and the Republicans. The Federalists pounced on Genet's blunders. They sought not only to build support for neutrality, but to also undermine the Republicans. Across the country, Federalists sponsored resolutions supporting the Washington administration; they also indicated their opponents were dangerous radicals. Not to be outdone, the Republicans suggested their opponents sought to create discord between France and the United States in order to restore a British-like monarchy in the United States. Partisan newspaper editors outdid themselves in attacking the opposition. Only respect for George Washington, says Gordon Wood, kept the partisan feuding from becoming completely unmanageable.[52] However, by the time John Jay went to London to deal with problems between the United States and Great Britain (some of which were caused by the Anglo-French conflict) the American people had clearly divided along pro-French and pro-British lines.

10.3.3 The Whiskey Rebellion

The Federalists and the Republicans found another reason to worry about the opposition's intentions: the Whiskey Rebellion. In 1790, the Washington administration sought to levy a direct tax on the American people to help defray the costs of Hamilton's financial program. The secretary of treasury knew indirect import duties would not entirely cover the costs of putting the nation on solid financial footing, so he proposed an excise tax on distilled spirits, which the Federalist-dominated Congress approved. However, several Republicans predicted the people would refuse to pay.[53]

As foreseen, the federal government struggled to collect the whiskey tax. Just as in the years leading up to the American Revolution, the people expressed hostility to a direct tax put in place by a faraway central government. Taxing distilled spirits meant the farmers farthest from the centers of commerce felt the burden most heavily. Perishable goods often did not survive the trip to market; however, when turned into alcohol, grain became portable. In cash-strapped areas of the country, people also used whiskey as a form of currency. Therefore, people in states south of New York began almost immediately to protest the excise tax. They tarred and feathered tax collectors, sent petitions to Congress requesting a repeal of the tax, and attacked fellow citizens who paid the tax.[54]

Federalists concluded that in order to preserve the union they must enforce the tax. Such public outbursts against legitimate laws passed by the central government would lead to anarchy. Hamilton decided to focus on four counties in western Pennsylvania.

With Philadelphia the home of the central government, it looked bad that the government could not even collect the tax in the Pittsburgh area. Furthermore, government officials at least attempted to collect the tax in Pennsylvania. Anti-tax sentiment was so high the Washington administration could not find people to take jobs as tax collectors in most other states. In 1792, at Hamilton's urging, Washington issued a proclamation to condemn the efforts to resist the tax and to threaten strict enforcement. However, not until 1794 did the federal government attempt to back up the proclamation when the violence in Pennsylvania escalated.[55]

That summer, federal officials had attempted to enforce the whiskey tax. In response, approximately 500 members of the local militia units converged on the home of General John Neville, the excise inspector for the region. They demanded he resign his position and stop all efforts to collect the tax. Neville tried to defend his home, but the attackers set the house on fire and escaped into the countryside. Two weeks later, on August 1, about 6,000 militiamen gathered outside of Pittsburgh to continue their protest against the tax. Some wanted to attack Neville's headquarters, but cooler heads prevailed and the group dispersed. However, western Pennsylvanians continued to meet in smaller groups where they set up mock guillotines and talked about attacking the nearby federal arsenal. Rumors of secession and civil war circulated through the region.[56]

Whatever sympathy the president possessed for the people's concern about direct taxes evaporated when militia units gathered and threatened an attack on the federal government. Washington vowed to defend the union—quickly and decisively. He noted, "Neither the Military nor Civil government shall be trampled upon with impunity whilst I have the honor to be at the head of them."[57] Washington issued a proclamation on August 7 suggesting he would call out the militia to enforce the law. Since the governor and legislature of Pennsylvania had not asked for assistance, Washington sought a judicial writ giving him the power to use force if necessary. Hamilton wanted to deploy troops immediately; however, the president decided to send a peace commission to negotiate an end to the insurrection. When that effort failed, Washington called up 12,000 troops from New Jersey, Pennsylvania, Maryland, and Virginia. On September 25, the troops set out for Pittsburgh under Washington's command. By the time they arrived in October, the resistance movement had all but collapsed. The government arrested twenty men and took them to Philadelphia for trial. The president later pardoned the two convicted for treason, and the crisis ended.[58]

Nevertheless, the incident inflamed partisan passions. Federalists firmly believed they had saved the nation from disunion. They saw the rebellion as a test of the government's strength; in crushing it so decisively, they had won. Washington, for example, thought European monarchies would take seriously the idea that a republican form of government could successfully enforce the laws and simultaneously protect liberty and property. On the other hand, Republicans saw the show of force as a sign Federalists planned to create a standing army and thwart democracy. Jefferson, who had already left the administration, implied in his public statements that the Federalists had conjured a rebellion to boost their power.[59]

10.3.4 The Election of 1796

By 1796 the aging George Washington, having served two terms, wanted to retire to Mount Vernon, and no one could change his mind. Four years earlier, Washington had threatened to retire because of the ideological divisions in his cabinet and the growing political partisanship among the people. His closest advisers talked him out of what they considered a dangerous action. During a meeting with the president, James Madison sympathized with the great sacrifices Washington had made but also encouraged him to stay on. When Washington consulted Alexander Hamilton and Thomas Jefferson a short while later, they concurred. All three felt as Jefferson did when he wrote, "The confidence of the whole nation is centered in you."[60] And so, Washington agreed to stand for reelection, and the Electoral College voted for him unanimously.

However, the partisan rancor in his second term convinced the president he must retire. In part, Washington believed one way to quell the dissent was to set a precedent for the regular rotation of public officials. Republicans long accused Federalists of being monarchists. If he left office by choice, then he could mute such criticism. On September 19, 1796, George Washington announced his decision not to seek reelection to the American people. His "Farewell Address" appeared in newspapers across the country; he never delivered it as a spoken address. The address had three main themes: maintaining national unity, denouncing partisanship, and steering clear of permanent alliances with foreign countries.[61]

The address incorporated not only George Washington's ideas about maintaining national unity, but those of James Madison and Alexander Hamilton. The president revived a draft Madison began in 1792 before their ideological differences drove them apart. Washington, according to historian Joseph Ellis, included Madison's thoughts because he wanted to stress the importance of "subordinating sectional and ideological differences to larger national purposes." He also thought the effect would be all the more potent since Madison had become one of the leaders of the opposition party. The president then passed his notes on to Hamilton, who took out the self-pitying remarks about partisanship. The former secretary of treasury (he had left the administration in 1795) believed Washington's statement needed to "wear well." Over the course of several months, they ironed out the final statement that unmistakably indicated the president would not seek a third term.[62]

Washington's decision to retire set the stage for the first partisan president election in American history. No one had even bothered to challenge Washington in 1788 or 1792; he was, for many, the symbol of independence. In 1796, the people considered a long list of men with revolutionary qualifications, including Samuel Adams, Alexander Hamilton, Patrick Henry, and James Madison. However, John Adams and Thomas Jefferson emerged as the top choices. For much of their early political careers, the pair had worked together to secure independence. In the 1780s, they grew closer when Adams served as the minister to Great Britain and Jefferson served as the minister to France. They had grown apart in the 1790s as their ideological differences became more apparent. Adams dutifully supported the Federalist agenda, while Jefferson helped lead the opposition against a stronger central government. In the minds of the American people, Adams and Jefferson earned their fame as a pair, making the contest in 1796 even more heated. As Joseph Ellis remarks, "choosing between them seemed like choosing between the head and the heart of the American Revolution."[63]

At the Constitutional Convention in 1787, the framers had created the Electoral College to choose the president and vice president. Each state had the same number of electors as the number of people that served in United States Congress from that state. They could choose their electors in any way they saw fit. The electors could vote for any two candidates, as long as one of those candidates was not from their home state. The candidate with the highest number of votes became president; the candidate with the second highest number of votes became the vice president. If no candidate received a majority, then the House of Representatives, voting by state, would decide. Many of the framers anticipated most elections would end up in the House, and the Electoral College would serve more like a nominating body—determining the most qualified candidates for the presidency. As the political factions developed, political leaders began to speak more forcefully for a specific candidate, and the Electoral College never quite worked as envisioned in 1787.[64]

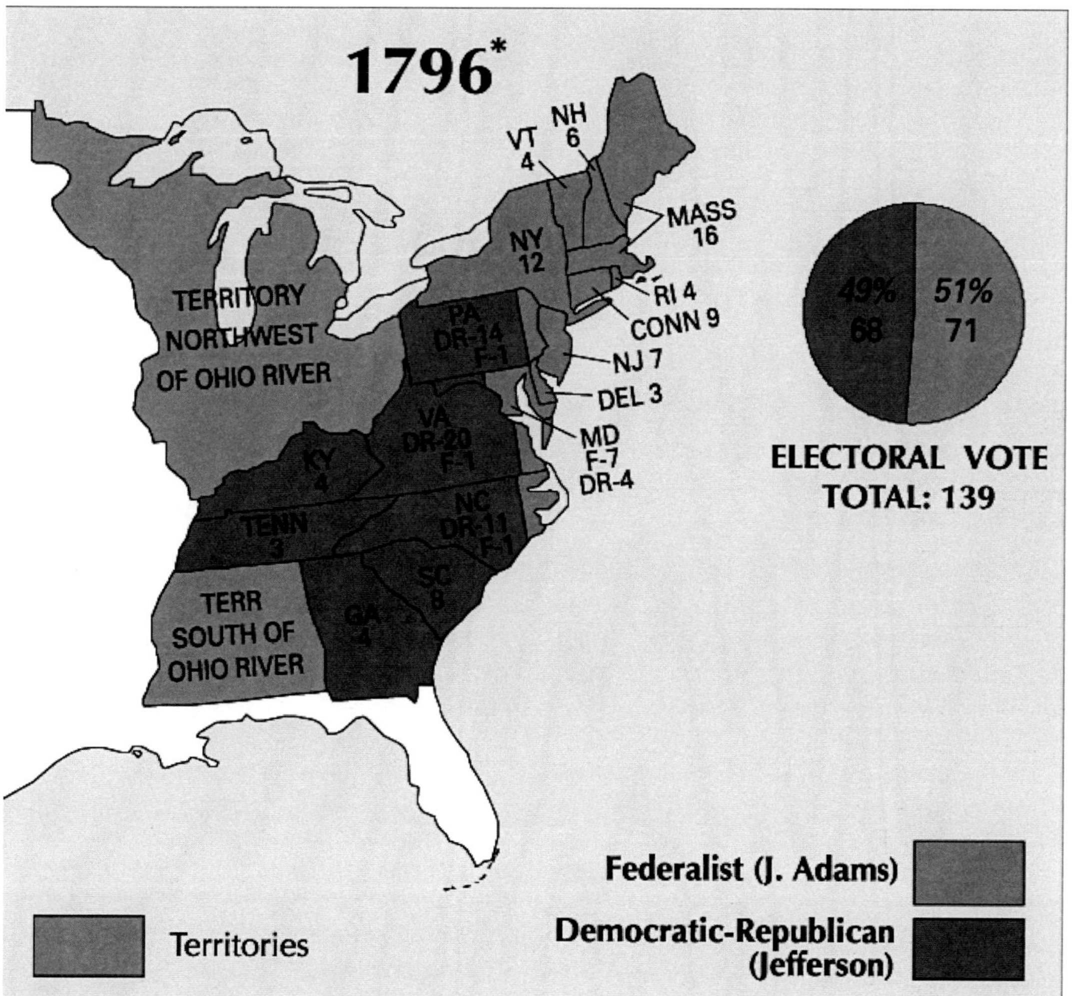

Figure 10.1 Presidential Election Map | 1796–George Washington's decision to retire set the stage for the first partisan president election in American history. Members of the Electoral College had to choose between John Adams, Aaron Burr, Thomas Jefferson, and Thomas Pinckney. The Federalist Adams triumphed, but the Republican Jefferson became the vice president.

Author: National Atlas of the United States
Source: Wikimedia Commons

While both John Adams and Thomas Jefferson wanted to be president, as disinterested gentlemen leaders they could not publicly say so. In 1796, political aspirations made a candidate seem less qualified, not more, for public office. Therefore, both men retired to their homes and allowed their supporters to speak on their behalf. The Federalists supported John Adams and Thomas Pinckney; the Republicans supported Thomas Jefferson and Aaron Burr. Electors cast ballots for two individual men and not a ticket of president and vice president, so the lead up to the election was somewhat chaotic, especially since behind the scenes. Alexander Hamilton schemed to encourage Federalists to choose Pinckney over Adams. As the election approached, hostility toward Jay's Treaty seemed to give Jefferson the edge. However, economic conditions in the country suggested to some people that the Federalist agenda had achieved positive results.[65]

When the electors cast their ballots, John Adams took seventy-one votes to Jefferson's sixty-eight, Pinckney's fifty-nine, and Burr's thirty. The remaining votes went to a smattering of other candidates. The votes lined up on sectional lines more so than party lines. Most voters in the North preferred Adams, and most voters in the South preferred Jefferson. The results also meant a Federalist would serve as president, and a Republican would serve as vice president. Some observers thought that because Adams and Jefferson worked together so well before, they would mend their political differences and help end the factionalism that characterized the Washington years. Initially, both men seemed willing to bridge the gap between the parties. Adams thought Jefferson could play a greater role in his administration than he had played during Washington's administration. But hopes faded quickly, and the factionalism grew worse in the Adams years.

10.3.5 Before You Move On...

Key Concepts

In the wake of the battle over ratification of the Constitution, most Americans accepted the new government it created. However, many still harbored suspicions about the possibility of the government abusing the considerable power placed in its hands. Therefore, a new debate arose over the Constitution's implementation, which led to the creation of the first party system. Federalists saw the federal government as a positive agent for change. If the nation's social and economic elite headed a strong central government, they believed all society would prosper. Republicans favored a less powerful central government and sought to place restrictions on its operation. They trusted the people to maintain a virtuous political system.

Inevitably, these two visions of the republic led to clashes between the leaders of both factions over the meaning of the French Revolution and the threat posed by the Whiskey Rebellion. As the Federalists looked at the farmers' revolt in western Pennsylvania, they saw the excesses of the French Revolution coming to the United States. Thus, the federal government needed to step in to eliminate such threats to order. However, the Republicans saw in Washington's decision to intervene in Pennsylvania the first signs of the federal government trampling on the people's liberty.

In 1796, the two parties vied to win the presidency in the nation's first partisan election. The two leading candidates—John Adams and Thomas Jefferson—both had the needed revolutionary credentials to run for president. Based on the provisions of the Electoral College, Federalist John Adams became president, and Republican Thomas Jefferson became vice president. Many people hoped the outcome would lessen political divisions, but during the Adams years tensions mounted as the two parties debated how to handle problems caused by the war between Great Britain and France.

Test Yourself

1. In foreign affairs, Americans became deeply divided in the 1790s over

   a. relations with Spain.

   b. the rise of Napoleon.

   c. the French Revolution.

   d. the banning of the international slave trade.

2. The Whiskey Rebellion in 1794 resulted in

   a. the repeal of the federal liquor tax.

   b. declining support for the Republicans.

   c. mass executions of the captured rebels.

   d. the sending of a massive army to western Pennsylvania.

3. In the election of 1796, the Federalist John Adams became president, and his vice president was

   a. the Republican Thomas Jefferson.

   b. the Federalist Charles C. Pinckney.

   c. the Federalist Alexander Hamilton.

   d. the Republican Aaron Burr.

See page 398 for answers

10.4 THE ADAMS YEARS: FEDERALISTS UNDER FIRE

John Adams ascended to the presidency in 1797 with a great deal of public service experience. As a lawyer in Massachusetts, he became involved in the American Revolution. He pushed for independence at a time when other delegates to the Continental Congress wavered. In the 1780s, he was a diplomat in Holland, France, and Britain. Finally, he served as the vice president for eight years. While well-respected by his peers, he lacked Washington's prestige. Adams's obsession with adopting the appropriate ceremonial features for the new government earned him the nick name "his Rotundity" in the

Washington years. Moreover, Adams had long supported the creation of a powerful chief executive. He felt conflict between the ordinary and the elite was inevitable, and only a strong president could effectively mediate disputes and preserve the rights of the people. His Republican critics associated his ideas with a desire to reinstate a monarchy in the United States, and members of his own party did not always trust his intentions. Thus, as he took the oath of office and gave his inaugural address, Adams sought to convey his republican simplicity, his desire for political unity, and his determination to avoid war with France or Britain.[66] Unfortunately, he realized none of his goals while in office. The growing crisis with France dominated his administration and, in turn, made partisan politics worse in the United States.

10.4.1 Adams, Jefferson, and Political Partisanship

With no precedent to follow, Adams opted to retain his predecessor's cabinet officers. Therefore, he had Timothy Pickering at the state department, Oliver Wolcott at the treasury department, and James McHenry at the war department. The new president thought the decision would lend greater prestige to his administration and help develop a civil service. Unfortunately, the holdovers proved problematic for two reasons. When Jefferson and Hamilton left government service, Washington found it difficult to find qualified appointees willing to serve given the bitter political climate. Therefore, his appointments possessed less political and administrative skill than needed for their positions. Moreover, all three owed their political careers to Alexander Hamilton. On political issues, they followed his lead publically even when it countered official administration policy. To some extent, Adams also experienced problems during his presidency because he prided himself on his independent action. Although he sought the advice of his secretaries, he often failed to inform them in advance of a pending decision, further driving them into Hamilton's camp.[67]

Beyond the challenges posed by retaining Washington's advisers, Adams had to deal with the fact that Thomas Jefferson, a member of the opposition party, became his vice president. After the election, Jefferson wrote to Adams, both to congratulate him and to suggest his willingness to serve the new president. The letter certainly convinced Abigail, Adams's wife, that the two men could work successfully together to lead the nation and develop bipartisan support for their policies. She encouraged her husband's belief that together they might just be able to fill Washington's shoes. To accomplish this, the president-elect looked to give Jefferson a greater role in his administration—possibly having him attend cabinet meetings and having him use his diplomatic skills. According to Joseph Ellis, Adams, unlike many of his contemporaries, seemed willing to negotiate political differences. For Adams, "intimacy trumped ideology."[68]

Jefferson learned about Adams's bipartisan plans through newspapers and conversations with his own supporters. The president-elect could not in the political climate of the day directly approach the vice president-elect to discuss the situation. Adams wrote letters and told his confidants his plans, knowing those plans would become public knowledge. Initially, as he learned of Adams's suggestions, Jefferson reacted somewhat favorably. However, his response changed when he heard the most controversial aspect of the plan:

Adams planned to send a special minister to France to help avert war and hoped that either Jefferson or James Madison would head the delegation. Jefferson seemed more inclined to accept the offer than Madison, but Madison convinced him that accepting would be politically unwise.[69]

In the end, Jefferson chose leadership of the Republican Party over his friendship with Adams. The two men had dinner in early March with Washington at the presidential mansion in Philadelphia. Jefferson implied during conversations that neither he nor Madison wanted to play a role in developing the nation's policy toward France. Politically, Jefferson made a wise decision because the public never associated him with Adams's controversial foreign or domestic policies. Thus, Jefferson remained a viable alternative to Adams in the presidential election of 1800. Meanwhile, Adams faced an uphill battle in his administration from the start, because he had no one among his advisers whom he could really trust for advice. Adams often turned to Abigail, who was quite politically astute. However, her skills could not make up for the fact Adams came into the presidency with few people rooting for his success.[70]

10.4.2 The Quasi-War with France

Although Adams did not have Jefferson's support, the new president decided he must attempt to resolve the growing problem with France. When France declared war on Britain, the United States tried to maintain a neutral stance. From the French perspective, the Americans abandoned their neutrality with Jay's Treaty in 1795. However, the French took little action until after the presidential election in 1796. They had hoped Jefferson would prevail and reverse the pro-British stance of the Federalists. When Adams won, they turned from political subterfuge to direct confrontation. Just as the British had done before, the French began to seize American ships engaging in neutral trade.

Hoping to repair the relationship with France, Adams sent Charles Pinckney, John Marshall, and Elbridge Gerry to Paris. The envoy, per the president's instructions, sought to reiterate American friendship and request compensation for the attacks on American commercial vessels. Unfortunately, nothing went according to plan. French Foreign Minister Charles Maurice de Talleyrand-Périgord saw no reason to negotiate with the American delegates, as the United States posed no real threat to France. At the same time, the French government needed money to support its war against Britain. So, Talleyrand's agents—later labeled as X, Y, and Z—outlined the steps required for negotiations to begin: Adams needed to apologize for anti-French statements he made, the United States needed to pay its outstanding debts to France, and the United States needed to arrange for a loan, akin to a bribe, of 50,000 pounds for Talleyrand's private use. Since the Americans refused to pay the French, negotiations broke down.[71]

When Adams learned of the attempted bribe, later labeled as the XYZ Affair, in March 1798, he informed Congress that the diplomatic mission had failed. Moreover, he proposed arming American merchant ships. At that point, however, he refrained from telling Congress about the attempted bribe. The president felt he needed some time to devise a response. Without a doubt, Talleyrand's demands upset him. However, France's decisions to attack any American ship carrying British goods and close their ports to any American ship that docked in a British port concerned him more. The move would put Americans at risk as well as undermine American trade. Adams then sought the advice of his cabinet. Secretary of State Timothy Pickering and Attorney General Charles Lee favored a declaration of war. Pickering also suggested expanding the Anglo-American alliance. Secretary of Treasury Oliver Wolcott and Secretary of War James McHenry (taking his cues from Alexander Hamilton) felt the Americans should pursue a moderate course by engaging in limited hostilities and seeking a negotiated settlement. The president mulled over their ideas but eventually decided against an all-out war.[72]

After Adams announced the mission had failed, his Republican critics pounced. They said he had acted too rashly because he favored Britain. Thomas Jefferson, who had not seen the communications from the ministers in France, encouraged fellow Republicans in Congress to delay any war-like measures. Most of the opposition, including the vice president, believed the decision not to release the contents of the ministers' dispatches was some kind of cover up. During the debates on whether to arm merchant ships, Republicans led the House of Representatives in passing a resolution to force Adams to share all the information he received from his ministers. The president complied in a restrained speech in April, much to the chagrin to the Republicans. The American people immediately expressed outrage over the XYZ Affair. War fever gripped the nation. Meanwhile, the Federalist Party, especially John Adams, became immediately popular with the public.[73]

Public outrage spurred Congressional support for Adams's policy of a limited, undeclared war with France—the so-called Quasi-War. In the following months, Congress approved by narrow margins measures for an embargo on all trade, increasing the size of the army and the navy, creating a Navy department, allowing naval vessels in the Atlantic to attack

Figure 10.2 The XYZ Affair | This British political cartoon from 1798 depicts the French attempt to force the Americans to pay for the right to negotiate a treaty to ease tensions between the two nations.

Author: S.W. Fores
Source: Library of Congress

French ships in the act of seizing American vessels, and formally ending all previous treaties with France. Congress also approved a new tax measure, the Direct Tax, to pay for the military buildup. The government levied taxes on official documents (similar to the Stamp Act of 1765) and private residences. Few people questioned the need to support a more effective navy, since the undeclared war with France was a naval conflict. American ships like the USS *Constitution* and the USS *Constellation*, equipped with the latest naval technology, had some success in destroying French ships in the Caribbean.[74]

The decision to provide additional funds for a standing army was more divisive. Republicans loathed the idea of a standing army, fearing the government would use it to suppress opposition. Some Federalists, led by John Adams, preferred to put money into the navy. Adams saw the navy both as important in the conflict with France and for the future of American trade. High Federalists, led by Alexander Hamilton, preferred to put money into the army because it would help them curb any possible domestic rebellion. In spite of Adams's opposition, the more conservative High Federalists in Congress won support for enlarging the army. Largely because of the actions of the cabinet, Hamilton became the inspector general—making him the de facto commander of the U.S. Army. Many Republicans feared that Hamilton planned to use the newly raised 20,000 man army against them, especially since he only appointed loyal Federalists to the officer corps.[75]

American naval victories in 1799, as well as Adams's fear of the High Federalists' plans, led him to send another diplomatic envoy to France. However, the cabinet encouraged fellow High Federalists in Congress to delay peace with France by preventing the diplomatic mission. In frustration, Adams retreated to his home in Massachusetts to await developments at home and abroad.[76] Before the end of the year, Napoleon Bonaparte came to power in France. His government indicated it would welcome the American ministers. With some Federalists still obstructing peace, Adams threatened to resign the presidency. Most accepted the decision to seek peace because they did not want Jefferson to become president. Adams then sent a new three-person delegation to Paris to negotiate a peace settlement.

In the Treaty of Mortefontaine, also known as the Convention of 1800, the Americans and the French pledged permanent friendship. They also cancelled their prior treaties relating to trade and mutual alliances. Furthermore, they agreed to uphold the principles of free trade. The Americans did not seek damages for the loss of ships or goods during the conflict. Adams sent the treaty and all the diplomatic communications relating to the treaty to the Senate in December. Republicans favored ratification, but High Federalists opposed an agreement with the French. The first time the Senate voted, the treaty did not pass. However, Adams tried again with a slightly modified

Figure 10.3 *Constellation* vs. French Frigate | This painting by Rear Admiral John William Schmidt (1906-1981) depicts the fighting between the USS Constellation (left) and French frigate L'Insurgente (right) on February 9, 1799 during the undeclared war with France.

Artist: John William Schmidt
Source: Naval History and Heritage Command

treaty in February. This time, the Senate approved the treaty by a narrow margin, officially ending the hostilities with France.[77]

10.4.3 Domestic Turmoil

The XYZ Affair and the Quasi-War led to the increase of partisan politics in the United States. Pro-French sentiments remained high among some Republicans, and many doubted the French threat. Albert Gallatin, a leading Republican Congressman, went so far as to suggest Adams created the crisis to increase his power. Therefore, Republicans did not want to engage in a war against France, even a limited one. Throughout the debates on the war measures, Congressional Republicans attempted to block their passage. While unsuccessful, many still spoke publicly about their opposition. Federalists, meanwhile, did not just fear the French threat on the seas. They wondered what side the Republicans would support if France launched an attack on the United States. Federalists like Harrison Gray Otis believed France's victories in Europe came because they effectively deployed French spies to other countries. Federalists saw their political opponents as the first wave of French collaborators in the United States. Their fear led to the passage of the controversial Alien and Sedition Acts—four laws that targeted immigrants and the Republican press. Although the president signed each measure into law, he was never the driving force behind their creation or their enforcement. Abigail Adams and the High Federalists drove him to accept the measures.[78]

The Alien Act

The three laws targeting immigrants focused on those people who had yet to become naturalized citizens. Large numbers of people arrived in the United States during the 1790s. Federalists feared French immigrants would side with their home country, and Irish immigrants would side with France because they hated Great Britain. Once naturalized, moreover, the French and the Irish tended to vote Republican.[79] The Naturalization Act of 1798 extended the residency requirement for citizenship from five years to fourteen years. It also required all aliens to register upon arrival in the United States and prevented citizenship for aliens from countries at war with the United States. The Alien Enemies Act of 1798 allowed the president to deport or imprison an alien from an enemy country in times of war. The Alien Friends Act of 1798 allowed for the deportation of any alien in peacetime without a hearing if the president deemed that person a threat to the safety of the nation. The Adams administration never deported any aliens under these statutes for two reasons: many French voluntary left the country even before the measures passed, and the president adopted a strict interpretation of the statutes. Still, the immigration acts proved politically disadvantageous to the Federalists.[80]

Federalists designed the immigration acts to target people who might pose a threat to the country and who sided against them in elections. However, the laws also affected German immigrants living in southeastern Pennsylvania who tended to vote for the Federalists. Highly insular, the German population cared most about securing their land, selling their grain, and obtaining fair tax rates. For much of 1790s, Federalists took the German voters for granted. However, the naturalization law, coupled with tax increases to pay for the Quasi-War, harmed the Germans' pride and their finances. By the end of the decade, they grew tired of such treatment. Perhaps unintentionally, the federal government exacerbated tensions in the German community when they appointed mostly Moravians as tax assessors. Since the American Revolution, Germans in the United States had divided into two camps: "church" Germans (mostly Lutherans) and "sectarian" Germans (Moravians, Mennonites, and Quakers). The "church" Germans represented the majority of the German population. Republican leaders in Pennsylvania took advantage of the situation created by the federal government's hiring of the tax assessors; at the state level in 1798, their party scored several decisive victories in the southeastern counties.[81]

In early 1799, the Germans began to take up arms against the government. Although the Adams administration had attempted to assess the new taxes fairly, most Germans felt aggrieved by the increase. They held town meetings to discuss the tax laws, and they petitioned Congress to repeal them. But when armed bands of men began to intimidate the tax collectors, it prompted the local U.S. Marshals to arrest eighteen men for obstructing the law. On March 7, the marshals prepared to move the prisoners to Philadelphia for trial. The Bucks County militia, led by John Fries, surrounded the Sun Tavern in Bethlehem where the marshals held the prisoners. Fries demanded the prisoners be tried in Bucks County per the Sixth Amendment; he also demanded the marshals release the prisoners. Rather than challenge the over 140 armed men gathered outside the tavern, the chief marshal complied with Fries's request. The militia dispersed peacefully, but the chief marshal reported how an unruly mob seized the prisoners.[82]

In the wake of the events at the Sun Tavern, tensions cooled in southeastern Pennsylvania. The German population, including John Fries, publicly began to state they would comply with the tax laws. To the Federalist leaders in Philadelphia, however, Fries's Rebellion spoke directly to the threat posed by immigrants. As Adams prepared to leave for Massachusetts in March, his cabinet convinced him to issue a proclamation promising to suppress the treasonous actions with force. Adams agreed to the proclamation and left his secretaries to implement it. Federal troops set out for Bucks County and the surrounding area in April. The forces scoured the countryside for men, including Fries, who participated in the rebellion. Upon their arrest, the government transported the sixty prisoners to Philadelphia for trial on treason and other offenses. When the trials began, the Federalist judges showed no mercy on the defendants. Juries convicted Fries and two others of treason, and the judges sentenced them to death. Juries also convicted most of the remaining defendants of lesser crimes.[83]

As the date of the executions approached, Adams queried his cabinet on whether or not the events in Bucks County actually constituted treason. His advisers all argued the convicted men had engaged in an insurrection and so had committed a treasonous act. Adams, however, disagreed. He saw the action as a rebellion, not an insurrection. He decided to pardon not only Fries but all of the other defendants. As historian John Diggins suggests, "The president's pardon was an act of courage." Adams knew it would be unpopular with members of his own party. Politically, the response to Fries's Rebellion also hurt the Federalists because they lost the support of much of the German population.[84] The heavy-handed response, coupled with the immigration laws, became a political liability for Federalists, especially the president.

The Sedition Act

In the 1790s, the number of newspapers in the United States increased significantly, especially those that supported the Republican Party. For Republicans, newspapers provided a means to criticize the Federalists' undemocratic tendencies. For Federalists, they became a means for their opponents to promote the cause of the enemy.[85] Fearing the influence of the Republican press, Federalists in Congress supported the Sedition Act of 1798, which they set to expire on March 3, 1801. The act made it a crime "to impede the operation of any law of the United States" or to intimidate an official agent of the government from carrying out their duty. Violators of this article faced a prison term of up to five years and a fine of $5,000. The act also made it a crime to write, speak, or publish "any false, scandalous and malicious writing or writings against the government of the United States, or either house of the Congress of the United States, or the President." Violators of this article faced a prison term of up to two years and a fine of $2,000.[86]

Federalists, led by Thomas Pickering, actively pursued newspaper publishers who criticized Adams or the Fifth Congress. All told, the government arrested twenty-five people, brought charges of sedition against seventeen, and convicted ten including Matthew Lyon, a member of the House of Representatives. Lyon emigrated from Ireland in 1764 and became a successful businessman in Vermont. After years of trying, Lyon was elected to serve in the House in 1797. The following year, he became somewhat notorious after he spat on Roger Griswold of Connecticut when Griswold insulted his honor. A few days later Griswold and Lyon engaged in a tavern-like brawl on the House floor. Lyon also founded his own newspaper once he entered Congress because he could not find a publisher for his more radical ideas. Federalists, already wary of him after the confrontation with Griswold, decided to use the Sedition Act against Lyon. The government arrested him, brought him to trial, and convicted him in October 1798. He faced four months in prison and a $1,000 fine. The conviction did not end Lyon's political career, much to the Federalists' dismay. While in prison he continued to promote the Republican cause, successfully ran for reelection, and became a martyr for the cause of freedom.[87]

Most Republicans found the Sedition Act extremely offensive. The act limited free speech, which some Republicans thought violated the First Amendment. Furthermore, it did not protect the vice president from abuse. Lyon's conviction, as well as the convictions of other editors, convinced Republicans they needed to stand up against the Federalists' excesses. Thomas Jefferson and James Madison worked secretly through the Virginia and Kentucky legislatures to oppose the Alien and Sedition Acts. Jefferson wrote a series of resolutions, which he passed along to John Breckinridge to introduce in Kentucky. The vice president argued the states had the final authority to determine if acts of the federal government exceeded the limits of the Constitution. When states deemed a federal statute as excessive, they could declare it to have "no force" in their state. In other words, they could nullify federal laws. Madison drafted slightly milder resolutions of protest, which he gave to John Taylor to introduce in Virginia.[88]

Kentucky passed the resolutions in November, and Virginia followed suit in December. Each legislature also encouraged the other states to join them in questioning the constitutionality of the Alien and Sedition Acts. None of the other state legislatures supported the measures, and several northern legislatures rejected them outright and suggested the judicial branch, not the states, should determine the constitutionality of federal laws. The Virginia and Kentucky Resolutions of 1798 did not at the time alter the prevailing notions about the relationship between the federal government and the states. They did provide a piece of political propaganda for Republicans to use as the nation drew closer to the next presidential election. In the future, states' rights activists would point back to the resolves when the debated the merits of nullification and secession.[89]

10.4.4 The Election of 1800

John Adams recognized his chances for reelection in 1800 were not good. By pursuing a moderate course, he had managed to alienate both Federalists and Republicans. His own party disliked his decision to settle with France and to pardon those involved in Fries's Rebellion. The opposition party disliked the emergence of a standing army and the passage of the Alien and Sedition Acts. Alexander Hamilton led the opposition to the president among the Federalists, even after the party endorsed Adams and Charles Pinckney. Hamilton suggested in a report leaked to the press that Adams did not have a talent for administration. Furthermore, he said "there are great defects to his character, which unfit him for the office of chief magistrate."[90]

The Republicans delighted at how the Federalists turned on one another because it made their favored candidate, Thomas Jefferson, appear as the only sensible choice. Of course, the Republicans did not remain free of controversy. They paired Jefferson with Aaron Burr—a talented New York politician who possessed a reputation for self-promotion—in hopes of picking up votes in Burr's home state. Republicans thought they had a good chance to win the presidency given the Federalists' antics. However, no one expected the counting of the Electoral College to play out quite like it did. Adams and Pinckney, as expected, did well in New England. Jefferson and Burr, not surprisingly, did well in the South. But in the end, the election turned on the votes of New York and Pennsylvania, which both went to the Republicans. Jefferson and Burr each took seventy-three votes, Adams took sixty-five, and Pinckney took sixty-four. The Federalists lost the election, but because the Republican candidates took the same number of votes, the House of Representatives would determine the victor.[91]

To win, Jefferson or Burr needed the support of nine of the sixteen states within the House of Representatives. The Federalists controlled six delegations, while the Republicans controlled eight. Vermont and Maryland's delegations split between the two parties. In essence, Federalists in Congress would have the final say on whether Jefferson or Burr would become president. Some Federalists so disliked and distrusted Jefferson that they considered throwing the election to Burr. He seemed the safer choice because for much of his political career he had promoted himself, not a political philosophy. Burr seemed less likely to dismantle the Federalists' economic program. Once again, Alexander Hamilton stepped in to sway his fellow party members. Hamilton never trusted Burr; therefore, he encouraged the Federalists in the House to vote for Jefferson. Burr, meanwhile, knew the Republicans had intended for Jefferson to become president, but he would not step aside or defer to Jefferson.[92]

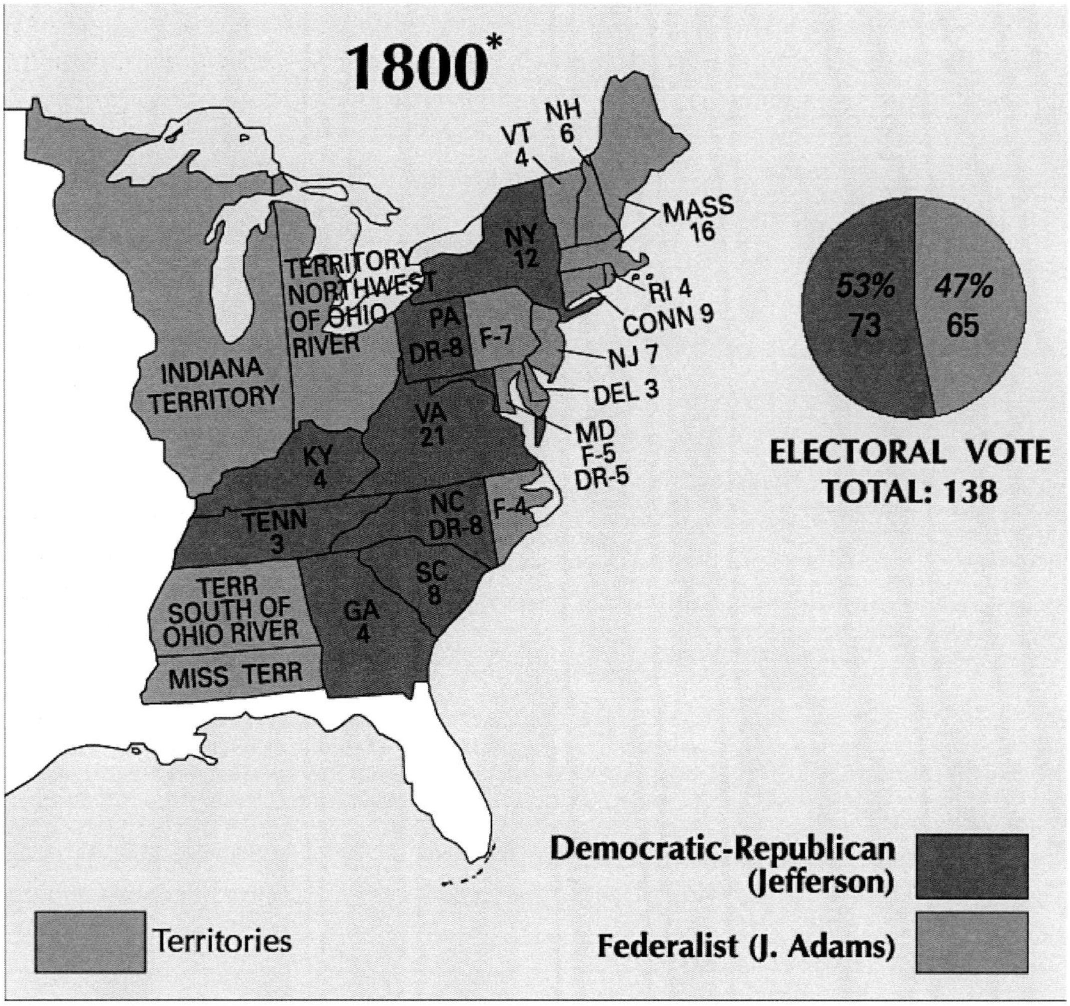

Figure 10.4 Presidential Election Map, 1800 | Thomas Jefferson challenged incumbent John Adams for the presidency in 1800. Jefferson defeated Adams, but he tied with fellow Republican Aaron Burr in the Electoral College voting. The House of Representatives decided in favor of Jefferson after his longtime opponent Alexander Hamilton swayed some Federalist votes against Burr. Many people have referred to the election as the "Revolution of 1800" because of the peaceful transfer of power from one political party to another.

Author: National Atlas of the United States
Source: Wikimedia Commons

The House voted thirty-five times in early February but neither candidate received a majority. Fears that Republicans might call for a new constitutional convention, coupled with increasing threats of mob violence, pushed Federalists to turn toward Jefferson. On February 17, 1801, Jefferson received a majority of votes when several delegates abstained from voting. Republican newspapers celebrated Jefferson's victory as well as the party's victories in numerous congressional elections. Many suggested the election had revolutionary undertones because it marked the first time in modern history when a popular election led to a peaceful transfer of power. Jefferson echoed those sentiments in an 1819 letter, suggesting his victory "was as real a revolution in the principles of our government as that of 76" because it was achieved by a "rational and peaceable instrument of reform." Moreover, it marked the dismissing of one political philosophy in favor of another.[93]

John Adams was hardly surprised by the election's outcome. During his final months in office, he did work to promote one more initiative. In 1799, he had encouraged Federalists in the Senate to expand the federal judiciary; however, few paid attention to his request. When Adams lost the election, Federalists in the outgoing or lame-duck Congress began to feel differently about the future of the judicial branch. If they created more positions, the president could fill those positions with loyal Federalists before he left office. Those judges could thus help preserve the Federalist agenda when Jefferson took over. In February, only days before the House chose Jefferson, Congress passed the Judiciary Act of 1801. It created twenty-three new district and circuit court positions eliminating the need for Supreme Court justices to hear district court cases. The president signed the measure and began to make appointments for the Senate to approve before their session ended. By the time he left office, Adams had made recommendations to fill all of the new positions. However, the most notable of the so-called midnight appointments went to John Marshall, who became the Chief Justice of the Supreme Court.[94]

On March 4, 1801, John Adams left Washington, D.C., where the federal government had moved the previous year, without attending his successor's inauguration. Adams felt let down by his own party, abused by the opposition party, and most definitely not appreciated for the contributions he had made to the nation throughout his public career. His departure, for all practical purposes, spelled the end of the Federalists as a national party. While they retained a presence in the Northeast until 1815, they attracted few new voters to their cause. For much of their history, the Federalists had run against the tide of democracy, and their actions in the Adams years further underscored that fact. However, their program of economic development lived on as future nationally-minded leaders proposed protective tariffs, a national bank, and support for internal improvements, among others.

10.4.5 Before You Move On...

Key Concepts

During his presidency, John Adams struggled to manage the growing crisis with France and handle the domestic divisions stemming from his foreign policy. Adams initially sought to negotiate a treaty with France to protect American shipping from attacks. Unfortunately, the attempt led only to the XYZ Affair in which the French attempted to bribe the American negotiators in Paris. After Adams disclosed the duplicity, the majority of the American people appeared to want to defend American honor, leading to the Quasi-War.

Republicans vocally opposed the conflict with France and even suggested Adams created the conflict to increase his power. Angered by the accusations against the president, Federalists responded with the controversial Alien and Sedition Acts in 1798, which curbed the rights of immigrants and the freedom of speech. Frustrated Republicans felt they needed to respond to the Federalist threat. As a result, Thomas Jefferson and James Madison secretly made an impassioned plea for states' rights with the Virginia and Kentucky Resolutions of 1798, arguing that states should determine the constitutionality of federal laws. While the resolutions did little to change the relationship between the federal government and the state governments, they did serve as an important piece of propaganda for the Republicans as the election of 1800 approached. Thomas Jefferson defeated John Adams, bringing the Federalist Era to an end.

Test Yourself

1. The Federalists designed the Sedition Act of 1798 primarily to
   a. safeguard civil liberties.
   b. smother political opposition.
   c. ensure public safety.
   d. encourage the flow of European immigrants.

2. The Virginia and Kentucky Resolutions asserted that
   a. the Republicans had betrayed the spirit of the Constitution.
   b. the federal government had the right to void state laws.
   c. the Supreme Court had no constitutional authority to invalidate federal laws.
   d. states had the right to nullify federal laws.

3. The election of 1800 did all of the following except
   a. mark the first time an opposition party came to power.
   b. cause Federalist rioting in the streets of the capital.
   c. show the emergence of a more democratic politics.
   d. elevate Jefferson to the presidency.

4. Federalists passed the Judiciary Act of 1801 in order to
   a. deny Republicans full control of the government.
   b. replace the principles of English common law.
   c. establish the doctrine of judicial review.
   d. reduce the number of federal courts and judges.

See page 398 for answers

10.5 Conclusion

During the Federalist Era, the American people and their leaders sought to define the character of their nation. The country transitioned from a loose confederation of states to a stronger coalition under the new national government. Nevertheless, many facets of the relationship between the people, the states, and the federal government still needed to be determined. Two political parties—the Federalists and the Republicans—emerged to debate the implementation of the Constitution. Federalists supported a strong central government, whereas Republicans favored a more limited central government. The 1790s became quite contentious because political leaders found it difficult to accept differences of opinion. Regardless of their party, they believed the nation was engaged in a life-and-death struggle for its future.

George Washington tried to implement Alexander Hamilton's ideas for strengthening the nation at home and abroad in order to build respect for the new country. Questions about supporting economic development and developing a pro-French or pro-British foreign policy emerged during his tenure. Washington's response to the Whiskey Rebellion suggested he most definitely leaned towards the Federalist outlook; it also increased opposition to his policies. By 1796, political divisions created a tense atmosphere as the nation sought to select a new president. In the nation's first partisan election, Federalist John Adams defeated Republican Thomas Jefferson, but Jefferson became the vice president because Electoral College voters did not vote by party simply for two candidates.

Political divisions continued to afflict the nation when John Adams took over. The United States became involved in the Quasi-War after the XYZ Affair exposed the nefarious nature of the French government. Republicans disliked the war, but they opposed the Alien and Sedition Acts (an effort by the Federalists to curb the Republicans' power) even more. In 1800, Thomas Jefferson won the presidency for the Republican Party. Many Americans believed the nation experienced a second revolution of sorts because power had transferred peacefully from one political party to another.

As the United States entered a new century, the true revolutionary character of Jefferson's election remained unclear. Washington and Adams had done much in their presidencies to shape the character of the presidency and of the nation. When Jefferson took office, people wondered how much their relationship to the central government really would change. Would Jefferson truly abandon a strong national government and defer to the states, or would his changes be more cosmetic than substantial? Republicans anticipated future changes, while Federalists dreaded them.

10.6 CRITICAL THINKING EXERCISES

- Throughout American history, international developments have affected domestic public policy. How did they alter the nation's course in the Federalist Era? How might the experiences of George Washington and John Adams compare to the presidents of the twenty-first century?
- Political parties in the United States have constantly evolved. How do Federalists and Republicans in the first party system compare to the Democrats and Republicans today? What similarities and differences do you see between these parties in terms of political philosophy and important public policy issues?
- The popular press played an active role in the political debates of the 1790s. What did the newspapers provide to national leaders, and why did they become so important? How do the papers of 1790s compare to modern social media? Do they play the same role?

10.7 KEY TERMS

- Alien and Sedition Acts of 1798
- Bill of Rights
- Aaron Burr
- Citizen Genet
- Compromise of 1790
- Democratic-Republican Clubs
- Farewell Address
- Federalists (Federalist Party)
- French Revolution
- Fries's Rebellion
- *Gazette of the United States*
- Alexander Hamilton
- Indian Intercourse Acts
- Jay's Treaty
- Thomas Jefferson
- Judiciary Act of 1801
- Little Turtle
- James Madison
- John Marshall
- Midnight Appointments
- *National Gazette*
- Northwest Indian War
- Thomas Pickering
- Charles Pinckney
- Pinckney's Treaty
- Quasi-War with France
- Report on Public Credit
- Report on the Bank
- Report on Manufactures
- Republicans (Republican Party)
- Revolution of 1800
- Treaty of Greenville
- Treaty of Mortefontaine
- Virginia and Kentucky Resolutions of 1798
- George Washington
- Anthony Wayne
- Whiskey Rebellion
- XYZ Affair

10.8 CHRONOLOGY

The following chronology is a list of important dates and events associated with this chapter.

Date	Event
1788	Electoral College chose George Washington as the first president
1789	French Revolution began; James Madison drafted the Bill of Rights; Congress approved ten amendments to the Constitution; Congress passed the Judiciary Act of 1789; John Fenno began publishing the Gazette of the United States to support the Washington administration's policies

Date	Event
1790	Alexander Hamilton sent the Public Report on Credit and the Report on the Bank to Congress; Hamilton and Madison agreed to the Compromise of 1790; Congress approved the Assumption Bill and the Residence Bill; Congressed passed an excise tax on distilled spirits (the whiskey tax)
1791	Congress chartered the First National Bank of the United States; Philip Freneau began publishing the National Gazette to oppose the Washington administration's policies; Hamilton sent the Report on Manufacturers to Congress
1792	Washington issued a proclamation supporting the enforcement of the whiskey tax
1793	Reign of Terror began in France; France declared war on Great Britain; Washington issued the Neutrality Proclamation; First Democratic-Republican clubs began to meet; Citizen Edmond Charles Genet arrived in the United States as the new ambassador from France
1794	French government recalled Genet because of American complaints; Battle of Fallen Timbers occurred in the Ohio Valley; Whiskey Rebellion occurred in western Pennsylvania; Washington led the militia forces to put down the attack on the government
1795	The United States concluded the Treaty of Greenville with various tribes in the Northwest; The United States concluded Jay's Treaty (Treaty of Amity, Commerce and Navigation) with Great Britain
1796	The United States concluded Pinckney's Treaty (Treaty of San Lorenzo) with Spain; Washington decided not to seek a third term and issued his Farewell Address; John Adams defeated Thomas Jefferson in the presidential election
1798	XYZ Affair prompted an undeclared war with France (the Quasi-War); Congress passed the Alien and Sedition Acts; Virginia and Kentucky Resolutions passed by the respective state legislatures to oppose the Alien and Sedition Acts
1799	Fries's Rebellion (a tax revolt) occurred in western Pennsylvania
1800	The United States concluded the Treaty of Mortefontaine (Convention of 1800) with France to end the Quasi-War; Thomas Jefferson defeated John Adams in the presidential election

10.9 BIBLIOGRAPHY

Appleby, Joyce. *Capitalism and the New Social Order: The Republican Vision of the 1790s*. New York: New York University Press, 1984.

Brown, Ralph Adams. *The Presidency of John Adams*. Lawrence: University of Kansas Press, 1975.

Burns, James McGregor and Susan Dunn. *George Washington*. New York: Times Books, 2004.

Diggins, John Patrick. *John Adams*. New York: Times Books, 2003.

Elkins, Stanley and Eric McKitrick. *The Age of Federalism*. New York: Oxford University Press, 1993.

Ellis, Joseph J. *Founding Brothers: The Revolutionary Generation*. New York: Vintage Books, 2002.

McDonald, Forrest. *The Presidency of George Washington*. Lawrence: University Press of Kansas, 1974.

Miller, John C. *The Federalist Era*. New York: Harper & Row, 1960.

Outline of U.S. History. Washington: U.S. Department of State, 2005, 2010.

Staloff, Darren. *Hamilton, Adams, Jefferson: The Politics of Enlightenment and the American Founding*. New York: Hill and Wang, 2005.

Sturgis, Amy H., ed. *Presidents from Washington through Monroe, 1789-1825: Debating the Issues in Pro and Con Primary Documents*. Westport, CT: Greenwood Press, 2002.

Wood, Gordon S. *Empire of Liberty: A History of the Early Republic, 1789-1815*. New York: Oxford University Press, 2009.

Wood, Gordon S. *The Radicalism of the American Revolution*. New York: Vintage Books, 1993.

10.10 END NOTES

1 James McGregor Burns and Susan Dunn, *George Washington* (New York: Times Books, 2004), 48.

2 Burns and Dunn, *George Washington*, 48; Gordon S. Wood, *Empire of Liberty: A History of the Early Republic, 1789-1815* (New York: Oxford University Press, 2009), 51-58.

3 John Adams to Jabez Brown, 26 June 1789 in *Presidents from Washington through Monroe, 1789-1825: Debating the Issues in Pro and Con Primary Documents*, ed. Amy H. Sturgis (Westport, CT: Greenwood Press, 2002), 22.

4 Wood, *Empire of Liberty*, 83-85.

5 Wood, *Empire of Liberty*, 53-54, 84-85; Burns and Dunn, *George Washington*, 56-57.

6 Stanley Elkins and Eric McKitrick, *The Age of Federalism* (New York: Oxford University Press, 1993), 59-60.

7 Elkins and McKitrick, *The Age of Federalism*, 61-62; Wood, *Empire of Liberty*, 67-69.

8 Burns and Dunn, *George Washington*, 44, 52, 58.

9 Woods, *Empire of Liberty*, 78.

10 Burns and Dunn, *George Washington*, 53-55.

11 George Washington to John Armstrong, 25 April 1788, *The Papers of George Washington*, University of Virginia, April 19, 2012, http://gwpapers.virginia.edu/documents/constitution/1788/armstrong.html.

12 George Washington to James McHenry, 13 July 1796, *The Writings of George Washington*, Volume XI, ed. Jared Sparks (New York: Harper & Brothers Publishers, 1848), 147-148.

13 Wood, *Empire of Liberty*, 86-89.

14 Wood, *Empire of Liberty*, 95-97; Elkins and McKitrick, *The Age of Federalism*, 116-117.

15 Elkins and McKitrick, *The Age of Federalism*, 116; Wood, *Empire of Liberty*, 103-104; Burns and Dunn, *George Washington*, 79.

16 Wood, *Empire of Liberty*, 141; Joseph J. Ellis, *Founding Brothers: The Revolutionary Generation* (New York: Vintage Books, 2002), 56-57.

17 Wood, *Empire of Liberty*, 141, 148-149; Ellis, *Founding Brothers*, 58.

18 Wood, *Empire of Liberty*, 142; Ellis, *Founding Brothers*, 48-49.

19 Ellis, *Founding Brothers*, 50-52, 78-80.

20 Wood, *Empire of Liberty*, 149.
21 Darren Staloff, *Hamilton, Adams, Jefferson: The Politics of Enlightenment and the American Founding* (New York: Hill and Wang, 2005), 79-80.

22 Wood, *Empire of Liberty*, 98-99, 144-145; Staloff, *Hamilton, Adams, Jefferson*, 97-98.

23 Elkins and McKitrick, *The Age of Federalism*, 229-230; James Madison, "Speech on the Bank Bill." 2 February 1791 in *Liberty and Order: The First American Party Struggle* ed. Lance Banning (Indianapolis: Liberty Fund, 2004), The Online Library of Liberty, April 19, 2012, http://oll.libertyfund.org/title/875/63865.

24 Fisher Ames, *Annals of Congress*, I Cong., 3 Sess. quoted in Elkins and McKitrick, *The Age of Federalism*, 230-231.

25 Wood, *Empire of Liberty*, 144-145; Burns and Dunn, *George Washington*, 81-82.

26 Wood, *Empire of Liberty*, 101-102.

27 Burns and Dunn, *George Washington*, 83-84.

28 Elkins and McKitrick, *The Age of Federalism*, 276-277.

29 Burns and Dunn, *George Washington*, 98.

30 Wood, *Empire of Liberty*, 88-89, 198-199.

31 Northwest Ordinance (1787), The National Archives and Records Administration, January 30, 2012, http://www.ourdocuments.gov/doc.php?flash=true&doc=8.

32 *Johnson v. M'Intosh,* 21 U.S. 543 (1823).

33 Wood, *Empire of Liberty*, 112-113.

34 Elkins and McKitrick, *The Age of Federalism*, 392, 397.

35 Wood, *Empire of Liberty*, 197-198.

36 Burns and Dunn, *George Washington*, 104; Wood, *Empire of Liberty*, 131.

37 Wood, *Empire of Liberty*, 150-151.

38 Wood, *Empire of Liberty*, 162-163.

39 Wood, *Empire of Liberty*, 104; Burns and Dunn, *George Washington*, 90.

40 Wood, *Empire of Liberty*, 161; Burns and Dunn, *George Washington*, 90; *Outline of U.S. History* (Washington: U.S. Department of State, 2005, 2010), 79, January 11, 2012, http://www.america.gov/publications/books/history-outline.html.

41 Wood, *Empire of Liberty*, 164-173, 251-252.

42 John Marshall, *The Life of George Washington*, Volume 5 (Philadelphia: C.P. Wayne, 1807) quoted in Elkins and McKitrick, *The Age of Federalism*, 310.

43 Wood, *Empire of Liberty*, 177-178.

44 Burns and Dunn, *George Washington*, 105.

45 Wood, *Empire of Liberty*, 182-183.

46 George Washington, "A Proclamation," April 22, 1793, *The Avalon Project*, Yale Law School, January 9, 2012, http://avalon.law.yale.edu/18th_century/neutra93.asp.

47 Wood, *Empire of Liberty*, 183.

48 Wood, *Empire of Liberty*, 184-185.

49 Elkins and McKitrick, *The Age of Federalism*, 340-341.

50 Wood, *Empire of Liberty*, 186-187; Elkins and McKitrick, *The Age of Federalism*, 350.

51 Elkins and McKitrick, *The Age of Federalism*, 351-352.

52 Wood, *Empire of Liberty*, 187-188.

53 Wood, *Empire of Liberty*, 134-135.

54 Wood, *Empire of Liberty*, 136.

55 Elkins and McKitrick, *The Age of Federalism*, 462.

56 Elkins and McKitrick, *The Age of Federalism*, 463; Wood, *Empire of Liberty*, 137.

57 George Washington, *Writings*, Volume 32, ed. John Clement Fitzpatrick (Washington: U.S. Government Printing Office, 1931-1944), George Washington Resources, University of Virginia, April 19, 2012, http://etext.virginia.edu/washington/fitzpatrick/.

58 Elkins and McKitrick, *The Age of Federalism*, 463; Wood, *Empire of Liberty*, 137-138.

59 Wood, *Empire of Liberty*, 138-139; Ellis, *Founding Brothers*, 140-141.

60 Thomas Jefferson, *Writings*, Volume 6, ed. Paul Leicester Ford (New York: G.P. Putnam's Sons, 1892-1899) quoted in Burns and Dunn, *George Washington*, 94.

61 Ellis, *Founding Brothers*, 121, 128-129; Burns and Dunn, *George Washington*, 129.

62 Ellis, *Founding Brothers*, 149-151.

63 Ellis, *Founding Brothers*, 163-164.

64 Wood, *Empire of Liberty*, 210.

65 Wood, *Empire of Liberty*, 200, 211.

66 John Patrick Diggins, *John Adams* (New York: Times Books, 2003), 89; Wood, *Empire of Liberty*, 215.

67 Diggins, *John Adams*, 91-92.

68 Ellis, *Founding Brothers*, 179-180.

69 Ellis, *Founding Brothers*, 182-183.

70 Ellis, *Founding Brothers*, 184-185.

71 Diggins, *John Adams*, 96-97; Wood, *Empire of Liberty*, 241-242.

72 Elkins and McKitrick, *The Age of Federalism*, 582-583, 586.

73 Elkins and McKitrick, *The Age of Federalism*, 587-588; Wood, *Empire of Liberty*, 243-244.

74 Wood, *Empire of Liberty*, 245; Diggins, *John Adams*, 106, 130, 141.

75 Diggins, *John Adams*, 107-108.

76 Diggins, *John Adams*, 144-145.

77 Diggins, *John Adams*, 147; Ralph Adams Brown, *The Presidency of John Adams* (Lawrence: University of Kansas Press, 1975), 173-174.

78 Wood, *Empire of Liberty*, 246-247.

79 Elkins and McKitrick, *The Age of Federalism*, 694-695.

80 Diggins, *John Adams*, 111-113; Wood, *Empire of Liberty*, 249-250, 260.

81 Elkins and McKitrick, *The Age of Federalism*, 695-696.

82 Elkins and McKitrick, *The Age of Federalism*, 697; Diggins, *John Adams*, 131-132.

83 Elkins and McKitrick, *The Age of Federalism*, 697-698.

84 Diggins, *John Adams*, 136-137.

85 Wood, *Empire of Liberty*, 251, 256-257.

86 "An Act for the Punishment of Certain Crimes Against the United States [The Sedition Act]," July 17, 1798, General Records of the United States Government, Record Group 11, National Archives, January 27, 2012, http://www.ourdocuments.gov/doc.php?doc=16&page=transcript.

87 Wood, *Empire of Liberty*, 227-229, 262; Elkins and McKitrick, *The Age of Federalism*, 710-711.

88 Elkins and McKitrick, *The Age of Federalism*, 719.

89 Elkins and McKitrick, *The Age of Federalism*, 720-721.

90 Alexander Hamilton, *The Public Conduct of John Adams, Esq., The President of the United States* (New York: E.G. House, 1809), The New York Public Library Internet Archive, April 19, 2012, http://archive.org/details/letterfromalexan00hami2.

91 Diggins, *John Adams*, 148-149.

92 Wood, *Empire of Liberty*, 283-284; Ellis, *Founding Brothers*, 43.

93 Wood, *Empire of Liberty*, 285-286; Thomas Jefferson to Spencer Roane, 6 September 1819. Thomas Jefferson Papers, Library of Congress Manuscript Division, Washington, DC, January 27, 2012 http://www.loc.gov/exhibits/jefferson/137.html.

94 Brown, *The Presidency of John Adams*, 199-200.

ANSWER KEY FOR CHAPTER TEN: THE FEDERALIST ERA

Check your answers to the questions in the Before You Move On Sections for this chapter.

Correct answers are **BOLDED**

Section 10.2.4 - p369

1. The Bill of Rights did all of the following except
    - a. constitute the first ten amendments to the Constitution.
    - b. appease some initial critics of the Constitution.
    - c. safeguard freedoms such as press, speech, and assembly.
    - **D. SETTLE ALL QUESTIONS ABOUT FEDERAL VERSUS STATE AUTHORITY.**

2. Madison and Jefferson objected to the national bank in the 1790s primarily because
    - **A. THEY BELIEVED IN STRICT CONSTRUCTION WHEN INTERPRETING THE CONSTITUTION.**
    - b. they felt it was not powerful enough to meet the nation's financial needs.
    - c. it would cost the government too much money.
    - d. it would be located in New York rather than Virginia.

3. The Treaty of Greenville was an agreement between the United States and
    - a. Great Britain.
    - **B. INDIANS ON THE NORTHWEST FRONTIER.**
    - c. Spain.
    - d. Canada.

4. Jay's Treaty, ratified by the Senate in 1795,
    - a. guaranteed the right of Americans to trade in the West Indies.
    - b. forced Hamilton's resignation from the cabinet.
    - **C. INFURIATED AMERICAN PEOPLE FOR ITS CONCESSIONS TO THE BRITISH.**
    - d. was most strongly opposed in New England.

Section 10.3.5 - p379

1. In foreign affairs, Americans became deeply divided in the 1790s over
    - a. relations with Spain.
    - b. the rise of Napoleon.
    - **C. THE FRENCH REVOLUTION.**
    - d. the banning of the international slave trade.

2. The Whiskey Rebellion in 1794 resulted in
    - a. the repeal of the federal liquor tax.
    - b. declining support for the Republicans.
    - c. mass executions of the captured rebels.
    - **D. THE SENDING OF A MASSIVE ARMY TO WESTERN PENNSYLVANIA.**

3. In the election of 1796, the Federalist John Adams became president, and his vice president was
    - **A. THE REPUBLICAN THOMAS JEFFERSON.**
    - b. the Federalist Charles C. Pinckney.
    - c. the Federalist Alexander Hamilton.
    - d. the Republican Aaron Burr.

Section 10.4.5 - p390

1. The Federalists designed the Sedition Act of 1798 primarily to
    - a. safeguard civil liberties.
    - **B. SMOTHER POLITICAL OPPOSITION.**
    - c. ensure public safety.
    - d. encourage the flow of European immigrants.

2. The Virginia and Kentucky Resolutions asserted that
    - a. the Republicans had betrayed the spirit of the Constitution.
    - b. the federal government had the right to void state laws.
    - c. the Supreme Court had no constitutional authority to invalidate federal laws.
    - **D. STATES HAD THE RIGHT TO NULLIFY FEDERAL LAWS.**

3. The election of 1800 did all of the following except
    a. mark the first time an opposition party came to power.
    B. CAUSE FEDERALIST RIOTING IN THE STREETS OF THE CAPITAL.
    c. show the emergence of a more democratic politics.
    d. elevate Jefferson to the presidency.

4. Federalists passed the Judiciary Act of 1801 in order to
    A. DENY REPUBLICANS FULL CONTROL OF THE GOVERNMENT.
    b. replace the principles of English common law.
    c. establish the doctrine of judicial review.
    d. reduce the number of federal courts and judges.

Chapter Eleven:
The Early Republic

Contents

Chapter Eleven: The Early Republic

11.1 INTRODUCTION

The United States at the beginning of the nineteenth century was a young nation searching for its place in the world. Federalist domination of government was over, as Thomas Jefferson and his new party, the Republicans, came into power. They believed in a limited Federal government with more control in the hands of the states and the people. However, events would demonstrate the need for balance between the two differing visions of how the U. S. should be governed.

During his presidency, Jefferson, and then James Madison, faced the challenge of trying to protect the country from the fallout of the Napoleonic Wars. Although the U. S. was not directly involved, Americans often felt the impact of the battling European giants. These difficulties would lead into another war.

The War of 1812 helped the United States gain international respect as well as launch the political career of Andrew Jackson. Jackson was a victor in the war; the Federalist Party and the Indians were not so fortunate. As America grew across the continent, the Indians were increasingly in the way of the expansion with nowhere to go.

The war and the events leading up to it drastically altered the U.S. economy from one depending on imports and exports to one focused here at home in the Market Revolution. The Cotton Revolution would be a great step in the industrialization of New England and a major change in the way goods were manufactured in America.

11.1.1 Learning Outcomes

After completing this chapter, you should be able to:

- Explain why Jefferson's first term was such a success and his second was such a failure.
- Understand the causes of the War of 1812.
- Explain the forces that produced the market revolution in the United States.

11.2 JEFFERSON

In Thomas Jefferson's vision of the Federal government, less was more. A smaller government meant less strain on, and more freedom for, the people. To this end, Jefferson set about shrinking the government during his first term in office. He cut back on anything he considered unnecessary, such as the army and navy. At the same time, he funded exploration and expansion to give the young country room to grow.

11.2.1 Jefferson's Values

These acts reflected Jefferson's values. Jefferson's well-known love of farming was more than just his personal hobby; it also reflected the tremendous value he placed on an agrarian society. Jefferson believed that the United States would best be served by a strong agricultural base with as many land owners as possible. He believed land ownership supported good citizenship by giving people a tangible reason to be invested in the success and security of their state.

Jefferson's values included the relationship of a nation's government and its citizenry. Jefferson differed from his Federalist predecessors in his view that government should be limited. To Jefferson's mind, citizens should be allowed to pursue life, liberty, and happiness with minimal interference from the Federal Government. Because of this view, Jefferson opposed the Alien and Sedition Acts of 1798; when he became president, he pardoned those arrested under them. The Kentucky and Virginia Resolutions were drafted secretly by Jefferson and James Madison in response to the Acts. These Resolutions, which declared that states had the right to judge the constitutionality of Acts of Congress, also provided that states had the right to declare such Acts null if they were found to be unconstitutional. Although the Alien and Sedition Acts expired, the ideas expressed in the Resolutions continued to be supported by states-rights advocates and would eventually contribute to the founding principles of the Confederacy.

The Napoleonic Wars also called for Jefferson to act upon his values. These wars had been a cause of concern for the United States. Some, such as Adams, wanted ties with Great Britain; others, such as Jefferson, favored France. With the two nations in question at war, many believed the United States would inevitably be drawn into the fray. This very fear had led to Congress authorizing the Direct Tax of 1798 to raise funds to support the military when the conflict came to American shores. Jefferson not only repealed the tax as unnecessary, he also reduced the army to just two regiments, preferring to rely on militia instead; he additionally cut back the navy. By reducing the professional military, Jefferson slashed the defense budget. Although Jefferson felt a large standing army was an expense the nation did not need, he understood the need for professional officers. One of the early problems during the revolution had been the lack of well-trained officers. The solution was the establishment of the United States Military Academy at West Point in 1802. The cadets who attended West Point were drawn from all states in the United States.[1]

Careful diplomacy kept the United States largely out of the international wars, the exception being the War in Tripoli which was a conflict with the Barbary Pirates of the North African coast. During his first term, therefore, it seemed that Jefferson was right. On the home front, Jefferson also deftly dealt with several issues, including relations with Indians.

11.2.2 Forging a New Indian Policy

As a new nation, the United States faced the problem of negotiating a new relationship with the many Indian nations of the region. The most important question that the government faced was a matter of precedence. Should the government follow the patterns established by the British, or should the U.S. forge a new path in Indian policy? The Constitution established that the federal government was the authority in Indian relations. Indian tribes were regarded as foreign powers; Congress held the power to negotiate treaties and set rules for the sale of Indian lands. In 1787, the Northwest Ordinance created the Northwest Territory in the Great Lakes area, the first organized territory in the United States. The Ordinance addressed the relationship between the government and Indian nations, stating that the government would observe the "utmost good faith" in its negotiations; the United States would inevitably expand, but Congress desired expansion with honor.[2] In 1790, Congress passed the first in a series of acts that came to be known as the Indian Intercourse Act, which established that no individual or state could trade or negotiate land sales with Indians without the permission of the federal government. Ultimately, the United States held one clear goal that shaped the structure of Indian relations: to assert their claim to the lands east of the Mississippi River while avoiding war with Indians.

When Thomas Jefferson came to the presidency, he had two main goals for federal Indian policy. First and foremost, he wanted to assure the security of the United States and sought to ally Indian groups with the United States through treaties. Such treaties would prevent the encroachment of European powers through native alliances. These treaties also sought to gain land and promote trade.

Second, Jefferson sought to acculturate Indian populations through "civilizing" programs, a policy begun under the Federalists. Jefferson believed that the essence of U.S. policy was coexistence with the Indians, which would result in their gradual acculturation to "American" ways. Contact with "civilization," Jefferson believed, would transform native peoples and bring peace between Indians and settlers. Jeffersonian views were consistent with earlier U.S. Indian policy in that concern about land and expansion deeply informed his ideas. As Indians became "civilized" by replacing hunting with farming, Jefferson argued, they would require less land as their lifestyle and subsistence patterns changed, thereby freeing up land for white settlers. Although Jefferson's views were progressive for his time, they failed to take into account that many native groups were already highly productive agriculturalists, albeit agriculturalists who did not use Euro-American technology and methods. Instead, Jefferson's vision for Indians closely resembled his ideal for Americans: the yeoman farmer.

Jeffersonian Indian policy focused its greatest efforts on this idea of civilizing Indians. To this end, civilizing programs were established to educate native peoples in Euro-American farming methods. Artisans such as blacksmiths worked with Indian apprentices to maintain plows and farming equipment. Jefferson encouraged missionaries from protestant churches to take part in the civilizing process, and hundreds of missionaries established themselves among many groups all over the country and in the territories. Finally, he authorized the dispatch of Indian agents to educate and civilize Indians by persuading them to adopt American agricultural methods. The civilizing programs met with its greatest success in the South.

While the president did honestly seek coexistence with many native groups, he also recognized that, inevitably, some groups would resist encroachment by white settlers. Jefferson understood that all Indian relations eventually came down to matters of land and expansion, and some groups would be pushed aside in favor of white settlers. Indeed, this was already happening. Individuals and tribes alike were falling into debt with private trading houses. As a result, they were forced to sell their lands bit by bit to pay their debts. For example, in 1773 the Creeks had agreed to cede land to Georgia to cover debts owed to traders. In a letter to William Henry Harrison, governor of the Indiana Territory, Jefferson wrote,

> When they [the Indians] withdraw themselves to the culture of a small piece of land, they will perceive how useless to them are their extensive forests, and will be willing to pare them off from time to time in exchange for necessaries for their farms and families. To promote this disposition to exchange lands, which they have to spare and we want, for necessaries, which we have to spare and they want, we shall push our trading uses, and be glad to see the good and influential individuals among them run in debt, because we observe that when these debts get beyond what the individuals can pay, they become willing to lop them off by a cession of lands. At our trading houses, too, we mean to sell so low as merely to repay us cost and charges, so as neither to lessen or enlarge our capital. This is what private traders cannot do, for they must gain; they will consequently retire from the competition, and we shall thus get clear of this pest without giving offence or umbrage to the Indians. In this way our settlements will gradually circumscribe and approach the Indians, and they will in time either incorporate with us as citizens of the United States, or remove beyond the Mississippi.[3]

This method would not be the only means of obtaining Indian lands. Jefferson was the first president to propose removal of tribes to lands west of the Mississippi River. In cases where tribes resisted the civilizing programs, Jefferson argued, their removal to lands west of the Mississippi was the best course of action. He recommended that the Shawnee and the Cherokee be among the tribes removed to the west. Although these groups were not removed under Jefferson, the idea of removal became an important part of the Indian policy of the United States, and ultimately was carried out under the presidency of Andrew Jackson.

11.2.3 The Louisiana Purchase

Jefferson was opposed to unnecessary expenditures, yet at the same time, with the value he placed on land, he could not pass up a bargain when it came along. The Louisiana Territory had been claimed by Spain and was ceded to France in 1800 during the Napoleonic Wars. While under Spanish control, the United States had been denied access to New Orleans. Jefferson and Congress were in agreement that control of New Orleans and the Mississippi was of vital interest to the United States. The reason why is clear—the Mississippi and its contributing rivers provide access to the interior of the North American continent from the Gulf of Mexico almost to Canada. Any westward expansion of the country would involve the Mississippi. Even so, did Jefferson have the right to make the purchase? Nothing in the Constitution granted Jefferson the power to make such an arrangement. This fact troubled Jefferson and others whose political philosophy was marked by their strict adherence to the Constitution. But Jefferson's dream of an agrarian society depended on having farmable land for the masses, and that desire outweighed any Constitutional considerations. Jefferson assigned Robert Livingston and James Monroe the task of completing the purchase for the United States. Napoleon, the seller, was motivated to sell, helping to ease the transaction along. On behalf of the United States, Livingston and Monroe signed the Louisiana Purchase Treaty and Conventions in Paris on April 30, 1803. The purchase was essentially concluded late in 1803. For $15 million, which worked out to mere pennies per acre, the United States gained enough territory to double in size.

11.2.4 The Lewis and Clark Expedition

At the same time that the Louisiana Purchase was being debated in Congress, Jefferson asked for a much smaller sum of money, only $2,500, to fund a mission of exploration led by Captain Merriwether Lewis and Lieutenant William Clark. Jefferson was clear about the mission at hand and, with his typical attention to detail, gave instructions covering everything from where the expedition should begin and end, to what equipment and supplies they should have, to how they should take notes and how to handle the natives and even how to organize the leadership of the expedition in the event that the original leaders perished on the journey. What follows are excerpts from Jefferson's rather lengthy letter:

> 20 June 1803
>
> To Meriwether Lewis esq. Capt. of the 1st regimt. of infantry of the U. S. of A.
>
> Your situation as Secretary of the President of the U. S. has made you acquainted with the objects of my confidential message of Jan. 18, 1803 to the legislature; you have seen the act they passed, which, tho' expressed in general terms, was meant to sanction those objects, and you are appointed to carry them into execution.
>
> ...
>
> The object of your mission is to explore the Missouri river, & such principal stream of it, as, by its course & communication with the waters of the Pacific Ocean, whether the Columbia, Oregan, Colorado or and other river may offer the most direct & practicable water communication across this continent, for the purposes of commerce.
>
> Beginning at the mouth of the Missouri, you will take *careful* observations of latitude & longitude, at all remarkeable points on the river, & especially at the mouths of rivers, at rapids, at islands, & other places & objects distinguished by such natural marks & characters of a durable kind, as that they may with certainty be recognised hereafter. The courses of the river between these points of observation may be supplied by the compass the log-line & by time, corrected by the observations themselves. The variations of the compass too, in different places, should be noticed.
>
> The interesting points of the portage between the heads of the Missouri, & of the water offering the best communication with the Pacific ocean, should also be fixed

by observation, & the course of that water to the ocean, in the same manner as that of the Missouri.

...

In all your intercourse with the natives, treat them in the most friendly & conciliatory manner which their own conduct will admit; allay all jealousies as to the object of your journey, satisfy them of its innocence, make them acquainted with the position, extent, character, peaceable & commercial dispositions of the U.S. of our wish to be neighborly, friendly & useful to them, & of our dispositions to a commercial intercourse with them; confer with them on the points most convenient as mutual emporiums, and the articles of most desireable interchange for them & us. If a few of their influential chiefs, within practicable distance, wish to visit us, arrange such a visit with them, and furnish them with authority to call on our officers, on their entering the U.S to have them conveyed to this place at the public expense. If any of them should wish to have some of their young people brought up with us, & taught such arts as may be useful to them, we will receive, instruct & take care of them. Such a mission, whether of influential chiefs or of young people, would give some security to your own party. Carry with you some matter of the kinepox; inform those of them with whom you may be, of it'[s] efficacy as a preservative from the small-pox; & instruct & incourage them in the use of it. This may be especially done wherever you winter.

As it is impossible for us to foresee in what manner you will be recieved by those people, whether with hospitality or hostility, so is it impossible to prescribe the exact degree of perseverance with which you are to pursue your journey. We value too much the lives of citizens to offer them to probable destruction. Your numbers will be sufficient to secure you against the unauthorised opposition of individuals or of small parties: but if a superior force, authorised, or not authorised, by a nation, should be arrayed against your further passage, and inflexibly determined to arrest it, you must decline its further pursuit, and return. In the loss of yourselves, we should lose also the information you will have acquired. By returning safely with that, you may enable us to renew the essay with better calculated means. To your own discretion therefore must be left the degree of danger you may risk, and the point at which you should decline, only saying we wish you to err on the side of your safety, and to bring back your party safe even it if be with less information.

...

Given under my hand at the city of Washington this 20th day of June 1803.

Th. Jefferson

Pr. U.S. of America[4]

Figure 11.1 Lewis and Clark | This image shows Lewis and Clark while on their journey to find the Northwest Passage.

Artist: Frederic Remington
Source: Library of Congress

The three-year expedition would travel from the Mississippi across the Northwest to the Pacific. They failed to find the Northwest Passage, a waterway that could be navigated all the way to the Pacific, as none exists, but Lewis and Clark brought back a wealth of other information on the Indians, geography, and the flora and fauna of the areas they explored. Their achievement was quite notable, and yet in their own time, largely ignored.

11.2.5 Judicial Issues

The bad blood and immense distrust between the Federalists and the Republicans created some judicial controversies. Federalists dominated Congress; to stop Jefferson from being able to appoint a Republican to the Supreme Court, they reduced the number of justices from six to five with the Judiciary Act of 1801. This act also created many new judicial positions further down the system, many of which were filled with Adams's appointees. These included lifetime appointments that Adams filled with one of his last actions as president; however, not all the commissioning documents were delivered before the end of Adams's term. James Madison, the incoming Secretary of State for Jefferson's administration, refused to deliver those remaining commissions, in this way keeping several Federalists out of office. One of the last-minute appointees was William Marbury, a rich Federalist. Marbury was determined to have his appointment, and so took his case to the Supreme Court. The Supreme Court, which was packed with Federalists, was led by the Federalist Chief Justice John Marshall. Marshall, Adams's Secretary of State was himself one of the last and most significant judicial appointments Adams made. Marshall's court heard the landmark case of Marbury v. Madison. The court agreed with Marbury that Madison should have delivered the commissions yet ultimately ruled against Marbury because the Court also found that the law under which Marbury made his petition to the Supreme Court, the Judiciary Act of 1789, was unconstitutional. The court's 1803 decision in that case established the Supreme Court as the final defense of the Constitution with the power to review and strike down any law or portion of a law that it rules as being unconstitutional. With this decision, the Court also demonstrated that although it too is the head of a branch of the Federal Government, it could rise above politics and stand apart from the legislative and executive branches of government, setting the tone for Marshall's long and distinguished service as Chief Justice.

11.2.6 Jefferson's Second Term

Jefferson's first term in office was a great success. The nation enjoyed peace, its territory doubled, its debt almost halved, and taxes were reduced. Jefferson's renomination by his party was assured, though he would choose a new running mate, Governor George Clinton of New York. The glaring problem with the election process that had left Jefferson contending with his own vice-presidential running mate for office in 1800 had been fixed with the Twelfth Amendment to the Constitution. Jefferson won by a landslide.

The one dark cloud for Jefferson and his party was his first-term vice president, Aaron Burr. Burr, who had never enjoyed a close relationship or the confidence of Jefferson, and understanding that he would not be considered for the vice-presidency in 1804, looked elsewhere to continue his political career. He set his sights on being governor of New

York but lost the election. One figure who contributed to that loss was staunch Federalist Alexander Hamilton, who despised Burr. Their personal enmity dated back over a decade to the time when Burr ran against Hamilton's father-in-law for a seat in the Senate and won. Burr was so angered by Hamilton's interference in his career that he challenged him to a duel. Hamilton accepted for honor's sake, and they met on the morning of July 11, 1804 in Weehawken, New Jersey.

Although illegal in both New York and New Jersey, duels were not uncommon. The duel between Burr and Hamilton followed classic rules: two men, each with a second; two single-shot pistols which they loaded themselves; then, standing 10 paces apart, they fired at will when given the command. Hamilton's shot missed; Burr's did not. From the letters and statements of the time, it seems Hamilton intentionally missed. He fell to the ground, mortally wounded. Burr moved towards him but then turned and departed, as was proper. The witnesses agreed the duel was well done. Hamilton sat on the ground with the support of his second and told the attending physician the injury was fatal before passing out. Hamilton was removed to a boat for the trip back to New York with the doctor working to revive him. Hamilton did not die an easy death, lingering until the afternoon of the following day. Hamilton lost his life, but Burr lost his political career. For all his accomplishments, Burr became known primarily as the man who killed Alexander Hamilton. He finished out his term as vice president, then left Washington.

During Jefferson's second term, Burr became involved in a scheme that resulted in his being charged with treason in 1806. Burr was determined to make a fortune and looked for opportunity in the territory of the Louisiana Purchase. In various conversations with many different people, both American and foreign, Burr expressed the idea that the people of Louisiana were unhappy with American control. He also looked to a possible revolt by Mexico against the Spanish and possible war between the Spanish and Americans as opportunities to gain personal control over territory that belonged to the United States. Some of the people Burr shared his ideas with were alarmed and believed he was talking treason. This news reached Jefferson who then demanded that Burr be charged with treason. He was eventually arrested and brought to Richmond, Virginia for trial, with Supreme Court Chief Justice John Marshall presiding.

Burr was acquitted due to lack of evidence. There were neither sufficient witnesses nor physical evidence against him, particularly as the most important letter from Burr was lost. Among the evidence the prosecution wanted to use were documents held by Jefferson. The case is interesting because Jefferson argued that the right of executive privilege gave him the power to determine what documents he should turn over to the court for the trial, rather than simply handing over anything the attorneys in the case requested. Jefferson wanted Burr convicted, but felt that defending the independence of the executive branch was of greater importance.

11.2.7 Foreign Pressures

One of the reasons for the success of Jefferson's first term as president was his ability to steer the United States well clear of the conflicts consuming Europe. Jefferson had managed to limit the military engagements to relatively small encounters with Barbary

Pirates in the Mediterranean. The Napoleonic Wars, particularly between France and Great Britain, threatened the neutrality of the United States. Both Great Britain and France repeatedly stopped U.S. merchant ships, seizing cargo and sailors. Britain was the worst offender, using the excuse of searching for deserters from the Royal Navy. Many sailors indeed deserted from the Royal Navy due to the miserable conditions on British ships: bug-infested food, bad water, harsh punishments, and long voyages all made service in the Royal Navy a difficult experience even for those sailors who had freely enlisted. Many had been forced into the Royal Navy by press gangs under a policy known as Impressment. Impressed men were kidnapped from bars, streets, and other ships because the Royal Navy was desperately short on labor. The gangs were not picky about a new recruit's nationality. When they boarded the American ships and took sailors away, they claimed to be taking English citizens; in fact, they captured Americans as well. The British captains could not afford to care about the origins of their crews; lacking a full crew could cost a ship a victory, and defeat often meant death for most, if not all, on board.

The American people were increasingly outraged by stories of American ships being boarded and Americans being impressed into British service. They expected Jefferson to respond. In 1807, the *HMS Leopard* approached an American military vessel, the frigate *USS Chesapeake,* and demanded to search the ship for deserters. The captain of the *Chesapeake*, James Barron, refused. The *Leopard* opened fire, damaging the *Chesapeake*, killing three members of the crew, and wounding several others. Barron responded with one shot before surrendering. Members of the *Leopard* boarded the *Chesapeake* and removed four men they said were deserters. While all the men had in fact served in the Royal Navy, three were Americans who had been previously press-ganged. The one who was British was subsequently hung for desertion by the Royal Navy.

Jefferson wanted to avoid warfare if at all possible. He continued to try diplomacy without success. So, rather than go to war, Jefferson proposed instead to fight an economic battle with the Embargo Act of 1807. The Act was expected to have a negative economic impact on both Great Britain and France of such a degree as to cause both countries to cease their harassment and abuse of American shipping. Instead the Act had little impact on either country, and both continued to ignore American neutrality. American shipping, however, was devastated by the embargo: American merchants were unable to sell their American-produced goods to Britain and France, thus creating economic hardship at home. Jefferson and the Republicans consequently lost favor with the people, who blamed them for not defending American shipping and for causing the financial crisis. The Federalist Party, which had been in decline, suddenly revived, and even Jefferson realized the embargo was a failure, leading to its repeal in 1809. The repeal of the embargo came too late to salvage Jefferson's second term as president, which was an unexpected disappointment following the tremendous success of his first term.

Although damaged by the problems of Jefferson's second term, the Republicans still managed to win the White House once again in the election of 1808, placing James Madison, another Virginian and close confidant of Jefferson, in the presidency. Jefferson retired to his estate, Monticello, while Madison was left to find a solution to the ongoing conflict with Britain and France that had so vexed Jefferson.

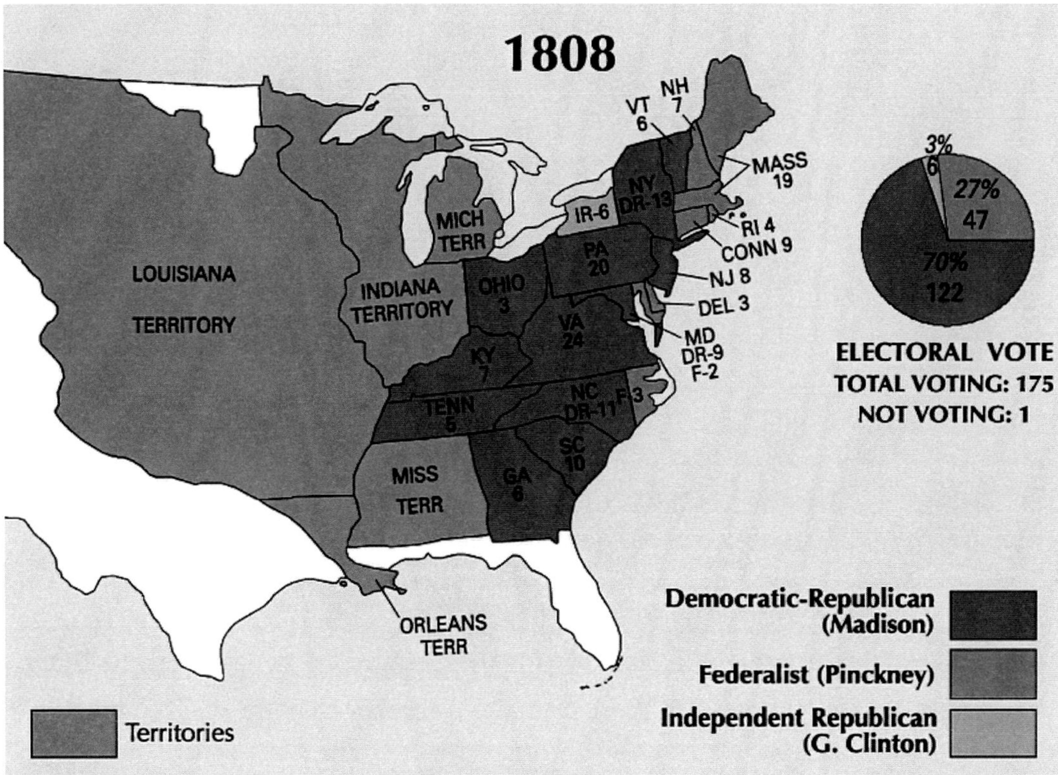

Figure 11.2 Presidential Election Map, 1808 | In the 1808 election, Republican James Madison of Virginia easily defeated Federalist Charles Pinckney of South Carolina as well as an independent Republican George Clinton of New York.

Author: National Atlas of the United States
Source: Wikimedia Commons

11.2.8 Before You Move On...

Key Concepts

Jefferson believed in small government and supporting an agrarian society. He felt that proper use of diplomacy would avoid international conflicts, making a standing army unnecessary. His first term in office seemed to bear out his ideas, but his second term exposed their flaws, especially in international affairs. Jefferson believed expansion of territory was necessary for the nation to grow. He realized that something had to be done about the Indians, as there was no way to expand the nation without entering Indian territory. Jefferson hoped that the Indians could be drawn peacefully into American society, thereby making territorial expansion a natural outcome for all concerned.

Test Yourself

1. Jefferson believed in Big Government.

    a. True

    b. False

2. Acquisition of land was the most important motivating factor in the formulation of early U.S. Indian policy.

a. True

b. False

3. Jefferson's efforts to use economic pressure to solve the situation with Britain and France were successful.

a. True

b. False

4. Lewis and Clark found the Northwest Passage.

a. True

b. False

5. The Louisiana Purchase doubled the territory of the United States.

a. True

b. False

6. Jefferson's second term was as successful as his first.

a. True

b. False

See page 430 for answers

11.3 MADISON

As Jefferson's Secretary of State, James Madison did not have success in convincing the French and British to leave Americans alone. Now as president, his role had changed, but the problems he faced were still the same. Although neither France nor Britain wanted to harm the United States, neither cared what damage they inflicted on the Americans as long as they were able to continue fighting one another. America could not avoid the conflict; Madison had to try something new. The previous attempt to use economics had not only failed but had unintentionally harmed the United States. In place of the Embargo Act, Madison began his presidency with the Nonintercourse Act, which allowed American trading with all nations excepting France and Great Britain. In practice, this move was little better than the previous Embargo Act, and the economy still suffered.

On May 1, 1810, a new plan, Macon's Bill Number 2, was put forward by Congress. It opened trade again with whichever nation was first to recognize American neutrality and cease attacking American ships while refusing trade with the other warring nation. Madison did not like the plan, but since Congress passed the bill, he had to enforce it. Napoleon Bonaparte of France quickly accepted the terms. For Napoleon, it marked an opportunity to offend the British and hopefully cause them some economic damage at the same time. It worked to a certain extent. The British were offended, worsening their already tense relations with the Americans. The economic impact, though, never manifested.

Figure 11.3 James Madison | This image is a portrait of President James Madison, painted by Gilbert Stuart in the 1820s.

Artist: Gilbert Stuart
Source: National Gallery of Art

Meanwhile, Madison faced a war with the Indians of the Northwest. Many Indian leaders of the tribes in the Northwest had tried to adapt to the American ways. They signed treaties ceding lands in Ohio and Indiana to the United States, thus allowing for American settlers to move in and slowly expand American territory. These chiefs who supported peace with the United States dominated the Indians of the area, such as the Shawnee, Miami, and Lenape, until 1805 when illness, smallpox, and influenza swept through the tribes. Among the dead was a Lenape leader, Buckongahelas, who had led his tribe from Delaware to Indiana to escape American expansion years before. He and others like him did not trust the Americans and did not want contact with them, due in part to the history of violent conflict between the two peoples. With the death of Buckongahelas, new leaders rose from the tribes in the region, including two brothers from the Shawnee: Tenskwatawa, also known as The Prophet, and his brother Tecumseh.

Tenskwatawa and Tecumseh both were opposed to the Americans and what they saw as an unhealthy American influence on their people. Tenskwatawa had himself been a heavy drinker before having a transformative experience during the time of illness in 1805. From then on, he began to promote a return to the old ways, following strictly Indian customs, promoting Indian culture, and rejecting American, or "white," things such as alcohol. As the brothers rose to prominence and attracted followers, they created problems for the nearby Indians who were pro-American and who were trying to peacefully co-exist with the settlers.

In 1808 the brothers and their followers were forced to move further toward the northwest into lands inhabited by other tribes in Indiana. They established Prophetstown on the Wabash River where it joins the Tippecanoe River, south of Lake Michigan and not far from the Indiana-Illinois border. The village was named after Tenskwatawa, who was seen as a prophet by many who believed in his spiritual/cultural revival. This time was one of great trouble for the Indians of the area. Deadly bouts of illness continued to occur, bringing misery to the tribes. Many remained pro-American or pro-British, wanting to trade with, and learn to live with, the whites, while others were drawn to Tenskwatawa. The differences of opinion crossed tribal lines, creating a sense of uneasiness both for the

Indians and American settlers of the area. These white settlers were concerned about the growing influence of Tenskwatawa and his anti-white view. Still more settlers were ready to move into the fertile lands, and, in 1809, William Henry Harrison negotiated the Treaty of Fort Wayne in which he purchased millions of acres of land from the Indians of the area. The Indians were not all in agreement about the sale, a fact that added to the troubles.

Tenskwatawa and his followers were particularly determined in their opposition to the sale. Tecumseh, who was emerging from his brother's shadow, was outraged. He argued that no one tribe owned the land and so no tribe could sell it unless all Indian tribes agreed to the sale. Harrison had been successful in negotiating the sale because he was able to get several tribes to agree to it, for example, by getting one tribe to persuade others until enough had agreed and the sale went forward. Tecumseh spoke of killing the chiefs who had signed the treaty and of killing Harrison as well.

By 1811 Prophetstown's population had grown to around 3,000 Indians from various tribes of the Algonquian group, including Shawnee, Winnebago, Iroquois, Kickapoo, Sauk, Fox, and Potawatomi, among others. With Tecumseh and Tenskwatawa actively opposing the Americans, Harrison had to act. He led a force to Prophetstown in November, 1811. At this time, Tecumseh was away in the South, encouraging the Creeks and others to rise against the Americans. While Harrison said he wanted to negotiate with Tenskwatawa, and Tenskwatawa said he wanted to meet with Harrison, both were prepared for a fight. Tenskwatawa struck first but was defeated. He was not a military leader, unlike his brother, but a spiritual one. While his followers attacked the Americans, Tenskwatawa prayed for their safety and victory. When they lost, he was blamed and denounced by his own followers, who believed that he did not have the spiritual powers he had claimed. Prophetstown was burned by the Americans, and Tenskwatawa was abandoned by his followers. This event was the Battle of Tippecanoe and was hailed by the Americans as a great victory for Harrison. In reality, it was not so much the military victory but rather the destruction of the Indian alliance that followed Tenskwatawa that proved significant. Harrison would later successfully run for president with the slogan, "Tippecanoe and Tyler Too." Although Tenskswatawa was disgraced, Tecumseh's reputation and influence continued to grow as he worked to create an Indian alliance to resist the Americans. He fought on, becoming an ally of the British. The Indian conflicts with the Americans that he encouraged would become part of the War of 1812.

Meanwhile, the British continued to harass American shipping, and Madison faced enormous pressure at home to do something to alleviate this situation, even if any action meant war. Madison knew that on paper the United States was militarily no match for Great Britain. But Britain's continuing attacks on American ships fueled the calls for action from the War Hawks in Congress, particularly Henry Clay and John C. Calhoun. Madison, having done all he could to find a non-military solution, was finally pushed to call for a declaration of war on June 1, 1812, a declaration that won Congress's subsequent approval.

11.3.1 The War of 1812

The war began with the Americans facing several obstacles. First, the British had military superiority. Under Jefferson, the American army had been reduced as a cost-cutting measure. Now it needed to be expanded, and quickly. Second, raising funds for the war was inhibited by the lack of a national bank. The late Federalist Alexander Hamilton had been a proponent of a national bank and helped create it with a twenty-year charter in 1791. To the Federalists, having a national bank was vital for the health of the nation. To Democrat-Republicans such as Jefferson and Madison, a national bank was unnecessary and might even be dangerous to economic liberty. The charter for the bank expired in 1811 and was not renewed, as the Congress and the president were not pro-bank Federalists. The timing was truly unfortunate for Madison. In not renewing the bank's charter in 1811, Madison stood on his political principles. In 1812, the virtues of having a national bank became clear to Madison, albeit too late. The final obstacle concerned the primary battlefield, the Atlantic Ocean: the American fleet consisted of less than 20 warships to face the most powerful navy in the world.

The one saving grace for the United States was the other half of the Napoleonic Wars. Britain was deeply entangled against Napoleon, having committed large parts of both its army and navy to the effort. For this reason, Britain was not prepared to turn the full force of its military might on the United States. In fact, the British Government had not wanted a war with the Americans at all. The actions of British naval captains on the high seas reflected the needs of the British navy, not the desires of the British government.

The War in the North

The Americans could not attack Great Britain directly; an invasion of the British Isles was out of the question. To conduct the war, the Americans had to find British military targets at sea, in the form of the British navy, and on land in North America, where the first obvious target was Canada.

During the American Revolution, the Americans had hoped to convince at least some Canadians to join their cause in revolt against the British Crown. Those hopes were doomed, as most French and British Canadians stayed loyal to Britain. After the American Revolution, many Loyalists who had remained in the American Colonies in hopes of a British victory moved to Canada to continue as British subjects rather than becoming citizens of the new United States. By 1812, some Americans believed that this time an American invasion of Canada would finally trigger a Canadian revolt and help ensure an American victory, which might even bring the war to a quick end. They were wrong. The war in the north went badly for the Americans at every stage.

Although the U.S. had declared war, Britain was better able to inform their colonists in North America about the official hostilities. For this reason, the American garrison at Fort Mackinac, Mackinac Island, Michigan was surprised when a British force arrived in July, 1812 and demanded their surrender. The British force was small, consisting of the garrison from St. Joseph Island along with Indians from several tribes and some Canadians. Fort Mackinac was on the southern end of Mackinac Island, off the northern tip of the main Michigan Territory between Lake Huron and Lake Michigan. The location was remote in relation to the rest of the American territory and states, but of strategic importance in that area of the Great Lakes. The American commander of the fort, Lieutenant Porter Hanks, had no warning or instructions from his superiors concerning the war and the British. He had no way of knowing what sort of force he faced, as he could not actually see the British troops. His only information was one shot from a British cannon, followed by a demand for surrender presented on behalf of the British by some of the island inhabitants who apparently told Hanks that the British force had a great number of Indians. Hanks would have been aware of the Indian troubles from the previous year with Tecumseh and knew that the ill feelings continued. He surrendered his fort without firing a shot.

The British Commander, Captain Charles Roberts, let the American garrison go. He then took over the fort as his new base, which gave the British the first victory in the war, a toehold in American territory, and new Indian allies as news of the British victory spread.

The American troubles continued further south on the Michigan peninsula at Detroit. Indians from the battle at Fort Mackinac traveled south after that victory to join with Tecumseh. Brigadier General William Hull commanded the Americans at Detroit. Hull had served in the Revolution and was an experienced officer now at the end of a long career; perhaps he had served too long and was not fit to command. He invaded Canada but stayed on the coast and never moved on into Canadian territory. Rather than convince Canadians to revolt against the British and join the Americans, Hull's actions served only to offend the Canadians and firm up their support for the British. Hull then returned to the American side of the Great Lakes where he learned that Indians were approaching, along with the British. The British were leading what was intended to be an attack against Hull, but the Indians were what Hull feared. He surrendered without a fight. In his defense, it should be noted that he was concerned not only for the lives of his men, but also for the many civilians in the fort. He feared that if he tried to fight and lost, the Indians, along with the British, would overrun the fort and a massacre might ensue. The British had done what they could to keep this thought in Hull's mind, telling him they would not be able to control their Indian allies and trying to make their force seem larger than it actually was. Hull had no reports of his own as to the actual size and nature of the British force. This first stage of the war was a disaster for the Americans. The news of the fall of Detroit emboldened more Indians to rise against the Americans and support the British, while it increased British confidence in their ability to win.

The United States Navy

Although the United States Army failed abysmally in their efforts in Canada and Michigan, the United States Navy surprisingly found success. The British Navy was the greatest navy in the world at that time. The U. S. Navy, meanwhile, was greatly underdeveloped. In theory, the campaign was fully skewed towards the British. Although the bulk of the British Navy was occupied with the Napoleonic Wars, the British were able to commit about eighty-five ships to fight the Americans. The entire American fleet numbered less than twenty, probably only about a dozen ships, most of which were small. The Americans had three forty-four-gunfrigates, the largest ships at American disposal, and six frigates, three large and three smaller ones which were designed to carry between thirty-six and forty-four guns, although they could carry more. They were designed somewhat differently than European frigates with an emphasis on strength of hull and speed. They had three masts with full rigging and one actual gun deck. The American frigates carried crews of between

340 to 450 sailors and Marines, depending on the size of the ship. They could out run many enemy ships due to an innovative design using diagonal ribbing which provided a unique hull support and a slimmer frame that made the ships faster in the water. The best of the British fleet were the larger ships of the line, designed to form a line in the ocean and sail past the enemy, firing until one fleet or the other won. These heavy warships had multiple gun decks, carrying sixty-four or seventy-two or more guns. They could unleash devastating fire power at targets on land, such as in a harbor, or at ships at sea.

With their superior numbers, the British established a blockade of American ports. The Americans did not have the ships to break the blockade but did manage some naval victories which improved American morale. The star of the American fleet was the *USS Constitution*, "Old Ironsides," as she came to be known, an American-designed and constructed frigate made from American oak. She first brought a cheer to the Americans under Captain Isaac Hull when she evaded a pursuing group of British ships for fifty-seven hours. Running away successfully may seem an odd victory, but for warships, speed was a source of pride. So, when the *Constitution* out-sailed the best navy in the world in 1812, the Americans rejoiced.

A month later, the *Constitution* found the *HMS Guerriere* alone out in the Atlantic, a situation that gave Hull the perfect opportunity to show that the *Constitution* was built to fight, not run away. Officially, the *Constitution* carried forty-four guns. Hull added more. The *Guerriere* was originally a French frigate carrying thirty-eight guns that was captured by the British and put into British service. Her commander, Captain James Richard Dacres, was confident of his ship's ability to take the *Constitution,* so when she was sighted, he ordered his ship to close with her in typical fashion of the day. As they approached, each ship fired at the other, even though shots from the forward cannons were not expected to have any real effect. The real damage would be done by the broadsides fired from the guns mounted down the sides of the ships. If the gunners were good, they could target the masts of the other ships; without masts, the enemy ship would be unable to maneuver or flee. To bring these guns into play, the two ships would sail past each other as close as each captain dared. After each pass, they turned to bring the guns back into position and fire again. Ultimately, the *Constitution* blasted the mizzen mast from the *Guerriere*; it fell overboard but was still attached to the ship, acting as a drag and preventing the British ship from moving properly. The American ship followed with more shots, dangerously damaging the *Guerriere's* canvas and rigging.

Figure 11.4 The *Constitution* and the *Guerriere* | Depiction of the *Constitution* and the *Guerriere*. The damage to the *Guerriere* was considerable.

Artist: Anton Otto Fischer
Source: Naval History and Heritage Command

Then a shot was fired from the *Guerriere* straight into the side of the *Constitution*. The American sailors who saw the shot coming were amazed when they saw the cannon ball bounce off and fall into the water, thus giving the ship her nickname of "Old Ironsides." The sign of surrender was to strike the colors, that is, to bring down the flag of your ship. *Guerriere* was so badly damaged she had no colors left to strike. Eighty members of her officers and crew, including the captain, were killed or wounded. American losses were comparatively light. The *Guerriere's* crew was taken on board the *Constitution*, and what remained of the *Guerriere* was burned at sea.

The Land War Moves South

The year 1813 brought more good news for the Americans. The U.S. Navy in the Great Lakes proved it had more than one fighting ship by winning control of Lake Erie. The army under the command of General William Henry Harrison then defeated the combined British and Indian forces at the Battle of the Thames. Tecumseh, the leader who had brought the Indian tribes together, was killed. Without his strong leadership, his confederation did not last. Although some Indians would continue to fight for the British, most returned home. The British lost their best allies, the Americans regained control of the Great Lakes, and the focus of the war moved south.

The Creek Nation was divided into Upper Creeks and Lower Creeks. Generally, the Lower Creeks were on good terms with the Americans, while the Upper Creeks favored the British. Tecumseh, whose own mother reportedly was a Creek, had traveled south in 1811 to encourage the Southern Indians to join his alliance and fight the Americans. While leaders were not keen to be involved, younger men, especially of the Upper Creeks, responded. The ideas of Tecumseh and his brother resonated with them, these ideas being the rejection of white influence, resistance to white expansion, a return to the old ways, and the preservation of their culture. These Indians formed a group referred to as the Red Sticks. Their fight against the Americans, the Creek War, soon became part of the larger War of 1812. It ended with a defeat in 1814 at the Battle of Horseshoe Bend in Alabama, at the hands of Colonel Andrew Jackson.

The American actions in the north, that is, the attempts to invade Canada and the destruction of Canadian property, were offensive to the British. They realized that the American defenses were stretched thin, particularly along the Atlantic coast, thanks to the U.S.'s small navy. While the Americans might be able to win an occasional victory at sea, they could not adequately defend all of their seaports at the same time. In 1814, with the end of the Napoleonic Wars, the British could finally turn their attention to the war with the United States. The time was right to avenge the American actions in Canada.

The British first struck at Washington, D. C., which was under the command of Major General Robert Ross. They attacked with precision and discipline, destroying only public buildings, such as the Capitol and the White House, while leaving personal property alone. This decision brought mixed opinions in England; some approved, while others believed harsher treatment was justified in light of what the Americans had done in Canada. First Lady Dolly Madison famously stayed at the White House as the British worked their way through the town; she directed the removal of many valuables to save them from destruction. Both the Capitol Building and the White House were completely gutted by fires. Their sandstone exteriors survived, although blackened, even as their interiors went up in flames. One terrible loss for the nation was the Library of Congress, which had been housed in the Capitol and was burned. Thomas Jefferson's personal library of over 6,000 books would serve as the core of the new Library of Congress in 1815.

In September, 1814, the British Army struck Baltimore again under the command of Ross in a combined action with the British Navy under Admiral Alexander Cochrane. Cochrane's fleet attacked Fort McHenry, which was the main defense of Baltimore harbor. The plan was simply to bombard the fort until its defenders surrendered. The British continued the attack for twenty-five hours without success. As Francis Scott Key famously wrote, when it was over, our flag was still there. The defenders of Fort McHenry survived and flew a huge American flag, the Star Spangled Banner, to prove it. Cochrane tried landing a small force to attack on land, but that attack also failed.

Meanwhile, Ross personally led 5,000 British troops on their march to Baltimore, until he was shot down by American snipers, sent to hold off the British and allow more time for Baltimore's defenders to secure their positions. Ross, mortally wounded, was carried back to the ships and died along the way. The British continued their advance until halted by stiff resistance from the Americans, who had artillery as well as defensive works. The British then retreated back to their ships. With both attacks by the army and navy having failed and the commander of the army dead, the British broke off their attack and sailed for New Orleans.

The Battle of New Orleans, the last and arguably the most famous battle of the War of 1812, actually happened when the war was nearly over. The Treaty of Ghent was signed on December 24, 1814 but not actually ratified by the American Government until February, 1815. The British attacked New Orleans on January 8, 1815.

The British fleet had reached the Gulf of Mexico on December 12, 1814 and set about removing the American naval forces in the area. By December 14th, their way was clear, and the British were able to build a garrison on an island thirty miles out from New Orleans, close enough to prepare for their eventual attack yet far enough away to be somewhat safe from an attack by the Americans. On December 23, a British advance group under the command of General John Keane moved inland along the Mississippi, drawing to within nine miles of New Orleans. Keane met no opposition but halted his advance to wait for the arrival of the rest of the British forces.

The Americans at New Orleans were commanded by Major General Andrew Jackson. Jackson, known for his decisive nature, reacted quickly when he learned of the British arrival. He organized a night attack on their camp. The attack was fairly brief before Jackson pulled his forces back, but it served its purpose. Jackson had made it clear he intended to defend New Orleans, and the British were caught off-guard by the attack. After Jackson withdrew back to New Orleans and prepared the defenses, Keane waited, unsure of what to do next. Days passed until a meeting of the British commanders settled the matter; meanwhile, the American defenses had been strengthened by the hour. The British made their first move on December 28th, with small attacks along the defensive works as they sought weak points. They then withdrew, and the Americans continued improving their defenses and placing a variety of artillery pieces. The British began their first real attack on New Year's Day with an artillery barrage. They could not sustain their attack due to a lack of ammunition; still, they damaged some of the defensive works and destroyed a few American cannons. It was not enough to pave way for the next phase of the British plan, so Pakenham canceled the rest of the intended assault.

By January 8, more British troops had landed and joined Pakenham's force, and an attack was launched early that foggy and wet morning. The British had not made proper preparations, leaving their troops to struggle in the mud of the canals instead of advancing along a prepared path. The British approached the American defensive works under the cover of fog, only to have the fog lift at the worst possible moment. The Americans, surprised to see British standing in front of their guns, did not hesitate to open fire. Many officers as well as soldiers were killed or wounded, while those who survived were confused and leaderless. Keane was among the wounded. Other British troops moved forward; without support, they failed to hold any positions they captured. Jackson's artillery continued firing with grape shot. Some British never made it out of the canals; they were pinned down, unable to advance or retreat. Pakenham himself was mortally wounded. Caught in the open, the British suffered horrific casualties as the Americans mercilessly continued their fire. Finally, General John Lambert took command of the British and withdrew his infantry from the field. The British suffered over 2,000 casualties, killed or wounded, including their commander, compared to seventy-one killed or wounded Americans. Lambert ordered his men back to the fleet and left New Orleans. He planned to continue the campaign in Mississippi, until he received news of the Treaty of Ghent, declaring an end to the hostilities.

The End of the War

Most of the war went poorly for the Americans, a fact that demoralized those on the home front in general but in particular those in New England, the Federalist stronghold where the war was never popular. By 1814 feelings were running so high that some even suggested having New England secede from the United States and negotiate a separate peace with Great Britain. In response to the rising bitterness, Connecticut, Massachusetts, Rhode Island, New Hampshire, and Vermont all sent delegates to Hartford, Connecticut to meet and consider what should be done. Their timing proved unfortunate for their purposes. Unknown to the delegates at the Hartford Convention, Andrew Jackson was in the midst of a smashing victory in New Orleans. News of Jackson's victory reached Washington just in time to thwart any proposals from the Federalist Hartford Convention. Moderates had dominated the convention and had kept the more radical ideas at bay, but still the fact that the Federalists in New England convened to even discuss secession while Americans were fighting for victory in New Orleans seemed unsavory to the American public. The Federalists would never regain the trust and confidence of the American people, and the party would fade from the political scene.

The Treaty of Ghent officially ended the War of 1812. With the treaty, each side returned any territory and property it had taken in the war. All borders were returned to their 1811 state. The Indians were also promised to have their lands as of 1811 returned. This particular agreement, however, was not honored. The Americans, particularly Andrew Jackson, were not interested in honoring any agreement with the Indians that would ultimately limit

American expansion. While Great Britain and the United States regained their former borders, the Indians would never be restored to their former condition. Indeed, from 1814 onwards, the Indians would continually be pushed aside by the United States: the United States was expanding, and the Indians were in the path with nowhere to go. The war had one other casualty: the Federalist Party. On the verge of death once before, their opposition to the war dealt them a fatal blow. American success cost the Federalists public approval. Some of their ideas survived, however, as the war gave James Madison reason to reconsider his own political views.

11.3.2 Before You Move On...

Key Concepts

Madison inherited Jefferson's foreign relations problems, and, although personally opposed to war, he was unable to find a peaceful solution, thus leading to the War of 1812. The War of 1812 was a costly solution to a diplomatic problem: the lack of respect for the sovereignty of the United States by the British, particularly the British sea captains who, due to the Napoleonic Wars, were desperate to find crew members for their ships. The Americans were beaten when they attempted to invade Canada; also, much of the capital, Washington, D.C., was burned. Although overall the British fared better in the War of 1812, it was seen as an American victory, particularly due to the Battle of New Orleans—despite the fact that that battle actually occurred after the war was technically over. Concerns over the course of the war and the fear of defeat at the hands of the British led the Federalists in New England to organize the Hartford Convention where the more radical members considered secession. This action led the demise of the Federalist Party. The War of 1812 officially ended with the Treaty of Ghent, which essentially returned American property to the Americans and British property to the British.

Test Yourself

1. Madison was much better at finding a peaceful solution for the problems with the British and French than Jefferson.

   a. True

   b. False

2. Madison was enthusiastic about declaring war on the British.

   a. True

   b. False

3. The British Navy was the greatest in the world in 1812.

   a. True

   b. False

4. Andrew Jackson led the Americans at the Battle of New Orleans.
   a. True
   b. False

See page 430 for answers

11.4 ECONOMIC AND SOCIAL CHANGES

The end of the war seemed almost a cathartic moment for the nation. The squabbles with Britain that had dominated the landscape for so long were now over. A new national bank was in place, and Americans could look within their own borders for consumer goods and necessities. Trade with foreign nations was a luxury Americans could enjoy but did not need to depend on any longer. The United States was ready to enter a new phase of history, one in which it would truly stand on its own feet.

The war changed political opinions as well. Madison and many members of his party realized that some national institutions in the Federalist style were necessary to build a nation, even if such institutions were not in keeping with the traditional principles of the Republicans. A new national bank, tariffs to protect American industry, and a standing professional army and navy able to defend the nation when needed were all ideas Madison now embraced.

The American people thus experienced the market revolution in the early nineteenth century as the nation transitioned from home production to factory production. During this period, traditional controls over production, distribution, and exchange gave way to market transactions. Supply, demand, and price became far more important in economic transactions than did social relationships. In the colonial period, emotional attachments often dictated economic transactions. As historian John Lauritz Larson notes, "who you were, where you were, and what you were" shaped "how you bought, sold, and prospered." In the nineteenth century, customary social practices did not play a role in economic transactions. In essence, "money alone mobilized goods and people" in a system of anonymous transactions. Individuals' good names came from their willingness to honor their contracts.[5]

On the positive side, these changes encouraged greater mobility among the American people. Increasingly, they spread into the territory beyond the Appalachian Mountains in an attempt to better their social and economic position. Throughout the Old Northwest and the Old Southwest, settlers staked claim to land and put that land into production, thereby providing raw materials for the increasing number of factories in the Northeast. The social changes that occurred also prompted political changes as states throughout the country moved toward universal white male suffrage. On the negative side, when a pioneer's wife gave up spinning in the home, he needed to produce more cash crops to purchase cloth, or when a slaveholder moved west, the demands on those slaves often increased. Meanwhile, as more young men and women took positions in workshops and factories, they found themselves working for wages for most of their lives. Lastly, greater settlement in less populated regions caused problems between the settlers and the Indians living on the land. Because expansion was considered vital to the interests of the country, the Indians' rights to land were seen as an obstacle.[6]

11.4.1 Market Revolution

The market revolution largely stemmed from an availability of resources. As the United States acquired more territory, like the Louisiana Purchase, it attained more natural resources and land to produce raw materials. As the nation's population increased, it gained more workers and ultimately more consumers. American entrepreneurs also had access to monetary resources; in other words, they found investors willing to support their new businesses. Furthermore, recognizing the importance of transportation and communication to economic growth, state governments supported internal improvement projects. At the same time, the market revolution occurred because the American people largely embraced the changes. They willingly pulled up stakes and ventured into new regions. They also possessed a spirit of enterprise that spurred the expansion of transportation and industry. And more unfortunately, they seemed content in many cases to exploit workers—slave or free—to bring their economic vision to life.[7]

Prior to the War of 1812, the United States exported raw materials such as cotton and tobacco, and imported manufactured goods such as cotton fabric and fine smoking tobacco. Thomas Jefferson had attempted to use the need for the exports to put economic pressure on Britain and France, with disastrous economic results for the United States. During the war, exports were not essential for either European nation, so the farmers continued to suffer financially. Buyers in England and France were forced to look for new sources of raw materials, and American farmers needed to find new buyers for their produce. After the war, industrialization was on the rise in the United States, creating homegrown markets for raw materials and a new American source for quality manufactured goods for American consumers. The Northeast became the manufacturing center of the country with many factories and mills located there. The earliest mills depended on reliable sources of water power, on rivers flowing with enough force to turn the water wheels that in turn powered the machinery. The advent of steam broke the bonds tying the mills to the rivers and instead bound them to any site of water and coal.[8]

Good transportation was needed to move the raw materials to the mills and factories and the manufactured goods out to the shops for sale, as well as to connect the agricultural regions of the nation with the manufacturing region. Transportation was also important for the expansion of the nation. Between 1816 and 1821, six new states joined the Union: Indiana, Mississippi, Illinois, Alabama, Maine, and Missouri. Before the War of 1812, there were roads, often old Indian trails that had been widened but not paved, and a few canals. There were also ships that would sail up passable rivers and around the coast, yet overall traveling was inefficient and quite expensive. According to some estimates, it cost as much to ship a ton of material thirty miles overland in the United States as it did to ship that material to Europe.[9] Problems moving goods and people especially during the war prompted American leaders to support improvements.

State governments helped to build turnpikes by chartering private corporations and granting them the exclusive right to construct a road. Then they would invest some state money in the corporation's securities; the rest of the money came from private stockholders. The number of investors in these projects, according to historian Daniel Walker Howe, showed "the extent of grass-roots enthusiasm for improved transportation." Given the slow pace of travel on these roads, people also clamored for other forms of transportation. Many northern states turned to extending their canal system. In 1817, the New York legislature decided to support the construction of the Erie Canal—a forty-foot-wide canal with a twenty-foot-wide towpath. When it opened in 1825, the canal stretched 363 miles from Buffalo on Lake Erie to Albany on the Hudson River and connected the Northwestern territories to global markets. Moreover, it made the state a good deal of money. Robert Fulton's invention of the steam engine in 1807 made steamboats and later railroads possible. Steam allowed boats to navigate up rivers as well as down rivers. Flat-bottom paddleboats became especially important for travel on the Mississippi River, thereby allowing the Southwestern territories access to global markets as well. Ultimately, canals, steamboats, and railroads improved the comfort and speed of travel and provided for economic growth.[10]

As evidenced by the improvements in transportation, innovation became a key factor in the market revolution. Eli Whitney, known best for inventing the cotton gin, also developed the idea of interchangeable parts so that, if a part on a machine broke, it could easily be replaced with an identical part. Prior to Whitney's new system, everything was made by hand and was therefore unique. Replacements consequently had to be custom-fitted to each machine. This system was time-consuming and costly. With Whitney's interchangeable parts, machines and products could be produced more quickly, each part being an exact duplicate of every other like part, each machine as a whole an exact duplicate of every other machine of the same type and manufacture.[11]

The impact was enormous for the process of moving from home to factory production and ultimately to massive industrialization later in the century. Inventors continued to churn out new creations for both industry and agriculture as evidenced by the fact that the number of patents issued by the federal government went up significantly. For example, Elias Howe, a machinist in Massachusetts, created the sewing machine, while Cyrus McCormick, a blacksmith in Virginia, developed the reaper. Moreover, entrepreneurs looked for new ways to market their products. Chauncey Jerome, a clockmaker in Connecticut, not only developed new techniques for making timepieces, he also found markets by pricing his products so consumers could buy them and by convincing consumers they needed them.[12]

11.4.2 Cotton Revolution

Cotton became a cash crop for the South thanks to Eli Whitney's cotton gin, invented in 1793. Cotton has two forms: the long staple, which has long fibers and relatively easy-to-remove seeds, and short staple, which has shorter fibers and a difficult-to-remove seed. The long staple cotton was most desirable but could only be grown along the coast. Inland cotton planters had to grow the less-valuable short staple cotton. The only way to make any profit from growing the short staple cotton was to produce large quantities of it. Whitney's gin made this possible because it removed the seeds quickly, making production faster. Thanks to Whitney's gin, the short staple cotton supply soon dominated the market. As Americans moved into the Old Southwest, they also found the soil well-suited to grow short-staple cotton. With the price of cotton rising on the international market, new land was quickly put into production in an effort to make a profit. From 1800 to 1820, cotton production increased significantly, from somewhere around 73,000 bales to 730,000 bales, and the numbers continued to rise throughout the century. By mid-century, the United States produced roughly 68 percent of the world's cotton.[13]

As the production of cotton increased, Americans began to think more about domestic production. In the 1790s, British immigrant Samuel Slater, with the support of merchant Moses Brown, built the first American textile mill in Pawtucket, Rhode Island. Using water power, workers spun cotton into thread, which was then woven into fabric in rural homes. Slater then created in Slatersville, Rhode Island, the first mill village, complete with a factory, houses, and a company store. Before the War of 1812, the number of spinning mills did increase; by 1809, eighty-seven mills dotted the Northeastern landscape.[14] Still, in the first decade of the nineteenth century, most Southern cotton flowed to British mills.

This situation only began to change when Francis Cabot Lowell established in 1814 the Boston Manufacturing Company and built a textile mill at Waltham, Massachusetts. The mill relied on the Charles River for its power source. It was an integrated mill, meaning that all parts of cotton fabric production were integrated into one building, making it the first of its kind in the United States. Workers brought in raw cotton, which they spun, dyed, and wove into finished cotton fabric. They even built looms for the mill on-site in their own machine shop and also produced looms for sale to other mills. While Lowell died in 1817, his company lived on. Using the Waltham System, the company built factories for Lawrence and Lowell by 1821.[15] Textile mills, like those run by the Boston Manufacturing Company, provided a new market for southern cotton, making cotton fabric truly an all-American product.

To operate their mill, the Boston Manufacturing Company employed women. Lowell, who had travelled to Britain where he learned about cotton production, worried about the creation of a permanent working class. He felt young women could work for a few years to earn money for their dowry, and then they would return to their rural communities, marry, and raise a family. These young, single women worked eighty hours a week in a noisy and hot factory filled with particles of thread and cloth. They also lived in company-owned boarding houses, which one worker described as "a small, comfortless, half-ventilated apartment containing some half a dozen occupants." Moreover, the company provided the girls with "wholesome" activities such as concerts, dances, church services, classes, and lectures to fill their time when not at work, and were given chaperones to help ensure the protection of their reputation. They could be fired for not performing their work properly or for not obeying company rules when not working. Finally, they were paid less than men

Figure 11.5 Lowell's Mill | This photograph of Francis Cabot Lowell's mill at Waltham, Massachusetts.

Author: Wikipedia User "Daderot"
Source: Wikimedia Commons

for the same work; still, the mill gave young women the opportunity to leave the farm life behind with socially acceptable employment. Lowell's mill was thus able to attract workers despite its dismal conditions. However, increasingly the workers did not come from the American countryside; rather, new Irish immigrants, who were willing to work for low pay, took positions in the mills.[16]

These new American mills provided unwanted competition to the English, who could sell their cotton fabric for a lower price in the United States. In 1816, Lowell successfully lobbied Washington for a tariff to protect the new American textile industry. Although the practice of having underpaid workers living in a controlled environment would eventually fail, the integrated mill itself would be the model followed for textiles and other factories. Just as importantly, the development of manufacturing in the North, while the South focused on agriculture, would widen the cultural gap between the two regions as the nineteenth century progressed.

11.4.3 Before You Move On...

Key Concepts

The War of 1812, and the events leading up to it, resulted in major economic and social changes in the United States, producing the market revolution fueled by the availability of resources and an entrepreneurial spirit. As the United States moved from home production to factory production, it ceased to depend on imports/exports and instead developed a domestic market. American farmers produced more cotton and other raw materials, which American manufacturers turned into finished products. The market revolution took a major step forward with the development of interchangeable parts and the integrated mill. The differences between Northern and Southern society increased with the industrialization of the North and the increasing focus on agriculture in the South.

Test Yourself

1. The market revolution brought many social and economic changes to the United States.

   a. True

   b. False

2. Eli Whitney created the Cotton Gin.

   a. True

   b. False

3. Short staple cotton was preferred to long staple prior to the invention of the cotton gin.

   a. True

   b. False

4. Francis Cabot Lowell built the first integrated textile mill in New England.
   a. True
   b. False

See page 430 for answers

11.5 Conclusion

John Adams's exit from the presidency was not without controversy, particularly in the judiciary. However, his appointment of Chief Justice John Marshall would prove to be significant for the United States for decades to come. Jefferson's first term was decidedly positive, perhaps the most successful first term of any president, as he reduced the debt and doubled the size of the nation. His second term was just as disastrous as his first was successful, leaving a diplomatic tangle for Madison to navigate, and leading to the War of 1812.

These events in the early nineteenth century led the Republicans to realize that not all Federalist policies were bad; some were even necessary for the welfare of the nation as a whole. Madison was able to blend the best of the Federalist ideas, such as a national bank, with the best of the Republicans, as in limiting government so that it did not become a burden to the people. His skills led the nation towards the Era of Good Feelings. The War of 1812 brought the United States new respect as a nation and helped to create a new economy for the country while triggering the end of the old Federalist Party. Along with these changes, the Market Revolution's impact on manufacturing in the United States altered the American lifestyle in the North and widened the social gap between the North and South.

11.6 CRITICAL THINKING EXERCISES

- Why did Jefferson want to avoid a military conflict?
- Why did the British and French not care that they were violating American rights?
- Was there anything either Jefferson or Madison could have done that would have solved the conflict with the British and avoided the War of 1812?
- Were the British right or wrong to burn Washington D.C.? Why?

11.7 KEY TERMS

- Baltimore
- Aaron Burr
- Civilizing agents
- Cotton Gin
- Cotton—Long Staple
- Cotton—Short Staple
- Dueling
- Federalists
- Fort McHenry
- Frigate
- Indian Intercourse Act
- Interchangeable parts
- Integrated Mill
- Alexander Hamilton
- William Henry Harrison
- Andrew Jackson
- Thomas Jefferson
- Judiciary Act of 1801
- Francis Scott Key
- Lewis and Clark
- Library of Congress
- Loom
- The Louisiana Purchase
- Francis Cabot Lowell
- James Madison
- Marbury v. Madison
- Market Revolution
- Mill girls
- Napoleonic Wars
- New Orleans
- Press Gang
- Red Sticks
- Republicans
- Samuel Slater
- Star Spangled Banner
- Tecumseh
- Textile mill
- USS Constitution “Old Ironsides”
- War of 1812
- Washington
- Eli Whitney

11.8 CHRONOLOGY

The following chronology is a list of important dates and events associated with this chapter.

Date	Event
1790	Indian Intercourse Act passed
1793	Eli Whitney invented the Cotton Gin
1794	Samuel Slater opened the first textile mill the United States
1801	Thomas Jefferson began his first term as president; Judiciary Act of 1801 passed
1803	Louisiana Purchase
1805	Thomas Jefferson began his second term as president
1809	James Madison began his first term as president
1812	War of 1812 began
1813	Death of Tecumseh
1814	Treaty of Ghent signed; Lowell opened his textile mill
1815	Battle of New Orleans; Treaty of Ghent ratified; War of 1812 ended
1816	Protective tariffs enacted

11.9 BIBLIOGRAPHY

American Social History Project, directed by Herbert Gutman. *Who Built America? Working People and the Nation's Economy, Politics, Culture and Society*, Volume 1. New York: Pantheon Books, 1989.

Bernstein, Peter L. "The Erie Canal: The Waterway That Shaped a Great Nation." In Stephen B. Oates and Charles J. Errico, *Portrait of America*, Volume 1, Ninth Edition. Boston: Houghton Mifflin, 2007).

Friend, Craig Thompson. "Liberty is Pioneering: An American Birthright." *OAH Magazine of History* (May 2005): 16-20.

Howe, Daniel Walker. *What Hath God Wrought: The Transformation of America, 1815-1840*. New York: Oxford University Press, 2007.

Larson, John Lauritz. "The Market Revolution in Early America: An Introduction." OAH *Magazine of History* 19 (May 2005): 4-7.

Rilling, Donna J. "Liberty is Innovation: Sources of Energy and Enterprise." *OAH Magazine of History* (May 2005): 12-15.

Rockman, Seth "Liberty is Land and Slaves: The Great Contradiction." *OAH Magazine of History* (May 2005): 8-11.

Rockwell, Stephen J. *Indian Affairs and the Administrative State in the Nineteenth Century*. Cambridge: Cambridge University Press, 2010.

Tucker, Barbara M. "Liberty is Exploitation: The Force of Tradition in Early Manufacturing." *OAH Magazine of History* (May 2005): 21-24.

Wood, Gordon S. *Empire of Liberty: A History of the Early Republic, 1789-1815*. New York: Oxford University Press, 2009.

Yaeger, Dan. "Francis Cabot Lowell: Brief Life of an American Entrepreneur: 1775-1817." *Harvard Magazine*, (September 2010). http://harvardmagazine.com/2010/09/vita-francis-cabot-lowell.

Digital History. http://www.digitalhistory.uh.edu/.

PBS.org. The War of 1812. http://www.pbs.org/wned/war-of-1812/essays/naval-battleships/.

The Library of Congress. http://www.loc.gov/index.html.

Eli Whitney Museum and Workshop. http://www.eliwhitney.org.

Lowell Mill Girl. Tsongas Industrial History Center and Center for Lowell History. http://www.uml.edu/tsongas/bringing-history-home/page_00/index.htm.

U. S. Navy. USS Constitution. http://www.history.navy.mil/ussconstitution/history.html.

Dan Yaeger. Francis Cabot Lowell. Harvard Magazine. http://harvardmagazine.com/2010/09/vita-francis-cabot-lowell.

11.10 END NOTES

1 West Point. *A Brief History of West Point*. http://www.usma.edu/wphistory/SitePages/Home.aspx.

2 Northwest Ordinance (1787), http://www.ourdocuments.gov/doc.php?flash=true&doc=8.

3 Stephen J. Rockwell, *Indian Affairs and the Administrative State in the Nineteenth Century* (Cambridge: Cambridge University Press, 2010), 88.

4 Catherine Lavender. *President Thomas Jefferson's Instructionsto Captain Meriwether Lewis (June 20, 1803) http://www.library.csi.cuny.edu/dept/history/lavender/jefflett.html.*

5 John Lauritz Larson, "The Market Revolution in Early America: An Introduction," OAH *Magazine of History* 19 (May 2005): 4.

6 Larson, "The Market Revolution in Early America: An Introduction," 5.

7 Larson, "The Market Revolution in Early America: An Introduction," 5. For more information, see Craig Thompson Friend, "Liberty is Pioneering: An American Birthright," *OAH Magazine of History* (May 2005): 16-20; Donna J. Rilling, "Liberty is Innovation: Sources of Energy and Enterprise," *OAH Magazine of History* (May 2005): 12-15; Barbara M. Tucker, "Liberty is Exploitation: The Force of Tradition in Early Manufacturing," *OAH Magazine of History* (May 2005): 21-24; Seth Rockman, "Liberty is Land and Slaves: The Great Contradiction," *OAH Magazine of History* (May 2005): 8-11.

8 Daniel Walker Howe, *What Hath God Wrought: The Transformation of America, 1815-1840* (New York: Oxford University Press, 2007), 535-536.

9 American Social History Project, *Who Built America? Working People and the Nation's Economy, Politics, Culture and Society*, Volume 1 (New York: Pantheon Books, 1989), 224.

10 Howe, *What Hath God Wrought*, 213-217; Peter L. Bernstein, "The Erie Canal: The Waterway That Shaped a Great Nation," in Stephen B. Oates and Charles J. Errico, *Portrait of America*, Volume 1, 9/e (Boston: Houghton Mifflin, 2007), 244-250.

11 The Factory." Eli Whitney Museum and Workshop, September 8, 2012, http://www.eliwhitney.org/new/museum/about-eli-whitney/factory; Howe, *What Hath God Wrought*, 532-534.

12 Howe, *What Hath God Wrought*, 534-535; Rilling, "Liberty is Innovation," 13-14.

13 Howe, *What Hath God Wrought*, 128.

14 Gordon S. Wood, *Empire of Liberty: A History of the Early Republic, 1789-1815* (New York: Oxford University Press, 2009), 702-703.

15 Howe, *What Hath God Wrought*, 132-133.

16 American Social History Project, *Who Built America*, 252-254; Howe, *What Hath God Wrought*, 133-134; "Factory Tracts. Factory Life as it Is. By an Operative," *History Matters*, George Mason University, October 20, 2012, http://historymatters.gmu.edu/d/6217.

ANSWER KEY FOR CHAPTER ELEVEN: THE EARLY REPUBLIC

Check your answers to the questions in the Before You Move On Sections for this chapter.

Correct answers are **BOLDED**

Section 11.2.8 - p410

1. Jefferson believed in Big Government.
    a. True
    B. FALSE

2. Acquisition of land was the most important motivating factor in the formulation of early U.S. Indian policy.
    A. TRUE
    b. False

3. Jefferson's efforts to use economic pressure to solve the situation with Britain and France were successful.
    a. True
    B. FALSE

4. Lewis and Clark found the Northwest Passage.
    a. True
    B. FALSE

5. The Louisiana Purchase doubled the territory of the United States.
    A. TRUE
    b. False

6. Jefferson's second term was as successful as his first.
    a. True
    B. FALSE

Section 11.3.2 - p420

1. Madison was much better at finding a peaceful solution for the problems with the British and French than Jefferson.
    a. True
    B. FALSE

2. Madison was enthusiastic about declaring war on the British.
    a. True
    B. FALSE

3. The British Navy was the greatest in the world in 1812.
    A. TRUE
    b. False

4. Andrew Jackson led the Americans at the Battle of New Orleans.
    A. TRUE
    b. False

Section 11.4.3 - p425

1. The market revolution brought many social and economic changes to the United States.
    A. TRUE
    b. False

2. Eli Whitney created the Cotton Gin.
    A. TRUE
    b. False

3. Short staple cotton was preferred to long staple prior to the invention of the cotton gin.
    A. TRUE
    b. False

4. Francis Cabot Lowell built the first integrated textile mill in New England.
    A. TRUE
    b. False

Chapter Twelve: Jacksonian America (1815-1840)

Contents

Chapter Twelve: Jacksonian America (1815-1840)

12.1 INTRODUCTION

After the War of 1812, a number of significant transformations took place in the United States. Cities became the center of commerce and manufacturing in order to meet the demand for finished goods from the nation's ever-increasing population. Simultaneously, the countryside became the source for raw materials, launching calls for territorial expansion. The market revolution wove local life together with regional, national, and international developments at a time when American men became more politically active. Between 1816 and 1828, most states stopped tying the right to vote to property ownership. Therefore, the number of white men voting more than doubled. The framers' vision of a republic led by enlightened elites faded from view as politicians embraced a democracy guided by the will of the people expressed in popular elections.

Many leading politicians sought to deal with deficiencies in the nation's financial and transportation systems exposed by the war. During the Era of Good Feelings, which coincided with James Monroe's presidency, a new generation of leaders such as John C. Calhoun, Henry Clay, and Daniel Webster committed themselves to a program of nationally-minded growth to further the market revolution. However, a number of tensions in American society emerged to undermine their programs and the unity of the period. Economic, population, and territorial growth resulted in much change; these changes prompted public debates over tariffs, banking, internal improvements, the extension of slavery, and Indian removal. Most Americans supported continued growth, but they differed on the best means to achieve that growth.

Their debates laid the groundwork for the emergence of new political parties in the Age of the Common Man, which coincided with Andrew Jackson's presidency. As Americans divided over the president's policies, the second party system emerged to replace the first party system. The Democrats supported Jackson's views on the relationship between the people and their government. They believed the government should reflect the will of the majority and should work to promote the interests of the common citizen. The Whigs preferred the nationalist tendencies of the postwar years because they thought the government played an important role in economic growth. By the early 1840s, most Americans recognized how much the United States had changed economically and socially since the days of the Revolution, and those changes affected their political outlook.

Learning Outcomes

After completing this chapter, you should be able to:

- Describe and analyze the factors that contributed to the Era of Good Feelings, especially the nationalist tendencies of the government and the sectional tensions those tendencies caused.
- Explain Andrew Jackson's democratic vision and analyze the role Jacksonian Democracy played on public policy debates in the 1830s.

- Describe the reasons behind the collapse of the first party system and analyze the factors that led to the development of the second party system.
- Explain and evaluate the causes of the Panic of 1819, the Missouri Compromise, Indian Removal, the Nullification Crisis, the Bank War, and the Panic of 1837.

12.2 THE ERA OF GOOD FEELINGS

Marking the end of the War of 1812, The Treaty of Ghent ushered in an era of heightened nationalism in the United States. Patriotic sentiments ran high as Americans delighted in their "victory" over the British and looked for ways to make their nation even stronger. People all over the country celebrated Virginian James Monroe's election to the presidency in 1816. Meanwhile, Monroe struck an optimistic tone in his first inaugural address, noting the "present happy condition of the United States" and "the happy Government under which we live."[1] To further promote the happy condition, he launched a goodwill tour to mend the regional divisions that had grown during the war since the New Englanders never really supported the war. In the postwar euphoria, however, the Republican president even received a warm reception in the old Federalist stronghold of Boston in 1817, prompting a local newspaper to comment on the emergence of an "era of good feelings." Given his popularity, it came as no surprise to most voters when Monroe won nearly unanimous reelection in 1820.

James Monroe, like many other leaders in the nation's early years, opposed the development of political parties and believed the nation's elite should govern the country. They felt the elites better understood what could make the country successful over time, and they could mediate the will of the people. Therefore, Monroe worked to eliminate party politics during his two terms in office. After the ill-timed Hartford Convention in 1814, where delegates from several England states met to draft several Constitutional amendments to weaken the power of the southern states, the Federalist Party faded from the political scene. In the Era of Good Feelings, only the newly-christened National Republicans remained. Within this one-party system, Federalists like John Quincy Adams and Republicans like John C. Calhoun and Henry Clay worked to promote a stronger, self-sufficient United States. In the end, however, James Monroe found it as difficult to avoid factionalism as George Washington had in the 1790s. Two major events—the Panic of 1819 and the Missouri Compromise—undermined National Republican unity and paved the way for Andrew Jackson to become a major figure in American life.

Figure 12.1 James Monroe | People all over the country celebrated Virginian James Monroe's election to the presidency in 1816. During his presidency, Monroe worked to eliminate party politics.

Artist: Gilbert Stuart
Source: National Portrait Gallery

12.2.1 Promoting a Nationalist Vision

Even before James Monroe ascended to the presidency, nationally-minded leaders began to think about ways to improve the three sectors of the American economy: agriculture, commerce, and manufacturing. During the War of 1812, the lack of both a national bank to help secure credit to finance the war and a functioning nationwide transportation network to help move troops and goods hindered the effort to defend the country from British attacks. Realizing the potential of the budding market revolution and the interconnectedness of the nation's postwar economy, a majority of Congress accepted a larger role for the federal government in economic matters. At the same time, the Supreme Court deemed much of the government's expansion as wholly in line with the Constitution. Finally, the diplomatic corps worked after 1817 to foster trade, to support territorial expansion, and to increase American influence over other countries in the Western Hemisphere.[2]

Congressional Nationalism

In 1816, while James Madison was still president, Congress eagerly began to resurrect much of Alexander Hamilton's economic vision for the country and to adapt it to meet the needs of a growing nation. Led by Henry Clay of Kentucky in the Senate and John C. Calhoun of South Carolina in the House of Representatives, Congress considered proposals for a national bank, a protective tariff, and internal improvements. Supporters believed the program, which Clay labeled the "American System" in 1824, would benefit all regions of the country. The bank would create a more stable currency system by checking the money and credit supply. The tariff would protect nascent American factories from foreign competition, make the nation less dependent on foreign trade, and raise additional revenue for the government. Finally, internal improvements would allow raw materials and finished goods to move around the country at a faster pace.

To many nationally-minded leaders, addressing the banking issue was of prime importance because the war and its aftermath suggested the potential problems of unregulated currency. As the market revolution took hold, the practice of bartering tapered off. Banks allowed people to purchase goods and services with their notes as opposed to the often cumbersome gold or silver coins (i.e., specie). In 1811 Congress refused to recharter the Bank of the United States, claiming it exceeded what was a necessary power of the government. After the demise of the national bank, the number of state banks began to rise precipitously.

During the war, financial problems pushed most state banks to suspend specie payments (meaning note holders could not exchange paper currency for its equivalent in coin). Since there was no expectation of convertibility, banks issued currency well in excess of the amount of specie they possessed. It became increasingly difficult to determine the real value of the currency in circulation; furthermore, state banks showed no indication they planned to resume specie payments after 1815. Many people feared the speculative bubble would burst; to those concerned, the best way to prevent an economic downturn was to create a new national bank.

James Madison sent a message to Congress requesting it consider a proposal for a national bank in 1816. Five years before, questions about the constitutionality of such a venture derailed the recharter effort, but after the War of 1812, few people mentioned such considerations in the debate about the new bank because the fight with the British convinced many American leaders of the necessity of supporting economic development. Members voted to charter the Second Bank of the United States (the "BUS" or the "bank") for a period of twenty years. Under the terms of the charter, the government would deposit government funds in the bank, accept the bank's notes as payment for government transactions, and buy one-fifth of the bank's stock. The bank, a private corporation, agreed to transfer Treasury funds without charge, to allow the federal government to appoint five of the bank's twenty-five directors, and to pay the government a fee of $1.5 million.[3] The BUS could open branches anywhere it saw fit; therefore, its notes became the only currency accepted all over the country. It could also demand the state bank notes it accepted be redeemable in specie, a policy which could help curb inflation.

After settling the banking question, John C. Calhoun, with the backing of Henry Clay, pushed Congress to consider implementing an openly protective tariff (import tax). Calhoun and Clay saw the tariff as having two functions: protecting manufacturers from foreign competition by making it cost-prohibitive for consumers to buy anything other than American made goods and providing the government the revenue necessary to fund internal improvements.[4] The potential for uneven economic benefits had, in previous years, prevented Congress from enacting the tariff. Opponents of the tariff maintained that while the commercial sector would benefit from protection, the agriculture sector would suffer. Protected industries would see their profits increase, while farmers would find it more difficult to sell raw materials on the international market and more expensive to purchase goods in an uncompetitive market. Thus, a small segment of the American population would gain at the expense of the rest of the population.

Although Calhoun and Clay worried about the reaction of frontier farmers who traditionally opposed federal taxes, they persevered in their effort to increase the tariff rate. They convinced enough members of both chambers to support the Tariff of 1816, which set the rate at 20 percent for most goods and 25 percent for textiles. As with the bank, the war provided the impetus for this measure. With foreign trade virtually cut off by the British blockade, it became apparent to most Americans that some measure of self-sufficiency in manufactured goods was important. Even delegates in western and southern states, usually hostile to tariffs, could see the connection between manufacturing and commercialized agriculture.

Figure 12.2 Second Bank of the United States | In 1816, Congress chartered the Second Bank of the United States for a period of twenty-five years in an attempt to further their nationalist vision for the country. William Strickland designed the headquarters of the BUS in Philadelphia.

Author: Independence National Historical Park Collection
Source: Wikimedia Commons

Finally, Congress took up the question of internal improvements—by far the most controversial issue on the nationalist's agenda. Federal support for roads, canals, and other transportation improvements would help develop the nation's economic capacity by cutting the costs and time of shipping raw materials to markets and manufactured goods to consumers. Moreover, rising revenues from federal land sales and tariffs provided the government surplus revenue to fund such ventures. In late 1816, Calhoun and Clay supported the Bonus Bill, designed to use the revenue from the Second National Bank to fund internal improvements. The question of the constitutionality of the measure, specifically that it might not be a necessary function of the government, colored the debate.[5]

While National Republican leaders secured enough votes to pass the bill, James Madison vetoed it shortly before leaving office. Although Madison had bent his strict constructionist views to support the bank, he told Calhoun he would not do the same for internal improvements. The outgoing president suggested introducing a constitutional amendment that would give the government the power to fund improvements. Once in office, James Monroe did encourage Congress to adopt an amendment for funding roads and canals. However, Henry Clay, convinced that Congress already had the power to fund improvements, prevented the consideration of an amendment. Thus, internal improvements became the purview of the state governments. Some wholly embraced the development of a transportation network, while others seemed reluctant to commit funds to such projects in the 1820s and 1830s.

Judicial Nationalism

In 1801, John Adams (in one of his final acts as president) appointed John Marshall, his fellow Federalist, to head the nation's top court; he hoped to protect his party's nationalist agenda after he left office. During the Jefferson and Madison years, the Supreme Court worked to establish itself as the authority over constitutional matters at the federal level in *Marbury v. Madison* (1803) and at the state level in *Fletcher v. Peck* (1810). However, the chief justice thought the time was not right to decide major constitutional questions on the "necessary and proper" clause as it related to government support for economic development. Only in the Era of Good Feelings did Marshall and the associate justices issue a series of decisions strengthening the role of the federal government and bolstering the turn toward manufacturing and commercial agriculture.

Figure 12.3 John Marshall | Shortly before leaving office in 1801, John Adams appointed John Marshall to serve as Chief Justice of the Supreme Court in an attempt to preserve some of the Federalist agenda once Thomas Jefferson became president. This image by Saint-Mémin depicts Marshall as he looked in 1808.

Artist: Charles Balthazar Julien Fevret de Saint-Mémin
Source: Library of Congress

The first major decision addressing these issues, *Dartmouth College v. Woodward* (1819), related to the sanctity of contracts. During the colonial era, Dartmouth received a royal charter to conduct its business in New Hampshire; however, in 1816 the state legislature passed a law to convert the private college into a public university by granting the governor the right to appoint a new Board of Trustees. After the state implemented the change, the old trustees sought to reverse the statute. Their case made it to the Supreme Court. Daniel Webster, an alumnus of Dartmouth, made an impassioned plea to the justices about how the college, like all corporations, should be protected from shifts in the public mood. The majority opinion in favor of the college suggested that the government could not modify (or regulate) corporate charters or other contracts once issued without the consent of both parties.

The second major decision, *McCulloch v. Maryland* (1819), related to the constitutionality of the Second Bank of the United States. The state of Maryland decided to tax the bank at a high rate in an effort to give preference to state chartered banks. The BUS refused to pay, prompting the state to file a suit in federal court in an effort to collect the taxes. The Marshall Court sided with the bank, not with the state. Their decision noted "that the act to incorporate the Bank of the United States is a law made in pursuance of the constitution, and is a part of the supreme law of the land." Moreover, the justices indicated a state did not have the power to impede the legitimate actions of the federal government.[6] In making its decision, the Supreme Court finally weighed in on the "necessary and proper" clause by supporting the concept of implied powers.

The third major decision, *Gibbons v. Ogden* (1824), related to the interstate commerce. After Robert Fulton invented the steamboat in 1807, New York state legislature granted Fulton and Robert Livingston exclusive control over ferry traffic on the Hudson River for twenty years. As such, they had the right to grant permits to any ferry operator they chose. They granted a permit to Thomas Gibbons but not to Adam Ogden to transport passengers and freight across the river. Thus, Ogden sued Gibbons to challenge his monopoly of the ferry traffic. The case eventually made its way to the Supreme Court because it involved traffic going from New York to New Jersey. The Marshall Court deemed the New York monopoly law "repugnant" to the Constitution since the power to regulate commerce between two or more states went to Congress, not the individual states.[7]

Collectively, these three decisions suggested the federal government had a rightful role to play in promoting economic development. *Dartmouth College v. Woodward* suggested the government could not legitimately regulate private businesses, which encouraged free enterprise in the United States. *McCulloch v. Maryland* and *Gibbons v. Ogden* supported a broad interpretation of the federal government's power in relation to the states.

Diplomatic Nationalism

While Congress and the Supreme Court promoted economic development, John Quincy Adams, James Monroe's secretary of state, sought to formulate an imperial rhetoric for the United States that fit with the president's nationalism. Skilled in diplomacy during his father's administration, Adams believed in the unique virtue of the United States, in the necessity of remaking the world in the American image, and in the nation's God-given right to expand. Based on his beliefs, the secretary of state (with the president's blessing) sought to promote foreign trade, to pursue continental expansion, and to lessen the influence of European powers in Latin America.[8]

In the wake of the War of 1812, both Great Britain and the United States sought ways to improve their relationship, largely because the war settled none of their differences. The

British reached out to the Americans to address issues not resolved in the Treaty of Ghent; their effort led to several agreements that brought long-term peace between the two nations. The Rush-Bagot Agreement of 1817 demilitarized the Great Lakes region; the Congress of 1818 provided for American fishing rights off the coast of Canada, restricted British travel on the Mississippi River, ended British trade with the Indians in the Louisiana Purchase, and set the boundary between the United States and Canada at the Rocky Mountains. The Anglo-American rapprochement also tacitly gave American shippers the protection of the British Navy in the Atlantic. Thus, the Americans could spend less on their own navy and devote those resources to other projects. The agreements improved foreign trade and helped both nations improve their economic health.

The American government had long wanted to acquire Spanish Florida (a haven for runaway slaves), and members of the Monroe administration were no different. During the War of 1812, the Americans had seized West Florida (the panhandle). After the war, Andrew Jackson—in his attempt to quell the Indians in the Southeast—took American forces into Spanish-controlled East Florida under dubious circumstances. Rather than apologize for Jackson's violation of Spanish territorial integrity, Adams used the incident to put pressure on the Spanish foreign minister Don Luis de Onís to return to the negotiating table. In 1819, with the Adams-Onís Treaty, the United States took control of Florida in

Figure 12.4 Adams-Onís Treaty Map | This treaty, concluded in 1819, set the border between the United States and New Spain and gave the United States complete control over Florida.

Author: Bill Rankin

exchange for $5 million. Spain relinquished its claim to Oregon, and the United States renounced, at least temporarily, its claim to Texas. The treaty helped pave the way for further expansion across the continent.

Spain's reluctance to complete an agreement with the United States over Florida stemmed from its fear of losing control over its entire New World Empire. Since the turn of the century, a series of revolutions had shaken Latin America. The United States seemed both sympathetic to these revolutions and concerned about the ability of the new republics to maintain their independence. As a show of support, the Americans opted to recognize the revolting governments as a means to undercut European influence, to assist commerce, and to nominally encourage the growth of republicanism.[9] By the early 1820s, American leaders feared the possibility that even if Spain could not regain its hegemony, other European powers might try to expand their influence in the Western Hemisphere.

Initially, Monroe considered issuing a joint declaration with the British pledging to protect the fledgling governments in Latin America. However, Adams convinced him that the United States should chart its own course. In his annual message to Congress in 1823, the president outlined the Monroe Doctrine. Adams, who drafted the statement, believed the Americans had to make a forceful statement suggesting that future European colonization would not be welcome in the Western Hemisphere. Moreover, since American and European political systems were different, neither side should meddle in the affairs of the other.[10] Most Americans praised the doctrine for its assertion that the United States was unique among nations. Few people realized their government would have found it difficult to back up the Monroe Doctrine had the Europeans challenged its provisions.

12.2.2 The Retreat from Nationalist Tendencies

During the Era of Good Feelings there was only one political party; however, differences of opinion on the role of the federal government never completely disappeared. Most national leaders believed the government should serve the interests of the common good, but they disagreed on what exactly the common good meant. The Republicans had never spoken with one voice. Moderates tended to support the same programs to promote commercial development as the Federalists. Radicals, or Old Republicans, opposed any talk of loose construction, preferring a very limited federal government. By 1820, an economic crisis and a debate on slavery in the territories underscored existing differences within the National Republican coalition.[11]

Panic of 1819

The market revolution created a remarkable amount of economic growth in the United States as commodity prices rose after the war. Simultaneously, inflation and speculation also increased. State banks issued notes in excess of their reserves and made somewhat risky loans. When Congress chartered the Second Bank of the United States, supporters hoped its policies would lead to deflation. The bank's Board of Directors, like most Americans during this era, found the opportunity to make money too appealing. Rather than working to limit the amount of money in circulation, their policies only led to more inflation and speculation. Furthermore, Congress had hoped to make the United States more self-sufficient through the bank and the tariff. To some extent, those measures achieved their goal, but the American economy was never completely divorced from the European economy. If anything, the market revolution made the American business cycle more sensitive to the world market.[12]

After 1815, rising prices had encouraged the inflation and speculation, but most financial experts realized any excessive demand for specie could destabilize the entire credit system. In late 1818, the Second Bank of the United States shifted from an inflationary policy to a deflationary policy to stave off a drop in their specie reserves. It began to demand repayment of outstanding loans, and it required state banks to convert their notes held by the BUS to specie. The BUS clearly acted to save itself. In the process, it brought ruin to numerous state banks and, in turn, the American people.[13] International developments compounded the American credit problems. The American speculative boom had rested on the expectation that commodity prices would continue to rise, but they began a steep decline in 1819 as Europe recovered from the Napoleonic Wars, lessening their need for American foodstuffs. Moreover, pent-up European demand for cotton had caused the price to rise after 1815. English manufacturers then began to look for a cheaper source from which to obtain raw cotton, causing a collapse in the American market. Finally, European nations adopted the gold standard, leading to a drain on world gold reserves.[14] The combined domestic and international problems caused the Panic of 1819 and a subsequent depression in the United States.

During the panic, American cities faced the direst circumstances, but farmers far from commercial centers also felt the strain. Around 500,000 urban residents could not find work. For example, in Philadelphia approximately 75 percent of workers remained idle. The number of paupers rose dramatically as did the numbers of debtors imprisoned for nonpayment. People who owned their own homes faced foreclosures, and those who did not own homes stopped believing they someday could. Rural landowners, even those considered well off, struggled to pay back their debts when banks called in their loans. For example, in Nashville the number of reported bankruptcies reached 500 in 1819 alone.[15] Throughout the crisis, the BUS avidly pushed its debtors to repay their outstanding loans, leading to more business failures, more property seizures, and more unemployment. Across the nation, popular protest became common. Some debtors called for "stay laws" to provide more time to pay back their creditors. Others sought the abolition of debtor's prisons. Finally, many voters sought to reduce state and federal expenditures in order to cut the people's tax burden. It would take several years for the economy to recover, and those harmed by their creditors never lost their suspicion of financial institutions, which they thought did more damage than good for the American economy.

Missouri Compromise

In the years after the Revolutionary War, states in the North, inspired by the egalitarian sentiments of the fight for independence, began to rethink the merits of bound labor. By the mid-1780s, all northern states had ended slavery or had made plans to end slavery in their states. At the same time, the Northwest Ordinance of 1787 prohibited slavery in the territories north of the Ohio River. Some northerners thought the South would turn away from slavery as well. Manumission (freeing slaves on an individual basis) was not unheard of in the years immediately following the revolution. However, after the invention of the cotton gin, most southern states committed themselves to maintaining slavery. Moreover, as the nation expanded westward, so too did slavery, especially in areas where cotton grew well. Kentucky, Tennessee, Alabama, Mississippi, and Louisiana all joined the union as slave states. Through the years, the country maintained a balance of slave and free states in the Senate by chance more than anything else; however, the free states had an advantage in the House of Representatives because more people lived in the North than the South.

In 1819, the sectional balance nearly came unhinged when Missouri petitioned to become the first state carved out of the unorganized portions of the Louisiana Purchase. As a territory, Missouri had allowed slavery and would continue to do so as a state. Amidst concerns about an uneven balance in the Senate, James Tallmadge—an anti-slavery representative from New York—introduced a measure designed to prohibit slavery in Missouri and provide for the gradual emancipation of the 10,000 slaves living there. While Tallmadge feared the expansion of slavery, most members of Congress expressed more concern about the balance of power in the national government. Rufus King, in support of the Tallmadge Amendment, attacked the morality of slavery, suggesting laws protecting slavery went against the "law of God." However, Old Republicans distrusted the motives of the Old Federalists who seemed to want to use the debate to revive their party. King and other former Federalists had long opposed the boost in representation the slave states received because of the "three-fifths" rule allowed them to count slaves toward their total population. Forcing Missourians to free their slaves would cut southern political power.[16] Ultimately, the House opposed statehood for Missouri unless accompanied by the Tallmadge Amendment, while the Senate supported it. As the end of the congressional session approached in March, no decision had been made.

Led by Speaker of the House Henry Clay, nationally-minded leaders hoping to avoid disunion worked toward an agreement as the new Congress gathered in December. The resulting Missouri Compromise (Compromise of 1820) brought Missouri in as a slave state and Maine in as a free state, since Maine had petitioned for independent statehood shortly after Missouri. To soothe northern concerns about the expansion of slavery, the compromise also included the Thomas Proviso (named for Jesse Thomas of Illinois) that banned slavery north of the southern boundary of Missouri, the 36°30' line, for the rest of the land within the Louisiana Purchase.

Both sides believed they managed to divert a major crisis. Southerners, however, thought they had won a major victory with the Missouri Compromise. Although the vast northern regions of the Louisiana Purchase would bar slavery, most people assumed no one would settle in the "Great American Desert." From his home in Virginia, however, Thomas Jefferson worried about the compromise. In a letter to John Holmes, the former president predicted the growing divisions on the question of slavery might be "the knell of the Union" because "the angry passions of men, will never be obliterated; and every new irritation will mark it deeper and deeper."[17]

The Corrupt Bargain

By James Monroe's second term, divisions about economic development and the expansion of slavery were setting the stage for the presidential election of 1824. Meanwhile, Martin Van Buren, an upstate New York lawyer and politician, took a seat in the United States Senate in 1821. As a senator, he hoped to develop a strong political party to promote a limited government. In an age where more white men gained the right to vote because many states abandoned property qualifications for voting, he quickly realized the role public opinion played in the political system. While the nation's founders seemed to think political parties served no lasting purpose, Van Buren saw them as a necessary function of government and as a means to draw power away from privileged insiders. Seeking out other likeminded politicians, he began to dwell on how to use the election in 1824 to build a solid political organization committed to Jeffersonian principles such as a strict construction.

Most people expected James Monroe would support John Quincy Adams, his secretary of state and son of a former president, for president in 1824. However, Monroe said nothing about his choice of a successor, which left Van Buren control over the Congressional Caucus and the party's nominee. At Van Buren's behest, the National Republicans nominated William H. Crawford, the secretary of treasury from Georgia, known for his support of states' rights. To Van Buren, Crawford's southern roots could help build a regionally balanced political party. Fearing their constituents more than Van Buren, many Republicans failed to show up for the caucus vote. Therefore, more candidates entered the race, including John Quincy Adams, Henry Clay, and Andrew Jackson. Each candidate appealed to voters in their home region, but it seemed unclear if any could develop nationwide support. John C. Calhoun also considered running, but he opted to be the only nominee for vice president.

In many ways, the election of 1824 was the battle of the favorite son candidates. Adams polled well in New England, Crawford and Jackson split the South, and Clay and Jackson split the West. Jackson led in the popular (42 percent) and Electoral College (38 percent) votes, but he did not have the needed majority in the Electoral College. Per the Constitution, the House of Representatives would choose from the top three candidates—Jackson, Adams, and Crawford. Jackson assumed the House would choose him; he did not expect that Clay, the Speaker of the House, would actively work to deny him the presidency. Clay did not think Jackson had the necessary qualifications to be president. On the other hand, Adams and Clay shared many of the same principles on the government's role in economic development. In the end, Adams won thirteen states to Jackson's seven.

Just days after the voting in the House, Adams announced Clay was to serve as his secretary of state. What seemed normal politics to Adams and Clay seemed to the defeated Jackson a sure sign the two men had conspired to steal the presidency. Not one to be slighted easily, Jackson frequently complained about the "corrupt bargain." While little evidence surfaced to suggest Clay had in fact made a blatant deal with Adams by giving his support in the House vote for a position in the cabinet, the prevailing rumors made it quite difficult for Adams to govern effectively.[18] Once in office, Adams set out to complete the National Republic agenda, which only confirmed the opposition's suspicions.

In his first message to Congress, the new president outlined a grandiose plan for national development, including support for roads, canals, a national university, and a national astronomical observatory, among others. He also suggested Congress support such programs for the "common good" regardless of what their constituents thought best.[19] Most members of Congress found Adams slightly audacious for even making the proposal, as it seemed contrary to what the people wanted. In the recent election, more voters chose Jackson and Crawford with their calls for a smaller government than Adams or Clay with their calls for a larger government. Adams lacked the political skill to implement much of his program. As a result, Congress never acted on any of his proposals.

12.2.3 Before You Move On...

Key Concepts

After the War of 1812, patriotic feelings ran high in the United States, leading to the emergence of the Era of Good Feelings. During this time of one-party rule, American leaders worked to promote a stronger, self-sufficient United States. Congress chartered the Second Bank of the United States and approved a protective tariff. The bank created a more stable currency system by checking the money and credit supply. The tariff protected American factories from foreign competition, raised additional revenue for the government, and theoretically made the nation less dependent on foreign trade. The Supreme Court issued a series of decisions designed to enhance the power of the federal government and support economic development. These decisions, *Dartmouth College v. Woodward*, *McCulloch v. Maryland*, and *Gibbons v. Ogden*, supported a broad interpretation of the federal government's role in relation to the states and to economic development. Finally, James Monroe and John Quincy Adams developed foreign policy that protected American rights in the Western Hemisphere, especially with the Monroe Doctrine. Although political divisions faded from view, the president could not eliminate differences of opinion about the role of government. The Panic of 1819, the Missouri Compromise, and the "corrupt bargain" all suggested that a new era of partisan politics would soon emerge because economic, social, and political concerns continued to divide the American people. The expansion of democratic sentiment helped bring Andrew Jackson to the forefront of those developments.

Test Yourself

1. Which of the following did not represent the government's nationalist tendencies in the Era of Good Feelings?

   a. Second Bank of the United States

   b. Tallmadge Amendment

   c. Tariff of 1816

   d. *Gibbons v. Ogden*

2. The Panic of 1819 increased the American people's faith in the Second Bank of the United States.

a. True

b. False

3. As a result of the "corrupt bargain,"

a. Henry Clay's plans for economic development were defeated.

b. John Quincy Adams became president.

c. the protective tariff rate increased.

d. Congress approved the Monroe Doctrine.

See page 476 for answers

12.3 THE AGE OF THE COMMON MAN

The power of Andrew Jackson's personality stamped his name indelibly on American history during the 1830s. Then and later, Jackson received credit for many of the trends that emerged during this period; however, it is more accurate to say that he was a manifestation of the social and cultural currents of the time. He was a war hero, an Indian fighter, and in the minds of many, a representative of the common man—particularly since he was the first American president not born to an elite family. When Jackson took office, he sought to assert the power of the executive branch. As such, he used presidential powers such as patronage and the veto to promote his vision for the nation, a trend that would help define the modern presidency in the early twentieth century. On the major issues of the day—Indian removal, nullification, and the bank—Jackson vowed not only to win the battles but destroy his political enemies. Opposition to Jackson's vision would eventually lead to the emergence of the second party system.

The extension of democracy to nearly all white men characterized the Age of the Common Man, sometimes called the Age of Jackson. By the late 1820s, almost all adult white men had gained the right to vote, and more government positions became elective rather than appointive. The very image of the "common man" came to be glorified. The ideal of equality among white males became a pervasive theme, even if it did not reflect social and economic realities, since the disparity of wealth increased from 1815 to 1840. Furthermore, the era saw the mass removal of Indians from their homelands and increasing sectional tensions over slavery. These developments called into question the meaning of democracy for minorities. Nevertheless, for most white Americans, life seemed relatively good; therefore, few people questioned the political, social, and economic inequality that emerged in the 1830s.

12.3.1 The Emergence of Jacksonian Democracy

With the help of a growing number of political supporters, Andrew Jackson used the four years after his defeat in 1824 to build up his reputation with the people as a common man and to outline his vision for the nation. Since voters thought it unseemly for candidates to campaign for themselves, Jackson spent most of his time in Tennessee at his home, the Hermitage, carefully watching how his followers worked to develop broad support for his nomination. After William Crawford failed to win national support in 1824, Martin Van Buren switched his allegiance to Jackson. The New Yorker increasingly saw his own view on the importance of political parties match up with Jackson's view on a more limited government. Van Buren enlisted the support of John C. Calhoun (Adams's vice president) to woo southern voters. Calhoun, who was extremely politically ambitious, thought switching parties would improve the likelihood that someday he would become president. Next, Jackson targeted other voters alienated by the Adams's policies. Local Hickory Clubs—a reference to Jackson's nickname, Old Hickory—appeared all over the country to raise funds for the campaign and encourage people to vote. Meanwhile, partisan newspapers began praising Jackson's vision for the country. Politicians involved in the Jackson campaign hoped to reap the rewards of their loyalty; they fully expected to be the beneficiaries of the federal patronage system, sometimes called the spoils system by its opponents.[20]

Jackson's democratic vision was firmly rooted in his own triumph over humble beginnings, but it also reflected the ongoing changes in American life since the days of the fight for independence. In a series of private letters, which he fully expected to be published, Jackson outlined the problems facing the nation in the 1820s. His musings promoted a states' rights philosophy based on the will of the majority. In other words, Jackson believed that certain powers fell outside the scope of the federal government. Furthermore, national leaders should serve as stewards of what the majority of Americans indicated they wanted in state and national elections. Jackson saw conflict, not consensus, in American society—a conflict between the producers and the non-producers. He sought ways to refocus the federal government's actions to benefit farmers and laborers at the expense of the business community. For Jackson, the government's main purpose was to address problems of artificial inequality because it could do little about natural inequality. The former resulted when certain segments of the population sought to use the government for their own benefit at the expense of the majority; the latter stemmed from a person's innate abilities.[21]

As the Jackson camp busied itself preparing for the contest in 1828, Adams did very little to develop popular support. As president, he could have used federal patronage to develop loyalty; moreover, he could have pushed Congress to consider at least some of the measures he proposed in 1825. Meanwhile, politicians who shared his views on using the federal government to promote economic growth, including Henry Clay and Daniel Webster, tried to reach out to supporters through partisan newspapers and organizations. But overall, Adams's supporters seemed ineffective in presenting their candidate's vision to potential voters.

Although the two candidates presented different visions for the United States, those issues did not dominate the campaign. Questions about the candidates' fitness for office and rumors of scandal seemed more important to voters, but those concerns did take their cues from broader concerns about the nation's moral decline. Jackson's team focused on the allegedly-corrupt way in which Adams achieved the presidency. Furthermore, they painted the president as a monarchist bent on undermining the wave of democratic sentiment spreading across the country. They frequently indicated that because his father served as president, Adams clearly sought to establish an unelected dynasty. Finally, they called his morality into question. They implied he was a gambler who installed gaming tables in the White House at the public's expense. Moreover, they charged that while Adams served as the American minister to Russia he found a young American girl to satisfy the czar of Russia's sexual desires.[22] However, what Jackson's supporters accused Adams of was nothing compared to the charges leveled by Adams's team against Jackson.

Using his military exploits and past duels, Adams's followers suggested that Jackson would become a tyrant once in office. In turn, his actions would destroy the American democratic experiment. The papers also repeated rumors that Jackson was the mulatto son of a prostitute. The most flagrant accusations about Jackson centered on his marriage to Rachel Donelson in 1794. Rachel believed her estranged husband, Lewis Robards, filed for divorce. She and Jackson only found out after their wedding that he had not, and they had to re-exchange their vows two years later. In the hands of the partisan papers, Jackson became an adulterer who kidnapped Rachel from her husband and forced her to live in a licentious state.[23]

Throughout the campaign, Jackson's supporters found it easier to paint their candidate as a hero of the common man, as accusations about his lawlessness increased his standing

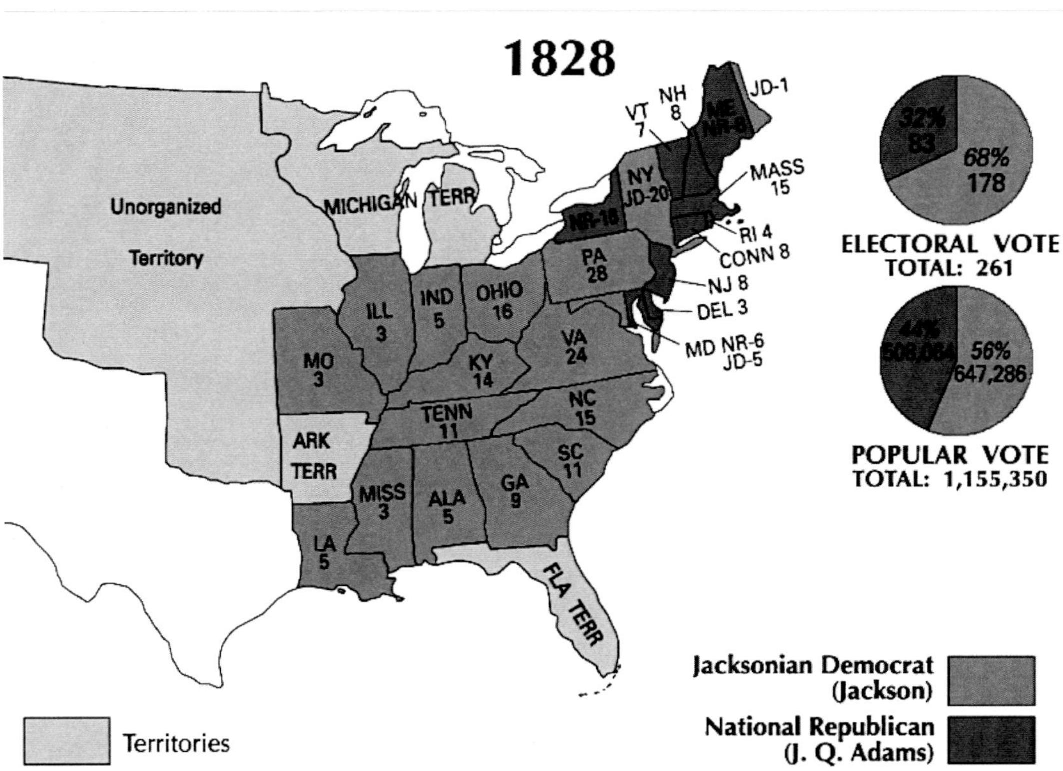

Figure 12.5 Presidential Election Map, 1828 | Andrew Jackson triumphed in the popular and Electoral College votes in 1828 because his supporters successfully portrayed him as a champion of the common man and a defender of states' rights.

Author: National Atlas of the United States
Source: Wikimedia Commons

with many voters. However, Adams's supporters could not overcome concerns that their candidate was an elitist. Jackson won a sweeping victory in the popular (56 percent) and the Electoral College (68 percent) votes. His commanding majority clearly came from widespread support among urban workers, small northern farmers, southern yeomen, and southern planters. The election also showed the concerns the nation's founders had about political factions for the most part had disappeared. Candidates for local, state, and national office increasingly depended on parties to build support and deliver votes.

12.3.2 Jackson in Office

Although Andrew Jackson expressed satisfaction with his victory, he arrived in Washington for his inauguration in deep mourning. In December, Rachel Jackson had travelled to Nashville to do some Christmas shopping where, for the first time, she read about the opposition's criticisms of her marriage. She fainted on the spot and died not long after. Mrs. Jackson had not been in good health before her trip, but none of Jackson's friends could convince him that his political opponents were not responsible for his beloved wife's death. In his younger years, the president-elect might have challenged those responsible to a duel. But in his advancing age, he vowed to demolish his enemies through the political system by destroying the American System.

In honor of their hero's ascension to the presidency, Jackson's supporters followed him to Washington. After taking the oath of office on the steps of the Capitol, Jackson gave a vague inaugural address promoting states' rights, pledging respect for the Constitution, and promising to correct the abuses of power by the privileged. Most people remembered the day not for what Jackson said about his plans for reform, but for the boisterous celebration of his well-wishers. Thousands of people (perhaps as many as 20,000) lined Pennsylvania Avenue. Jackson insisted on opening the presidential mansion, recently christened the White House, to the public for a reception. The numbers quickly overwhelmed the staff as they attempted to stop people from breaking the china and standing on the furniture. Jackson escaped the mayhem, and the staff finally restored order by moving the refreshments to the lawn. After the festivities, partisan papers commented on the events. Jackson's supporters saw it as a sign the new president truly represented the American people. His opponents saw it as an omen of the mayhem to come under Jackson's leadership.

Figure 12.6 Inaugural Festivities, 1833 | Jackson's supporters descended on the capitol city in March to celebrate their hero's victory. This print shows the crowd of well-wishers during the inaugural reception at the White House.

Artist: Robert Cruikshank
Source: Library of Congress

Andrew Jackson chose Martin Van Buren to become his secretary of state because the New Yorker had been so instrumental in building a coalition to support him. Van Buren then encouraged Jackson to make use of the federal patronage system not only to reward his loyal followers but to build support for his democratic agenda. At all levels of the civil service, the new administration began to fill posts with Jacksonians. Numerically speaking, Jackson's overall replacement rate was similar to Thomas Jefferson who had also used patronage to develop political support. Politics partly dictated Jackson's move to bring in loyal supporters. But to the new president, a regularly rotating civil service would ward against the abuses of power seen in the Federalist and National Republican years and prevent a permanent government.[24]

In time, Van Buren also became Jackson's most influential political adviser and likely successor, although during the early years of the administration he competed with Vice President John C. Calhoun for the president's ear. Philosophically, Calhoun began to move away from his support for a nationalist agenda by the late 1820s; he committed himself to promoting states' rights, something that Jackson and Van Buren also supported. However, each man understood the concept of states' rights slightly differently. Calhoun supported an extreme version of states' rights philosophy where states had the right to check power of the federal government. Van Buren, as a strict constructionist, believed the Constitution delegated some powers to the federal government and some powers to the states. In time, Jackson found his views matched those of Van Buren more than those of Calhoun. Politics aside, the Jackson administration would find itself mired in personal controversy, driving Jackson and Calhoun farther apart.[25]

In 1828, Jackson's close friend Senator John Eaton married Margaret ("Peggy") O'Neale Timberlake, the daughter of a Washington innkeeper, not long after her first husband, a naval officer, died. Rumors abounded that Peggy's dalliances with Eaton led John Timberlake to commit suicide. After the wedding, Jackson named Eaton as his choice for secretary of war because he wanted one close associate in the cabinet. Polite Washington society, including the vice president's wife, Floride Calhoun, recoiled at the idea they would have to invite the lowly Mrs. Eaton to their functions. Jackson saw the attacks on his friend as similar to the attacks on his own marriage. Moreover, Jackson firmly believed the Calhouns were responsible for the snubbing. Jackson, along with the help of Van Buren, did everything in his power to support the Eatons.

The issues surrounding the Eaton affair festered until 1831. At that point, the president decided to remove the members of his cabinet he perceived as loyal to Calhoun. To keep up appearances, Jackson also asked Eaton and Van Buren to resign, with the intention of shifting them to other positions in the government. In the coming years, Jackson relied less on the cabinet for advice and more on his political friends who did not serve in any official capacity, in what his opponents labeled the "Kitchen Cabinet."[26] Only after the cabinet shakeup did Andrew Jackson fully devote his attention to promoting his democratic agenda and addressing the major public policy issues of the day: Indian removal, the tariff, and the bank.

12.3.3 Indian Removal

The roots of Jackson's Indian removal policy stretched back to the Jeffersonian era. Jefferson had reasoned that too much land was a bad thing for Indians, as the abundance of land gave them no reason to become "civilized." Instead, they would continue to utilize the land in a way which white society considered inefficient, wasteful, and "uncivilized." To this end, his administration stressed a policy of assimilating native peoples into American ways of life. In particular, he sought to transform Indians into sedentary, intensive agriculturalists like the American yeoman farmer. Jefferson saw this policy as beneficial in two ways: first, it would “speed up” what he saw as a natural and inevitable process as Indian ways and beliefs gave way to American ones. Secondly, converting Indians to intensive agriculture would mean that thousands of acres across the east coast would be freed for white settlement.

Jackson came to the presidency as a renowned Indian fighter with knowledge of nations like the Cherokee and Creek. He quickly set the tone for his administration’s Indian policy, calling for all Indian groups living east of the Mississippi River to be moved west of the river. Civilization and progress, he argued, demanded that Indians be removed. At Jackson’s urging, Congress passed the Indian Removal Act of 1830 by a narrow margin, an indication of developing tensions between Whigs and Democrats in Congress. Theoretically, removal was supposed to be voluntary for native peoples, but in reality, tremendous pressure was applied to groups all over the east coast to remove. This was especially true in the South, where white Americans cast a keen eye to lands held by the Five Civilized Tribes: the Cherokee, Creek (Muskogee), Choctaw, Chickasaw, and Seminole.

Removal in the South

The Five Civilized Tribes were thus called because, in response to Jefferson’s policies, they had in many ways acculturated to American society. The Cherokee provide an excellent example of the ways in which the nations acculturated in the interests of survival. In 1827, the Cherokee adopted a government modeled on the American system. They adopted a written constitution which outlined a three-branch system of government including a principal chief, a two-house legislature, and an independent judiciary with a Supreme Court. Most Cherokee lived and dressed like the average American, and some converted to Christianity. Most Cherokee, moreover, became literate after the development of a written Cherokee syllabary; the nation published their own newspaper, *The Cherokee Phoenix* (ᏣᎳᎩ ᏧᎴᎯᏌᏅᎯ). The wealthiest Cherokee owned plantations and slaves and grew cotton. Like their American counterparts, the group developed and improved the land, building grist mills, saw mills, blacksmith shops, and tanning yards. By most standards and measures, the Cherokee had acculturated in all significant ways to an American way of life; instead of ensuring the survival of the group, however, it intensified the desire of white settlers for this improved Indian land. Georgians and the state of Georgia were among the biggest proponents of removal, and the pressure that the state exerted on the Cherokee to relocate was tremendous. Moreover, Indian removal would further the economic development of the region, as Tennessee and Georgia sought to implement internal improvements, such as easier river navigation, which would more closely connect the region and stimulate the economy.

The Choctaw, however, were the first of the Five Civilized Tribes to agree to move. For decades, the Choctaw had been pressured to give up lands to white settlers; in the period between 1801 and 1825, the nation signed seven treaties with the U.S. government, ceding some 15,000,000 acres. On September 15, 1830, the nation met with Secretary of War John Eaton and General John Coffee to negotiate the terms for removal west of the Mississippi. The Treaty of Dancing Rabbit Creek was the result. It guaranteed that in exchange for Choctaw lands east of the Mississippi (about 11 million acres), the nation would receive

15 million acres in what is now the state of Oklahoma, then known as Indian Territory. It also established the boundaries of the relationship between the U.S. government and the government of the Choctaw nation. It also agreed to continue to pay annuities established in previous treaties the Choctaw had made with the United States; for instance, Choctaw who had fought in the American Revolution would continue to receive annuities. After the signing of the treaty, many reluctantly prepared to leave the Choctaw homeland. In his "Farewell Letter to the American People," George Harkins voiced this frustration, saying, "We as Choctaws choose to suffer and be free, than live under the degrading influence of laws, where our voice could not be heard in the formation...Much as the state of Mississippi has wronged us, I cannot find in my heart any other sentiment than an ardent wish for her prosperity and happiness."[27] Removal began in the fall of 1831 and was scheduled to end in 1833. Since this was the first, Jackson was anxious to make this the model for Indian removal. Nearly 15,000 Choctaw made the trip; some 2,500 died on the journey. The Choctaw removal came to be called "the trail of tears and death," a phrase which was used to describe the removal of other nations as well.

Other nations did not remove as willingly. After initial negotiations with the U.S. government, many of the leaders of the Seminoles of Florida renounced their agreements, saying that they had been forced to sign the documents. A few groups and villages did remove to Indian Territory, but most chose to remain in Florida. In late December 1835, a group of Seminole ambushed a U.S. Army company, killing 107 of 110 men; the event became known as the Dade Massacre and began the Second Seminole War, with the Third Seminole War following a few years later. Over the next ten years, the Seminole attempted to resist removal with mixed success. Under the leadership of Osceola, the war was largely fought using guerilla tactics against the army, which vastly outnumbered the Seminole forces. Ultimately, some 4,000 people were forcibly removed to Indian Territory, but between 100 and 400 Seminoles remained in the Everglades, having resisted and eluded the American military. The wars were tremendously expensive for the United States, costing approximately $40,000,000.[28]

The Cherokee chose very different means of resisting removal. They had been under increasing pressure from the state of Georgia since the 1790s, which intensified in the wake of the discovery of gold in 1827, resulting in the nation's first gold rush as prospectors and settlers began pouring into Cherokee land. The state responded by passing a resolution that declared its sovereignty over Cherokee lands within the state and asserted that state laws were to be extended to Cherokee land. Georgia passed a series of laws specifically targeting the Cherokee and created a special police force called the Georgia Guard to patrol Cherokee lands and harass and intimidate the population. The Guard arrested principal chief John Ross and closed down and seized the press for the *Cherokee Phoenix*. The state simultaneously attempted to undermine and weaken the Cherokee governing structure, closing down the tribal courts and preventing the council from meeting. Finally, in 1832, after the Indian Removal Act but before the Cherokee had signed any treaties ceding land, Georgia created a state land lottery to distribute Cherokee lands to white settlers.

The Cherokee decided to contest removal legally, asserting that it was illegal for Georgia to enforce state laws on Cherokee lands. But the Marshall court found that *Cherokee Nation v. Georgia* (1831) was out of their jurisdiction, as the Cherokees were not U.S. citizens and were a "domestic dependent nation" to the United States. The nation tried again the next year when a missionary from Vermont was arrested by the Georgia Guard. Since the plaintiff was a U.S. citizen, the Court could rule in the case of *Worcester v. Georgia* (1832). The Court decided in favor of the Cherokee, ruling that only the national government, not the states, had authority in Indian affairs.

Despite this ruling, both Jackson and the Georgia state government were determined to enforce removal for the Cherokee and continued to pressure the Cherokee to migrate. After the landslide reelection of Jackson in 1832, a minority of Cherokee leaders began to question how long the nation could hold out against Jackson and Georgia. A small group, mostly elite Cherokee, decided that they now had no choice but to remove. This group, known as the Treaty Party, led by Major Ridge, his son John, and family members Elias Boudinot, editor of the *Cherokee Phoenix,* and Stand Watie, began unauthorized talks with Washington. Principal Chief John Ross, the majority of Cherokees, and the Cherokee government remained staunchly against removal. The Ridges and their followers responded by forming a breakaway council government, and in December 1835 they signed the Treaty of New Echota. The treaty gave up all Cherokee lands east of the Mississippi in return for lands in Indian Territory, five million dollars, and compensation for property left in the east. It also provided for a two-year period to voluntarily leave. Soon after the signing, members of the Treaty Party, along with a few hundred Cherokee, migrated to the new lands. John Ross and the majority of the Cherokee population remained, protesting that the Treaty Party had no authority and the document was a fraud. Of 17,000 members of the nation, only about 500 had joined the Treaty Party. Ross and his followers refused to migrate. Many Americans were deeply uneasy about the nature of the treaty. This was reflected in the Senate's vote to approve the treaty, which passed by only one vote. In

Figure 12.7 John Ridge and John Ross | John Ridge (left), along with his father Major, believed the Cherokee had no choice but to accept removal and concluded the Treaty of New Echota with the United States in 1835. As principal chief, John Ross (right) led the fight against removal after 1835.

Author: John Bowen (both images)
Source: Library of Congress

the spring of 1838, Martin Van Buren, Jackson's successor, sent General Winfield Scott and 7,000 troops to Georgia. Over a period of almost a month, troops forcibly removed thousands of Cherokee from their homes at gunpoint. Most were held in internment camps for much of the summer, awaiting removal. Hundreds died of dysentery and other diseases. Several hundred Cherokee managed to escape to the mountains of North Carolina, evading removal. Some 17,000 people were removed over what became known as the Trail of Tears. An estimated 2,000-6,000 people died along the Trail. Although we cannot know with absolute certainty how many died, 4,000 deaths, nearly one-fourth of the tribe in total, is the most cited and well-supported figure.[29]

The aftermath of removal was dramatically played out on the new Cherokee lands near Tahlequah, Oklahoma. Soon after the majority of the Cherokee arrived in Tahlequah, John Ross was once again elected as principal chief. On the night of his election, many of the leading members of the Treaty Party were assassinated, including Major Ridge, John Ridge, and Elias Boudinot.

Aftermath of Indian Removal

Native peoples all over the East Coast were relocated, voluntarily and forcibly. In the North, groups such as the Sauk, Shawnee, and Ottowa signed agreements to relocate to Indian Territory. Some, like the Potawatomi, experienced significant casualties along the

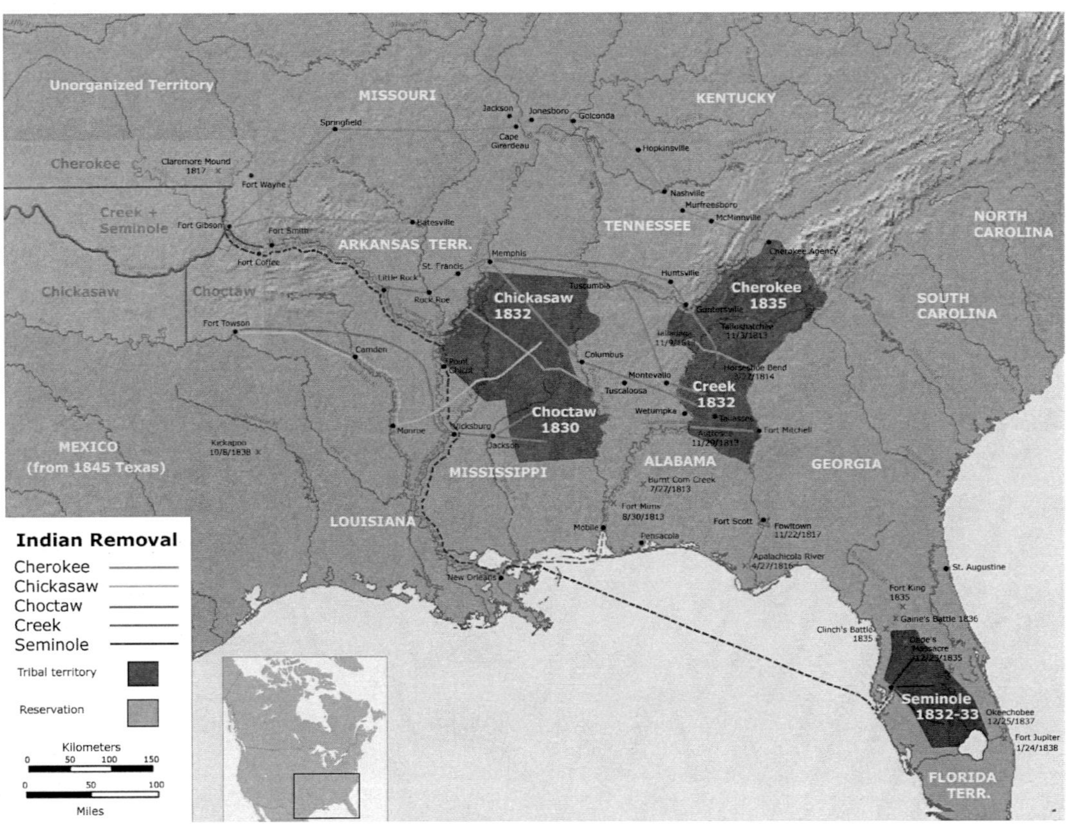

Figure 12.8 Indian Removal | This map shows the paths the southern tribes took in the 1830s as they made their way to their new homes in Oklahoma.

Author: Wikipedia User "Nikater"
Source: Wikimedia Commons

route of removal. Others, like the Iroquois (Haudenosaunee), were able to escape when the land company that was supposed to purchase land in the west failed to do so. This allowed the Iroquois to renegotiate and keep most of their reservations. Others attempted to escape removal, such as Sauk leader Black Hawk, who attempted to lead a breakaway group of Sauk, Fox, and Kickapoo back to Illinois homelands. Settlers claimed that they were being invaded, and the militia and federal troops were called in. Most of Black Hawk's followers were defeated at the Battle of Bad Axe as they tried to cross back over the Mississippi River. Fragmentation of many groups was a lasting legacy of the Indian Removal Act of 1830. As groups resisted removal, they often broke apart geographically, resulting in two separate groups. These groups include the Oklahoma Cherokee Nation (those that removed, forcibly and voluntarily) and the Eastern Band of Cherokee (those that escaped and remained in North Carolina), and the Oklahoma Seminole (those who willingly removed and those who were captured by the Army) and the Florida Seminole (those who resisted, fled the Army, and remained in the Everglades).

12.3.4 The Nullification Crisis

In 1829, the members of the Jackson administration began to divide over the future of the Tariff of 1828. Martin Van Buren pushed Congress to adopt higher import taxes in 1828. The new tariff increased duties on raw wool, flax, molasses, hemp, and distilled spirits, which assisted farmers in the North. Van Buren reasoned that the South would vote for Jackson regardless of the tariff. However, without the tariff the North might vote for Adams. Grumbling could be heard throughout the South about the "tariff of abominations." Many southerners thought tariffs harmed their interests because they sold their cotton on the unprotected world market, whereas most northerners sold goods on the protected national market. Southerners also believed tariff revenues funded government projects that benefitted only the North. John C. Calhoun quieted the protests in 1828 by suggesting he could push Jackson to reverse the tariff once he took office. Van Buren's risk and Calhoun's promises proved effective, and southerners turned out for Jackson in November.[30]

After the election, the South began to demand a reduction of the tariff. To southerners, import taxes only brought economic misery. Furthermore, they worried about the potential consequences for slavery if the North and the West banded together against the South. Frustrated southerners turned to Calhoun to help them make a reasoned argument against the measure. The vice president secretly drew up the *South Carolina Exposition and Protest*. He maintained the tariff was unconstitutional because it did not set uniform duties and it clearly benefited one region over another. Far more importantly, he suggested how states could fight objectionable federal laws. Calhoun argued that the Constitution was a compact between sovereign states, based on Article VII indicating that the states, not the people, would ratify the document. Therefore, the states had a right to determine the constitutionality of federal laws. When a state found a law objectionable, a special state convention could declare said law null and void within its borders. The other states then had the right to clarify the law's validity through a constitutional amendment. If one or more states still objected, they had the right to secede from the union.[31] Calhoun believed once the *Exposition and Protest* emerged, he could work with Jackson to reduce the tariff rates and avoid the need for nullification. The vice president, however, could not have known that the Eaton affair would drive a wedge between himself and the president. Moreover, he misread Jackson's views on the relationship between the federal government and the states. For Jackson, any talk of nullification or secession undermined the principles of the American Revolution.[32]

In 1830, a congressional discussion on the sale of federal lands sharpened the debate between the supporters and opponents of nullification. In assessing the merits of a bill covering the sale of federal land, Robert Y. Hayne of South Carolina and Daniel Webster raised the issue of states' rights. Hayne suggested the southern opposition to the tariff reflected a desire "to preserve, not destroy the union" from "federal dominance." Webster, on the other hand, thought that in affirming the Constitution, the states agreed the laws of the United States would be the "supreme law of the land."[33] After the Hayne-Webster debate, Jackson and Calhoun outlined their position on nullification and made public their growing feud at a Lincoln Day banquet in April. After a series of speeches on the importance of states' rights, Jackson rose to give a toast. The president intoned, "Our federal union, it must be preserved." The vice president, seemingly stunned by his assertion, responded, "The Union, next to our liberties most dear." Jackson publically challenged Calhoun because he saw an important political issue at stake. The president shared Calhoun's concern about reducing the tariff, but he could not acquiesce in labeling the tariff unconstitutional or in suggesting states could nullify federal laws.[34]

Once Andrew Jackson stated his preference for a strong union, he needed to work out a compromise before he ran for reelection in 1832. If he could secure a reduction in the tariff levels that still supported the principle of protectionism, then he could paint himself as a moderate should the nullifiers choose to act. In July, Congress passed the Tariff of 1832, cutting tariff levels in half.[35] Jackson's plan worked brilliantly up to a point; he placated enough people to win reelection, but he did not entirely silence the concern of some southerners. To them, the tariff was only one of many signs of their growing isolation in the union and their growing concern about the interference of outside authority.

That same year, John C. Calhoun, realizing he no longer had the president's support, resigned the vice presidency to seek a seat in the Senate, where he hoped to destabilize Jackson's political agenda. Even after his break with the president, Calhoun remained reluctant to publicly support his own doctrine. He thought the South needed more time to build its case before taking drastic action. However, radical sentiment was rising in his home state, so Calhoun joined the radicals rather than lose his political influence. The South Carolinians moved one step closer to nullification when they elected their new state legislature in November; two-thirds of the members supported calling for a state convention to discuss nullifying the Tariffs of 1828 and 1832. Once in session, the convention approved an ordinance of nullification scheduled to take effect on February 1, 1833. They also suggested they would reaffirm the union, if Congress instated a non-protective tariff. South Carolina hoped once they took action, other states would follow suit.[36]

Fully expecting South Carolina to move toward nullification, the president increased the naval presence in Charleston to collect tariff revenues before the ships docked. Then in his annual message, Jackson rejected nullification but also proposed to lower the tariff to only cover necessary federal expenses such as national defense. When the nullifiers opted not to back down, Jackson released a special proclamation on December 10, 1832 declaring South Carolina on the "brink of insurrection and treason." While the president supported the principle of states' rights, at heart his vision for the nation centered on majority rule. He had pledged himself to follow the will of the people not long after he took office. South Carolina's nullification, if allowed to stand, would allow the minority to dictate public policy. Jackson also hoped his proclamation would isolate South Carolina. To that extent it succeeded, as no other southern states joined in the protest, though some states expressed sympathy for the doctrine of nullification.[37]

Andrew Jackson also called on Congress to give him direct power to collect the tariff revenues, which his critics labeled the Force Bill. Meanwhile, Henry Clay and Daniel Webster, delighted for once with Jackson's strong support for nationalism, began to lay the groundwork for a compromise with John C. Calhoun who publicly would not back down but privately wanted a compromise. By the end of December, Congress was debating a proposal to drastically lower the tariff over two years. When the members deadlocked over continuing protectionism, Clay introduced a compromise measure to gradually lower the tariff over ten years and give manufacturers some time to adjust to an unprotected market.[38]

Henry Clay's proposal eventually won support from all sides of the debate. On March 2, 1833, the president signed both the Tariff of 1833 and the Force Act into law. Calhoun headed to South Carolina to present the measures to the state convention, which subsequently withdrew its nullification of the tariff. In a final move to support minority rights, it nullified the Force Act. The federal government simply ignored the latter move, and the crisis passed peacefully. Both sides, however, claimed victory. Jackson had defended the union, while South Carolina showed a single state could force Congress to revise objectionable laws. However, according to historian Harry Watson, neither side emerged clearly victorious given that the "underlying constitutional questions" remained unanswered, paving the way for another, perhaps larger crisis in the future.[39]

12.3.5 The Bank War

While Andrew Jackson strongly supported the federal union during his first term, he made a bold statement on interpreting the Constitution's "necessary and proper" clause when it came to the future of the Second Bank of the United States. The country's business community, centered in the Northeast, liked the bank because it provided a stable currency system and provided easier access to credit. Yet many average Americans, especially in the South and West, despised the BUS; as a privately run institution, it concentrated too much power in the hand of too few and was not accountable to the people. Jackson, who had distrusted banks for years, sided with the common people and looked for ways to destroy the BUS. To Jackson, both the bank and the paper currency it issued were unconstitutional. He thought the only safe currencies were gold and silver (specie). Jackson's war on the bank fit perfectly with his view that the government served to protect the majority, not the privileged few.

Although the bank helped bring general prosperity to the nation after the Panic of 1819, political divisions in the 1820s increased hostility toward any form of national authority. To some extent, the anti-bank coalition was correct that the bank and its director, Nicolas Biddle, wielded an enormous amount of power. In 1830, the Second Bank of the United States issued just under 20 percent of the nation's loans and 40 percent of the nation's currency. Those percentages only increased in the 1830s. Additionally, the bank had the ability to determine the overall amount of money in circulation by demanding the state bank notes it accepted be redeemable in specie. When Biddle took over the bank in 1823, he worked to rebuild its reputation after the Panic of 1819 as well as to limit the federal government's control over his institution. Although the bank's charter allowed the government to appoint five of the twenty-five directors, Biddle minimized the involvement of the government's directors in decisions about the bank's operations.[40]

Jackson's attack on the bank started slowly, as initially the Easton affair, Indian removal, and other issues required his attention; additionally, the bank's charter did not expire until 1836, giving him time to develop a plan for the future of government deposits. In 1831, after replacing his Cabinet, Jackson began to focus on the bank issue. Louis McLane, his new secretary of treasury, proposed a compromise that would not eliminate the bank, but restructure it. McLane tied it to the president's desire to reduce the national debt, and the president approved the scheme. Jackson asked only that McLane wait until after his reelection campaign to follow through. Inadvertently, McLane undermined his own proposal in December when he penned his annual report that called for re-chartering the bank and raising the tariff. The anti-bank members of the Kitchen Cabinet opposed McLane's proposal because it included a tariff proposal. The window for compromise quickly passed, and Jackson recommitted himself to oppose the bank in any form.[41]

Around the same time, the National Republicans chose Henry Clay to oppose Andrew Jackson in the upcoming presidential election. In 1830, Biddle had approached Clay and Daniel Webster for help in working out an agreement with the Jackson administration that would preserve the Second Bank of the United States. With the hopes of compromise waning in early 1832, Clay and Webster convinced Biddle to apply for re-charter early, rather than waiting for the bank's charter to expire in 1836. Biddle, knowing that Jackson wanted to keep the bank out of the campaign, hesitated at first. But Clay and Webster convinced him Congress would vote in favor of the bank, and asserted Jackson would not risk vetoing the measure because the bank was so popular with the American people. If he took that risk, Congress would override the veto, and Clay would win the presidency. Biddle acquiesced. On June 11, the Senate voted in favor of the measure. On July 3, the House did the same. From Clay's perspective, all seemed to be going according to plan.[42]

Figure 12.9 The Bank War | This political cartoon (from the early 1830s) shows Andrew Jackson seeking to destroy the Second Bank of the United States, the "Many Headed Monster."

Author: H.R. Robinson
Source: Anne S.K. Brown Military Collection, Brown University Library

When Andrew Jackson learned about the vote, he decided not just to veto the measure but to prematurely destroy the bank, reportedly telling Martin Van Buren "The bank...is trying to kill me, *but I will kill it*."[43] Over the next several days, Jackson's advisers drafted the text of his veto message in such a way as to appeal to diverse political groups who only had hatred for the bank in common. The administration decided to speak directly to the people in order to prevent Congress from overriding Jackson's veto. The message, says historian Sean Wilentz, "combined Jackson's constitutional views with his larger democratic outlook" especially as it related to the president's desire to eliminate artificial inequality in American life.[44] On the bank question, Jackson better understood the desire of the American people. Congress decided not to override the veto, leaving Clay without an issue on which to campaign. Thus, the National Republicans opted to paint the president as a power-mad executive. Try as they might, they could not undermine the popularity of Andrew Jackson and his running mate, Martin Van Buren. Not even the presence of a third-party candidate, William Wirt representing the Anti-Masonic Party, could derail Jackson's reelection. He easily won the popular (55 percent) and the Electoral College (77 percent) votes.

After his reelection, Andrew Jackson made it his personal mission to destroy not only the bank, but also Nicolas Biddle. To speed the bank's demise, Jackson proposed withdrawing the government deposits (totaling about $10 million) from the BUS before its charter expired in 1836. Jackson planned to deposit the government's money in carefully-selected state banks, later called the "pet banks" by their opponents. The plan, in Jackson's

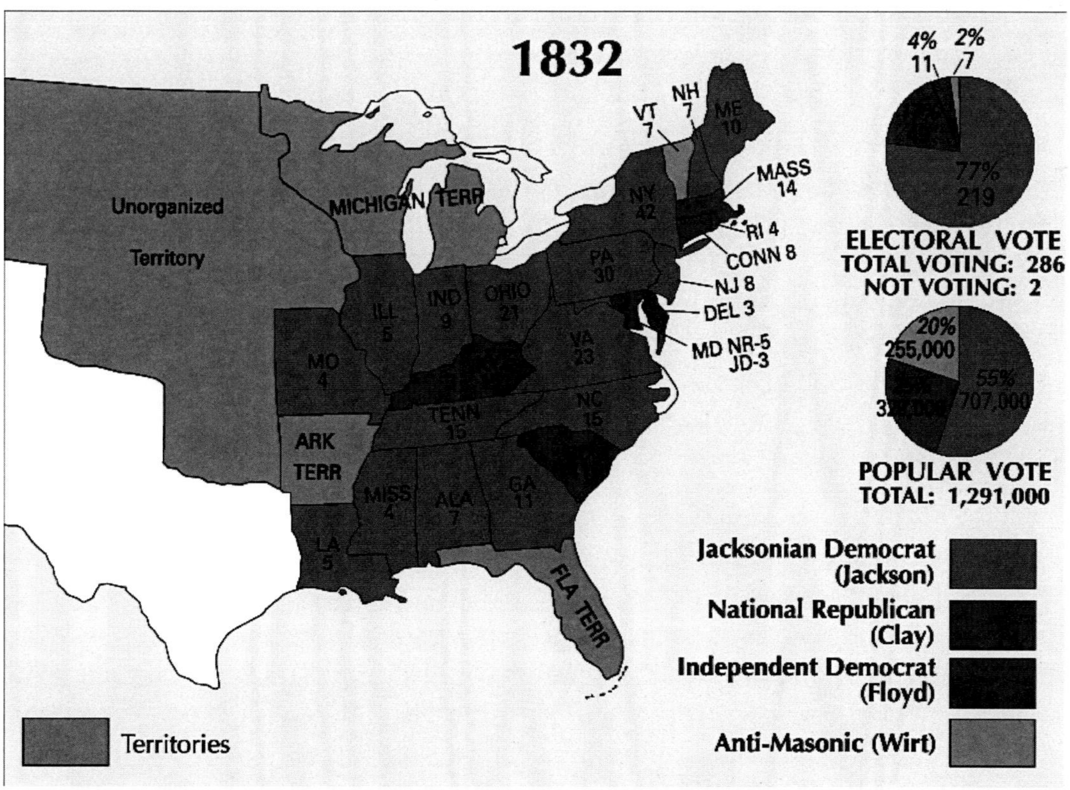

Figure 12.10 Presidential Election Map, 1832 | Henry Clay had hoped to use the issue of the bank to his advantage in 1832, but Andrew Jackson easily won the popular and Electoral College votes. After his reelection, he vowed to destroy the BUS and its director Nicolas Biddle.

Author: National Atlas of the United States
Source: Wikimedia Commons

opinion, would end the bank's ability to control the nation's currency and credit system, as well as prevent Biddle from mounting an effective challenge to the veto.[45]

Most of Jackson's cabinet worried about his decision, but the president was determined to follow through with his plan. When Louis McLane refused to withdraw the government's funds from the Second Bank of the United States, Jackson shifted him to the vacant position of secretary of state and appointed William J. Duane to fill the vacancy in the treasury department. When Duane refused to remove the funds, Jackson fired him. Finally, Jackson appointed Roger B. Taney, his attorney general, to head the treasury department. Slowly, Taney began to remove the federal government's deposits and shift them to the state banks. Biddle did not go down without a fight. As soon as the withdrawals began, he began to contract the bank's credit, claiming he needed to put the bank's books in order before the charter expired. His efforts caused a slight economic downturn but did not derail the effort to kill the bank.[46]

Although Jackson would feel the sting of the Senate's censure and their rejection of Taney as the secretary of treasury in his second term, Congress did begin a shift toward a hard money policy, something Jackson supported, when it passed the Coinage Act in 1835. The measure substituted gold coins for paper currency in commercial transactions. For Jackson, shifting to hard money was a more equitable system because it helped avoid the boom and bust cycle caused by speculation and inflation, which had increased after the federal deposits moved to state banks. Jackson also encouraged Congress to pass legislation that would ban banks from issuing paper currency worth less than five dollars. When Congress declined to follow through, the treasury department told its deposit banks not to accept small bills; later they required on-demand convertibility of paper notes to specie.[47]

The end of the Second Bank of the United States and Jackson's proposal to shift to hard money certainly did not please all of his supporters. Even so, several factions approved of his decisions, at least in part. Western farmers disliked the bank because it tended to limit the amount of paper currency in circulation and, in turn, the amount of credit available. They wanted a currency system based on cheap money, or paper currency, not backed by specie. Diehard states' rights advocates sought an end to the bank because they viewed it as an unconstitutional exercise of power, and they distrusted paper currency. Working people in Northeastern cities also disliked all banks in general. They believed that paper currency brought economic misery to the working class; thus, they wanted to end the use of all paper currency.[48]

Conservative Democrats, who supported the maintenance of paper currency, increasingly found themselves at odds with the president. They seemed to have more in common with the economic nationalists. The president's opponents tried to stop his move to hard money policies after 1835 by supporting a proposal Henry Clay made during Jackson's first term. Clay had proposed to keep the price of land high so the government could disperse the revenue back to the states for internal improvements. Simultaneously, John C. Calhoun proposed a measure to regulate the pet banks. The Senate wove the two proposals together in the Deposit Bill, which Congress passed in mid-1836. After the act took effect, speculation began to rise, which worried Jackson's hard money supporters. The president responded with the Specie Circular, which required payment in hard currency for all federal land transactions and made millions of dollars of currency almost worthless.[49] The currency debate was far from over as Jackson's presidency ended. One thing seemed clear by 1836: the bank war helped pave the way for the second party system.

12.3.6 Before You Move On...

Key Concepts

In 1828, Andrew Jackson defeated John Quincy Adams in the presidential election. His victory ushered in the era of Jacksonian Democracy—a time that promoted the common man, states' rights, and strict construction. During his presidency, personal and political issues meshed in Jackson's mind as he strove to address questions about Indian removal, concerns over the tariff and nullification, and the future of the BUS. Fully living up to his southern supporters' expectations, Jackson oversaw the removal of the Five Civilized Tribes from the Southeast. Given the controversial nature of the Tariffs of 1828 and 1832, Jackson helped reduce tariff rates. At the same time, he took a strong stand in favor of the preservation of the union when South Carolina claimed the states had the right to nullify federal laws. Finally, Jackson underscored his belief in a literal interpretation of the Constitution when he worked to destroy the Second Bank of the United States. In 1832, largely based on his stance regarding the bank, Jackson defeated Henry Clay in the presidential election. However, the bank issue also increased hostility to his vision, paving the way for the creation of the second party system.

Test Yourself

1. Andrew Jackson's action in regard to the Indians was to

   a. oppose their removal to the West.

   b. refuse to enforce a Supreme Court decision in the Indian's favor.

   c. defend Indian rights to disputed lands in Georgia.

   d. send troops to slaughter the Indians.

2. Who was the author of the *South Carolina Exposition and Protest*?

   a. John C. Calhoun

   b. Henry Clay

   c. Robert Hayne

   d. Daniel Webster

3. Many critics of the Second Bank of the United States, including Andrew Jackson, charged that

   a. it failed completely to meet its financial obligations.

   b. it was a tool of the Democratic Party.

   c. it was mismanaged by Nicholas Biddle.

   d. it concentrated too much power in the hands of the privileged.

See page 476 for answers

12.4 THE SECOND PARTY SYSTEM

In the 1820s, many states expanded the electorate when they dropped the property qualifications associated with voting rights. Aside from South Carolina and Delaware, the voters instead of state legislators chose their representatives to the Electoral College by 1882. Together these developments made people believe they possessed a greater say in their state and national governments. This expansion of democratic sentiment, coupled with the social and economic developments in the 1820s and 1830s, led to the rise of the second party system in the United States. Political leaders increasingly believed that parties served to mobilize voters behind certain candidates and policies. Nevertheless, it took time for these leaders to appreciate the full potential of partisanship as well as the possible problems of trying to build a national coalition of voters when local issues dominated the minds of most voters.[50]

The Democrats emerged in 1828 to campaign for Andrew Jackson and continued during his presidency to define their vision and expand their support through partisan newspapers and patronage. The Whigs materialized in 1834 to oppose Jackson and his vision. These two parties dominated the political scene for almost twenty years, although several third parties captured the voters' attention for brief periods. However, the question of slavery and its expansion westward proved the death knell of the Whigs and the second party system in the early 1850s.

12.4.1 Democrats and Whigs

When Andrew Jackson ran for president in 1828, the campaign served not just as a vehicle to promote his election but as a vehicle for creating a lasting political coalition committed to the state's rights philosophy that had guided the Old Republicans in the Jeffersonian era. For supporters like Martin Van Buren, the creation of a national party would help keep political issues on the forefront of the common voter's mind in the years between national elections. Furthermore, it would ensure that Jackson's vision outlasted his own presidency.

While during the campaign and in his first inaugural address Jackson promised to reform the national government, his statements had been somewhat vague. Therefore, partisan newspapers, especially the *Washington Globe*, helped define and spread the Democrats' message using Jackson's actions during the nullification crisis and the bank war as a guide. Historian Sean Wilentz observes that Democratic thought brought together three interrelated themes. One, they supported a "robust nationalism on constitutional issues" while also exercising some "restraint on federal support for economic development." Two, they distrusted the wealthy and the powerful, especially those people who possessed undue economic power. Three, they believed in the power of the people or that the will of the majority reigned supreme.[51] In essence, the Democrats wanted the freedom to pursue individual interests with as little government interference as possible.

The opposition party took longer to develop in the early 1830s because Henry Clay, Daniel Webster, and others struggled to find an effective means to arrest Jackson's growing support. According to historian Michael Holt, these men had the difficult task of "uniting the opponents of the majority and broadening that coalition until it was competitive."

Initially, they thought they could wait Jackson out; they assumed incorrectly that once the people realized Jackson wanted to dismantle the American System his coalition would fall apart. As Jackson's popularity grew, Clay and Webster looked for a way to bring all of the president's opponents into one party. However, such an effort proved quite difficult. The question of the tariff affected their ability to appeal to southern voters. Meanwhile, the emergence of the anti-Masons (who tended to distrust all political leaders) made it difficult to appeal to northern voters.[52]

Clay and Webster hoped to use the question of the bank to build up an opposition party going into the election of 1832. However, that effort failed when Jackson vetoed the re-charter bill and won a resounding reelection. Although Clay lost the election, he did not give up his effort to oppose Jackson. When Jackson moved to destroy the bank, Clay led a successful effort to censure the president in 1834, which helped lay the groundwork for a legitimate opposition party. The Whig Party finally found common ground in their opposition to Jackson—"King Andrew the First," as he had been labeled during 1832. The party took its name from a group of British politicians who had sought to defend their liberties from a power-hungry king, and whose writings had done much to inspire the American Revolution.[53] Whig thought centered on defending liberty against power. Moreover, the party supported the maintenance of the economic and judicial nationalism seen in the Era of Good Feelings.

The two parties clearly differed on the meaning of the Constitution and the role of the federal government. The Democrats believed in a strong central government as evidenced by Jackson's position during the nullification crisis, but one that left most decisions to the states. When it came to the "necessary and proper" clause of the Constitution, they believed in strict construction. The Maysville Road veto in 1830 demonstrated the party's view on limiting the role of the government. Jackson saw the bill, which provided federal funding to build a road entirely in Kentucky, as beyond the scope of the powers granted to the federal government. The Whigs, on the other hand, saw a larger role for the federal government, especially when it came to economic development. In their view, funding for projects like the Maysville Road did not exceed the powers delineated to the federal government in the Constitution. Such funding would benefit the entire nation, making it a necessary and proper exercise of federal power.[54]

For both parties, questions about territorial expansion complicated their ability to build national coalitions. The Democrats tended to favor territorial expansion, especially in terms of acquiring territory from Mexico (such as Texas, New Mexico, and California). The Whigs believed before the nation acquired more territory, the government should focus on the economic development of the existing states and territories. Complicating the question of territorial expansion was the expansion of slavery in new territories. The Missouri Compromise seemingly settled the issue of slavery in the existing territories, but not what might happen in any new territories. Both the Democrats and the Whigs in the 1830s wanted to avoid questions about slavery, whether in terms of expansion or abolition. The Whigs found themselves stymied by the slavery question; their economic program appealed to many large slaveholders, but their reform outlook appealed to many abolitionists. Opposing territorial expansion became the easiest way for the Whigs. If the

United States did not acquire any more territory, then the question of the future of slavery in those territories could not divide their coalition.

To attract southern supporters, the Democrats avoided questions of slavery by emphasizing that states had the right to choose to allow slavery or to abolish slavery, which seemed to appease most supporters. Andrew Jackson, Martin Van Buren, and their followers looked for other ways to diffuse the slavery question, especially as antislavery sentiments began to increase in the 1830s and activists looked to the federal government to take a stand against the extension of slavery. Jackson gave tacit agreement for the postal service to interfere with the delivery of antislavery tracts to the southern states. Meanwhile, Congress implemented what became known as the "gag" rule. As the antislavery cause gained ground in the North, the number of petitions requesting legislation to end slavery in federal territories, especially the District of Columbia, increased. Southern legislators despised these petitions, even though they knew the proposals would never amount to anything. They wanted to turn all antislavery petitions away without consideration, but Democratic Party leaders knew if they allowed that to happen then their opponents would charge them with impeding free speech. Therefore, Van Buren proposed a solution to the quandary; Congress would accept the petitions, but would table them without discussion.[55]

As the Democrats and the Whigs built their coalitions, they attracted diverse voters to their parties. Voter loyalty stemmed from a complex set of factors. Voters in the South and the West tended to support the Democrats, whereas voters in New England, the Mid Atlantic, and the upper Midwest preferred the Whigs. Small farmers, urban workers, and artisans looked to the Democrats to represent their economic interests, whereas large southern planters, wealthy business owners, and middling farmers chose the Whigs. Immigrants tended to appreciate the Democrats' ability to separate political and moral questions. This ability also made them appealing to Catholics, Baptists, Methodists, and free thinkers. Native-born Americans, especially those associated with the Presbyterian, Congregationalist, and Quaker churches, leaned in the other direction because the Whigs saw nothing wrong with the government weighing in on questions of morality. Sometimes regional or class factors determined voting patterns, but in other cases ethnic, religious, or cultural factors influenced party choice. In the end, the voters' decisions came down to which party would best represent their interests at the local and national level.

After the Whig coalition emerged, both parties began to prepare for the presidential election in 1836. Martin Van Buren of New York easily won the Democratic nomination. By all accounts, Van Buren had the political experience to be president. Not only had he been instrumental in the creation of the Democratic Party, but he also advised Jackson on a host of issues in the 1830s. For as influential as Van Buren was in his home state and in the nation's capital, however, he was not particularly well-known by voters around the country. The Whigs decided to run three candidates with strong regional bases—Daniel Webster of Massachusetts to appeal to the Northeast, Hugh Lawson White of Tennessee to appeal to the South, and William Henry Harrison of Indiana to appeal to the West. Given Van Buren's lack of popular appeal, the Whigs hoped to throw the election into the House of Representatives, where they could unite behind a single candidate.

Table 12.1

Second Party System: Leaders, Supporters, and Beliefs

	Democrats	Whigs
Leaders	• Andrew Jackson • John C. Calhoun • Martin Van Buren	• Henry Clay • Daniel Webster • William Henry Harrison
Supporters	• Region: South and West • Class: Small farmers and urban laborers/artisans • Ethnicity: Scots-Irish, French, German, and Canadian • Religion: Catholics, Baptists, Methodists, and free thinkers	• Region: New England and Upper Midwest • Class: Large southern planters, wealthy businessmen, and middling farmers • Ethnicity: English, New England Old Stock (WASPS) • Religion: Presbyterians, Congregationalists, and Quakers
Political Beliefs	• Supported States' Rights • Opposed government support for monopoly • Committed to Indian Removal • Wanted aggressive territoral expansion • Favored low-cost sale of federal land • Stressed class conflict • Opposed reform movements like prohibition	• Supported National Power • Wanted government support for tariffs and internal improvements • Opposed territorial expansion • Opposed low-cost sale of federal land • Stressed harmony of interests among social classes • Supported reform movements like prohibition

During the campaign, the Whigs harkened back to the fears of partisanship among the nation's founders as an explanation for presenting voters with three candidates. The Democrats countered such anti-party sentiment by arguing their unity would help promote their principles and discourage abuses of power. The Democrats also implied to voters that the Whigs sought another "corrupt bargain" that would deny the will of the majority. Van Buren won the popular (51 percent) and Electoral College (58 percent)

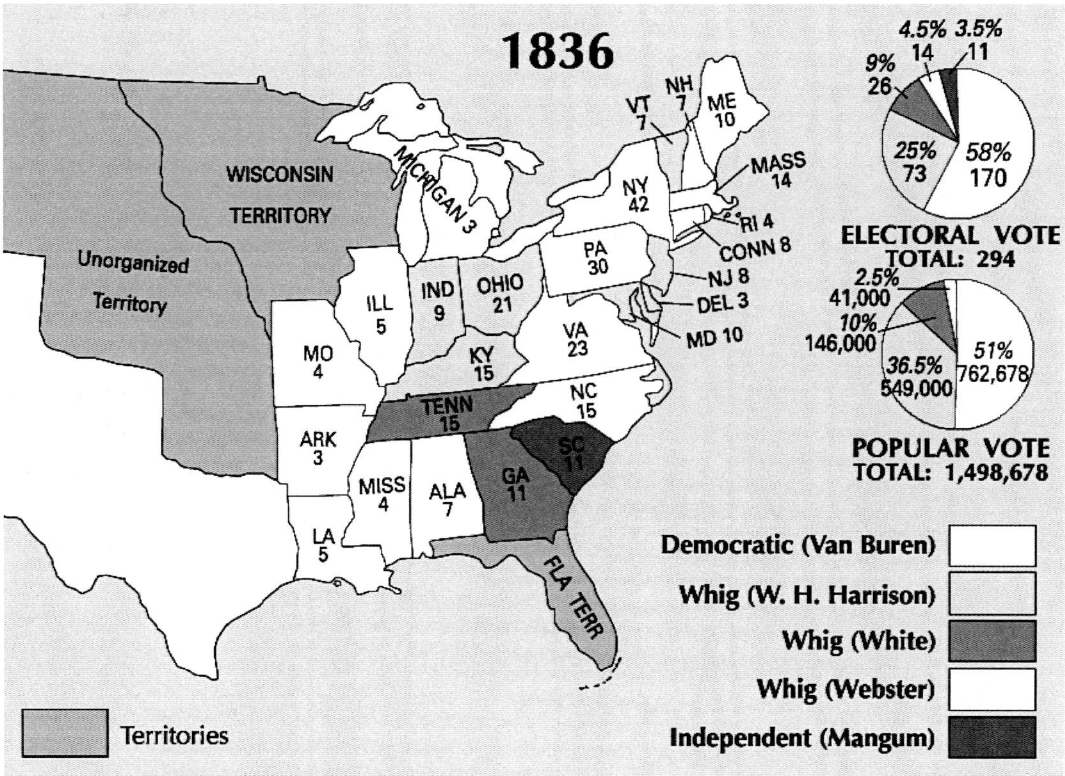

Figure 12.11 Presidential Election Map, 1836 | In an attempt to throw the election to the House of Representatives, the Whigs nominated three favorite son candidates—Daniel Webster, Hugh Lawson White, and William Henry Harrison. However, their strategy backfired and Democrat Martin Van Buren defeated all three opponents.

Author: National Atlas of the United States
Source: Wikimedia Commons

votes. Since Van Buren won just over a majority of the popular votes, the Democrats and the Whigs appeared almost evenly matched. The results further suggested that the two-party system had become firmly entrenched in American life.[56] Nevertheless, the future of both parties seemed to rest on how well Martin Van Buren served as a custodian of Jacksonian principles.

12.4.2 The Trials of Martin Van Buren

A major economic depression prompted by the Panic of 1837 dominated Martin Van Buren's presidency. Not long after he took office, the mid-1830s economic boom went bust, and the new president struggled in vain to come up with a solution to remedy the decline. Andrew Jackson's attack on the bank planted the seeds for the crisis, but other factors played a role as well. Even before the bank's demise, the amount of money in circulation was rising because Nicolas Biddle had hoped the inflation would help him fight the president's initiative. When Jackson deposited the federal government's revenue in the pet banks, all brakes on credit expansion disappeared and inflation followed.[57] Like the Panic of 1819, international factors also contributed to the economic collapse in late 1836 and early 1837. Rising commodity prices, especially cotton, worried British bankers. They began to demand payment in specie from firms that conducted business in the United States in order to stop the flow of British gold across the Atlantic. The decision caused a decline in the price of cotton. To cope with the bust, by 1837 leading banks in New York suspended specie payments and banks around the country followed suit.[58]

Even before the banks suspended specie payments, the public felt the pressure of rising prices for flour, pork, coal, and rent. For example, flour sold for approximately $7.75 a barrel in March 1836 and $12.00 in March 1837, bringing distress to many workers who could not afford to feed their families. In New York City, a protest meeting organized by the Loco Foco faction of the Democratic Party quickly turned into a riot. The angry mob began to storm businesses and private residences to liberate hoarded flour. After several hours, the police finally managed to restore order. Although many people feared outbreaks in other cities, those protests never materialized. However, the suffering continued around the country.[59] Newspapers reported high levels of unemployment, perhaps as high as 30 percent by the end of 1837. For people who managed to hold onto their positions, wages declined anywhere from 30 to 50 percent.

As people agitated for relief, Martin Van Buren publicly blamed "luxurious habits founded too often on merely fancied wealth." The president also recognized the people's suffering, but he never considered putting more power in the hands of the federal government to deal with the problem.[60] Privately he weighed three options for ending the panic. One, he could reverse Jackson's hard money by repealing the Specie Circular and by advocating for the creation of a new national bank. Two, he could retain his predecessor's state deposit system but also promote more stringent government regulation of banks. Three, he could attempt to enact a complete separation of the government's fiscal affairs from the private banking system by creating an independent treasury system to hold federal government deposits.[61]

Van Buren called for a special session of Congress to convene in September; over the summer, he agonized over which proposal to recommend. While the president clearly wanted his policy to promote economic recovery, he also needed to find a plan all factions of the Democratic Party could accept. Not all Democrats supported the hard money banking policies that Jackson instituted after he destroyed the national bank; some preferred paper currency solutions. When Congress came into session, Van Buren recommended several measures to put the nation's financial house in order, including measures to allow for the deferment of tariff payments and to issue treasury notes to meet the government's obligations. He then called on Congress to create an independent treasury system. When Congress began to debate the bill, John C. Calhoun amended the proposal to require the government to only take payments in specie. Van Buren, a hard-money man, found the amendment perfectly acceptable, but the move slowed Congressional action.[62]

Van Buren's proposal dominated political discourse for several years. The president perceived his policy to be an appealing solution to the country's currency and banking issues, but many conservative Democrats banded together with the Whigs to oppose the measure. Conservative Democrats tended to support continued use of the state banks, whereas the Whigs leaned toward the creation of a new national bank. However, they all agreed that Van Buren's solution had potentially dangerous consequences for the nation's financial health. Van Buren's supporters in Congress worked diligently to garner support for the Independent Treasury bill until it finally won approval in 1840. Meanwhile, according to historian Harry Watson, Van Buren "seemed to concentrate on the pleasures of being President," as opposed to working to further Jackson's agenda.[63]

12.4.3 The Whigs Triumphant

The debate over the Independent Treasury bill set the stage for the presidential election of 1840. It provided the Whigs an opportunity to develop a cohesive statement on what they stood for that moved beyond their hatred of Andrew Jackson. Whig leaders suggested the independent treasury would lead to further economic misery; they also depicted Martin Van Buren as nearly as power hungry as his predecessor in his attempts to push Congress to accept the proposal. Finally, the Whigs painted the federal government as a force for positive change, especially in times of economic crisis. They believed the government needed to take steps to stimulate economic growth by creating a sound currency managed by private banks. The depression also helped the Whigs draw in new supporters among conservative Democrats. With the exception of their position on a national bank, the conservatives had more in common with the Whigs than they did with the radicals in their own party.[64]

The Democrats re-nominated Martin Van Buren for president, but since the economic crisis still plagued the nation, his chances for reelection seemed slim. Meanwhile, the Whigs concentrated on finding the most electable candidate. Henry Clay looked like a front-runner for the nomination; he could draw support from pro-development forces because he was the architect of American System and from southern Whigs because he was a Kentucky slaveholder. However, a younger generation of Whig politicians saw those qualities as negatives when voters looked for a candidate who could represent the common man; instead, they looked to Daniel Webster of Massachusetts, William Henry Harrison of Ohio, and Winfield Scott of Virginia. The Whigs eliminated Webster early on since it appeared he would not do well outside of the Northeast. Harrison (who had fought in the War of 1812) and Scott (who had eased tensions during a border conflict with Canada in 1838) could both draw on their military records to develop support.[65]

William Henry Harrison eventually won the nomination after his supporters used some underhanded tactics to paint Scott as an abolitionist in order to break the deadlock at the Whigs' convention. To placate Henry Clay's supporters, the convention nominated Clay's longtime friend John Tyler for vice president. Tyler brought sectional balance to the ticket, but few of the delegates knew or seemed to care that his political views were more in tune with Andrew Jackson than with Henry Clay. In 1840, the Whigs relied on many of the same techniques the Democrats had used in 1828 to secure Jackson's election. An offhand comment by a Clay supporter about Harrison drinking hard cider in his log cabin turned into a major advantage for the Whigs. The party knew they needed to shed their elitist reputation and the image of Harrison as a frontiersman (even if the description did not fit) and a war hero aided in that effort. The Whigs held rallies around the country, including in Baltimore during the Democratic convention, to promote "Tippecanoe and Tyler Too." The Democrats certainly tried to overcome the support for Harrison, but it became increasingly difficult after the Whigs christened the president "Martin Van Ruin."[66]

William Henry Harrison won both the popular (53 percent) and the Electoral College (80 percent) votes in an election that drew record numbers of voters to the polls. Approximately

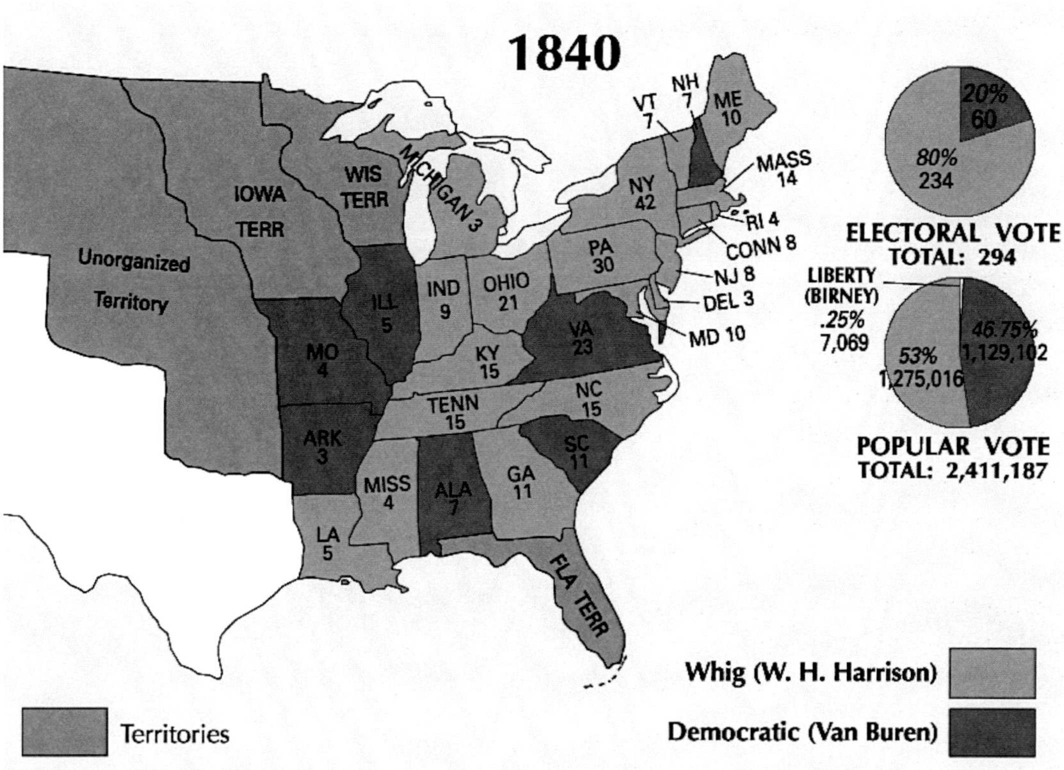

Figure 12.12 Presidential Election Map, 1840 | During the 1840 campaign, the Whigs held rallies around the country to promote "Tippecanoe and Tyler Too" over "Martin Van Ruin." The tactic clearly proved effective when William Henry Harrison defeated Martin Van Buren on election day.

Author: National Atlas of the United States
Source: Wikimedia Commons

80 percent of eligible voters cast ballots, which far exceeded the average of 57 percent in the three previous presidential elections. The Whigs had much to celebrate when Harrison arrived in Washington to take the oath of office in 1841. They had shown they could be a majority party, not simply an opposition party.[67] Unfortunately, their victory was short-lived. Harrison unwisely chose to give a two hour inaugural address in the freezing rain without a coat or hat. He contracted pneumonia and died a month later.

John Tyler, who disregarded all concerns about the legitimacy of his succession, took the oath of office shortly after Harrison's death. Then he proceeded to oppose the entire Whig legislative agenda since he was a committed states' righter and strict constructionist. Congressional Whigs were furious with Tyler when he vetoed their proposal for a new national bank twice and disregarded suggestions for increasing the tariff and providing federal funds for internal improvements. Tyler became a president without a party, while the Whigs lost their momentum when the Democrats took control of Congress after the midterm elections in 1842. By the mid-1840s, the Democratic agenda of territorial expansion replaced the Whig agenda of economic development, setting the stage for the Civil War.

12.4.4 Before You Move On...

Key Concepts

While early American leaders seemed hostile to permanent political factions, by the 1830s parties appeared to be an integral part of the political process. The Democratic Party emerged in 1828 to support Andrew Jackson's bid for president. The Whig Party emerged in 1834 to oppose Jackson's vision and policies. The core difference between the two parties was how they interpreted the Constitution's "necessary and proper" clause. The Democrats wanted the freedom to pursue individual interests with as little government interference as possible. They deferred to the states on most issues. The Whigs promoted economic and judicial nationalism, which required a larger role for the federal government. By 1836, the second party system had taken hold as the Democrats and the Whigs squared off in the presidential election that year. Martin Van Buren, the Democrat, defeated his three Whig opponents, and he looked forward to promoting his predecessor's vision. However, the Panic of 1837 undermined his efforts because the crisis seemed tied directly to Jackson's decision to crush the Second Bank of the United States. Moreover, Van Buren struggled to come up with an effective solution to end the depression. In 1840, the Whigs triumphed at the national level, turning their party from an opposition party to a majority party. However, William Henry Harrison's death and the emergence of questions about territorial expansion and slavery left the future of the second party system unclear.

Test Yourself

1. The Second Party System consisted of which two political parties?

   a. Federalists and Democrats

   b. Democrats and Republicans

   c. Democrats and Whigs

   d. Republicans and Whigs

2. After the Panic of 1837, Martin Van Buren supported _________ to remedy the nation's economic problems.

   a. the Second Bank of the United States

   b. the Independent Treasury System

   c. the Specie Circular

   d. a new protective tariff

3. William Henry Harrison's defeat over Martin Van Buren in the presidential election of 1840 was a victory for the Democratic Party.

   a. True

   b. False

See page 476 for answers

12.5 Conclusion

In many ways, both James Monroe and Andrew Jackson—both of whom lived through the Revolutionary Era—served as symbols for their age. Monroe represented the political elite of that generation who hoped through their government service to preserve some semblance of order in the United States. While good feelings pervaded his time in office, his presidency harkened back to the ceremony of the Federalist Era. Jackson represented the common individual of that generation who saw the break from Great Britain as an opportunity for social and economic mobility for average Americans. True, Jackson had travelled quite far from his humble origins, but he still managed to speak to and for those Americans who wanted democratic principles to mean something in their own lives.

From 1815 to 1840, the United States came of age economically and politically. The market revolution changed the way the American people related to one another and to their government, especially as that government sought to promote economic growth. The emergence of the second party system composed of the Democrats and the Whigs helped the American people to make sense of the changes affecting the nation. By 1840, they had accepted the idea that permanent political parties would help define the important political and economic issues of the day and provide a means for public debate on those issues. Moreover, they saw the political parties as the best way to safeguard democratic principles and personal liberties. However, the central debates over the rights of the states and the rights of the federal government left one question—the future of slavery—unanswered. And unanswered, that question became a dangerous and poisonous element in American life.

12.6 CRITICAL THINKING EXERCISES

- From 1815 to 1840, American leaders managed to limit the growing impact sectional differences had on economic and political issues. However, the fear of disunion remained an underlying threat. What major issues divided the nation in this period, and how were they resolved? In spite of efforts to minimize the divisions, why did these divisions ultimately bring disunion in the 1860s?
- For years, historians have pondered whether "Age of the Common Man" is an appropriate label for this period in American history. At the heart of the debate lies questions about the real level equality achieved by average Americans as the much-heralded democratic trends swept the nation. Who in American society benefitted most from the political and economic changes of the decade and why? What was the reality of the common citizen from the 1820s to the 1840s? Based on your responses to these questions, do you think we should continue to use "Age of the Common Man," or should we attach another label to this period (and what should it be)?
- Oftentimes, when we think of political parties in the American past we draw parallels to our modern political parties. How do the Democrats and Whigs in the second party system compare to the Democrats and Republicans today? What similarities and differences do you see between these parties in terms of political philosophy and important public policy issues?

12.7 KEY TERMS

- John Quincy Adams
- Adams-Onís Treaty of 1819
- American System
- Bank War
- Nicholas Biddle
- John C. Calhoun
- The Cherokee Phoenix
- Henry Clay
- Coinage Act of 1835
- Corrupt Bargain
- Dartmouth College v. Woodward
- Democratic Party
- Distribution Act of 1836
- Eaton Affair
- Era of Good Feelings
- Five Civilized Tribes
- Force Bill
- "Gag" Rule
- Gibbons v. Ogden
- William Henry Harrison
- Robert Hayne
- Independent Treasury Act of 1840
- Indian Removal Act of 1830
- Andrew Jackson
- Jacksonian Democracy
- Kitchen Cabinet
- Martin Van Buren
- Maysville Road Veto
- McCulloch v. Maryland
- Missouri Compromise
- James Monroe
- Monroe Doctrine
- Nullification Crisis
- Panic of 1819
- Panic of 1837
- John Ross
- Rush-Bagot Agreement of 1817
- Second Bank of the United States
- South Carolina Exposition and Protest
- Specie Circular of 1836
- Tariff of 1816
- Tariff of 1828 (Tariff of Abominations)
- John Tyler
- Daniel Webster
- Whig Party

12.8 CHRONOLOGY

The following chronology is a list of important dates and events associated with this chapter.

Date	Event
1816	Congress charted the Second Bank of the United States; Congress adopted the Tariff of 1816, an overtly protective tariff; James Monroe elected President
1819	Supreme Court issued Dartmouth College v. Woodward decision; Supreme Court issued McCulloch v. Maryland decision; Adams-Onís Treaty signed by the United States and Spain; Panic of 1819 caused economic distress throughout the nation
1820	Congress approved the Missouri Compromise; James Monroe reelected President
1823	James Monroe issued the Monroe Doctrine
1824	Supreme Court issued *Gibbons v. Ogden* decision; John Quincy Adams elected President
1828	Congress adopted the Tariff of 1828 (Tariff of Abominations); Democratic Party formed to support Andrew Jackson; John C. Calhoun secretly published the *South Carolina Exposition and Protest*; Andrew Jackson elected President
1830	Congress passed the Indian Removal Act; Hayne-Webster Debate occurred in Congress; Andrew Jackson vetoed the Maysville Road Bill
1831	Supreme Court issued *Cherokee v. Georgia* decision
1832	Supreme Court issued *Worcester v. Georgia* decision; Andrew Jackson vetoed the Second Bank of the United States Re-charter Bill; Congress adopted the Tariff of 1832; Andrew Jackson reelected President; South Carolina issued the ordinance of nullification for the Tariffs of 1828
1833	Congress approved the Tariff of 1833 and the Force Act; South Carolina withdrew its nullification of the tariffs
1834	The Senate, led by Henry Clay, censured Andrew Jackson; Whig Party formed to oppose Andrew Jackson
1835	Congress passed the Coinage Act

Date	Event
1836	Congress adopted the Deposit Act; Andrew Jackson issued the Specie Circular; Martin Van Buren elected President
1837	Panic of 1837 launched an almost four-year long depression
1840	Congress approved the Independent Treasury Act; William Henry Harrison elected President
1841	William Henry Harrison died; John Tyler succeeded him as President

12.9 BIBLIOGRAPHY

Calloway, Colin G. *First Peoples: A Documentary Survey of American Indian History*. Boston: Bedford/St. Martin's, 2004.

Covington, James W. *The Seminoles of Florida*. Gainesville: University Press of Florida, 1993.

Ellis, Richard E. "The Market Revolution and the Transformation of American Politics, 1801-1837." In *The Market Revolution in America: Social, Political, and Religious Expressions, 1800-1880*, eds. Melvin Stokes and Stephen Conway. Charlottesville: The University of Virginia Press, 1996.

Ellis, Richard E. *The Union at Risk: Jacksonian Democracy, States Rights' and the Nullification Crisis*. New York: Oxford University Press, 1987.

Forbes, Robert Pierce. *The Missouri Compromise and Its Aftermath*. Chapel Hill: University of North Carolina Press, 2007.

Freehling, William W. *The Road Disunion: Secessionists at Bay, 1776-1854*. New York: Oxford University Press, 1990.

Harkins, George "Farewell Letter to the American People." In *Great Documents in American Indian History*, ed. Wayne Moquin with Charles Van Doren. New York: Praeger, 1973. 152.

Holt, Michael. *The Rise and Fall of the American Whig Party: Jacksonian Politics and the Onset of the Civil War*. New York: Oxford University Press, 1999.

Perkins, Bradford. *The Cambridge History of American Foreign Relations, Volume I: The Creation of a Republican Empire*. Cambridge: Cambridge University Press, 1993.

Schlesinger, Jr., Arthur M. *The Age of Jackson*. New York: Little Brown, 1945.

Sellers, Charles. *The Market Revolution: Jacksonian America, 1815-1846*. New York: Oxford University Press, 1991.

Watson, Harry L. *Liberty and Power: The Politics of Jacksonian America*. New York: Hill and Wang, 1990.

Weeks, William Earl "Early American Foreign Relations." In *Paths to Power*, ed. Michael J. Hogan. Cambridge: Cambridge University Press, 2000.

Wilentz, Sean *Andrew Jackson*. New York: Times Books, 2005.

Wilentz, Sean. *The Rise of American Democracy: Jefferson to Lincoln*.New York: W.W. Norton, 2005.

12.10 END NOTES

1 James Monroe, "Inaugural Address, March 4, 1817," *The American Presidency Project* [online] edited by Gerhard Peters and John T. Woolley, November 5, 20122, http://www.presidency.ucsb.edu/ws/?pid=25807.

2 Charles Sellers, *The Market Revolution: Jacksonian America, 1815-1846* (New York: Oxford University Press, 1991), 70-71, 84, 97; Bradford Perkins, *The Cambridge History of American Foreign Relations, Volume I: The Creation of a Republican Empire* (Cambridge: Cambridge University Press, 1993), 147.

3 Sellers, *The Market Revolution*, 72.

4 Sellers, *The Market Revolution*, 74-75.

5 Sellers, *The Market Revolution*, 77-78.

6 *McCulloch v. Maryland* decision, 1819, Minutes of the Supreme Court of the United States, Record Group 267, National Archives, November 7, 2011, http://ourdocuments.gov/doc.php?doc=21.

7 *Gibbons v. Ogden* decision, 1824, Records of the Supreme Court of the United States, Record Group 267, National Archives, November 7, 2011, http://ourdocuments.gov/doc.php?doc=24.

8 William Earl Weeks, "Early American Foreign Relations," in *Paths to Power* edited by Michael J. Hogan (Cambridge: Cambridge University Press, 2000), 32-33.

9 Perkins, *The Creation of a Republican Empire*, 157-158.

10 "The Monroe Doctrine," December 2, 1823, *National Archives and Records Administration*, November 23, 2011, http://www.ourdocuments.gov/doc.php?doc=23&page=transcript.

11 Michael Holt, *The Rise and Fall of the American Whig Party: Jacksonian Politics and the Onset of the Civil War* (New York: Oxford University Press, 1999), 2-4.

12 Richard E. Ellis, "The Market Revolution and the Transformation of American Politics, 1801-1837," in *The Market Revolution in America: Social, Political, and Religious Expressions, 1800-1880* edited by Melvin Stokes and Stephen Conway (Charlottesville: The University of Virginia Press, 1996), 160-162.

13 Sellers, *The Market Revolution*, 135-136.

14 Ellis, "The Market Revolution and the Transformation of American Politics, 1801-1837," 163.

15 Sellers, *The Market Revolution*, 137-139.

16 Rufus King quoted in Robert Pierce Forbes, *The Missouri Compromise and Its Aftermath* (Chapel Hill: University of North Carolina Press, 2007), 83-84.

17 Letter from Thomas Jefferson to John Holmes, April 20, 1820, Thomas Jefferson Papers, Library of Congress Manuscript Division, Washington, DC, November 8, 2011, http://www.loc.gov/exhibits/jefferson/159.html.

18 Sean Wilentz, *Andrew Jackson* (New York: Times Books, 2005), 48.
19 John Quincy Adams, "First Annual Message to Congress, December 6, 1825," *The American Presidency Project* [online] edited by Gerhard Peters and John T. Woolley, November 22, 2011, http://www.presidency.ucsb.edu/ws/index.php?pid=29467#axzz1eSLGGg13.

20 Wilentz, *Andrew Jackson*, 50-51; Holt, *The Rise and Fall of the American Whig Party*, 9.

21 Arthur M. Schlesinger, Jr., *The Age of Jackson* (New York: Little Brown, 1945), 306-307; Wilentz, *Andrew Jackson*, 11-12.

22 Daniel Walker Howe, *What Hath God Wrought: The Transformation of America, 1815-1815* (New York: Oxford University Press, 2007), 278.

23 Harry L. Watson, *Liberty and Power: The Politics of Jacksonian America* (New York: Hill and Wang, 1990), 91-93.

24 Wilentz, *Andrew Jackson*, 56-57.

25 Richard E. Ellis, *The Union at Risk: Jacksonian Democracy, States Rights' and the Nullification Crisis* (New York: Oxford University Press, 1987), Chapter 1.

26 Wilentz, *Andrew Jackson*, 60-62.

27 George Harkins, "Farewell Letter to the American People," in *Great Documents in American Indian History*, ed. Wayne Moquin with Charles Van Doren (New York: Praeger, 1973), 152.

28 James W. Covington, *The Seminoles of Florida* (Gainesville: University Press of Florida, 1993), 144-146.

29 Colin G. Calloway, *First Peoples: A Documentary Survey of American Indian History* (Boston: Bedford/St. Martin's, 2004), 213-217.

30 Wilentz, *Andrew Jackson*, 63; Watson, *Liberty and Power*, 88-89.

31 Wilentz, *Andrew Jackson*, 64; Watson, *Liberty and Power*, 117.

32 Wilentz, *Andrew Jackson*, 64.

33 Watson, *Liberty and Power*, 118-120; Robert Hayne, "Second Speech - January 21, 1830," and Daniel Webster, "Second Reply - January 26, 1830," The Hayne-Webster Debate edited by Hal Morris, The Constitution Society, November 19, 2011, http://www.constitution.org/hwdebate/hwdebate.htm.

34 Andrew Jackson and John C. Calhoun as quoted in William W. Freehling, *The Road Disunion: Secessionists at Bay, 1776-1854* (New York: Oxford University Press, 1990), 270; Watson, *Liberty and Power*, 122. Other sources suggest that Jackson's toast did not include the word "federal" because in his excitement he spoke more bluntly than intended. See Wilentz, *Andrew Jackson*, 65.

35 Wilentz, *Andrew Jackson*, 89.

36 Wilentz, *Andrew Jackson*, 93-94; Freehling, *The Road to Disunion*, 277.

37 Andrew Jackson, "Nullification Proclamation, December 10, 1832," *The Avalon Project*, Yale University, November 19, 2011, http://avalon.law.yale.edu/19th_century/jack01.asp; Wilentz, *Andrew Jackson*, 97.

38 Watson, *Liberty and Power*, 128-129.

39 Watson, *Liberty and Power*, 129.

40 Wilentz, *Andrew Jackson*, 76-77.

41 Wilentz, *Andrew Jackson*, 79-80.
42 Wilentz, *Andrew Jackson*, 80; Schlesinger, *The Age of Jackson*, 86-87.

43 Schlesinger, *The Age of Jackson*, 89.

44 Wilentz, *Andrew Jackson*, 82.

45 Schlesinger, *The Age of Jackson*, 98.

46 Wilentz, *Andrew Jackson*, 107-108.

47 Wilentz, *Andrew Jackson*, 116-117.

48 Schlesinger, *The Age of Jackson*, 76-79.

49 Wilentz, *Andrew Jackson*, 117-118.

50 Watson, *Liberty and Power*, 172.

51 Wilentz, *Andrew Jackson*, 112.

52 Holt, *The Rise and Fall of the American Whig Party*, 10-13.

53 Holt, *The Rise and Fall of the American Whig Party*, 17, 25-28.

54 Wilentz, *Andrew Jackson*, 71-72.

55 Wilentz, *Andrew Jackson*, 132-134.

56 Watson, *Liberty and Power*, 204-205.

57 Schlesinger, *Age of Jackson*, 217-218; Sellers, *The Market Revolution*, 344-345.

58 Sean Wilentz, *The Rise of American Democracy: Jefferson to Lincoln* (New York: W.W. Norton, 2005), 456.

59 Schlesinger, *Age of Jackson*, 218-220.

60 Martin Van Buren as quoted in Watson, *Liberty and Power*, 207.

61 Wilentz, *The Rise of American Democracy*, 457-458.

62 Holt, *The Rise and Fall of the American Whig Party*, 65.

63 Watson, *Liberty and Power*, 209.

64 Holt, *The Rise and Fall of the American Whig Party*, 66-68.

65 Watson, *Liberty and Power*, 212-214.

66 Watson, *Liberty and Power*, 214-216.

67 Watson, *Liberty and Power*, 226.

ANSWER KEY FOR CHAPTER TWELVE: JACKSONIAN AMERICA (1815-1840)

Check your answers to the questions in the Before You Move On Sections for this chapter.

Correct answers are **BOLDED**

Section 12.2.3 - p443

1. Which of the following did not represent the government's nationalist tendencies in the Era of Good Feelings?
    a. Second Bank of the United States
    B. TALLMADGE AMENDMENT
    c. Tariff of 1816
    d. Gibbons v. Ogden

2. The Panic of 1819 increased the American people's faith in the Second Bank of the United States.
    a. True
    B. FALSE

3. As a result of the "corrupt bargain,"
    a. Henry Clay's plans for economic development were defeated.
    B. JOHN QUINCY ADAMS BECAME PRESIDENT.
    c. the protective tariff rate increased.
    d. Congress approved the Monroe Doctrine.

Section 12.3.6 - p459

1. Andrew Jackson's action in regard to the Indians was to
    a. oppose their removal to the West.
    B. REFUSE TO ENFORCE A SUPREME COURT DECISION IN THE INDIAN'S FAVOR.
    c. defend Indian rights to disputed lands in Georgia.
    d. send troops to slaughter the Indians.

2. Who was the author of the South Carolina Exposition and Protest?
    A. JOHN C. CALHOUN
    b. Henry Clay
    c. Robert Hayne
    d. Daniel Webster

3. Many critics of the Second Bank of the United States, including Andrew Jackson, charged that
    a. it failed completely to meet its financial obligations.
    b. it was a tool of the Democratic Party.
    c. it was mismanaged by Nicholas Biddle.
    D. IT CONCENTRATED TOO MUCH POWER IN THE HANDS OF THE PRIVILEGED.

Section 12.4.4 - p468

1. The Second Party System consisted of which two political parties?
    a. Federalists and Democrats
    b. Democrats and Republicans
    C. DEMOCRATS AND WHIGS
    d. Republicans and Whigs

2. After the Panic of 1837, Martin Van Buren supported _________ to remedy the nation's economic problems.
    a. the Second Bank of the United States
    B. THE INDEPENDENT TREASURY SYSTEM
    c. the Specie Circular
    d. a new protective tariff

3. William Henry Harrison's defeat over Martin Van Buren in the presidential election of 1840 was a victory for the Democratic Party.
    a. True
    B. FALSE

Chapter Thirteen: Antebellum Revival And Reform

Contents

Chapter Thirteen: Antebellum Revival and Reform

13.1 INTRODUCTION

The period between 1820 and 1860 was a time of great change in society, religion, and culture in the United States. The Second Great Awakening, a religious revival movement, saw evangelical Christianity supplant the established religious patterns of the colonial and Revolutionary eras: the Methodist and Baptist churches grew and spread. Others turned to "rational" religious denominations, such as Unitarianism. They based their religious beliefs and practices on rationalism, downplaying the miracles of scripture and concentrating instead on the morals it imparted and the historical events it recounted, arguing, "my rational nature is from God." The mid-nineteenth century also witnessed the appearance of a number of millennial sects such as the Mormons, Shakers, and Millerites, advocating that the Second Coming of Jesus was at hand. Socially, society was in a period of great upheaval because of the changes spurred by the market revolution: increasing urbanization and industrialization, the growth of immigration, and growing inequality between classes. As a result, the reform impulse and its subsequent movements, such as abolitionism and the movement to reform prisons and asylums, were strongest in the northern United States, the area most affected by the social upheaval of the market revolution as reformers sought to impose order on a changing society. Socially and culturally, the period was also a time of experimentation. More than 100 Utopian communities sprang up all over the country. Some of these, such as the Shakers, were religious communities. Others, like Brook Farm, considered themselves to be social experiments.

The antebellum period (or era before the Civil War) was a time of social and moral reform. Moral reform groups promoted temperance, or abstinence from alcohol. Others worked to make basic education available to all or sought to improve conditions in prisons and asylums. Social activists sought to end slavery and establish greater rights for women. American intellectualism and literature flowered, in part under the transcendentalist movement. Each of these movements, religious, moral, and reform, stressed a belief in the basic goodness of human nature, and in its own way, each of the movements sought to perfect humankind and society.

13.1.1 Learning Outcomes

After completing this chapter, you should be able to:

- Evaluate the broad social implications of the Second Great Awakening.
- Analyze the "perfectionist" tendencies of the movements of the 1820-1860 period.
- Explain how the cultural movements of the nineteenth century (transcendentalism, Utopian communities, and the Cult of Domesticity) influenced American culture.
- Explain how The Second Great Awakening influenced the anti-slavery movement and the women's rights movement.

13.2 RELIGIOUS REFORMS IN THE ANTEBELLUM UNITED STATES

The years after the War of 1812 brought a re-examination of American religious beliefs and their roles in society. Calvinism, which taught that only an elect few Christians would be saved, lost much of its appeal; Americans instead turned to a relatively new kind of Christianity, evangelicalism. Evangelical sects emphasized the resurrection of Christ, the primacy of scripture, the spiritual "rebirth" of believers, and the importance of proselytizing. The movement began in Europe in the 1700s with the growth of the Baptist movement and the foundation of the Methodist church. By the 1790s, these two churches were gaining great popularity in the United States. Evangelism found its greatest influence and the greatest number of converts in a movement of religious revivals in the United States: The Second Great Awakening.

13.2.1 The Second Great Awakening

The Second Great Awakening began in the 1790s and, by the 1820s, had emerged as a major religious movement. Evangelical in nature, it stressed that salvation was available to all through free will. Religious reformers preached that individuals were responsible to seek out their own salvation and hoped to regenerate and perfect society through individual conversions. Because it was generally inclusive of everyone, the message was spread to men and women, to rich and poor, and among slaves and free blacks alike. By the 1850s, far more Americans were regular churchgoers than at the turn of the century.

The most successful denominations of the Second Great Awakening were the Methodist and Baptist churches. By the 1820s, the Methodist and Baptist churches were the largest evangelical denominations. Both were popularly-rooted movements that emphasized conversion and a spiritual rebirth through personal religious experiences. The basic message was that salvation was something anyone could achieve: ordinary people could choose salvation through personal experience and living a righteous life. Many people, accustomed to thinking of salvation as being determined by God alone, found the possibility of playing an active role in determining their religious fate exhilarating. Evangelical churches became tightly-knit communities that sought to transform society first as a force that determined and enforced values, morality, and conduct, and second, by outreach through moral reform societies that concentrated on reforming personal vices such as drinking, sexual misconduct, and gambling. Through these moral reform societies, churches hoped to change society by putting individuals on the "path to righteousness." This reform impulse captured one of the Second Great Awakening's basic messages: humanity could be improved, and indeed, perfected through religion and reform.

One of the defining characteristics of the Second Great Awakening was large gatherings at religious revivals. The meetings typically lasted three to five days and were meant to reawaken or "revive" one's religious faith through an intense, emotional experience. In part, this was achieved by a certain theatricality of preaching. Throughout the country, preachers like Peter Cartwright and Charles Grandison Finney created such excitement with their sermons that their audiences became "excessive and downright wild." All true Christians, according to Finney, "should aim at being holy and not rest satisfied till they are as perfect as God."[1] The religious music and hymns written during the era also helped draw crowds to the revivals; they appealed the common individual by using familiar melodies from popular music and featured folk instruments that many could play, such as the fiddle. Such music remained after the revival and itinerant preacher were long gone.

Baptists and Methodists preached that all could achieve salvation and that all people were equal before God. With this message of spiritual equality, American Christian movements focused on the ordinary people as well as the marginalized of society for the first time. The message held the greatest appeal for those without power in society. Far more women than men were converted during the revivals of the Second Great Awakening. For some women, church membership and the new Christian message offered more personal power and greater personal freedom, as becoming active in the church was considered to be acceptable feminine conduct. The early message also empowered African Americans, free and enslaved. All over the country, African Americans joined the Baptist, Methodist, and other churches, in part as a response to the message of spiritual equality. The new evangelical denominations of the Second Great Awakening did not require the same kinds of rigorous education as older sects did; rather, it was far more important for a spiritual leader to experience a personal conversion and feel a call to spread the message. Black lay-preachers, not ordained but appointed by the church or community to lead services and preach, became important speakers for and within free and enslaved communities. However, there were limits to spiritual equality; although all were spiritually equal in the eyes of God, for many believers, African Americans and women were still inferior to white men in all other ways. As a result, some African American congregants left the evangelical churches because of racial discrimination or because they were barred from leadership positions within the church and founded their own evangelical denominations, such as the African Methodist Episcopal (AME) church. Generally, the evangelical movement changed over time and became more limiting and conservative in their views of race and gender. The Second Great Awakening swept through most of the country, but it took differing forms in the North and the South.

The Second Great Awakening in the South and in Appalachia

In Appalachia and the South, the Second Great Awakening brought a sense of community and provided entertainment in isolated rural and frontier areas. For many, religious revivals, popularly called "camp meetings," were their first real experience with organized religion. Camp meetings were so called because, on the sparsely populated frontier, many attendees had to travel long distances to the meeting and camp out at the location. Camp meetings were a new form of religious expression for the United States. Their intense and emotional atmosphere inspired a tremendous number of conversions. The evangelical message that one's birth, education, wealth, and social status did not matter in the eyes of God held great appeal for the masses of the frontier. Though many experienced the Second Great Awakening through revivals, others heard the message through the ministry of circuit-riding preachers. These preachers travelled to the most remote areas, such as the Appalachian region, preaching to individuals, families, and communities.

Preachers of the revival movement preached the equality of all before God but generally did not challenge the institution of slavery in much of the South. For some, the issue initially boiled down to access to the slave population and the ability to bring the message to a wider audience. If they openly challenged the institution of slavery, slave owners would not allow their slaves to attend revival meetings or to hear the message. Indeed, many slave owners feared the message of spiritual equality, so they kept the evangelists out. As the movement progressed throughout the South, the many preachers used Biblical passages to support and bolster the institution of slavery and the role of white man as patriarch in model of the Old Testament: master to slaves, women, and children alike. Simultaneously, the slaves, women, and children were told that obedience to their master was their Christian duty. Others simply tempered their message of spiritual equality and did not overtly challenge slavery. Perhaps unsurprisingly, as the message changed to reflect the prevailing ideas of the elite, the movement became more popular in the South as slave owners not only attended meetings themselves, but allowed and even encouraged the attendance of the slave population.

Throughout the South, slaves attended camp meetings. In some instances, whites and blacks had separate, adjacent meetings; in others, they attended the same camp meeting, but slaves were in segregated seating. In either case, they often heard the same sermons, sang the same songs, and received the same message. Revivals also created a widely known group of respected black leaders, many among them preachers associated with the movement. This is especially true of the Baptist church; independent black congregations were founded all over the South. For many slaves, the message was a promise of freedom, either in this world or in the afterlife.

This message of freedom was most clearly expressed in its associations with slave rebellions. Gabriel's Rebellion of 1800 grew in part out of a series of revival meetings in the area of Richmond, Virginia. Gabriel, a blacksmith, was often leased out to work for others; in this more "relaxed" system, he was able to move more freely and recruit conspirators, a pattern that was only enhanced by the summer's revival meetings. Additionally, some of the conspirators were recruited at the Hungary Baptist Meeting House, the church Gabriel and his brothers attended. Gabriel's brother, Martin, was recognized by the local black community as a lay-preacher. When one of the conspirators proved hesitant to rebellion, Gabriel called on his brother to speak at a meeting of the conspirators to encourage them to action: outright rebellion. Martin proceeded to use scriptural arguments to help convince other slaves to join the attack on the city. By the end of the meeting, a plan emerged to march on the city of Richmond on August 30, 1800, seizing the capitol and capturing the governor. Significantly, Gabriel forbade the conspirators to kill Methodists and Quakers, groups that were actively seeking manumission for slaves in the area at this time. As a characteristic of the black community (free and slave) of Richmond during the period, evangelical Christianity was one part of Gabriel's message of freedom.[2]

Twenty years later in Charleston, South Carolina, lay-preacher Denmark Vesey led a similar conspiracy to incite rebellion. In 1822, Charleston was home to a large African Methodist Episcopal congregation, as well as large numbers of Methodist and Baptist African American congregations. Many of the congregants were literate, including Vesey himself. Historian James Sidbury has argued that Vesey and his conspirators "sought to build their liberation movement through their access to books and their skill in interpreting them."[3] The most important of these texts by far was the Bible; Vesey and church leaders argued that the Bible did not sanction slavery or command obedience from slaves. Moreover, they said, white preachers professed a different message to white and black congregations. Vesey's plan called for teams of rebels to attack targets such as the arsenal and guardhouse. Afterward, the rebels would flee to the newly-freed nation of Haiti. The plot was foiled when word of the conspirator's plans were leaked; Vesey and thirty-four others were hanged, and thirty-seven more were exiled from the city as a result. After the conspiracy was quelled, white Charlestonians accused black congregations of the same offense: falsifying and misinterpreting the Bible. The African Methodist Episcopal Church where Vesey preached was destroyed.[4]

Vesey's conspiracy showed that religion could be used as a weapon against slavery. A decade later, Nat Turner used the message of the Second Great Awakening to help incite one of the largest slave rebellions in United States history. Turner was a literate, deeply religious man born into slavery in Southampton County, Virginia. Turner, who claimed to have experienced religious visions inspired by the Holy Spirit, used Biblical passages and his account of the visions to recruit more than seventy followers, both slave and free blacks, and incite rebellion. In late August of 1831, Turner and his followers launched the rebellion. Over the next two days, the insurrectionists killed some sixty white men, women, and children. The rebellion was quelled by a local militia, who killed or captured many of the insurrectionists. Fifty-five slaves were tried for insurrection, murder, and treason. They were subsequently executed. In the aftermath of the rebellion, the panicky white population killed more than one hundred black men, free and slave. Rumors spread across the South that the rebellion was not limited to Virginia; more African Americans were killed or arrested in Alabama, Virginia, and in other slaveholding states. Turner himself evaded capture for months. Eventually, however, he was captured, tried, and executed. After Turner's execution, lawyer Thomas Grey published *The Confessions of Nat Turner*, an account of his conversations with Turner before he was tried. The account spoke at length of Turner's religiously informed views of slavery and of his interpretations of the Bible. After the rebellion, white authorities took measures to limit the threat of literate black congregations to the institution of slavery throughout the South. For example, Virginia passed legislation making it illegal to teach slaves, free blacks, or mulattoes to read or write. Moreover, black congregations could not hold religious meetings without a licensed white minister present, presumably to assure that the "right" messages on slavery and freedom were the only ones presented from the pulpit.[5]

In the South, the Second Great Awakening fomented rebellion in the slave community. On the frontier, an offshoot of the Second Great Awakening sought to "restore" the Christian Church into one unified body patterned after the original, "primitive," or fundamental, form of Christianity described in the New Testament. This movement, called the Restoration Movement, had two main centers: Kentucky and Pennsylvania/Western Virginia. Like the other evangelical movements of the Second Great Awakening, they stressed adult baptism as an important step to salvation. Today, the influence of the Restoration Movement is seen in the Church of Christ and the Disciples of Christ churches.

The Second Great Awakening in the North

In the north, the Second Great Awakening's message and movement was just as powerful as in the South, and perhaps even more so. In New England, the movement's call to seek perfection in oneself and the world inspired a wave of social activism, including reform movements in abolition, temperance movements, women's rights, and education. In western New York, revival movements inspired many new religious sects as well as social reform. Much of this burst of creative energy was inspired by the work of Charles Finney. In 1821, Finney set out to preach in western New York. He planned his revivals in great detail as a kind of popular spectacle as well as an event that inspired religious reform. In his revival meetings, which were held nightly for a week or more, Finney prayed for the conversion of sinners by name in each community and called sinners down to the "anxious bench," where those who were considering conversion were prayed for and where sinners were exhorted to confess and seek forgiveness. Finney also encouraged women to speak publicly in "witness" or "testimony" in these mixed-sex gatherings. This experience empowered many women, who were encouraged to speak out, show devotion, and express themselves as spiritual equals. Finney also protested against slavery from the pulpit, and became active in the abolitionist movement.

Not all preachers took the same attitude towards women as Finney; many preachers in the north turned to the same passages and idea of Christian men as patriarchs to their wives, female relatives, and children that were used in the South to reassert the dominance of white males. Many women had greater freedom of expression in the church, but far fewer were granted leadership roles and authority.

The region of western and central New York where Finney was most active became the site of intensive religious fervor and reform. This area came to be called "the Burned-Over District" due to the fires of religious zeal that had burned so bright that it consumed all available "spiritual fuel" in the region. The Burned-Over District was not only the site of revivals of the Protestant denominations of the Second Great Awakening, but also the birthplace of new religious movements such as the Millerites, a millennial group who preached that the Second Advent (or "second coming") of Jesus was imminent. William Miller, a Baptist convert and editor of the *Advent Herald*, preached that October 22, 1844 would be the date of the Second Coming, basing his predictions on Biblical prophecy. Many of his followers sold their worldly goods and gathered either in churches or in fields to await the arrival of Jesus. The movement experienced what became to be known as "the Great Disappointment" when the morning of October 23 arrived rather than Jesus. Soon after, the movement disintegrated. However, the modern-day Seventh Day Adventist Church later grew out of the Millerite movement. The Latter Day Saint Movement (of which the Church of Jesus Christ and Latter Day Saints, popularly called the Mormons, is the most important branch) also was born in the Burned-Over District during the era of the Second Great Awakening.

The Mormons

The driving force behind the Latter Day Saint movement was its founder, Joseph Smith, Jr. In 1823, Smith recounted that an angel named Moroni had visited him. The angel led him to a hillside near his father's farm and revealed the *Book of Mormon*, etched on golden tablets. Smith described Moroni as a son of the prophet Mormon and the last of the Nephites, descendants of Hebrews who had travelled to the Americas sometime around 500 BCE. The book reports that there, Jesus visited the Nephites after his crucifixion and resurrection. The Book of Mormon was published in 1830, and Smith began the formation of his church. Like many religious movements of the day, Mormons believed in the imminent Second Coming of Jesus. Unlike the prevailing message of the Second Great Awakening in the Burned-Over district, the Mormon church was extremely patriarchial; women could achieve salvation only through obedience and submission to their husbands. Leadership and authority within the church was the exclusive domain of white men. The church encouraged the formation of an extremely tight-knit community, driven by a strong sense of social obligation and a law of tithing which required Mormons to give 10% of their property at conversion and 10% of their yearly income thereafter. Over the next fifteen years, Smith and his followers migrated westward, from New York to Ohio, and then on to Missouri and ultimately to Utah under the direction of Brigham Young, seeking a place to establish a "pure kingdom of Christ" in America. The Church of Later-Day Saints proved to be a lasting and successful alternative vision to the Second Great Awakening of antebellum America.

The Unitarian Movement

Evangelical Christianity was certainly the most powerful religious movement in the antebellum United States, but it was not the only one. Throughout New England, many Christians began to espouse Unitarianism, a sect based on the importance of human reason. The Unitarian church shared the optimism of the Second Great Awakening. Unitarians stressed the inherent goodness of humankind. Everyone was eligible for salvation, and a loving God embraced all. Dr. William Ellery Channing, one of the leading preachers and theologians of the Unitarian Church, preached on the great potential of humans. In 1828, his "Likeness to God" sermon argued that true religion is marked by the believer becoming more and more like God. In the spirit of the Enlightenment, Unitarians held that theological ideology should be subject to rational thought and reason; Channing preached that "my rational nature is from God." Unitarians attested to the "oneness of God." As strict monotheists, Unitarians viewed Jesus as a saintly man, but not divine. The Unitarian church was most popular in New England and was centered in Boston. For the most part, it appealed to the elite of society. The Unitarian movement spread through many of the Congregationalist churches of the area. Channing's 1819 "Unitarian Christianity" sermon, which outlined many of the core beliefs of the new American sect, such as a belief in human goodness and rejection of the Trinity, inspired many churches to adopt Unitarianism.

13.2.2 Before You Move On...

Key Concepts

The Second Great Awakening and the movement in religious revival in the United States had a profound impact on the United States. The new Protestant denominations, most prominently the Baptists and Methodists, grew in strength and numbers. The Second Great Awakening encouraged this impulse to reform by emphasizing individual responsibility and the desire to seek perfection. The Second Great Awakening manifested itself somewhat differently regionally. In the South, the movement became more conservative over time, and generally supported the system of slavery. Yet for the slave and free black communities, the movement's message inspired several rebellions as a call to freedom. In the north, the movement reached its zenith in the "Burned-Over District" of Charles Finney. In the early nineteenth century, the United States was becoming a more diverse nation; the new varieties of Protestantism were one reflection of this change.

Test Yourself

1. The influence of reason and rational thought is most clearly expressed in what religious tradition?

   a. Unitarians

   b. Mormons

   c. Methodists

   d. Puritans

2. The ______________ refers to an area of New York that was so affected by the Second Great Awakening that there "was no more fuel to burn" for the fire of religion.

   a. Burned-Over District

   b. "anxious bench"

   c. Moroni

   d. Millerites

See page 502 for answers

13.3 CULTURAL MOVEMENTS: TRANSCENDENTALISM, UTOPIAN COMMUNITIES, AND THE CULT OF DOMESTICITY

Like the Second Great Awakening, other American movements professed a deep-held belief in the goodness of mankind. Transcendentalists and members of Utopian communities emphasized the perfectibility of humanity and took steps to live their lives and create communities so as to achieve some measure of human perfection. These movements transformed American culture in distinct ways. The transcendentalists had a lasting effect as part of a greater, global movement in Romanticism, which emphasized elevation of the spirit over reason. Transcendentalists also had a powerful effect on the development of a distinctly American field of literature.

More than a hundred Utopian communities were established throughout the United States during the nineteenth century; each of these communities sought to perfect the human experience, though they took differing views on how this could be achieved.

13.3.1 Transcendentalism

The transcendentalists were an intellectual community mostly centered in New England. They emphasized the dignity of the individual and exalted American ideals of freedom, optimism, and self-reliance. They sought to "transcend" the limits of reason and intellect and allow the soul to attain a relationship, a mystical oneness, with the universe. Many important American transcendentalists were writers who set about establishing an "American literary independence," producing a flowering of literature. Much of their literature reflected transcendental beliefs, praising Nature, a simple life, and self-reliance. In *Walden, or Life in the Woods*, Henry David Thoreau wrote of his experiences supporting himself living on Walden Pond, Massachusetts; he begins his narrative by declaring, "I went to the woods because I wished to live deliberately, to front only the essential facts of live, and see if I could not learn what it had to teach, and not, when I came to die, discover I had not lived."[6] In his address "The American Scholar," fellow Massachusetts resident Ralph Waldo Emerson similarly wrote that "We will walk on our own feet; we will work with our own hands; we will speak our own minds...A nation of men will for the first time exist, because each believes himself inspired by the Divine Soul which also inspires all men."[7] Many transcendentalists, including Emerson and Thoreau, were also reformers who worked in the abolitionist and women's rights causes.

13.3.2 Utopian Communities

Other groups held similar beliefs to the transcendentalists and focused their efforts on establishing ideal communities that would work to perfect the human experience in a social Utopia. Over the course of the century, some 100 Utopian communities were founded. Many focused on religion as the center of its community and activities; others were secular in nature. Utopian movements withdrew from the larger society and focused their efforts on the creation of a perfected new social order, not a reformed older one. Most of the communities stressed hard work and commitment to community ideals as a means of achieving this perfected new society. Many collapsed after years or even months; however, taken together, Utopianism was a significant movement that introduced new ideas to American society. In some cases, the transcendental and Utopian movements overlapped.

In 1840, leading transcendentalist George Ripley of Boston announced his intention of creating a place based on communal living and transcendental values. He and his followers established Brook Farm, where intellectuals pursued both hard physical and mental work as a way of life. Each member of the community was encouraged to work at the farming tasks that they liked best; every member was paid the same wage, including women. The community supported itself not only through farming, but also selling handmade goods and charging admission to the farm to curious visitors; they also earned money through the tuition raised by the excellent school run on the farm by Ripley. Brook Farm was to serve as an example in the perfection of living for the rest of the world. By 1844, community members had formally adopted a socialist societal model. They wrote and published a journal to promote and promulgate their views. However, the general public paid little attention to both the journal and the farm itself. Like many other Utopian communities, the experiment at Brook Farm came to an end in part because it had little to no real effect on the outside world. The final factor in its ending was when part of the farm caught fire; the community was unable to rebuild because the buildings were uninsured. By 1847, the experiment in communal living was over, and the farm closed down.

One of the longest-lasting Utopian traditions was the Shaker community. The United Society of Believers in Christ's Second Appearing established multiple communities devoted to living a simple life and developing one's talents through hard work. They were popularly called Shakers because of their practice of worship through music and dance, sometimes in twitching, "shaking" movements. Shakers worked to perfect themselves and their communities in anticipation of Christ's return.

Shakers, who lived a celibate life, added to their community through adoption and conversion, by taking in orphans, the homeless, and poor. The sexes lived and worked separately but held property in common. They practiced equality of the sexes, and at each level of the church hierarchy, both men and women held leadership positions. Since men and women were equal in the eyes of God, they argued, men and women should be treated equally on Earth. In fact, the founder of the American Shaker church was a woman: "Mother" Ann Lee. Shakers believed that God had both male and female aspects, and that Mother Lee was the female counterpart to Christ. For these reasons, more women joined the Shakers than men. At their height, the movement had about 6,000 members; however, the movement's rule of celibacy brought about its decline as few people joined the Shakers after mid-century.

Ultimately, the Shaker community's most lasting influence on the American public was not religious, but through design aesthetics. The Shaker emphasis on simplicity, functionality, and craftsmanship held broad appeal for many Americans. Shaker-designed and produced products and furniture, such as chairs, boxes, and cabinetry, remain a staple of the design world to this day.

Utopian socialist communities formed as a reaction to growing industrialization and its effects on the working class. The most prominent example of this is the community at New Harmony, Indiana. Established in 1825 by Scottish business owner and social reformer Robert Owen, the community's goal was to create a new social order where cooperation and the needs of the community superseded the interests of individuals. To this end, the community adopted a constitution which required that members of the community work for the community in exchange for credit at the town store. Those who did not wish to work could purchase credit instead. The town was to be governed by a committee of seven: four chosen by Owen, three elected by the community. Within the year, complaints of discrepancies between workers and non-workers arose. Additionally, the community had been unable to become self-sufficient and was overcrowded. Nevertheless, many members remained hopeful that the experiment world work and the community adopted a new constitution that espoused equal rights and equal duties for all. Although the constitution aspired to lofty goals, it proved too short on detailed specifics on how the community was to function on a day-to-day basis. The community limped along for several more months, but by 1827, it was subdivided and socialism gave way to individualism.

13.3.3 The Cult of Domesticity and Separate Spheres

Though many of the Utopian communities such as the Shakers called for relative equality of the sexes and women were viewed as spiritual equals in the Second Great Awakening, the American elite and middle class held a very different idea of the nature of women and their role in society. The "Cult of Domesticity" declared that the sphere of a "true woman" was her household. Publications such as *Godey's Lady Book* and *A Treatise on Domestic Economy* instructed women on how to create a refuge for their husbands and children, sheltering them from the cruel world outside. Moreover, women were to be the moral compass for their families. The Cult of Domesticity provided a powerful ideology of gender roles for many Americans. While not all regions and classes were adherents to this ideology, it was a movement that profoundly influenced American culture.

The ideology of the Cult of Domesticity took shape in the early 1800s. It viewed women and men as complete and total opposites, with almost no characteristics in common. Sex was the ultimate divisor, and gender roles and American society and culture were shaped with this division at its heart. Men and women inhabited two completely different "spheres": the public world of work and politics, belonging exclusively to men, and the private world of home and family, the domain of women. Although the spheres were completely separate, they were complimentary. The Cult of Domesticity built upon this notion of separate spheres and asserted that true women were centered exclusively in the domestic world of home and family; childrearing and caretaking was not work for women, but a natural expression of their feminine nature. True womanhood was found in selfless service to others. True women were to be pure and pious as well as skilled practitioners of the domestic arts, such as needlecraft. The Cult of Domesticity was upheld as the ideal among the mainstream American culture; however, many women were effectively excluded from "true womanhood" by virtue of their social status, race, or religion. True women, the underlying message proclaimed, were white, Protestant, and did not work outside of the home; it was a middle-class social ideology resting on the assumption that a woman was married to a man who was able and willing to support her. Living the ideals of the Cult of Domesticity and true womanhood allowed the middle class to distinguish themselves from the working class as increasing industrialization, urbanization, and immigration in the 1820-1850 period resulted in the first emergence of female wage laborers.

The Cult of Domesticity served a religious as well as social and cultural role. Through their devotion and sacrifice as wife, and more importantly, as mother, women were serving as a Christian ideal for their family. She served as a representative of Christ in daily life and made her sphere of domesticity a kind of sacred territory, creating a home which was a "haven from the heartless world" for her husband and children. Historians Ellen Carol DuBois and Lynn Dumenil argue that "true womanhood was a fervently Protestant notion, which gave to female devotion and selfless sacrifice a redemptive power."[8] It is no coincidence that this ideology came to prominence in the same era as the Second Great Awakening.

Both the influence of the Cult of Domesticity and the role that women played in the Second Great Awakening ultimately allowed and even encouraged women to participate in the moral reform efforts that came to characterize the antebellum period in the United States. Beginning in the 1820s, women participate in female benevolent associations that sponsored international Christian missionary efforts. Other organizations worked closer to home to uplift the poor, spiritually and morally. Middle class women were involved in these organizations because adherents of the Cult of Domesticity viewed the absence of separate spheres and family values as the cause of poverty. Since the mother and wife worked outside of the home in the corrupt public world, they reasoned, how could it be a place of refuge and purity? Middle class women worked to "educate" the poor in how they should live. Belief in the moral superiority of the Cult of Domesticity allowed for women of the middle class to engage in good works outside of the home, in the public world. In essence, the moral outreach and female benevolent societies expanded the private, domestic sphere and allowed the middle class to view itself as superior to the working class not only economically, but also socially. By the early 1830s, middle class women played an important role in the many reform movements of the age, including the temperance movement as well as the reform of education and prisons.

13.3.4 Before You Move On...

Key Concepts

The nineteenth century saw cultural movements that, like the Second Great Awakening, perceived humanity as basically good and imminently perfectible. The transcendentalists, the United States' first organized intellectual community, expressed this notion in their writings. American literature flourished in part because of the activities of the transcendentalists. Secular and religious utopian communities sought to live their lives and create communities that achieved some measure of human perfection. Utopian movements focused their efforts on the creation of a perfected new social order, not a reformed older one. Most of the communities withdrew from society, stressing the value of hard work and commitment to community ideals as a means of achieving this perfected new society. The Brook Farm community was an intellectual experiment that overlapped with the transcendental movement. The Shakers sought perfection of humanity in religion, stressing the equality of the sexes and celibacy. Finally, the utopian socialist community of New Harmony tried to create a more perfect society through communal work and property.

Finally, the Cult of Domesticity sought to perfect family life through the maintenance of a home run by a moral, domestically-skilled wife and mother. The home (and, by extension, the woman of the house) came to represent a place of morality, in sharp contrast to the corrupt public world. The Cult of Domesticity provided a powerful ideology of gender roles for many Americans. While not all regions and classes were adherents to this ideology, it was a movement that profoundly influenced American culture.

Test Yourself

1. Transcendentalists viewed _________ as the key to the human experience.

   a. transcending nature to attain reason

   b. equality of nations

   c. self-reliance

   d. dystopian communities

2. Shakers and Millerites were ______ movements, because they thought that the second coming of Jesus was approaching.

   a. millennial

   b. diurnal

   c. reform

   d. utopian

3. The notion of separate spheres and the Cult of Domesticity allowed the American middle class to distinguish themselves as separate from and superior to the working class.

   a. True

   b. False

See page 502 for answers

13.4 AMERICAN ANTEBELLUM REFORM

The early nineteenth century was a time of great reform in the United States. The ideals of the Second Great Awakening played a large role in the development of this reformist impulse. Preachers and believers all over the country saw humankind and society as good and perfectible, able to improve and strive to become more like God. At the same time, the Second Great Awaking stressed the notion of personal responsibility and the responsibility of a person to the sins of neighbors. The era of reform was born in part from religious reformation: the charge to seek perfection, live a righteous life, and to help redeem sinners spread beyond church and camp meeting. The antebellum reform movements were based in a network of voluntary, church-affiliated reform organizations. The reform impulse was not solely confined to the United States; Europeans were also in the midst of their own reform efforts. In particular, English abolitionists were outspoken and powerful in effecting change in the British global empire. Many types of reform movements existed during this period in the United States, and groups and causes only grew more splintered over time. Many different kinds of Americans worked in the reform movement. In particular, women played a large role in various aspects of reform. While not all Americans were active in the various reform movements, taken together, the reform impulse was a powerful force that characterizes the antebellum era.

13.4.1 The Temperance Movement

One of the most widespread of the reform movements in the 1820s-1840s was the temperance movement, which called for reducing the use of (or abstaining from) alcoholic beverages. Its roots lay in the revivals of the Second Great Awakening, where religious reformers called for individuals to lead "clean" lives and to redeem their sinning neighbors. The reformist impulse also stemmed from new social conditions. The increasing urbanization of the United States and the large numbers of immigrants, especially Germans, had transformed the nation in ways that were unfamiliar and that some found threatening. Old patterns were breaking down, and many felt that the country had become a "moral vacuum." Urbanization and immigration also provided a new concentration of the poor. The emerging American middle class participated in reform not only for religious reasons, but also to confirm their new social status. By helping others, they asserted their worth while at the same time alleviating social ills.

Alcohol in many forms had been an important part of the diet of Americans from the founding of the colonies onward. The Mayflower carried barrels upon barrels of beer for its passengers. Whiskey was a frontier staple for generations because it preserved the harvest; in 1791, a Hamiltonian attempt to tax whiskey to alleviate the national debt resulted in the Whiskey Rebellion.[9] By the 1830s, Americans were drinking more than ever; in the 1830s, the average American consumed more than 1.5 bottles of liquor a week. Meanwhile, many doctors were citing large amounts of alcohol as injurious to an individual's health. Chief among these physicians was Dr. Benjamin Rush of Pennsylvania. Ministers such as Connecticut Presbyterian Lyman Beecher also spoke out against alcohol as a societal evil.

The response to these conditions was the 1826 creation of the American Temperance Society in Boston, Massachusetts. The Society grew quickly and soon had spread across the country. Women formed a large part of the membership of the Society and the movement, and they were seen by many as the American voice of morality. Much of this perception stems from the "Cult of Domesticity." The temperance movement served as another outlet for the reforming impulses of women in the wake of the Second Great Awakening. Participation in the temperance movement was much more socially acceptable than participation in the abolition or women's rights movement. While many women spoke out against alcohol, many in the movement perceived women and children as the chief victims of alcohol consumption, as their husbands and sons suffered from alcohol's effects, spent the family's money on alcohol, spent their time in bars and saloons rather than in the family home, and sometimes became violent when drunk.

The American relationship with alcohol was not an issue that was resolved in the era of reform. The temperance movement and organizations had more than a million supporters who enthusiastically held rallies and distributed pamphlets on the evils of "demon rum." By the 1860s, their efforts had indeed slowed, but certainly did not stop, the average American's consumption of alcohol. Over the course of the nineteenth century, many towns and counties became "dry." Perhaps the greatest legislative victory for the temperance movement during the era of reform was Maine's short-lived total ban on alcohol from 1851-1856.

13.4.2 Reform of Prisons, Asylums, and Schools

Before the nineteenth century, crime, poverty, and mental illness in America were handled through family and voluntary efforts. Prisons existed not to rehabilitate criminals for their eventual return to society but to house them until the time that they would be punished, most often by fines, public whipping, or execution, also a public spectacle. Debtors were punished by imprisonment. Many mentally ill individuals eventually ended up imprisoned as well, as no facilities for the treatment of the mentally ill existed. Reformers worked to create public institutions to deal with the social problems. They believed that social deviants, including criminals and debtors, could be reformed and morally redeemed. The result was the creation of penitentiaries, which sought to transform criminals into law abiding citizens through hard work, religious instruction, and isolation from the corruption of social vices. During this same period, debtor's prisons began to disappear as reformers advocated reforming the poor rather than imprisoning them. Workhouses were established to keep the poor from drunkenness, idleness, and gambling. Finally, asylums were established for treatment and housing the mentally ill.

Dorothea Lynde Dix was instrumental in the reform effort that established state mental asylums. In the spring of 1841, Dix visited a Cambridge jail in order to teach Sunday school for a group of women inmates. There she found the inmates, some of them mentally ill (whom Dix refers to as lunatics), housed in filthy conditions in unheated cells. Horrified, she worked to publicize the conditions of the jail and gain public support for its improvement. She conducted an eighteen month study of the jails and almshouses of Massachusetts and, in 1843, made a presentation to the Massachusetts legislature, reporting that the mentally ill were housed in "cages, closets, cellars and pens...Chained, naked, beaten with rods, and lashed into obedience."[10] A movement for change was already underway when Dix began her campaign for reform; for instance, Quakers had already founded several asylums for treatment. Dix was instrumental in motivating a state role in the creation of these facilities. Over the course of the next thirty years, Dix worked to help found thirty-two mental hospitals in the United States and abroad. Moreover, her reports on jails also aided in the efforts to reform prisons.

American reformers also sought to implement school reform. Before the early 1800s, education for most Americans was very basic. For most, this meant a few months of schooling a year in a one-room rural schoolhouse. The wealthy engaged private tutors and academies. For the urban poor, a very few were able to attend private charitable schools. Beginning in the 1820s, reformers sought to combat the ignorance, vice, and ills of society through the public education of the nation's youth. Moreover, the rising numbers of immigrants in the northeast combined with near-universal white male suffrage convinced cities and states that education was essential to maintain a democracy. Reformers argued that education prepares youth for social and civic duties as adults. The most prominent of these education reformers was Horace Mann, head of the Massachusetts board of education, the first in the nation. Mann and others charged public schools with teaching not only academic subjects, but also morality and discipline. One means of teaching these values was through the series *McGuffey's Readers*, a series of texts that taught not only spelling and vocabulary, but also punctuality, frugality, and temperance. Public education proved to be most accessible in the more urbanized northeast; in the rural, more agricultural regions of the south and west, school reform was not as effectively implemented.

Women played a large role in education reform. Young female teachers staffed many of the schools. It is also during this time that higher education began to open to women. The earliest women's colleges were founded in the 1830s: the Georgia Female College in Macon, Georgia (now Wesleyan College), founded in 1836, and Mount Holyoke Female Seminary in South Hadley, Massachusetts (Now Mount Holyoke College), founded in 1837. Oberlin College in Oberlin, Ohio became the first co-educational institution when it admitted four women in 1837.

13.4.3 Abolitionism and the Women's Rights Movements

Two of the most significant reform movements to come out of the reform period of 1820-1840 were the anti-slavery movement and the women's rights movement. Each of these movements worked for freedom and emancipation and to grant a greater body of rights to two of the groups on the periphery of American society. The movements shared a common support base: many abolitionists supported or were active in the women's rights movement, or vice versa. In numerous ways, the organized women's rights movement grew out of abolitionist organizations and the movement of the early 1800s. Although neither group saw their cause's ultimate goals achieved during the era of reform, each movement saw great advances. Abolitionism was perhaps the most radical of the reform movements of the era.

The struggle to end slavery has a long history both globally and in the United States; indeed, the struggle to end slavery emerged at roughly the same time as slavery itself. However, abolitionism developed significantly over the 1800s. In the early decades of the century, several groups emerged as "colonizationists." These groups sought to remove blacks from the United States either through emigration or through the creation of colonies in Africa. The end of slavery would come about gradually under this ideal. For the most part, colonizationists accepted the idea of black inferiority. For some members of the movement, the idea meant the end of slavery; for others, it was an answer for racial tensions in the United States. Kentucky Congressional representative Henry Clay argued for colonization because of the "unconquerable prejudice" against blacks in the United States. Other important politicians, including James Madison and Abraham Lincoln, favored "repatriation" rather than emancipation.

For the most part, the African American community did not see colonization or repatriation as a viable alternative to emancipation and abolition. David Walker, an African American abolitionist, called for a unified global black voice against slavery in his *Appeal to the Colored Citizens of the World.* Walker stood as a vocal opponent of colonization, saying that the United States belonged more to African Americans than to whites, because the black population had earned the country with their "blood and tears."

Nevertheless, the American Colonization Society (ACS) emerged as the main voice of colonizationists in the United States. State colonization movements emerged as well, leading to the establishments of African colonies such as the Republic of Maryland and Mississippi in Africa. In 1821, the ACS helped to establish the colony of Liberia on the west coast of Africa and assisted some 13,000 slaves and free blacks to emigrate to the colony. The experiment in Liberia proved to be, in many ways, a failure; hundreds died from disease soon after emigrating. Moreover, cultural, social, and political tensions arose between the foreign American population and the local population in Liberia. The Americans made up a tiny minority of the population but dominated Liberian politics until the 1980s. Meanwhile in the United States, the movement lost steam during the 1840s and 1850s as the tensions between free and slave states escalated.

One of the most prominent abolitionists of the era was William Lloyd Garrison, publisher of the abolitionist newspaper *The Liberator*. Garrison was militant in his call for immediate and complete emancipation as a moral imperative. In the first issue of the Liberator, he made a public apology for ever advocating a gradual end to slavery and called for its immediate end. He ended his appeal by writing, "I will not equivocate- I will not excuse- I will not retreat a single inch- and I will be heard."[11] Along with an immediate end to slavery, Garrison also espoused racial equality as an absolute necessity to ending the institution without massive bloodshed. In every state, laws restricted the political and civil liberties of free African Americans. Many Americans found this radical notion of racial equality and the call to end these restrictive laws intimidating or even frightening. Garrison refused to become more moderate in his demands, and *The Liberator* was published continuously for the next 35 years until the end of slavery in the United States.

In 1833, Garrison was among the group that founded the American Anti-Slavery Society. They were inspired in part by the success of British abolitionists. Abolitionists differed in their ideas about how to effectively bring about the end of slavery. Some, like Garrison, favored fiery calls and "no moderation"; at a rally in 1854, Garrison asserted that there could be "no union with slaveholders" and called the U.S. Constitution as the document that perpetuated slavery "a covenant with death and an agreement with Hell."[12] Others were convinced that their best strategy was to convince the public that slavery was a sin. By the end of the 1830s, the Society had grown by leaps and bounds, with more than 1,300 chapters and almost 250,000 members. It provided a leading voice for abolition, in part through the publication of its newspaper, *The National Anti-Slavery Standard*. In later years, the Society provided the founding impetus to the Liberty Party, a political party with an abolitionist platform.

The Anti-Slavery Society was home to white and black abolitionists. Many prominent African American abolitionists such as Frederick Douglass were members of the Society. Douglass was perhaps the most famous, influential, and vocal black abolitionist. Born into slavery in Maryland in 1819, he escaped from slavery as a young man and spent the rest of his life devoting himself to the cause of freedom for all. Douglass was a skilled orator and a prolific writer. His many autobiographies, including *Narrative of the Life of Frederick Douglass, an American Slave*, were instrumental in giving voice to the enslaved and black Americans and inspired generations of black leaders and reformers who called for freedom for all populations.

Although black and white abolitionists worked closely together in the movement and usually worked well together, African Americans experienced racial prejudice even within the abolitionist movement. Some of this came from a lack of understanding; in other cases, it was overt prejudice. White abolitionists tended to see free and slave as two polar opposites; black abolitionists knew that there were varying degrees of freedom and slavery. Often, white abolitionists knowingly or unknowingly exploited stereotypes in their abolitionist efforts. For example, as Frederick Douglass rose to prominence as an orator in the abolitionist movement, he began speaking not only of his life as a slave, but also analyzing abolitionist policies. White abolitionists warned him that people would cease to believe that he had ever been enslaved if he sounded too educated and advised him to leave the complex analysis to the whites. Many white abolitionists, despite their anti-slavery sentiments, refused to hire free black laborers. Even anti-slavery and abolitionist groups refused to grant full rights to black members. Eventually, the American Anti-Slavery Society itself split into factions over social issues.

Figure 13.1 Fredrick Douglass (1879) | Frederick Douglass, author, orator, and abolitionist, was a leading voice in the abolitionist movement of the early nineteenth century.

Author: Frank W. Legg
Source: National Archives

The abolitionist sentiment was also present in the South. An important example of the abolitionist voice in the South came from sisters from Charleston, South Carolina who had migrated north and become Quakers because of their abolitionism. The Grimké sisters, Sarah and Angelina, spoke out against the system of slavery in many forums. In 1837, Angelina wrote to William Lloyd Garrison's *The Liberator*. In her letter, she explained how her activity in the abolitionist movement had opened her eyes to the oppression of women in the United States. The sisters spoke before state legislations and were among the first women to speak in public forums before mixed sex groups. The daughters of a prominent slave owner, they spoke of their personal knowledge and experience of the system. Angelina later married Theodore Dwight Weld, a prominent abolitionist preacher. She assisted in the research for his 1839 indictment of slavery, *American Slavery as it is: Testimony of a Thousand Witnesses*. The Grimké sisters were one example of the overlap in the reformist impulse between abolitionism and women's rights.

The Women's Rights Movement

To the eyes of many reformers, the movements in abolition and women's rights had much in common; many who worked to end slavery also called for the "emancipation of women." Indeed, the women's rights movement had largely grown out of the anti-slavery movement. Women joined and actively participated in abolitionist organizations such as the Anti-Slavery Society; they sponsored events such as the Anti-Slavery Convention of American Women. A key moment came in 1840, when the Anti-Slavery Society split after a woman, Abigail Kelley, was nominated to serve on one of the Society's committees. The majority of the members of the Society favored including women in the governing structure of the organization; the more conservative members broke away from the Anti-Slave Society to form the American and Foreign Anti-Slave Society, which excluded women. Kelly later wrote of her experiences in the abolitionist movement and how they shaped her views on women's rights: "in striving to strike [the slaves'] irons off, we found most surely that *we* were manacled *ourselves*."[13]

Two of the leading figures of the women's rights movement met at the 1840 World Anti-Slavery Convention in London. There, the convention refused to seat the American female delegates. Lucretia Mott and Elizabeth Cady Stanton, two of the excluded delegates, united to form an organization that would speak for oppressed women.

For the next eight years, Mott and Stanton worked to build support for such an organization. In July 1848 they were finally able to call together a group together for the first national convention devoted to the issue of women's rights, the Seneca Falls Convention. Three hundred delegates, both men and women, attended the meeting. Over the course of two days, the delegates discussed the role of women in society and debated the issue of women's right to vote. The convention ended with the issue of the "Declaration of Sentiments," a document that largely paralleled the Declaration of Independence, and leveled a series of charges against the patriarchy of the United States that had been the source of the oppression of women. It declared that "all men and women are created equal," and went on to list the "repeated injuries and usurpations on the part of man toward

Figure 13.2 Lucretia Mott and Elizabeth Cady Stanton | These two women were instrumental in organizing the Seneca Falls Convention and writing the Declaration of Sentiments, which would articulate the goals of the women's rights movement.

Author: Unknown (Mott), Carol M. Highsmith (Stanton)
Source: Library of Congress

women," including that "He has compelled her to submit to laws, in the formation of which she had no voice," and "He has taken from her all right in property, even to the wages she earns."[14] The Declaration of Sentiments formed the basis of the goals of the women's rights movement that lasted throughout the rest of the century. The first and foremost of these goals was achieving the right to vote as an inalienable right of full, republican citizenship. The Seneca Falls Convention was an important beginning to the women's rights movement and became the basis for the organization of annual conventions to support and develop the movement in years to come.

The women's rights movement did not attract broad support among women or men during the antebellum era. Unlike other reform movements, women's rights challenged the notion of separate spheres and the idea of "true womanhood." Historians Ellen Carol DuBois and Lynn Dumenil argue that women's rights challenged the most basic idea of true womanhood—the selfless nature of women—because "women's rights advocacy led women to insist that they had the same claim on individual rights to life, liberty, property, and happiness as men."[15] The work to achieve the vote made no substantive progress in the antebellum period. The most significant success was that by 1860, more than a dozen states had granted women greater control over the wages they earned, and some even allowed women to sue husbands and fathers who tried to deprive them of their wages.

13.4.4 Before You Move On...

Key Concepts

Early nineteenth-century America was a time of reform. Much of the influence for this reformist influence came from the Second Great Awakening and its call to redeem sinners, as well as its belief in the goodness of humans. Like the preachers of the revivals, the temperance movement reformers called for individuals to lead "clean" lives and to redeem their sinning neighbors. Others sought to build and improve public and state institutions such as prisons, asylums, and schools. Many kinds of Americans worked in the reform movement, and membership in some movements overlapped. Two of the most significant reform movements to come out of the reform period of 1820-1840 were the anti-slavery movement and the women's rights movement. Each of these movements worked for freedom and emancipation and to grant a greater body of rights to two of the groups on the periphery of American society. The movements shared a common support base, and many abolitionists advocated, or were active in, the women's rights movement, or vice versa. In many ways, the organized women's rights movement grew out of abolitionist organizations and the movement of the early 1800s. Although neither group saw their cause's ultimate goals achieved during the era of reform, each movement saw great advances. Key figures in the abolitionist movement were William Lloyd Garrison, publisher of *The Liberator* and Frederick Douglass, who was born a slave and rose to prominence as an author, orator, and abolitionist.

Test Yourself

1. The colonizationist scheme of the early 1800s proved to be popular among black abolitionists.

   a. True

   b. False

2. The Seneca Falls Convention worked to establish____

   a. women's rights.

   b. a utopian community.

   c. the end of slavery.

   d. a national temperance society.

3. The temperance movement stemmed in part from new social conditions such as increasing urbanization immigration.

   a. True

   b. False

See page 502 for answers

13.5 Conclusion

The period between 1820 and 1860 reflected a national mood of experimentation and rebellion. Americans experimented in new ways of thinking and believing, and rebelled against injustices to women and the enslaved. The mid-nineteenth century was also a time of change in religion. Older religious denominations were supplanted in many areas by new religious sects such as the Methodists and Baptists. Others were deeply influenced by the Enlightenment and rational thinking. Convinced of the perfection of nature defined and popularized by scientists of the sixteenth and seventeenth centuries, these new theologians believed that this very perfection argued for the existence of a rational creator. They based their religious beliefs and practices on this rationalism, downplaying the miracles of scripture and concentrating instead on the morals it imparted and the historical events it recounted, arguing, "my rational nature is from God." However, these rational religions had limited appeal for the vast majority of Americans, who, in the mid-nineteenth century, were attracted to the preaching of the Second Great Awakening, a religious revival movement. Preachers like Peter Cartwright and Charles Grandison Finney created such excitement with their sermons that their audiences became "excessive and downright wild."

The mid-nineteenth century also witnessed the appearance of a number of millennial sects advocating that the Second Coming of Jesus was at hand. The Mormons called themselves the "latter day" saints and spoke continually of an approaching new dispensation; the official name of the Shakers was "the United Society of Believers in Christ's Second Appearing." The followers of William Miller, a Baptist convert and editor of the *Advent Herald*, established 1844 as the year of the Second Coming, sold their worldly goods, and gathered either in churches or in fields to watch the descent of Jesus. When he failed to appear, the movement disintegrated.

Just as the millennial sects looked forward to a new and better life introduced by the Second Coming of Jesus, so also did a group of men and women who participated in one of the many utopian experiments of the mid-century. The Shakers created a religious community that bound their residents to each other and to God. Brook Farm was one of the best-known communities and included among its participants literary figures like Ralph Waldo Emerson. Closely linked to the emotional outpouring behind revivalism and the creation of new, often millennial, sects was the appearance of a movement known as Romanticism. Manifested in transcendentalism and in the literature of mid-eighteenth century, American Romanticism embodied a revolt against the rationalism of the Enlightenment, of Deism and Unitarianism, and emphasized the victory of heart over head. Utopian movements focused their efforts on the creation of a perfected new social order, not a reformed older one. Most of the communities withdrew from society, stressed the value of hard work and commitment to community ideals as a means of achieving this perfected new society. The Brook Farm community was an intellectual experiment that overlapped with the transcendental movement. The Shakers sought perfection of humanity in religion, stressing the equality of the sexes and celibacy. Finally, the utopian socialist community of New Harmony tried to create a more perfect society through communal work and property.

The Cult of Domesticity provided a powerful ideology of gender roles for many Americans. While not all regions and classes were adherents to this ideology, it was a movement that profoundly influenced American culture. In the ideology of separate spheres, the home (and, by extension, the woman of the house) came to represent a place of morality, in sharp contrast to the corrupt public world.

Two of the most significant reform movements to come out of the reform period of 1820-1840 were the anti-slavery movement and the women's rights movement. Each of these movements worked for freedom and emancipation and to grant a greater body of rights to two of the groups on the periphery of American society. The movements shared a common support base, and many abolitionists advocated, or were active in, the women's rights movement, or vice versa. In many ways, the organized women's rights movement grew out of abolitionist organizations and the movement of the early 1800s. Although neither group saw their cause's ultimate goals achieved during the era of reform, each movement saw great advances.

13.6 CRITICAL THINKING EXERCISES

- Which reformist impulse changed the United States more deeply: religious or political reform?

13.7 KEY TERMS

- Abolitionism
- Anti-Slavery Society
- Brooke farm
- Burned-Over District
- William Ellery Channing
- Cult of Domesticity
- Dorothea Dix
- Frederick Douglass
- Charles Grandison Finney
- The Liberator
- Mormons
- Lucretia Mott
- Second Great Awakening
- Separate Spheres
- Seneca Falls Convention
- Shakers
- Joseph Smith
- Elizabeth Cady Stanton
- Temprance movement
- Transcendentalism
- Unitarianism
- Utopianism
- Brigham Young

13.8 CHRONOLOGY

The following chronology is a list of important dates and events associated with this chapter.

Date	Event
1800	Gabriel's Rebellion
1820s	Height of Second Great Awakening
1821	Foundation of the colony of Liberia
1826	Foundation of the American Temperance Society
1830	Publication of the Book of Mormon
1833	American Anti-Slavery Society established
1840	Brook Farm establisted
1840	Seneca Falls Convention
1847	Mormon trek to Utah

13.9 END NOTES

1 Charles G. Finney, *Lectures on Revivals of Religion* (New York: Leavett, Lord & Co., 1835), 374.

2 James Sidbury, *Plowshares into Swords: Race, Rebellion, and Identity in Gabriel's Virginia, 1730-1810* (New York: Cambridge University Press, 1997), 76; 73-80.

3 James Sidbury, "Reading, Revelation, and Rebellion: The Textual Communities of Gabriel, Denmark Vesey, and Nat Turner," in *Nat Turner: A Slave Rebellion in History and Memory*, ed. Kenneth S. Greenburg (New York: Oxford University Press, 2003), 124

4 Sidbury, "Reading, Revelation, and Rebellion," 123-127.

5 Sidbury, "Reading, Revelation, and Rebellion," 127-133.

6 Henry David Thoreau, *Walden, or Life in the Woods*_(USA: Dover Thrift Edition, 1995 edition), 59.

7 Ralph Waldo Emerson, *The Complete Works of Ralph Waldo Emerson, Volume 1* (American Scholar Digital Editions, 2008).

8 Ellen Carol DuBios and Lynn Dumenil, *Through Women's Eyes: An American History with Documents* (Boston: Bedford/St. martin's Press, 2005), 139.

9 For more information on the Whiskey Rebellion, see chapter 10.

10 Dorothea Dix, "Memorial, to the Legislature of Massachusetts" American Journal of Public Health, v.96 (4), April 2006; 622-624.

11 Bryan Paul Frost and Jeffery Sickkenga, *History of American Political Thought*_(Oxford: Lexington Books, 2003), 398.

12 Paul Finkelman, *Slavery and the Founders: Race and Liberty in the Age of Jefferson*_(New York: M.E. Sharpe, 2005), 3.

13 Teresa Zackodnick, *Press, Platform, Pulpit: Black Feminist Publics in the Era of Reform*_(Knoxville, Tennessee: University of Tennessee Press, 2011) , 104.

14 Sue Davis, *The Political Thought of Elizabeth Cady Stanton* (New York: New York University Press, 2008).

15 DuBois and Dumenil, *Through Women's Eyes*, 222-223.

ANSWER KEY FOR CHAPTER THIRTEEN: ANTEBELLUM REVIVAL AND REFORM

Check your answers to the questions in the Before You Move On Sections for this chapter.

Correct answers are **BOLDED**

Section 13.2.2 - p. 485

1. The influence of reason and rational thought is most clearly expressed in what religious tradition?
    - **A. UNITARIANS**
    - b. Mormons
    - c. Methodists
    - d. Puritans

2. The _____ refers to an area of New York that was so affected by the Second Great Awakening that there "was no more fuel to burn" for the fire of religion.
    - **A. BURNED-OVER DISTRICT**
    - b. "anxious bench"
    - c. Moroni
    - d. Millerites

Section 13.3.4 - p. 490

1. Transcendentalists viewed _____as the key to the human experience.
    - a. transcending nature to attain reason
    - b. equality of nations
    - **C. SELF-RELIANCE**
    - d. dystopian communities

2. Shakers and Millerites were _____ movements, because they thought that the second coming of Jesus was approaching.
    - **A. MILLENNIAL**
    - b. diurnal
    - c. reform
    - d. utopian

3. The notion of separate spheres and the Cult of Domesticity allowed the American Middle class to distinguish themselves as separate from and superior to the working class.
    - **A. TRUE**
    - b. False

Section 13.4.4 - p. 498

1. The colonizationist scheme of the early 1800s proved to be popular among black abolitionists.
    - a. True
    - **B. FALSE**

2. The Seneca Falls Convention worked to establish_____
    - **A. WOMEN'S RIGHTS.**
    - b. a utopian community.
    - c. the end of slavery.
    - d. a national temperance society.

3. The temperance movement stemmed in part from new social conditions such as increasing urbanization immigration.
    - **A. TRUE**
    - b. False

Chapter Fourteen: Westward Expansion

Contents

Chapter Fourteen: Westward Expansion

14.1 INTRODUCTION

The expansionist movement in the United States gained tremendous momentum in the 1840s. The movement, coined "manifest destiny" in the mid-1840s, justified expansion with a sense of mission and purpose, viewing American expansion as inevitable, just, and divinely foreordained. This expansion led to the addition of Texas and Oregon to the Union and was an underlying cause of war with Mexico, which resulted in the acquisition of vast territories in the Southwest, including the prize of California.

However, expansion came at a price. The Mexican-American War further incited resentment of the United States by not only Mexico, but also the region of Latin America. In the aftermath of the war, tensions grew between the American and Mexican populations of Texas and California as Hispanics were pushed further and further out of the dominant society, dispossessed of their land, and politically disenfranchised in the new states of Texas and California. Westward expansion also led to increasing hostilities between the United States and Native Americans, resulting in a series of disturbances, massacres, and wars. Finally, the expansionist movement further ignited the debate over slavery in the wake of the Missouri Compromise.

14.1.1 Learning Outcomes

After completing this chapter, you should be able to:

- Trace the expansion processes that completed the continental United States.
- Explain the underlying causes of the expansion of the United States.
- Describe the legacies of expansion.

14.2 WESTWARD EXPANSION AND MANIFEST DESTINY

The American expansionist movement did not begin with Manifest Destiny and the push westward in the 1840s. Americans had been pushing boundaries since the colonial era, most notably across the Appalachian Mountains. Jefferson set the stage for expansionism with the Louisiana Purchase; the movement grew in the 1830s with the Indian Removal program under Jackson, "freeing" land east of the Mississippi for the expanding population. At the turn of the century, the overwhelming majority lived east of the Appalachian Mountains; just fifty years later, about half of all Americans lived west of the mountains, a tremendous demographic shift.[1]

The rapid western expansion of the 1840s resulted in great part from demographic, economic, and political pressures. The population of the United States grew rapidly in the period from 1800-1850, rocketing from about five million to over twenty million in a fifty-year period.[2] Americans were increasingly land-hungry as populations grew. Throughout many of the overworked farms of the east, soil fertility was declining, making the cheap land of the west more and more attractive. Politically, many feared that if the United States did not occupy the West, then the British would. Some reasoned that westward expansion would counterbalance the increasingly industrialized and urbanized northeast, assuring that the republic of the United States would continue to be rooted in the ideals and values of Jefferson's yeoman farmer. Expansion deeply influenced U.S. foreign policy; to the south, tensions arose with Mexico as thousands of Americans immigrated into the Mexican state of Coahuila y Tejas, hereafter referred to as Texas. Expansion was also deeply economically motivated. For example, Eastern merchants wanted control of west coast ports to trade with Asia. Overall, many Americans envisioned the same end, even though they favored expansion for different reasons; many, however, came to equate the idea of "spreading freedom" with spreading the United States.

The westward expansion movement continued in the 1840s. During this period, the concept of Manifest Destiny arose to give a religious and cultural justification to American expansion across the continental United States. Millions of Americans professed the belief that the destiny of the United States was to spread democratic institutions "from sea to shining sea." Manifest Destiny asserted that Americans would expand to the limits of North America, taking political and economic control of the continent. In the process, the inhabitants of North America, including Indians and Mexicans, would be Americanized. Any attempt to resist would be forcibly extinguished. Some would even argue that, in effect, God had chosen Americans to control the Western Hemisphere. These viewpoints are evident in the speech of Senator Thomas Hart Benton, one of the leading proponents of Manifest Destiny:

> I know of no human event, past or present, which promised a greater, and more beneficent change upon the earth than the arrival of...the Caucasian race...It would seem that the white race alone received the divine command, to subdue and replenish the earth! for it is the only race that has obeyed it—the only one that hunts out new and distant lands, and even a New World, to subdue and replenish...the Caucasian race now top[s] the Rocky Mountains, and spread[s] down the shores of the Pacific. In a few years a great population will grow up there, luminous with

> the accumulated lights of the European and American civilization...The Red race has disappeared from the Atlantic coast: the tribes that resisted civilization met extinction...For my part, I cannot murmur at what seems to be the effect of divine law...Civilization, or extinction, has been the fate of all people who have found themselves in the track of advancing Whites, and civilization, always the preference of the Whites, has been pressed as an object, while extinction has followed as a consequence of its resistance.[3]

However, the issue was certainly not that simple. The issue of expansion raised challenging and hotly-debated questions that were taken up by both the American government and the American population. Was expansionism moral, and moreover, could a government accept and even promote expansion through moral action, or were the two mutually exclusive? Would the nation fundamentally change with the incorporation of distant lands and new populations (perceived by many as "unable to assimilate" into the U.S. population)? Would unchecked expansionism threaten American military and economic security? Was the expansion of the United States synonymous with the expansion of freedom? Finally, how was the growing nation to expand without upsetting the precarious balance between free and slaveholding states? In the first half of the nineteenth century, the Southwest Ordinance of 1790 mandated the Ohio River as a dividing line: states to the south of the river would be open to slavery. Consequently, the area north of the river was largely characterized by family farms and free labor, and to the south, largely characterized by slave labor. As the expansionist movement grew in the 1840s, the nation struggled to maintain a stalemate of sorts as territories were incorporated into the nation as states. By 1850, seven states (California, Illinois, Indiana, Iowa, Maine, Michigan, and Wisconsin) had entered the union as free states, and six as slaveholding states (Alabama, Arkansas, Florida, Mississippi, Missouri, and Texas). As the concept of manifest destiny developed throughout the 1840s, it became increasingly apparent that it was for white Americans only, not only because of the spread of slavery as a part of westward expansion, but also because of American attitudes and policies towards the Indian and Mexican populations of areas such as Texas and California. Manifest destiny also became a justification for the aggressively expansionist policies of President James Polk.

14.2.1 Texas

The first movement of American settlers outside of the boundaries set by the Missouri Compromise was into the Mexican province of Texas, an area that had been sparsely populated since the early colonial era. As a newly independent country, Mexico was in a politically tumultuous state. Agustín I, emperor of the short-lived Empire of Mexico (1821-1823), hoped to populate the land that had been home to mostly Indians and Franciscan missionaries, so he invited Americans to populate Texas. At first, the invitation was extended to 300 families; however, there was no official maximum set for the future. Families were to be of good moral character, agree to abide by the laws of Mexico, and be Roman Catholic. In 1821, Stephen F. Austin led the 300 families into Texas. In the years that followed, the American population in the Mexican province exploded; by 1827, 12,000 Americans lived in Texas, outnumbering the Mexican population by 5,000.

In later years, the American population in Mexico grew even more. The American immigrants brought hundreds of slaves with them, making Texas very different from the rest of turn-of-the-century Mexico; the institution of slavery had died out in the late 1700s throughout much of Mexico, and slavery was no longer an economic foundation of the country. However, the government seemed willing to make exceptions in order to attract immigrants to the state. Cheap land was one of the many draws for Americans, slaveholding or no; immigrants to Texas paid 10 cents an acre for land. Comparable land was selling for $1.25 an acre in the United States. Moreover, each male colonist was allowed to purchase 640 acres for himself and up to 320 additional acres for his wife, up to 160 acres for each of his children, and up to 80 acres for each slave that he brought into the province. Finally, colonists were given a ten-year exemption from paying Mexican taxes.[4]

Figure 14.1 Stephen Fuller Austin | Portrait of Stephen Fuller Austin.

Author: Flickr user "cliff1066"
Source: Flickr

The Mexican government, believing that the Americans could be integrated into the Mexican community, passed a battery of laws. All official transactions were to be in Spanish. Colonists were to settle deep into Texas; no foreigner was to settle within 60 miles of the U.S. boundary. Finally, foreigners who married Mexican citizens would be eligible for extra land. All of these laws, the government believed, would facilitate the acculturation of Americans into Mexican society. However, all efforts failed, and political, cultural, and economic tensions emerged between the Mexican government and the "Texans," as opposed to the Mexican "tejanos." From a Mexican point of view, the Texans were a growing threat. Culturally, the Texans had remained distinct from the Mexican population, due in great part to the fact that, although the colonists were required to be Catholic in order to settle in Mexico, only a very small percentage of Texans professed Catholicism. Politically, Texans dominated local government. The Mexican government also felt that the Texans were an economic threat to the tejanos. In one instance, an American settler even threatened to illegally confiscate the land of any Mexican who could not produce a deed. When the Mexican government moved to stop him, he led a revolt, which was ultimately unsuccessful. Slavery emerged as an important issue of contention in Texas; the institution of slavery was tacitly illegal in Mexico, having been a part of the revolutionary ideals, and limited by a series of restrictive laws. Though many of the Anglo immigrants were not slaveholders, some slaveholding Texans circumvented this expectation by classifying their slaves as servants indentured for life. Although the expansion of slavery into Texas had started small, the population had quickly grown and became a major source of irritation and concern for the government. An 1829 government

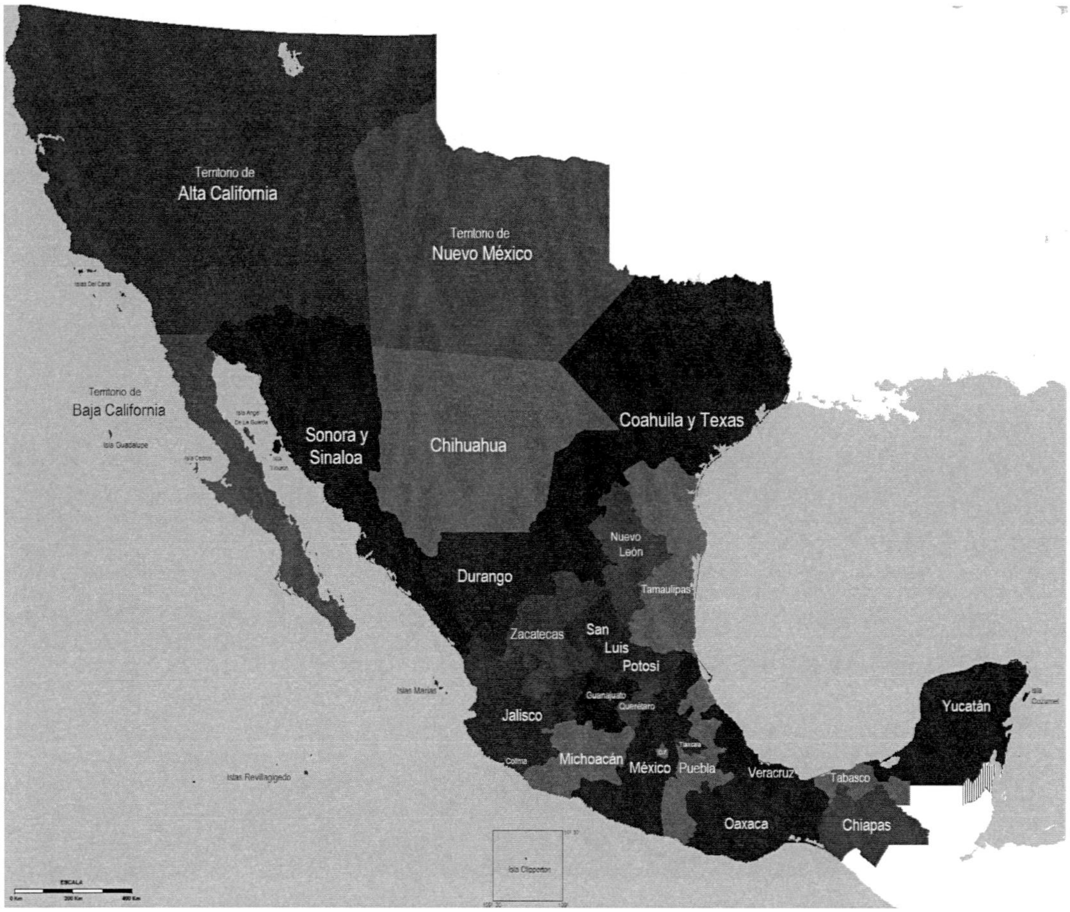

Figure 14.2 Map of Mexican States and Territories in 1825 | Map of Mexican states and territories in 1825, showing Coahuila y Texas.

Author: Wikipedia User "Hpav7"
Source: Wikimedia Commons

report confirmed that the colonization efforts were ultimately unsuccessful because many Texans refused to be naturalized as Mexican citizens, remaining socially and culturally distinct and isolated. The final straw, the report concluded, was the way in which the Texans ignored slavery laws.

The government sought to weaken the influence of the Texans in a variety of ways. In 1829, President Vicente Guerrero officially outlawed slavery in Mexico; as slavery was not economically important anywhere in Mexico except for Texas, the proclamation intended directly to weaken the position of the Texans. The government also encouraged Mexican immigration into the state while simultaneously arresting further American immigration and strengthening the Texas garrisons. None of these measures succeeded; indeed, they further incited the Texans and American expansionists, who called for the incorporation of Texas into the United States through one means or another. In fact, many of the Texans had immigrated with the firm idea that Texas would eventually become part of the United States. Two presidents had even offered to purchase Texas from Mexico and were twice rejected.

The United States was not the only foreign power with an eye to taking part of Mexico; in 1829, Spain invaded in an attempt to retake the country as a colony. The invasion failed, and General Antonio López de Santa Anna Pérez de Lebrón (Santa Anna for short) gained great popularity as the "hero of Tampico." He helped to lead a coup against the Mexican president and was himself elected president in 1833. The conservative Santa Anna overturned the Mexican Constitution of 1824, which was based on the U.S. Constitution, in favor of a new, conservative constitution called the Siete Leyes (Seven Laws). The Siete Leyes dissolved Congress and invested power in a centralized government backed by the military. This act was the last straw for the Texans; the centralization of government was alien to the Americans, who were used to separation of powers, and meant that Texans would have no political voice at all. They revolted, raising the "Federal Army of Texas" to defend the Constitution of 1824 against Santa Anna and the centralists. Expansionists in the United States and Mexican liberals opposed to Santa Anna alike encouraged the revolt. The revolt culminated in Texas's declaration of independence on March 2, 1836 and the formation of the Republic of Texas, or the Lone Star Republic (1836-1846). Texas was not the only Mexican state to declare independence; Santa Anna also faced rebellions in the Zacatecas and the Yucatán.[5]

The Texas Revolution and the Lone Star Republic

Santa Anna successfully quelled the other rebellions but faced a greater challenge in Texas. In the winter of 1835, the president himself led an army of 6,000 soldiers into Texas. He reached San Antonio in late February of 1836, roughly coinciding with the Texans' declaration of independence from Mexico. Santa Anna found that the Texans, including notables such as Davy Crockett and Jim Bowie, had taken shelter in an old mission building known as the Alamo. The events that followed have been presented in a variety of ways, most often reflecting the nationalist views of the historian. After holding the mission under siege, on March 5 Santa Anna sounded the *degüello*, a bugle call used by the Spanish since the earliest days of colonization to signal that the enemy was to be given no quarter; that is, they declared a battle to the death. Inside the mission, the Texans may or may not have heard and understood the bugle call. The defenders' understanding of the upcoming battle, nevertheless, matched with Santa Anna's as commander of the Alamo, W.B. Travis, declared there would be no surrender or retreat.

The following morning, the Mexicans began throwing wave after wave of troops against the wall; hundreds died under heavy artillery fire from the Texans. After about an hour, however, the numerical superiority of the Mexican army prevailed, and they breached the walls of the mission. The defenders suffered catastrophic casualties. Seven men survived the battle to surrender; they were executed as prisoners. Thirty noncombatants inside the mission were spared, including several slaves of the Texans. Santa Anna hoped thereby to convince other slaves to support the Mexicans in the rebellion. The high casualty rates on both sides reinforced the idea that peaceable settlement was impossible. Another hard Texan defeat followed on the heels of the Alamo. Again, Santa Anna ordered that all survivors taken as prisoners be executed, despite the protests of his commanding general.

After the Alamo, Americans flocked from the United States to aid and avenge their Texan compatriots. In cities such as New York and New Orleans, "Texas committees" organized volunteers to join the cause. Texans traveling to these cities gathered even more volunteers with tales of the vast acreage of available land in Texas. Up until this time, several companies of tejanos were active in the war effort and fought for independence. Indeed, largely ignored today is the fact that some of the defenders at the Alamo were tejanos. But as more and more Americans came to join in the war effort, and as more and more evident the anti-Mexican rhetoric within Texas became, most tejanos left the Texas Revolution.

Tejanos were not the only ones fleeing the Revolution; the costly defeats at Goliad and the Alamo resulted in an exodus of civilians out of Texas to Louisiana, an exodus known as the Runaway Scrape. The Texas army under the leadership of Sam Houston was also on the run from the larger army of Santa Anna. The Revolution finally came to an end at the Battle of San Jacinto, where Houston pulled off a stunning and definitive victory when he took Santa Anna by surprise. The Texans forced Santa Anna to sign not one, but two treaties: one public, one private. The public Treaty of Velasco declared the hostilities between Mexico and Texas over but did not go so far as to recognize the Republic; the private Treaty of Velasco, however, stated that in return for Santa Anna's freedom, Mexico would accept the independence of the Lone Star Republic. After returning to Mexico City, Santa Anna repudiated the private treaty, saying that he signed it under duress and as an individual rather than dictator of Mexico. The "Texas problem" remained an issue for Mexico, although the nation was so racked with internal problems that it never launched another full-scale invasion to retake Texas. The greatest point of dispute was the border; Texas claimed the Rio Grande as the border, while Mexico held the Nueces River as the true boundary.

After the Revolution ended, Texas elected Sam Houston as its first president. The Lone Star Republic remained an independent nation from 1836 to 1846. During these years, tens of thousands more American immigrants poured into Texas. Some, both in Texas and the United States (particularly expansionists in the slaveholding South), considered that the annexation of the Republic to the Union was imminent; others took advantage of the plentiful land that the new government was giving to heads of immigrant households. While the U.S. recognized Texas as an independent nation, some feared that this annexation talk would inflame political tensions with Mexico. Indeed, the annexation of Texas and its boundary with Mexico would later become a causal factor of the Mexican-American War.

14.2.2 Oregon

The second area of great expansion for the continental United States was the Oregon Territory, comprising present-day Oregon, Washington, Idaho, and British Columbia, stretching from the 42nd parallel, the northernmost boundary of California, to the 54th, the southernmost boundary of Alaska. Originally, Spain, Russia, Britain, and the United States all claimed the Oregon Territory. Eventually, Spain and Russia dropped their claims, leaving Britain and the U.S. as remaining contenders. British claims were based on prior discovery, exploration, and treaty rights; additionally, the most important colonizing agency was the Hudson Bay Company, which engaged in active trade with the Indians of the Pacific Northwest. The U.S. claims were also based on discovery, exploration, and treaty rights; additionally, a small number of Americans, including missionaries trying to convert Pacific Northwest Indians, joined the claim of occupation to the American list. The two countries temporarily resolved the matter with an 1818 agreement to a ten-year joint occupation, renewed in 1827, but the matter was far from settled. In the period from 1816 through the 1840s, few Americans and Europeans settled in Oregon. But beginning in the early 1840s, "Oregon Fever" gripped the United States. Oregon was touted as a land of pleasant climates and fertile soil. Several thousand American settlers began a great westward migration over the Oregon Trail. By the mid-1840s, some 5,000 Americans had populated the Territory, thus strengthening the U.S. claim to Oregon. "Oregon Fever," moreover, fueled the idea of Manifest Destiny, popularizing it at the national level.

The famed Oregon Trail traveled by westward pioneers grew from rough trails cut by trappers, traders, and explorers. It ran for about 2,000 miles from Independence, Missouri, across the western plains and the Rocky Mountains, ending in the valleys of Oregon, most notably the Willamette Valley. As more and more immigrants came, other cities such as St. Joseph, Missouri, and Council Bluffs, Iowa, vied for business as "jumping off points" onto the trail, as outfitting the westward-bound immigrants was a profitable business in food and supplies, wagon repairs and fittings, and livestock. The journey over the trail was slow, taking somewhere around five to six months to complete. Most people walked beside their wagons much of the way to reduce the load on the oxen and wagon, and because the wagons were loaded to capacity with goods. The journey was dangerous; accidents, including drowning during river crossings, were frequent. Diseases such as cholera and dysentery were the most common killers on the journey. Although Hollywood later popularized the idea of pioneers "circling the wagons" against Indian attack on the trail, such skirmishes were actually very rare and most often provoked by

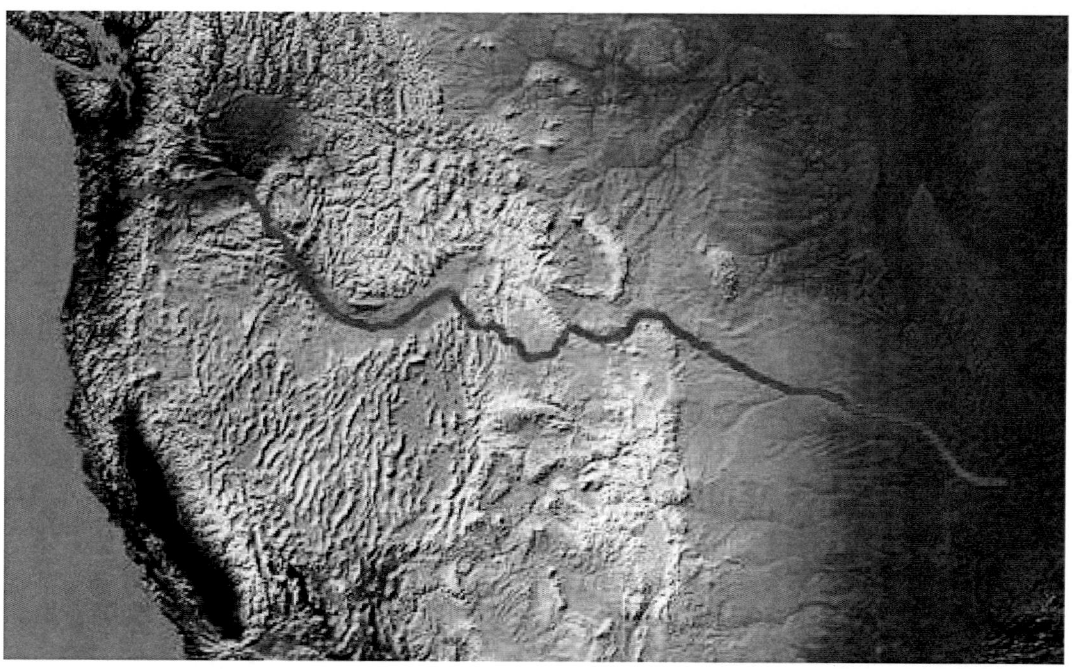

Figure 14.3 The Oregon Trail | The route of the Oregon Trail is shown on a map of the western United States from Independence, Missouri in the east to Oregon City, Oregon in the west.

Author: Matthew Trump
Source: Wikimedia Commons
License: CC BY SA 3.0

the immigrants themselves. While thousands of immigrants died from disease and injury over the course of the 1840s, fewer than 120 were killed in altercations with Indians. Cooperation and coordination was very important to the success of each group traveling the trail. For this reason, many groups of immigrants drew up a formal document outlining the responsibilities and work assignments of each wagon in the group. The timing of the group's departure and their daily progress was of pivotal importance as well; they needed to be sure that they would reach the plains late enough to have adequate grazing for the livestock, but reach the western mountains early enough to avoid the winter snows. As the movement into the west expanded, new routes branched off from the original Oregon Trail. The California Trail extended the Oregon Trail south into California, the Mormon Trail into Utah, and the Bozeman Trail north into Montana.

14.2.3 The Election of 1844

The issue of territorial expansion became one of the paramount issues of the election of 1844. Democrat James K. Polk, Speaker of the House and protégé of Andrew Jackson, defeated Jackson's old enemy Henry Clay in an election that revolved largely around the issues of the possible annexation of Texas and acquiring some or all of Oregon. Polk, a more vocal expansionist, won the election by a narrow majority. The Democrats also took both houses of Congress, causing many to read the election as a mandate of expansionism.

Many Americans, Polk among them, set their sights on taking the Mexican provinces of New Mexico and California in addition to Oregon. Polk hoped to obtain New Mexico and California peacefully but was prepared to use force to take them. To this end, Polk settled with the British on the issue of Oregon in order to conserve American strength for obtaining further territory from Mexico. The issue was further complicated by speculations and indications that Britain was considering signing an alliance with Texas, which would forestall any hopes of annexation to the U.S.

Upon taking office, Polk therefore began talks with Britain. In the months after the election, the rhetoric over Oregon had grown increasingly heated. Expansionists demanded that the United States take all of Oregon Territory, threatening war with the slogan "Fifty-four forty or fight!" referring to the northernmost latitude of Oregon. Polk publicly embraced the demand for "all of Oregon." However, he was more than willing to accept a boundary line along the 49th parallel, splitting Oregon between the U.S. and Britain. By accepting the 49th parallel boundary, the U.S. acquired Puget Sound, the first Pacific deepwater port held by the U.S. Acquiring part of Oregon also brought territory that would become free states into the Union, counterbalancing the possible annexation of Texas, sure to become slaveholding. By accepting less of Oregon, Polk and the nation could prepare for the coming war with Mexico. This compromise displeased many of the more militant expansionists, but others saw its pragmatism. Why "all of Texas" but not "all of Oregon"? Senator Thomas Hart Benton of Missouri reportedly observed, "Because Great Britain is powerful, and Mexico is weak."[6]

14.2.4 The Mormon Trek

For one group, the Mormons, westward expansion was closely linked with religious beliefs. In a migration that paralleled the early westward movement of the American population, Joseph Smith led his followers, the Latter-Day Saints (or Mormons), from New York to Ohio and then on to Missouri. In each place, they were met with skepticism and, often, hostility. Non-Mormons were mistrustful of Mormon secret rituals, because the "new gospel" reopened the canon of the Bible, and because, led by Smith, the group denied the authority of local governments. Non-Mormons also feared that the Mormon block voting would lead to the creation of a local quasi-theocracy. The Mormons were expelled from northwest Missouri in the 1838 Mormon War. They came to settle in a town in Illinois that they renamed Nauvoo, where the Saints set to construct a temple and create their new Zion. The city charter established independent courts and a Nauvoo militia. These institutions and a boom in local commerce allowed the Mormons great autonomy in the region. During this period, Smith became increasingly powerful. He expelled from the Church dissidents and many who spoke out against him. His practice of "plural marriage," whereby he (and other Mormon leaders) was husband to multiple wives, attracted the attention and outrage of many Americans. Smith's growing power in northwestern Missouri did not sit well with his Protestant neighbors, who feared that Mormons would come to politically dominate the region. In 1844, these concerns led to the arrest of Joseph Smith. Smith and his brother were killed by a mob as they were held for trial.

In the aftermath of Smith's death, Brigham Young emerged as new church leader. Young oversaw the journey over the Mormon Trail, a 1,300-mile journey westward from Nauvoo to the "promised land," an area near the Great Salt Lake in Utah, a sparsely-populated outlying province of Mexico. The first 12,000 Mormons made the trek in 1846-1847; more came later in the period from 1848-1860. From 1856-1860, the church promoted the use of handcarts, rather than wagons pulled by draft animals, as a more affordable means of migration. Many of these so-called "handcart pioneers" were new converts to the church who had recently emigrated from Europe and now were on the last leg of their migration. Over the four-year period, ten companies of handcarts made the journey along the trail; two of the ten had significant causalities.

Soon after the 1847 trek, Mormons found themselves once again residents of the United States after the defeat of Mexico in the Mexican-American War. The signing of the Treaty of Guadalupe Hidalgo ceded much of the modern-day American Southwest, including Utah, to the United States. Utah was incorporated into a territory by Congress in 1860, and President Millard Fillmore appointed Brigham Young territorial governor.

14.2.5 Before You Move On...

Key Concepts

Americans increasingly embraced the concept of Manifest Destiny in the 1840s. Manifest Destiny was associated not only with land expansion, but also with the idea of Americanization of Indians and Mexican residents of areas such as Texas, Oregon, and California. Moreover, many Americans likened the idea of the physical spread of the boundaries of the United States with spreading freedom. The debate over expansionism was not a simple one, but raised complex questions about the nature of freedom and republicanism and the role of the state in expansion. Many feared that expansionism was a threat to the nation, whether in the form of overextension, national security, or a changing population. Private individuals engaged in commercial and agrarian enterprises at the frontiers of expansion proved to be one of the greatest sources of pressure for expansionism, as their economic activities often preceded national expansion into the territory.

The first major movement of Americans was into the Mexican province of Texas. Beginning in 1821, American settlers poured into the region, with Americans soon outnumbering Mexicans. Cultural and religious differences and the American reliance on slave labor led to rising tensions in Texas and, ultimately, to the Texas Revolution in 1835-1836. In 1836, Texas declared independence as the Republic of Texas, or the Lone Star Republic.

In the early 1840s, thousands of Americans pushed westward into Oregon Territory over the Oregon Trail. The United States and Great Britain both laid claim to Oregon Territory; however, the greater numbers of American settlers helped to bolster U.S. claims to the region. In 1844, James K. Polk was elected president. Although he was an expansionist and courted the American public with talk of taking "all of Oregon" for the United States, he negotiated with Great Britain to accept the 49th parallel as the boundary between U.S. and British holdings. It should be noted that expansion into both Oregon and Texas meant that the delicate balance between free and slaveholding states remained intact for the meantime. Finally, the Mormon Trek was part of a greater movement in the westward expansion of the United States in the nineteenth century.

Test Yourself

1. The concept of Manifest Destiny embraced the idea(s) that

   a. the United States would expand "from sea to shining sea."

   b. residents of areas under expansion would be Americanized.

   c. spreading the boundaries of the United States was equivalent to spreading freedom.

   d. all of the above.

2. American settlers in the Mexican province of Texas were typically unlike tejanos in that

a. many were slave owners.

b. they remained religiously distinct from the Roman Catholic tejanos.

c. they demanded popular sovereignty for all, including women.

d. A and B.

e. all of the above.

3. "Fifty-four forty or fight!" refers to

a. the border dispute between the United States and Mexico: the U.S. claimed the Rio Grande as the border, Mexico claimed the Nueces River.

b. American desires to expand to take "all of Oregon," despite the British claims to the territory.

c. the struggles of the settlers as they traveled over the Oregon Trail.

d. the American desire to expand into California.

See page 526 for answers

14.3 THE MEXICAN-AMERICAN WAR

In the days after the election of 1844 before Polk's inauguration, at the behest of lame duck President Tyler, Congress passed a resolution to annex Texas. Although Mexico had finally recognized Texas's independence in 1845, it held that the border between Mexico and Texas was the Nueces River, as it had been from the colonial era. Texas—and now the United States—held the border as the Rio Grande. The area between the two rivers was not the real point of contention for the two countries. The Rio Grande wanders aimlessly for hundreds of miles far into New Mexico and present-day Colorado; in effect, claiming the Rio Grande as the boundary tacitly laid claim to hundreds of thousands more acres. Mexico responded to annexation by cutting off diplomatic relations with the U.S.; both countries prepared for war. As a last-ditch effort to avoid war, Polk sent emissary John Slidell to Mexico City to resolve the border dispute. His secondary mission, however, was to secure California and New Mexico for the United States. Slidell was authorized to pay $5 million for New Mexico and as much as $25 million for Alta (Upper) California. Soon after Slidell's arrival in Mexico City, the Mexican press learned of his mission to attempt buying so much Mexican territory. Newspapers and journals denounced Slidell and the United States, and leaflets appeared all over the city threatening rebellion if the government negotiated. Slidell was sent away.

Polk seized this opportunity to provoke war with Mexico. He ordered General Zachary Taylor into the disputed territory between the rivers. When a skirmish broke out between Taylor and the Mexican general assigned to patrol the disputed territory, Polk declared war, saying that he had tried every effort at reconciliation. "Mexico," he stated, "has passed the boundary of United States, invaded our territory, and shed American blood upon the American soil."[7] Despite opposition from some Whigs, most notably Abraham Lincoln, Congress overwhelmingly approved the declaration of war. The view from Mexico City was very different, however. Mexico contended that the United States had not only taken Texas, but also tried to double Texas's size. Moreover, when Mexico tried to defend its territory, the United States claimed that Mexico had invaded U.S. land.

The U.S. strategy for the Mexican-American War called for a three-pronged attack on Mexico. The Army of the West was to take and occupy New Mexico; the Army of the Center, to remain in northern Mexico. In anticipation of war with Mexico, the United States assembled a Navy fleet off the coast of California, deploying Marines to the ships. In June of 1846, a small group of mostly American settlers seized the garrison at Sonoma, California. The takeover was peaceable; in fact, no shots were fired. Many of the settlers and californios, or Mexican residents of California, supported the rebellion, as the government of the California territory was ineffectual and notoriously unstable: in the twenty-five year period before the revolt, leadership had changed hands more than forty times. Upon taking the garrison, the rebels proclaimed a new government of the California Republic. This Republic was very short-lived, lasting less than a month; indeed, few Californians knew of its existence. Twenty-six days after the birth of the California Republic, an army corps of engineers under the command of John Frémont marched into Sonoma. The Republic disbanded, and Frémont and the U.S. took over.

Meanwhile, the third prong of the U.S. attack on Mexico, the Army of Occupation, was to take Mexico City. General Winfield Scott led an amphibious assault against the port city of Veracruz and, after taking the city, began his march to the capitol. Scott's arrival in Mexico coincided with great political turmoil in the nation; in the time since the outbreak of war, the Mexican president had been overthrown by a general. The general then tried to abrogate the constitution, declare martial law, and take power himself; consequently, he was overthrown in a rebellion. The army then invited Santa Anna back from exile to resume the presidency. By the time that Scott took Veracruz, Santa Anna had only just arrived and taken command.[8]

Scott's army was successful in taking much of the city. On August 20, Scott asked for surrender from Santa Anna; Santa Anna agreed to negotiate. Rather than seriously negotiating surrender, however, Santa Anna used the time to shore up the city defenses. By the time the armistice was at an end, Santa Anna was ready for battle, with his forces concentrated at Chapultepec Castle at the center of the city. The defenders of the Castle, about 1,000 men and the cadets from the military academy, laid land mines all over slopes of the steep hill upon which the Castle was located. The land mines failed to explode. After a fierce battle, Scott's

Figure 14.4 Monument of the Boy Heroes | Monument to the boy heroes in Mexico City, Mexico.

Author: Wikimedia User "Thelma Matter"
Source: Wikimedia Commons

forces prevailed. Mexican sources attest that by the time Scott's forces reached the Castle, only a handful of cadets remained to defend it. After the death of his comrades, the last remaining cadet wrapped himself in the Mexican flag and jumped from the palace terrace, plummeting to his death on the steep rocks below.

14.3.1 The Treaty of Guadalupe Hidalgo and the Aftermath of the War

The Treaty of Guadalupe Hidalgo, which ended Mexican-American War, was signed in February of 1848. The treaty confirmed the U.S. title to Texas and ceded the Alta California and New Mexico territories to the United States, some 525,000 square miles. Mexico was allowed to keep everything south of the Rio Grande. The United States agreed to pay $15 million and to assume the claims of Americans against the Mexican government, about $3,250,000. In short, Mexico lost more than half of its territorial landmass in the Treaty of Guadalupe Hidalgo. The land ceded to the United States eventually became the states, or part of the states, of California, Arizona, New Mexico, Texas, Utah, Nevada, Colorado, Wyoming, and Kansas, tremendously increasing the U.S. holdings and stoking the fires of Manifest Destiny. The most radical adherents of Manifest Destiny had gone so far as to demand the annexation of not only "all of Texas," but all of Mexico as well. Why, given the expansionist climate of the era, did the United States not lay claim to all of Mexico? Perhaps the best answer to this question lies in an examination of the problems that arose from the Mexican Cession itself.

Through the Treaty of Guadalupe Hidalgo, the United States acquired about 55% of Mexico. Of course these lands were not "empty" but (sparsely) populated with indigenous peoples and Mexican citizens who suddenly, and through no choice of their own, found themselves residents of the United States. It is estimated that there were 80,000 Mexican citizens in California in the late 1840s. Many of the families had been residents of the California or New Mexico territories for generations, since the Spanish colonial period. Mexico was keenly interested in ensuring that these Mexicans would be provided for under the Treaty of Guadalupe Hidalgo, which stated that all Mexican citizens who remained in the ceded lands for more than one year could become naturalized U.S. citizens. Moreover, the original version of the treaty guaranteed that Mexican and Spanish land deeds and grants would be recognized by the United States, allowing resident Mexicans to retain ownership of their lands. Later amendments and interpretations of the treaty weakened this provision.

However, racial tensions emerged as the conquest of the territories of the Cession set a pattern for violence and racial antagonism that still resonates today. Over the next decades, Mexicans and Mexican-Americans alike (some having become citizens, some having declined the offer and remaining Mexican citizens) lost their lands as Texas, California, New Mexico, and the United States government itself declared the Mexican and Spanish land deeds "imperfect," questioned their veracity, and ultimately took the lands of tejanos, californios, and others. Before the Treaty of Guadalupe Hidalgo, Mexicans owned all lands valued over $10,000 in California; by the 1870s, they owned only one-quarter of these lands; by the 1880s, californios were relatively landless. Thousands went from being landowners to laborers, sometimes on the very land they had once owned. Much of the work was migratory in nature, and Mexican laborers were paid as much as two-thirds less

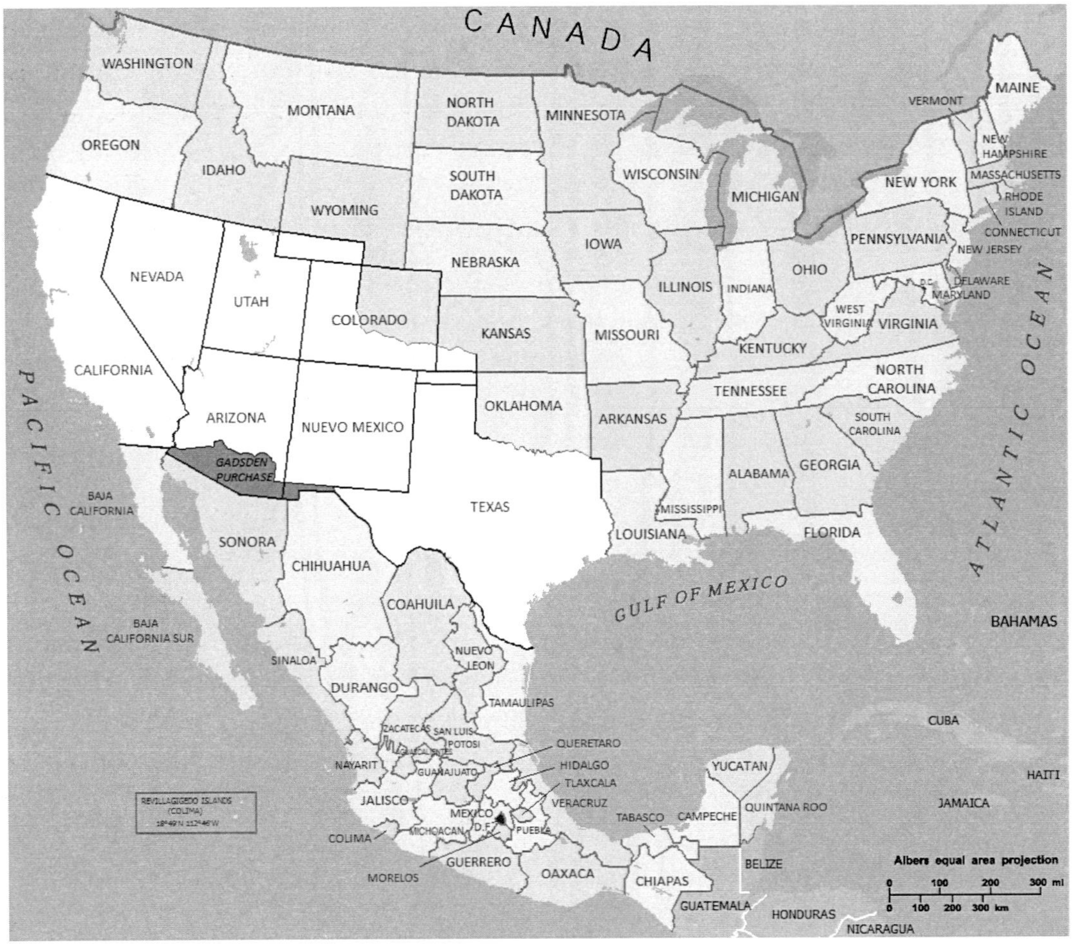

Figure 14.5 Mexican Cession | The Mexican Cession of the Treaty of Guadalupe Hidalgo, shown in white. The lands of the Gadsden Purchase are shown in brown.

Author: National Atlas of the United States
Source: Wikimedia Commons

than white laborers.[9] California, Texas, and other soon-to-be states also passed laws that targeted and politically unempowered Mexican-Americans. A good example of this type of legislation was California's Greaser Act, enacted in 1885. Technically, the Greaser Act was an anti-vagrancy law. However, "vagrants" were defined in the law as "all persons who are commonly known as 'Greasers,' or the issue of Spanish and Indian blood...and who go armed and are not peaceable and quiet persons."[10] In general, Hispanics became more and more alienated from the dominant society in the decades after Guadalupe Hidalgo.

So why didn't the United States acquire "all of Mexico" after conquering Mexico City? Some historians argue that racism played a large role. It was one thing to take the thinly-populated portions of Mexico that could be populated with many more Caucasian Americans and another thing entirely to take over a country, or "uncontrolled dominion," with a turbulent history, populated with people of mixed ancestry, whom many Americans considered to be "mongrels."[11] Ultimately, Mexico would have been an expensive, complicated problem for the United States. In taking the California and New Mexico territories, the U.S. increased its land mass by some 20% and gained the important ports of San Diego and San Francisco, thus allowing for trade with Asia, a much more pragmatic and manageable arrangement.

Because the Mexican Cession delineated by the Treaty of Guadalupe Hidalgo represented a tremendous increase to the land mass of the United States, it did much to further manifest destiny. The last major territorial acquisition of the continental United States followed on the heels of the Mexican Cession of 1848. In 1854, the United States and the Mexican government, once again under the control of the corrupt Santa Anna, signed the Mesilla Treaty, confirming the Gadsden Purchase. The United States paid $10 million for Arizona's Mesilla Valley, approximately 30,000 acres. The purchase also clarified and finalized the border between the United States and Mexico. The U.S. desired this land for two additional reasons. First, the Mesilla Valley offered the best terrain for building a transcontinental railroad along a deep southern route. Second, by securing the land south of the Gila River, the United States finalized the border between California and Baja California (now the U.S. and Mexico) as south of the San Diego Bay, offering an excellent harbor. Plans were made for building the trans-continental railroad from Texas to San Diego, but nothing ever materialized.[12]

The war was a tremendous military victory for the United States. The American military gained much experience. West Point and the Naval Academy claimed that their training were the key to success and justified their existence with the war's success. The Marines won prestige as well and still sing of the conquest of "the halls of Montezuma." The British and foreign skeptics also reevaluated their opinion on American military strength in the war's aftermath. However, the war was also costly. Some 13,000 Americans died, most from disease. The war's monetary cost was about $100,000,000. The war also influenced foreign relations in Latin America, especially with Mexico, in lasting ways. Mexico, and much of Latin America, considered that the United States had deliberately provoked the war and that American greed was its primary underlying cause. The war intensified what has been referred to as "Yankeephobia" in Latin America, leading to distrust and suspicion. The United States, many contended, was untrustworthy, considered itself superior to others, and was a bully. It was called the "Colossus of the North." Perhaps most significantly, the war upset the carefully-maintained domestic political truce over slavery. Some felt that the war would lead to a severe sectional crisis; poet Ralph Waldo Emerson observed, "Mexico will poison us!"[13] Many Whigs opposed the war on principle, believing that the U.S. had no legal right to the land south of the Nueces River, the original boundary dispute between Texas and Mexico; many abolitionists believed that the war was provoked by the South in order to expand slavery. The sheer amount of possible slaveholding territory coming into the Union upset the balance established by the Missouri Compromise, reignited the slavery debate, and threatened stability. In response to this, Congressman David Wilmot introduced a bill, called the Wilmot Proviso, which would have banned slavery in any territory acquired from Mexico in the war. The measure was eventually defeated and never became law. However, it was strongly supported by representatives of Congress from the free states. Ultimately, the Mexican War represented the looming question of slavery's future.

Technological Development and Manifest Destiny

As the United States expanded geographically, it also underwent a period of growth and development in technology. Many advocates of manifest destiny saw a clear link between territorial growth and technological development; internal development, the mechanism that would spread American influence, followed on the heels of expansion. Two technologies were particularly important in facilitating communication and travel across the great distances from coast to coast: the telegraph and the railroad.

The development of a railroad infrastructure had begun in the 1830s in a limited area and proved to be viable and profitable. Rail travel transformed the American economy in the 1840s and 1850s, linking port cities to the interior. Before the advent of rail, the main route of commerce was along canal lines, which remained rail's biggest competitor for quite some time. Although the steam locomotive was faster, shipping costs were cheaper by canal. By the 1850s, however, the railroad network had grown into the dominant means of transport by far. The growth of the telegraph and railroads also provided stability to the growing nation. The United States had become so big that critics doubted its ability to effectively govern so much land and so many people. Railroads and the telegraph provided one solution. Moreover, they facilitated the emergence of a national market system.

The expansion of railroads and the telegraph was not just an effect of manifest destiny. It was a continuation of an ongoing discussion in the American government: the debate over internal improvements. The issue was first raised under Jefferson and focused on the building of canals to better connect the trans-Appalachian frontier to the United States. The debate changed with evolving technology and was raised again and again, most notably during the Madison and Jackson presidencies. A constant in the debate was the discussion of whether or not it was appropriate to use federal money to fund these internal improvements. Manifest destiny and its accompanying technological advances was simply the latest incarnation of this debate.

The significance of these technological advances to the concept of Manifest Destiny appears in various cultural artifacts. In John Gast's "American Progress" (1872), for example, the floating figure above the landscape resembles an angel and symbolizes the American belief that Manifest Destiny was divinely ordained. How does the angel express the concept of Manifest Destiny as espoused by John O'Sullivan? The paragraph below is from a nineteenth century description of the painting by George Crofutt, who widely distributed his engraving of it.

In "American Progress," a diaphanously and precariously-clad America floats westward through the air with the "Star of Empire" on her forehead. She has left the cities of the east behind, and the wide Mississippi, and still her course is westward. In her right hand she carries a school book—testimonial of the national enlightenment, while with her left she trails the slender wires of the telegraph that will bind the nation. Fleeing her approach are Indians, buffalo, wild horses, bears, and other game, disappearing into the storm and waves of the Pacific coast. They flee the ponderous vision—the star "is too much for them."[14]

Figure 14.6 American Progress (1872) | John Gast painted American Progress in 1872.

Artist: John Gast
Source: Library of Congress

Technology enabled American expansionism throughout the North American continent by facilitating travel and communication. Americans were not the only ones to harness this technological power towards an expansionist goal; during the 1800s, these technologies further enabled European powers such as France, Britain, and Germany to establish a new kind of colonialism: imperialism. The telegraph and railroad, along with other new technologies such as the steamboat and the Maxim gun, one of the first machine guns, allowed a small number of Europeans to dominate large areas and great numbers of people and fuel their own Industrial Revolutions. In this way, Manifest Destiny became a part of a greater nineteenth century movement in expansionism.

14.3.2 Before You Move On...

Key Concepts

In 1845, the United States annexed Texas and admitted it to the Union. Tensions arose between the U.S. and Mexico over the boundary; the U.S. claimed the Rio Grande as the border, with Mexico claiming the long-established boundary at the Nueces River. The real reason for this border dispute was deeply linked to the expansionist desires of the United States; establishing the Rio Grande as the border would lay claim to a substantial portion of Mexico outside of the confines of Texas. John Slidell's mission to Mexico exemplifies this intent; although his formal mission was diplomatic, he was secretly charged with buying a substantial portion of the Mexican northwest for the United States. When Mexicans responded to this offer with outrage, Polk took advantage by provoking war. The Mexican-American War, fought from 1846 to 1848, culminated with General Winfield Scott's invasion of Mexico City.

The Treaty of Guadalupe Hidalgo ended the Mexican-American War. The treaty confirmed the U.S. title to Texas and ceded the Alta California and New Mexico territories to the United States, some 525,000 square miles. Mexico lost more than half of its territorial land mass. This ceded land eventually became all of, or part of, the U.S. states of California, Arizona, New Mexico, Texas, Utah, Nevada, Colorado, Wyoming, and Kansas, tremendously increasing U.S. holdings and stoking the fires of Manifest Destiny. In 1848, the Gadsden Purchase finalized the present border between the United States and Mexico with the purchase of Arizona's Mesilla Valley.

The incorporation of so much Mexican territory and so many Mexican citizens into the United States led to great problems. The conquest of the territories of the Mexican Cession set a pattern for violence and racial antagonism that still resonates today. Over the next decades, Mexicans and Mexican-Americans alike lost their lands in Texas, California, and New Mexico; the United States government declared the Mexican and Spanish land deeds "imperfect," questioning their veracity and ultimately taking the lands of tejanos, californios, and others.

The Mexican-American War adversely and lastingly influenced foreign relations in Latin America. Mexico, and much of Latin America, believed that the United States deliberately provoked the war, with American greed being its primary underlying cause. The war intensified Latin American "Yankeephobia," leading to distrust and suspicion. The war also upset the carefully-maintained domestic political truce over slavery. Some felt that the war would lead to a severe sectional crisis. The sheer amount of potential slaveholding territory coming into the Union upset the balance established by the Missouri Compromise, reignited the slavery debate, and threatened stability.

Finally, the growth of technologies such as the telegraph and the railroad accompanied and enhanced the growth of Manifest Destiny, connecting the burgeoning country in communication and ease of travel. Rail linked the ports and the interior, facilitating trade and propelling the emergence of a national market system.

Test Yourself

1. The "Greaser Act" is an example of

a. a law that targeted and politically unempowered Mexican-Americans.

b. "Yankeephobia" in Mexico.

c. an attempt to maintain the balance between free and slaveholding states in the aftermath of the Mexican-American War.

d. an attempt to settle territorial disputes between the United States and Mexico.

2. The Wilmot Proviso is an example of

a. a law that targeted and politically unempowered Mexican-Americans.

b. "Yankeephobia" in Mexico.

c. an attempt to maintain the balance between free and slaveholding states in the aftermath of the Mexican-American War.

d. an attempt to settle territorial disputes between the United States and Mexico.

3. As a result of the Treaty of Guadalupe Hidalgo, Mexico lost more than half of its territorial land mass.

a. True

b. False

4. The growth of rail and telegraph was hailed by expansionists as a means to

a. spread American influence.

b. enhance internal development.

c. facilitate trade.

d. all of the above.

See page 526 for answers

14.4 Conclusion

The era of expansionism in the United States gained great momentum in the 1840s and saw the finalization of the boundaries of the continental United States. Manifest destiny justified expansion with a sense of mission and purpose. It portrayed American expansion as inevitable, just, and divinely foreordained. Expansion added Texas and Oregon to the Union and was an underlying cause of war with Mexico, which resulted in the acquisition of vast territories in the Southwest, including California. Although it was a popular movement, it further antagonized the divisions between free and slaveholding states. As the country grew and incorporated more and more territory, the delicate balance established by the Missouri Compromise became increasingly tenuous. Finally, the era of Manifest Destiny profoundly influenced foreign relations, as some of the great European powers such as Great Britain reevaluated their opinion of U.S. military strength, and Mexico and much of Latin America came to regard the United States with increasing suspicion.

14.5 CRITICAL THINKING EXERCISES

- Why did the United States eventually incorporate "all of Texas," but not "all of Oregon" or "all of Mexico"? What factors in the decision were similar, and which were different? What problems would the U.S. have faced if it had incorporated all of these regions?
- Using John Gast's painting *American Progress*, explain how Americans viewed Manifest Destiny. Consider the role of "progress" in technology, culture, and economy.

14.6 KEY TERMS

- Antonio López de Santa Anna
- Stephen F. Austin
- Battle of Goliad
- Battle of the Alamo
- John Frémont
- Gadsden Purchase
- Greaser Act
- Vicente Guerrero
- Manifest Destiny
- Mexican Cession
- Oregon Fever
- James K. Polk
- Republic of California
- General Winfield Scott
- John Slidell
- General Zachary Taylor
- Texas Republic
- Texas Revolution
- Treaty of Guadalupe Hidalgo

14.7 CHRONOLOGY

The following chronology is a list of important dates and events associated with this chapter.

Date	Event
1821	Stephen F. Austin led the first 300 families into Texas
1829	Mexican president Vicente Guerrero outlawed slavery in Mexico in an effort to weaken the influence of American settlers in the Mexican province of Texas
1835-1836	Texas Revolution
1836	Formation of the Republic of Texas, or the Lone Star Republic
1840s	"Oregon Fever"--expansion into Oregon Territory explodes
1844	James K. Polk elected President of United States
1846	Senator Thomas Hart Benson's "Manifest Destiny" speech
1846-1848	Mexican-American War
1848	Treaty of Guadalupe Hidalgo
1854	Gadsden Purchase

14.8 END NOTES

1 Lesli J. Favor, *A Historical Atlas of America's Manifest Destiny* (New York: Rosen Publishing Group, 2005), 41-44.

2 Favor, *Historical Atlas*, 18.

3 Sarah Mytton Maury, *The Statesmen of America in 1846* (Philadelphia: Carey and Hart, 1847), 64-65. Accessed November 28, 2011, http://books.google.com/s?id=4xxBAMJoMZcC&printsec=frontcover&dq=the+statesmen+of+america+in+1846&hl=en&ei=vr7TTuuSIYK4twfS04y5DQ&sa=X&oi=book_result&ct=result&resnum=1&ved=0CC8Q6AEwAA#v=onepage&q=the%20statesmen%20of%20america%20in%201846&f=false.

4 Michael C. Meyer, William L. Sherman, and Susan M. Deeds, *The Course of Mexican History* (New York: Oxford University Press, 2011), 252.

5 Philip L. Russell, *The History of Mexico: From Pre-Conquest to Present* (New York: Routledge Press, 2010), 150-153.

6 Frederick Merk, *Manifest Destiny and Mission in American History* (USA: Alfred A. Knopf, 1963), 42.

7 Thomas Hart Benton, Abridgement of the Debates of Congress, from 1789-1856. (New York: D. Appleton & Co, 1868), 462. Accessed November 29, 2011, http://books.google.com/books?id=jsdCAAAAYAAJ&pg=PA1&dq=abridgement+of+the+debates+of+congress+from+1789&hl=en&ei=flDVTqGuDIu-tgeckbWvAg&sa=X&oi=book_result&ct=result&resnum=4&ved=0CD4Q6AEwAw#v=onepage&q&f=false.

8 Meyer et.al, *Course of Mexican History*, 256-258.

9 Ronald Takai, *A Different Mirror: A History of Multicultural America* (New York: Little, Brown and Co, 2008), 186-187.

10 Steven W. Bender, *Greasers and Gringos: Latinos, the Law, and American Immigration* (New York: New York University Press, 2005), xiii-xiv.

11 Merk, *Manifest Destiny and Mission*, 156-159.

12 Meyer et.al, *Course of Mexican History*, 262-263.

13 Ralph Waldo Emerson, *Journals of Ralph Waldo Emerson, 1820-1872* (Boston: Houghton Mifflin, 1912), 206.

14 George A. Crofutt, "Description of American Progress," ca. 1873.

ANSWER KEY FOR CHAPTER FOURTEEN: WESTWARD EXPANSION

Check your answers to the questions in the Before You Move On Sections for this chapter.

Correct answers are **BOLDED**

Section 14.2.5 - p514

1. The concept of Manifest Destiny embraced the idea(s) that
    a. the United States would expand "from sea to shining sea."
    b. residents of areas under expansion would be Americanized.
    c. spreading the boundaries of the United States was equivalent to spreading freedom.
    D. ALL OF THE ABOVE.

2. American settlers in the Mexican province of Texas were typically unlike tejanos in that
    a. many were slave owners.
    b. they remained religiously distinct from the Roman Catholic tejanos.
    c. they demanded popular sovereignty for all, including women.
    D. A AND B.
    e. all of the above.

3. "Fifty-four forty or fight!" refers to
    a. the border dispute between the United States and Mexico: the U.S. claimed the Rio Grande as the border, Mexico claimed the Nueces River.
    B. AMERICAN DESIRES TO EXPAND TO TAKE "ALL OF OREGON," DESPITE THE BRITISH CLAIMS TO THE TERRITORY.
    c. the struggles of the settlers as they traveled over the Oregon Trail.
    d. the American desire to expand into California.

Section 14.3.2 - p522

1. The "Greaser Act" is an example of
    A. A LAW THAT TARGETED AND POLITICALLY UNEMPOWERED MEXICAN-AMERICANS.
    b. "Yankeephobia" in Mexico.
    c. an attempt to maintain the balance between free and slaveholding states in the aftermath of the Mexican-American War.
    d. an attempt to settle territorial disputes between the United States and Mexico.

2. The Wilmot Proviso is an example of
    a. a law that targeted and politically unempowered Mexican-Americans.
    b. "Yankeephobia" in Mexico.
    C. AN ATTEMPT TO MAINTAIN THE BALANCE BETWEEN FREE AND SLAVE-HOLDING STATES IN THE AFTERMATH OF THE MEXICAN-AMERICAN WAR.
    d. an attempt to settle territorial disputes between the United States and Mexico.

3. As a result of the Treaty of Guadalupe Hidalgo, Mexico lost more than half of its territorial land mass.
    A. TRUE
    b. False

4. The growth of rail and telegraph was hailed by expansionists as a means to
    a. spread American influence.
    b. enhance internal development.
    c. facilitate trade.
    D. ALL OF THE ABOVE.

Chapter Fifteen: The Impending Crisis (1848-1861)

Contents

Chapter Fifteen: The Impending Crisis (1848-1861)

15.1 INTRODUCTION

Most Americans rejoiced in their country's victory over Mexico when the U.S. Senate approved the Treaty of Guadalupe Hidalgo in 1848. However, the acquisition of new territory in the West raised questions about the expansion of slavery in the United States. Southerners believed the government should allow slavery in places like California and New Mexico. Northerners disagreed. Their differences had very little to do with humanitarian concerns about slavery. Rather, they centered on the economic and political implications of the so-called peculiar institution. National political leaders tried to quiet the division with the Compromise of 1850. However, sectional tensions mounted throughout the remainder of the decade. With each passing year, a new crisis drove the wedge deeper. The Fugitive Slave Act, Kansas-Nebraska Act, the *Dred Scott* decision, and other events increased sectional hostilities and left leaders with little hope for compromise. While the North and the South shared many intellectual, social, political, and economic beliefs, they seemed unable to come to an agreement about whether the nation should be slave or free. Abraham Lincoln's election as president in 1860 ultimately led to the secession of several southern states and paved the way for a civil war.

15.1.1 Learning Outcomes

After completing this chapter, you should be able to:

- Discuss the different solutions proposed to deal with the issue of slavery in the territories and the major terms of the Compromise of 1850.
- Describe the major events in the movement toward secession after the Compromise of 1850.
- Describe and analyze the major political developments of this period, especially the emergence of new political parties and the presidential contests.

15.2 THE SECTIONAL BALANCE BEGINS TO UNRAVEL

Northerners and southerners alike saw the territories in the West as a place of opportunity to improve their quality of life. People from both regions wanted to ensure social mobility, but their views of social mobility differed significantly. For northerners, it meant small, family homesteads where they could ensure self-sufficiency and participate in the market economy. For southerners, it meant the opportunity to acquire more land and more slaves on which to build their life. In the late 1840s and early 1850s, political leaders struggled to balance the interests of their constituents and maintain national unity. They managed to halt the sectional conflict with the Compromise of 1850, but their efforts provided only a temporary solution to the problem of a nation half slave and half free.

15.2.1 Slavery in the Territories

For at least some Americans, the Mexican-American War and the potential territorial expansion spelled trouble for the future of the United States. An aging John C. Calhoun opposed the war because it would bring slavery back into the national political discourse. A young Abraham Lincoln had similar misgivings. From the mid-1830s to the mid-1840s, the Democratic Party had managed to keep debates about slavery in Congress to a minimum with the gag rule. Calhoun and Lincoln realized, however, that any discussion over a treaty with Mexico or the question of slavery in newly acquired territories would raise challenging issues. Poet Ralph Waldo Emerson also recognized the potential problem, when he noted, "Mexico will poison us." These men, of course, were correct since the sectional divide only intensified after the Treaty of Guadalupe Hidalgo.[1]

The Wilmot Proviso

Before the end of the war, Democrat Representative David Wilmot of Pennsylvania brought up the question of slavery in the territories. Wilmot proposed to ban slavery and involuntary servitude in the territory acquired from Mexico. The Wilmot Proviso passed in the House of Representatives, but not in the Senate. The measure came before Congress several times over the next few years; in every instance, northerners voted for the compromise and southerners voted against it.[2] Party affiliation, it seemed, mattered little when it came to the debate over slavery in the territories.

Figure 15.1 The Wilmot Proviso | In 1846, Democrat David Wilmot, a member of the U.S. House of Representatives, introduced a proviso to an appropriations bill that would have barred slavery in any territory acquired as a result of the Mexican-American War. His suggestion reintroduced the issue of slavery into national politics.

Artist: Unknown
Source: Library of Congress

Wilmot introduced the measure because he opposed slavery and because he opposed southern control of the Democratic Party. As northerners lined up to support the measure, both reasons motivated their decision.

Northern Democrats worried the question of slavery in the territories would drive antislavery voters to the Whigs; taking the lead on banning slavery in the Southwest would lessen that possibility. Meanwhile, true abolitionists found the proposal appealing. It fell short of their ultimate goal to end slavery as quickly as possible, but it allowed them to duck charges of extremism. Many northerners believed they were fulfilling the wishes of the founding fathers by fighting the extension of slavery. They maintained that the Revolutionary generation compromised on slavery in order to provide a decent interval for the institution to die out naturally. As such, supporters of the Wilmot Proviso invoked the Revolution's legacy.[3]

Few southerners expected slavery to take hold in most of the Mexican Cession because the climate was inhospitable to plantation slavery. However, they objected to the Wilmot Proviso because it would limit their ability to dominate national politics. While they held a majority in the Senate in 1846, they could not compete in the House. The North's population grew at a much faster rate than did the South's. If Congress legislated on the status of slavery in the territories, then it might also pass laws on the status of slavery in the states in the future. Calhoun, hoping to halt further debate on the issue, introduced a measure suggesting that the Fifth Amendment prevented Congress from excluding slavery from the territories. The Senate did not pass Calhoun's resolution because the Northwest Ordinance of 1787 and the Missouri Compromise had set a precedent for Congressional authority.[4] After the Treaty of Guadalupe Hidalgo went into effect, it became more important for Congress to set up territorial governments. Thus, the future of slavery in the territories became a major issue in the next presidential election.

The Election of 1848

The extension of slavery proved problematic for both the Democrats and Whigs. Both parties had always been a coalition of diverse voters, and they had won national elections by holding those voters together in support or opposition of issues like the tariff. Slavery had always been the issue leaders wanted to avoid at all costs, but that no longer seemed possible in 1848. First, the Wilmot Proviso made the issue a matter of national public debate. Until the national government resolved the issue, it would continue to dominate politics. Second, antislavery advocates worked hard to keep the expansion of slavery on the minds of voters. Northern "Free Soilers" sought to prevent the expansion of slavery. Most Free Soilers did not worry much about the effect of slavery on the slaves. Rather, they worried about how slavery undermined the dignity of free labor. Southern proponents of slavery hardly could understand the Free Soil arguments. Slavery provided blessings to the slave and to the master, and thus should be spread to the new territories.[5]

James K. Polk opted not to run again in 1848, so potential Democratic candidates James Buchanan and Lewis Cass proposed solutions on the extension question in their attempt to win the nomination. Buchanan, Polk's secretary of state, supported the administration's plan to extend the Missouri Compromise line (the 36°30' line) to the Pacific Ocean. The Senate voted to support the proposal several times before the election, but the House voted it down. Lewis Cass, a Michigan senator, proposed letting the people who actually settled in the territories decide slavery's fate. Popular sovereignty's most appealing feature was the ambiguity about the precise moment when settlers needed to decide slavery's fate. The doctrine won Cass the Democratic nomination because, as long as the timing remained vague, it gave both sides hope they could win new territories to their cause.[6]

Meanwhile, the Whigs hoped to maintain party unity by adopting no platform at all. They also decided to bypass longtime Whig leader Henry Clay because of his association with the Whig's efforts to oppose territorial expansion during the war. The Whigs needed to accept and deal with the Mexican Cession because peace came before they nominated a candidate. So, they chose General Zachary Taylor, a Mexican-American War hero. Historian James M. McPherson suggests his nomination "illustrated...the strange bedfellow nature of American politics." Taylor hardly looked presidential; he often appeared in a simple uniform and a straw hat when in battle. At the same time, his image of "Old Rough and Ready" had great appeal to the average voter. Furthermore, Taylor owned plantations in Louisiana and Mississippi, ensuring that southern Whigs would not abandon the party after their northern brethren supported the Wilmot Proviso.[7]

Antislavery Whigs could not accept Taylor's nomination. Therefore, they left the party. New Yorker William H. Seward proclaimed the time had come to create "one grand Northern party of Freedom."[8] They joined with the Barnburners, who were a group of Democrats opposed to Cass's nomination, as well as members of the Liberty Party. In August, the new Free Soil Party met in Buffalo. It nominated Martin Van Buren for president and Charles Francis Adams for vice president. The Free Soil platform called for no more slave states and no more slave territories. At the same time, delegates carefully chose a former president and the son of a former president to give their ticket more appeal to voters.[9]

The presence of the Free Soil candidate in 1848 meant the Whigs and the Democrats could not ignore the issue of slavery. The Whigs promoted statements made by Taylor that he would not veto any decisions Congress made about slavery in the North; they also highlighted Taylor's status as a war hero and a slaveholder in the South. The Democrats, meanwhile, embraced the doctrine of popular sovereignty. Taylor won both the popular and the Electoral College votes. He was stronger in the South than in the North.[10] However, Van Buren took ten percent of the popular vote, throwing many northern states into the Taylor column. As it turned out, Taylor shared the Free Soilers' ideas about preventing the extension of slavery. Moreover, the Free Soilers elected nine representatives and two senators, Salmon P. Chase (OH) and Charles Sumner (MA). Their influence far exceeded their numbers when the new Congress began to address California's application for statehood.

Figure 15.2 Zachary Taylor | This portrait captures Zachary Taylor, the successful presidential nominee in 1848. The Whigs chose him because he was war hero and a plantation owner.

Artist: Unknown
Source: National Archives US Presidents in the Census Records

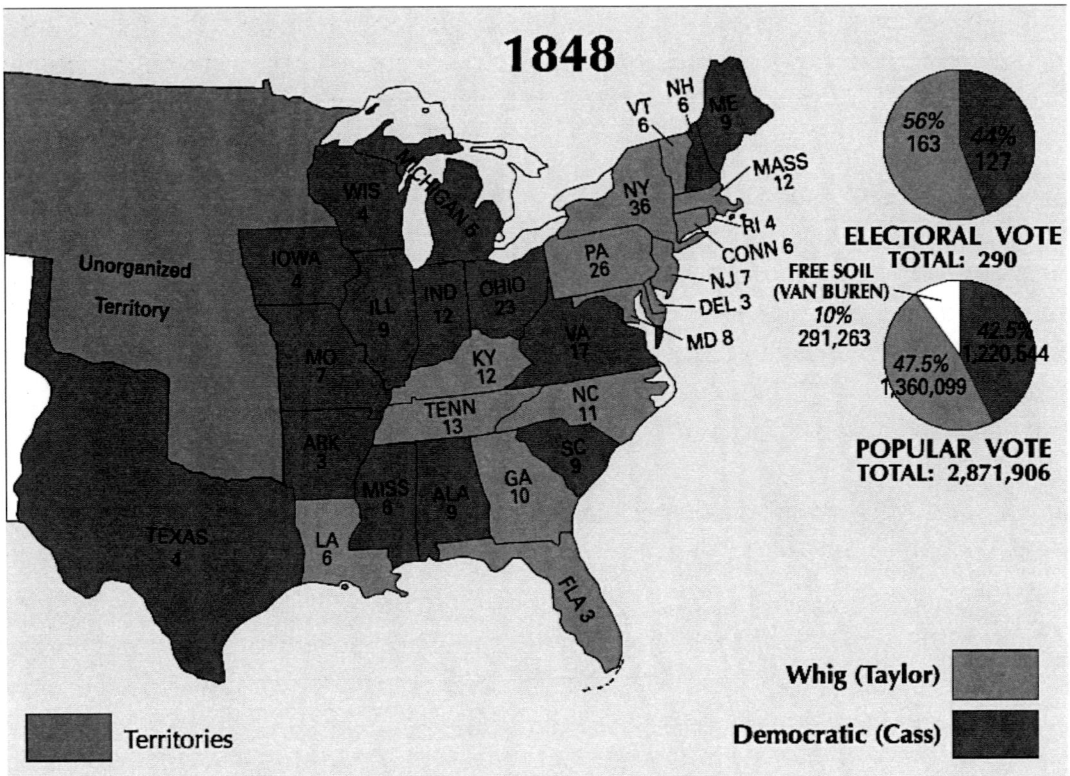

Figure 15.3 Presidential Election Map, 1848 | The central issue of the 1848 election related to the extension of slavery in the territories. Both the Democrats and the Whigs hoped to avoid the issue, but the presence of the Free Soil candidate meant the parties had to take a stand. The Democrats promoted popular sovereignty. The Whigs, meanwhile, did not unite on a single position; they ran different campaigns in the North and the South. Ultimately, the Whigs triumphed.

Author: National Atlas of the United States
Source: Wikimedia Commons

The Question of California

While the presidential election played out, an unexpected discovery in California quickened the pace of the sectional divide. In January 1848, a worker at John Sutter's sawmill in northern California stumbled upon gold. Word spread quickly to San Francisco about the discovery. Within days, the city appeared empty as people poured into the gold fields. By the end of the year, gold fever had shifted to the East coast. The so-called "forty-niners" migrated to California to make their fortune. The population grew so quickly that military authorities called for an organized territorial government. Before Congress acted, California had enough people to consider applying for statehood. Throughout the debate on the extension of slavery, politicians assumed they would have plenty of time before any of the areas of the Mexican Cession would apply for statehood. The gold rush, of course, changed that assumption.

As California's population rose, national leaders weighed the question of whether the new state would be slave or free. Southerners saw California as the most suitable territory acquired from Mexico for cotton production. Northerners refused to accept the idea that its suitability preordained it as a slave state. Meanwhile, the residents of California grew impatient since the lame-duck Polk did little to encourage a divided Congress to appoint a territorial government before they adjourned. In fact, tensions ran so high in the Senate that late one night several rather drunk members began to exchange not only insults, but punches too. When Zachary Taylor took office, he made it clear he wanted to resolve the issue. He proposed to skip the creation of a territory and move directly to the application for statehood. So, the military authorities in California issued a call for a state constitutional convention.[11]

The president worked under the assumption that California, as well as New Mexico, would become free states. Although he owned slaves, Taylor supported a Free Soil solution for the Mexican Cession as the best way to preserve the Union.[12] The settlers in California also opposed slavery, which worked in Taylor's favor. In July 1849, a group of Texas slaveholders arrived in the gold fields. After staking out their claim, they set their slaves panning for gold. White miners did not like the idea of competing with slave labor. Hence, they held a meeting to discuss slavery in the gold fields. The miners resolved that "no slave or Negro should own claims or even work in the mines." Not long after forcing the Texans out, a delegate to the state constitutional convention from the mining region proposed a ban on slavery and involuntary servitude in California. The other delegates supported the measure unanimously and began to draft a constitution that barred slavery.[13] Although California's application for statehood seemed the perfect the opportunity to test the real meaning of popular sovereignty, it instead provoked a crisis in Congress.

15.2.2 The Compromise of 1850

Tensions between northern and southern leaders were quite high when the new Congress convened in December 1849. The House could not even decide on a new speaker, much less on the more substantial questions about slavery once Zachary Taylor proposed to admit California to the Union. The president, wanting to play on the members' devotion to the Union, asked them not to discuss the "exciting topics of a section character" that "provided the painful apprehensions in the public mind." According to historian Michael A. Morrison, Taylor hoped non-action in Washington would allow people in the West to take the initiative with respect to becoming a free or a slave state. However, few members of Congress—Whig or Democrat—wanted a quick solution.[14]

Northern Whigs saw the president's move as rejecting his support for the Wilmot Proviso. Southern Whigs saw the president as a traitor to the slaveholding class. Southern Democrats maintained the president wanted to harm the South on purpose. Southerners, regardless of party affiliation, believed they would, perhaps permanently, lose control of the Senate with California's admission as a free state. Taylor's request did little to quell the debate. According to one northerner, it seemed that slavery affected every public policy issue in 1850. Henry Clay once again decided to step in to promote a compromise. Denied the Whig nomination in 1848, Clay wanted to seize the initiative from the president and preserve national unity as he had done with the Missouri Compromise. Daniel Webster and Stephen A. Douglas aided him in working out the details and finally getting Congressional approval. At the same time, John C. Calhoun and William H. Seward led the opposition to any compromise.[15]

The Road to the Compromise

On January 29, 1850, Henry Clay rose before the Senate to introduce a series of measures to relieve the sectional tension. Throughout much of his career, the Kentucky senator had

Figure 15.4 Henry Clay Promotes Compromise | Questions surrounding the extension of slavery in Mexican Cession, especially California, created a major rift between the North and South. Longtime unionist, Henry Clay, promoted a series of measures in 1850 designed to resolve the differences of opinion.

Artist: Engraving by Robert Whitechurch of painting by Peter Rothermel
Source: Library of Congress

promoted economic growth and national unity at the expense of slavery, even though he owned slaves. He proposed measures that required both sides to give a little in the increasingly tense debate. First, California would enter the Union as a free state; the rest of the Mexican Cession would organize without restriction on slavery, or along the lines popular sovereignty. Second, Texas would abandon its claim to territory in New Mexico; in return, the federal government would cover debts incurred by Texas when it was an independent republic. Third, Congress would abolish the slave trade but not slavery in the District of Columbia. Finally, Congress would adopt a stronger fugitive slave law, but it would not regulate the interstate slave trade.[16] Clay's proposals touched off an eight-month debate in Congress. Southern and northern radicals opposed the measures for a variety of reasons.

John C. Calhoun spoke ardently for the southern position. Calhoun, who was too ill to deliver his own speech, blamed the North for the crisis. He implied only the North could save the Union "by conceding to the South an equal right in the acquired territory, and to do her duty by causing the stipulations relative to fugitive slaves to be faithfully fulfilled." Moreover, the North needed to "provide for the insertion of a provision in the Constitution...which will restore to the South in substance the power she possessed of protecting herself, before the equilibrium between the sections was destroyed by the action of this Government." If the North failed to respond to the South's concerns, Calhoun indicated the South could not stay in the Union.[17]

In his first speech before the Senate, William H. Seward explained the northern opposition to compromise. Seward denied the Constitution protected the right to own human property and, even if it did, slavery was "repugnant to the law of nature and of nations." While the Constitution did recognize slavery, he implied the institution was incompatible with the nation's founding principles. "Freedom is...in harmony with the Constitution of the United States...You may separate slavery from South Carolina, and the state will still remain; but if you subvert freedom there, the state will cease to exist." Finally, he suggested Americans, though subject to the Constitution, were subject to a higher law as well. Clay, Taylor, and others lambasted the radical and inflammatory nature of Seward's comments, but to some extent, he represented the feelings of much of the upper North.[18]

While the radicals set the tone of public debate, moderates from the lower North and upper South worked toward a compromise. In a speech supporting the compromise, Daniel Webster said, "I speak to-day for the preservation of the Union...I speak to-day out of a solicitous and anxious heart for the restoration to the country of that quiet and harmonious harmony which make the blessings of this Union so rich, and so dear to us all."[19] Many moderates shared his opinion and hoped to gain support for Clay's scheme. A special Congressional committee combined the proposals into the one measure. The supporters of compromise hoped the desire to preserve the Union would outweigh sectional interests so they could pass the "Omnibus Bill." Unfortunately, they hoped in vain.

Figure 15.5 Millard Fillmore | This photograph captures Millard Fillmore who ascended to the presidency after Zachary Taylor unexpectedly died.

Author: Unknown
Source: National Archives US Presidents in the Census Records

Radicals, who composed nearly two-thirds of Congress, did not intend to accept the compromise. Neither, for that matter, did Zachary Taylor. He wanted to see California, New Mexico, Oregon, Utah, and Minnesota admitted to statehood before the question of slavery was addressed, a proposal that would have given the North a ten-vote majority in the Senate.[20] A sudden turn of events changed the debate over the compromise. Zachary Taylor died unexpectedly on July 9, 1850. Millard Fillmore, a New Yorker who ardently supported a compromise, succeeded him. Even with Fillmore's support, the Omnibus Bill failed to win a majority in either chamber.

While Clay gave up on the compromise, other members of Congress decided to try a different tactic. Led by Illinois Senator Stephen Douglas, supporters of compromise worked to salvage the situation. Douglas broke Clay's proposal into separate parts. By introducing the measures one at a time, he managed to gather support from varying coalitions of Whigs and Democrats and Northerners and Southerners on each issue. In September, Fillmore signed each bill—collectively known as the Compromise of 1850—into law. California entered the Union as a free state. New Mexico and Utah territories were organized, but Congress deferred the question of slavery until their admission as states. Texas gave up a portion of its western boundary to New Mexico in return for $10 million. Congress abolished the slave trade in the District of Columbia. Finally, Congress passed a more stringent fugitive slave law.[21]

The Impact of the Compromise

People around the country rejoiced at how the compromise saved the Union; the president even called it "a final settlement" of sectional differences. However, radicals on both sides maintained the battle would continue, especially when the Fugitive Slave Law went into effect. Few members of Congress had paid much attention to the provisions of the measure designed to assist slaveholders capture runaway slaves. The nation's first fugitive slave law came in 1793 because Article IV of the Constitution said "No person held to service or labor in one state, under the laws thereof, escaping into another, shall, in consequence of any law or regulation therein, be discharged from such service or labor, but shall be delivered up on claim of the party to whom such service or labor may be due." However, the 1850 version made the law much harsher than it had been in the past.[22]

The Fugitive Slave Law of 1850 required all citizens to help in the capture of fugitive slaves. U.S. Marshalls had the ability to deputize citizens to aid in seizing runaways. Those who refused to help or interfered in the effort to capture slaves faced stiff fines and jail time. Furthermore, those accused of being runaways had no right to a jury trial and no right to testify in their own defense. Federal commissions could send blacks, runaway or free, back to slavery solely on the sworn statement of individuals claiming to be their owners. The law also said the government would pay commissioners a $10 fee if they found in favor of the claimant, but a $5 fee if they found in favor of the accused. Frustrated about the preference the law gave to southern slaveholders, northerners began to obstruct its implementation. While the law did not turn all northerners into antislavery advocates, many believed that accepting it would undermine their states' freedom of choice.[23]

In northern communities, blacks and whites banded together to protect runaways. They passed "personal liberty laws" denying federal officials the use of state facilities. They formed vigilance committees to warn blacks when slave catchers arrived in town and to obstruct their efforts in capturing runaways. In Boston, abolitionists helped fugitives William and Ellen Craft of Georgia escape capture by harassing the slave catchers in the streets. They also freed Shadrach, who fled his master in Virginia, from a federal courtroom. Abolitionists saved some runaways with such daring stunts, but they could not save them all. In the 1850s, commissioners returned over three hundred blacks to the South and set only eleven free. Most fugitives opted to head to Canada rather than wait to see whether a slave catcher would come after them.[24]

In Christiana, a small Quaker community near Gettysburg, a slaveholder died in an attempt to capture his runaways. Millard Fillmore, under pressure from southerners to enforce the law, sent the marines to find the runaways and those responsible for the slaveholder's death. The federal government tried the resisters for treason, but the case fell apart. Local juries would simply not convict those accused of violating the law. Southerners expressed horror at the open defiance of the law, even though most northerners complied with it. Historian William W. Freehling remarks that white southerners happily relied on the use of federal power "whenever necessary to sustain the Peculiar Institution," even as they promoted states' rights. Historian Vernon Burton indicated southerners expected the federal government to protect their right to property even when it came at the expense of northerners' right to free speech.[25]

With tensions already on the rise, the antislavery movement stepped up their efforts to persuade the northern population (and if possible some southerners) about the evils of slavery. They relied heavily on slave narratives and novels designed to highlight the worst aspects of slavery. *Uncle Tom's Cabin*, written by Harriet Beecher Stowe, became the most widely known of these efforts. The book, published in 1852, caused a sensation in the North. In the first year alone, it sold 300,000 copies. Most people were moved by the pain and suffering of the book's main characters, Uncle Tom and Eliza. More than ever before, they began to think about the moral implications of slavery because Stowe successfully managed to link the antislavery cause with the preservation of the family. Stowe clearly criticized the southern way of life. However, in making the villain, Simon Legree, a northern transplant, she also blamed northerners for their complicity in perpetuating slavery.[26]

Figure 15.6 Uncle Tom's Cabin | Harriet Beecher Stowe's novel featuring the horrors of slavery incensed both northerners and southerners. People in the North reacted to the abuse slaves faced, while people in the South claimed the book contained many falsehoods about slavery.

Author: Unknown
Source: *Pictures and Stories from Uncle Tom's Cabin*

While it would be hard to quantify the impact of Stowe's book, James McPherson maintains that few contemporaries "doubted its power." Influential political leaders both at home and abroad read *Uncle Tom's Cabin*. Moreover, the "vehemence of the southern denunciations" of the book served as "best gauge of how close they hit home." Most southerners considered Stowe's book slanderous. The *Southern Literary Messenger* thought the South had every right to criticize the book because it contained so many false accusations. Pro-slavery authors responded with dozens of books designed to counter the images presented in the antislavery literature. Most of their efforts suggested that slaves lived far better lives than workers in the North did; they focused on the goodness and gentility of life on the plantation. They suggested that slavery's shortcomings came not from deficiencies in the institution, but from an unequal union.[27]

As national elections approached in 1852, much like in 1848, Whigs and the Democrats sought to close the sectional rifts that had opened within their parties. Both parties chose moderates who had not inflamed voters' passions on the question of slavery. The Whigs needed to find a candidate other than Millard Fillmore, because antislavery Whigs would not vote for him after he ardently upheld The Fugitive Slave Law. Southern Whigs refused to support William H. Seward because of the "Higher Law" speech. To maintain party unity, they selected Winfield Scott, a Mexican War hero and non-slaveholding Virginian. The Democrats also bypassed their better-known members, including James Buchanan, Lewis Cass, and Stephen Douglas. They settled on Franklin Pierce, a former New Hampshire senator.[28]

The Democrats and the Whigs wanted to avoid the issue of slavery but had no other issues on which to campaign. A healthy economy meant no one cared much about the tariff, a national bank, or internal improvements. Therefore, the campaign descended into a series of vicious personal attacks. The Whigs implied Pierce had no talent for governing; moreover, he was a cowardly drunk. In return, the Democrats, painted Scott as a nativist, which prevented him from picking up votes among immigrants. Pierce triumphed in both the popular and the Electoral College votes. Free Soil candidate Nathan P. Hale siphoned off some of Scott's popular votes, but most Democrats returned to the party fold, thus giving Pierce the edge. Moreover, most southern Whigs could not accept Scott as a candidate because he seemed less than devoted to the Compromise of 1850. The sectional divide for the Whigs did not bode well for the party's future. The Democrats, at least temporarily, papered over their divisions. After the election, many people believed the tensions had finally subsided.[29]

15.2.3 Before You Move On...

Key Concepts

When Ralph Waldo Emerson proclaimed, "Mexico will poison us," he quite accurately captured the effect territorial acquisition from the Mexican-American War had on the United States. New territories raised new questions about the extension of slavery that political leaders could not easily answer in the late 1840s and early 1850s. The Wilmot Proviso, proposing to bar slavery in territories acquired from the war, touched off debate in Congress that took over four years to resolve. The gold rush forced a quick decision on the slave issue because California petitioned for statehood in 1849. Californians desired to enter the Union as a free state, and many southerners stood aghast at the real possibility of the Senate tilting in favor of the free states. Southerners threatened secession. In response, Senator Henry Clay proposed a series of measures, collectively known as the Compromise of 1850, to preserve the Union. After months of debate, Congress passed the compromise. Slavery, however, was not a matter that would disappear. Concerns about the response of those opposed to slavery to the Fugitive Slave Law and the publication of *Uncle Tom's Cabin* to promote the end of slavery kept North and South divided into 1852 when Democrat Franklin Pierce triumphed over Whig Winfield Scott in the presidential election.

Test Yourself

1. The Wilmot Proviso

   a. was unconstitutional.

   b. would prohibit slavery in lands acquired from Mexico.

   c. passed both houses of Congress.

   d. would extend the Missouri Compromise line to the Pacific.

2. The Compromise of 1850

   a. postponed California statehood.

   b. gave Texas more territory.

   c. ended slavery in Washington, D.C.

   d. strengthened the fugitive slave laws.

3. Harriet Beecher Stowe's novel *Uncle Tom's Cabin*
   a. was perhaps the most effective piece of antislavery propaganda.
   b. was perhaps the most effective piece of proslavery propaganda.
   c. ended section hostilities after its publication in 1852.
   d. presented a picture of happy, well-treated slaves and benevolent masters.

See page 572 for answers

15.3 THE COLLAPSE OF THE SECOND PARTY SYSTEM

Many Americans believed Franklin Pierce's election in 1852 would end the sectional problems that emerged after the Mexican-American War. Southerners expected the new president to uphold the Fugitive Slave Law and protect slavery; for the most part, Pierce lived up to their expectations. Democrats also looked for ways to maintain the sectional balance and promote economic development that would benefit all Americans. However, the resulting efforts to annex Cuba and spread slavery to Kansas raised concerns about the future direction of the nation, especially among those opposed to slavery. As North and South once again pulled apart, the Whigs entered a period of decline. After the election of 1852, they ceased to exist as a national party. Several new parties emerged to take their place—most notably the Know-Nothing Party, or the American Party, and the Republican Party. Events in 1856 ultimately paved the way for the Republicans to supersede the Whigs as the second largest party in the nation. Showing the clear divide of the nation, all of the Republicans' support came from the North.

15.3.1 The Possible Expansion of Slavery

Southerners, when surveying the national landscape in 1852 and 1853, continued to worry about their weakening power in the Union. Utah and New Mexico allowed slavery, but low levels of slaveholding did little to strengthen the southern hold on the national government. Moreover, although slavery remained profitable because of a cotton boom in the 1850s, the prices of slaves rose steadily since the ban on the international slave trade went into effect in 1807. Slaveholders, especially in the lower South, had bristled for years about the laws restricting the international slave trade. Some suggested states adopt laws allowing landowners to acquire "apprentices" from Africa. Others simply broke the law. Late in the decade, Charles Lamar sent the *Wanderer* to Africa. Federal authorities stopped the importation of these slaves, but southern juries acquitted Lamar and his cohorts of all charges, an acquittal which resembled the actions of northern juries in dealing with fugitive slave cases.[30] The slaveholder's desire for more territory, particularly in Latin America and later in Kansas, proved far more significant than their defiance of the ban on the international slave trade.

Young America and Cuba

Acquiring new slave territory in the 1850s fit well with a nationalistic movement in the Democratic Party known as Young America. For several years, some slaveholders had looked to Cuba. James Polk offered to purchase the territory, but the Spanish refused. When that effort failed, many expansionists were more than willing to go to war to win the island. Narciso Lopez, a Cuban exile, encouraged these efforts by recruiting pirates to attack Cuba. His expeditions failed, but the desire to obtain Cuba did not abate. During 1852, the Young Americans made acquiring Cuba from Spain part of the Democratic Platform. Pierce's victory increased the possibility of territorial expansion, especially after he appointed numerous southern expansionists to his administration.[31]

Although Pierce sent Pierre Soulé, a devoted expansionist, to Spain as minister, he seemed less than confident the Spanish would sell. So, the president encouraged John Quitman to plan a piracy expedition. Pierce hoped the effort would spark an uprising against Spanish rule in Cuba. The revolution would lead to an independent republic, which, like Texas, would apply to enter the Union. Since slavery was legal in Spanish Cuba, it would remain so after annexation. By 1854, Quitman recruited enough volunteers for an invasion. Louisiana Senator John Slidell then introduced a measure to suspend the neutrality law so Americans could sell weapons to Cubans. At that point, the Pierce administration began to have second thoughts about supporting Quitman because of developments in Kansas and Nebraska.[32]

Since the president still wanted Cuba, he instructed Soulé to offer the Spanish $130 million for the territory. Failing that, Soulé should "detach the island from the Spanish dominion." Soulé encouraged James Buchanan, the minister to Great Britain, and John Mason, the minister to France, to join him in issuing the Ostend Manifesto. Their memorandum stated, "We firmly believe...the vital interests of Spain are as seriously involved in the sale, as those of the United States in the purchase, of the island and that the transaction will prove equally honorable to both nations." They further declared that Spanish control of the island harmed the United States. If Spain would not sell, then the United States would "be justified in wresting it from Spain." The European and American press savaged the Ostend Manifesto. By the end of the year, the administration gave up any hope of acquiring Cuba, though they later flirted with acquiring Nicaragua through similar means.[33] Although the Pierce administration ultimately failed to acquire Cuba, it did complete the continental expansion of the United States. In 1853, the president appointed James Gadsden as the minister to Mexico. When he arrived in Mexico City, Gadsden had one goal—to negotiate the purchase of land in northern Mexico so the United States could complete a rail line from New Orleans to southern California. Gadsden offered Santa Anna $50 million for 250,000 square miles. Even though the Mexican leader needed the money, he would not part with one-third of his territory. Instead, he negotiated the sale of 55,000 square miles for $15 million. The Senate approved the Gadsden Purchase only after northern members cut the acquisition to 46,000 square miles.[34] While many southerners did not give up their desire to acquire more slave territory, after 1854 they turned their attention to Kansas.

The Kansas-Nebraska Act

As southern politicians supported expansionist ventures, northern politicians looked for ways to promote national unity. Stephen Douglas, the "Little Giant" who successfully shepherded the Compromise of 1850 through Congress, saw economic expansion as the best means to bridge the gap between the sections. To facilitate that growth, Douglas looked to Congress to grant land concessions to the Illinois Central Railroad in order to complete a transcontinental railroad from Chicago to San Francisco. Since the route would go through the central part of the country, Congress also needed to organize new territories out of the Louisiana Purchase. As an investor in the railroad, Douglas stood to gain financially upon the line's completion. But more than personal gain motivated the senator. Douglas believed, according to Vernon Burton, his plan "offered something for everyone" and the spirit of manifest destiny would prevail. Unfortunately, the plan had the opposite effect.[35]

As the chair of the Senate committee on territories, Douglas introduced a bill in 1853 to organize the Nebraska territory based on the terms of the Missouri Compromise. His counterpart in the House did likewise. While the House passed the measure, opposition from southern senators derailed it. Leading southern senators made it clear that, if Douglas wanted their support, he would have to allow slavery in the territory. He, of course, knew opening the territory to slavery would undermine northern support. When Douglas proposed a revised bill in 1854, he used the same phrase Congress used with respect to New Mexico and Utah. The southerners, however, indicated he had not gone far enough to meet their needs. They insisted on a stated repeal of the Missouri Compromise. By 1854, southerners grew frustrated with northern defiance of the Fugitive Slave Law. The case of Anthony Burns in Boston, where leading abolitions supported his failed rescue attempt from the federal courthouse, made southerners want stronger federal protection for slavery. Douglas acquiesced to their demands when he introduced the Kansas-Nebraska bill. The measure proposed to create two territories instead of one; it also supported the use of popular sovereignty in both territories.[36]

Figure 15.7 Stephen A. Douglas | This photograph of Douglas (the "Little Giant") was taken sometime after the passage of the Kansas-Nebraska Act. The Illinois Democrat hoped to promote economic growth when he introduced the measure to organize two new western territories. However, the bill only reignited sectional tensions.

Author: Unknown
Source: Library of Congress

The Kansas-Nebraska bill ended the sectional peace. When the Pierce administration tried to propose a bill that would not repeal the Missouri Compromise, southern senators literally stormed the White House in protest. The president backed down because they told him he would lose southern support if he did not support the measure as proposed. The administration then put pressure on northern Democrats to vote for the measure. However, regardless of their party, many northerners could not accept the bill. The Free Soilers' frequent warnings of a slave power conspiracy no longer seemed so farfetched. State legislatures across the North passed resolutions opposing the Kansas-Nebraska bill. In response, Douglas claimed that the Compromise of 1850 had already repealed the Missouri Compromise. But most northerners found the argument disingenuous since the 1850 measures only applied to the Mexican Cession, not the Louisiana Purchase.[37]

Congress narrowly approved the Kansas-Nebraska Act in 1854 after Douglas found enough northerners to support the bill. At the same time, southerners prevented the simultaneous passage of a homestead act to provide settlers with 160 acres of free land in the newly-organized territories. James McPherson maintains the Kansas-Nebraska Act "may have been the most important single event pushing the nation toward civil war." It undermined the Whigs as a national party and cut the strength of Democrats in the North.[38] After the measure passed, most people assumed Nebraska would be a free territory because its climate was not suitable for plantation slavery. Kansas, on the other hand, would be up for grabs. Whichever side controlled the process of writing the state constitution would make the decision. In the coming years, the confrontation in Kansas turned violent.

15.3.2 The Emergence of New Parties

After the election of 1852, Whigs across the country thought that they could mount a comeback if they exploited the Democrats' mistakes, a recovery that would come so long as the Whigs did not draw attention to themselves. Historian Michael Holt, however, maintained their strategy had serious flaws. By 1853, the Whigs had broken into five factions, ranging from those who wanted to create a new antislavery party to those who wanted to create a new union party. Try as they might, the Whigs could not find an issue in 1853 to unite their national party.[39]

Although the Kansas-Nebraska debate weakened the Democrats, it did not benefit the Whigs. The rising concern about immigrants and about slavery hurt them. The Whigs' wait-and-see strategy backfired because time was not on their side, as they believed. Moreover, they failed to consider other parties might gain more from voter backlash against the Democrats.[40] While dozens of new political organizations vied for voters' attention, two emerged as true contenders. One focused on concerns about immigration; the other focused on concerns about slavery. The party realignment that occurred in the 1850s did not rest solely on the issue of slavery; nativism played a significant role as well.

The Know-Nothing Party

During the 1830s, anti-immigrant sentiments in the United States began to rise. Protestant Americans viewed Catholic immigrants as ignorant and superstitious and so perceived their growing number as harmful to the nation's republican form of government. At first, nativist tendencies influenced the workplace more than political debates. Employment advertisements often featured the phrase, "No Irish Need Apply." When the potato famine sent thousands of Irish people to American shores, nativist organizations rose in both popularity and political power. In the 1840s, the Order of United Americans and the Order of the Star Spangled Banner, two secret organizations, formed in an effort to preserve native-born political power. They merged in 1852 to form the Know-Nothing Party, sometimes known as the American Party. Their name derived from member's standard response to questions about the party: "I know nothing." With over one million members, the group became an important political force in the North.[41]

Men who gravitated toward Know-Nothingism tended to be in their twenties and to work in lower white-collar or skilled blue-collar positions. More than anything else, in light of the Market Revolution, they wanted to preserve their place in American society. Their political positions stemmed from their hostility to foreigners. They linked the poverty and ignorance of the Irish in Ireland and the United States to drink and to Catholic education. Therefore, the party supported the temperance movement and opposed tax support for parochial schools in order to assimilate the Irish into American culture. However, more than anything else, Know-Nothings wanted to undermine the political power of naturalized citizens. They proposed to lengthen the naturalization period from five to twenty-one years. They also called for public office to be restricted to the native born.[42]

In 1854, the Know-Nothings did well in local and state elections. They controlled state governments in California, Connecticut, Massachusetts, New Hampshire, and New York. By 1855, the party spread southward, as they made significant inroads in Maryland, Kentucky, and Tennessee. These victories stemmed less from nativist sentiment and more from the desire of southern Whigs to find a new home before the next presidential election. As the strength of the party shifted, slavery became a divisive issue. Northern Know-Nothings tended to oppose the spread of slavery. They thought slavery, like Catholicism, stemmed from ignorance and tyranny. They did well in the 1854 and 1855 elections in some states because they banded with Free Soil candidates. Southern Know-Nothings, however, could not accept a party that denounced the expansion of slavery into the territories. Northern delegates walked out of their 1855 national convention after southern delegates asked the party to endorse the Kansas-Nebraska Act. Antislavery advocates looked for other options; thus, the American Party grew stronger in the South and weaker in the North.[43]

The Republican Party

After Stephen Douglas introduced the Kansas-Nebraska bill, some northerners thought they needed to create a new political coalition to stop the spread of slavery. As the nation approached the midterm elections in 1854, people opposed to the extension of slavery aligned in hopes of undermining the Democrats' control of the national government. In time, disgruntled Democrats, disillusioned Free Soilers, distraught Whigs, and discouraged Know-Nothings united in what supporters eventually called the Republican Party, though until 1856 it had several different names. The results of the 1854 elections showed a great deal of resentment toward the Democrats among northern voters, but it did not guarantee a party hostile to slavery could be successful. Party organizers therefore looked for a way to unite their rather heterogeneous group of voters.[44]

Efforts to build the Republican Party into a cohesive group began in earnest after the 1854 elections. Leaders sought to outline a political philosophy or ideology that could speak to former Democrats and former Whigs as well as appeal to nativists and immigrants. They needed to find a way to package their antislavery views to as many northerners as possible, since they did not expect to draw much support from southerners. Historian Eric Foner maintains "the concept of 'free labor' lay at the heart" of Republican ideology. It provided a "coherent social outlook" that allowed the party to suggest why slavery harmed American society. Republicans believed, as William Seward indicated, slavery was "morally unjust, politically unwise, and socially destructive" because it undermined a person's ability to achieve economic independence and social mobility. Free labor allowed Republicans to focus on the effects of slavery on non-slaveholders as opposed to the slaves; thus, they could better blunt criticism that they favored racial equality.[45]

Republicans expanded on their platform of free labor by promoting "free soil" and "free men." Free soil referred to the old Free Soil Party that hoped to stop the spread of slavery in the territories and to the crisis in Kansas following the Kansas-Nebraska Act. Republicans wanted to spread free labor to the West. For that to happen, those territories needed to be free of both slaves and free blacks. Free men referred to a belief that all men, black or white, deserved the right to their own labor. Few Republicans supported equality between the races, but they believed in basic human rights for all. The number of Republicans who supported the American Colonization Society's efforts to encourage migration of former slaves to Africa suggested widespread racism in the party. At the same time, most Republicans fought efforts to make the legal and social position of blacks worse than it was in the 1850s.[46]

Free labor ideology helped to bridge the gap between the radical, conservative, and moderate wings of the party. Regional variations in the North helped shape Republican policy and programs as well as determined which part leaders chose to focus on. When dealing with radical members, leaders addressed the need to end slavery. When dealing with conservative members, leaders focused on the need to preserve the Union. As the party grew in strength, moderates held the party together and tried to find a way to meet both of their goals.[47] Although the Kansas-Nebraska Act helped form the party, it would be events in 1856 that helped the Republicans become the dominant alternative to the Democrats by the end of the decade.

15.3.3 The Tremors of 1856

Throughout 1854 and 1855, it seemed unclear whether the Know-Nothings or the Republicans would successfully manage to succeed the Whigs in the traditional two-party system. However, two events paved the way for the Republicans to rise in strength. After the passage of the Kansas-Nebraska Act, both sides vowed to triumph in Kansas. New Englanders sent money and weapons to the antislavery settlers; meanwhile, Missouri slaveholders pledged to burn the abolitionists out of Kansas. In 1856, the conflict between proslavery and antislavery elements turned violent, leading to a civil war in Kansas and an attack on Charles Sumner in Washington. Combined, the two events made the threat of slavery seem far more serious than the threat of immigrants.[48]

Bleeding Kansas

At first, antislavery and proslavery advocates in Kansas hoped to use the ballot box to swing the territory to slave or free. Initially, slaveholders outnumbered Free Soilers. Nevertheless, proslavery leaders wanted to ensure victory in elections for a representative to Congress and for the territorial legislature. Led by David Atchison, who was a Missouri senator, proslavery forces from Missouri cast ballots in the Kansas elections. On May 30, 1855, the slaveholders secured a majority in the territorial legislature, though almost 5,000 illegal ballots were cast. Andrew Reeder, the territorial governor, ordered new elections in many districts, which the Free Soilers won. However, when the legislature met in July, it refused to seat those elected in the second election. Then it passed a series of laws to undermine the influence of the Free Soilers, including one that made it a crime to express antislavery statements. When Missourians cast ballots in Kansas, according to William Freehling, they created a new issue there. It became less about legalizing slavery and more about "whether Kansas could abide antirepublican repression of whites."[49]

When Reeder traveled to Washington to meet with the president about the fraud, Franklin Pierce backed the proslavery forces in Kansas. He replaced Reeder with William Shannon, whom he instructed to uphold the laws passed by the proslavery legislature. At the same time, Free Soilers made it clear they had no intention of living under the laws of a legislature they considered fraudulent. They continued to move into Kansas to press their cause and soon outnumbered the slaveholders. Free Soilers held a convention in Topeka, where they adopted a constitution that barred slaves and free blacks from Kansas. Moreover, they proposed to select a new state legislature and a new governor. As 1856 began, Kansas had two constitutions and two legislatures: one representing proslavery forces in Lecompton, and one representing antislavery forces in Topeka.[50]

Kansas descended into violence in 1856. Hoping to encourage Free Soilers to leave the territory, hundreds of proslavery forces, mostly from Missouri, marched into Lawrence on May 21, 1856. Their purpose was to arrest the leaders of the antislavery government for treason. Although the leaders did not resist arrest, the posse burned the local hotel, looted a number of houses, destroyed two antislavery printing presses, and killed one man. Less than a week later, the antislavery forces responded in kind. John Brown, who believed he had a personal duty to overthrow slavery, became quite agitated when he heard about what happened in Lawrence. He vowed to "fight fire with fire" and to "strike terror in the hearts" of the proslavery forces. Along with four of his sons and three other supporters, Brown headed to a neighborhood near Pottawatomie Creek on May 24, 1856. They killed five proslavery men and proceeded to cut off their heads and hands during the course of the night. The "Pottawatomie Massacre" coupled with the "Sack of Lawrence" led to a guerilla war that lasted for much of the rest of the decade.[51]

Bleeding Sumner

Given the situation in Kansas, Congress opened debates on its statehood in a heated atmosphere. However, both sides knew neither a proslavery nor an antislavery constitution would win approval because the Republicans controlled the House and the Democrats controlled the Senate. Thus, both sides saw the debates as an opportunity to attack the opposition before the next presidential election. David Atchison had previously indicated if the South won Kansas, slavery would spread successfully to the Pacific. However, if the South failed, it would lose Missouri, Arkansas, and Texas. In other words, the South was playing "for mighty stakes." South Carolina Representative Preston Brooks tied the fate of the South to the Kansas issue, noting it was a "point of honor."[52]

At the same time, Republicans highlighted the infringement of the rights of the Free Soil settlers. On May 19, 1856, Massachusetts Senator Charles Sumner began his "Crime against Kansas Speech." Sumner hoped to inflame passions about the situation in Kansas when he stated, "It is the rape of a virgin Territory, compelling it to the hateful embrace of slavery; and it may be clearly traced to a depraved longing for a new slave State, the hideous offspring of such a crime, in the hope of adding to the power of slavery in the national government." Democrats heavily criticized the speech, while Republicans remained muted in their praise because Sumner's remarks showed so much hostility to the South. However, no one quite expected that one man's response to the speech would revive political abolition.[53]

During the speech, Charles Sumner made a passing reference to Andrew Butler, his aging colleague from South Carolina. Sumner accused Butler of not only defending but also lusting after the "harlot, Slavery" for most of his public life. Southerners were furious about this personal attack on one of their elder statesman, none more so than Butler's cousin, Preston Brooks. The young representative felt compelled to defend the honor of both his cousin and the South. Under normal circumstances, Brooks would have challenged Sumner to a duel. However, he did not consider Sumner worthy of a duel, nor did he think Sumner would accept. On May 22, 1856, Brooks did what he considered the next best thing. After the Senate adjourned, he approached Sumner who was working at his desk. Brooks declared Sumner had libeled his state and his relative, and he planned to punish him for it. As the senator looked up from his desk, Brooks began to assault him with his cane and did not stop until Sumner lay bleeding and unconscious on the floor.[54]

In the wake of the caning, southerners labeled Brooks a hero. A Charleston newspaper praised him for "standing forth so nobly in defense of...the honor of South Carolinians." Northerners in the House hoped to expel him, but southern support blocked the attempt. Brooks then resigned his seat; he returned home only to have the people of South Carolina reelect him unanimously. Fellow southerners also sent him gifts of new canes with inscriptions like "Hit Him Again" and "Use Knock Down Arguments." Simultaneously, northerners turned Sumner into a martyr for the antislavery cause. Brooks's assault symbolized the barbarity of the slave system. Moreover, it showed southerners would not tolerate free speech anywhere, even in the halls of Congress, when it criticized their beloved institution of slavery. Southern praise for Brooks proved even more damaging than the attack itself. Northern conservatives began to concede that southern society might be as bad as the radicals had suggested. The combined effects of "Bleeding Kansas" and "Bleeding Sumner" convinced many northerners of the necessity of curbing slave power.[55]

The Election of 1856

As the election of 1856 approached, once again the future of slavery and the future of freedom dominated public discourse. "Bleeding Kansas" and "Bleeding Sumner" set the stage for the election as the Know-Nothings, the Republicans, and the Democrats looked to find candidates who could hold their fragmented coalitions together. In the end, the ongoing sectional tensions shaped the outcome. The election also paved the way for the continuation of those divisions as the Republican Party grew stronger in the North.

In 1856, Know-Nothing leaders hoped to bridge the gap between the two regions that had grown in the wake of their split over slavery the previous year. Once again, southerners called for support of slavery, and many northerners refused. The southern delegates nominated former president Millard Fillmore, who had cast his lot with the Know-Nothings when the Whigs fell apart in New York. Fillmore ran on a platform that did not specifically endorse slavery; rather, it endorsed popular sovereignty and respect for existing laws. The northerners who left the convention chose to support Speaker of the House Nathaniel Banks; however, Banks intended to pull out of the race so that antislavery Know-Nothings would have to support the Republican nominee.[56]

Republican leaders chose not to use the name Republican when they called their convention. Instead, they held an antislavery convention in Philadelphia open to all those opposed to the Kansas-Nebraska Act and the Pierce administration. Party leaders looked to draft a platform and select a candidate that would help broaden their constituency in the North. The platform opposed the expansion of slavery. Republicans also supported Whig ideas about internal improvements and left their commitment to nativism ambiguous. The party selected John C. Frémont as their presidential nominee. His reputation as a notable explorer, known as the "Pathfinder," served to enhance his political standing. His marriage to Missouri politician Thomas Hart Benton's daughter helped him appeal to antislavery Democrats. Finally, his support for a free California and a free Kansas demonstrated his antislavery credentials. Throughout the campaign, the Republicans used the slogan "Free Soil, Free Speech, Free Men, Frémont!"[57]

Democratic leaders shied away from incumbent Franklin Pierce and from Stephen Douglas because in the public's mind both bore a great deal of responsibility for reigniting sectional hostilities. So, they turned to James Buchanan, then serving as the minister to Great Britain, because he seemed like a safe choice. Buchanan, who hailed from Pennsylvania, had made few political enemies in a long career of public service. The best thing Buchanan had going for him in securing the nomination and campaigning for president was he had been out of the country while it divided over Kansas. Southern delegates preferred Douglas, but they conceded to Buchanan's selection. The party platform also helped mollify their concerns about choosing a northerner. The Democrats pledged to uphold popular sovereignty and states' rights.[58]

Since Frémont did not appear on the ballot in most southern states, two races occurred in 1856. Buchanan and Fillmore contested for votes in the South, while Buchanan and Frémont contested for votes in the North. Pennsylvania, New Jersey, Indiana, and Illinois were the battleground states. The Democrats, especially in these key states, focused on the sectional nature of the Republican Party. Given the fact that many southerners threatened secession if Frémont won, Democrats could claim a vote for Buchanan was a vote for the Union. Moreover, the Democrats suggested

Figure 15.8 Republican Political Cartoon, 1856 | The Republican Party ran its first presidential candidate, John C. Frémont in 1856. This political cartoon supporting his candidacy pokes fun at James Buchanan's support for popular sovereignty.

Artist: John L. Magee
Source: Library of Congress

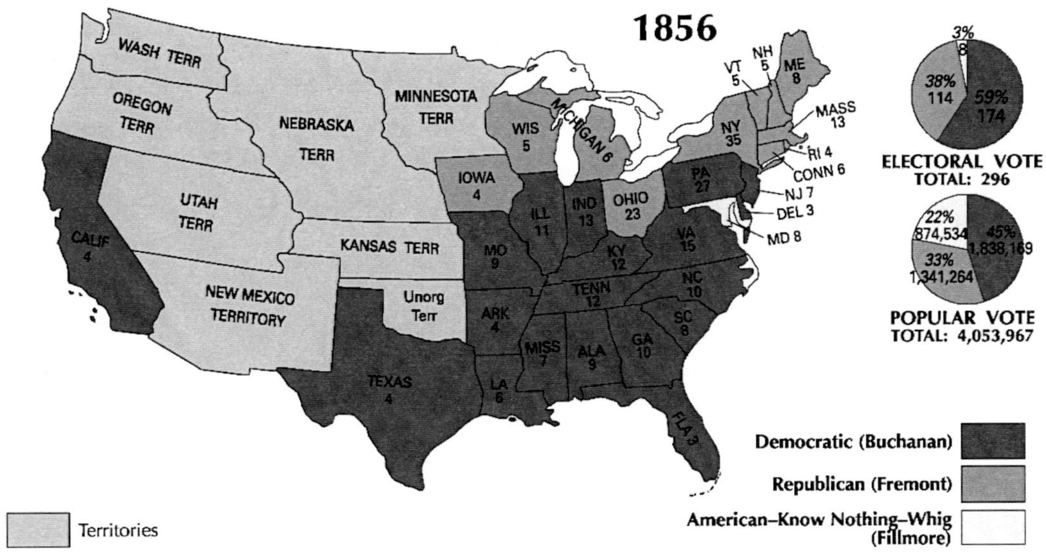

Figure 15.9 Presidential Election Map, 1856 | Democrat James Buchanan defeated Republican John C. Frémont and Know-Nothing Millard Fillmore because southerners threatened secession if Frémont won. However, Frémont's victories in the North showed the strength of the Republican Party.

Author: National Atlas of the United States
Source: Wikimedia Commons

the Republicans wanted to end white supremacy and enact racial equality. The Republican Party found it very difficult to counter the charges, even though they were not true.[59]

James Buchanan defeated John C. Frémont and Millard Fillmore by winning both the popular and Electoral College votes. He took the entire South, plus the battleground states. Southerners vowed to use their support of Buchanan to exact future concessions on the question of slavery. Astute politicians across the country, however, realized the potential for an entirely sectional candidate to triumph in 1860. If the Republicans could hold the North as well as take Pennsylvania and Illinois, then they could win the election without a single Electoral College vote from the South. The results cemented the strength of the Republican Party, but they spelled trouble for union in the future.[60]

15.3.4 Before You Move On...

Key Concepts

Many Americans believed Franklin Pierce's presidency would help lessen the sectional divide, but the opposite happened. From 1853 to 1856, a series of events stemming from the southern desire to expand slavery and the northern desire to curb slavery made the resentment worse. Southerners, with the backing of the Young America movement, promoted the expansion to the South—looking to Cuba and Mexico. Their attempts raised concerns in the North, concerns which Stephen Douglas further exacerbated when he proposed to organize the Nebraska territory. The resulting Kansas-Nebraska Act, repealing the Missouri Compromise line, pleased southerners who wanted federal protection for slavery and angered northerners who opposed its extension into new territories.

The measure contributed to the end of the second party system. The Whigs could no longer find common ground and disintegrated into several factions. The Know-Nothings rose to prominence by opposing the influence of immigrants on the country in light of the fact that the rate of immigration rose in the late 1840s and early 1850s, whereas the Republicans began to gather support by expressing concern about the expansion of slavery especially in terms of how it affected non-slaveholding whites. As the two parties vied for support, the outbreak of violence in Kansas over the implementation of popular sovereignty, as well as Preston Brooks's attack on Charles Sumner, set the stage for the presidential contest in 1856. Democrat James Buchanan defeated Republican John C. Frémont and Know-Nothing Millard Fillmore because the Democratic Party successfully managed to portray him as the only viable option to disunion and to racial equality. However, most people also realized his election would not bring sectional harmony.

Test Yourself

1. The Ostend Manifesto was

   a. an agreement by the United States, Britain, and France to free oppressed Cubans.

   b. a diplomatic dispatch suggesting that Cuba be taken from Spain to protect American interests.

   c. an attempt to gain Cuba as a colony for freed American slaves.

   d. a plot by slaveholders to gain more slave territory.

2. Stephen Douglas's proposed Kansas-Nebraska Act

   a. strengthened his presidential prospects.

   b. showed his enthusiastic support of slavery.

   c. strengthened the Missouri Compromise.

   d. might allow slavery in Kansas and Nebraska.

3. During the presidential campaign of 1865, the Republican Party

   a. nominated William H. Seward for president.

   b. opposed the further spread of slavery.

   c. supported states' rights.

   d. condemned nativism.

See page 572 for answers

15.4 THE SECTIONAL BALANCE COMES UNDONE

The last few years of the 1850s paved the way for the sectional breakdown that resulted in a civil war. Following the Mexican-American War, disunion seemed like an unlikely prospect even though North and South disagreed on the future of slavery. In the past, national leaders had managed to compromise on divisive issues like the tariff and the bank; most people expected them to do so when it came to slavery. Unfortunately, by the time James Buchanan took office in 1857, few people wanted to compromise. The new president also seemed unwilling or incapable of bringing the North and the South together. Southerners, who worried about Buchanan's northern sympathies, found him disposed to accept their demands for federal support of the extension of slavery. Then a financial panic, the *Dred Scott* decision, and John Brown's raid on Harper's Ferry made tensions between proslavery and antislavery advocates worse. Finally, Abraham Lincoln emerged as a forceful speaker for the Republican Party as Buchanan tilted the Democratic Party further to the South.

15.4.1 Northern and Southern Perspectives

Northerners and southerners in the 1850s increasingly felt the need to defend their position on slavery, whether they opposed it or they favored it. Slavery drove the two sides apart, but not because either side had many moral concerns about the peculiar institution. Both sides saw their freedom at stake, namely, their freedom to the political and economic liberties they believed the Constitution guaranteed. Both sides saw themselves as fighting for liberty and for what they perceived to be the legacy of the American Revolution. They simply had very different viewpoints about what the Revolution had meant.

Northerners believed a vast slave power conspiracy dominated national politics. Meanwhile, southerners saw an influential abolitionist element trying to eliminate slavery all over the country. Few people on either side fell into these extremist categories. But, northern and southern spokesmen felt compelled to criticize the other side and defend their position. As tensions mounted toward the end of the decade, people began to wonder if they could ever mend their differences. In 1858, William H. Seward outlined the notion of irrepressible conflict, in which the nation would have to choose to be all slave or all free. Northerners and southerners nonetheless did not necessarily think their differences would lead to a war.

The Northern Perspective

Northerners increasingly turned to ideas about free labor to explain the benefits of their society. A free labor system in which employers paid workers wages led to economic growth. New Yorker William Evarts suggested that labor was "the source of all our wealth, of all our progress, of all our dignity and value." The system also provided opportunity for social mobility. The goal for most northerners was not great wealth, but economic independence. If they worked hard enough, they could improve their lives and enter the ranks of the middle class. Pennsylvanian Thaddeus Stevens recorded how "the middling classes who own the soil, and work it with their hands are the main support of every free government."[61] In the nineteenth century, most northerners also believed progress came from developing the economy, increasing social mobility, and spreading democratic institutions.

To the proponents of free labor, slavery robbed labor, both slave and free, of its dignity. Slavery denied workers social mobility. Since workers had no incentive, they became less productive. Economically speaking, they believed slavery led to mass poverty. However, northerners worried more about the effect a slave-based economy had on non-slaveholders than on slaves. They frequently commented on the lack of opportunity for poor whites to improve their social and economic standing. From the northern perspective, people born poor in the South remained poor. Northerners believed all the best qualities about a free labor society, such as hard work, frugality, and a spirit of industry, were lacking in the South. Many northerners, especially the Republicans, sought to create a free labor system in the South. They looked for government action to promote free labor; however, southern dominance of national political institutions, referred to sometimes as slave power, prevented that option.[62]

The Southern Perspective

Southerners found the criticism of their lifestyle unwarranted. They believed courtesy, hospitality, and chivalry were the hallmarks of their way of life. When antislavery advocates became more vocal in the 1830s, southerners began to highlight the positive nature of slavery. Thomas R. Dew, a professor at William and Mary, relied on biblical and historical evidence to suggest how slavery benefited the master and the slave. To justify why only blacks became slaves in the South, Dew suggested the institution helped Africans become more civilized. Moreover, enslaving blacks brought greater liberty and equality to whites. By the 1850s, southern theorists like George Fitzhugh focused even more on racial inferiority to justify slavery. Fitzhugh argued in favor of the paternalistic nature of slavery, noting that "He the Negro is but a grown up child, and must be governed as a child, not as a lunatic or criminal. The master occupies toward him the place of parent or guardian."[63]

To the proponents of slavery, free labor did not benefit anyone. Alluding to the paternalistic nature of slavery, Virginian Edmond Ruffin suggested northern employers held their workers "under a much more stringent and cruel bondage, and in conditions of far greater...suffering than our negro slaves." Slaves, moreover, did not have to worry about securing food, clothing, or shelter, since their masters provided those commodities. James Henry Hammond, basing his justification for slavery on the so-called mudsill theory, further suggested the benefits of slavery for southern whites. All societies had, he noted, a "mudsill class" or working class. In the South, slaves performed the menial and thankless tasks, leaving whites to pursue the fruits of civilization. In the North, the wage labor system meant whites performed the tasks of slaves and therefore had no real opportunity for advancement.[64]

The Panic of 1857

The debate between the North and the South intensified after a financial panic hit the nation in 1857. American exports of grain increased between 1854 and 1856 because of the Crimean War in Europe. When the war ended, the market slumped. The war also pushed investors in Europe to sell off their American stocks and bonds. Both developments hurt the American economy. For much of the decade, economic growth caused a rise in western land prices, the overextension of the railroads, and risky loans by banks. When grain exports declined and European investment stopped, American banks began to fail. By the end of the year, hundreds of thousands of northern workers lost their jobs. Relief efforts helped the jobless to survive the winter and prevent a much-feared class war. By spring, the economy was on its way to recovery.[65]

Southerners for the most part escaped the economic downturn. So, they boasted about the superiority of the plantation economy. Many even suggested cotton saved the North from financial ruin. Frustrated northerners blamed the South, with its constant demand for low tariffs, for the crisis. After the panic, a coalition of northern Republicans and Democrats pushed for an increase in the tariff, as well as land grant measures for farmers, the railroads, and colleges, to help prevent future economic problems. Southern obstruction of these efforts only made the sectional tensions worse.[66] Southerners saw the measures as a way to promote a federally-backed antislavery agenda; northerners, on the other hand, saw the slave power conspiracy at work.

15.4.2 The Crisis Continues

As northerners and southerners staked their claim to the Revolution's legacy, the dispute about the future of slavery in the United States continued. The Supreme Court, under the leadership of Roger B. Taney, decided to step into the debate on the rights of slaves and slaveholders. Moreover, questions about Kansas's proposed statehood continued to affect territorial authorities and national leaders. The sectional tensions also provided politicians with new challenges and opportunities, as evidenced by Abraham Lincoln's reentry into politics as a Republican after the Kansas-Nebraska Act. In 1858, Lincoln challenged Stephen Douglas to a series of debates before the fall elections. He hoped to win a Republican majority in the state legislature in order to secure a position in the U.S. Senate.

The Dred Scott Decision

In 1846, Dred Scott sued for his freedom after his master Dr. John Emerson died. White friends encouraged Scott to file the suit because his master had taken him to live for a significant period in the free state of Illinois and the free territory of Wisconsin in the 1830s before returning to Missouri. Scott, his wife Harriet, and their daughter claimed residing in free territory made them free. Scott initially won freedom for his family in the Missouri courts. But on appeal, the Missouri Supreme Court reversed the decision. The court had previously awarded slaves their freedom in similar cases. Scott's lawyers therefore took his suit to the federal courts. In 1854, the Missouri district court agreed to hear the case and subsequently upheld the decision to return the family to slavery.[67]

The U.S. Supreme Court agreed to hear the case in 1856. Chief Justice Roger B. Taney hoped their decision in the case would be the final word on the constitutionality of the institution of slavery. The justices decided to delay their ruling until after the presidential election. According to James McPherson, the Court had three questions to answer in their decision. One, did Scott have the right to sue in federal court; in other words, was he a U.S. citizen? Two, did residence in a free territory for almost four years make him free? Three, did Congress have the authority to bar slavery in any territory; in other words, was the Missouri Compromise constitutional? Before James Buchanan's inauguration, a majority of the Court seemed inclined to rule that Missouri law determined Scott's status as a slave and to say nothing more.[68]

However, Roger B. Taney encouraged his fellow southerners to issue a decision in order to put the matter of slavery in the territories to rest. Taney, a native of Maryland, had long wanted to write this decision; he had waited for years for the right opportunity to protect the southern way of life. The chief justice also knew the southern majority on the Court would need one northerner to go along as well. So, one of the southern justices asked the president-elect to put pressure on one of the northern justices. Whatever Buchanan felt about the impropriety of such a move, he shared with Taney a desire to settle the issue. He knew how poisonous the debate about slavery could be to his administration. Buchanan, in his inaugural address, suggested that the issue of the extension of slavery belonged with the Supreme Court, not Congress.[69]

Two days after the inauguration, the Court issued its ruling in *Dred Scott v. Sandford*. Speaking for the majority, Taney declared Scott had no standing to sue in federal court because blacks could not be citizens of the United States. Technically, the decision should have ended there since, as once he declared Scott a non-citizen, nothing else mattered. However, Taney decided to address the remaining issues before the court in order to settle portions of the ongoing slavery debate. The chief justice said that residence in free territory did not make a slave free once he or she returned to slave territory. He further indicated that the Constitution upheld slavery because it protected private property and slaves were a form of property. Finally, he said Congress had no authority to bar slavery in the territories, making the Missouri Compromise unconstitutional.[70]

Figure 15.10 Dred Scott | In 1858, the Supreme Court issued a decision in the Dred Scott v. Sandford case. Scott claimed his residence in a free territory made him free. The court declared blacks could not be citizens of the United States, residence in a free territory did not make a slave free, and Congress had no authority to bar slavery in the territories

Artist: Unknown
Source: Library of Congress

According to Vernon Burton, "The *Dred Scott* ruling was pure joy for southerners." Not only did the decision grant them protection for their human property, but also it confirmed their right to take slaves anywhere in the country. In other words, slavery was a national institution; the distinction between slave and free states no longer existed. After the decision, northerners could only destroy slavery through a constitutional amendment, and no southerner expected that to happen.[71] The South also delighted in the idea that the decision would crush the hated Republican Party. Republicans, however, refused to accept Taney's decision.

Republican papers lambasted the ruling. The *Cleveland Leader* called it "villainously false," and the *New York Tribune* said it had "as much moral weight...the majority of those congregated in any Washington bar-room." Moreover, Republicans argued the decision was not binding because it addressed matters not before the court, a practice known as *obiter dictum*. Northern legislatures with Republican majorities responded by passing laws reaffirming the citizenship of their black residents. The decision additionally gave many northern Democrats pause. It occurred to them that Taney also undermined popular sovereignty because the chief justice indicated voters could not exclude slavery from a territory. The decision hurt the Democrats more than the Republicans, especially in light of what happened in Kansas.[72]

Whatever Roger B. Taney hoped to accomplish with his ruling, he certainly did not remove the question of slavery from politics. The decision in *Dred Scott v. Sandford* only made the sectional divide greater. From the northern perspective, everything they feared about southern slave power seemed to be coming true. From the southern perspective, the decision secured them from the onslaught of northern abolitionists and preserved the institution of slavery.

Kansas Again...

Before the presidential election of 1856, Franklin Pierce sent John W. Geary to Kansas as the new governor, since Wilson Shannon proved unable to end the conflict. Geary managed to quell the violence before the election, but the peace did not last. Looking at the election returns of 1856, southerners believed they needed more slave territory in order to prevent a Republican victory in 1860. They set their sights on Kansas, where the proslavery legislature still controlled the territory, even though the Free Soilers had a commanding majority in population. To maintain the peace, Geary asked the proslavery legislature to revise the antislavery acts. In response, the legislature made plans to revise the state constitution but indicated they would not seek a statewide referendum on the changes. Geary, shocked by their audacity, resigned his position.[73]

After the *Dred Scott* decision, James Buchanan persuaded Mississippian Robert J. Walker to become governor of Kansas. The president asked him to oversee an orderly drafting of a constitution, which the people had an opportunity to vote on. Surprisingly, Walker had no real desire to see Kansas become a slave state. He encouraged the slaveholders to submit the Lecompton Constitution to the people for a vote, but they refused and sent the constitution to Congress, along with their petition for statehood. Walker then journeyed to Washington to consult with Buchanan and explain the situation, especially since the president told him to secure a referendum. Buchanan, facing pressure from his proslavery advisers, refused to accept that the majority of people in Kansas wanted to become a free state. Instead of rejecting the Lecompton Constitution, Buchanan asked Congress to admit Kansas as a slave state based on the provisions of the *Dred Scott* decision. At the time, the president firmly believed opposing the South would lead to secession.[74]

Southerners who wanted a victory in Kansas believed they could win approval of the Lecompton Constitution, since the Democrats controlled Congress and they controlled the Democratic Party. At the same time, enough recognized the risk of their plan and encouraged the Kansas legislature to put the constitution to vote. What seemed like a major concession proved nothing more than a face-saving device. Voters could choose from a constitution with slavery or a constitution with no slavery that protected slave property in Kansas forever. Free Soil residents called it the "great swindle," and criticism of the South's malfeasance mounted in the North. Walker resigned when he realized that Buchanan no longer supported a fair referendum in Kansas.[75]

Many northern Democrats opposed admitting Kansas as a slave state because it was not what the people wanted. Stephen Douglas met with Buchanan in December and pled with him not to support the Lecompton Constitution; otherwise, he would have to oppose the president in Congress. Buchanan apparently told Douglas to "remember that no Democrat ever yet differed from an administration of his own choice without being crushed." In spite of the threat, Douglas knew he had to stand up to Buchanan over Kansas. If he did not, his future political career would be quite short since he staked his political reputation on the validity of popular sovereignty. Douglas worked with Republicans to defeat the Lecompton Constitution. Then the Kansans held two separate elections; one where only the proslavery forces voted, and one where only the antislavery forces voted. These elections made it apparent that the Free Soilers held a two-to-one majority and northerners could not accept Kansas as a slave state. In the wake of the vote, Kansas once again descended into violence.[76]

The Lincoln-Douglas Debates

Into the 1850s, Illinois was one of the most southern-like northern states because so many southerners migrated there early in the century. Southern folkways pervaded the lower part of the state. Moreover, it had been a stronghold for the Democratic Party. Most residents, especially in the more rural regions of the state, loathed the idea of an active government. From the 1830s to the 1850s, the Democrats usually held a majority in the state legislature, and the state consistently voted Democrat for president.[77] However, the debates on slavery by the mid-decade allowed the newly-formed Republican Party to gain some ground among Illinois voters. In 1858, the Republicans very much wanted to secure a seat in the U.S. Senate. If they could win a majority in the state legislature, then they could replace Stephen Douglas with someone opposed to slavery. Abraham Lincoln hoped the Republicans would choose him. Douglas, of course, looked for ways to prevent that outcome.

Kentucky-born Abraham Lincoln moved to Indiana as a boy and to central Illinois as a young man. Lincoln decided not to become a farmer like his father. He wanted to find work more in tune with the modern capitalist world, so he worked as a storekeeper, surveyor, and lawyer. By the 1840s, Lincoln was prosperous and respectable. Given his views about the market economy, Lincoln found his political beliefs more in line with the Whigs than the Democrats. Eric Foner asserts that Lincoln "saw government as an active force in promoting opportunity and advancement." Although the Democrats dominated Illinois, Lincoln served four terms in the state legislature and one term in the U.S. House of Representatives. In the early 1850s, he returned to his law practice. However, the Kansas-Nebraska Act reinvigorated his desire to run for office.[78]

With the Whigs in decline, Lincoln eventually found a home in the Republican Party. In a series of speeches in late 1854, Lincoln called slavery a "monstrous injustice" and suggested that slavery undermined "the very fundamental principles of civil liberty."

While he admonished slavery, Lincoln was no abolitionist. Like many Republicans, he had moderate racial views. He opposed human bondage, but he also opposed political or social equality for blacks. To Lincoln, slavery threatened the human ability to succeed; it robbed individuals of the freedom to better their condition. Thus, like other Republicans, he believed in free labor principles. His public pronouncements against slavery helped him win a seat in the state legislature in 1854. However, he resigned that seat so he could seek election to the U.S. Senate. The state legislature did not award Lincoln the position. His failure pushed him more toward the Republican Party as he cast his eye on Stephen Douglas's seat in 1858.[79]

As Douglas looked toward the elections in Illinois in 1858, he knew that, in order to retain his spot in the Senate, he needed to stand up to the president's policy on the Lecompton Constitution. He purposely broke with Buchanan and precipitated a sectional divide in the Democratic Party because he needed to come across as anti-southern to Illinois voters. He also tried to reach out to Republican voters, but he failed to win the Republicans over. Rather, when party leaders met in June, they criticized popular sovereignty and *Dred Scott*. Moreover, they publicly supported Lincoln for the U.S. Senate seat, which parties did not normally do until after the state elections. In support of his campaign, Lincoln noted, "A house divided against itself cannot stand...this government cannot endure, permanently, half slave and half free. I do not expect the Union to be dissolved...but I do expect it will cease to be divided." In other words, Lincoln asked the voters of Illinois to decide whether to support freedom or to support slavery.[80]

Lincoln also challenged Douglas to a series of debates so he could expose the failings of his opponent's position on slavery. Douglas agreed to seven meetings so he could do likewise. Lincoln focused his attention on how, during his career, Douglas had undermined the intentions of the Founding Fathers by supporting an extension of slavery into the territories. He forced Douglas to reconcile popular sovereignty with *Dred Scott*. In the Freeport Doctrine, named for the town where the second debate occurred, Douglas suggested residents of a territory could bar slavery by enacting "local police regulations," a position he had made public several times before. Contemporaries argued the Freeport Doctrine helped drive a wedge in the Democratic Party. However, both James McPherson and Eric Foner point out that Douglas's position on the Lecompton Constitution already caused a rift.[81]

Meanwhile, Douglas exploited the race issue by labeling Lincoln a "Black Republican" and by telling voters about how free blacks such as Frederick Douglass were campaigning on his behalf. He further argued it was a "monstrous heresy" to suggest the Founding Fathers intended to make blacks citizens with equal rights. Finally, only those who believed in black equality would vote for Lincoln. Countering the race issue became of major importance for Lincoln. In the fourth debate he said, "I will say then that I am not...in favor of bringing about in anyway the social and political equality of the white and black races...I am as much as any other man in favor of having the superior position assigned to the white race." At the same time, he continued to argue against the dehumanization of blacks.[82]

Douglas managed to retain his seat in the Senate. However, Republicans did quite well in the elections. Had the state apportionment actually reflected the growth of the northern districts, Lincoln might have won. Nevertheless, Douglas reinforced his position as the leader of the northern Democrats. Still, Lincoln gained a great deal from the 1858 campaign. The debates highlighted the differences between Democrats and Republicans in the North. They also catapulted Lincoln into the national spotlight. Finally, they showed that Lincoln was more than up to the challenge of taking on Douglas in the presidential election of 1860.[83]

Figure 15.11 The Lincoln-Douglas Debates (1858) | In preparation for state elections in Illinois, Republican Abraham Lincoln challenged Democrat Stephen Douglas to a series of debates, so he could expose the failings of his opponent's positions. Douglas agreed to seven meetings so he could do the same to Lincoln. Lincoln became a nationally-known Republican figure even though he did not win a seat in the U.S. Senate.

Author: U.S. Government, Post Office Department
Source: Wikimedia Commons

15.4.3 The Road to Secession

By 1859, James Buchanan knew the issue of slavery had ruined his administration. Although he had hoped a Supreme Court ruling could quiet concerns about slavery, the *Dred Scott* decision poisoned the political atmosphere and ensured the next presidential election would focus on the future of slavery. The Lincoln-Douglas debates deepened the national division over slavery. But nothing proved more inflammatory than John Brown's attempt to foment a widespread southern slave rebellion with his attack on Harper's Ferry. As the election of 1860 approached, the Democratic Party stood as one of the few remaining national institutions. It too proved unable to maintain unity in the face of the slavery debate as it split into three factions. This division presented an opportunity for the Republican Party to win the presidency, which they did with the nomination of Lincoln. The election of a purely sectional party prompted South Carolina and six other states from the Lower South to secede from the Union.

John Brown's Raid on Harper's Ferry

In the years following his attack on proslavery forces at Pottawatomie Creek, John Brown's devotion to the antislavery cause grew. While traveling around the North to raise funds for the Free Soil effort in Kansas, Brown developed a scheme to launch a guerilla attack against slavery. With a small band of men, both black and white, he planned to attack the federal arsenal at Harper's Ferry, Virginia, where the Potomac and the Shenandoah Rivers meet. With the arsenal secure, Brown's forces would move southward to incite slaves to rebel against their masters with the weapons from the arsenal. In 1858, he approached several abolitionists for financial support for the raid. The "Secret Six" agreed to help him purchase weapons.[84]

Meanwhile, Brown looked for recruits, especially free blacks, to join his mission. In August, he approached Frederick Douglass about participating in the raid. Douglass, like many other black abolitionists, had concluded that slaves would only truly be free if they fought for their own emancipation. Brown reportedly told Douglass, "When I strike, the bees will begin to swarm, and I shall need you to help hive them." Whatever Douglass thought about the use of violence, he said no because the plan seemed suicidal. Although many of his recruits never showed up, Brown decided to proceed anyway. He had twenty-two men: five blacks and seventeen whites, including three of his sons; with these men, he would launch his war against slavery.[85]

On October 16, 1859, Brown and his raiders crossed from Maryland into Virginia. They quickly captured the arsenal. However, then things began to fall apart. Brown sent several men into the countryside to inform the slaves the time for a rebellion had come and to kidnap some prominent whites. The expected slave uprising never occurred. Local slaves might have wanted to rebel against their masters, but they would have been suspicious of any stranger supporting an insurrection. For all they knew, their owners could have been testing their loyalty. Moreover, word spread quickly to the white community of the impending attack. Local militia units converged on Harper's Ferry; several raiders and locals died in the exchange of fire. On October 18, 1859, the U.S. marines, under the command of Colonel Robert E. Lee and Lieutenant J.E.B. Stuart, arrived on the scene. They stormed the firehouse where Brown and his troops retreated during the confrontation with the locals. The marines killed two of the raiders and captured the rest, including Brown.[86]

While Brown accomplished nothing he set out to do, his attack inflamed passions in both the South and the North. Southerners called for Brown's blood. Even though the attack happened on federal property, he stood trial for treason, murder, and incitement of a slave insurrection before the end of the month in Virginia. The judge sentenced him to death after the jury returned a guilty verdict. Brown was executed in early December. Southerners also wanted an investigation into the rumors that prominent northerners funded the raid. They saw the attack as a clear sign of the lengths abolitionists would go to undermine the southern way of life. For some time after the incident, anyone in the South who did not support the maintenance of slavery faced a real risk of coming to a violent end. Southerners did take comfort in several things after the raid. One, no slave flocked to Brown's cause. Two, slaveholders and non-slaveholders united to fight off the invaders. Three, the federal government defended slavery.[87]

The majority of northerners criticized John Brown's raid, but his composure during his trial and when facing execution transformed public opinion. Brown, according to James McPherson, "understood his martyr role and cultivated it." He refused to plead insanity and suggested he would forfeit his life to help end slavery. On the day of his execution, church bells tolled and guns fired salutes in his honor. Preachers gave eulogies emphasizing his martyrdom. People did not condone his tactics. Rather, they agreed the time had come to do more about southern power, as opposed to doing something about slavery.[88]

Democrats in the North condemned the incident in order to rebuild their ties with the South and to undermine support for the Republicans. They realized the distinction between thought and action did not impress most southerners; Stephen Douglas and others implied that Brown's actions stemmed directly from Republican ideology. In response, leading Republicans, including William H. Seward and Abraham Lincoln, condemned Brown's actions. Lincoln suggested that "John Brown was no Republican." Without a doubt, Harper's Ferry furthered the hostility between the North and the South. It also set the stage for the presidential election.[89]

The Election of 1860

In April 1860, the Democratic Party met in Charleston, South Carolina, home of the "fire-eaters," or those who claimed they would die defending slavery. John Brown's raid had convinced many southerners the time had come to draw a line in the burgeoning conflict; they no longer saw northern Democrats as their ally. In fact, a few southern delegates hoped for a Republican victory because then southerners would have to choose submission or secession. Meanwhile, northern delegates felt constantly under attack as proslavery speakers extolled the virtue of slavery throughout the city.[90] Given these feelings, the gathering began with an auspicious start.

Before choosing a candidate, party members had to agree on a party platform. Speaking for many southerners, Alabama's William L. Yancey presented a proslavery platform to the convention delegates. It called for the nomination of a proslavery candidate. Furthermore, it demanded the adoption of a congressional slave code to protect slaveholders' constitutional right to take their property to the territories. Speaking for many northerners, Stephen Douglas introduced an alternative platform. His platform supported the principle of popular sovereignty as well as respect for the *Dred Scott* decision. The platform committee leaned toward a proslavery platform; however, the delegates still had to vote. When Yancey linked the platform to the defense of southern honor, many delegates heartily cheered his assertion. Douglas's supporters refused to yield.[91]

In the end, the party delegates adopted the northern platform. Northerners outnumbered southerners in the polling because the party based state delegations on population. At that point, many of the southerners walked out of the convention. The meeting adjourned because there were not enough members present to nominate a presidential candidate. Two months later, northern Democrats met in Baltimore, Maryland; southern Democrats met in Richmond, Virginia. The two groups conferred with each other but were unable to resolve their differences. The northern Democrats nominated Stephen Douglas. The southern Democrats nominated Kentucky's John C. Breckenridge, who was the vice president at the time. A third group of Democrats, along with some former Whigs, formed the Constitutional Union Party in an attempt to throw the election to the House of Representatives. They nominated Tennessee's John Bell.[92]

The split in the Democratic Party presented an excellent opportunity for the Republican Party to secure victory. They met in Chicago, Illinois. To win, however, the party needed to build on their showing in 1856. Somewhat expecting to lose California, Oregon, and possibly New Jersey, they directed the most attention to Pennsylvania, Illinois, and Indiana. Therefore, party leaders worked to develop a platform that dealt with more than just slavery. They also set out to choose a nominee who could reach the widest range of northern voters. Few Republicans expected to have any presence in the South. With respect to the platform, the party retained their stance against the expansion of slavery but condemned John Brown's raid. They also promoted free homesteads in the West, a protective tariff, and a transcontinental railroad. Moreover, they supported immigrant political rights in order to ward off any lingering concerns about their ties to the nativist movement.[93]

Most delegates knew the selection of a candidate was more important than the platform. The Republicans had a tough choice to make because they needed to find someone who could appeal to conservative and radical voters. Leading contenders for the nomination included Illinois's Abraham Lincoln, Missouri's Edward Bates, New York's William H. Seward, Ohio's Salmon P. Chase, and Pennsylvania's Simon Cameron. Seward appeared strong going into voting. Nevertheless, some leaders hoped to nominate a candidate who could help the party in its weaker states. They knew the Republicans would carry New York regardless of whether the party nominated the state's favorite son. Moreover, many voters linked Seward with the radical abolitionist sentiments because of his "Higher Law" speech. On the third ballot, Lincoln defeated Seward. Three things worked in Lincoln's favor: party members saw him as a moderate, his humble origins gave him a good political personality, and he came from the crucial state of Illinois.[94]

The election disintegrated into two separate contests: Lincoln versus Douglas in the North and Breckinridge versus Bell in the South. Lincoln focused all of his efforts on the North; he did not even appear on the ballot in most southern states. Breckinridge, likewise,

Figure 15.12 Two Races in 1860 | Given the division over slavery, the presidential election disintegrated into two separate contests: Abraham Lincoln (top left) versus Stephen Douglas (top right) in the North and John Breckenridge (bottom left) versus John Bell (bottom right) in the South.

Authors: Alexander Gardner (Lincoln), Mathew Brady (Douglas, Bell, & Breckenridge)
Source: Library of Congress

focused all of his attention on the South. Bell attempted to reach out to other unionists. Douglas broke with tradition and campaigned on his own behalf. He traveled all over the eastern part of the country before the election. In speech after speech, Douglas claimed only he could prevent disunion. Douglas's effort, however, could not overcome the split in the Democratic Party, which guaranteed a Republican victory. Lincoln took all the free states except New Jersey, which he split with Douglas. Lincoln won just under 40 percent, which was only a plurality of the popular vote; combined, the opposition nevertheless could not stop him from winning the Electoral College.[95]

The Secession Crisis

Before the 1860 election, southern leaders proclaimed disunion would follow if Lincoln won. William Yancey even toured the North in October. At his speaking engagements, he described how an end to slavery would destroy the southern way of life, even if the Republicans did not intend to abolish slavery where it already existed. Kentucky's John J. Crittenden, a longtime unionist, echoed this sentiment. He noted many southerners concluded they had no choice but to secede if the Republicans triumphed. Many northerners, who had heard the threats before, discounted the possibility. Heeding them in the past only made the South more demanding. Buchanan won in 1856 because northern Democrats feared secession; his presidency led to the *Dred Scott* decision and the Lecompton Constitution. Some Republicans asked Lincoln to issue a statement to calm southern fears, but he chose not to. He reasoned little he might say would placate them.[96]

South Carolina voted to secede from the Union in December. For years, secessionists in the state had waited for the right moment to leave the Union. Lincoln's victory allowed the separatists to triumph at the state's secession convention. Mississippi, Florida, Alabama, Georgia, Louisiana, and Texas soon followed suit. In each of these states, the debate over

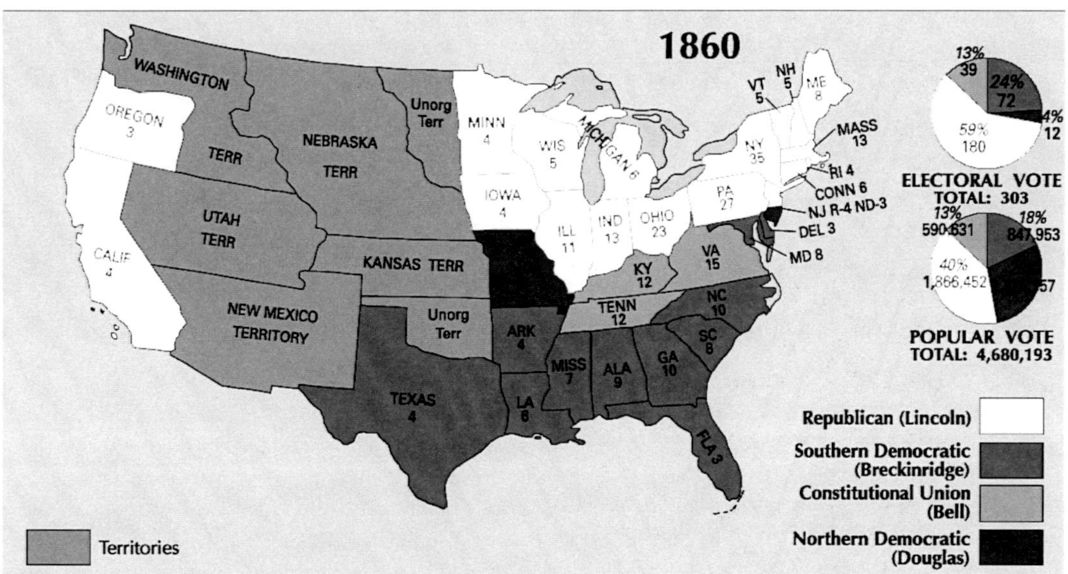

Figure 15.13 Presidential Election Map, 1860 | Since the Democrats split, Abraham Lincoln, the Republican candidate, won the presidential election of 1860 with just under 40 percent of the popular vote. However, he took a majority of the Electoral College votes.

Author: National Atlas of the United States
Source: Wikimedia Commons

secession hinged on when and how, as opposed to whether they should. The southerners who left the Union believed they had the legal right to do so. Secessionists, as Jefferson Davis put it, sought to defend the liberty their fathers and grandfathers fought for during the Revolution. They championed the idea of states' rights, noting the federal government should never infringe on their right to own property or to take that property anywhere in the country. To encourage non-slaveholders to support secession, they also used the ideas of white supremacy. Slavery made all whites, even poor whites, superior to blacks.[97]

In February 1861, the seven seceded states met in Montgomery, Alabama to form the Confederate States of America. Four additional southern states, Virginia, North Carolina, Tennessee, and Arkansas, gave a warning to the federal government that if the government used force against the seceded states, then they too would leave the Union. Meanwhile, James Buchanan denied the southern states had the right to secede. He noted that "the Union shall be perpetual" and further suggested that preservation of the alliance trumped states' rights. Nevertheless, he declared that the federal government had no authority to coerce a sovereign state. The president apparently hoped to encourage the two sides to compromise before he left office, since most northerners remained unsure as to the appropriate response to the southerners' move.[98]

Before Lincoln's inauguration, various individuals and groups worked on some form of compromise to end the crisis. Senator John J. Crittenden led one of the most important efforts. His plan called for a constitutional amendment, which would recognize slavery as existing in all territories south of the Missouri Compromise line, the 36°30' line. The amendment would also guarantee that the federal government would not attempt to tamper with the institution of slavery in the future. However, the compromise required the support of the president-elect. Lincoln refused to support the plan because it contradicted one of the main principles of the Republican Party, which was to stop the further spread of slavery into the territories. The Crittenden Compromise went nowhere, nor did any of the other proposals to avoid disunion. Every suggestion required the North, or the Republicans, to make all the concessions. In early 1861, the Republicans would not submit.[99] Thus, the nation waited for Lincoln's inauguration on March 4, 1861 to see whether secession would lead to war.

15.4.4 Before You Move On...

Key Concepts

After James Buchanan took office, the United States continued down the road to disunion. While the country dealt with a financial crisis and the ongoing question of Kansas, the Supreme Court weighed in on the matter of slavery in the *Dred Scott v. Sandford* (1857) decision. Much to the delight of southerners, the Court asserted the right of slave owners to transport their slaves anywhere within the territories, whether that territory was free or permitted slavery. Likewise, the decision created a storm of protest in the northern states. The famous debates between Republican Abraham Lincoln and Democrat Stephen Douglas in 1858 as they vied for a position in the

U.S. Senate deepened the national division over slavery. John Brown and his cohorts riveted national attention upon Harper's Ferry with their failed attempt to foment a widespread southern slave rebellion in 1859.

As the critical presidential election of 1860 approached, the Democratic Party stood as one of the few remaining national institutions. It too proved unable to maintain unity in the face of the slavery debate as it split into three factions after its convention in Charleston, South Carolina. This three-way division among Stephen Douglas, John Breckinridge, and John Bell presented the Republican Party an opportunity to win the presidency, which they did with the nomination of Abraham Lincoln. After Lincoln's election, South Carolina, followed by six other southern states, seceded from the Union. In February 1861, these states met in Montgomery, Alabama, and formed the Confederate States of America, setting the stage for a civil war.

Test Yourself

1. In the *Dred Scott v. Sandford* decision, the Supreme Court
    a. ruled that slaves who were taken to free states were free.
    b. ruled that slaves who escaped must be returned to their owners.
    c. stated that blacks did not have federal citizenship and could not bring suit in federal courts.
    d. declared the Missouri Compromise constitutional.

2. In the Kansas territory, the proposed Lecompton Constitution showed the dominance of the Free Soilers.
    a. True
    b. False

3. What significant event occurred at the 1860 Democratic Convention in Charleston?
    a. Southern delegates walked out.
    b. Northern delegates walked out.
    c. Delegates nominated Abraham Lincoln for the presidency.
    d. Delegates nominated Jefferson Davis for the presidency.

See page 572 for answers

15.5 Conclusion

By 1850, Americans recognized the divisions that questions about slavery in the territories had caused, but few expected those divisions would lead to a crisis of union by 1860. However, that was precisely what happened. Throughout the 1850s, sectional tensions mounted. Increasingly, northerners and southerners concluded they had little in common. Northerners saw the extension of slavery into the territories as a threat to their way of life based on the principles of free labor. Southerners, however, thought they needed to expand slavery to preserve their way of life built on the institution of slavery. When California applied to the Union as a free state, both sides felt compelled to press their interests at the national level. The Compromise of 1850 resolved the question of California's status, though it hardly lessened the tensions.

Questions about slavery in Kansas only reinvigorated the debate. After 1854, southerners sought federal protection of slavery. The *Dred Scott* decision seemingly gave them that protection. As northerners embraced the antislavery positions of the new Republican Party, they refused to accept the legitimacy of the Supreme Court's ruling. John Brown's raid on Harper's Ferry in 1859 convinced southerners that northerners would go to any lengths to abolish slavery. Therefore, Abraham Lincoln's victory in the presidential election of 1860 prompted the secession of the lower South and the creation of the Confederate States of America.

15.6 CRITICAL THINKING EXERCISES

- Historian James McPherson maintains the Kansas-Nebraska Act "may have been the most important single event pushing the nation toward civil war." Do you agree or disagree with this statement? Why?
- Ever since the Civil War, historians have debated the causes of the conflict. Slavery clearly seems to have played a role in the coming of the war; however, other factors also contributed to the tensions. How much of a role did economic differences between the two regions play in the conflict? What influence did religion, culture, and ethnicity have?
- Historians have also debated whether the Civil War was avoidable or not. At what point (if any) did civil war become inevitable? In other words, did the nation need the war to determine whether it would be slave or free? What might it have taken to avoid the Civil War?

15.7 KEY TERMS

- Bleeding Kansas
- Bleeding Sumner
- John Bell
- John Breckinridge
- John Brown
- James Buchanan
- John C. Calhoun
- Lewis Cass
- Democratic Convention(s) of 1860
- Henry Clay
- Compromise of 1850
- Crittenden Compromise
- Jefferson Davis
- *Dred Scott v. Sandford*
- Stephen A. Douglas
- Millard Fillmore
- "fire eaters"
- Free Soil Party
- John C. Fremont
- Fugitive Slave Act of 1850
- Gadsden Purchase
- Harper's Ferry
- Kansas-Nebraska Act
- Know-Nothing Party (American Party)
- Lecompton Constitution
- Abraham Lincoln
- Ostend Manifesto
- Panic of 1857
- Franklin Pierce
- Popular sovereignty
- Republican Party
- Republican Convention of 1860
- Winfield Scott
- Harriet Beecher Stowe
- Zachary Taylor
- Daniel Webster
- Wilmot Proviso

15.8 CHRONOLOGY

The following chronology is a list of important dates and events associated with this chapter.

Date	Event
1846	David Wilmot attempted to ban slavery in territory acquired from Mexico in the Wilmot Proviso
1848	Treaty of Guadalupe-Hidalgo ended the Mexican-American War; Whig Zachary Taylor elected president
1849	California applied for admission to the Union as a free state

Date	Event
1850	Henry Clay introduced the Compromise of 1850 to resolve questions about slavery in the Mexican Cession; Zachary Taylor died and Millard Fillmore succeeded him as president; Compromise of 1850 approved by Congress
1851	Fugitive Slave Act (part of the Compromise of 1850) heightened concern about slavery in the North
1852	*Uncle Tom's Cabin* heightened concern about abolition in the South; Democrat Franklin Pierce elected president
1853	Pierre Soulé, James Buchanan, and John Mason issued the Ostend Manifesto suggesting the United States planned to acquire Cuba by force if necessary; James Gadsden negotiated the purchase of additional land from Mexico in the Gadsden Purchase
1854	Stephen A. Douglas introduced a bill to organize the Kansas and Nebraska territories, which opened the territories to slavery contrary to the Missouri Compromise; Congress approved the Kansas-Nebraska Act; Second party system collapsed as the Know-Nothings and the Republicans formed to replace the Whigs
1856	Antislavery and proslavery advocates fought to win Kansas in the Sack of Lawrence and the Pottawatomie Massacre (Bleeding Kansas); Preston Brooks caned Charles Sumner in the Senate chamber (Bleeding Sumner); Democrat James Buchanan elected president
1857	Supreme Court issued its decision in the Dred Scott v. Sandford, which stated blacks could not be citizens of the United States; North suffered the effects of the Panic of 1857; Kansas applied for statehood as a slave state with the Lecompton Constitution prompting a split in the Democratic Party
1858	Lincoln-Douglas debates highlighted the problem of slavery and paved the way for the next presidential election
1859	John Brown launched an attack on the federal arsenal at Harper's Ferry, Virginia

Date	Event
1860	Democratic Party nominated two candidates for president, Stephen A. Douglas and John C. Breckenridge; Constitutional Union Party nominated John Bell for president; Republican Party nominated Abraham Lincoln for president; Abraham Lincoln elected president; South Carolina seceded from the Union
1861	Mississippi, Florida, Alabama, Georgia, Louisiana, and Texas seceded from the Union; Southern states formed the Confederate States of America; Crittenden Compromise proposed in an effort to prevent further disunion

15.9 BIBLIOGRAPHY

Ashworth, John. *Slavery, Capitalism and Politics in the Antebellum Republic: The Coming of the Civil War, 1850-1861*, Volume 2. New York: Cambridge University Press, 2008.

Burton, Orville Vernon. *The Age of Lincoln*. New York: Hill and Wang, 2007.

Foner, Eric. *Free Soil, Free Labor, Free Men: The Ideology of the Republican Party Before the Civil War*. New York: Oxford University Press, 1995.

Foner, Eric. *The Fiery Trial: Abraham Lincoln and American Slavery*. New York: W.W. Norton, 2010.

Freehling, William W. *The Road to Disunion: Secessionists at Bay, 1776-1854*, Volume I. New York: Oxford University Press, 1990.

Freehling, William W. *The Road to Disunion: Secessionists Triumph, 1854-1861*, Volume II. New York: Oxford University Press, 2007.

Gienapp, William E. *The Origins of the Republican Party, 1852-1856*. New York: Oxford University Press, 1988.

Holt, Michael. *The Rise and Fall of the American Whig Party: Jacksonian Politics and the Onset of the Civil War*. New York: Oxford University Press, 1999.

McCardell, John. *The Idea of a Southern Nation: Southern Nationalists and Southern Nationalism, 1830-*1860. New York: W.W. Norton, 1979.

McPherson, James M. *Battle Cry of Freedom: The Civil War Era*. New York: Oxford University Press, 1988.

Mintz, Steven. "The Impending Crisis." *Digital History*, accessed February 28, 2012. http://www.digitalhistory.uh.edu/database/subtitles.cfm?TitleID=58.

Morrison, Michael A. *Slavery and the American West: The Eclipse of Manifest Destiny and the Coming of the Civil War*. Chapel Hill: The University of North Carolina Press, 1997.

Oates, Stephen B. *The Approaching Fury: Voices of the Storm, 1820-1861*. New York: HarperCollins, 1997.

15.10 END NOTES

1 Orville Vernon Burton, *The Age of Lincoln* (New York: Hill and Wang, 2007), 29-30; Eric Foner, *The Fiery Trial: Abraham Lincoln and American Slavery* (New York: W.W. Norton, 2010), 54; Ralph Waldo Emerson as quoted in James M. McPherson, *Battle Cry of Freedom: The Civil War Era* (New York: Oxford University Press, 1988), 53.

2 McPherson, *Battle Cry of Freedom*, 52-54.

3 William W. Freehling, *The Road to Disunion: Secessionists at Bay, 1776-1854*, Volume I (New York: Oxford University Press, 1990), 458-459; Michael A. Morrison, *Slavery and the American West: The Eclipse of Manifest Destiny and the Coming of the Civil War* (Chapel Hill: The University of North Carolina Press, 1997), 56-57.

4 Freehling, *The Road to Disunion*, Volume I, 461-462; Morrison, *Slavery and the American West*, 58-59.

5 McPherson, *Battle Cry of Freedom*, 54-56.

6 McPherson, *Battle Cry of Freedom*, 58.

7 McPherson, *Battle Cry of Freedom*, 58-59.

8 William H. Seward as quoted in McPherson, *Battle Cry of Freedom*, 60.

9 McPherson, *Battle Cry of Freedom*, 60-61.

10 McPherson, *Battle Cry of Freedom*, 62-63.

11 Morrison, *Slavery and the American West*, 96-97, 101-104.

12 McPherson, *Battle Cry of Freedom*, 66-67.

13 Steven Mintz, "The Crisis of 1850," *Digital History*, accessed February 22, 2012, http://www.digitalhistory.uh.edu/database/article_display.cfm?HHID=325.

14 Zachary Taylor as quoted in *Slavery and the American West*, 105.

15 Morrison, *Slavery and the American West*, 106-108; Freehling, *The Road to Disunion*, Volume I, 487, 493-493.

16 McPherson, *Battle Cry of Freedom*, 70-71.

17 John C. Calhoun, "The Compromise," *Congressional Globe* [1850], Library of Congress, accessed February 23, 2012, http://www.loc.gov/rr/program/bib/ourdocs/Compromise1850.html.

18 William S. Seward, "Freedom in the Territories," March 11, 1851, *United States Senate*, accessed February 23, 2012, http://www.senate.gov/artandhistory/history/resources/pdf/SewardNewTerritories.pdf; McPherson, *Battle Cry of Freedom*, 73.

19 Daniel Webster, "The Constitution and the Union," March 7, 1851, *United States Senate*, accessed February 23, 2012, http://www.senate.gov/artandhistory/history/resources/pdf/Webster7th.pdf.

20 McPherson, *Battle Cry of Freedom*, 73-74.

21 McPherson, *Battle Cry of Freedom*, 75.

22 McPherson, *Battle Cry of Freedom*, 76; Burton, *The Age of Lincoln*, 62.

23 McPherson, *Battle Cry of Freedom*, 80.

24 McPherson, *Battle Cry of Freedom*, 80-83.

25 McPherson, *Battle Cry of Freedom*, 84-85; Freehling, *The Road to Disunion*, Volume I, 502, 536; Burton, *The Age of Lincoln*, 60; John McCardell, *The Idea of a Southern Nation: Southern Nationalists and Southern Nationalism, 1830-1860* (New York: W.W. Norton, 1979), 166-169.

26 McPherson, *Battle Cry of Freedom*, 88-89; Burton, *The Age of Lincoln*, 66-68.

27 McPherson, *Battle Cry of Freedom*, 90-91; Burton, *The Age of Lincoln*, 68.

28 R.D. Monroe, "Campaign of 1852," *Getting the Message Out! National Political Campaign Materials, 1840-1860*, Northern Illinois University Libraries, accessed February 24, 2012, http://dig.lib.niu.edu/message/campaignhistory-1852.html.

29 Morrison, *Slavery and the American West*, 139-141; Monroe, "Campaign of 1852."

30 McPherson, *Battle Cry of Freedom*, 102-103.

31 McCardell, *The Idea of a Southern Nation*, 241-243, 252-253.

32 McCardell, *The Idea of a Southern Nation*, 256-258.

33 James Buchanan, J.Y. Mason, and Pierre Soulé, "The Ostend Manifesto," October 18, 1854, *South by Southwest: The Caribbean Slave Empire*, University of Virginia, accessed February 24, 2012, http://xroads.virginia.edu/~hyper/hns/ostend/ostend.html; McCardell, *The Idea of a Southern Nation*, 259-260, 269.

34 McPherson, *Battle Cry of Freedom*, 108.

35 Burton, *The Age of Lincoln*, 68-69.

36 McPherson, *Battle Cry of Freedom*, 122-123; Freehling, *The Road to Disunion*, Volume I, 537, 552-553.

37 McPherson, *Battle Cry of Freedom*, 123-124.

38 McPherson, *Battle Cry of Freedom*, 121, 125.

39 Michael Holt, *The Rise and Fall of the American Whig Party: Jacksonian Politics and the Onset of the Civil War* (New York: Oxford University Press, 1999), 766-767, 774-777.

40 Holt, *The Rise and Fall of the American Whig Party*, 804-805.

41 McPherson, *Battle Cry of Freedom*, 130-135.

42 McPherson, *Battle Cry of Freedom*, 136.

43 Holt, *The Rise and Fall of the American Whig Party*, 883-893, McPherson, *Battle Cry of Freedom*, 140-141.

44 Burton, *The Age of Lincoln*, 73; McPherson, *Battle Cry of Freedom*, 126, 129-130.

45 Eric Foner, *Free Soil, Free Labor, Free Men: The Ideology of the Republican Party Before the Civil War*, Revised Edition (New York: Oxford University Press, 1995), 11, 16-17, 40, 59.

46 Foner, *Free Soil, Free Labor, Free Men*, 56-58, 267-268, 284-285.

47 Foner, *Free Soil, Free Labor, Free Men,* 116-117, 188, 206-209.

48 McPherson, *Battle Cry of Freedom*, 144-146.

49 McPherson, *Battle Cry of Freedom*, 146-147; William W. Freehling, *The Road to Disunion: Secessionists Triumph, 1854-1861*, Volume II, (New York: Oxford University Press, 2007), 75.

50 McPherson, *Battle Cry of Freedom*, 146-148.

51 McPherson, *Battle Cry of Freedom*, 148-149; 152-153; Steven Mintz, "Bleeding Kansas and Bleeding Sumner," *Digital History*, accessed February 25, 2012, http://www.digitalhistory.uh.edu/database/article_display.cfm?HHID=332.

52 David Atchison as quoted in Freehling, *The Road to Disunion*, Volume II, 75; Preston Brooks as quoted in McPherson, *Battle Cry of Freedom*, 149.

53 Charles Sumner, "On the Crime Against Kansas," *The World's Famous Orations, America: II. (1818–1865)*, Great Books Online, accessed February 25, 2012, http://www.bartleby.com/268/9/14.html; McPherson, *Battle Cry of Freedom*, 150; Burton, *The Age of Lincoln*, 50.

54 Burton, *The Age of Lincoln*, 50-51.

55 McPherson, *Battle Cry of Freedom*, 150-151; Freehling, *The Road to Secession*, Volume II, 82-84.

56 Holt, *The Rise and Fall of the American Whig Party*, 964; McPherson, *Battle Cry of Freedom*, 154.

57 McPherson, *Battle Cry of Freedom*, 154-156, 161.

58 McPherson, *Battle Cry of Freedom*, 156-157.

59 McPherson, *Battle Cry of Freedom*, 157-159.

60 Monroe, "The Campaign of 1856."

61 William Evarts as quoted in Foner, *Free Soil, Free Labor, Free Men*, 12; Thaddeus Stevens as quoted in Foner, *Free Soil, Free Labor, Free Men*, 17.

62 Foner, *Free Soil, Free Labor, Free Men*, 38, 45-52.

63 McCardell, *The Idea of a Southern Nation*, 54-55; George Fitzhugh, "The Universal Law of Slavery," *Africans in America*, American Experience [PBS], accessed February 28, 2012, http://www.pbs.org/wgbh/aia/part4/4h3141t.html.

64 Edmond Ruffin as quoted in Burton, *The Age of Lincoln*, 82; James Hammond as quoted in Burton, *The Age of Lincoln*, 83.

65 McPherson, *Battle Cry of Freedom*, 189-191.

66 McPherson, *Battle Cry of Freedom*, 192-193.

67 Foner, *The Fiery Trial*, 98; McPherson, *Battle Cry of Freedom*, 170-171.

68 McPherson, *Battle Cry of Freedom*, 171.

69 McPherson, *Battle Cry of Freedom*, 172-173; Freehling, *The Road to Disunion*, Volume II, 115-117.

70 Foner, *The Fiery Trial*, 98; Burton, *The Age of Lincoln*, 85-86.

71 Burton, *The Age of Lincoln*, 87.

72 Foner, *The Fiery Trial*, 94; McPherson, *Battle Cry of Freedom*, 176-178.

73 McPherson, *Battle Cry of Freedom*, 161-163.

74 McPherson, *Battle Cry of Freedom*, 163-166.

75 McPherson, *Battle Cry of Freedom*, 165.

76 McPherson, *Battle Cry of Freedom*, 167-169.

77 Foner, *The Fiery Trial*, 33-35.

78 Foner, *The Fiery Trial*, 35-39.

79 Abraham Lincoln, "Peoria Speech," October 16, 1854, *National Parks Service,* U.S. Department of Interior, accessed February 26, 2012, http://www.nps.gov/liho/historyculture/peoriaspeech.htm; Foner, *The Fiery Trial*, 65-72, 74-78, 89.

80 Abraham Lincoln, "A House Divided," June 16, 1858, *Digital History*, Gilder Lehrman Collection, accessed February 26, 2012, http://www.digitalhistory.uh.edu/documents/documents_p2.cfm?doc=26; Foner, *The Fiery Trial*, 98-100.

81 McPherson, *Battle Cry of Freedom*, 183; Foner, *The Fiery Trial*, 106-107.

82 Stephen A. Douglas as quoted in McPherson, *Battle Cry of Freedom*, 184; Abraham Lincoln as quoted in Foner, *The Fiery Trial*, 107-109.

83 Foner, *The Fiery Trial*, 111; McPherson, *Battle Cry of Freedom*, 188.

84 Burton, *The Age of Lincoln*, 94; McPherson, *Battle Cry of Freedom*, 202-205.

85 McPherson, *Battle Cry of Freedom*, 205.

86 Burton, *The Age of Lincoln*, 94; McPherson, *Battle Cry of Freedom*, 206.

87 Burton, *The Age of Lincoln*, 95-96.

88 McPherson, *Battle Cry of Freedom*, 209-210.

89 Stephen A. Douglas and Abraham Lincoln as quoted in *Battle Cry of Freedom*, 211-212.

90 McPherson, *Battle Cry of Freedom*, 213-214.

91 McPherson, *Battle Cry of Freedom*, 214-215.

92 McPherson, *Battle Cry of Freedom*, 215-216, 221-222.

93 McPherson, *Battle Cry of Freedom*, 216, 221.

94 McPherson, *Battle Cry of Freedom*, 217-221.

95 McPherson, *Battle Cry of Freedom*, 224-225, 232-233.

96 Freehling, *The Road to Disunion*, Volume II, 336-337; McPherson, *Battle Cry of Freedom*, 230-231.

97 Freehling, *The Road to Disunion*, Volume II, 421-423; McPherson, *Battle Cry of Freedom*, 234-235, 240-241, 243.

98 McPherson, *Battle Cry of Freedom*, 246.

99 McPherson, *Battle Cry of Freedom*, 251-254.

ANSWER KEY FOR CHAPTER FIFTEEN: THE IMPENDING CRISIS (1848-1861)

Check your answers to the questions in the Before You Move On Sections for this chapter.

Correct answers are **BOLDED**

Section 15.2.3 - p538

1. The Wilmot Proviso
   a. was unconstitutional.
   B. WOULD PROHIBIT SLAVERY IN LANDS ACQUIRED FROM MEXICO.
   c. passed both houses of Congress.
   d. would extend the Missouri Compromise line to the Pacific.

2. The Compromise of 1850
   a. postponed California statehood.
   b. gave Texas more territory.
   c. ended slavery in Washington, D.C.
   D. STRENGTHENED THE FUGITIVE SLAVE LAWS.

3. Harriet Beecher Stowe's novel Uncle Tom's Cabin
   A. WAS PERHAPS THE MOST EFFECTIVE PIECE OF ANTISLAVERY PROPAGANDA.
   b. was perhaps the most effective piece of proslavery propaganda.
   c. ended section hostilities after its publication in 1852.
   d. presented a picture of happy, well-treated slaves and benevolent masters.

Section 15.3.4 - p549

1. The Ostend Manifesto was
   a. an agreement by the United States, Britain, and France to free oppressed Cubans.
   B. A DIPLOMATIC DISPATCH SUGGESTING THAT CUBA BE TAKEN FROM SPAIN TO PROTECT AMERICAN INTERESTS.
   c. an attempt to gain Cuba as a colony for freed American slaves.
   d. a plot by slaveholders to gain more slave territory.

2. Stephen Douglas's proposed Kansas-Nebraska Act
   a. strengthened his presidential prospects.
   b. showed his enthusiastic support of slavery.
   c. strengthened the Missouri Compromise.
   D. MIGHT ALLOW SLAVERY IN KANSAS AND NEBRASKA.

3. During the presidential campaign of 1865, the Republican Party
   a. nominated William H. Seward for president.
   B. OPPOSED THE FURTHER SPREAD OF SLAVERY.
   c. supported states' rights.
   d. condemned nativism.

Section 15.4.4 - p563

1. In the Dred Scott v. Sandford decision, the Supreme Court
   a. ruled that slaves who were taken to free states were free.
   b. ruled that slaves who escaped must be returned to their owners.
   C. STATED THAT BLACKS DID NOT HAVE FEDERAL CITIZENSHIP AND COULD NOT BRING SUIT IN FEDERAL COURTS.
   d. declared the Missouri Compromise constitutional.

2. In the Kansas territory, the proposed Lecompton Constitution showed the dominance of the Free Soilers.
   a. True
   B. FALSE

3. What significant event occurred at the 1860 Democratic Convention in Charleston?
   A. SOUTHERN DELEGATES WALKED OUT.
   b. Northern delegates walked out.
   c. Delegates nominated Abraham Lincoln for the presidency.
   d. Delegates nominated Jefferson Davis for the presidency.

Chapter Sixteen: The Civil War

Contents

Chapter Sixteen: The Civil War

16.1 INTRODUCTION

During the 1850s, tensions mounted between the North and the South over the issue of slavery and its relationship to political, social, and economic power. When Republican Abraham Lincoln won the presidential election of 1860, southerners firmly believed his victory would bring an end to the life they knew and loved. And so, seven states in the Lower South seceded from the Union before Lincoln's inauguration. Secession of these slave states ultimately led to a civil war between the South and the North that lasted from April 1861 to April 1865. Once the fighting began, several more states seceded from the United States of America to cast their lot with the newly formed Confederate States of America. Initially it seemed as though the South might win its bid for independence. But in time, the North's political and economic advantages helped it to secure victory.

Soldiers, according to historian James McPherson, fought for cause and comrades. They battled one another to preserve American values: to preserve liberty and freedom in a democratic nation. They also fought because they felt a sense of loyalty to their fellow soldiers.[1] However, the Civil War was not just about military victories and losses. The war divided family and friends in large numbers, and it caused numerous tensions on the home front. In the North, the fate of slavery continued to divide the people. In the South, funding the war exacerbated preexisting tensions between planters and yeomen. Ultimately, the North triumphed over the South and restored the Union. Nevertheless, no matter how you look at the war, the conflict brought profound social, political, and economic changes to the American people.

16.1.1 Learning Outcomes

After completing this chapter, you should be able to:

- Explain why the South and North eventually determined war was the only way to respond to their differences.
- Explain the difference between an army fighting another army and an army taking on civilians, such as in Sherman's March.
- Assess political and economic developments in the South and North during the Civil War.
- Explain the complex motives that went into the creation of the Emancipation Proclamation and analyze why the Proclamation applied only to those states still in rebellion against the Union, rather than freeing all slaves in both the North and South.
- Explain why conscription was necessary in both the North and the South.
- Describe the impact of the war on the Union and Confederate home front.
- Explain the issues that created political, social, and economic tension beginning in 1864 and 1865.
- Explain the use of African Americans in the Union and Confederate Armies.

16.2 THE ROAD TO WAR

Although seven states left the Union in the wake of Abraham Lincoln's victory in the presidential election of 1860, secession did not necessarily mean war between the South and the North. Between the election and the inauguration, people in the South and the North openly questioned how to respond to the formation of the Confederate States of America. Some people favored preserving the Union at any cost, while others seemed more inclined to let the Union fall apart. Ultimately, secession did lead to the Civil War, but only after people in the South and North resolved to fight for their cause. That moment only came after Confederate forces fired on Union forces at Fort Sumter in Charleston, South Carolina.

16.2.1 From Secession to War

After South Carolina, Mississippi, Florida, Alabama, Georgia, Louisiana, and Texas voted to secede, members of the newly formed Confederate government worked to present a moderate image in order to develop good will among reluctant southerners in other states, secure the future of the new nation, and avoid a costly war. At heart, the secessionists wanted to protect the rights of the states and of the citizens, which they believed Republican rule of the national government would undermine. Moderation seemed the best means to achieve those ends.[2] Meanwhile, northerners divided over whether to work toward a compromise to preserve the Union. Most Republicans and Democrats in the North saw secession as illegal, but they did not agree on the proper response. Business leaders seemed to prefer compromise, even if it meant accepting slavery in the territories. Antislavery Democrats, who joined the Republican Party in the 1850s, looked to fight to preserve the Union, not compromise with the South. Diehard abolitionists also wanted to avoid compromise because they thought secession would quicken the move toward emancipation.[3] As the debates raged, southerners and northerners waited to see the impact the forming of the Confederacy would have on Abraham Lincoln's policy toward the seceding states.

The Confederacy Takes Shape

On February 4, 1861, delegates from the seceded states convened the Montgomery, Alabama Convention to draft a provisional and a permanent constitution for the Confederate States of America. The atmosphere was euphoric as those gathered were there to promote the "Southern cause" of securing the rights of the South in the Union. Although radicals controlled the secession process at the state level, moderates quickly took control of the efforts to set up a government. Within days, delegates drafted and approved the provisional Constitution using the United States Constitution as a model. The delegates made only a few minor changes to what became the permanent Constitution, adopted on March 11, 1861. Both versions put the focus on the sovereignty not of the people but of the states and included language protecting slave property. The Confederate Constitution also limited the president to one six-year term, provided for the line item veto for appropriations, prohibited the use of a tariff for revenue, prohibited federal funding of internal improvements, gave the states the right to impeach federal officials working solely in their state, and banned the international slave trade. To most Confederates, the

U.S. Constitution was a sound document that the Republicans had corrupted. According to historian Vernon Burton, in mirroring the U.S. Constitution, the delegates hoped "to articulate specific areas of difference so resolution could proceed."[4] The delegates also selected a provisional president and vice president, and they agreed the delegates to the convention would serve as the provisional legislature until elections could be held.

Figure 16.1 The Inauguration of Jefferson Davis | On February 18, 1861, Jefferson Davis was sworn in as the provisional President of the Confederate States of America in Montgomery, Alabama.

Author: James Massalon
Source: Library of Congress

In choosing their provisional chief executives, the delegates voted unanimously for Jefferson Davis of Mississippi as president and Alexander Stephens of Georgia as vice president. Davis appeared to be the ideal choice. He supported southern rights, but was no radical. He had military experience should the North attack the South in an attempt to preserve the Union. He also seemed distinguished and looked presidential. The delegates selected Stephens because he brought balance to the Confederate government. As a one-time Whig and a late-comer to the secessionist cause, he helped project an image of moderation. On February 11, 1861, Stephens took the oath of office; then on February 18, 1861, Davis did so as well, his inauguration being delayed due to his having to travel to Montgomery. In his inaugural address, the new president tried to downplay the revolutionary nature of secession and suggested that the South took action only to preserve the status quo. He also said that "With a Constitution differing only from that of our fathers in so far as it is explanatory of their well-known intent...it is not unreasonable to expect that States from which we have recently parted may seek to unite their fortunes to ours under the Government which we have instituted."[5]

Lincoln Takes Over

In the months leading up to his inauguration, Abraham Lincoln received numerous pleas to issue a public statement on the future of slavery in the states so as to stem the tide of secession; however, he remained publicly silent. The president-elect, in fact, found the requests somewhat annoying. Lincoln thought he clearly stated his position during the campaign: he would not interfere with slavery where it already existed. Nothing about that had changed since he won, and he did not want to commit himself to a course of action before taking office. Moreover, he believed southern papers would misrepresent his position, thereby negating the effect of any statement.

Numerous correspondents also asked Lincoln to support a compromise with the slave states that might bring the seceded states back into the Union. Lincoln did not oppose compromise per se, but he remained unwilling to change his position on slavery in the territories. When Republican legislators queried Lincoln about the Crittenden Compromise, a proposal to extend the Missouri Compromise line to the Pacific, he told them not to support the measure. Responding to Congressman Nathan T. Hale, Lincoln said, "We have just carried an election on principles fairly stated to the people. Now we are told in advance, the government shall be broken up, unless we surrender to those we have beaten...if we surrender, it is the end of us, and of the government."[6]

While Lincoln did not want to surrender to the slave states' demands, he also recognized the importance of stemming the secessionist tide. So in the transition period, he focused on finding the appropriate advisers and drafting his inaugural address. Lincoln believed his Cabinet appointments and the tone of his first public speech as president would speak volumes about his policy toward the South. With respect to his Cabinet, the president-elect asked his four main political rivals to serve in his administration: William H. Seward at the State Department, Simon Cameron at the War Department, Salmon P. Chase at the Treasury Department, and Edward Bates as Attorney General. Some represented the conservative side and some the radical side of the Republican Party. He then filled the remaining positions with Republicans from different regions, most notably Montgomery Blair from the southern state of Maryland, a Border State, as the Postmaster General. Lincoln's choices underscored his belief in the importance of standing firm on the issue of slavery, while also entertaining a compromise to preserve the Union.[7]

The president-elect began working on his inaugural address in January and continued to do so even while he travelled to Washington. Lincoln's trip took twelve days because he wanted to meet the people and build good will for his presidency. The tour unfortunately did little to help him. James McPherson suggests that Lincoln so wanted to avoid saying anything controversial that his statements underscored his reputation "as a commonplace prairie lawyer." Moreover, when Lincoln learned of a possible threat to his life in Baltimore, he agreed to rearrange his schedule to pass through the city in the middle of the night. Newspaper editorials subsequently criticized Lincoln for sneaking into Washington. Therefore, the text of his inaugural address became even more important. In his early drafts, Lincoln offered both a sword and an olive branch to the seceded states. The sword centered on reclaiming federal property confiscated by the southern states; the olive branch focused on emphasizing the non-interference with slavery where it already existed. William H. Seward and Orville Browning, Lincoln's friend from Illinois, thought he needed to tone down the sword, so Lincoln conceded to their points.[8]

Figure 16.2 The Inauguration of Abraham Lincoln | On March 4, 1861, Abraham Lincoln was sworn in as the President of the United States of America in Washington, D.C.

Source: USCapitol Photostream (Flickr)

On March 4, 1861, a somber Washington gathered to witness Abraham Lincoln take the oath of office and deliver his inaugural address. The new president tried to calm southern fears and to mobilize unionists to support his government.[9] Lincoln started by noting he would not interfere with slavery where it already existed. Then he indicated he planned to administer the law on all federal property, but that he would not use violence unless forced to do so. More significantly, he repudiated secession, emphasized the permanent nature of the Union, and affirmed the importance of majority rule. Finally, he made a plea for reconciliation, noting "We are not enemies, but friends...Though passion may have strained it must not break our bonds of affection. The mystic chords of memory...will yet swell the chorus of the Union, when again touched, as surely they will be, by the better angels of our nature."[10]

The Firing on Fort Sumter

Lincoln believed his address would allow some time for reconciliation, but Davis and other Confederate leaders did not agree since he disavowed secession. On March 6, 1861, the Confederate Congress gave Davis the power to call up 100,000 troops to defend the South, suggesting war might be a real possibility. To make matters worse, Lincoln faced an immediate problem regarding Union forts in Confederate territory. While the seceding states confiscated most federal property, four forts remained in Union hands, Forts Taylor and Jefferson in the Florida Keys, Fort Pickens near Pensacola, and Fort Sumter in Charleston. If the Union wanted to retain the forts, then Lincoln would need to arrange to supply them. Doing so would follow the policy on federal property that the new president laid out in his inaugural address. However, only after he took office did Lincoln find out that Fort Sumter would soon run out of supplies and any attempt to resupply the fort would likely lead to a Confederate attack.[11]

Figure 16.3 Beauregard and Anderson | General P.G.T. Beauregard (left), was the Confederate commander at Charleston who fired on Fort Sumter, and started the Civil War, and Major Robert Anderson (right), served as the Union commander of Fort Sumter.

Authors: Matthew Brady, Unknown
Sources: National Archives, Library of Congress

After South Carolina seceded, Major Robert Anderson moved his forces from Fort Moultrie on the mainland to the unfinished Fort Sumter on a manmade granite island in the harbor. Anderson also requested reinforcements and supplies from the out-going Buchanan administration. At the same time, South Carolina's leaders approached the president requesting the transfer of Fort Sumter to their control. James Buchanan refused the request and decided to send Anderson reinforcements in January. To minimize the threat to South Carolina, the supplies and soldiers traveled on an unarmed merchant ship, the *Star of the West*. As the ship approached the harbor, the South Carolina militia opened fire, causing the ship quickly to turn around. Since neither side wanted war at that point, an implied agreement set in. So long as Buchanan did not send supplies, South Carolina would not fire on the fort. When Jefferson Davis took office, he sent another mission to Washington to negotiate for the transfer of the fort, and he dispatched General P.G.T. Beauregard to Charleston to command the South Carolina militia.[12]

When Lincoln found out about the situation at Fort Sumter, he had several options. One, he could scrape together enough warships to use force to enter the harbor and supply the fort, but that risked losing the Upper South. Two, he could cave in to South Carolina's demands and abandon the fort, but that meant accepting the South's independence. Three, he could try to find a solution that would avoid the downsides of the other options. Unsure of what to do, Lincoln polled his Cabinet. His advisers, except Montgomery Blair, seemed against starting a war over Fort Sumter. In fact, unbeknownst to the president, William H. Seward sent word to the Confederate commissioners in Washington that Anderson would evacuate the fort.[13]

Initially, Lincoln was leaning in that direction, but two factors changed his mind. For one thing, Northern public opinion seemed decidedly against pulling U.S. troops out of Charleston. Moreover, on March 28, 1861, Winfield Scott, the U.S. General-in-Chief, recommended pulling out troops from both Fort Sumter and Fort Pickens to prevent the remaining slave states from seceding. Scott's suggestion outraged the Cabinet because the proposal amounted to unconditional surrender to the South. With the support of his advisers, the president arranged to resupply Fort Sumter in the least aggressive way possible. On April 6, 1861, Lincoln sent a message to Francis W. Pickens, South Carolina's governor, indicating the United States would send unarmed ships to supply Fort Sumter with provisions. In warning Pickens of his intentions, Lincoln put the decision for war in Davis's hands. Lincoln had said on numerous occasions that he would defend the Union should the Confederacy attack; thus, should Davis tell Beauregard to fire on the supply ships, the war would begin.[14]

Figure 16.4 The Bombardment of Fort Sumter | On April 12, 1861, Confederate forces began to fire on Union forces stationed at Fort Sumter in Charleston's Harbor. The attack marked the beginning of the Civil War.

Author: Unknown
Source: US National Park Service

For Jefferson Davis, the presence of any Union troops at Fort Sumter and Fort Pickens called into question the sovereignty of the Confederacy. Missionaries from the Davis administration meeting with leaders in the Upper South heard repeatedly that secessionists would not gain enough support to leave the Union without proof that the Confederacy would defend its move toward independence. Therefore, Davis instructed Beauregard to demand the evacuation of Fort Sumter, “and if this is refused, proceed in such a manner as you may determine to reduce it.” On April 11, 1861, Beauregard made the request, and Anderson subsequently refused. However, he also noted he only had a few more days of supplies, hoping that Beauregard would hold off action until that point. Beauregard, knowing Davis wanted to oust Anderson before the Union ships arrived, gave the order for the militia to open fire on April 12. Within two hours, the federal troops had returned fire but did not put up much of a defense. After enduring a 33-hour bombardment, Major Anderson surrendered to General Beauregard. The formal transfer of the fort took place on the afternoon of April 14, which caused wild celebration in Charleston. The war had begun, and the first victory belonged to the South.[15]

16.2.2 Choosing Sides: The Dilemma of the Slave States

The day after the surrender of Fort Sumter, Abraham Lincoln called on the states to recruit 75,000 men for ninety days of service to put down the South’s rebellion. The response in most states was so overwhelming that the War Department hardly knew what to do with all the recruits. The firing on Fort Sumter convinced most northerners in the Republican and the Democratic Parties that the time had come to defend the Union. The abolitionist’s warnings about the difference between a free society and a slave society no longer seemed so far-fetched. However, Lincoln never mentioned slavery when he addressed the need to suppress the rebellion; he focused solely on the need to preserve the Union. The president feared talk of slavery would divide the northerners at this crucial stage and drive the remaining slave states out of the Union.

Meanwhile, the northern call for troops convinced many southerners that, contrary to his public statements, Lincoln planned to fight a war to undermine their way of life. Throughout the Confederate States, leaders began to organize troops. More importantly, the war reinvigorated the ongoing secessionist debates in the southern states that remained in the Union. The Confederacy needed the industrial resources and personnel of those states to have a better chance to win the war. As James McPherson points out, these states “contained most of the South’s resources for waging war; more than half its [white] population...three-quarters of its industrial capacity, half its horses and mules, [and] three-fifths of its livestock and food crops.” At the same time, the Union hoped to retain these states in order to isolate the rebellion.[16] Ultimately, Virginia, North Carolina, Tennessee, and Arkansas seceded from the Union, whereas Delaware, Maryland, Kentucky, and Missouri remained in the Union.

Delegates to Virginia’s secession convention voted to leave the Union on April 17, 1861. Of all the states that seceded after Fort Sumter, Virginia brought the most valuable resources to the Confederate war effort. The Tredegar Iron Works in Richmond was the only plant in the South capable of manufacturing heavy artillery. Virginia’s heritage, especially as the home to three presidents, also brought greater prestige to the Confederacy. And most importantly, Virginia’s secession brought the South Robert E. Lee. Although fiercely loyal to the United States, Lee would not take up arms against the place of his birth. His dilemma represented that of many southerners. While they had doubts about leaving the Union, their primary reason to join the Confederacy was defense of home.[17] After Virginia seceded, Arkansas, North Carolina, and Tennessee quickly followed suit.

While the majority of voters in the Upper South embraced secession, pro-Union sentiment remained high in the mountainous regions of western Virginia, western North Carolina, northern Arkansas, and eastern Tennessee. For the residents of western Virginia and eastern Tennessee, fighting for slavery was too much to ask. During the war, both regions mounted an effort for separate statehood; the Virginian's effort succeeded, whereas the Tennessean's effort failed.[18] Western Virginians reasoned if a state could legally secede from the national government, then a county could legally secede from a state government. They convened a meeting to vote on creating a new state. Voters eventually approved an "ordinance of dismemberment," and West Virginia joined the Union in January 1863.[19] When people in Tennessee went to the polls to vote on the state's declaration of independence, 70 percent of the residents in eastern counties voted against the measure. However, unionists in eastern Tennessee could not mount an effective challenge to secessionist control. The state government quickly moved to declare martial law in the region and imprison the opponents of secession. Still, over 30,000 people in Tennessee fled the state in order to fight in the Union Army.[20]

For the remaining southern states, the so-called Border States, the debate over secession was far more divisive. Maryland, Missouri, Kentucky, and Delaware realized that they would become the battleground of the war if they seceded, and so they hoped to adopt a neutral position in the struggle between the slave and free states. However, in reality, neutrality was not an option because of the natural and industrial resources located in these states. According to James McPherson, Maryland, Kentucky, and Missouri "would have added 45 percent to the...military manpower of the Confederacy, 80 percent to its manufacturing capacity, and nearly 40 percent to its supply of horses and mules." Therefore, both the Lincoln and Davis administrations sought to attract their loyalty. Delaware, given its small slave population, seemed more like a free state than a slave state. Before the war began, the state legislature expressed their disdain for secession and did not discuss the matter again. In the remaining Border States, devotion to the Union wavered throughout the war.[21]

In Maryland, a riot broke out in Baltimore in April 1861 over the issue of secession after Union troops from Massachusetts attempted to pass through the city. The city's mayor and board of police, who tilted toward the South, determined it would be unwise for additional northern troops to enter the city. So, with the governor's tacit approval, they destroyed the railroad bridges surrounding the city and cut the telegraph wires running to Washington. In the days after the riot, it appeared that the secessionists might triumph, but when additional Union troops arrived, the city settled down. Lincoln then took additional steps to stabilize the situation, which included having troops arrest southern-sympathizing members of the state legislature and suspending habeas corpus, meaning the government would not try the prisoners for their supposed crimes. When Maryland's legislature finally met in November to consider secession, it criticized Lincoln for his actions but did not call for secession. Approximately 66 percent of white men in Maryland fought for the Union during the Civil War.[22]

The battle over secession in Missouri was far more violent than Maryland. After Fort Sumter, Governor Claiborne Jackson, the former leader of proslavery fighters in Kansas, took measures to push the state toward the Confederacy. He refused to fulfill Lincoln's request for troops and sent the militia to take control of a federal arsenal near Kansas City. At the same time, Captain Nathaniel Lyon, the commander of the federal arsenal in St. Louis, very much wanted to keep Missouri in the Union. Knowing the governor wanted to seize the arsenal, Lyons prepared to attack before the secessionists could make their move. Violence broke out in St. Louis in May 1861, which sparked a guerilla war between pro-North and pro-South elements; in spite of the fighting, Union forces controlled the state for the rest of the war. Jackson resigned his position and proceeded to set up a pro-South government in exile. Shortly thereafter, Jefferson Davis accepted Missouri as the twelfth Confederate state. Nevertheless, nearly 75 percent of the white men in Missouri fought for the North in the Civil War.[23]

The people of Kentucky divided more evenly between the South and the North than in the other Border States because they had cultural and economic ties to both regions. Kentucky was also important symbolically because it was the birthplace of both Abraham Lincoln and Jefferson Davis. In May 1861, the legislature adopted a position of neutrality. Then, Governor Beriah Maffogin ignored both Lincoln and Davis's calls for troops. Since the governor privately tilted to the South, he let Confederate recruiting agents into the state. Lincoln opted to allow a neutral stance until unionist sentiments grew and even resisted tying the war to the issue of slavery so as not to upset the people of Kentucky. After Southern troops moved into Kentucky in September 1861, the legislature declared its loyalty to the Union and vowed to expel the Confederate invaders. Lincoln's patience paid off in the end. Governor Maffogin resigned his seat and convened a secession convention, which voted to split from the Union. Davis acknowledged Kentucky as the thirteenth Confederate state, but the pro-Southern government never effectively controlled the state.[24]

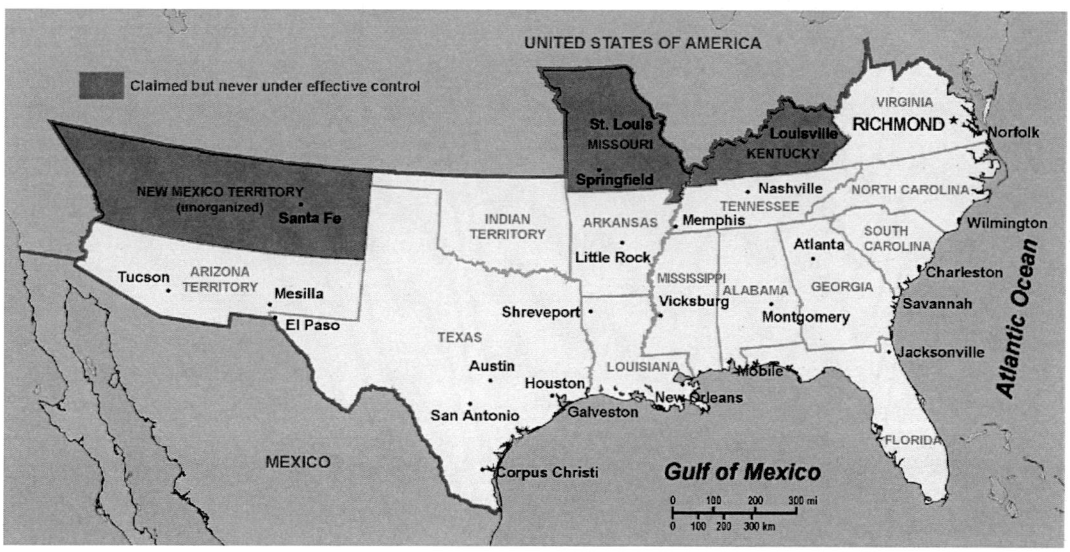

Figure 16.5 The Confederacy | Eleven states seceded from the Union to form the Confederate States of America. The Confederacy also claimed Kentucky and Missouri, but they never exercised control over those states during the war.

Author: Wikipedia User "Nicholas F"
Source: Wikimedia Commons

16.2.3 Before You Move On...

Key Concepts

When the states of the Lower South began to secede from the Union in late 1860 after Abraham Lincoln's election as president, it remained unclear whether their action would lead to a war between the South and the North. In his inaugural address, Lincoln denied the right of states to secede from the Union, but he also put the burden of war on the seceded states when he indicated the Union would only fight if the Confederacy attacked. Unfortunately, the need to resupply federal troops at Fort Sumter in Charleston made the possibility of that attack more likely. On April 12, 1861, Confederate forces attacked Fort Sumter before the United States could send supplies, and the Civil War began. Days later, Lincoln called for troops to put down the rebellion. In the following months, the states of the Upper South had to decide where their loyalties lay. Virginia, North Carolina, Arkansas, and Tennessee seceded from the Union; Delaware, Maryland, Missouri, and Kentucky did not.

Test Yourself

1. In his first inaugural address, Abraham Lincoln emphasized

    a. the moral wrongness of slavery.

    b. the permanent nature of the Union.

    c. the loyalty of southerners during the Mexican War.

    d. economic development.

2. The Civil War began when

    a. Union forces at Fort Sumter fired on nearby Confederate positions.

    b. Confederate forces at Fort Sumter fired on nearby Union positions.

    c. Union forces fired on Confederate troops stationed in Fort Sumter.

    d. Confederate forces fired upon Fort Sumter.

3. All of the following were slave states that remained in the Union except

    a. Tennessee.

    b. Maryland.

    c. Delaware.

    d. Missouri.

See page 638 for answers

16.3 THE MILITARY CONFLICT

As the South and the North prepared to do battle during the Civil War, both sides expected that the war would be short and that their side would win. These expectations derived from their faith in the cause: the right to secede from the Union and the necessity to preserve the Union. But they also stemmed from the unique advantages their side had.

The United States held a clear advantage when it came to population and to industrial capacity. The total population in the northern states was around 22 million people, whereas the population in the southern states was around 9 million. Moreover, 1.3 million northerners worked in factories as opposed to only 110,000 southerners. Those northern factories produced nine times as many industrial goods as southern factories. The North also had a much better rail system than the South, both in terms of total amount of track and operating efficiency. Thus, when it came to supplying the growing military and moving troops around the country, the North had a significant advantage.[25]

The Confederate States, in spite of their disadvantages in terms of population and industrial capacity, still had several advantages to draw on. In order to win the war, the South merely needed to defend itself against a northern attack. While a daunting task, it was not impossible since the Confederacy controlled over 750,000 square miles of territory and defensive wars usually require less manpower. Moreover, the Confederate Army could draw on skilled military leaders, many of whom attended West Point. Additionally, many of the southern recruits regularly used fire arms and rode horses while many of the urban northern recruits did not. Thus, to win, the South simply needed to wait the North out, and, with the advantages they possessed, that seemed entirely possible.[26]

From 1861 to 1865, after the bombardment of Fort Sumter, over 350 military engagements were fought in the Civil War. The vast majority were fought in the southern states, with others fought in the territories as well as in the northern states. Of all of these engagements, the following few stand out as having particular importance.

16.3.1 First Manassas or First Battle of Bull Run

- **Date**: July 21, 1861.
- **Location**: Prince William County, Virginia, along Bull Run, near Manassas, Virginia
- **Confederate Commanders**: Brigadier General P.G.T. Beauregard, Brigadier General Joseph E. Johnston
- **Union Commander**: Brigadier General Irvin McDowell
- **Confederate Force:** 32, 320
- **Union Force**: 28,450
- **Confederate Losses**: 1,982
- **Union Losses**: 2,896
- A Confederate Victory

For President Lincoln, allowing the secession issue to linger while the Confederates built up their military was unacceptable. He ordered his commanding general, Brigadier

Figure 16.6 First Manassas | General Joseph E. Johnston was one of the Confederate commanders at First Manassas

Author: Unknown
Source: Library of Congress

General McDowell, to advance south into Virginia. Brigadier General Beauregard had command of the Confederate forces near Manassas and had placed them along Bull Run, a small river in the area, and Brigadier General Joseph Johnston commanded additional Confederate forces further west.

McDowell hoped to flank Beauregard by coming around the left side of Beauregard's army, forcing it out of position thus making it vulnerable to attack, and then, after defeating Beauregard, marching on to Richmond, which was the Confederate Capitol. Beauregard was aware of McDowell's approach and devised his own strategy: he would attempt to flank McDowell, also on the left. This strategy left both armies attempting to turn the other. Although the Union forces were able to push the Confederates back early, the Confederate lines did not break. Colonel Thomas J. Jackson and his men were noted for holding their position, standing like a "stonewall." The nickname stuck to Jackson ever after. McDowell knew Johnston was in the west and expected he would be engaged by other Union forces and so unable to come to the aide of Beauregard. McDowell was mistaken; Johnston was able to get his army on a train and arrived in the afternoon to reinforce Beauregard. Confederate Calvary Colonel James Ewell Brown, "Jeb" Stuart arrived and charged into troops from New York who fled the field in what quickly became a rout. Union troops panicked and turned back for Washington in a confused mass. Civilians from Washington had come to watch the battle, now they and their buggies were in the way of their retreating army. McDowell's army was saved because Beauregard's and Johnston's armies were too tired and disorganized themselves to mount a pursuit. The Union Army reached Washington on April 22. McDowell lost his command.

First Manassas is significant as the first real battle of the war and because it proved to both sides that the war would not be quickly won. Lincoln, relieving McDowell marked the beginning of his long search for a general who would win. The Confederacy was bolstered by the victory, but personality conflicts between Beauregard and most others, including President Jefferson Davis, kept the issue of the Confederate command unsettled.

16.3.2 Shiloh

- **Date**: April 6-7, 1862.
- **Location**: Pittsburg Landing, Hardin County, Tennessee
- **Confederate Commander**: General Albert Sidney Johnston, General P.G.T Beauregard

- **Union Commander**: Major General Ulysses S. Grant, Major General Don Carlos Buell
- **Confederate Force**: 44,968
- **Union Force**: 65,085
- **Confederate Losses:** 10,669
- **Union Losses:** 13,047
- A Union Victory

Major General Ulysses S. Grant was the commander of the Union Army of the Tennessee, and Major General Buell was the commander of the Union Army of the Ohio. Grant, who had been successful in pushing the Confederates out of Tennessee, intended to continue pressing forward into Confederate territory. He camped at Pittsburg Landing in Tennessee to organize and await the arrival of Buell who planned to join Grant on the next part of the campaign.

General Albert Sydney Johnston (no relation to Brigadier General Joseph Johnston) knew Grant was waiting for Buell and understood his best chance of defeating Grant was to attack before Buell arrived. Weather delayed Johnston's plans, so he was unable to launch an attack until the morning of April 6. The Confederates caught the Union army by surprise and drove them back but were unable to completely break their lines. Union groups formed up in an area known as the Hornet's Nest and refused to be moved. The Confederates opened up with artillery, and still the Union troops held their ground. Johnston, an experienced commander, stayed in the front lines of his army. He was shot in the leg behind his knee and ignored the wound. Unknown to Johnston, his artery had been severed. By the time he and his officers realized his wound was serious, it was too late. Johnston bled to death. Command of the Confederates fell to Beauregard as Johnston's

Figure 16.7 Shiloh | General Albert Sydney Johnston (left) was Confederate commander at Shiloh, while Major General Ulysses S. Grant (right) was the Union commander.

Authors: Unknown, Mathew Brady
Sources: Library of Congress, National Archives

fears were realized: the Confederates were unable to break Grant's lines before the arrival of Buell. Beauregard continued to attack until it was apparent that victory was not possible, and then he withdrew from the field.

With over 23,000 total casualties, Shiloh saw the greatest loss of life of any battle in the war up to that point. The loss of Albert Sydney Johnston was a blow to the Confederacy. Although a Union victory, Northern newspapers did not sing Grant's praises; rather, they lambasted him and accused him of being drunk as the public digested the horrible cost of war.

Figure 16.8 Major General Don Carlos Buell | Buell helped Grant achieve a victory at Shiloh.

Author: Mathew Brady
Source: Library of Congress

16.3.3 Seven Days

- **Date**: June 25-July 1, 1862.
- **Location:** Virginia
- **Confederate Commanders**: General Robert E. Lee
- **Union Commander**: Major General George B. McClellan
- **Confederate Force**: 92,000
- **Union Force**: 104,000
- **Confederate Losses**: 20,000
- **Union Losses**: 15,000
- A Confederate Victory

The Seven Days refers to not one battle, but a group of six major battles conducted over a seven day period in 1862. McClellan planned to advance on Richmond, capture it, and end the war. Lee, in defending Richmond, became the aggressor and drove the Union Army down the Peninsula formed by the York and James Rivers and away from Richmond.

McClellan's original plan had been to land his army at Fort Monroe, Virginia, located at the end of the peninsula on the Chesapeake Bay. He thought he could take the Confederates by surprise attacking them from the east, rather than coming down from Washington to the north. His advance slowed when he encountered Confederate defenses, and then ground to a halt after engaging Confederates in battle and having the weather take a turn for the worse. During one battle, the Confederate commander, General Joseph Johnston was wounded and relieved of command, which was then given to General Lee. While McClellan waited for better conditions, Lee planned his attack, organized his army, and continued to develop the defenses of Richmond.

On June 25, McClellan began once again to advance. The terrain in any weather would be formidable—heavy forest broke into large swamps with small rivers running throughout. McClellan planned to advance along the Williamsburg Road, an old and

Figure 16.9 The Seven Days | During this week-long battle, General Robert E. Lee (left) was the Confederate commander and General George B. McClellan (right) was the Union commander.

Authors: Julian Vannerson, Mathew Brady
Sources: Library of Congress, National Archives

narrow road that ran from Richmond to Williamsburg. His goal was to draw close enough to Richmond to place his artillery batteries to threaten the city. He gained little ground and lost over 1,000 men before pulling back.

Lee was already on the move with his own plan, going on the attack to the north of Richmond at Beaver Dam in what would be the second of the six battles. Lee had intended to attack McClellan's right flank. Due to various organizational issues, including having Stonewall Jackson arrive late and one general attacking without orders, the battle did not go as Lee had planned; consequently, the Confederates suffered unnecessary casualties. Still, they forced the Union forces under Brigadier General Fitz John Porter to withdraw.

On June 27, Lee pressed on against Porter who had taken up a defensive position at Gaines Mill. Early Confederate attacks were unsuccessful, and the Confederates suffered losses. Late in the day, the Confederates were able to break Porter's lines, forcing a retreat. This battle, on the third of the seven days, led to McClellan's full withdrawal from the Richmond area and retreat back down the Peninsula.

McClellan's army was in full retreat by June 29, with Confederate forces in pursuit. The Confederates reached the Union rear guard and attacked at Savage's Station but were unable to prevent the Union forces from continuing their retreat. Lee had expected Jackson to come in, but Jackson remained north of the Chickahominy and was unable to aide in stopping McClellan's retreat. So determined was McClellan to escape Lee that he abandoned his wounded and supplies and retreated into White Oak Swamp.

On June 30, the armies continued to encounter each other as McClellan's main force retreated towards the James River. The main fighting occurred at Glendale with the Confederates attempting to split the Union force in half. Jackson was still in the north along the Chickahominy and engaged the Union rear guard there without much success. Throughout the Seven Days, both sides had suffered from poor execution of commands, resulting in failed plans and lost opportunities. Lee had hoped with his aggressive pursuit to be able to destroy the Union Army and possibly bring an early end to the war. Instead, the Union forces were able to continue their retreat to the James.

Malvern Hill would prove to be the last of the Seven Days Battles. On July 1, Union forces occupied a strong defensive position on the hill, forcing the Confederates to attack. Well-placed Union artillery destroyed the Confederate artillery batteries before they could be brought into play. Despite the obvious advantages of the Union, Lee ordered his forces to attack. The Confederates suffered over 5,000 casualties in this one battle, more than in any other battle of the Seven Days. Still, rather than stay and try to regroup for another attempt on Richmond, McClellan chose to continue his retreat, withdrawing his army to Harrison's Landing on the James River, where his army would be covered by Union gun boats as they made their way away from Richmond.

After the Seven Days, Lee felt Richmond was secure enough to turn his attentions north to Maryland. Both sides in the war wanted to end it quickly, and Lee believed victory was possible for the Confederacy if he could have a successful campaign in Maryland and threaten Washington. Although McClellan's decisions to retreat even when he held strong positions have been the subject of much debate, he continued to hold on to his command.

16.3.4 Antietam

- **Date**: September 16-18, 1862.
- **Location**: Antietam Creek, Sharpsburg, Washington County, Maryland
- **Confederate Commanders**: General Robert E. Lee
- **Union Commander**: Major General George B. McClellan
- **Confederate Force**: 45,000
- **Union Force**: 87,000
- **Confederate Losses**: 10,316
- **Union Losses**: 12,401
- A Draw

Lee's army took up a defensive position along Antietam Creek near Sharpsburg where it was engaged by McClellan's army on September 16. At dawn on September 17, Major General Joseph Hooker of the Union Army launched an attack on Lee's left flank held by Stonewall Jackson, opening the battle for the day, the day known as the bloodiest in American history. Although outnumbered, Lee gambled and threw all of his army into the battle. Rather than holding back behind his defenses, Lee launched aggressive counterattacks against the superior Union forces. The fighting around Jackson's position was an intense artillery battle that devastated both sides with Jackson holding firm. An area known as the Cornfield became a horrific killing ground as regiments marched in only to be cut down by a combination of artillery, bayonets, and vicious hand-to-hand combat. The Union forces advanced and almost broke Jackson's line, only to be pushed back by Confederate reinforcements.

Action continued in the center of the battle lines as the Union forces attacked the main part of Lee's army. McClellan's troops almost captured the center of the Confederates, but unlike Lee who had committed all of his force to the battle, McClellan held back and did not use his superior numbers to gain the victory. Because McClellan did not press the attack on all fronts, Lee was able to adjust to the threats from the Union forces by moving his troops as needed from one area to another. With nightfall, the fighting ended. Lee planned a retreat to Virginia, sending off his wounded and then the bulk of his army, while keeping units behind to cover the retreat on the 18th. McClellan did not press the attack, allowing Lee to slip away. Lincoln was angry as he needed a victory, and although Lee withdrew, this battle was far from a Union victory. Still, Lincoln declared it to be a victory and then issued the Emancipation Proclamation.

September 17, 1862 saw more casualties in a single day of battle than any other in the entire war. With his vastly superior numbers, McClellan probably could have defeated Lee, but his cautious strategy, which conserved troops, prevented the possibility of victory, thus allowing the war to continue. McClellan's failure to attack with all his force, to prevent Lee from crossing back into Virginia, and to then pursue Lee led to his dismissal by Lincoln later in the year.

16.3.5 Vicksburg

- **Date**: May 18-July 4, 1863.
- **Location**: Vicksburg, Warren County, Mississippi
- **Confederate Commanders**: Lieutenant General John C. Pemberton
- **Union Commander**: Major General Ulysses S. Grant
- **Confederate Force**: 33,000
- **Union Force**: 77,000
- **Confederate Losses**: 9,091
- **Union Losses**: 10,042
- Union Victory

Vicksburg held strategic importance for the war along the Mississippi. Situated on a bluff that overlooked the river at a point where the Mississippi is narrow, slow, and winding, whoever commanded Vicksburg would be able to control traffic on the river. Taking Vicksburg was essential to cutting the Confederacy in half, an important step for the Union to win the war.

After Shiloh, Grant had continued to use his Army of the Tennessee to push back the Confederates in the West. Opposing Grant for much of the way was Pemberton and the Army of Vicksburg. Effectively using his superior numbers, Grant forced Pemberton down the Mississippi to Vicksburg, a Confederate stronghold on the river.

Grant, along with occasional support from the Union Navy, tried several times to take Vicksburg without success and suffered casualties. Meanwhile the Union and Confederate armies continued to clash along the Mississippi. In May, Grant decided to lay siege to Vicksburg. Siege warfare, which was long, tedious, expensive, and without guarantee for success, was not considered to be the optimum choice for the day. While the defender is held in check, so too is the attacker, unable to leave and carry on with the war; instead his army is invested in taking a city, knowing that the advantage tends to be with the defender. Grant felt he had no other choice. A well-conducted siege could cause Vicksburg to fall with little loss of life, only a loss of time.

Grant encamped his army, and then his troops began digging their way to Vicksburg, slowly constructing lines of trench works that allowed them to move ever closer to the Confederate battlements without exposing themselves unnecessarily to enemy fire. The Union forces surrounded the city, blockading it, and cutting off its supplies. Union sappers tunneled under the Confederate fortifications and blew them up, leaving holes in the defenses vulnerable to attack. Union artillery shelled the city, forcing the civilian population to seek shelter. Even so, what defeated Vicksburg was not the overwhelming Union forces in battle, but starvation from the blockade. The siege soon had the citizens of Vicksburg eating whatever they could find, including pets. Pemberton was forced to surrender. Confederate losses from battle were few, but Pemberton surrendered almost 30,000 men, a terrible blow to the Confederacy. Grant generously paroled the Confederates, allowing them to surrender their weapons and leave.

The capture of Vicksburg gave Grant the advantage he sought in the Western Theatre of the war. Confederate forces there would never again mount a strong offensive. As for Grant, his victory helped him to gain the attention of Lincoln who was still looking for his one perfect general.

Sidebar 16.1: Prisoners of War

In the early days of the war, captured soldiers might well expect to be exchanged, that is returned to their own side as had happened at the surrender of Fort Sumter, rather than being kept as prisoners of war. As the war progressed attitudes among government officials changed and the exchanges stopped, leaving both sides with the problem of how to maintain the prisoners. For the South, the issue was not simply where to put the prisoners, but how to provide for them. As the war dragged on, the South had fewer and fewer resources for soldiers in the field and even less for prisoners of war. In the North, the reasons for the horrific neglect of prisoners are more difficult to determine.

In both North and South prisoners struggled to survive the lack of adequate medical care, clothing, shelter and food as they were packed into over-crowded camps. Starvation was not unusual in many places. Diseases such as scurvy due to lack of proper nutrition were common. Prisoners suffered terribly in the winter, particularly in the Union camps along the coast such as Point Lookout in Maryland and Fort Delaware in Delaware as the chilly damp winds blew off the Atlantic into the prison camps where the prisoners had little to no bedding and blankets or clothes to keep warm in the tattered tents.

The summers could be equally dreadful for prisoners such as those at Andersonville, the notorious Confederate prison in Georgia where there was often no shelter to be had from the scorching summer sun and no relief from the heat. A small creek ran through one corner of the camp, but it was a disease infested cesspool in the unsanitary camp. Andersonville's mortality rate was estimated to be 29 percent. Prison camps in the North such as Elmira in New York also had high mortality rates, losing a quarter of its prisoners. An estimated 56,000 prisoners total died from both sides.[122]

16.3.6 Gettysburg

- **Date**: July 1-3, 1863.
- **Location**: Gettysburg, Adams County, Pennsylvania
- **Confederate Commander**: General Robert E. Lee
- **Union Commander:** Major General George Gordon Meade
- **Confederate Force**: 75,054
- **Union Force**: 83,289
- **Confederate Losses**: 28,000
- **Union Losses**: 23,000
- A Union Victory

Lee invaded Pennsylvania with a desire to take the war to the enemy and hopefully to speed the way to peace by bringing the war to an end sooner. George Gordon Meade, the newly appointed commander of the Army of the Potomac, was determined to protect Washington while having to pursue Lee. He managed to do both by keeping his army between the Confederates and the Capitol.

Figure 16.10 Major General George Gordon Meade | Meade, the Union commander at Gettysburg, helped to prevent Confederate forces from moving the battleground to the northern states.

Author: Mathew Brady
Source: Library of Congress

This famous battle began almost by accident as units from both armies were maneuvering to their intended positions when they ran into each other on July 1. Each side, realizing they had stumbled upon the enemy, formed and prepared to fight. What began with a chance encounter soon developed into a full-blown battle with 30,000 Confederates facing 20,000 Union soldiers. The Confederates won the day, driving the Union forces back. The Union Army then formed up in defensive positions as more units from both armies arrived in the area.

By the morning of the second day, the bulk of each army was now in the area, and the Union had taken up the naturally defensive position along the crest of hills below Gettysburg. The Union had the advantage, forcing Lee to either attack or withdraw. Lee chose to position his army around the Union positions and attack, first on one flank and then the other in classic style. His attacks on the Union flanks ultimately failed, and the Union troops continued to hold their ground. A well-known military strategy was to try each of the opponent's flanks and, if those attacks failed, go up the middle.

On July 3, having failed to turn either flank of the Union forces, Lee ordered Lieutenant General James Longstreet to go up the middle, attacking the Union center on Cemetery Ridge. Major General George Pickett was given the honor of leading the attack which has ever since borne the name of "Pickett's Charge." The attack, being a classic military maneuver could not have been a surprise to Meade. The only things Meade did not know were who would lead the attack and when the attack would be launched.

As it turned out, Meade was not alone in wondering when the attack would begin. Lee had wanted to begin in the morning and to coordinate the attack with other offensive maneuvers he had planned. Instead there was a delay of several hours before the brigades involved in the attack were ready to go. Some blame Longstreet, who was known to be unenthusiastic about the plan. Finally, around 2:00 p.m., approximately 12,500 Confederate men began the march across the open fields towards the Union lines. Difficult to imagine today, the Confederate line was almost a mile wide as the men marched across the field. Facing artillery and gun fire, the Confederates marched in order until they were close enough to the Union lines to actually charge. Some of the Union forces retreated, creating gaps in their lines. Others stood their ground and engaged in fierce fighting.

Figure 16.11 Gettysburg | This photograph of the dead at Gettysburg after the battle captures the grim realities of the war.

Author: Timothy H. O'Sullivan
Source: Library of Congress

The Confederates faced several artillery batteries which continued to fire even as the Confederates were directly in front of the guns. The Confederates reached the Union lines but were thrown back. The point at which they breached the Union lines has been referred to as the "High Watermark of the Confederacy." Half the men who made Pickett's Charge were wounded or killed in the action, helping to give Gettysburg the highest casualty rate of the war. The survivors of the charge made their way back to the Confederate lines. On July 4, as Grant was declaring victory in Vicksburg, the Confederate and Union armies at Gettysburg collected their 50,000 dead from the field. Lee and his army retreated back to Virginia. Gettysburg marked the last time Lee would attempt to invade the North.

16.3.7 Chattanooga

- **Date**: November 23-25, 1863.
- **Location**: Chattanooga, Hamilton County, Tennessee
- **Confederate Commander**: General Braxton Bragg
- **Union Commander**: Major General Ulysses S. Grant
- **Confederate Force:** 44, 010
- **Union Force**: 56, 359
- **Confederate Losses**: 6, 670
- **Union Losses**: 5, 815
- A Union Victory

Chattanooga's location gave it a strategic importance in the Civil War. Union Major General William Rosencrans took the city from Confederate General Braxton Bragg in early September; Bragg was determined to recapture the city and the Union army stationed within it. The two armies had fought a few engagements before coming together at the Battle of Chickamauga where Rosencrans's army made a major mistake, allowing Bragg to win the battle and forcing Rosencrans to retreat back to Chattanooga. Bragg laid siege to the city and cut off its supplies. Rosencrans suffered from his defeat at Chickamauga, which was particularly brutal, and the subsequent siege at Chattanooga and became unable to command.

Figure 16.12 General Braxton Bragg | This photograph captures Bragg, who served as the Confederate commander at Chattanooga.

Author: Unknown
Source: Library of Congress

Bragg had problems of his own, as several of his subordinates disagreed with him so strongly that President Jefferson Davis had to travel to Chattanooga to settle matters personally. Davis decided in favor of Bragg, and left him with the task of retaking Chattanooga. Grant arrived and took over command of the Union forces from Rosencrans. Grant was able to establish a new supply line for the almost starving army of Rosencrans. The arrival of Major General William T. Sherman in November sparked a new offensive on the part of Union forces against the Confederates. The Union forces were successful in driving Bragg off and securing Chattanooga for their own use.

Bragg lost not only Chattanooga but ultimately his command as well. President Davis called on Bragg to leave the field and instead serve as Davis's military advisor in 1864. With Chattanooga in hand, Sherman had a strong position with access to the Tennessee River and rail lines useful for transporting supplies and troops. The city would become the launch point for Sherman's March to the Sea.

16.3.8 Atlanta Campaign

- **Date**: May 7-September 2, 1864.
- **Location**: North Georgia to Atlanta, Georgia
- **Confederate Commanders**: General Joseph E. Johnston, Lieutenant General John Bell Hood
- **Union Commander**: Major General William Tecumseh Sherman
- **Confederate Force**: 60,000
- **Union Force**: 100,000
- **Confederate Losses**: 34,979
- **Union Losses**: 31,687
- A Union Victory

After securing a base at Chattanooga, Tennessee, Sherman prepared for an assault on Georgia while Grant transferred his attentions to Virginia where he would face Lee. Sherman's mission was to demoralize the South, capture Atlanta, and drive another wedge between areas of the Confederacy, just as Grant had done at Vicksburg.

From Chattanooga, Sherman crossed into North Georgia where he faced Johnston. Sherman had the superior force; Johnston had the advantage of strong defensive positions. From May 7 into July, they fought a series of ten battles, Sherman attacking, Johnston holding, then Sherman flanking Johnston forcing Johnston to fall back to a new position further south towards Atlanta. Johnston was never able to mount a counter attack that would halt Sherman's progress, but he was slowly reducing Sherman's forces by inflicting casualties during the long retreat.

In July, with Sherman rapidly approaching the outskirts of Atlanta, President Davis replaced Johnston with John Bell Hood. Hood was seen as a more aggressive general, and Davis hoped that he could do something other than manage a fighting retreat. Hood assumed command with no time to organize or prepare his army to his liking and carried on with Johnston's plans to attack the Union forces at Peachtree Creek on July 20. Sherman had divided his army into three branches to attack Atlanta from the north and the east, forcing the Confederates to stretch their defenses. Although the attack went relatively well,

Figure 16.13 Major General William Tecumseh Sherman | During the Atlanta Campaign and later in the March to the Sea, Sherman led the Union forces in Georgia.

Author: Unknown
Source: Library of Congress

Hood was not able to commit enough troops to the attack to carry the day as he was forced by the Union strategy to spread his own forces to other areas. In the end, the Union was able to repulse the Confederate attack and resume their drive towards Atlanta. Atlanta, however, was not without its own defenses. A major railway hub for the South, Atlanta had been well fortified against Union attacks. Sherman's attempts to take Atlanta from the north and east both failed.

Sherman then redeployed his forces to the west, determined to cut Hood's supply lines and take Atlanta. The month of August was spent with both armies maneuvering around the Atlanta area: Sherman trying to find a way into Atlanta, Hood trying to disrupt Sherman's plans, and cavalry from both sides raiding behind the lines, destroying supplies and the railroads that brought them. Although disruptive, the cavalry raids did not do enough permanent damage since the railroads could be repaired. Sherman needed to permanently cut the supplies going to Hood and Atlanta.

Sherman moved the majority of his army out of its entrenched positions around Atlanta and concentrated them near Jonesborough on August 31 where they would be able to cut the two railroads still feeding Atlanta—the Macon & Western and the Atlanta & West Point. Hood moved to protect the vital lines, but misjudged the size of the Union force, resulting in a defeat for the Confederates. Sherman was able to cut the supply lines, but was unable to smash the Confederates, who fell back. Hood, understanding that Atlanta was now lost as the supply lines were cut with no chance of repair and there was no hope of any Confederate forces coming to their relief, felt the best he could do for his army and the people of Atlanta was to evacuate the city on September 1.

Hood was able to save his army, much to the disappointment of Sherman who had hoped to destroy it. By evacuating so soon after the last supply lines were cut, Hood saved the people of Atlanta, who had already suffered greatly in the war, from enduring the horrors of a siege. Hood ordered the military supplies that he could not carry away to be burned and military structures to be destroyed so as not to leave anything that might be of use to the enemy. Sherman took Atlanta on September 2, while Hood and his army moved back towards Tennessee. The capture of Atlanta was welcome news in the North, increasing Lincoln's popularity just two months before the presidential election of 1864.

After capturing Atlanta, Sherman went after Hood, who hoped to draw Sherman away from Atlanta, but Sherman did not cooperate and turned back to Atlanta to prepare for what would be his most famous action in the war, Sherman's March to the Sea.

Sherman remained convinced that to defeat the Confederacy quickly, it was necessary to demoralize the Confederates. His famous march was intended to do just that.

16.3.9 Sherman's March to the Sea

On November 14, having gathered his army, Sherman ordered Atlanta to be evacuated and burned. The pleas of the civilians there could not convince him to change his mind as this was part of his plan to destroy the Confederate will to fight. He cut the telegraph lines to Washington, set fire to the city, and headed to Savannah. His army was divided into two columns which stayed several miles apart. As they traveled, they destroyed railroads and raided and burned plantations and farms. Slaves who were freed as the army passed soon began gathering behind the columns, following them towards Savannah. The Confederates offered little resistance, Hood had taken the only large military force in the state and headed for Tennessee, leaving the Georgians essentially defenseless. Local militia and one cavalry unit under Major General Joseph Wheeler were all that was left. On November 22, at Griswoldville, near Macon, 650 militiamen were killed in a one-sided battle. The Union lost just 62 soldiers. On November 23, the state capitol at Milledgeville fell. Sherman then continued on towards Savannah.

Figure 16.14 Atlanta after Sherman | This photograph captures the city's rail depot in ruins.

Author: George N. Barnard
Source: Library of Congress

One exceptionally dark mark of Sherman's march is known as Ebenezer Creek. One of Sherman's officers, Brigadier General Jefferson C. Davis, who was no relation to the Confederate president, Jefferson Davis, took a controversial and tragic action. Although close to Savannah, the Union columns were still being pursued by Wheeler's cavalry. Wheeler could do little but harass the vastly superior Union force. Wheeler had a few thousand men, while the Union columns had over 60,000; nevertheless, Wheeler followed the Union army and took shots whenever the opportunity arose to do so.

Davis used Wheeler's pursuit as an excuse to rid the Union forces of the slaves that followed them. Sherman previously had encouraged the slaves to turn back, as he had no supplies to spare, but he had not forced them to move away from his army. Davis was in charge of the pontoon bridge being used on December 9 by the Union to cross Ebenezer Creek. A pontoon bridge is a temporary bridge made of floating sections tied together. It can be put in place and removed fairly quickly, allowing an army to cross a difficult body of water. As it was winter, Ebenezer Creek was cold. It was also deep and well over 100 feet wide. Accounts differ as to how many slaves were present, with the estimated numbers ranging from a few hundred to a few thousand. What observers agreed upon was what happened to them. Davis ordered the last of the troops crossing the bridge to halt and prevent the slaves from stepping onto the bridge. Then he had the bridge cut loose,

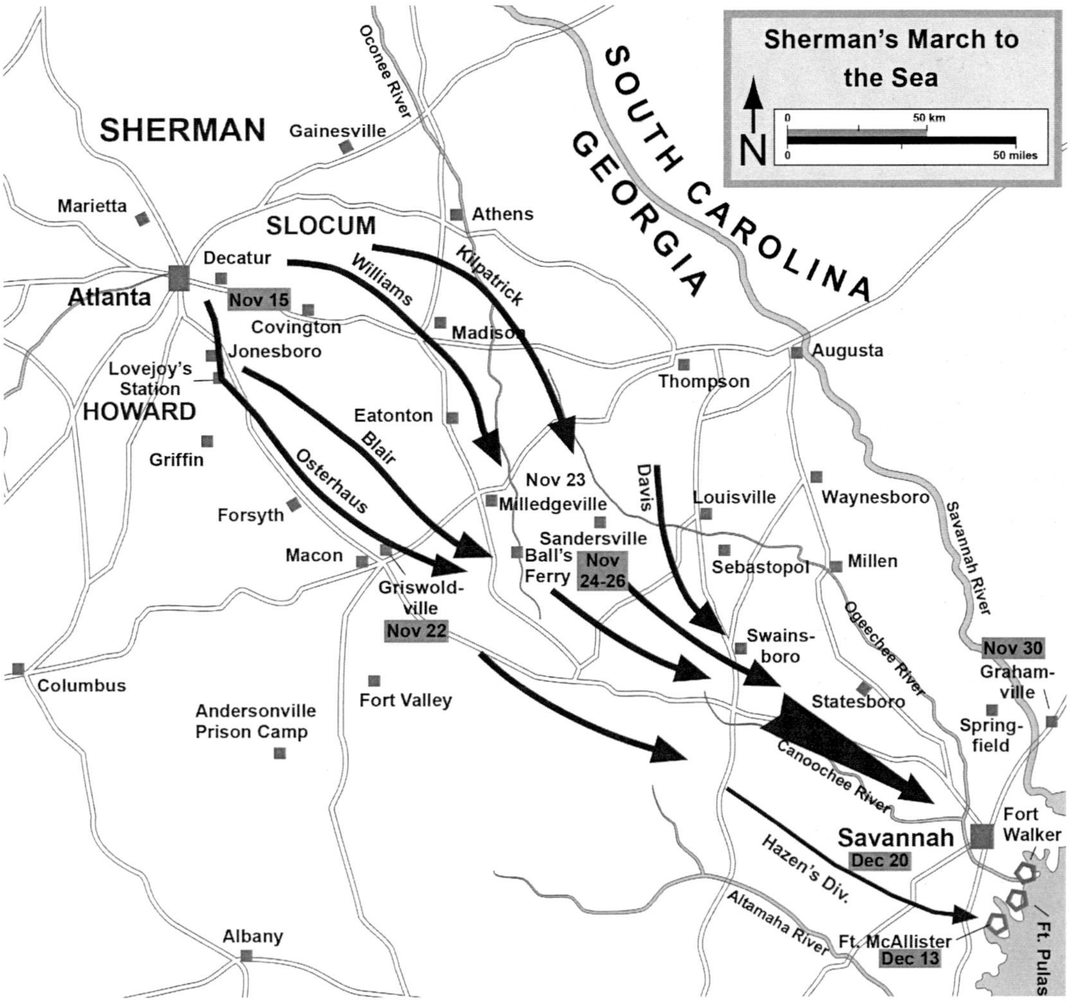

Figure 16.15 Map of the March to the Sea | After capturing Atlanta, Sherman proceeded to march across Georgia in an attempt to destroy the Confederate will to fight.

Author: Hal Jespersen
Source: Wikimedia Commons

thereby stranding the slaves on the far side. Wheeler's cavalry arrived soon after. The slaves, comprising men, women and children, panicked to see the Confederates bearing down on them, so many jumped into the creek to escape, only to drown in the freezing waters. Of those who did not jump, many were shot or cut down with swords. The fate of the rest is uncertain. While this tragedy took place, Davis and his soldiers marched away. Sherman defended Davis's actions, and no one was reprimanded for the incident which was called a military necessity.

On December 20, realizing that resisting Sherman would lead to the destruction of Savannah, Lieutenant General William J. Hardee withdrew his troops from the city and headed to South Carolina. This action enabled Savannah's mayor, Richard Arnold to surrender the city on December 22 and thereby preserve it. Sherman sent a message to Lincoln saying Savannah was his Christmas present. Sherman's famous march ended at Savannah. He continued to fight on, turning his army north to Charleston, still with the intent to demoralize the Confederacy.[27]

16.3.10 The End of the War

While Sherman marched to the sea, Grant and Lee continued the fight in Virginia. Lee knew that a long war was an advantage to the Union as the Confederacy did not have the resources to continue indefinitely. Marching across his home state, he witnessed first-hand the suffering the war brought to the people. The Confederate army was without food, many of the men going days with little or no nutrition. Disease ran rampant in the poorly equipped camps, and the quest for food became so desperate for the southerners that many resorted to going through horse dung, searching for undigested kernels of corn.[28] For almost seven months, from late summer 1864 to the winter of 1865, the coldest winter in memory, Lee's army lived in a series of trenches, thirty-seven miles long, stretching east of Richmond and southwest of Petersburg, as Grant repeatedly hurled his army at Lee's troops.

Realizing the desperate plight of his troops, Lee traveled to Richmond in winter 1865 to plead before the Confederate Congress for additional aid. However, he was met by a legislature which, the general confided to his son, Custis, "don't seem to be able to do anything except to eat peanuts and chew tobacco while my army is starving."[29] His requests were turned down. The standoff near Richmond between Lee and Grant continued as did starvation, disease, a plummeting morale, and general feeling of despair. General Lee said of the circumstances in 1864 and 1865 that he could live with privation and general hardship, but to sacrifice his men when the fight seemed futile and destined to end badly for the South, was beyond his endurance. In late winter Lee had fewer than 35,000 men present for duty. He believed that Grant had more than 150,000. If Grant's army were reinforced with General William T. Sherman's army from the south and General Philip Sheridan's from the west, Lee feared the Union commander would lead an army of 280,000, a number, it turned out, that was not far off the mark.

And so Lee came up with a new tactic: if the defense of Richmond were given up Lee's troops could then march southward, join General Joseph Johnston's army coming east from Tennessee, and perhaps stop Sherman's destructive move through the South. Lee did indeed evacuate Richmond on April 2, but by that time, sensing that the end was near, he was no longer willing to subject his men to continuing hardship. Grant had hoped to catch Lee at Petersburg, having extended his lines to surround the Confederate army, only to find that Lee and his army had slipped away in the night. Lee headed west to Lynchburg, another Confederate supply point with Grant in pursuit. As Lee retreated towards Lynchburg, his army and Grant's continued to clash notably on April 6 at Sailor's Creek and again on April 8 at Appomattox Station and finally on April 9 at Appomattox Court House.

Grant wrote to Lee on April 7, suggesting to Lee that to continue would be futile and so Lee should surrender. Lee replied asking for what terms Grant would offer and an exchange of letters ensued. Lee met with Grant at the McLean house in Appomattox Courthouse, Virginia, just one week later on April 9, and surrendered his Army of Northern Virginia. In his farewell address to his troops, Lee stressed that the Confederates had been beaten by superior forces and not undermined by internal failings: "After four years of arduous service, marked by unsurpassed courage and fortitude, the Army of Northern Virginia has been compelled to yield to over whelming numbers and resources."[30]

Figure 16.16 The Confederate Surrender | On April 9, 1861, Lee surrendered to Grant at the McLean House in Appomattox Courthouse, Virginia.

Author: Hal Jesperson
Source: Wikimedia Commons

News of Lee's surrender was slow in reaching the South; unlike in the North where a vast array of telegraphs and newspapers quickly provided their readers with the news, southern telegraph lines had largely been destroyed and its newspapers were pretty much nonexistent. Lee's surrender did not end the war, as there were still other Confederate armies in the field in other states. In an apparent "Appomattox Spirit," southern generals followed Lee's lead and surrendered their armies to their northern counterparts. Significant Confederate resistance ended with the surrender of Joseph E. Johnston's army on April 26, 1865. The last Confederate general to surrender his army was General Stand Watie, a Cherokee, in June 1865. As the Confederate army began to surrender, Jefferson Davis, President of the Confederacy, left an undefended Richmond the first week in April, traveling south by rail and horse and buggy.[31] On May 10, 1865, Jefferson Davis was captured by Union troops near Irwinville, Georgia and was charged with treason and imprisoned.

As southerners assessed the course and meaning of the conflict that had devastated their region, Gary Gallagher observes, "few believed the war had proved secession illegal. Armed might alone, rather than constitutional authority, lay behind the North's ability to label former Confederates as traitors."[32] Elizabeth Pendleton Hardin commented about her departure from Eatonton, Georgia: "We had been there two years and a half, watching with unfaltering hope our struggle for independence and life, and now that our hopes had come to naught, we returned to our homes with sad hearts, feeling we had left the brightest part of our lives behind."[33] Not all southerners looked favorably on the Confederacy nor were they unhappy to see it end. Mary Chesnut reported in her *Diary from Dixie*, that she had overheard a citizen of North Carolina declare, "Now they will have no Negroes to lord it over. They can swell and peacock about and tyrannize now over only a small parcel of women and children, those only who are their very own family."[34] The war had ended, and as Lee looked back on it in the late 1860s, he commented, "We lost nearly everything but honor, and that should be religiously guarded."[35]

16.3.11 Before You Move On...

Key Concepts

In the beginning of the war, people on both sides thought it would end quickly. The Union misjudged the anger in the Confederacy, while the Confederates misjudged the Union's determination not to allow the secession to go forward. The shots fired at Fort Sumter began the war, but the first real battle was First Manassas. At First Manassas, both sides realized that war was uglier than they imagined and that this war would not be over quickly. The North had greater resources in terms of men and supplies than the South. If the South had any real chance of winning, it would have been to end the war quickly. Great suffering was experienced by the civilians as well as the soldiers of the Confederacy as Union forces moved into Confederate territory.

Test Yourself

1. The battle with the most over-all casualties was ______and the battle with the most casualties on a single day was _______.

2. The general who devastated Georgia with his march to the sea was _______.

3 The only two land battles fought outside of Confederate territory were? _______ and _______.

4. Grant captured Vicksburg with an effective use of what tactic?

5. Maneuvering around the side of an army, rather than attacking directly from the front is called?

See page 638 for answers

16.4 WARTIME POLITICS

The four years during which the United States of America and the Confederate States of America waged a long, trying civil war were ones in which the governments in both regions attempted to deal with common issues: conscription, inflation, racial tension, financing the war, divisiveness between political parties and disparity of ideals and goals between the presidents of the regions and those they governed. Both Congresses passed conscription acts and attempted not only to raise armies but also to maintain and supply them. Both areas experienced elation in the beginning, which turned to fear and despair as the years passed. When the war ended, the Union had survived, and its capital city was spared; the Confederacy was destroyed, with nothing left of Richmond or, indeed, of most of the South.

16.4.1 Politics in the Union States

Northern unity in the first year of the war, like unity in the South, was tenuous, at best. The Republican Party was relatively new: a "coalition of men" according to James McPherson, "who a few years earlier had been Whigs, Democrats, Know-Nothings, Free Soilers or abolitionists."[36] When the Civil War began, the U.S. Congress was not to meet for eighty days; Lincoln thus began his presidency, as the head of a new, untried political party, "with a virtual monopoly of emergency powers."[37] Almost immediately he released a series of executive orders, some constitutionally based, some not. First, he declared that an insurrection existed and called out the state militias, increasing their number to number 75,000. Second, he issued two proclamations that created blockades of southern ports. Then, knowing that additional troops would be needed, he expanded the number of military troops, a power that the president did not hold under the Constitution as the Constitution gives the power to raise an army and navy to Congress. Ohio Representative John Sherman remarked at the time, "I never met anyone who claimed that the President could, by a proclamation, increase the regular army."[38] As a whole, Congress found these actions to be extra-constitutional. Lincoln's subsequent actions in the summer of 1861 with respect to paying Union soldiers and seizing transportation resources did not allay their fears as he once again seemed to step beyond the president's powers as laid out in the Constitution.[39]

As the new Congress assembled for a special session to deal with issues raised by the conflict with the seceded states, Lincoln assessed the coming struggle in his address to Congress when he explained:

> Our popular government has often been called an experiment. Two points in it, our people have already settled—the successful establishing and the successful administering of it. One still remains—the successful maintenance against a formidable [internal] attempt to overthrow it...And this issue embraces more than the fate of these United States. It presents to the whole family of man the question, whether a constitutional republic or a democracy—a government of the people, and by the same people, can maintain its territorial integrity against its own domestic foes.[40]

Congress then passed a declaration of war against the Confederate States, and John C. Crittenden added a resolution specifying that the purpose of the war on the part of the Union would be to "defend and maintain the supremacy of the Constitution."[41] In other words, no state could choose to nullify the Constitution, thus secession was not only unconstitutional, it was also treasonous. The war, in the words of Historian C. Vann Woodward, would be one "against secession, a war to maintain the Union—that and nothing more."[42] One last piece of legislation came out of this special session of Congress: a law authorizing the president to call for the enlistment of 500,000 troops to serve for a period of not less than six months or more than three years.

Civil Liberties Curtailed

When Congress met in regular session, it passed two confiscation acts that defined and specified punishment for treason and a separate, less severe punishment for insurrection.

The latter included as part of one's punishment the liberation of his slaves. All property held by the officers of the Confederate government and by those who supported the rebellion was to be seized after a sixty-day warning.

Neither of the confiscation acts, the second being the Treason Act, addressed the question as to what should be done to and about anti-war activities in the North, and Lincoln, instead of working through the courts and the legislative branch, decided to suspend habeas corpus, thus providing for arrest and punishment of "all Rebels and Insurgents, their aiders and abettors within the United States and all persons discouraging volunteer enlistments, resisting militia drafts or guilty of any disloyal practice."[43] In such cases the individual involved would lose his right to habeas corpus and would be subject to martial law. Historian David Donald comments that the numbers of those arrested was in the tens of thousands. And finally, before it adjourned, Congress abolished slavery in the District of Columbia.

Opposition from the Peace Democrats

Throughout the war, the political parties divided over Abraham Lincoln's leadership as it related to the war. The three main factions included the Republican Party from New England, New York, and Pennsylvania; the "Peace" Democrats, who drew their support mostly from the Midwest; and the "War" Democrats, who supported a more aggressive policy against the South. Northern Democrats, especially the Peace Democrats soundly criticized Lincoln for exercising powers that went far beyond those given to the president by the Constitution. While most historians say that Lincoln stopped short of creating a dictatorship in the twentieth century sense of the word, there was no doubt that the powers he claimed for the presidency were extraordinary. On the other hand, though he suspended habeas corpus, he did not suspend freedom of speech or the press, and so civil liberties continued to exist, even if they were curtailed during the enforcement of the treason and confiscation acts.

Lincoln also faced criticism throughout his first administration regarding emancipation from the "Peace" Democrats. Christened the "Copperheads" by their detractors, the "Peace" Democrats were a diverse socioeconomic group, drawing membership mainly from the southern Midwest and the immigrant Catholics of northern cities. One of the leading proponents of the Copperhead cause was the Ohio Representative Clement Vallandingham, who frequently denigrated Lincoln and emancipation in the same breath. And dislike of emancipation became the hallmark of most northern Democrats, who favored a United States that would be "the white man's home." Antislavery measures passed through Congress reflected a sharp division by party; on each bill, Republicans voted in favor of the measures, while Democrats stood firmly against them.

As the election of 1864 approached, the North was caught up in a peace movement that reflected the sentiments of a "war-weary and heartsick nation."[44] The peace movement gained wide recognition in 1863 and 1864, and as anti-war sentiment built in the Union, the Copperheads became the most vocal wing of the Democratic Party. They favored the Union, but demanded immediate peace and the ousting of Abraham Lincoln. At times they threatened violence, but none ever materialized. The Copperheads had several newspapers at their disposal, and when Horace Greeley became associated with the peace movement, other northerners also focused on the issue. Greeley wrote to Abraham Lincoln in spring 1864, "I venture to remind you that our bleeding, bankrupt, almost dying country also longs for peace; shudders at the prospect of fresh conscriptions, of further wholesale devastations, and of new rivers of human blood. And a widespread conviction that the government and its...supporters are...doing great harm."[45] Lincoln made public his own his own thinking about peace in a memo in July 1864:

> To Whom it may concern: Any proposition which embraces the restoration of peace, the integrity of the whole Union, and the abandonment of slavery, and which comes by and with an authority that can control the armies now at war against the United States will be received and considered by the Executive government of the United States, and will be met by liberal terms on other substantial and collateral points.[46]

Fearing that he would not be reelected, Abraham Lincoln submitted to his Cabinet on August 23 the following memorandum: "This morning, as for some days past, it seems exceedingly probable that this Administration will not be reelected. Then it will be my duty to cooperate with the President elect, as to save the Union between the election and the inauguration; as he will have secured his election on such ground."[47] Lincoln was sure that the Democrats would nominate retired Union general, George McClellan, whose opposition to the war and the Lincoln administration was well known.

The Election of 1864

The Democrats met in Chicago in August 1864. As Lincoln predicted they nominated George McClellan and adopted a platform that focused on bringing an end to the war. The platform, written by the Peace Democrats, denounced the practices of wartime: arbitrary military arrest;" "suppression of freedom of speech and the press;" and "disregard of State rights."[48] In his acceptance letter, McClellan stressed the need to preserve the Union as the nation's first priority.

For their part, the Republican Party worked toward greater unification, since half of their members were "opposed to the war and wholly opposed to emancipation." Looking at the Democratic platform, War Republicans suddenly realized that Lincoln was their "only alternative" to a disastrous defeat for the Union.[49] And so Abraham Lincoln was nominated by his party, with a platform that stressed abolition as a necessary precursor to peace. The Republican Party, in an effort to win the support of the "War" Democrats, changed its name to the National Union Party and nominated the incumbent president and "former" Republican Abraham Lincoln for president and "former" War Democrat Andrew Johnson for vice president. As a result, many War Democrats could support Lincoln's Civil War policies, while avoiding the "Republican" ticket.

During the fall campaigns, the Democrats touted the need for peace and the Republicans did their best to prove that their opponents were traitors to the future of the Union. General Grant was convinced that the South appeared set on holding out until after the election, relating in a dispatch from the front that "deserters come into our lines daily who tell us that the men are nearly universally tired of war...but that they believe peace

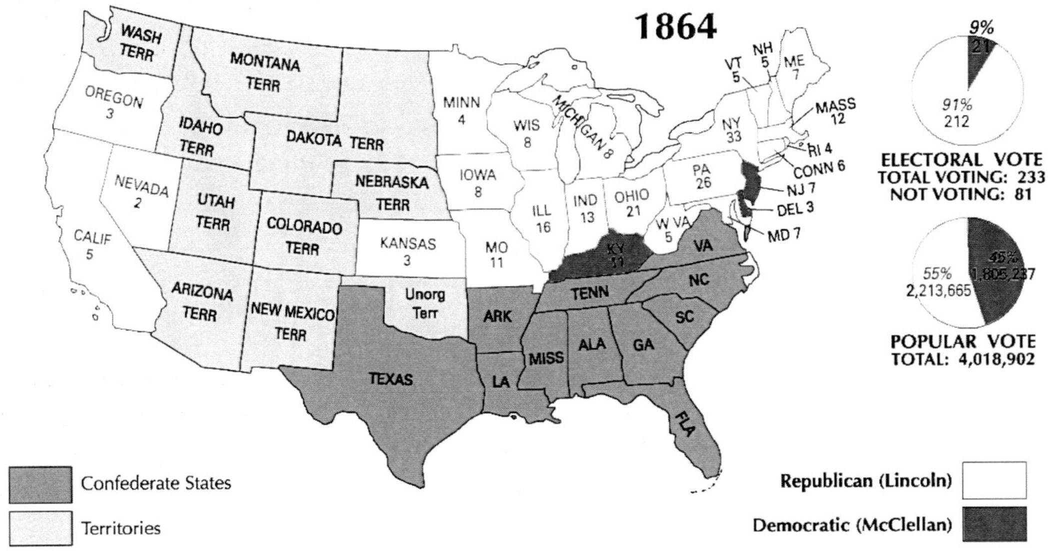

Figure 16.17 Presidential Election Map, 1864 | Abraham Lincoln easily won re-election in 1864.

Author: National Atlas of the United States
Source: Wikimedia Commons

will be negotiated after the fall elections."[50] Alexander Stephens, Vice President of the Confederacy, commented that the Democratic platform was "the first ray of light I have seen from the North since the war began," and a Confederate secret service agent wrote to Richmond from his post in Canada that the Democratic platform "means peace unconditionally...McClellan will be under the control of the peace men...At all events, he is committed by the platform to cease hostilities and to try negotiations."[51]

Much was made by Republicans of a series of "conspiracies" to which the Democratic leadership was linked, and headlines accused the Sons of Liberty, founded in 1864 and most of whom were Northern Democrats, of plots to overthrow the government and to create a diversion in the Northwest so that the Union would have to divert its troops from the South to defend the Union elsewhere. Headlines screamed, "REBELLION IN THE NORTH!! EXTRAORDINARY DISCLOSURE." Pamphlets provided additional details as they adopted such titles as *Copperhead Conspiracy in the Northwest: An Exposé of the Treasonable Order of the Sons of Liberty*.[52] Thus, Democratic "treason" became an additional focus of the Republican message.

When Atlanta fell to Sherman in September, 1864, it appeared that victory would go to the Republicans. On November 8, 1864, Lincoln won by over 400,000 popular votes and easily secured an electoral majority of 212 to 21 for McClellan. McClellan won just three states: Kentucky, Delaware, and his home state of New Jersey. Lincoln won almost two-thirds (64 percent) of the 1,118 counties in the 25 states where popular voting occurred; the Democrats claimed victory in the remainder.

16.4.2 Politics in the Confederate States

On February 4, 1861, the seceded southern states met to create a government for their new nation, the Confederate States of America. At that meeting, they drafted a constitution and elected provisional leaders, Jefferson Davis and Alexander Stephens. Throughout the summer, the provisional government worked in Montgomery, Alabama and, later, in Richmond, Virginia, where the capital moved, to manage the war effort. On November 6, 1861, voters in the Confederate states elected Davis as the permanent President of the Confederacy and Stephens as the permanent Vice President. As stated in the Constitution, they would serve for six years and could not stand for re-election. The Constitution also created a cabinet, along the lines of Lincoln's Cabinet, to help Davis manage the government's functions. However, Davis also had to work with the Confederate Congress and the state governors, a requirement which often proved problematic for the southern leader.[53]

Jefferson Davis and the Confederate Congress faced many issues from the outset as the new government began to examine its financial and political options. First, Davis sent emissaries to the North to purchase machinery and munitions. Second, it was necessary to raise and equip an army. In the opening months of the war, the Confederacy had been overrun with volunteers, almost too many to handle, as Southerners clung to the idea that the war would be short-lived. One volunteer from Virginia commented to his governor, "All of us are...ripe and ready for the fight...I shall be shoulder to shoulder with you whenever the fight comes off." Davis confirmed that volunteers were coming from all corners: "From Mississippi I could get 20,000 men who impatiently wait for notice that they can be armed." He regretted that he did not have enough arms to supply all of those who wanted to volunteer.[54]

Jefferson Davis, like Lincoln, did not glide smoothly through the war years, and, like Lincoln, he faced fierce political opposition, not from an opposing political party as was the case with some of Lincoln's opponents, but from states' rights supporters who had embraced secession and now guarded the rights of their states as ardently as they had against Union encroachment. The states' rights movement was centered in Georgia and North Carolina. Their governors, Joseph E. Brown of Georgia and Zebulon Vance of North Carolina, challenged Davis on everything from his reaction to the Bread Riots in Richmond to conscription, taxes, and the most onerous issue: suspension of habeas corpus.

In 1862, the Confederate Congress gave Davis the right to suspend habeas corpus when a situation dictated such action. Davis then proceeded to suspend the writ in several areas of the South. This action led to an outcry of "military despotism," especially in Georgia. Alexander Stephens, Vice President of the Confederacy, who devoted much attention to criticizing Davis's every move, decried the suspension of habeas corpus, insisting, "Away with the idea of getting independence first, and looking for liberty afterwards...Our liberties once lost, may be lost forever."[55] And most opponents of Davis "cloaked their opposition in the rhetorical garb of states' rights," arguing that they had joined the secession movement to "sustain the rights of the states."[56]

16.4.3 The Problems of Financing the War

During the Civil War, both the Confederate and Union governments faced difficult choices about what financial policies to implement since waging total war is an expensive undertaking. In order to pay for wars, governments have only so many options open to them. They can tax, borrow, print money, confiscate supplies, and conscript labor. All of these choices can have a negative effect on a nation's economy; however, printing money usually has the worst impact because it causes inflation, whereas taxation usually causes the least disruption to the people's lives. Confederate and Union leaders implemented a variety of these options, based on their military needs as well as the expectations the people had about the relationship between the government and its citizens.[57]

Southern Experiments in Financing

Jefferson Davis and his advisers, especially Treasury Secretary Christopher G. Memminger, needed to find a means to finance the effort to defend secession when the Confederacy had few resources to draw from. Some of the southern states gifted the new government money confiscated from the Union, but such donations provided only a short term solution. The Confederate Congress then authorized the sale of war bonds totaling $15 million. They sold quickly because of patriotic sentiment, but a second issue of $100 million did not, leaving the government short of needed funds to pay its bills. So in May, Congress permitted the Treasury Department to issue $20 million in treasury notes or paper currency, which people could not convert into specie (gold or silver coin) until two years after the conflict ended. The Confederate Congress, however, resisted making the treasury notes legal tender. Therefore, citizens did not have to accept the money as a form of payment. These events, in early 1861, set a precedent for the Confederacy; it constantly struggled to manage the economic issues brought on by war.[58]

Memminger hoped the bonds and the currency issued in 1861 would increase patriotism in the South by giving the people a stake in the success of the war effort. However, as the war dragged on southerners did not want to invest in their government. Fiat money, currency not backed by specie, only holds value when people have faith in the government, and the people's faith in their government declined.[59] Therefore, Confederate treasury notes lost value almost as soon as the government issued them. By war's end, $1 in Confederate currency equaled about $.02 in Union currency. To offset the problems of printing more money, Confederate leaders attempted to make war bonds more attractive and create a comprehensive tax policy, but nothing really improved the financial situation in the South.[60]

Loans, mostly in the form of war bonds, failed to bring in large amounts of revenue because of the nature of the cotton economy. In the antebellum years, cotton made southern landowners a good deal of money, which they reinvested in more land and more slaves. Therefore, when war came they did not have specie on hand to invest in the government. When they did purchase bonds, they paid with paper currency issued by the Confederate government or by the state governments.[61] The Confederacy also succeeded in setting up loans from European nations, especially France, but again the cotton economy impeded their efforts as the war dragged on. Cotton-backed bonds sold well to European investors when it looked as though the Confederacy might win the war and they needed southern cotton. When the fortunes of war changed and the demand for southern cotton decreased because the Europeans found other source of cotton, the bonds ceased to be a good investment, suggesting the limits of cotton diplomacy. War bonds, sold domestically or internationally, ultimately only accounted for about 21 percent of the South's wartime revenue.[62]

The Davis administration tried to adopt a comprehensive tax policy during the war to meet its financial obligations. In 1861, the Confederate Congress enacted a tariff, but because international trade declined it brought in little revenue. The government also placed a small direct tax on personal property, such as real estate. Seeing as southerners had no real tradition of paying taxes and they fervently supported states' rights, most people resisted paying the direct tax because it expanded the role of the national government. The majority of states paid by confiscating northern property or by printing state notes.[63] In 1863, the Confederate Congress approved a new tax program to raise revenue, which included a tax-in-kind on agricultural produce where farmers had to give the government 10 percent of what they raised. Not surprisingly, many farmers loathed the tax-in-kind because they paid more percentagewise in taxes than non-agricultural laborers. Not to mention, the yeoman disliked the fact that the government did not tax slave property; to them, the government was failing to spread the tax burden evenly. All told, taxes only accounted for about 10.5 percent of the South's wartime revenue and did not seem worth the price, given the hostility caused.[64]

Unfortunately, printing fiat money became the easiest way to finance the war effort when loans and taxation did not bring in enough revenue. In fact, the Confederacy financed over 60 percent of their war effort through the printing press. Southern leaders understood printing excess amounts of paper currency could lead to massive inflation and create economic hardship for the people. James M. McPherson, however, suggests, "the South resorted to this method of financing...from necessity, not choice." The treasury had a limited amount of specie on hand, so they could not back the currency. In 1863, the Confederate Congress approved a measure allowing treasury notes to be exchanged for interest bearing bonds, but the proposal required the government to issue more fiat money to be exchanged for the bonds. Given the declining faith in the Confederate war effort, the government only exchanged $21 million for bonds of the $500 million it printed for the program.[65]

Northern Experiments in Financing

When the Civil War began, financially speaking, the North had two things working in its favor. It had an established treasury and a source of income. However, Abraham Lincoln and his advisers, especially Treasury Secretary Salmon P. Chase, still faced challenges in financing the war against the South. Secession caused a slight economic downturn, making the Union government's financial situation tenuous because the nation was already spending more money than it made. While Chase knew little about the world of finance, he proved more adept as the country's fiscal manager than people expected. To raise money to support the war in 1861, Chase turned to financier Jay Cooke who arranged short-term bank loans and encouraged his wealthy friends to purchase long-term government bonds. Once it became clear the war would last longer than a few months, Chase laid plans that helped the government pay for the war while also providing for economic growth.[66]

The North financed the war by the same means that the South financed it, through loans, treasury notes, and taxes. However, the North relied more on loans and taxes than it did on treasury notes because it could rely on credit from European banks and the

American people. In fact, the Union financed almost 65 percent of the war through loans and bonds. The Lincoln administration believed loans provided the best means to finance the war without adding to the nation's pre-existing debt. While the Bank of England, as well as other European financial institutions, continued to loan money to the United States, Chase and Cooke developed a program to make the purchase of war bonds a patriotic venture. In February 1862, Chase made Cooke the official marketer of war bonds. Cooke's bond issues raised almost $1.2 billion. To encourage ordinary northerners to buy war bonds, Cooke sold them in denominations as low as $50 and almost 1 million northerners took advantage of the program. While contemporaries criticized Cooke for profiting off the war, James McPherson maintained it "was a cheaper and more efficient means of selling bonds to the masses than the government could have achieved in any other way."[67]

Figure 16.18 Salmon P. Chase | As Secretary of Treasury for the United States, Chase oversaw the Union's efforts to finance the war.

Author: Mathew Brady
Source: Library of Congress

In 1862, the Lincoln administration also reluctantly turned to printing treasury notes, often called greenbacks, to help finance about 16 percent of the war's costs. Beginning in the 1830s, the treasury only issued notes backed by specie. However, financing the war drained the gold reserves, which limited the amount of new currency the government could issue. The government tried to boost its specie reserves by requiring people to pay for their bonds in gold. When that failed, Chase worked with Congress to come up with a solution that would allow the government to issue more money without further draining the gold reserves from banks.[68] Republicans proposed a bill to make $150 million of newly printed fiat money legal tender in the United States in January 1862. Under the terms of the proposal, the government and the people had to accept treasury-issued paper currency as a form of payment for almost all business transactions except interest on government bonds and customs duties. Debate over the bill in Congress was fierce. Opponents, mostly Democrats, declared the measure unconstitutional. They tended to take the founders' permission to coin money literally. Supporters, mostly Republicans, saw the measure as a necessary and proper solution to the wartime financial crisis. Ultimately, Congress accepted the Legal Tender Act, and the president signed it into law on February 25, 1862. Later in the year, Congress approved issuing another $150 million.[69]

Alongside the efforts to fix currency problem, Congress worked to extend more federal control over the banking system because the Legal Tender Act did nothing about the numerous state notes that circulated alongside the new treasury notes. Congress passed the National Bank Acts of 1863 and 1864, which Salmon Chase encouraged Lincoln to

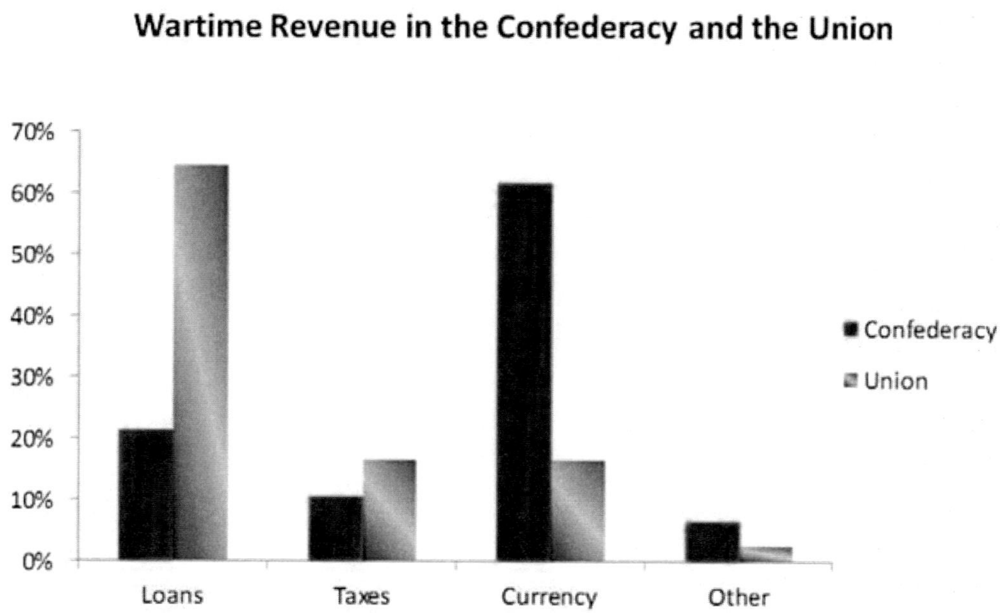

Figure 16.19 Wartime Revenue in the Confederacy and the Union | During the war, both the Confederate and Union governments struggled to come up with the best means to finance the war. This chart shows each side's revenue. Source: John Munroe Godfrey, Monetary Expansion in the Confederacy (New York: Arno Press, 1978), 14.

Author: Sarah Mergel
License: CC-BY-SA

sign. Collectively the measures created a national banking system and a uniform national currency. The laws allowed the federal government to charter banks and required those banks to purchase U.S. bonds equivalent to one-third of their lending capital. In return, the national banks could issue banknotes worth up to 90 percent of their bond holdings. The measures also helped finance the war because if a bank wanted to issue more notes, it had to purchase more government bonds.[70]

Finally, the U.S. government relied on taxes to finance a little over 16 percent of the war's costs. Congress avoided turning to taxes until 1862 because it wanted to steer clear of the political pitfalls taxes sometimes caused. In 1861, national leaders raised the tariff in order to bring in additional revenue. But with the financial situation still deteriorating, the Republicans considered additional taxes. Congress approved, and Lincoln signed the Internal Revenue Act of 1862, a comprehensive tax measure to revise the income tax and implement excise taxes. The measure also created the Bureau of Internal Revenue to collect the taxes. The revised income tax provisions set up a progressive rate structure; how much a taxpayer earned determined the percentage they paid. Moreover, the government also began to tax inheritances. The excise duties taxed luxury items not necessities; so northerners paid taxes on liquor, tobacco, playing cards, carriages, yachts, billiard tables, jewelry, and dividend income. They also paid on patents, professional licenses, and other official documents. However, the government did not make any of these taxes permanent.[71]

16.4.4 Before You Move On...

Key Concepts

The wartime political problems faced by the Confederate States of America and the Union were similar, as was the manner in which the two Congresses tackled the problems. Ultimately, however, despite the fact that the South was able to create a new Constitution and a new government, the overwhelming resources of the North were more than the Southern Confederacy could withstand. The Confederate and the Union governments also dealt with challenges in their effort to finance the Civil War. The South relied mostly on treasury notes to cover wartime expenses. While they attempted to use loans and taxes, political leaders found both too risky as they tried to hold their nation together. The North relied mostly on bank loans and war bonds to pay for wartime expenses. However, they also raised taxes and issued treasury notes.

Test Yourself

1. When the war broke out, Lincoln announced that the war was being fought to free those who were enslaved in the South.

   a. True

   b. False

2. The Copperheads were

   a. War Republicans.

   b. Peace Democrats.

   c. Southern deserters.

   d. Northern abolitionists.

3. Habeas Corpus, which is guaranteed in the Bill of Rights, is the right of individuals to:

   a. A speedy trial.

   b. Be charged with a crime if arrested.

   c. Bear arms.

   d. Practice the religion of his or her choice.

4. Lincoln's opponent in the 1864 Presidential election was

   a. General Grant.

   b. General Sherman.

   c. General McClellan.

   d. General Lee.

5. The South financed its war effort primarily through
    a. selling war bonds.
    b. seizing northern assets.
    c. printing money.
    d. implementing an income tax.

6. The North financed its war effort primarily through
    a. selling war bonds.
    b. implementing an income tax.
    c. securing foreign loans.
    d. printing money.

See page 638 for answers

16.5 SOCIAL DEVELOPMENTS

The Civil War was fought not only on the battlefields, but in the towns, villages, and cities of the North and South where tensions ran high as inflation skyrocketed and conscription threatened to take the bread winners to the front lines with little guarantee that they would return. Such tensions caused by the war were reflected in such events as the Richmond bread riots and the draft and race riots in northern cities, but especially in New York City, where hundreds were killed or wounded. In both cases, fear of the changes that would come with emancipation of the slaves was an important factor.

16.5.1 Wartime Economic Problems

The Confederate government's economic policies created many problems for the civilian population, especially shortages of goods and inflation. In the antebellum years, the South imported items such as wool, coffee, tea, salt, finished cotton, iron, nails, and shoes from the North or from Europe. While the Union blockade had little effect in the first year of the war, southerners failed to produce substitutes for needed goods, and prices began to rise. The price of salt, used to preserve meat, went from $2 per bag in 1861 to $60 per bag in 1862. As the blockade became more effective, smugglers provided some supplies. But they tended to focus on war materials and luxury items because they brought in higher profits.[72] The second reason for the shortages stemmed from the nature of the cotton economy. Before the war, the South grew mostly export crops, and it took time to convert to food production. After 1862, the Union controlled the best food-producing land in the South. Elsewhere near battlefields, many people stopped planting crops for fear they would be destroyed or confiscated. Furthermore, with so many men serving in the military, even with the use of slave labor, the agricultural economy became less productive. Lastly, lack of an internal transportation system made it hard to move goods around the country. Food supplies often rotted before they reached their intended destination.[73]

Early on, inflation became an issue for the Confederacy. Shortages obviously contributed to the problem of rising prices, but the government's monetary policy seemed to be the major culprit. With the government constantly infusing more treasury notes into the economy, the value of the money depreciated. In other words, a person needed $100 in Confederate currency in 1865 to buy what $1 purchased in 1861. Wages did rise for most workers; however, they did not keep pace with prices. In 1862, wages for paid laborers increased about 55 percent; prices increased about 300 percent. In 1864, the average family needed $68 to purchase food, but a private in the Confederate Army made only $11 per month. Moreover, since the Confederacy chose not to make its notes legal tender, creditors did not have to accept them as a form of payment. For a soldier paid in treasury notes, it became increasingly hard to use those notes, a fact which further lessened their value. Southerners suffered a great deal because of the rising prices on the limited number of available goods. By closing months of the war, the inflation rate in the South jumped to over 9,000 percent.[74]

Economically speaking, the North weathered the war better than the South, but northerners still faced economic hardships because of shortages and inflation. Government-issued greenbacks lost value at a time when consumer goods became hard to find, so prices rose. The North experienced an inflation rate of about 80 percent as prices slowly edged upward throughout the war. What might have cost about $100 before the war would cost about $180 after the war. However, the decision to make treasury notes legal tender helped keep inflation in check. Many people expected that as unemployment declined because of wartime production, wages would rise in proportion to prices. Unfortunately for northern workers, real wages declined by about 20 percent. In 1864, a six-member family needed $18.50 to live in New York City, but most only made $16.

16.5.2 Conscription during the Civil War

In the South, as in the North, the first months of the war witnessed an enthusiastic swell of voluntarism. However, as the war dragged on, both sides found it difficult to recruit the numbers needed to continue the military effort. A Confederate general wrote from Virginia in 1861 that "the full flush of patriotism led many a man to join who now regrets it. The prospect of winter here is making the men very restless and they are beginning to resort to all sorts of means to get home."[75] The Confederate government tried enticing men to re-enlist once their one-year service was up, promising $50 bounty and a one month's furlough. Enlistment still lagged, and so in March 1862, Robert E. Lee, who served as Davis's military advisor, recommended that the government pass a conscription law.

The Confederate government complied and became the first government in the nation's history to enact a mandatory draft; the *Conscription Act*, passed in April 1862, was amended almost immediately to exclude any man who owned more than 20 slaves. Exempted also were militia officers, civil servants, clergymen, and teachers. It was permitted for draftees to hire substitutes; by 1863 the usual substitution rate was $6,000 in confederate money or $600 in gold. A common saying in both parts of the country hinted at the resentment that was building: the struggle was "a rich man's war but a poor man's fight."[76]

By early 1863, it was obvious that the North, like the South, would have to adopt mandatory conscription, and on March 3, the U.S. Congress passed the *Enrollment Act* which made all physically fit citizens and aliens who had filed for naturalization eligible for the draft. It allowed no exemptions by occupation, as was the case with the similar Confederate law, but did include just as many instances of substitution. The *Enrollment Act* established quotas by district equal to the number of eligible soldiers in the district, minus the number who had already served; as enlistments declined, districts began to bid against each other to fill their quotas. Historian James McPherson comments, "By 1864 it was possible for recruits in some districts to parlay federal, state and local bounties into a total payment of more than $1,000."[77]

16.5.3 Protests and Rioting in New York

Almost as soon as Congress passed the *Enrollment Act* protests began throughout the North, particularly in light of the fact that the wealthy could fairly easily "buy" a replacement. Fanned by the fear (promoted by pro-slavery speakers) that free blacks would take the jobs of draftees who were away at the front, northerners began to riot against the unjustness of the draft; these riots reflected a great deal of racial tension. The Democratic governor of New York, Horatio Seymour, reminded a large crowd at a Fourth of July celebration that the national government was acting in an unconstitutional manner by "forcing men into an 'ungodly conflict' waged on behalf of the black man."[78] Seymour also sent emissaries to meet with Lincoln to convince the president that the draft would unfairly target Irish workers. The *New York Daily News* affirmed that the purpose of the draft was obviously "to kill off Democrats."[79] Other newspapers would ultimately join the fray, some denigrating the law, some denigrating those who became rioters. On July 11, 1863, the first draftees were selected by lottery in New York City; their names appeared in the newspapers the following day, the same day that the casualty lists arrived from Gettysburg. Within two days a heinous riot broke out which many historians regard as one of the worst race riots in U.S. history. Fed by racism, fear, and the fact that most men could not afford the $300 exemption fee, demonstrations broke out and quickly turned to violence. Much of this violence was directed at New York blacks whom whites feared would take the jobs of those who were conscripted. On July 13, the mob first attacked and burned a draft office in Manhattan and then turned on an orphanage that housed over 200 black children. A contemporary described the scene in this manner:

> Toward evening the mob, furious as demons, went yelling over to the Colored-Orphan Asylum in 5th Avenue...and rolling a barrel of kerosene in it, the whole structure was soon in a blaze, and is now a smoking ruin. What has become of the 300 poor innocent orphans I could not learn. They must have had some warning of what the rioters intended; & I trust the children were removed in time to escape a cruel death.

The children escaped, thanks to the work of the New York City fire fighters and a stander-by, identified only as an "unknown Irishman," who called out, "If there's a man among you with a heart within him, come and help these poor children."[80] Although the children slipped away, no one learned what happened to the "generous spirited man."[81] Other blacks were not as fortunate as those in the orphanage: "Many were stoned and beaten and several were lynched." The rioters went from the orphanage toward Harlem where they "burned the aged-Colored Woman's Home on 65th Street."[82] When a British visitor asked about the violence to American blacks, his response was "Oh, sir, they hate them here...they are the innocent cause of all of these troubles."[83]

The rioters also focused their destruction on wealthy New Yorkers, whom they thought must be Republicans, both in the streets and in their Manhattan mansions. The office of Horace Greeley, a noted abolitionist and peace supporter, was burned and the New York police force threatened as it attempted to quell the rioting. After four days, and the arrival of several thousand military troops, the rioting ended; eleven black men had been lynched, more than 100 people had been killed and 400 more injured. Property damage was estimated at $1.5 million. But the draft continued, and when the next round was announced, forty-three regiments were moved to New York City to maintain order.[84] The riot in New York was one of many in cities throughout the United States, as those enduring the war on the "home front" reacted to stress, scarcity, loss and fear. In the South, though there were protests, none rivaled that of the New York race riot.

16.5.4 Bread Riots in the Confederacy

For the civilian population of the Confederacy, the war brought more than the usual sufferings of having their families torn apart as the men went off to fight. The impact of the war on the Confederate home front was devastating, growing worse with each passing year. By 1863, the situation had become so dire in urban areas as to lead to the Bread Riots.

Early Bread Riots

In the spring of 1863, the Confederate economy was straining under the burden of war. The local, state, and national governments all made attempts to hold down prices and keep the economy moving but to no avail. Many farmers still focused on cash crops of tobacco and cotton which could be stored for later sale in the hopes things would improve rather than on growing food to sell. Other farmers had their crop production disrupted by the opposing armies marching through their area. Much of what food was produced was purchased by the Confederate government for the war effort as the troops in the field needed to be fed. Population levels rose in the cities as workers were needed for the factories, hospitals, and prisons. Outbreaks of smallpox, dysentery, and tuberculosis were common in the overcrowded hospitals and prisons and on occasion spread to the civilian population. Crowded conditions in the cities left few options for producing food. The result of these various factors was deprivation and even starvation among the civilian population in the cities of the South.

Atlanta, Georgia, Mobile, Alabama, Salisbury, North Carolina, and Petersburg, Virginia were all sites of bread riots in early 1863.[85] In the case of Salisbury, the first troops from the area tended to be young and unmarried, but the next wave of troops, taken in 1862, were the older, married men who were forced to leave their wives and children to fend for themselves. Within months these families were in dire straits, and the local government did nothing to aid them, leading to a bread riot on March 18, 1863.[86]

The Richmond Bread Riot

News of bread riots further south reached Richmond in late March. By April, a group of women were ready to have their own riot in Richmond. The core group of rioters gathered in Richmond's Capitol Square near the equestrian statue of George Washington with the intention of speaking to Governor John Letcher. A woman who witnessed the gathering wrote of the pitiful near-skeletal condition of one of the rioters and their intentions to gain bread.[87] Governor Letcher refused to speak with them, so the rioters marched away to the business district, attracting followers as they went, and swelling their number to the hundreds, possibly thousands. Realizing too late the serious intentions of the rioters, Governor Letcher, along with the mayor of Richmond Joseph Mayo, attempted to disburse the crowd with no real effect: the rioters would simply move off to a new location.

Homes as well as businesses were robbed. The large group of women who attacked the stores on Main Street was fairly calm, taking each store as they reached it. Others, such as boys, were more haphazard, smashing doors and windows, grabbing what they could and running away. Bystanders watched but generally did not interfere. A Confederate officer, Major John W. Daniel wrote an account several years later of what he experienced when he tried to stop one looting lady,

> "While I was gazing at the scene," said the Major, "I saw a captain of a cavalry regiment, with whom I had a slight acquaintance. We were both in uniform. We agreed that something ought to be done to restore order and stop the robbery. At his suggestion we stationed ourselves at the door of a store already overrun. In a few seconds a virazo[sic] [virago] tried to pass us. . . . She carried in her arms a half dozen bars of yellow soap, a piece of dress silk, a long box of stockings, and some raisins and herrings." I said: "'. . . These goods are not yours. You have not paid for them, and you will not be permitted to leave this store with them."
>
> "She looked at me," said the Major, "in a wild way . . . and then went to the counter and threw down the goods. As she came back she deliberately took me by the arm and slung me from her with such force that I went spinning around like a top, and struck the front of the building so hard that it took the breath out of me. She then quickly gathered up her load from the counter and walked out.[88]

It was left to Confederate President Jefferson Davis to personally handle the situation. According to various accounts, Davis addressed the group, offering sympathy, money from his own pockets, a promise to provide food, and a threat to have the City Guard open fire and shoot everyone if they did not clear the streets. Davis succeeded in persuading the rioters to leave, and calm was restored. Several of the rioters were arrested with their hearings dragging on through the summer and into fall.

While many had a legitimate cause, others did use the event to commit crime. According to the Richmond *Examiner*, the rioters wanted anything but bread. When offered flour and rice as promised by Davis, many of them dropped it in the streets, preferring to rob stores of clothing and other items instead. The Richmond *Examiner* described the rioters as "a handful of prostitutes, professional thieves, Irish and Yankee hags, gallows-birds from all lands but our own...with a woman huckster at their head, who buys veal at the toll gate for a hundred and sells the same for two hundred and fifty in the morning market..."[89]

The "huckster" was Mary Jackson, described in a later article in the *Examiner* as, "a good specimen of a forty year old Amazon, with the eye of the Devil" who came to town that day brandishing a bowie knife and later a pistol as well as the knife and demanding "bread or blood," exciting the crowd and threatening people.[90]

In fact not all of the rioters were of a notorious nature. One particularly prominent person arrested was Dr. Thomas Palmer, surgeon at the Florida or Davenport Hospital. During the war there was a designated hospital in Richmond for soldiers from each state. Dr. Palmer tended to the injured troops from Florida. He had been on the corner of 15th and Main when Governor Letcher arrived and ordered the crowd there to disburse. Those present did leave as ordered–except Dr. Palmer. Dr. Palmer was not rioting for bread, nor was he looting stores. He refused to obey first the Governor and then the Mayor in an apparent spontaneous protest against the government. When the rioters in the area moved on, they left Dr. Palmer alone to face the governor and mayor. He was arrested.[91]

More Bread Riots

The Bread Riots indicated the suffering felt by the common people and their frustration with governments that offered no effective solutions. While bread and other foods and goods were available, the cost to the average person was too high to be affordable. One tell-tale sign of the desperation of the times was a cookbook published in Richmond in 1863. The *Confederate Receipt Book. A Compilation of over One Hundred Receipts, Adapted to the Times* offered among its recipes directions for curing meat without salt, making apple pie without apples, and even coffee without coffee beans.[92]

Although the President of the Confederacy personally stepped in to quell the Richmond riot, bread riots continued to occur throughout the South for the duration of the war as localities struggled with the impossible task of providing for the war and providing for the people at the same time. Cities such as Savannah and Mobile saw women take to the streets to demand relief. The September 1863 bread riot in Mobile, Alabama was typical. The women took to the streets, shouting "Bread!" and demanding an end to their suffering. The Army, in this case the 17th Alabama, was ordered to put down the riot but refused to attack the families of fellow soldiers. Then the local Mobile Cadets were ordered to disburse the women but were themselves driven away instead.[93] The riots normally were small and did little to alleviate the suffering of the families beyond providing an outlet for their frustrations with the war. While there had been arrests made of the ringleaders in the Richmond riot which had been unusually large, most rioters in Richmond and elsewhere were allowed to just go home.

16.5.5 The Emancipation Proclamation

From the northern perspective, the first year and a half of the Civil War continued, to be a war for union. As the war dragged on, and particularly as the Union cause flagged in the field in mid-1862, Abraham Lincoln was already considering a move that would drastically change the character of the war. Shifting to a position that he would not have held a year earlier, Lincoln began to embrace emancipation of the slaves as a war measure. From the time the war broke out, free blacks had tried to enlist in the Union army, but the president, his cabinet, and most Republicans opposed this move. Lincoln commented in spring 1862 that "to arm the Negroes would turn 50,000 bayonets from the loyal border states against us that were for us."[94] William Lloyd Garrison, avid abolitionist and editor of the abolitionist newspaper *The Liberator*, dubbed Lincoln, himself evidently indecisive on the issue of emancipation "nothing but a wet rag."[95] In fact, one of the reasons that Lincoln was an attractive candidate for the Republicans in 1860, according to James McPherson was that "he was viewed neither as an abolitionist nor an advocate of racial equality."[96] Although he believed the phrase "all men are created equal" from the Declaration of Independence was accurate, he feared the outcome should large numbers of slaves become freedmen; the differences in the two races might be too severe to overcome. Indeed five months into the war, Lincoln had made the remark that the Negro "had nothing to do with" the war and should not be "dragged into it."[97] Perhaps the following comment sums up his vacillation on the topic of manumission: "If I could save the Union without freeing any slave, I would do it, and if I could save the Union by freeing all the slaves, I would do it, and if I could save it by freeing some and leaving others alone, I would also do that."[98] And in 1862, he mused, "unexpected and unplanned 'events,' not he, had controlled his policy toward emancipation."[99]

By July, Lincoln had concluded that he should move ahead with emancipation. One reason was military. Slaves working in the field freed up southerners to fight against the Union. The loss of its slaves would seriously cripple the South's ability to fight. The assumption, of course, was that southern states would pay any attention at all to an order issued by the Union president. Also, adding emancipation to the Union cause would open the door for the recruitment of African Americans as soldiers, augmenting the available manpower of the Union army. Another consideration was diplomacy. If the Union embraced emancipation, thus including the eradication of slavery in the Union cause, then British recognition of the Confederacy would become problematic; the anti-slavery British public and English attempts to suppress the slave trade over the previous decade would make supporting the pro-slavery South incongruous. As James McPherson notes, it was obvious that Lincoln could not satisfy everyone, but "he hoped that [proclaiming emancipation] would reenergize those citizens who might support emancipation and black enlistment if they thought that would help bring the Union victory."[100]

Lincoln waited for the Union victory at Antietam to issue the preliminary Emancipation Proclamation on September 22, 1862. It stated that the slaves in those areas still in rebellion against the United States were "henceforth and forever free," insisting that this move was a "military necessity...absolutely essential to the preservation of the Union."[101] The statement also endorsed voluntary colonization of freed slaves (in other words, sending them back to Africa) and called on loyal states to effect "gradual emancipation." On December 1, Lincoln addressed Congress and in his message recommended a Constitutional amendment providing for compensated emancipation, one that would be gradual (actually extending the termination date to 1900) to apply to "every state where it now exists."[102] Democrats mistakenly thought this pronouncement suggested that Lincoln was backing down on emancipation. This was not the case, however, and on January 1, 1863, final Proclamation was signed and put into effect. The document proclaimed that slaves were freed in those Southern states that were not occupied by Union troops.

Southern areas to which the Proclamation did not apply were several counties in Virginia, several parishes in Louisiana, and the whole state of Tennessee. These areas were occupied by Union troops and therefore considered to be part of the Union. It appears that in the Emancipation Proclamation Lincoln was not so much creating a general measure to end slavery, but one rather to punish those areas involved in rebellion.

Not surprisingly, reaction to the Emancipation Proclamation was mixed. In the North, while some abolitionists praised the measure, others pointed out that the Proclamation freed only those slaves in areas still in rebellion against the Union, and thus not all slaves in all areas. Was this really a strong statement on slavery? And in fact, by exempting those areas under Union control, including the North, what impact did it really have? Surely the areas of the South not under Union control had no intention of paying any attention to the Proclamation. Secretary of State, William Seward, stated the opinion of many when he said, "Where he could, he didn't. Where he did, he couldn't."[103] Southern leaders universally denounced the proclamation as an incitement to riot, calling it a typical Republican trick, while the London *Spectator* quipped that the Proclamation's message was "not that a human being could not own another, but that he cannot unless he is loyal to the United States."[104] James McPherson insists, however, that criticisms such as those of the *Spectator* missed the point. The Proclamation was a war strategy "directed against enemy resources,"[105] and re-defined a "revolutionary new war aim: the overthrow of slavery by force of arms...A new union without slavery."[106] Early in 1863, Lincoln approved the enlistment of freed slaves in the Union army, writing to Andrew Johnson, military governor of Tennessee, "The bare sight of fifty thousand armed, and drilled black soldiers on the banks of the Mississippi would end the rebellion at once. And who doubts that we can present that sight?"[107]

Ultimately, the Emancipation Proclamation had far-reaching effects. The British government moved even further away from possibly recognizing southern nationhood. In short order, nearly 200,000 black soldiers were raised to bolster the Union ranks and helped swing the tide of the war in the Union's favor. Finally, the death knell sounded for slavery. In Lincoln's Second Inaugural Address, he invoked Old Testament language when he proclaimed, "American slavery is one of those offences which in the providence of God...He now wills to remove [through] this terrible war, as the woe due to those by whom the offence came...Fondly do we hope-fervently do we pray-that this mighty scourge of war may speedily pass away."[108]

Although Lincoln did not live to see the passage of a Constitutional amendment, he realized that one would be necessary to give emancipation the force of law, and so from the time the Proclamation was released, had thrown his support toward such a move. By spring 1864, the movement for an amendment abolishing slavery in the country gained momentum. In early 1865, Congress passed the Thirteenth Amendment and sent it to the states. In December 1865, eight months after Robert E. Lee's surrender at Appomattox Courthouse and the assassination of Lincoln, the amendment became law and neither "slavery nor involuntary servitude, except as a punishment for crime whereof the party shall have been duly convicted, shall exist within the United States, or any place subject to their jurisdiction." Thus slavery ended in the United States.

16.5.6 Black Americans and the War

When the Emancipation Proclamation took effect in January 1863, there was little immediate impact on slaves in the South. The Proclamation freed only those slaves held in states still in rebellion against the Union and slave owners in those states had no intention of supporting widespread manumission for many reasons, including the fact that they did not recognize federal law. And the slaves themselves did not engage in the rioting and looting predicted by Southern political leaders. On the other hand, as 1863 progressed and the presence of Union troops was more common in the South, slaves became restive and began to seize and redistribute property. These "freedmen" also tended to flock to federal camps. General Ulysses S. Grant commented that with the approach of union forces slaves fled the plantations and "flocked in vast numbers—an army in themselves—to the camps of the Yankees." What the Union troops witnessed was a slave population "springing from barbarism...forsaking its local traditions and all the associations of the old plantation life... with feet shod or bleeding, individually or in families...an army of slaves and fugitives pushing its way irresistibly toward an army of fighting men."[109] The account of General H.W. Slocum, who accompanied Sherman, is similar:

> The advance of Sherman's army...was known far and wide many miles in advance of us. It was natural that these poor creatures (the slaves), seeking a place of safety, should flee to the army, and endeavor to keep in sight of it. Every day, as we marched on we could see, on each side of our line of march, crowds of these people coming to us through roads and across the fields, bringing with them all of their earthly goods, and many goods which were not theirs. Horses, mules, cows, dogs, old family carriages, carts, and whatever they thought might be of use...They were allowed to follow in the rear of our column, and at times they were almost equal in number to the army they were following.[110]

To take care of these swelling populations living among his army in Tennessee, Grant assigned a chaplain, John Eaton of the Twenty-seventh Ohio Infantry, to set up a camp that would provide housing, food, and medical care for the blacks. By July 1864, almost 115,000 previous slaves were employed and living in the camps. Able-bodied men were engaged in service: 41,000 in military service as cooks, soldiers, servants, or laborers; the rest were in private service as mechanics, farm laborers, or blacksmiths.

Blacks in the Military

Although African Americans did eventually serve in significant numbers in the Union army and navy, it was not until 1863 that this practice began. And while it is understandable that the Confederacy would be reluctant to employ black soldiers, it is somewhat harder to understand why that was the case in the Union. It appears that while Union troops were willing to accept blacks as laborers in the military, they were much less willing to accept them as fellow soldiers. In addition, the Union Congress was evidently concerned about the reaction of the Border States to black troops, so it "refused to enlist even free blacks."[111] In fact, until 1863, it was common practice in Union armies fighting in Virginia and Tennessee to return escaped slaves to their masters rather than enroll them in the ranks of the army.

The Second Confiscation and Militia Act of July 17, 1862 marked the first official authorization to employ African Americans in federal military service. This act allowed President Lincoln to receive into the military persons of African descent for any purpose "he may judge best for the public welfare." However, the President himself did not take advantage of this authority until the official issuance of the Emancipation Proclamation in January 1863.

Historian James Robertson maintains that "no blacks were officially accepted into Confederate military service."[112] His reason for saying this is that if there had been black units this would have inevitably surfaced in the voluminous military records of the war. He points out, however, that in the last months of the war, when troops were in short supply, the Confederate Congress authorized the recruitment of black soldiers. Only about three dozen men answered the call, and they never saw military action, nor were they allowed to carry weapons. Howell Cobb of Georgia commented on the issue of receiving blacks into military service, "Enlisting slaves as Confederate troops would be the beginning of the end of the Revolution. If slaves make good soldiers our whole theory of slavery is wrong."[113]

Some historians point out that though blacks in the Confederate army were not soldiers nor were there black Confederate regiments, both freedmen and slaves did serve as cooks, musicians, and common laborers. And others explain that some states, ignoring the official position of the Confederate government, called for the conscription of "free persons of color." There were also instances in which Union commanders reported witnessing blacks fighting with the armies of the Confederate States. Union Colonel John Gibson Parkhurst, for example, recorded about the battle at Murfreesboro, Tennessee, "The forces attacking my camp were the First Regiment Texas Rangers, a battalion of the First Georgia Rangers, ... and quite a number of Negroes attached to the Texas and Georgia troops, who were armed and equipped, and took part in the several engagements with my forces during the day."[114]

Violence against Blacks in the North and South

A good deal of violence occurred toward blacks during the Civil War. The draft riots that took place in New York City in July 1863 quickly turned into racial violence. In addition to the instances mentioned earlier, the *New York Times,* July 15, 1863 reported that a "colored seaman's boarding house" was attacked, its residents removed, robbed and burned, that a liquor store was burned "on account of a colored woman taking refuge there," and that "a gang of nearly 500 rioters attacked the colored people residing at Nos. 104 and 105 Park street [in the Sixth Ward], drove them into the street, assaulting them with stones and other missiles." Those who were attacked "look perfectly bewildered—they are unable to designate between friend or foe. Many have lost all they ever had in the world, and some of them may become charges on the county."[115]

Racial prejudice also reared its ugly head during military action, especially in several notorious battles. One of the worst massacres of black troops occurred at Fort Pillow, Tennessee, though this was not an isolated incident. When the Confederate Army began to have morale problems in 1864, soldiers took their frustration out on the enemy in what David J. Eicher, calls "one of the bleakest, saddest events of American military history."[116]

Confederate soldiers under the command of Major General Nathan Bedford Forrest mercilessly slaughtered black Union soldiers on April 12, 1864 after the battle of Fort

Pillow, Tennessee. The incident quickly became known throughout the North, fanning the flames of hatred of the South. The *New York Times* reported on April 24, "The blacks and their officers were shot down, bayoneted and put to the sword in cold blood...Out of four hundred Negro soldiers only about twenty survive! At least three hundred of them were destroyed after the surrender! This is the statement of the rebel General Chalmers himself to our informant."[117] Similar slaughters occurred at Poison Spring, Arkansas and Petersburg, Virginia. At Poison Spring the Confederates successfully routed the Union army under Colonel James M. Williams, whose forces included the First Kansas Colored Infantry. After the retreat, the colored infantry were massacred by the Confederates and their Indian allies.

In concluding this section on the experiences of African Americans in the war years, it might be enlightening to read the letter of a twenty-one year old black Union soldier serving in the 55th Massachusetts to his wife:

> Dear Wife i have enlisted in the army . . . and though great is the present national dificulties yet i look forward to a brighter day When i shall have the opertunity of seeing you in the full enjoyment of fredom i would like to no if you are still in slavery if you are it will not be long before we shall have crushed the system that now opreses you for in the course of three months you shall have your liberty. great is the outpouring of the colered peopl that is now rallying with the hearts of lions against that very curse that has seperated you an me . . . i am a soldier now and i shall use my utmost endeavor to strike at the rebellion and the heart of this system that so long has kept us in chains...[118]
>
> Samuel Cabble
>
> [sic]

16.5.7 Before You Move On...

Key Concepts

The war created stress on the home front as well as on the front lines, and the anxiety that the populations in both regions felt because of the fighting and the fear of losing loved ones was exacerbated by such issues as manumission (freeing of the slaves), conscription, and the abundance, or lack thereof, of food. The draft riots in New York combined two of the three as men, facing an arbitrary conscription, were afraid that the jobs they left would be taken by freedmen, who would inevitably, once freed, leave the South for the North. Nerves were raw and the slightest disturbance could turn into full-fledged rioting. Nowhere was this more evident than in New York City and Richmond, Virginia, as citizens protested the draft and the effects of a runaway inflation. All of these events occurred in the seven months between January 1 and July 11, 1863; the Emancipation Proclamation was made official January 1; the Richmond bread riots took place in April and the New York City draft riots in July. It appeared to many Americans that the world had indeed turned upside down.

Test Yourself

1. Which of the following statements is true of the *Emancipation Proclamation*?

a. It allowed Lincoln to follow through on his campaign promises and finally eliminate slavery from the Union.

b. It was a military measure based on the congressional power to confiscate the property of traitors.

c. It freed the slaves of any state in open rebellion against the Union, based on military necessity.

d. It freed all slaves, and was passed only reluctantly due to Lincoln's feeling that it would divide the Union.

2. During the draft riots in New York City, the rioters targeted the ______ population of New York City:

a. Irish

b. Polish

c. Catholic

d. Black

3. The main common feature of all the Bread Riots is that they were all led by women. Why?

a. Women are natural riot organizers.

b. There were few men around; most were off to war.

c. Bread is a domestic issue, women handle domestic issues.

d. Men did not want to be involved.

4. Bread Riots occurred in which of the following cities?

a. Boston, Washington, Richmond

b. Atlanta, Mobile, Richmond

c. New York, Chicago, Mobile

d. Atlanta, Washington, Baltimore

5. The incident at Fort Pillow, Tennessee, is an example of the _______ that was/were a constant problem during the war.

a. Abolitionism

b. Pacifism

c. Treasonous activities

d. Racism

See page 638 for answers

16.6 Conclusion

When the Civil War broke out in April 1861 after Confederate forces fired on Union forces at Fort Sumter in Charleston, no one expected the war to last more than a few months. Northerners thought they could quickly put down the southern rebellion; southerners believed they could quickly secure their independence. Unfortunately, the conflict dragged on for four years in which the South seemed initially poised for victory, but the North eventually turned the tide of war and marched to victory in 1865.

By the time Lincoln took the oath of office for a second time, much had changed in American life, as evidenced by the fact that blacks composed, according to some estimates, half of those at the inauguration. While Lincoln remained reluctant to speculate on the war's end, he did take the opportunity to suggest what the postwar world might look like. He focused, according to historian Eric Foner, on the entire "nation's obligation to the slaves" and "the process of reconciliation." However, only after Lee surrendered to Grant at Appomattox could Lincoln truly face the challenges of reuniting a broken nation. On April 11, 1865, the president addressed a Washington crowd celebrating the North's victory. Lincoln gave no specifics about his postwar plans, but he seemingly supported extending the right to vote to black men. After the speech, most observers thought Lincoln remained unsure about what to do. However, one man in attendance that evening, John Wilkes Booth, concluded the president wanted to make former slaves citizens.[119]

Booth and several other pro-Confederate sympathizers had for some time been planning an elaborate scheme to kidnap the president and other government leaders to exchange for Confederate prisoners of war. The idea that blacks might become citizens was too much for Booth to take, and he vowed to kill the president. On the evening of April 14, 1865, Good Friday, Abraham Lincoln attended a production at the Ford's Theater. Booth stepped out from behind the curtains in the presidential box, fired his derringer pistol, and mortally wounded Lincoln. After dropping the gun, Booth managed to escape. Meanwhile, a doctor in the audience took the president to a boarding house across the street where he tried to revive him. Unfortunately, the bullet entered the president's brain and caused too much damage. Shortly after 7:00 the next morning, Abraham Lincoln died from his wounds.[120]

A sense of mourning and anger swept over the nation. Millions of Americans viewed Lincoln's remains as the funeral train snaked across the country to his home in Springfield, Illinois. Meanwhile, federal authorities tracked Booth to a barn near Bowling Green, Virginia. After giving him the option to surrender, the authorities set fire to the barn. They later found Booth dead, apparently of a self-inflicted gunshot wound. The government then captured, tried, and executed several of his co-conspirators.

With Lincoln dead, Andrew Johnson, a unionist from Tennessee, became president. No one quite knew what the future would bring, but they certainly recognized the costs of the war had been great. Financially speaking, the war cost the two sides billions of dollars, with the South facing the worst property damage and loss. But the human toll seemed much worse. The South lost at least 260,000 people to battle death and disease; the North lost over 360,000 to the same. Collectively, approximately 472,000 people suffered from

Figure 16.20 Abraham Lincoln's Assassination | This Currier and Ives print from 1865 depicted John Wilkes Booth shooting Abraham Lincoln in the presidential box at Ford's Theater on April 14, 1865.

Author: Currier & Ives
Source: Library of Congress

battle-related wounds. At the same time, the war freed the slaves and nothing in American life would really be the same again.[121]

The Civil War brought significant changes to American life. Although the cause held people together, the war exposed political, economic, and social fissures in both the North and the South that would continue to play out during Reconstruction and beyond. Politically, the war ushered in an era where the federal government dominated the states. Economically, the war undermined the South's plantation economy and strengthened the North's industrial economy. Socially, the war created tensions between the rich and the poor, resulting in draft riots and bread riots. Moreover, it led to the emancipation of enslaved blacks. Little about American life was the same after the Civil War.

16.7 CRITICAL THINKING EXERCISES

- What was there about Abraham Lincoln's personality that made him an effective leader? Did Jefferson Davis have these same qualities? Why or why not?
- In the years following the Civil War, the United States underwent massive industrialization and economic growth. What policies enacted during the war, do you think, helped to contribute to that growth?
- Abraham Lincoln was convinced that freeing the southern slaves would bring a speedy end to the war. Why did he think this? Did the Emancipation Proclamation accomplish this end?
- Why do you think the Irish of New York City were so opposed to the Enrollment Act of 1863?
- What could the governments, local, state and Confederate, have done to prevent the Bread Riots?
- Why was there opposition to drafting African Americans to fight in the War by both Northerners and Southerners?
- What do you think made Lincoln release the following memo prior to the election of 1864? Does he intend to say that he was against continuing the war?

> To Whom it may concern: Any proposition which embraces the restoration of peace, the integrity of the whole Union, and the abandonment of slavery, and which comes by and with an authority that can control the armies now at war against the United States will be received and considered by the Executive government of the United States, and will be met by liberal terms on other substantial and collateral points.

16.8 KEY TERMS

- Antietam
- Appomattox Court House
- Atlanta Campaign
- Baltimore Riot
- Blockades
- John Wilkes Booth
- Bread Riot
- Bureau of Colored Troops
- Salmon P. Chase
- Chattanooga
- Confederate Confiscation Act
- Confederate Congress
- Conscription
- Constitution of the Confederate States of America
- Jefferson Davis
- Despot
- Draft Riots
- Election of 1864
- Emancipation

- Emancipation Proclamation
- Enrollment Act, 1863
- Executive order
- Federal
- Fiat Money
- First Manassas (Bull Run)
- Fort Pillow, Tennessee
- Fort Sumter
- Gettysburg
- Ulysses S. Grant
- Habeas Corpus
- Inflation
- Internal Revenue Act of 1862
- Mary Jackson
- Joseph E. Johnston
- Robert E. Lee
- Legal Tender Act of 1862
- Governor John Letcher
- Abraham Lincoln
- Lincoln's First Inaugural Address
- Lincoln's Second Inaugural Address
- Manumission
- March to the Sea
- Mayor Joseph Mayo
- Christopher G. Memminger
- Montgomery, Alabama Convention
- National Bank Acts of 1863 and 1864
- Peace Democrats/Copperheads
- "Radical" Republicans
- Richmond Bread Riot
- Richmond, Virginia
- Second Confiscation and Militia Act
- Seven Days
- William T. Sherman
- Shiloh
- States' Rights in the South
- Thirteenth Amendment
- Treason Act, Union
- Vicksburg
- "War" Democrats

16.9 CHRONOLOGY

The following chronology is a list of important dates and events associated with this chapter.

Date	Event
December 1860	South Carolina seceded from the Union; Mississippi, Florida, Alabama, Georgia, Louisiana, and Texas followed suit.
February 1861	Confederate States of America created at the Montgomery, Alabama Conference; Confederate States of America adopted a provisional Constitution; Jefferson Davis chosen as provisional President and Alexander Stephens for Vice President of the Confederacy

Date	Event
March 1861	Abraham Lincoln inaugurated for his first term as President of the United States of America Lincoln used emergency powers to a degree not yet seen in the U.S. Presidency; Confederate States of America adopted a permanent Constitution; Davis called for 75,000 volunteers to serve in the Confederate Army
April 1861	Confederate forces fired on Union forces at Charleston (Fort Sumter); Lincoln issued a Proclamation calling for 75,000 militiamen and summoned a special session of Congress for July 4; Baltimore Riot occurred on April 19 Virginia seceded from the Union
May 1861	Arkansas and North Carolina seceded from the Union; Confederate Congress recognized that a state of war existed between the Confederate States of America and the United States of America; Confederate government began to issue treasury notes (cheap currency) to pay for the war; Lincoln issued a Proclamation of Blockade against Southern ports
June 1861	Tennessee declared its independence, effectively seceding from the Union
July 1861	U.S. Congress assembled in a special session First Manassas or First Battle of Bull Run fought
August 1861	Confederate Congress enacted a direct tax on personal property; Union Congress enacted the nation's first income tax and raised the nation's tariff rates
February 1862	Union Congress approved the Legal Tender Act; Salmon P. Chase appointed Jay Cooke as the official marketer of U.S. war bonds
April 1862	First Confederate Conscription Act passed through Congress; Habeas Corpus suspended in the Union and the Confederate States; Shiloh fought
July 1862	Union Congress enacted the Internal Revenue Act Preliminary Emancipation Act presented to Lincoln's Cabinet; Confiscation and Militia Act of July 17, 1862: the first official authorization to employ African Americans in federal service; Seven Days fought
September 1862	Antietam fought

Date	Event
January 1863	Final *Emancipation Proclamation* introduced into Congress; First black regiment in the North raised by Governor John Andres of Massachusetts
February 1863	Union Congress approved the National Banking Act, sometimes referred to as the National Currency Act
March 1863	John Slidell negotiated a loan for the Confederacy secured by future cotton sales; Confederate Congress passed the Impressment Act; Bread riots began the South including in Atlanta, Mobile, and Salisbury; First Union *Conscription Act* adopted
April 1863	Richmond Bread Riot occurred on April 2; Confederate Congress enacted a comprehensive tax policy including an income tax and a tax-in-kind on agricultural products
May 1863	Bureau of Colored Troops, under the War Department, established to coordinate and organize regiments; Black troops performed admirably at the assault on Fort Hudson; Vicksburg began
June 1863	West Virginia, composed of the western counties of Virginia, admitted to the Union
July 1863	54th Massachusetts Colored Regiment showed its bravery in the assault on Fort Wagner; Draft Riots occurred in New York City; Gettysburg fought
November 1863	Chattanooga fought
Spring 1864	Peace movements gained momentum in the Union and the Confederate States
April 1864	Massacre at Fort Pillow, Tennessee; Battle at Poison Spring where many men of the 1st Kansas Colored Infantry massacred by Confederate troops
May 1864	Atlanta Campaign began
June 1864	Union Congress passed the National Banking Act of 1864
August 1864	Democrats nominated George B. McClellan for president to run against Republican incumbent Abraham Lincoln

Date	Event
November 1864	Abraham Lincoln was re-elected president, defeating Democrat George B. McClellan. Lincoln carried all but three states with 55 percent of the popular vote and 212 of 233 electoral votes.
December 1864	March to the Sea began
March 1865	Abraham Lincoln inaugurated for his second term as President of the United States of America
April 1865	Confederate government, including Jefferson Davis, fled Richmond; Lee surrendered to Grant at Appomattox Court House; John Wilkes Booth assassinated Abraham Lincoln; Andrew Johnson became president

16.10 BIBLIOGRAPHY

Abraham Lincoln Papers. American Memory Collection, Library of Congress, May 28, 2012. http://memory.loc.gov/ammem/alhtml/alabout.html.

Baker, Gary. "First Blood in the Streets of Baltimore." *Civil War Interactive*, May 27, 2012. http://www.civilwarinteractive.com/ArticleFirstBloodInTheStreetsofBaltimore.htm.

"Bread Riot in Richmond, 1863." *Eyewitness to History* (2009), May 28, 2102. http://www.eyewitnesstohistory.com/breadriot.htm.

Burton, Orville Vernon. *The Age of Lincoln*. New York: Hill and Wang, 2007.

Carwardine, Richard. *Lincoln: A Life of Purpose and Power*. New York: Aflred A. Knoft, 2006.

Chesnut, Mary Boykin. *A Diary from Dixie*. Cambridge, Massachusetts: Harvard University Press, 1962.

City College of New York: *Virtual New York City*. http://www.virtualny.cuny.edu/.

Civil War Trust, June 12, 2012. http://www.civilwar.org/.

Clark, Victor S. "Manufacturing Development During the Civil War." In *The Economic Impact of the American Civil War*, second edition, ed. Ralph Andreano. Cambridge: Shenkman Publishing, 1967.

Confederate Receipt Book: A Compilation of over One Hundred Receipts, Adapted to the Times. Richmond, Virginia: West and Johnston, 1863. Academic Affairs Library, UNC-Chapel Hill, May 28, 2012. http://docsouth.unc.edu/imls/receipt/receipt.html.

Curry, Leonard P. *Blueprint for Modern America: Non-Military Legislation of the First Civil War Congress*. Nashville: Vanderbilt University Press, 1969.

DiLorenzo, Thomas J. *The Real Lincoln: A New Look at Abraham Lincoln*. New York: Random House, 2002.

Eicher, David J. *The Longest Night: A Military History of the Civil War*. New York: Simon & Schuster, 2001.

Faust, Drew Gilpin. *This Republic of Suffering*. New York: Alfred A. Knopf, 2008.

Foner, Eric. *The Fiery Trial: Abraham Lincoln and American Slavery*. New York: W.W. Norton, 2010.

Gallagher, Gary W. *The Confederate War*. Cambridge, Massachusetts: Harvard University Press, 1997.

Goodwin, Doris Kearns. *Team of Rivals: The Political Genius of Abraham Lincoln*. New York: Simon and Schuster, 2005.

Gorman, M. D., Civil War Richmond, May 28, 2012. http://www.mdgorman.com/Events/richmond_bread_riot.htm.

Historynet.com. Weider History Group, June 12, 2012. http://www.historynet.com/.

Hyslop, Stephen G. *Eyewitness to the Civil War*. Washington, D.C.: National Geographic, 2000.

Jones, Terry L. *The American Civil War*. New York: McGraw Hill, 2010.

Lerner, Eugene, M. "Money, Prices, and Wages in the Confederacy, 1861-1865." In *The Economic Impact of the American Civil War*, second edition, ed. Ralph Andreano. Cambridge: Shenkman Publishing, 1967.

McKown, Harry. *This Month in North Carolina History March 1863 -- The Salisbury Bread Riot.* 2005. http://www.lib.unc.edu/ncc/ref/nchistory/mar2005/index.html.

McPherson, James M. *Abraham Lincoln and the Second American Revolution*. New York: Oxford University Press, 1991.

McPherson, James M. *Battle Cry of Freedom: The Civil War Era*. New York: Oxford University Press, 1988.

McPherson, James M. *For Cause and Comrades: Why Men Fought in the Civil War*. New York: Oxford University Press, 1997.

McPherson, James M. *Ordeal by Fire: The Civil War and Reconstruction*. New York: Alfred A Knopf, 1982.

Morison, Samuel Eliot, Henry Steele Commager and William E. Leuchtenbury. *A Concise History of the American Republic*, vol. 1. New York: Oxford University Press, 1977

CWSAC Battle Summaries. American Battlefield Protection Program. Historic Preservation Services, National Parks Service, June 12, 2012. http://www.nps.gov/hps/abpp/battles/tvii.htm.

New Georgia Encyclopedia. Georgia Humanities Council, June 12, 2012. http://www.georgiaencyclopedia.org.

Padgett, Vernon. "Did Blacks Confederates Serve in Combat?" Dixie Sons of Confederate Veterans, May 30, 2012. http://www.dixiescv.org/fact_did-blacks-serve.html.

Peters, Gerhard and John T. Woolley, eds. *The American Presidency Project*, May 28 2012. http://www.presidency.ucsb.edu/inaugurals.php.

Potter, David M. "Jefferson Davis and the Political Factors in Confederate Defeat" in David Donald, ed. *Why the North Won the Civil War*. New York: Touchstone, 1960.

Randall, J.G and David Donald. *The Civil War and Reconstruction*, second edition. Boston: D.C. Heath, 1965.

Robertson, James. *The Untold Civil War: Exploring the Human Side of War*. Washington, D.C.: National Geographic, 2011.

Salsbury, Stephen. "The Effect of the Civil War on American Industrial Development." In *The Economic Impact of the American Civil War*, second edition, ed. Ralph Andreano. Cambridge: Shenkman Publishing, 1967.

The New York Times Archives. *THE BREAD RIOT IN MOBILE; Two Outbreaks in One Day. Arrivals in the City*. http://www.nytimes.com/1863/10/01/news/the-bread-riot-in-mobile-two-outbreaks-in-one-day-arrivals-in-the-city.html.

Thomas, Emory M. *The Confederate Nation: 1861-1865*. New York: Harper Torchbooks, 1979.

Thornton, Mark and Robert B. Ekelund Jr. *Tariffs, Blockades, and Inflation: The Economics of the Civil War*. Wilmington: SR Books, 2004.

Virtual New York City. City College of New York, May 28, 2012. http://www.virtualny.cuny.edu/.

Walthall, Major W.T. "The True Story of the Capture of Jefferson Davis." *Southern Historical Society Papers* (1877), May 28, 2012. http://www.civilwarhome.com/daviscapture.htm.

Weidman, Budge. "The Fight for Civil Rights: Black Soldiers in the Civil War." *Teaching with Documents*, National Archives, http://www.archives.gov/education/.

Winik, Jay. *April 1865: The Month that Saved America*. New York: Harper-Collins, 2001.

16.11 END NOTES

1 James M. McPherson, *For Cause and Comrades: Why Men Fought in the Civil War* (New York: Oxford University Press, 1997).

2 Emory M. Thomas, *The Confederate Nation: 1861-1865* (New York: Harper Torchbooks, 1979), 56-57; James M. McPherson, *Battle Cry of Freedom: The Civil War Era* (New York: Oxford University Press, 1988), 241, 257.

3 Eric Foner, *The Fiery Trial: Abraham Lincoln and American Slavery* (New York: W.W. Norton, 2010), 145-147.

4 Thomas, *The Confederate Nation*, 56-58, 63-64; Orville Vernon Burton, *The Age of Lincoln* (New York: Hill and Wang, 2007), 123.

5 Thomas, *The Confederate Nation*, 59-62; Jefferson Davis, "Inaugural Address of the President of the Provisional Government [February 18, 1861]," *The Avalon Project*, Yale Law School, May 25, 2012, http://avalon.law.yale.edu/19th_century/csa_csainau.asp.

6 Foner, *The Fiery Trial*, 151-153; McPherson, *Battle Cry of Freedom*, 253; Abraham Lincoln to Nathan P. Hale, 11 January 1861, *The Collected Works of Abraham Lincoln*, Volume 4 (Ann Arbor: University of Michigan Digital Library Production Services, 2001), May 25, 2012, http://quod.lib.umich.edu/l/lincoln/lincoln4/1:268?rgn=div1;view=fulltext.

7 McPherson, *Battle Cry of Freedom*, 259-261.

8 McPherson, *Battle Cry of Freedom*, 261-262.

9 Foner, *The Fiery Trial*, 157.

10 Abraham Lincoln, "Inaugural Address," March 4, 1861, *The American Presidency Project*, ed. Gerhard Peters and John T. Woolley, May 25, 2012, http://www.presidency.ucsb.edu/ws/?pid=25818.

11 Foner, *The Fiery Trial*, 161; McPherson, *Battle Cry of Freedom*, 264.

12 McPherson, *Battle Cry of Freedom*, 264-267.

13 McPherson, *Battle Cry of Freedom*, 267-268.

14 McPherson, *Battle Cry of Freedom*, 269-272; Terry L. Jones, *The American Civil War* (New York: McGraw Hill, 2010), 59.

15 McPherson, *Battle Cry of Freedom*, 273; Jones, *The American Civil War*, 59-60; L.P. Walker to P.G.T. Beauregard, 10 April 1861, *The Political History of the United States of America, During the Great Rebellion*, ed. Edward McPherson (Washington: James J. Chapman, 1882), 113.

16 Foner, *The Fiery Trial*, 162-163; Burton, *The Age of Lincoln*, 138; McPherson, *Battle Cry of Freedom*, 284.

17 McPherson, *Battle Cry of Freedom*, 278-281.

18 McPherson, *Battle Cry of Freedom*, 283-284, 297.

19 McPherson, *Battle Cry of Freedom*, 298, 303-304.

20 McPherson, *Battle Cry of Freedom*, 304-306.

21 McPherson, *Battle Cry of Freedom*, 284, 297.

22 McPherson, *Battle Cry of Freedom*, 284-287, 293; Jones, *The American Civil War*, 66-67; Gary Baker, "First Blood in the Streets of Baltimore," *Civil War Interactive*, May 27, 2012, http://www.civilwarinteractive.com/ArticleFirstBloodInTheStreetsofBaltimore.htm.

23 McPherson, *Battle Cry of Freedom*, 290-293; Jones, *The American Civil War*, 68; Thomas, *The Confederate Nation*, 94-95.

24 McPherson, *Battle Cry of Freedom*, 293-297; Jones, *The American Civil War*, 67; Thomas, *The Confederate Nation*, 94.

25 Jones, *The American Civil War*, 61-65.

26 Jones, *The American Civil War*, 65-66.

27 For more information on the various battles of the Civil War, including information on the commanders, summaries of the action, and statistics on casualties, see CWSAC Battle Summaries, The American Battlefield Protection Program, National Parks Service, Historic Preservation Services, September 27, 2012, http://www.nps.gov/hps/abpp/battles/tvii.htm.

28 Jay Winik, *April 1865: The Month that Saved America* (New York: Harper-Collins, 2001), 33.

29 Lee quoted in Winik, *April 1865,* 32.

30 Lee quoted in Gary W. Gallagher, The Confederate War (Cambridge, Massachusetts: Harvard University Press, 1997), 158.

31 Major W.T. Walthall, "The True Story of the Capture of Jefferson Davis," *Southern Historical Society Papers*, 1877, Confederate States of America, Civil War Home, May 25, 2012, http://www.civilwarhome.com/daviscapture.htm.

32 Gallagher, *The Confederate War*, 165.

33 Quoted in Gallagher, *The Confederate War*, 164.

34 Mary Boykin Chesnut, *A Diary from Dixie* (Cambridge, Massachusetts: Harvard University Press, 1962), xix.

35 Quoted in Gallagher, The Confederate War, 169.

36 James M. McPherson, *Ordeal by Fire: The Civil War and Reconstruction* (New York: Alfred A Knopf, 1982), 216.

37 McPherson, *Battle Cry of Freedom*, 216-218.

38 Quoted in J.G. Randall and David Donald. *The Civil War and Reconstruction*, second edition (Boston: D.C. Heath, 1965), 275.

39 Randall and Donald, *The Civil War and Reconstruction*, 276.

40 Quoted in Randall and Donald, *The Civil War and Reconstruction*, 279.

41 Randall and Donald, *The Civil War and Reconstruction*, 280.

42 Woodward quoted Randall and Donald, *The Civil War and Reconstruction*, 280.

43 Treason Act quoted in McPherson, *Ordeal by Fire*, 294.

44 Randall and Donald, The Civil War and Reconstruction, 470.

45 Randall and Donald, *Civil War*, 471.

46 Lincoln quoted in Randall and Donald, *Civil War*, 471.

47 McPherson, Ordeal by Fire, 440.

48 McPherson, *Ordeal by Fire*, 441.

49 McPherson, *Ordeal by Fire*, 441.

50 McPherson, *Ordeal by Fire*, 447.

51 Quoted in McPherson, *Ordeal by Fire*, 448.

52 McPherson, *Ordeal by Fire*, 448.

53 Jones, *The American Civil War*, 308-314.

54 McPherson, *Ordeal by Fire*, 251.

55 Stephens quoted in McPherson, *Ordeal by Fire*, 367.

56 Governor Brown of Georgia quoted in McPherson, *Ordeal by Fire*, 367.

57 Mark Thornton, and Robert B. Ekelund Jr., *Tariffs, Blockades, and Inflation: The Economics of the Civil War* (Wilmington: SR Books, 2004), 66-67.

58 Thomas, *The Confederate Nation*, 72-73; McPherson, *Battle Cry of Freedom*, 439.

59 Fiat Money: Money that is not backed by anything other than a government trust. Fiat money has no intrinsic value; it only has value at all because all participants in an economy agree to trust the government issuing the currency. While deflation is possible for fiat money, it is much more susceptible to inflation. See, "Fiat Money," *Farlex Financial Dictionary*, May 28, 2012, http://financial-dictionary.thefreedictionary.com/Fiat+Money.

60 McPherson, *Battle Cry of Freedom*, 439; Jones, *The American Civil War*, 266.

61 McPherson, *Battle Cry of Freedom*, 438.

62 Jones, *The American Civil War*, 267-268; Thorton and Ekelund, *Tariffs, Blockades, and Inflation*, 31-32, 75.

63 Thorton and Ekelund, *Tariffs, Blockades, and Inflation*, 32-33; McPherson, *Battle Cry of Freedom*, 438.

64 Jones, *The American Civil War*, 270; McPherson, *Battle Cry of Freedom*, 615-616; Thomas, *The Confederate Nation*, 198-199; Thorton and Ekelund, *Tariffs, Blockades, and Inflation*, 75.

65 Thomas, *The Confederate Nation*, 73, 138, 197; McPherson, *Battle Cry of Freedom*, 438-439; Jones, *The American Civil War*, 266.

66 McPherson, *The Battle Cry of Freedom*, 442-443.

67 Burton, *The Age of Lincoln*, 216; Thornton and Ekelund, *Tariffs, Blockades, and Inflation*, 75; Jones, *The American Civil War*, 259; McPherson, *Battle Cry of Freedom*, 443.

68 Jones, *The American Civil War*, 259; McPherson, *Battle Cry of Freedom*, 444.

69 Jones, *The American Civil War*, 260-261; McPherson, *Battle Cry of Freedom*, 4445-447.

70 Richard Grossman, "US Banking History, Civil War to World War II," *EH.Net Encyclopedia*, ed. Robert Whaples, May 22, 2102, http://eh.net/encyclopedia/article/grossman.banking.history.us.civil.war.wwii; Edward Flaherty, "A Brief History of Central Banking in the United States," *From Revolution to Reconstruction*, University of Groningen, May 22, 2012, http://www.let.rug.nl/usa/E/usbank/bank10.htm; McPherson, *Battle Cry of Freedom*, 444-445, 593-594.

71 Burton, *The Age of Lincoln*, 218; Jones, *The American Civil War*, 262; McPherson, *Battle Cry of Freedom*, 447-448.

72 Thorton and Ekelund, *Tariffs, Blockades, and Inflation*, 34-38; McPherson, *Battle Cry of Freedom*, 440.

73 Thomas, *The Confederate Nation*, 199-201; Burton, *The Age of Lincoln*, 203.

74 Thornton and Ekelund, *Tariffs, Blockades, and Inflation*, 73; McPherson, *Battle Cry of Freedom*, 440; Burton, *The Age of Lincoln*, 203-204; Eugene, M. Lerner, "Money, Prices, and Wages in the Confederacy, 1861-1865," in *The Economic Impact of the American Civil War*, second edition, ed. Ralph Andreano (Cambridge: Shenkman Publishing, 1967), 35.

75 McPherson, *Ordeal by Fire*, 181.

76 Quoted in McPherson, *Ordeal by Fire*, 182.

77 McPherson, *Ordeal by Fire*, 356.

78 Quoted in Goodwin, *Team of Rivals,* 356.

79 Goodwin, *Team of Rivals,* 356.

80 Quoted Stephen G. Hyslop, *Eyewitness to the Civil War* (Washington, D.C.: National Geographic, 2000), 248.

81 Anna Shotwell, mistress of the orphanage, quoted in Hyslop, Eyewitness to the Civil War, 248.

82 John Torrey to Asa Gray, July 13, 1863 quoted in Hyslop, *Eyewitness to the Civil War*, 248.

83 Quoted in Hyslop, Eyewitness to the Civil War, 248.

84 Drew Gilpin Faust, *This Republic of Suffering* (New York: Alfred A. Knopf, 2008), 141.

85 Richmond *Examiner*, Saturday, 4/4/1863, Civil War Richmond, May 28, 2012, http://www.mdgorman.com/Written_Accounts/Examiner/1863/richmond_examiner_441863f.htm.

86 Harry McKown, "The Salsbury Bread Riot," This Month in North Carolina History (2005), UNC Libraries, May 28, 2012, http://www.lib.unc.edu/ncc/ref/nchistory/mar2005/index.html.

87 "Bread Riot in Richmond, 1863," The Confederate Home Front, EyeWitness to History (2009), May 28, 2012, http://www.eyewitnesstohistory.com/breadriot.htm.

88 "OUR RICHMOND MOBS SOME EXPERIENCES IN THIS CITY WITH UNRULY MASSES. Two Governors Threatened - The "Bread Riot" - Burning of the Penitentiary and More Recent Exploits," The Richmond Dispatch, 12/16/1888, Civil War Richmond, May 25, 2012, http://www.mdgorman.com/Written_Accounts/Dispatch/Postwar/richmond_dispatch_12161888.htm.

89 The Richmond *Examiner*, Saturday, 4/4/1863, Civil War Richmond, May 28, 2012, http://www.mdgorman.com/Written_Accounts/Examiner/1863/richmond_examiner_441863f.htm.

90 The Richmond *Examiner*, Saturday, 4/4/1863, p.1, Civil War Richmond, May 28, 2012, http://www.mdgorman.com/Written_Accounts/Examiner/1863/richmond_examiner_441863e.htm.

91 The Richmond *Examiner*, Saturday, 4/4/1863, p.1, Civil War Richmond, May 28, 2012, http://www.mdgorman.com/Written_Accounts/Examiner/1863/richmond_examiner_441863e.htm.

92 *Confederate Receipt Book. A Compilation of over One Hundred Receipts, Adapted to the Times* (Richmond, Virginia: West and Johnston, 1863), Academic Affairs Library, UNC-Chapel Hill, May 28, 2012, http://docsouth.unc.edu/imls/receipt/receipt.html.

93 "THE BREAD RIOT IN MOBILE; Two Outbreaks in One Day. Arrivals in the City," The New York Times Archives, May 28, 2012, http://www.nytimes.com/1863/10/01/news/the-bread-riot-in-mobile-two-outbreaks-in-one-day-arrivals-in-the-city.html.

94 Quoted in James Robertson, *The Untold Civil War: Exploring the Human Side of War* (Washington, DC: National Geographic, 2011), 180.

95 Robertson, *Untold Civil War,* 180.

96 Ibid, 180-81.

97 Quoted in Carwardine, *Lincoln*, 191.

98 Quoted Hyslop, *Eyewitness to the Civil War*, 170; Doris Kearns Goodwin, *Team of Rivals* (New York: Simon and Schuster, 2005), 471.

99 Robertson, *Untold Civil War,* 191.

100 Goodwin, *Team of Rivals,* 471;McPherson, Ordeal by Fire, 441.

101 Quoted in Robertson, *Untold Civil War*, 180.

102 McPherson, *Ordeal by Fire*, 297.

103 Quoted in Robertson, *Untold Civil War*, 180.

104 Quoted in McPherson, *Ordeal by Fire,* 298.

105 McPherson, *Ordeal by Fire,* 298.

106 James M. McPherson, Abraham Lincoln and the Second American Revolution (New York: Oxford University Press, 1991), 34.

107 Quoted in McPherson, *Second American Revolution*, 34-35.

108 Abraham Lincoln, "Inaugural Address," March 4, 1865, The American Presidency Project, ed. Gerhard Peters and John T. Woolley, May 28, 2012, http://www.presidency.ucsb.edu/ws/?pid=25819.

109 Grant quoted in Randall and Donald, *The Civil War and Reconstruction*, 38-86.

110 Slocum quoted in Randall and Donald, *The Civil War and Reconstruction*, 384.

111 Samuel Eliot Morison, Henry Steele Commager, and William E. Leuchtenburg. A Concise History of the American Republic, volume 1, (New York: Oxford University Press, 1977), 283.

112 McPherson, *Ordeal by Fire*, 184.

113 Cobb quoted in McPherson, *Ordeal by Fire*, 185.

114 Vernon Padgett, "Did Blacks Confederates Serve in Combat?" http://www.dixiescv.org/fact_did-blacks-serve.html. Padgett includes in his paper a number of eyewitness accounts of blacks in service to the Confederates.

115 "The Reign of Rabble," *New York Times*, July 15, 1863.

116 David Eicher, *The Longest Night: A Military History of the Civil War* (New York: Simon & Schuster, 2001), 23.

117 *New York Times*, April 24 1864.

118 Samuel Cabble to his Wife, *Teaching with Documents*, National Archives, May 30, 2012, http://www.archives.gov/education/lessons/blacks-civil-war/.

119 Foner, *The Fiery Trial*, 325-326, 331-332.

120 Foner, *The Fiery Trial*, 332; "The Assassination of President Abraham Lincoln," *Abraham Lincoln Papers*, American Memory, Library of Congress, May 27, 2012, http://memory.loc.gov/ammem/alhtml/alrintr.html.

121 Foner, *The Fiery Trial*, 332-333; McPherson, *Battle Cry of Freedom*, 854; "The Assassination of Abraham Lincoln."

122 Yancy Hall. *U.S. Civil War Prison Camps Claimed Thousands*, National Geographic, September 26, 2012, http://news.nationalgeographic.com/news/2003/07/0701_030701_civilwarprisons.html.

ANSWER KEY FOR CHAPTER SIXTEEN: THE CIVIL WAR

Check your answers to the questions in the Before You Move On Sections for this chapter.

Correct answers are **BOLDED**

Section 16.2.3 - p584

1. In his first inaugural address, Abraham Lincoln emphasized
   a. the moral wrongness of slavery.
   B. THE PERMANENT NATURE OF THE UNION.
   c. the loyalty of southerners during the Mexican War.
   d. economic development.

2. The Civil War began when
   a. Union forces at Fort Sumter fired on nearby Confederate positions.
   b. Confederate forces at Fort Sumter fired on nearby Union positions.
   c. Union forces fired on Confederate troops stationed in Fort Sumter.
   D. CONFEDERATE FORCES FIRED UPON FORT SUMTER.

3. All of the following were slave states that remained in the Union except
   A. TENNESSEE.
   b. Maryland.
   c. Delaware.
   d. Missouri.

Section 16.3.11 - p602

1. The battle with the most over-all casualties was **GETTYSBURG** and the battle with the most casualties on a single day was **ANTIETAM.**

2. The general who devastated Georgia with his march to the sea was **SHERMAN**.

3 The only two land battles fought outside of Confederate territory were? **ANTIETAM** and **GETTYSBURG**.

4. Grant captured Vicksburg with an effective use of what tactic? **A SIEGE**

5. Maneuvering around the side of an army, rather than attacking directly from the front is called? **A FLANKING MANEUVER**

Section 16.4.4 - p612

1. When the war broke out, Lincoln announced that the war was being fought to free those who were enslaved in the South.
   a. True
   B. FALSE

2. The Copperheads were
   a. War Republicans.
   B. PEACE DEMOCRATS.
   c. Southern deserters.
   d. Northern abolitionists.

3. Habeas Corpus guaranteed in the Bill of Rights is the right of individuals to:
   a. A speedy trial.
   B. BE CHARGED WITH A CRIME IF ARRESTED.
   c. Bear arms.
   d. Practice the religion of his or her choice.

4. Lincoln's opponent in the 1864 Presidential election was
   a. General Grant.
   b. General Sherman.
   C. GENERAL MCCLELLAN.
   d. General Lee.

5. The South financed its war effort primarily through
    a. selling war bonds.
    b. seizing northern assets.
    C. PRINTING MONEY.
    d. implementing an income tax.

6. The North financed its war effort primarily through
    A. SELLING WAR BONDS.
    b. implementing an income tax.
    c. securing foreign loans.
    d. printing money.

Section 16.5.7 - p624

1. Which of the following statements is true of the Emancipation Proclamation?
    a. It allowed Lincoln to follow through on his campaign promises and finally eliminate slavery from the Union.
    b. It was a military measure based on the congressional power to confiscate the property of traitors.
    C. IT FREED THE SLAVES OF ANY STATE IN OPEN REBELLION AGAINST THE UNION, BASED ON MILITARY NECESSITY.
    d. It freed all slaves, and was passed only reluctantly due to Lincoln's feeling that it would divide the Union.

2. During the draft riots in New York City, the rioters targeted the _________ population of New York City:
    a. Irish
    b. Polish
    c. Catholic
    D. BLACK

3. The main common feature of all the Bread Riots is that they were all led by women. Why?
    a. Women are natural riot organizers.
    B. THERE WERE FEW MEN AROUND; MOST WERE OFF TO WAR.
    c. Bread is a domestic issue, women handle domestic issues.
    d. Men did not want to be involved.

4. Bread Riots occurred in which of the following cities?
    a. Boston, Washington, Richmond
    B. ATLANTA, MOBILE, RICHMOND
    c. New York, Chicago, Mobile
    d. Atlanta, Washington, Baltimore

5. The incident at Fort Pillow, Tennessee, is an example of the ________ that was/were a constant problem during the war.
    a. Abolitionism
    b. Pacifism
    c. Treasonous activities
    D. RACISM

Chapter Seventeen: Reconstruction

Contents

Chapter Seventeen: Reconstruction

17.1 INTRODUCTION

Even before the Civil War officially ended with the surrender of the last Confederate forces in 1865, Americans thought about what the reunited nation would look like. Issues not contemplated at the beginning of the war took center stage as the nation began transitioning from war to peace. National leaders had to decide the terms of peace, especially who would control southern governments and how the rebelling states would return to the Union. They also needed to address the legal and social status of former slaves and the development of a new labor system to replace slavery. Finally, they needed to determine what branch of government would handle the process: the executive branch or the legislative branch. During Reconstruction, from 1865 to 1877, the federal government took responsibility for making many administrative decisions for the southern states until residents formed new governments. Once that happened, the federal government sought to ensure the new governments protected the legal rights of the freedmen.

Andrew Johnson, who became president after Abraham Lincoln, shared his predecessor's view that the executive branch should control Reconstruction. He devised a plan for readmitting the southern states to the Union and proceeded to implement that plan in 1865. Many Republicans in Congress, however, disagreed because white southerners appeared determined to maintain slavery in any way possible. So, Congress asserted their control over Reconstruction by enhancing the federal government's protection of the freedmen in late 1866. The battle between Johnson and Congress ultimately led Republicans to impeach the president. Although Johnson remained in office, the ongoing debate soured many northerners and southerners on the efforts to reconstruct the South. In 1868, Republican Ulysses S. Grant won the presidential election based on his promise to bring peace to the country.

During Reconstruction, Republicans controlled the state governments in the South, but struggled to maintain this control. First, they represented a diverse group of voters, and they could not find a means to balance the interests of their black and white supporters. Second, conservatives, mostly members of the Democratic Party, sought to regain control of their state governments. They used threats and violence to keep Republicans away from the polls when elections rolled around. The problems associated with reconstructing the southern states seemed only to get worse during Grant's presidency. People began to lose patience with the constant focus on southern issues; many Americans wanted national leaders to focus on more pressing issues, such as the depression that followed the Panic of 1873. In the end, neither the executive branch nor the legislative branch found an effective means to reunite the nation and to protect the rights of the freedmen. Reconstruction officially ended in 1877 after Republican Rutherford B. Hayes became president and pulled the last of the federal troops out of the South.

17.1.1 Learning Outcomes

After completing this chapter, you should be able to:

- Examine the challenges the Lincoln administration confronted in its attempts to reconstruct the Border States and Union-occupied territory during the Civil War.
- Analyze the economic and political problems facing the nation at the conclusion of the Civil War.
- Demonstrate an understanding of Reconstruction and its impact on race relations in the United States.
- Analyze the positions of Abraham Lincoln, Andrew Johnson, and the Radicals in Congress on the nature and course of Reconstruction and the rights of the freedmen.
- Explain the effects of Reconstruction, the Black Codes, and the actions of the Freedmen's Bureau on African Americans in the South and North.
- Examine the social fears that helped give rise to groups such as the Ku Klux Klan.
- Assess the problems the Grant administrations faced in its attempts to deal with the political and economic issues confronting the nation.

17.2 WARTIME RECONSTRUCTION

Before the Civil War began, rumors spread in many southern communities that Abraham Lincoln planned to free the slaves. Slowly, a small number of slaves made their way to Union forts and camps seeking refuge. Initially, Union leaders returned the slaves, pursuant to the Fugitive Slave Act of 1850. However, General Benjamin Butler, at Fortress Monroe in Virginia, decided to put the slaves to work for the Union cause once the war broke out. For the remainder of the war, these "contrabands of war," as Butler called them, continued to flock to Union lines. At first, the Lincoln administration allowed individual commanders to determine how to handle the runaway slaves. As the war progressed, it became necessary for the government to adopt a more standard policy.[1]

Lincoln struggled to find a policy that would meet the demands of the refugees for freedom while also placating the needs of Border State slaveholders. Initially, his administration focused on the military uses of black labor in the Confiscation Acts. They did not develop a long-term policy for dealing with the former slaves. However, the Emancipation Proclamation, coupled with Union victories, contributed to the disintegration of slavery. Moreover, it meant when southern states, either by choice or by force, returned to the Union, they had to accept abolition. Therefore, Lincoln developed a policy for restoring the rebelling states that took into consideration the transition from a slave labor system to a free labor system. At the same time, the Congressional Republicans did not always approve of the president's approach. By 1864, Congress actively sought to challenge Lincoln for control of the process of reunifying the nation.[2]

17.2.1 Lincoln and Restoration

As Abraham Lincoln approached the interrelated questions of emancipation and reconstruction, he needed to balance the Union's political and military goals. In other words, Lincoln had to pursue a policy on emancipation that would not drive the Border States toward secession. So initially, he supported gradual compensated emancipation in the Border States. If successful, the plan would serve as a model for reconciling the rebelling states to the Union. Lincoln believed voluntary acceptance of emancipation would have better long-term results than a forced arrangement. In 1862, the president sent Congress a measure to enact his proposal, but most Republican members opposed compensation, so the bill died.[3] Lincoln also had to devise a policy that would not increase anti-war sentiment in the North. If he moved too fast on emancipation, then Democrats, who favored a more limited war, might begin to criticize his war-related policies. Such criticism could easily undermine the effort to preserve the union.[4]

In spite of these concerns, Lincoln increasingly saw emancipation as a military necessity. By freeing the slaves in the rebelling states, which he considered still part of the union, he hoped to undermine their ability to wage war. In July 1862, he raised the issue with his cabinet. According to Gideon Wells, the secretary of the navy, the president moved toward blanket emancipation because of the Union's military defeats and the failure of his plans for compensated emancipation in the Border States. While the cabinet initially split over his proposal, the president decided in favor of the move and announced the Emancipation Proclamation in September 1862, which was scheduled to take effect on January 1, 1863 unless the southern states ended their rebellion. Not only did Lincoln's decision effectively make the abolition of slavery a war aim, but it also raised questions about how occupied territories would implement emancipation and return to the Union.[5]

In 1863, Lincoln encouraged military governors in the occupied South to push residents to accept the end of slavery. However, he did not require immediate emancipation. The president told one governor that southern states could "adopt systems of apprenticeship for the colored people, conforming substantially to the most approved plans of gradual emancipation."[6] To Lincoln, a slower transition to freedom would benefit the black and the white population. Moreover, the president continued to support the possibility of colonization for former slaves in order to ease concerns about the post-emancipation relationship between blacks and whites. Lincoln hoped that by allowing for gradual emancipation and suggesting possible colonization, he could encourage pro-Union sentiments in the South, thereby shortening the conflict. By late 1863, the Lincoln administration's effort to increase loyalty in the southern states had accomplished little. Therefore, Lincoln decided the time had come to outline a policy for restoration.[7]

On December 8, 1863, Abraham Lincoln issued the "Proclamation of Amnesty and Reconstruction" and then explained the initiative in his annual message to Congress. In the proclamation, the president offered southerners who participated in the rebellion a "full pardon…with restoration of all rights of property, except as to slaves" if they would "take…an oath, and thenceforward keep and maintain said oath." He did exclude from amnesty all persons who served in "the so-called Confederate government" as well as those who served as high-ranking officers in the Confederate military. Furthermore, once ten percent of the number of voters in the 1860 presidential election took the oath, a state could establish a government, which the Union would recognize "as the true government of the state." Finally, he noted only Congress could decide whether to seat new members from the loyal governments. In his annual message, Lincoln suggested his plan followed the Constitution's provisions on presidential pardons. To quell possible concerns among the Radical Republicans, he also reinforced the idea that amnesty and restoration would not undermine the Emancipation Proclamation.[8]

Lincoln based the Ten Percent Plan on the principle that the "so-called Confederate" states had never really left the Union. As historian James McPherson noted, for Lincoln "the task of reconstruction was one of restoration rather than revolution." He designed the plan to shorten the war, not to launch major social and political changes in the South. The president proposed moderate, some even said lenient, terms in order to encourage enough southerners to declare their fidelity to the Union. If he imposed draconian terms or promoted black rights, lukewarm secessionists would never declare their loyalty. Additionally, any policy needed to respect the states' authority to determine the civil and political rights of their residents because they had never left the Union. Therefore, under the proclamation, loyal southern states had to accept the end of slavery, but they could set the pace at which it happened. The president also thought state action on slavery, as opposed to federal action, would help avoid questions about the constitutionality of the Emancipation Proclamation as it related to reconstruction. Lincoln hoped the procedures he set forth during the war would provide a model for the postwar era, but nothing quite turned out as planned since the Border States seemed reluctant to adopt emancipation and the Union-occupied territories struggled to establish loyal governments.[9]

17.2.2 Emancipation in the Border States

Although the Border States never left the Union, they still underwent a process of reconstruction during the war. The Lincoln administration encouraged Delaware, Kentucky, Maryland, and Missouri to adopt a policy of gradual compensated emancipation, which it hoped to use as a model for restoring the states in rebellion. Delaware and Kentucky firmly resisted the pressure to abolish slavery. However, discussions about emancipation led to significant political changes in Maryland and Missouri. There, whites excluded from power in the antebellum era made their voice heard. They managed to increase their own political power in the new state constitutions, but they did little to change the political status of the freedmen. Two factors seemed to make the difference between the move toward and the resistance to emancipation. At the beginning of the Civil War, federal troops moved into both Maryland and Missouri to help secure the loyalty of the population. The presence of those troops helped to undermine slavery, which caused support for abolition to grow.[10]

Lincoln offered Delaware a plan for gradual, compensated emancipation financed by the federal government early in the war. He expected leaders there to accept the plan given the small number of slaves in the state. While some residents supported abolition, Delaware never acted on the president's offer. Lincoln did not count on the white population's hostility to any suggestion of equality between the races. Once people heard about the proposal, some began to worry that emancipation would in turn produce demands for political rights. Supporters could not convince opponents otherwise, and Delaware retained slavery until the ratification of the Thirteenth Amendment in December 1865.[11]

Resistance to emancipation in Kentucky proved even greater than in Delaware. Early on, leaders suggested any attempt by the Lincoln administration to undermine slavery would affect their loyalty to the Union. Throughout the war, the planter class retained political power and no opposition movement emerged to challenge that control. The Emancipation Proclamation and the enlistment of runaways in the Union army weakened slavery, but did not destroy it in Kentucky. Masters only freed their slaves because of the Thirteenth Amendment, which the state never ratified.[12]

Early in the war, free black support for abolition, along with a rise in the number of slaves enlisting in the army, weakened the institution of slavery in Maryland. Most Unionists accepted emancipation, but they disagreed about when and how. Led by Henry Winter Davis, radicals wanted to enact immediate emancipation. Led by Montgomery Blair, conservatives embraced Lincoln's ideas for a gradual, compensated program. In 1863, supporters of immediate action won a majority of seats in the legislature because the army required all voters to take a loyalty oath, thereby curbing planter power. The legislature then called for the convention to write a new state constitution. Lincoln privately and publicly supported immediate emancipation if the convention chose to move in that direction. The resulting constitution abolished slavery immediately. It also cut the power of the planters in state politics, limited future voting to those who took a stringent loyalty oath, and created a tax-supported school system. However, it excluded the black population from political rights and access to education. By the end of the year, voters approved the new constitution, but the future of the freedmen in the state was far from certain.[13]

Like Maryland, Unionists in Missouri also divided over the issue of emancipation and therefore experienced political reconstruction during the war. Both conservatives and radicals pushed Lincoln to back their position, while the president tried to find a policy to reconcile their differences. In 1863, conservative unionists, who tended to be slaveholders, encouraged the adoption of gradual compensated emancipation. In response, radicals, who tended to be non-slaveholders, launched an effort to promote an immediate end to slavery. In 1864, voters chose as Governor Thomas C. Fletcher, a radical, a choice which led to a constitutional convention. The new constitution provided for an immediate end to slavery and granted the freedmen some political and educational rights. In order to secure its ratification, the radicals relied on laws restricting the political participation of Confederate sympathizers. The limited electorate approved the constitution in June 1865. However, their actions left the state bitterly divided as the war ended.[14]

17.2.3 Reconstruction in Union-Occupied Territory

Early in the war, Lincoln seized the initiative on restoring the southern states when he placed occupied territory under the control of a military governor. In so doing, he took the first step in moving toward presidential reconstruction. He planned to use executive decisions, not Congressional legislation, to shape the government's policy on the return of the rebelling states.[15] In Virginia, Arkansas, Tennessee, and Louisiana, the president sought to encourage the formation of loyal governments to help shorten the war. While Lincoln ascribed publicly to the Ten Percent Plan, he was more than willing in these states to be flexible on the means of restoration.

Both Virginia and Arkansas established loyal governments in 1864 under the auspices of the Ten Percent Plan. Loyalists in Virginia held an election for representatives and then a convention to draft a new constitution. Adopted in April, it barred slavery, restricted suffrage to white men, and created a system of public education for whites. At no point before the end of the war, however, could this government claim to represent ten percent of the states' population. Lincoln hoped the situation would be better in Arkansas because residents in the northern regions seemed more likely to declare their loyalty. Nevertheless, unionists there bypassed any elections under the Ten Percent Plan and moved directly to creating a constitution. The delegates proposed to end slavery gradually through a system of indentured servitude and to limit suffrage to the white population. In March, unionist voters approved the constitution. Although neither Virginia nor Arkansas followed the Ten Percent Plan exactly, Lincoln recognized the new governments as the legitimate authority in both states in order to show the success of his restoration policy.[16]

After Confederate forces withdrew from Tennessee in 1862, the president appointed Andrew Johnson as the military governor and instructed him to establish a new government. While Johnson convinced Lincoln to exempt Tennessee from the Emancipation Proclamation, the issue still divided the state. Some people renewed their commitment to slavery, and others became more vocal in their opposition to it. Johnson eventually sided with those who wanted to abolish slavery, and he took action to undermine the conservatives by expanding on the loyalty oath outlined in the Ten Percent Plan. In Tennessee, potential voters had to declare loyalty to the Union, vow to fight the Confederacy, and support the end of slavery. Johnson's support for abolition had more to do with a desire to punish the state's slaveholders, whom he long resented, than to do with a desire to help the state's slaves. His approach to restoration and amnesty did little to support the creation of a pro-Union government in 1864. After his election as Lincoln's vice president, Johnson followed the Arkansas model of restoration. He endorsed a constitutional amendment ending slavery drafted by a convention of unelected unionists. People permitted to vote under Johnson's loyalty oath approved the amendment in February 1865.[17]

Lincoln was optimistic about the restoration in Louisiana because many reluctant Confederates, immigrants from Europe and the northern states, and free blacks lived in the occupied area, and they appeared likely to support a constitution barring slavery. Partly because of the slow pace of change in Louisiana in 1863, Lincoln proposed the Ten Percent Plan. He thought it would encourage the residents to overcome their differences about how to approach reconstruction, particularly their questions on the future status of blacks. Conservatives and moderates preferred abolition but not equality; they feared mentioning equality would undermine unionism in the region. On the other hand, many of the radicals came from the wealthy free black community in New Orleans. They possessed more civil liberties than did most free blacks in the antebellum South, and they wanted to maintain those rights and secure voting rights.

The demand for black suffrage complicated the effort to create a loyal government in Louisiana. In 1863, the Lincoln administration supported the free black community's desire to vote in elections pertaining to the new state government. Edwin Stanton, the secretary of war, instructed General Nathaniel P. Banks to allow all loyal citizens to vote. Banks, however, ignored the order because he shared the moderates' opinion on how black suffrage would affect unionism. He supported the creation of a government under the old state constitution, which maintained slavery, rather than calling directly for a new state constitution. So, Banks used his patronage power, or power to appoint loyal supporters to public office, to help the moderates win a majority of seats in the elections in February 1864.

Lincoln accepted this move in Louisiana because he wanted a loyal government as quickly as possible, but he also continued to encourage Banks to support the drafting of a new constitution. After meeting with two representatives from the free black community who presented a petition regarding voting rights, the president also wrote soon-to-be governor, Michael Hahn, suggesting the possibility of voting rights for well-educated blacks. The president's work to please both factions led to a new constitution in July 1864 abolishing slavery, undermining the power of the planters, and providing tax-supported schools. It also granted the legislature the authority to extend the right to vote and for blacks to receive an education in the future. Ten percent of the voters in the 1860 presidential election supported the new government and constitution, somewhat validating Lincoln's plans for reconstruction.[18]

17.2.4 The Possibility of Land Redistribution

Elsewhere in the Confederacy, the advance of the Union troops forced military leaders to continue to address the issue of what to do about slaves who had fallen under union control. In some areas, Union military commanders experimented with land redistribution as a possible plan for reconstruction. Such instances occurred on South Carolina's Sea Islands, in Mississippi's Davis Bend, and along Georgia's coastline. These experiments represented an atypical approach to reconstruction. Nevertheless, they raised important questions about the nature of rebuilding the South. Should the loss of land be a form of punishment for those who rebelled against the Union? Should the granting of land be a means to provide for former slaves and compensate them for past abuses by their owners?

Late in 1861, Union forces occupied parts of the South Carolina Sea Islands. White residents fled to the mainland, leaving some 10,000 slaves behind. The slaves ransacked their masters' homes and then set about planting foodstuffs to support themselves. However, soon U.S. officials, missionaries, and reporters descended on the region, and they had their own ideas about how to help slaves transition to a life of freedom. Although the slaves had begun to disperse the land among themselves, treasury officials decided to organize land sales to cover the back taxes on the abandoned property. The missionaries hoped to secure some of the land for the freedmen, but most of it went to northern investors. They in turn hired the black residents to work as wage laborers on the plantations, a move which provided an opportunity to test the merits of free labor. Relatively quickly, the free labor experiment on the Sea Islands showed how whites and blacks understood the term differently. For the white landowners, free labor meant they would pay their workers wages; however, for the black workers, free labor meant the opportunity to own land and grow the crops of their choice. The misunderstanding on the

Sea Islands very much foreshadowed the problems that emerged in the postwar transition from slave to free labor.[19]

In Louisiana, and later Mississippi, Union commanders struggled to devise a policy to manage occupied plantations along the Mississippi River. They came up with a system to lease abandoned lands to northern investors who would pay slaves to work that land; while the workers technically remained in bondage and they remained subject to the whims of white investors, the payment of wages suggested a move toward free labor. However, military commanders occasionally allowed blacks to farm abandoned land independently. The best known of these experiments happened at Davis Bend on the Mississippi River, the former plantations of Jefferson Davis and his brother Joseph. Prior to the war, the Davis brothers developed a model slave community based on the ideas of British socialist Robert Owen where the slaves had a good deal of control over their own lives. Nevertheless, when the war forced Joseph Davis to abandon the plantation, his slaves refused to accompany him. Instead, they transitioned their experiences with utopian self-government into a successful self-run commercial enterprise. General Ulysses S. Grant instructed John Eaton Jr., the commander in the area, to lease the land to the freedmen. In November 1863, Eaton began distributing the land and instilling free labor principles among the residents. By 1865, under the leadership of former slave Benjamin Montgomery, Davis Bend produced 2,000 bales of cotton and made a profit of $160,000, suggesting to some observers that, given a chance, the freedmen and their families could become part of the market economy.[20]

The question of land and labor also came to Georgia in the waning days of the war. As General William T. Sherman launched his March to the Sea in September 1864, slaves took the opportunity to seize their own freedom by following the Union troops across the state. When Union forces reached Savannah in December, approximately 20,000 men, women, and children had joined the advance, and they refused the army's orders to disperse. Edwin Stanton, the secretary of war, travelled to Georgia to assess the situation. He recommended that Sherman arrange a meeting with black leaders. Stanton thought it important to understand how the freedmen conceived of their freedom. On the evening of January 12, 1865, Sherman and Stanton met with twenty representatives of Savannah's black community.[21] As former slave and Baptist minister Garrison Frazier noted,

> Slavery is receiving by irresistible power the work of another man, and not by his consent. The freedom, as I understand it, promised by the proclamation, is taking us from under the yoke of bondage and placing us where we could reap the fruit of our own labor, and take care of ourselves, and assist the Government in maintaining our freedom. The way we can best take care of ourselves is to have land, and turn in and till it by our labor...and we can soon maintain ourselves and have something to spare...We want to be placed on land until we are able to buy it and make it our own.[22]

Several days after that meeting, Sherman released Special Field Order No. 15, which set aside confiscated land south of Charleston, running thirty miles in from the Atlantic coast and totaling about 400,000 acres, for the settlement of the freedpeople in forty-acre plots. Sherman later indicated he would distribute some of the army's old mules to any freedpeople who cared to take advantage of the offer. For Sherman, the field order represented a temporary wartime measure designed to deal with the refugee problem. For the former slaves, conversely, it set up the expectation that the U.S. government supported land redistribution with a policy of granting "forty acres and a mule."[23]

17.2.5 Congress and Reconstruction

While the Lincoln administration proceeded with its efforts to promote wartime reconstruction through the Ten Percent Plan, Congress began to question his methods. By 1863, as historian Eric Foner notes, for Lincoln and the Radical Republicans, "the definition of Southern loyalty...encompassed not merely a willingness to rejoin the Union, but an acceptance of the slaves' freedom." Yet, they did not agree on the best method to end slavery. The president preferred a more moderate approach directed by the states. Radical Republicans wanted reconstruction to do more than just end slavery.[24]

The Radicals thought the federal government should have a greater say in the process of reconstruction. They wanted to ensure real Unionists controlled the process and to somewhat protect the rights of the freedpeople. To justify more federal control, Senator Charles Sumner of Massachusetts contended that when the southern states seceded they committed "state suicide." Therefore, they had to apply for readmission to the Union, and only Congress had the right to set the terms. Concerns about Louisiana, where the control of genuine Unionists seemed slim and the rights of the freedpeople seemed tenuous, prompted Radical Republicans in Congress to introduce an alternate approach to reconstruction that would forestall any decisions until after the war ended.[25]

In mid-1864, Congress considered numerous plans on how to improve Lincoln's approach to restoration. They finally settled on a measure sponsored by Senator Benjamin (Ben) Wade of Ohio and Representative Henry Winter Davis of Maryland. The proposed Wade-Davis bill required fifty percent of voters to declare their loyalty before reconstruction could begin. The first step in the process would be the drafting a new constitution that abolished slavery, barred Confederates from voting and serving in the new government, and repudiated the Confederate government's debt. Only voters who could swear an "iron-clad" oath of past and future loyalty could vote for delegates to the constitutional convention. The bill also contained provisions for federal courts to enforce the maintenance of the freedpeople's liberty. Congress would only readmit the reconstructed states to the Union if they followed these steps.[26]

Radicals won support for the bill from a majority of Congress on July 2, 1864, just before it adjourned for a break. To ensure support among moderates, Wade and Davis decided to leave out any provisions for black suffrage, even though they supported such a move. Therefore, similar to Lincoln's plan, observes James McPherson, the measure "confined the reconstruction process to white voters." The sponsors recognized most Republicans wanted to exert greater control over the process of reconstruction, but, for some, political equality went too far. Wade-Davis never became law because Abraham Lincoln decided to pocket veto the measure. In other words, he did not sign the measure before Congress adjourned. The president viewed the proposed law as unconstitutional because it would force states to abolish slavery. He also worried it would undermine the governments created under the Ten Percent Plan and it would limit his options for creating loyal governments.[27]

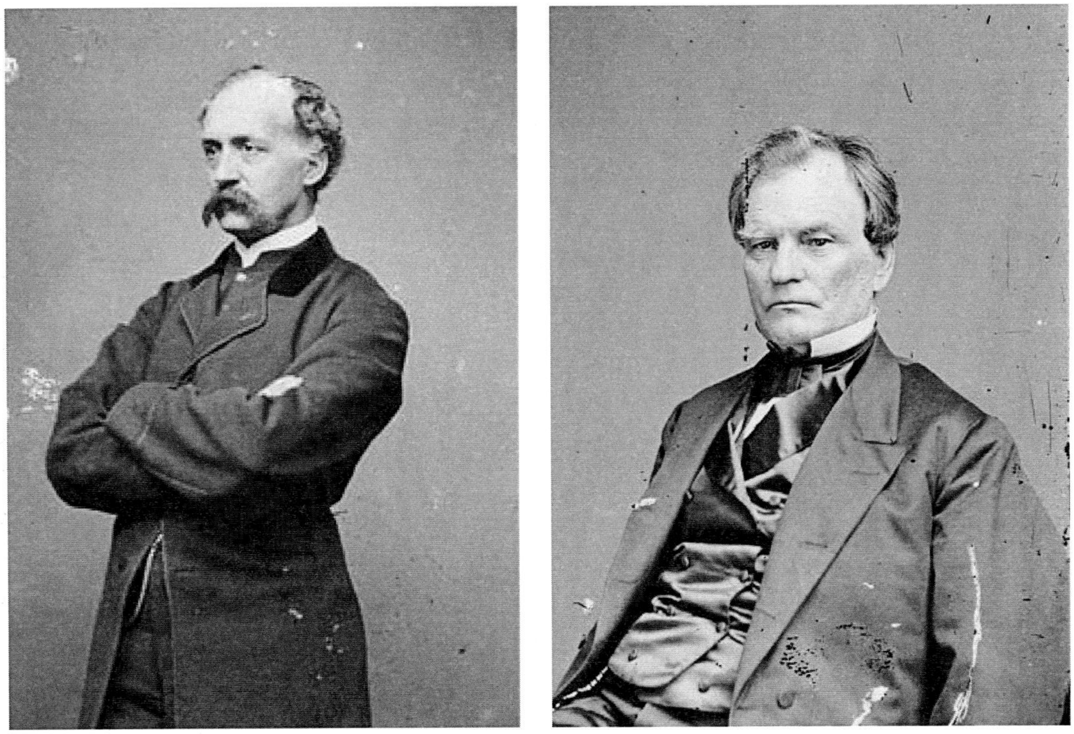

Figure 17.1 Senator Benjamin Wade and Representative Henry Winter Davis | In 1864, Congress tried to reassert control over the reconstruction process. Radical Republicans Benjamin Wade and Henry Winter Davis sponsored a bill to require at least fifty percent of voters in an occupied state to swear an oath of loyalty before restoration could begin.

Author: Mathew Brady (both)
Source: Library of Congress

Although the Wade-Davis bill died, the debate about the future of reconstruction continued throughout the presidential campaign of 1864. The Republican Party, rechristened the National Union Party, ultimately chose Abraham Lincoln as their presidential nominee, pairing him with Andrew Johnson, and the party adopted a moderate platform. While the party came together to support the president and win the election, their divisions over the future of reconstruction remained. When Congress reconvened in December after the election, Lincoln hoped to mend fences with the Radical Republicans. He decided to appoint Salmon P. Chase, his radical opponent for the Republican nomination, as the Chief Justice of the Supreme Court. Then, Lincoln and Congressional leaders tried to work out their differences. Congress agreed to accept the reconstructed governments of Louisiana and Arkansas; the president agreed to support harsher terms for the unreconstructed states. However, Congress repeatedly defeated versions of the compromise because some members wanted to include support for black suffrage and others did not.[28]

Meanwhile, Congress took another step toward inserting the federal government into the reconstruction process. For some time, Republicans had considered creating a government agency to assist former slaves in making the transition to freedom. However, they could not come to an agreement on the details about the management and functions of the agency. After the House of Representatives approved the Thirteenth Amendment on January 31, 1865 (the Senate had approved it in 1864), and it went to the states for ratification, Congress became determined to finish their work on a bill to create the

Freedmen's Bureau. Their reason for doing so was that, in addition to abolishing slavery, the Thirteenth Amendment enabled Congress to use legislation to guarantee that freedom.[29]

The Freedmen's Bureau bill was an attempt by Congress to define their authority over the former slaves as well as over the process of reconstruction. The measure, approved in March 1865, created the Bureau of Refugees, Freedmen, and Abandoned Lands to provide relief for loyal refugees, black and white, for the period of one year. The Freedmen's Bureau administered by the War Department distributed clothing, food, fuel, and land, as well as ran schools for the freedmen to help prepare them for citizenship. Although Congress envisioned the measure as a temporary solution to the problem of refugees in the South, it significantly expanded the power of the federal government over the states. Moreover, as historian Randall M. Miller maintains, "the act carried an implied promise of government aid to blacks and Unionists in staking new lives as independent farmers in a reconstructed South."[30] The creation of the Freedmen's Bureau showed Congress intended to exert more authority over reconstruction; however, until the war actually ended, no decisions about reconstruction were final. Moreover, policymakers in Washington rarely considered the needs and wants of blacks or whites in the South.

17.2.6 Before You Move On...

Key Concepts

Throughout the Civil War, Republican leaders in the North debated how to bring the Confederate states back into the Union. For Abraham Lincoln, the process of restoration fit into his desire to win the war as quickly as possible. He pursued a cautious policy on emancipation in the Border States to secure their loyalty. As for the rest of the South, he hoped to outline a policy that would encourage unionists to declare their loyalty to the United States. With the "Proclamation on Amnesty and Reconstruction" issued in December 1863, the president made emancipation a precondition for restoration, but allowed the states to determine how exactly to end slavery. Moreover, he required only ten percent of voters in a state to take a loyalty oath. In 1864, Lincoln worked with unionists in Virginia, Arkansas, Tennessee, and Louisiana to create loyal governments. Radical Republicans in Congress, however, found the president's Ten Percent Plan too lenient. Therefore, they tried to reassert their control over reconstruction with the Wade-Davis Bill. The measure set forth additional qualifications for readmission to the Union, so Lincoln pocket vetoed it. In 1865, after Congress sent the Thirteenth Amendment to the states for ratification, it created the Freedmen's Bureau to help the South transition from a slave labor to a free labor system. Although Congress had asserted its authority over reconstruction, it remained unclear whether the president or Congress would control the process in the postwar years since the war had not ended.

Test Yourself

1. Which of the following statements best describes Abraham Lincoln's "Proclamation on Amnesty and Reconstruction"?

a. The policy was consistent in the Union-occupied territories.

b. The policy was designed to promote the rights of the freedmen, not to help end the war.

c. The policy was fairly lenient toward the southern states.

d. The policy was widely supported by the Radical Republicans in Congress.

2. The Border States quickly accepted Lincoln's proposals for gradual compensated emancipation and willingly implemented the Thirteenth Amendment.

a. True

b. False

3. Which of the following measures did Republicans in Congress promote in 1864 to counter Lincoln's Ten-Percent Plan?

a. The Military Reconstruction Bill

b. The Louisiana Bill

c. The Civil Rights Bill

d. The Wade-Davis Bill

4. Congress envisioned the Freedmen's Bureau created in March of 1865 as a permanent solution to dealing with the problems of African Americans after the Civil War.

a. True

b. False

See page 699 for answers

17.3 RECONSTRUCTION AFTER THE ASSASSINATION OF LINCOLN

At the time of Abraham Lincoln's assassination, Vice President Andrew Johnson assumed the presidency. He also assumed the role that both he and Lincoln believed belonged to the executive branch: reconstructing the South. Johnson was a unique figure in American politics and more than one historian has characterized him as one of the most unfortunate men ever to take the Presidency. He was grim-faced and taciturn, and was about as ill-prepared as anyone could be to lead the nation in a time of crisis. Prior to becoming President, Johnson had had a varied career. He was a slave owner before the War; the only southern senator to remain in that body after his state, Tennessee, had seceded from the Union; he served as military governor of Tennessee in 1862; and, during the early years of the war, he was a Southern War Democrat. Johnson's success as governor of Tennessee led to Lincoln's choosing him as running mate in 1864 on the National Union Party ticket. Johnson had no strong allies in either the North or South, did not learn how to read until taught by his wife, and did not enjoy a significant following in either party.

Figure 17.2 Andrew Johnson | After Lincoln's assassination, Andrew Johnson, the new president, attempted to "restore" the South using the plan begun by Lincoln.

Author: Unknown
Source: National Archives

Johnson's opinion about reconstructing the South changed over the first few months of his Presidency. At first, he tended to agree with the Radicals in Congress that the South should be punished for seceding from the Union and was famous for remarking in the spring of 1865, "Treason is a crime and must be...made infamous, and traitors must be impoverished."[31] He was particularly hostile toward Southern aristocrats, whose attachment to slavery he blamed for the war. A staunch Jacksonian, he distrusted banks, corporations, and the New England states generally. Shortly after he came to the presidency, Ben Wade, an ardent Radical Republican, declared, "Johnson, we have faith in you. By the gods, there will be no trouble now in running this government."[32]

On the other hand, Johnson did not share the Radical Republican idea that the freedmen should be assured of constitutional equality with white Americans. As a previous slave owner who believed in white supremacy, and despite the fact that he told Tennessee blacks in 1864 that he would be their "Moses," he commented earlier, "Damn the Negroes! I am fighting these traitorous aristocrats, their masters." Two years later he remarked, "As for the Negro I am for setting him free but at the same time I assert that this is a white man's government...If whites and blacks can't get along together arrangements must be made to colonize the blacks."[33] He was equally blunt in 1866 when a delegation, led by Frederick Douglass, visited the White House to make a plea for black suffrage, remarking that not only did he have no interest in black suffrage, but also he distrusted Douglass, who "would sooner cut a white man's throat than not."[34]

Despite Ben Wade's optimism, trouble came soon enough, because Johnson, like Lincoln, believed that reconstruction, which he labeled "restoration," fell within the purview of the executive branch of the national government. Because of a conviction that he could proceed without the "advice and consent" of Congress, Johnson did not call for a special session when Lincoln was assassinated; instead, he moved to accomplish the restoration of the Confederate states before Congress was scheduled to assemble in December 1865. Following another line of Lincoln's reasoning, Johnson took the position that it was individuals who had rebelled and not states; therefore, individuals should be punished but not states, as they retained their constitutional rights. Thus, the states could quickly be brought back into a proper relationship with the Union.

17.3.1 Andrew Johnson Undertakes Reconstruction, 1865

In May 1865, Johnson issued two proclamations that would go far to define his approach to reconstructing the South. The first offered amnesty and restoration of property (except slaves) to anyone who took an oath of loyalty to the United States. Excepted from this offer were Confederate officials, army officers above the rank of Army Colonel, and Navy lieutenant; any men who had held positions in the Union government before the war and had left their posts to join in the rebellion; and all who owned property worth $20,000 or more. The first proclamation was similar to that issued by Lincoln in December, 1863, with the exception of the last category. In order for states to be readmitted to the union, they must repudiate their war debts, accept the Thirteenth Amendment, declare secession null and void, and draft a constitution. The second proclamation appointed a provisional governor for North Carolina and called for the state to create a constitution. In the ensuing weeks, Johnson made similar offers to six additional southern states and recognized the Lincoln-sponsored governments of Louisiana, Arkansas, and Tennessee. By the fall of 1865, "regular civil administrations" were thereby functioning in all of the former Confederate states except Texas. When Congress convened in December 1865, ten of the eleven Confederate states had therefore been readmitted to the Union.[35]

In neither proclamation did Johnson address the issue of civil rights for freedmen; the only requirement for the new constitutions was that they must specify that suffrage was limited to white men who had taken an oath of loyalty to the national government and received amnesty. None of the constitutions deviated from this instruction, so no state granted blacks the right to vote.

17.3.2 The South Reacts

Though the North was distrustful of Johnson's reconstruction measures, white southerners were jubilant. Southerners had braced themselves for a harsh retaliation, especially in light of the earlier utterances of the president, and at first, they could not believe their good fortune. On September 11, 1865, a delegation of Southerners met with the president to express their thanks for his "desire and intention to sustain Southern rights in the Union." Johnson was equally solicitous, declaring his "love, respect and confidence" in the Southern people.[36]

The measures of the President had an unintended lulling effect on the South, and within months Southern leaders began to show their previous irascible independence. Some of state legislatures ratified the Thirteenth Amendment; some did not. Some began to argue about war debts, and, while some declared secession null and void, others merely "repealed" their articles of secession. And if this were not enough to alarm the Radical Republicans, old Confederate leaders were elected to the state constitutional conventions, and the states even sent ex-Confederate generals, colonels, and congressmen to Washington, among these including the Vice President of the Confederacy, Alexander Stephens.

The worst offense of the newly reconstructed states, however, was the creation of Black Codes in every state; these were based on the pre-emancipation Slave Codes. Designed to create a supply of cheap labor and to prevent integration of the races, these codes regulated every aspect of the lives of "blacks, mulattos, or other persons of color." Although the

Codes varied from state to state, in most, marriage among blacks was recognized, and the newly freed-men could sue and be sued in court. But here the rights of the freemen ended, as the Codes denied basic rights, including the following: the right of freedmen to bear arms or vote; serve on juries; co-mingle with whites; leave the premises of an employer without permission; own property except in designated areas of a state, city, or town; and testify in court except in cases involving other blacks. Rules also prohibited miscegenation. According to the Black Code of Florida, for example, any black man guilty of sexual relations with a white woman would be fined $1000 and whipped (not to exceed 39 lashes); the woman would be similarly punished. In Mississippi, the punishment was even harsher; any person convicted of intermarriage would be sentenced to life in prison.

Because a primary goal of the Codes was to provide a constant source of subservient labor in the post-emancipation South, most contained sections dealing with free labor. All terms between laborer and employer were spelled out in contracts that specified the number of hours to be worked and amount of wages to be paid. Most Codes also contained clauses that children of freedpeople could be arbitrarily bound out by the state as apprentices; some of these listed obligations that the master owed the apprentice such rights as education, religious instruction, and housing; some did not. The monies gained from the apprentice's employment belonged to the master, except for a "small allowance" given the apprentice at the end of his tenure "with which to begin life." Similarly, freedpeople living in "idleness," such as gamblers and the unemployed, could be bound out to a master for a period of time "no longer than a year." Most states defined "person of color" as any man or woman who had one-eighth "or more Negro blood."[37]

17.3.3 The Issue of Equality

The North voiced outrage at the Codes, but it is interesting to look closely at the issue of black equality in the North as well as in the South. As early as 1863, Frederick Douglass, an abolitionist and former slave, warned that emancipation was only the first step toward black equality, and his words were echoed by Thaddeus Stevens and Charles Sumner, the authors of a radical plan of reconstruction, as they urged integration be adopted in southern society. But the fact is that the majority of Northerners were no more in favor of racial equality than were those in the South. In the North, only seven percent of the black population was allowed to vote and that was in the five New England states. All public facilities were segregated, including schools, prisons, hospitals, churches, and cemeteries; also, most states had housing and job restrictions. Moreover, many northern states still had laws against the immigration of blacks from state to state. But if Northerners, like Southerners, were not in favor of social and economic equality, most did want a reconstruction that would bring a better life for southern blacks, one in which they would enjoy equality before the law, freedom of movement, the right to sit on juries, and like punishment for like crimes.[38]

17.3.4 Congress Intervenes, 1865-1866

Radicals in the North looked with dismay as the South apparently returned to its pre-War social structure, with the exception of an established institution of slavery. The election of Confederate leadership to positions of importance in state and national offices was bad enough, but the Black Codes looked very much like a return to slavery. James G. Blaine, then Speaker of the House of Representatives, wrote in the early 1870s, "If the Southern men had intended as their one special desirable aim, to inflame public opinion of the North against them, they would have proceeded precisely as they did."[39]

When Congress convened in December 1865, its members acted to forestall the effects of the Black Codes and remind Southerners that the Confederacy had indeed been defeated. First, Congress created a Joint Committee on Reconstruction. Although the committee was not controlled by the Radicals, it did have among its membership one of the most influential Radicals in Congress: Thaddeus Stevens of Pennsylvania. Stevens and Charles Sumner, who was the Republican leader in the Senate, were the most outspoken proponents of radical reconstruction. The irascible Stevens made clear his position on Presidential Reconstruction when he remarked, "The punishment of traitors has been wholly ignored by a treacherous Executive and a sluggish Congress."[40] The Joint Committee eventually created the plan for reconstruction that Congress would ultimately adopt.

While the Joint Committee was getting to work, Congress acted on its determination to wrest control of reconstruction from the executive branch. In February 1866, the body tried to extend the life and powers of the Freedmen's Bureau, though this measure was vetoed by Johnson. In April, Congress passed the Civil Rights bill of 1866, which struck at the Black Codes and foreshadowed the provisions of the Fourteenth Amendment by specifying that "all persons born in the United States...of every race and color, without regard to any previous condition of slavery" would be entitled to the full protection of the Constitution. Further, the federal government could intervene in the affairs of the states to see that civil rights for all citizens were upheld and that any law designed to deprive citizens of their rights would be considered unconstitutional. Johnson vetoed the *Civil Rights Act*, but his veto was overridden, a sign of the solidarity of opinion that was beginning to become apparent in Congress.[41] The *Civil Rights Act* was the first act passed over a Presidential veto.

Meanwhile, the Joint Committee drafted and sent the Fourteenth Amendment to the states for ratification. This Amendment echoes the intent and language of the *Civil Rights Act* by proclaiming that "all persons born or naturalized in the United States are citizens of the United States and of the states wherein they reside." No state could "deprive any person of life, liberty, or property, without due process of law; nor deny to any person within its jurisdiction the equal protection of the laws." Moreover, suffrage could not be denied to any adult male citizen; if this denial of suffrage was accomplished by state law, then that state's representation in Congress would be decreased. And lastly, the Amendment disqualified from any state or national office anyone who had been involved in an "insurrection or rebellion against the [United States]." The still undeterred white South would not accept the third provision, and the Amendment did not pass at that time.[42]

Race Riots in the South

To make matters worse, violence against blacks began to sweep through the South. In Memphis, trouble broke out in May 1866 when carriages driven by a white man and a black man collided. What began as a fight between the two men evolved into violence when a group of whites stormed the black quarter and began burning houses and killing their inhabitants. A more serious riot occurred in New Orleans when a peaceful procession of blacks was fired upon. When the smoke cleared, 119 blacks and seventeen of their supporters had been injured, and thirty-seven blacks and three white friends were killed. It was in the context of this unrest that the Congressional campaigns of 1866 began.[43]

The Radical Cause Strengthens

The Southern refusal to ratify the Fourteenth Amendment strengthened the Radical position in Congress as northerners became more convinced than ever that the South was unreconstructed and unrepentant and that the plans of Johnson and Lincoln were failures. Northern opinion shaped the Congressional elections of 1866, as Johnson and the Radicals squared off before the American public. Johnson made what he called a "Swing around the Circle," an eighteen-day tour in which he went from Washington to New York to Chicago, south to St. Louis and then back to the nation's capital. While he did not declare a party allegiance, his rhetoric was decidedly pro-Democratic. Despite his efforts, the Republicans won by a landslide, taking thirty-seven additional seats in the House, which gave them a total of 173 seats in that body; the Democrats were left with forty-seven. In the Senate, the Republicans held fifty-seven seats and the Democrats held nine. Not until the 1930s' New Deal would the Democrats enjoy a similar majority.[44]

Radical Reconstruction

The Radicals now had a firm base of support in both the House and Senate, and they moved to adopt the plans outlined by the Joint Committee, including the First Reconstruction Act of March 1867. Historian Samuel Eliot Morison calls this act "the most important legislation of the entire period."[45] Thaddeus Stevens, an important contributor to the act's wording, commented, somewhat incorrectly, "I was a Conservative in the last session of this Congress, but I mean to be a Radical henceforth."[46] The basic premise of the act was that "no legal state governments or adequate protection for life and property now exists in the southern states," with the exception of Tennessee, which had accepted the Fourteenth Amendment in July 1866.[47] The Act, which passed over Johnson's veto, divided the ten unreconstructed states into five military districts, each under a federal military commander "not below the rank of brigadier-general, and to detail a sufficient military force to enable such officer to perform his duties and enforce his authority within the district to which he is assigned."[48] The responsibilities of the commanders were to establish new requirements for voting, set up new state governments, and oversee the drafting of state constitutions.

When a convention was elected by all citizens of a state (with the exception of those disenfranchised because of participating in "the rebellion" or those who had been convicted of a felony), a constitution created in keeping with the language and intent of the Constitution of the United States, and the Fourteenth Amendment ratified, then the states could apply for reentry into the union. The constitutions of the states must guarantee black suffrage. An addendum to this act was passed in July; it stated, "no

Figure 17.3 The Radical Republicans | Thaddeus Stevens and Charles Sumner were the main authors of Radical Reconstruction.

Authors: Mathew Brady, Julian Vannerson
Sources: National Archives US Presidents in the Census Records, Library of Congress

district commander... shall be bound in his action by any opinion of any civil officer of the United States."[49] This addendum was of dubious constitutionality because it infringed on the powers of the as Commander in Chief by keeping him from removing the commanders of the military districts.[50]

The state constitutions established under the direction of the military commanders were more egalitarian than those they replaced. In South Carolina, for example, property qualifications for voting were removed, thus allowing universal manhood suffrage; the Bill of Rights was expanded; all reference to "distinctions on account of color" were removed; women's rights were expanded; and imprisonment for debt ended.[51] By the summer of 1868, six of the previous confederate states, Arkansas, North Carolina, South Carolina, Louisiana, Alabama, and Florida, had met all requirements and been accepted back into the Union. The remainder of the states were reconstructed in 1870, at which time they had to ratify the Fifteenth Amendment as well as the Fourteenth; the former specified that "the right of citizens of the United States to vote shall not be denied or abridged by the United States or by any State on account of race color or previous condition of servitude." Once the conditions of the Reconstruction Act had been met, Congress formally readmitted the states to the union.

17.3.5 A Constitutional Imbalance: The Impeachment of Andrew Johnson

As the Radicals in Congress attempted to solidify Congressional power, an important aspect of this goal was to bring the Presidency into a position inferior to that of Congress. The *Reconstruction Act* began this process when it included the provision that "no district commander...shall be bound in his action by any opinion of any civil officer of the United States."[52] A second attempt came with the passage of the *Tenure of Office Act* in 1867 which

Figure 17.4 Johnson's Impeachment | Andrew Johnson was impeached by the House of Representatives in 1867 for disobeying the Tenure of Office Act, itself clearly unconstitutional. He was narrowly acquitted.

Author: Theodore R. Davis
Source: Library of Congress

denied the president the right to remove civil officials, including his own cabinet, without the approval of the Senate. The immediate goal of this legislation was to keep President Johnson from removing the Secretary of War, Edwin Stanton, who was the last remaining Radical in his cabinet. The next goal was to remove Johnson through impeachment; if Johnson were impeached and convicted, then his replacement would be the president pro-tempore of the Senate, the Radical Benjamin Wade. Falling in line with the Radical plan, Johnson did in fact dismiss Stanton and appointed to his place in the War Department General Lorenzo Thomas. On February 24, 1867, the House voted to impeach Johnson for "high crimes and misdemeanors." According to the Constitution, once impeached, or indicted, a president is tried by the Senate with the Chief Justice of the Supreme Court presiding. Seven Senators voted against conviction, so Johnson was not removed from office. Had one more Senator voted to convict, Wade would have become the President of the United States.

17.3.6 Before You Move On...

Key Concepts

With the death of Abraham Lincoln, the presidency passed to his Vice President, Andrew Johnson, who, like Lincoln, believed that the process of restructuring the South lay in the hands of the Presidency. Johnson's *Amnesty Proclamation,* delivered shortly after he came to office, was mild, and, within eight months of the death of Lincoln, all but one of the previous Confederate states had been brought back into the Union. When white Southerners displayed attitudes and political policies reminiscent of those in place before the beginning of the War, the Radicals in Congress seized the reins of reconstructing the South and created a series of Reconstruction Acts designed to punish as well as reconstruct the South. Congress also attempted to secure Congressional supremacy over the executive branch by passing the Tenure of Office Act and then bringing articles of impeachment against Johnson. Though he was indeed impeached, Johnson was not convicted. The last of the southern states fulfilled the dictates of the Congressional reconstruction acts, including the acceptance of the Thirteenth, Fourteenth, and Fifteenth amendments, and were returned to the union in 1870.

Test Yourself

1. The Black Codes passed in most southern states in 1865-1866 were based on the Slave Codes common in the period before emancipation.

   a. True

   b. False

2. The purpose of the Tenure of Office Act was to:

   a. Force Andrew Johnson into a position that could lead to his impeachment.

   b. Allow the presidency greater freedom in appointing officials to his Cabinet.

   c. Limit the number of terms members of the Supreme Court could serve.

   d. Keep previous confederate officials from holding office in southern states.

3. According to the First Reconstruction Act passed in 1867, the South was divided into military districts.

   a. True

   b. False

4. The Fifteenth Amendment specifies that no citizen of the United States will be:

   a. Deprived of the right of due process.

   b. Forced into servitude.

   c. Deprived of the right to vote.

   d. Kept from the occupation of his/her choice.

See page 699 for answers

17.4 THE RECONSTRUCTION EXPERIENCE

Life in the South during Reconstruction was often not easy for anyone. Among the obvious problems, the South was physically devastated by the war. Anywhere the armies had clashed, terrible destruction ensued, and where the armies had not advanced, there was still suffering from deprivation due to the shortages during and after the war. Almost everyone in the South, no matter their race, gender, social standing, or political views, suffered during and immediately after the war. The war had been physically and emotionally difficult; for many, Reconstruction would also prove to be a painful, even traumatic, experience.

Uncertainty prevailed in the South after the end of the war. What would the future bring? President Lincoln had not laid out concrete plans for reconstruction before his assassination. After his assassination, anger in the North became a key component of the reconstruction equation. Was the South to be accepted back and the nation healed, or was the South to be punished and brought to heel? Differing opinions among the public and the politicians held sway at various times as the Union decided what to do with the defeated Confederacy.

President Jefferson Davis's experience was atypical, but it does illustrate on a very personal scale the impact of the wrangling in the North following Lincoln's assassination. Davis had been captured in Georgia in 1865 as he tried to make his way to Texas in hopes of joining with Confederates still in the field. Davis was taken to Fort Monroe, Virginia while the investigation into Lincoln's assassination was conducted. Many believed that the Confederate government, and thereby Davis, had been behind, or at least connected to, the assassination. The investigation proved otherwise, but with feelings running high, Davis could not be released. Magazines and papers such as *Harper's Weekly* called for Davis to be charged with treason, tried, and, if convicted, executed.

General Ulysses S. Grant had given a parole to General Robert E. Lee and his army; however, Davis was not a part of the military, so he received no such parole. He was charged with treason. He was kept in a small cell and, at one point, shackled, not due to any order for such from Washington or fear of his escape, since his health was failing. Rather, the officer in charge of Davis's care, General Nelson Miles, who was given full authority and discretion to do as he thought best, chose to do so. When the officer in charge of Davis changed, so did Davis's treatment. Eventually he was moved into officer's quarters, and his wife and children were allowed to live at the fort with him. Davis was released on bond after two years, having never been brought to trial, and the charges were dropped. New charges of treason were brought in Richmond in 1868, and Davis was finally brought to trial, a proceeding that soon became entangled in constitutional issues. The trial simply ceased to continue, and the prosecution eventually dropped the case.

17.4.1 The Shared Experience

Focusing on the Reconstruction experience of one group or another in the South carries the danger of overlooking the shared experience. For many in the South before, during, and after the war, life was not a case of simple segregation.

For example, Joel M. Lax, of Halifax County, Virginia, was a white, slave-owning tobacco farmer with personal property valued at over $4,000 in 1860. In 1861 two of his sons, John and William A., joined the Confederate army. John stayed healthy and served throughout the war, while William A. contracted dysentery early on and spent most of the war moving from one army hospital to another until, at last, he came to the Confederate hospital at Chimborazo in Richmond, one of the largest hospitals in history. John was surrendered at Appomattox and returned home; William A. was captured along with the other hospital patients when Richmond fell and was shipped north to Point Lookout, Maryland, a Union prisoner of war camp known for its horrific conditions. William A. died there in May, still a prisoner a month after Lee's surrender. Like most families of soldiers in the war, William A.'s family had to wait to find out what had happened to their son. By the time they learned of his death, his body had long been buried in a mass grave.

Along with such uncertainties as the Lax family faced, came the uncertainty regarding the treatment of former slaves. At the end of the war, slaves were freed; however, entities responsible for their rights were unidentified. Although set free by law, many had nothing and were given nothing except their freedom. Some, whether by choice or necessity, stayed on their old plantations. Two such were Linda, age 25, and Sallie, age 45, who lived on the Lax farm. They almost certainly had been slaves previously but were listed in 1865 as servants. By the end of the war, both women had consumption, known more commonly today as Tuberculosis, a common disease in Virginia and other areas at the time. For people weakened by lack of proper food, clothes, and shelter, the chances of surviving this disease were slim. Sallie died in May, the same month as did William A. Linda survived until August, often a humid month in Southside Virginia, which is an unfavorable environment for consumptives. Although the war in Virginia had been over for months, Linda was still at her home, being provided for not by Federal officials but by her former owners, who were now her employers. If Sallie and Linda had had families, they might have left, but having none, they remained.

The 1870 Federal Census gives one more snapshot of the Lax family during Reconstruction. In the decade since the previous census, Joel Lax's personal property value had been cut in half to $2000. All of his living children, except his son John, remained at home. By the time of his death in 1887, Joel's personal property value had reached just below $4,000, still under its 1860 value.

In one respect, Joel Lax was fortunate: he was a tobacco farmer. Although the war impoverished many, he worked a crop that would continue to sell; consequently, barring natural disasters, such as the flood that hit his county, Lax would be able to have an annual income. Further south, from Georgia to Texas, the cash crop was cotton. The cotton economy had suffered during the war, as Southern cotton planters could not sell their cotton either to the North or overseas. With a lack of cotton coming from the South, overseas buyers, such as those in England, were forced to look elsewhere for a supply. By the time the war was over, the damage was done, and cotton prices fell. Many farmers in the Cotton Belt turned to cotton production to try to earn money only to fail because they could not sell their crop at prices high enough to cover their debts.

Being "land poor" was not a new condition for farmers and planters across the South. They produced much of what they needed on their own land and often did not have much available actual cash money. Seeds for crops and supplies could be purchased on credit with the debt being paid when the crop came in. The war strained this system of debt and harvest. Farm production had been reduced during and immediately after the war. Supplies, even when the farmers had cash, were short. Even General Lee, who still owned two farms after the war, had to cover his uniform buttons with cloth since he could not afford a new coat or buttons but had to conform to the law forbidding anyone wearing Confederate insignia in public.

17.4.2 Forty Acres and a Mule!

Post-war farmers potentially included former black slaves. In many parts of the South, former black slaves who had the skills and desire to farm often, however, did not have the opportunity to purchase land of their own. As whites tried to hold on to their land, blacks struggled to acquire land of their own. Because few opportunities for them to buy land existed, blacks were forced to find land to rent in order to farm for themselves. To earn money as farm hands, they had to find white farm owners who would hire them. Many blacks, as well as poor whites who lost their property and were economically devastated, became sharecroppers, paying the owner of the land with a portion of the crops they raised.

One means of obtaining land in the United States had long been through land grants from Jamestown colonists who were given grants of land if they paid the passage for themselves or other colonists, to Revolutionary War soldiers who were given land grants in return for military service. Land grants historically have played a part in the settlement of this country. In 1865, General Sherman devised a land grant program as a means to provide former slaves with land of their own. With Special Field Order No. 15, Sherman established white-free, black-only zones on the islands from Charleston, South Carolina down the coast to St. Johns River in Florida. The freedmen would be able to establish their own homesteads and communities and have self-governance. The homesteads were restricted in size to forty acres, and the freedmen could use old government mules if they were available to help work the land. In one sense, the program was a success: approximately 40,000 freedmen flocked to the islands and built their homes. However, the land Sherman gave away had been plantations before the war confiscated from their previous owners.

President Johnson did not support the forced confiscation of property, so in 1866 he ordered the land be returned to its previous owners. For the Radical Republicans in Congress, Sherman, not Johnson, had the right idea. They believed it was necessary, or at least desirable, to destroy the old plantation system and Southern aristocrat class. Breaking up the plantations and redistributing the land was an ideal means of achieving this goal. Some Radical Republicans even wanted to expand the program, seeing it as a way to crush the planter class they blamed for the war, generate revenue to pay off the war debts, and attach the freedmen to the Southern landscape, where they would be motivated by property ownership to remain.

Johnson prevailed, and, by 1867, the Sea Islands experiment in freedmen land grants was essentially over. The freedmen were forced to give up their land and encouraged instead to go to work for the "real" landowners. In many cases, these were the very plantation owners who had owned the freedmen as slaves. Even so, some freed people did manage to retain their holdings, but, within a couple of generations, being divided among heirs or sold off piecemeal reduced these holdings until they were also reduced to sizes too small to support families, thus resulting in communities held in a state of near perpetual poverty.

17.4.3 Interracial Relationships

The uncertain and problematized place of freed people in the United States after the war reflected a long history of uncertain relations between different races. Indeed, since the earliest European explorers arrived in the Americas, interracial relationships have existed between whites and Indians, whites and blacks, and blacks and Indians. These relationships were not always accepted and were often frowned upon, yet were found in many communities. Anti-miscegenation laws in the colonies date back to the seventeenth century, although these laws could often be ignored if the couple in question did not marry.

What changed with Reconstruction was a heightened awareness by some Southerners of, and objection to, these relationships, particularly those between whites and blacks. White men with black women were more likely to be left alone than were black men with white women. Returning to the example of the Lax family, two of Joel Lax's brothers raised families with black women in Virginia during Reconstruction, leaving their portion of the family farm to them in their wills. Not all white male-black female relationships were so accepted; discretion was one key to avoiding trouble, while another was luck.

Black men having relationships with white women was a great risk at that time. In 1871, John Walthall, a black man in Haralson County, Georgia, was accused of sleeping with white women after he had stayed in a house of four white sisters who were probably prostitutes. Although warned to leave the area, Walthall remained, married a black woman, and settled down. A group of men from the Ku Klux Klan, known as the "KKK," targeted him. The Ku Klux Klan was founded early in Reconstruction. Many of the leaders and rank and file members were Confederate veterans. It comprised one of several secret organizations formed in the face of rapid social change and fallout from the war. The Klan willingly used violent tactics to achieve their ends which were to preserve white supremacy in the South, keep blacks "in their place," and keep Northerners out. Late one night, the KKK entered Walthall's home and beat his wife with a pistol. Walthall himself tried to hide under the floorboards of his home, but was found, shot, and pulled up from the floor and dragged out. The KKK accused Walthall of sleeping with white women and of stealing, then they whipped both him and his wife. Walthall later died of his injuries.

That same night, the KKK also beat, threatened, and whipped nearby residents, including Jasper and Maria Carter, a couple who lived in a house the KKK first entered before reaching Walthall's. Jasper was taken away and whipped severely then allowed to return to his frightened wife who had been threatened with a pistol. Walthall's neighbors had known the KKK was looking for him and had tried to protect him by telling him to leave the area. By assaulting them with such public violence that their treatment would reach other black communities in the area, to the KKK intended to intimidate black communities with a demonstration of the risks of protecting their own.

17.4.4 Social Violence

The goals of the KKK and like-minded individuals were to keep blacks, and to a lesser degree "low" whites, "in their place" and thereby protect the pre-war social order. In the days of Reconstruction, many white Southerners therefore viewed the Klan in a positive light, as a source of order and means of protection against what they deemed as dangerous "trouble-makers" and criminals of all colors.

In many areas of the South, white southerners thought that the Federal authorities put in charge of the Reconstruction, and who were supposed to provide law and order, were unresponsive to the needs of many white citizens, thus resulting in what they saw as lawlessness. In other areas, southerners perceived Federal authorities as being biased in favor of blacks and such "disreputable" whites as carpet baggers, that is, northerners who came to the South to make a fortune during Reconstruction, and scalawags, that is, white southerners who cooperated and allied themselves with carpet baggers, blacks, and those in charge of Reconstruction, in order to profit from the troubles of other white Southerners. Of course, not all northerners who came South were carpetbaggers, nor were all white southerners who tried to improve conditions for blacks scalawags; indeed, many of these people had the very best of humanitarian intentions. They supported the Republican ideals of creating a postwar South that would not be under the control of the old Confederates. The question of equality for blacks was not as fervently embraced but definitely supported by large numbers of the Republicans. Many southern and northern whites in the South and blacks risked their lives for these causes. To the southerners who wanted to restore the antebellum social order, these people were disruptive and dangerous.[53]

Regulators were volunteers who took it upon themselves to restore law and order, and the Klan was originally seen by some as a group of Regulators. In some areas, where the Klan did little, that reputation continued. In other regions, the Klan acted with such violence that they earned the terrorizing reputation that continues to this day. Some of these acts of violence included lynchings, which were not uncommon. The Klan, Regulators, or groups of unconnected citizens, might lynch someone, often a black male accused of "crimes" against a white female; the practice continued into the twentieth century. Whites as well as blacks might be lynched, but white men accused of similar "crimes" against black women were unlikely to be lynched or even arrested.

During Reconstruction, Federal officials tried to make a fuller place in Southern society for blacks. These officials therefore encouraged blacks to take public jobs and government positions, and to vote. White supremacists found these actions unacceptable. Even while encouraging blacks to advance themselves and pursue political power, Federal authorities often did little to protect blacks from the Klan or other angry whites. The laws known as Black Codes that were established in the South, in some cases, sought to prevent blacks from exercising their free individual rights to property, to education, and to vote. These codes varied from state to state. In Georgia, the codes did not seem too harsh; some actually protected blacks. However, they did define "persons of color," and declared interracial marriage as a crime, two points that were common among the codes.[54] Southern whites who feared blacks being given political power sought to limit their political ability by supporting the passage of these laws. Blacks who were outspoken not only offended the white supremacists but also stood out, making themselves targets for vigilante violence. Jack Dupree of Mississippi was one such man. He became involved in his local Republican Party, stood for black rights, and so was murdered by Klansmen who cut his throat and disemboweled him. His wife, who was forced to witness this murder, was intentionally left alive to proclaim the horrific price Dupree paid for his political activities.[55]

Blacks were not the only victims of violence during the Reconstruction period. White on white violence was also common in some areas, violence that even spawned family feuds such as the famous one between the Hatfields and McCoys. These two families lived in Virginia at the start of the war, only to have their home made part of the new Northern state of West Virginia while they were absent fighting in the war. Their political and socio-economic differences soon led to a long-term violent feud. Typically in the case of feuds, leading members of the families would be on opposite sides politically or socially, or had fought on opposite sides during the war. From there, anything from a verbal dispute to a conflict over property could set off a feud that would begin a cycle of violence and retaliation that could span years.

In other cases, the crimes could be more personal. Two such involved were Dr. George Darden of Warren County, Georgia, and Senator Joseph Adkins of Georgia. In 1869, Darden murdered the local newspaper editor Charles Wallace. He then turned himself over to the authorities in fear for his life, rightly believing that friends of his victim would seek vengeance. His jailer allowed Darden to keep weapons for his defense in case anyone attempted to remove him from the jail. As he had expected, a crowd of men came for Darden and forced him from his cell. They allowed him to write a note to his wife before taking him away and shooting him. They were actuated by a vigilante desire for justice, fearing Darden would not be convicted of murder and punished. His being shot rather than lynched may have been due to Darden's high standing in his community, since lynching was an ugly death reserved for "outcasts" of white Southern society.

Soon after Darden's murder, Senator Joseph Adkins was also murdered. The white Adkins supported the Radical Republicans and associated with blacks, particularly with black women. He was thought to incite blacks against whites. Considered by white planters and those of their class as a "scalawag," Darden's being a state senator made him someone who had "risen above his station" and therefore unacceptable. His and Darden's murders were reported in the North where there was an assumption that the motive for murder was political. Newspapers of the day make it clear that, while politics played its part, the behavior of the murder victims, consorting with blacks, possibly inciting them, behaving like a so-called low person, all motivated their murderers.

17.4.5 Black Politics

Besides such white politicians as Adkins, black politicians particularly faced danger and violence; the Klan and others murdered at least thirty-five black politicians. Nevertheless, many blacks engaged in political activity. Approximately 2,000 held political office at the national, state, or local level during Reconstruction. The majority of black politicians were in South Carolina and Louisiana. While blacks from all backgrounds, that is, slave and free, prosperous and impoverished, participated in the political process, those who rose to the highest offices often had the benefit of education. One such was Hiram Revels, who became the first black U.S. Senator when elected from Mississippi. Another was Blanche K. Bruce, a senator from Mississippi. Revels was born free; Bruce was born a slave. Both had been received educations atypical for average black Americans of that time, but which were not uncommon among blacks elected to office. In all, sixteen blacks served in the U.S. Congress during Reconstruction and approximately 600 served in the state legislatures.[56]

17.4.6 The Legacy of Reconstruction

While Reconstruction policies and officials may have had unforeseen effects, such as causing rather than preventing violence or pain, they did point to a direction for the South. Blacks continued to face discrimination from not only Southern whites, but also those officials intended to help them. At the same time, other Southern planters and farmers with a more progressive view reached out to help. For every blanket assumption about any group in the South, there were always exceptions where individuals stepped outside the predicted boundaries of behavior for their social class and status and did something different, either good or ill.

Reconstruction was intended to bring the former Confederate states back into the Union as equal members once again. But the uneven efforts at Reconstruction contributed to a perpetual poverty in many Southern states, handicapping them for generations to come. Before the war, the South had been a largely agrarian society; after the war it remained so, with the difference that now most farmers did not own their own land. In the decades following the war, sharecropping would grow and fewer farmers, white as well as black, could afford to own land.

Progress for blacks was slow but still visible. Schools, both public and private, were established across the South. Some faced opposition, even being destroyed, but in the end they achieved a measure of acknowledged success. Augusta Institute, today known as Morehouse Academy, was founded in 1867. Maggie Walker, the first African American and the first woman to be a bank president in the history of the United States, began her journey to success in Reconstruction era schools in Richmond, Virginia.

17.4.7 Before You Move On...

Key Concepts

In 1865, the South was in a state of utter devastation due to the long years of war. Everyone from the most prominent citizens to the least experienced deprivation. In the middle of this universal suffering, the Federal Government implemented Reconstruction, which included an attempt at radical social change. The people of the South, no matter their social, racial, or economic status, had to adapt to defeat in war, economic hardship, and societal changes. Some reacted with violence; others attempted to help change society for the better. Still, poverty and racism continued to plague the South long after the end of Reconstruction.

Test Yourself

1. To whites in the South, all whites were the same.

   a. True

   b. False

2. Jefferson Davis was convicted of treason.

   a. True

   b. False

3. Sharecroppers were tenant farmers who paid their rent with shares of their crops.
   a. True
   b. False

4. Cotton formed a strong economic basis for the South during Reconstruction.
   a. True
   b. False

See page 699 for answers

17.5 RETREAT FROM RECONSTRUCTION: THE GRANT YEARS

When Ulysses S. Grant ascended to the presidency in 1869, the nation's commitment to Reconstruction had started to fade. With only three states, Virginia, Mississippi, and Texas, unreconstructed and still under military supervision, northerners and southerners concluded that, once Congress seated representatives from those states, the federal role in rebuilding the South would end. At the same time, conservative southerners worked to wrest control from the Republican governments established after the war. Moderates or conservatives redeemed the state governments and began to chip away at the rights granted to the freedpeople during Congressional Reconstruction. Their efforts repeatedly prompted national leaders to return to the issue of reconstruction. The Grant administration struggled to find a coherent policy for dealing with developments in the South, as well as with the other problems the nation faced in the 1870s.

17.5.1 Grant Comes to Power

During the Johnson administration, Ulysses S. Grant continued in his wartime role as general-in-chief. As such, he oversaw the military commanders stationed in the southern states. Initially, Grant worked with Andrew Johnson to implement the Congressional mandates; however, the general increasingly found himself at odds with the president. By 1866, he concluded any attempts to impede the smooth transition from slavery to freedom would undermine the Union victories, something he could not abide. As Republicans prepared for the presidential election of 1868, Grant emerged as their mostly likely candidate. Not only did he endorse the Radicals' plans for the South and publicly break with the president, but also he seemed universally respected by the American people because of his wartime service. Grant had some misgivings about running for president, especially in terms of the effect it might have on his reputation and his family's long-term financial security. At the same time, he felt obligated to accept the nomination in order to save the Union victories from professional politicians. When Grant formally accepted the nomination, he closed his acceptance letter with a sentiment many Americans found appealing: "Let us have peace."[57]

While the Republicans easily settled on Grant, the Democrats faced a more difficult choice in selecting a nominee in 1868. Andrew Johnson hoped the party would choose him;

however, his political baggage ruled out that possibility. At the convention, a consensus to back Horatio Seymour, the former governor of New York, emerged on the twenty-second ballot. Like Grant, Seymour had misgivings about running. However, his friends convinced him to accept the nomination. The Democrats, especially the vice presidential nominee, Francis C. Blair, then launched an attack against Congressional Reconstruction, which played on southern whites' fear of black rule. Blair, for example, claimed that southern whites had been "trodden under foot by an inferior and barbarous race." Meanwhile, the Republicans focused their campaign on Grant's plea for peace. They argued that the Democrats' calls to end Republican rule would bring more, not less, violence to the South.[58]

As voters prepared to cast ballots in the fall, events in the South underscored the Republican campaign message. Throughout the region, the Ku Klux Klan as well as other like-minded organizations threatened and attacked Republican voters in hopes of keeping them away from the polls. According to James McPherson, "the Klan had evolved from a harmless fraternal order into a hooded terrorist organization dedicated to the preservation of white supremacy." The state militias and the federal troops in the South could do little to stop the violent rampage in 1868. In Georgia, for example, Klan threats and beatings kept Republican voters from the polls. In state elections earlier in the year, the Republicans outpolled the Democrats by about 7,000 votes. However, in the presidential election, the Democrats outpolled the Republicans by about 45,000 votes. Throughout the South, the violence cut Republican majorities. At the same time, though, many northerners concluded the southerners hoped to use terrorism to reverse the results of the war. Thus, Grant defeated Seymour in both the popular (53 percent) and Electoral College (73 percent) votes.[59]

The nation seemed quite relieved after Grant won the election, and they waited expectantly for some sign of his plans. However, the president-elect said very little about

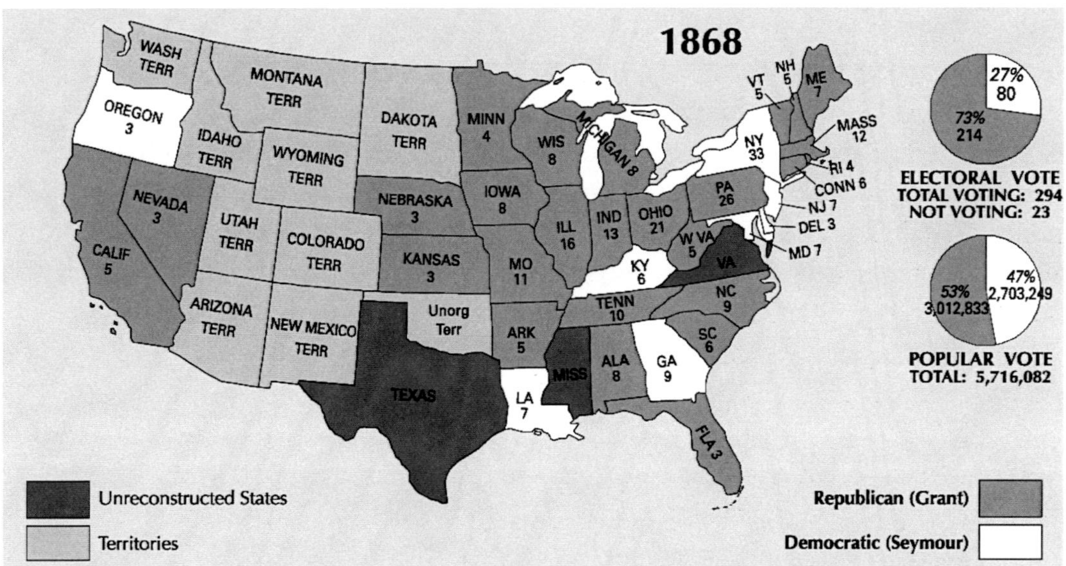

Figure 17.5 Presidential Election Map, 1868 | In 1868, Republicans easily chose Ulysses S. Grant as their candidate; the Democrats settled on Horatio Seymour. Grant defeated Seymour because of his military reputation and his call for peace when accepting the nomination.

Author: National Atlas of the United States
Source: Wikimedia Commons

his advisers or initiatives before inauguration day; in fact, he spent most of the time in Washington attending to his duties as general-in-chief.[60] In his inaugural address, Grant reiterated his campaign theme, but he noted the peace must be "approached calmly, without prejudice, hate, or sectional pride, remembering that the greatest good to the greatest number is the object to be attained." Thus, he vowed to work for the security of all citizens and to execute faithfully all laws. He also called on the states to ratify the Fifteenth Amendment, protecting the voting rights of all citizens. Moreover, he pledged to pay the nation's debt in gold and to limit government spending. His remarks struck a chord with the American people; as one southern editor noted, Grant expressed a "winning spirit toward the whole country."[61] The challenge for Grant throughout his presidency was to live up to the nation's expectations.

17.5.2 Problems in the First Term

During his first term, Ulysses S. Grant faced several foreign and domestic policy challenges. On the foreign policy side, he managed to resolve problems with Great Britain lingering from the *C.S.S. Alabama* claims. During the Civil War, British shipbuilders made several cruisers for the Confederacy including the *Alabama*. For numerous years, the American government sought to recover the losses caused by those ships. In the Treaty of Washington (1871), the British agreed to pay an indemnity to the Americans for the damages done by the *Alabama* and other British-made Confederate ships. However, Grant failed to secure the annexation of Santo Domingo when the opportunity presented itself. In spite of his lobbying effort, his poor relationship with Charles Sumner, the chairman of the Foreign Relations Committee, led the Senate to reject the treaty. On the domestic side, Grant outlined a policy for the "proper treatment of the original inhabitants" of the land. The president hoped to encourage humane treatment of Indians in the West, leading to their citizenship. However, hostility between Euro-Americans and Indians more often than not led to violence, making his policy less than successful.[62] However, the biggest challenges Grant faced as president stemmed from the effort to reconstruct the southern states and the emergence of Liberal Republicanism.

Figure 17.6 Ulysses S. Grant | The American people held high expectations for former Civil War hero turned president, Ulysses S. Grant. He promised to end to the strife caused by the war and by reconstruction but also to protect the rights of all citizens. However, he struggled to achieve his goals and live up to people's expectations.

Author: Mathew Brady
Source: Library of Congress

Restoring the Unreconstructed States

Although Congressional Reconstruction brought most of the southern states back into the Union before 1868, Ulysses S. Grant still had to address the southern problem. Virginia, Mississippi, and Texas remained unreconstructed when he took office, and

Republicans at the national level remained undecided about what to do about problems in Georgia regarding the seating of new black legislators. Reconstruction posed a challenge for Grant because of the goals he hoped to accomplish. Grant sought to protect the political and civil rights of blacks, but he also wanted to maintain a Republican presence in the South. Protecting blacks inherently would drive many whites away from the Republican Party; convincing whites to remain with the Republican Party would require abandoning the blacks to the mercy of the state governments. Moreover, to preserve the national Republican Party at a time when fighting slavery and rebellion no longer gave members a common cause likely would mean refocusing the party's interests away from the South. Finally, policies adopted during Presidential and Congressional Reconstruction limited Grant's options for dealing with problems in the southern states.[63]

Virginia, Mississippi, and Texas failed to ratify their state constitutions and reenter the Union before 1869 because of the so-called proscriptive clauses, which prevented former Confederates from participating in the government. Grant hoped to make Virginia a test case for his spirit of peace. Moderates there approached the president with a possible solution to end the impasse over the proposed constitution: whites would accept black suffrage only if they could reject the proscriptive clauses. Grant agreed to allow Virginians to vote on the proscriptive clauses separately from the rest of the constitution. He then recommended the solution to Congress for not only Virginia, but Mississippi and Texas as well. Congress approved the recommendation, but also required the states to ratify the Fifteenth Amendment before readmission. Voters in all three states ratified their state constitutions as well as the Fifteenth Amendment, without the proscriptive clauses, and Congress seated their representatives in 1870. Conservatives and moderates applauded the policy because it seemed as though Reconstruction was finally ending; radicals, on the other hand, criticized the president for selling out the freedpeople and the party. Through his moderate policy, Grant managed to preserve Republican rule in all three states, but only temporarily. By the mid-1870s, the Democrats had regained power, "redeeming" their states from Republican rule.[64]

While Grant followed a moderate policy in the unreconstructed states, he treated the situation in Georgia differently because of events that happened in 1868. In the state elections held in April, the Republicans won a majority of seats in the legislature. However, once the legislature convened, conservative whites voted to expel the twenty-eight black members. The Johnson administration did nothing about the problem, even though twenty-four of the whites who voted for the expulsion should not have been elected to the legislature because, as ex-Confederates, the Fourteenth Amendment barred them from government service. In response, Republicans in Georgia banded together with Democrats who opposed black suffrage to prevent ratification of the Fifteenth Amendment. They hoped such a turn of events would force Congress to protect black rights and the Republican Party in Georgia. Congress refused to seat Georgia's new representatives but did nothing else about the situation.[65]

Grant postponed any action until December 1869, when he asked Congress to return Georgia to military rule until the governor could remedy the problems with the legislature; Congress agreed. Most members believed the state brought the action on itself when the legislature took no action to reverse their decision about seating black members, even though a state court ruled blacks had the right to serve in the government. Congress further mandated that Georgia ratify the Fifteenth Amendment, a move Grant supported because he believed granting blacks full political rights would allow them to protect themselves in the future. Furthermore, the president saw his tougher stand in Georgia as a counterweight to his more lenient policy in the unreconstructed states. In 1870, the Republicans, with the military's support, ousted the conservative ex-Confederates, seated the black legislators, ratified the Fifteenth Amendment, and returned the state to the Union. However, the Republican gains in Georgia did not last long. In 1871, the Democrats won control of the state legislature and the governor's office and slowly chipped away at the gains the freedpeople made. Although asked to help, Grant did nothing.[66]

Table 17.1 Reconstruction and Redemption

State	Military District	Commander	Readmission	Redemption
Alabama	3	Pope	1868	1874
Arkansas	4	Ord	1868	1874
Florida	3	Pope	1868	1877
Georgia	3	Pope	1870	1871
Louisiana	5	Sheridan	1868	1877
Mississippi	4	Ord	1870	1876
North Carolina	2	Sickles	1868	1870
South Carolina	2	Sickles	1868	1876
Tennessee	N/A	N/A	1866	1869
Texas	5	Sheridan	1870	1873
Virginia	1	Schofield	1870	1869

Dealing with Klan Violence

While the Grant administration worked to reconstruct the final southern states, the process of ending Republican rule, what southern Democrats called redemption, had already begun. Throughout the South, Republican governments struggled to hold onto their power in the face of the divisions within the party, the growth of conservative sentiment, and the use of political terrorism. The Democratic Party in concert with the Ku Klux Klan hoped to restore white supremacy in economic, social, and political life. Georgian Abram Colby, when testifying before a Congressional Committee on Klan violence, noted how, when he refused a bribe to vote for the Democrats, the Klan pulled him out of his house in the middle of the night and whipped him repeatedly. Though hooded, Colby recognized the voices of his assailants: a local lawyer, a local doctor, and several farmers.[67]

Figure 17.7 The Ku Klux Klan in Mississippi | This image first appeared in Harper's Weekly in January 1872. It accompanied a story about the Justice Department's attempts to crack down on Klan intimidation and violence in the South.

Author: Unknown
Source: Library of Congress

Republican leaders in the South struggled to deal with such violence. If they did nothing, then the Democrats would triumph. If they tried to fight back with the state militia, composed mostly of blacks, then they might start a race war. At the same time, national Republican leaders seemed reluctant to involve the federal government. They worried about federal authority over Klan violence since murder, arson, and assault traditionally fell under the jurisdiction of the states. However, state governments could or would not stop the reign of terror against the signs of black power and advancement. In Mississippi, one case involving Klan violence fell apart when all five witnesses for the prosecution ended up dead before the trial. Thus, Congress, with Grant's support, passed several measures, collectively known as the Enforcement Acts, based on the terms of the Fourteenth and Fifteenth Amendments.[68]

The First Enforcement Act, approved on May 31, 1870, made it a federal crime to interfere with the right to vote, made it a felony to deny an individual's political or civil rights, and allowed the president to use federal troops to keep order at the polls. Then Congress created the Department of Justice, supervised by the Attorney General who to that point only served as the president's legal adviser to uphold the federal laws in the South. While Grant hoped the threat of the measure would curb the violence, many southerners seemed unconcerned about the new law. Therefore, Grant sent troops to North Carolina in late 1870; however, he would not declare martial law, so the troops did nothing to stop the violence. The president insisted that the governor, William W. Holden, mobilize local resources first. In essence, says historian Brooks Simpson, in North Carolina "the Republicans could not win unless they suppressed the violence, and the Democrats could not win unless their campaign of intimidation triumphed." Neither prospect looked good for the future of Reconstruction.[69]

Under the direction of Amos T. Ackerman, a Georgian appointed as Attorney General in late 1870, the Justice Department worked to prosecute individuals for violating the First Enforcement Act, but that did not bring much peace to North Carolina or the other southern states. Thus, Grant petitioned Congress for stronger laws to protect voters from intimidation and violence. The Second Enforcement Act, approved on February 28, 1871, created a federal mechanism to supervise all elections. The Third Enforcement Act, approved on April 20, 1871, strengthened the felony and conspiracy provisions for suffrage cases; moreover, it gave the president the authority to suspend the writ of habeas corpus and use the army to uphold the law. Shortly after he signed the last measure, popularly known as the Ku Klux Klan Act, Grant issued a proclamation asking white southerners to comply with the law.[70]

When that failed to happen, the Justice Department, assisted by the army, worked to arrest, indict, and prosecute Klansmen. The president only suspended habeas corpus in nine South Carolina counties in October 1871. Some of the federal government's prosecutions ended in convictions, but it dropped a majority of cases to clear the federal court dockets. As James McPherson notes, "the government's main purpose was to destroy the Klan and to restore law and order in the South, rather than secure mass convictions." To that end, they achieved a short-term victory in that "the 1872 election was the fairest and most democratic presidential election in the South until 1968."[71] Grant's judicious use of the Enforcement Acts, however, did become one of the issues of the presidential election campaign in 1872. Moreover, the administration's policy did not forestall the process of redemption.

Growing Criticism from the Liberal Republicans

Patronage for years served as a means for political parties to develop loyalty and raise money. People in government jobs felt fidelity to the party that put them there, and they usually gave a percentage of their salary to the party, a policy known as assessment. In 1865, reformers first introduced legislation to create a civil service commission that would determine how to identify the most qualified individuals for government service. When Grant took office, he appeared to share the reformers' concern about the effect the spoils system had on the quality of the nation's government. Grant certainly found himself beleaguered by the number of people seeking jobs after his election, and he expressed concern about the issue to those close to him. Moreover, Grant showed an air of independence when he selected his cabinet. He chose men he thought he could work well with, not those who had the most political clout. While Republicans in the Senate, who had to confirm his nominees, expressed dismay, the press seemed to appreciate Grant's decision to take politics out of the equation. Some of his choices turned out better than did others. Hamilton Fish, the secretary of state, served as an able steward of American foreign policy and worked well with the president. However, William Belknap, the secretary of war, mired the administration in scandal when it came out he accepted a bribe in exchange for a government contract.[72]

On the issue of civil service reform, Grant's early decisions about his own appointments caused the reformers to expect him to embrace change. Furthermore, the heads of the Treasury Department, the Interior Department, and the Justice Department began a system of extensive vetting for new hires and competitive exams for promotions. In his annual message to Congress in 1870, Grant recommended pursuing reform that would address "not the tenure, but the manner of making all appointments." Congress responded by creating a commission to study the issue and recommend changes in 1871. Grant appointed George Curtis, a noted reformer, to head the commission. After completing its review, the commission recommended examinations for all positions and an end to the practice of salary assessments. The president began to apply the changes in 1872.[73]

Two factors prevented Congress from adopting a permanent civil service system in the 1870s. First, Grant disliked patronage, but he also realized it served a political purpose. Unlike many reformers, the president did not equate patronage with corruption. In his support for reform, therefore, he never expected patronage to go away entirely. Grant even chose relatives and friends, including his father, for lower-level appointments to give them the prestige of holding a government position. Second, some Republicans in Congress turned against supporting civil reform when Grant became president. Calls for civil service reform in the mid-1860s partly came from concern about Andrew Johnson's appointments, and Republicans hoped to use reform to curb Johnson's power. With solid Republican control of the legislative and executive branches after 1869, reform seemed more harmful than helpful to the interests of the party.[74] In the end, Grant's mixed reputation for appointments and failure to fight for civil service reform after Congress lost interest disheartened many reformers.

Alongside questions about civil service reform, some Republicans began to question the Grant administration's approach to Reconstruction. Reformers, who adopted the name "Liberal Republican" in 1872, doubted there was much more the federal government could do to bring peace to the South. To them, the ratification of the Fifteenth Amendment suggested an end to federal involvement. Nevertheless, Grant, with the support of Radical Republicans, continued to intervene in the South. Liberal Republicans believed the time had come to let the southern states decide their own future so that the nation could focus on issues like civil service and tariff reform. Furthermore, they believed only a policy of full amnesty for former Confederates would end the violence and strengthen the Republican Party. In 1870, the Liberals and the Democrats joined forces in Missouri to defeat a Radical Republican administration. In 1872, the Liberal Republicans, composed of a variety of interest groups opposed to Grant's leadership, hoped to build on that momentum in the presidential election.[75]

Winning Re-Election in 1872

Liberal Republicans initially hoped to deny Grant the Republican nomination; however, when they realized that likely would not happen, leaders of the movement called for an independent nominating convention. The diversity of the delegates who gathered in Cincinnati in May 1872 demonstrated the dramatic changes within the Republican Party in the years after the Civil War. Some attendees seemed truly committed to reform; others sought to regain the political power they lost to Grant's supporters in the party. Thus, only two issues really brought the coalition together: their antipathy toward Ulysses S. Grant and their desire to adopt a new southern policy. Then again, those issues might just make the Liberal Republican nominee appealing to Democrats who also wanted to unseat Grant. In a series of backroom deals, the convention chose Horace Greeley, the publisher of the *New York Tribune*, as their presidential candidate. Greeley had name recognition across the country, and he had long supported amnesty and reconciliation. Adopting the motto "Anything to beat Grant," the Democrats also nominated Greeley for president, even though Greeley had spent much of his public career attacking them. For many Democrats, a fusion with Liberal Republicans would help end the nation's obsession with Reconstruction and, in turn, allow the party to rebuild its image after the Civil War. The Democrats, however, never unified themselves completely behind Greeley.[76]

Grant never really doubted his ability to win reelection, so he chose not to campaign. He did not want his lack of public speaking skills to undermine his candidacy. To counter the appeal of the Liberal Republican-Democrat coalition in 1872, the Republican Party worked diligently in the months before the election to support Grant's candidacy. As Eric Foner says, "Faced with this unexpected challenge, Republicans...moved to steal their opponents' thunder." Republicans in Congress reduced the tariff, then they passed an amnesty measure for Confederates barred from voting under the Fourteenth Amendment that had failed to win support in both 1870 and 1871. The party also effectively used political cartoons drawn by Thomas Nast that depicted Greeley shaking hands with the ghost of John Wilkes Booth over Abraham Lincoln's grave and with a conservative southerner standing over the victims of political terrorism.[77]

Grant easily won both the popular and Electoral College votes; in fact, he won every state he predicted he would take before the balloting began. His victory reflected the fact that public opinion on the ability of southern whites to manage Reconstruction lagged behind the Liberal Republican view. For Grant, the election was somewhat of a personal vindication, given the criticism he constantly faced in his first term. The results showed that voters liked Grant and continued to trust him to preserve the achievements of the

Figure 17.8 Republican Propaganda, 1872 | Noted political cartoonist, Thomas Nast, frequently attacked Horace Greeley, the Liberal Republican and Democratic nominee. In this drawing, Greely shakes hands with a Georgia Democrat standing over the bodies of the his victims, supporters of the Republican Party.

Author: Thomas Nast
Source: Wikimedia Commons

Civil War and Reconstruction. Though his reelection seemed to demonstrate public affection, according to political scientist Jean Edward Smith, it "marked the highpoint of Grant's presidency."[78]

17.5.3 Problems in the Second Term

In his second inaugural address, Ulysses S. Grant pledged to promote political equality through government action and encouraged social opportunity for all Americans, noting his "efforts in the future will be directed to the restoration of good feeling between the different sections of our common country." He also hoped to focus on the nation's economic health by restoring the "currency to a fixed value as compared with the world's standard of values—gold." Along the same lines, he wanted to promote the extension of the railroads and an increase in manufacturing to improve the nation's balance of trade.[79] The president desired to put the questions of reconstruction to rest and help rebuild the Republican Party around economic development. Grant achieved these goals to some extent, but not as he expected. Reconstruction ultimately ended in 1877, but the rights of blacks mattered very little to most whites. The Republican Party embraced economic development, in spite of a depression that the president seemed unable to handle.

Coping with the Panic of 1873

When Grant first came to office, he hoped to address the nation's economic problems. Financing the war and reconstruction left the federal government with a $2.8 billion debt and about $356 million worth of unbacked greenbacks in circulation. Republicans felt it important to pay the debt in full because failure to pay the debt would make it nearly impossible for the government to secure additional credit. Therefore, Grant proposed and

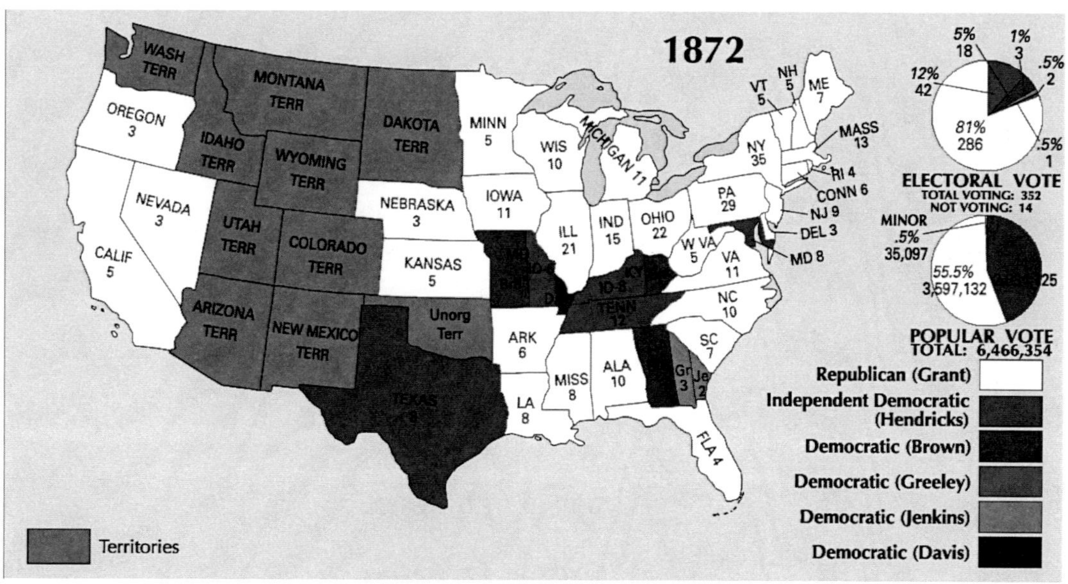

Figure 17.9 Presidential Election Map, 1872 | In 1872, Ulysses S. Grant easily secured victory over Greeley. The results showed voters liked Grant and they continued to trust him to preserve the achievements of the Civil War and Reconstruction.

Author: National Atlas of the United States
Source: Wikimedia Commons

Congress passed the Public Credit Act of 1869, which promised to pay all bondholders in specie. Meanwhile, George S. Boutwell, the secretary of treasury, worked to make his department more efficient in collecting government revenue. Boutwell, though, inadvertently caused a crisis when he began to sell the government's gold surplus in an attempt to reduce the debt. Speculators Jay Gould and Jim Fisk attempted to corner the gold market or manipulate the price in a way to make a healthy profit by using Abel Corbin, the president's brother-in-law, as an intermediary. Their maneuverings led to "Black Friday," September 24, 1869, where the price of gold and stocks declined and brokerage houses failed.[80]

However, it was a short-term setback. Over the next few years, the nation's economy grew, especially because of the expansion of the railroads, and the Grant administration reduced the debt. The booming economy in the early 1870s caused many businesses and investors to take risks, which led to a depression in 1873. The financial crisis stemmed from the general overexpansion of industry, but more specifically from the rapid growth of the railroads. Efforts to recover from the Civil War at home and the Franco-Prussian War abroad did not help either. In the mid-1860s, the country entered a railroad building boom, most notably in the southern and western states. The demand for money to finance new business ventures, while also paying old debts in the United States and Europe, prompted bankers to lend money irresponsibly and brokers to market worthless securities. Furthermore, railroad developers saturated the market; there simply were not enough customers to keep the railroads operating at a profit. By September 1873, the failure of Jay Cooke & Co., which was attempting to finance the Northern Pacific Railroad, spurred the Panic of 1873.[81]

After the panic began, Congressmen, especially from the Western states, called on Grant to inflate the currency by releasing retired greenbacks into circulation. Wary that that solution would cause rampant inflation, he traveled to New York City to seek the advice of leading businessmen and bankers. The businessmen supported currency inflation to relieve the crisis; the bankers did not. Grant sided with the bankers and pursued a tight money policy. Rather than release the retired greenbacks, the government as a temporary solution began to purchase bonds. In time, New York banks began to issue certificates usable as cash. Grant's response ended the immediate crunch for cash without decreasing the value of the dollar. From a strictly financial perspective, his policy ended the panic, but a depression set in around the country. In the next few years, over 18,000 businesses failed, unemployment reached 14 percent, and banks foreclosed on a large number of farms. Poverty spread across the country; unemployed workers went on strike and disgruntled farmers fused political alliances to attack business interests. The country at times seemed on the verge of a class war.[82]

Facing pressure from their constituents, Congress still sought to address the financial crisis through currency inflation, even though Grant made his preference clear for a tight money policy. In March 1874, Congress passed a measure to add about $100 million to the amount of money in circulation: half in greenbacks and half in specie-backed currency. Most people expected the president would not dare veto it. However, Grant had his doubts and he vetoed the inflation bill.[83] The financial community praised the veto; surprisingly, once he made the decision, the American people endorsed it as well. Congress then worked on a bill to support the president's push for specie-backed currency. The resulting Specie Resumption Act of 1875 proposed to redeem greenbacks in circulation for gold beginning on January 1, 1879. Grant happily signed the measure, which did not end the financial crisis so much as reorient the Republican Party toward conservative financial principles. In the meantime, Benjamin H. Bristow, appointed as the secretary of treasury during the crisis, worked to put the nation on the slow road to economic recovery by refinancing the federal government's debt by issuing new government bonds. Full recovery finally came 1878, leaving many Americans, especially in the North, frustrated that Reconstruction seemed to take greater precedence than financial recovery.[84]

Facing the Scandals

Even before Grant had to deal with the Panic of 1873, he faced the fallout of a variety of scandals linked to his administration; as the financial crisis set in, further revelations seemed to weaken his ability to act on important issues. After the gold crisis in 1869, people speculated about possible improprieties among Grant's advisers and even the president himself. While no evidence surfaced to tie Grant to any of the scandals involving his underlings, devotion to his staff prevented him from doing more to stop the behavior once he found out about the problems.[85] Grant's difficulties began in September 1872 when the *New York Sun* published a story about the Crédit Mobilier affair where several members of Congress took bribes to ignore the company's shady financial practices during the construction of the Union Pacific. Revelations about the Back Pay Grab, the Whiskey Ring, and the Indian Trading scandals soon followed. While the Grant administration had nothing to do with Crédit Mobilier, the same was not true of the other scandals.

At the end of its session in March 1873, the Forty-Second Congress inadvertently planted the seeds of a scandal when it voted to include a pay raise for the president, vice president, Supreme Court justices, cabinet officers, and members of Congress as part of the government's general appropriations bill. Few people quibbled about raising salaries for the executive and judicial branches, and the legislative increases were not inherently controversial since salaries for members had not gone up since 1852. However, members voted to make the pay increase retroactive, essentially giving each member a bonus of $5,000. Grant signed the appropriations bill, because if he failed to do so government agencies would not have any operating funds until the next session of Congress met. The public outcry, against both Democrats and Republicans, came quickly. When the Forty-Third Congress met, they immediately repealed the salary increases for Congress, but public trust in the government further declined.[86]

When Benjamin H. Bristow took over as secretary of the treasury in June 1874, he sought to implement civil service reforms within the department. Furthermore, he wanted to increase collections, especially from the liquor industry that for years evaded their taxes by bribing treasury agents. The problem seemed most acute in St. Louis, where Bristow focused the Whiskey Ring investigation. In the process, he turned his attention on General Orville Babcock, the president's confidential secretary, who was friends with General John A. McDonald, the revenue supervisor in St. Louis. Bristow maintained that two cryptic telegrams showed Babcock's collusion in the attempt to defraud the government.

To clear his name, Babcock requested a military court of inquiry look into the matter. Grant appointed the board after checking with his cabinet. However, the board never made a ruling because prosecutors in St. Louis refused to turn over any paper evidence; the case therefore went to civil court. Grant, convinced that the secretary of the treasury targeted his aide unfairly, gave testimony in 1876 for the trial in his Babcock's favor, and the jury later acquitted him. However, Babcock could no longer serve the president as his confidential secretary, and so Grant shifted him to another government position.[87]

Finally, William Belknap, the secretary of war, embroiled Grant in another scandal relating to the Indian trade. The problem began in 1869, not long after Belknap took office. Apparently, his wife Carrie, constantly short of money because she liked to live lavishly, discovered that the War Department contracted with private individuals to run military trading posts. Mrs. Belknap asked her husband to award the contract for Fort Sill to a friend, Caleb P. Marsh, who would share the profits of the lucrative Indian trade with the family. However, John S. Evans, who held the Fort Sill contract, did not want to give it up. Therefore, Marsh and Evans worked out a deal. Evans kept the contract and paid Marsh $12,000 per year, half of which he planned to give to the Belknaps. By 1876, William Belknap collected about $20,000 as part of the arrangement. Early that year, a House committee began to look into the military contracts and discovered Belknap's malfeasance. Lyman Bass, the head of the House committee, told Bristow the House planned to launch impeachment proceedings against Belknap. On Bristow's recommendation, Grant made an appointment with Bass for later that day. As he was departing the executive mansion to have his portrait painted, he learned from a steward that Belknap wanted to see him. The secretary of war tendered his resignation effective immediately, and Grant accepted it. Even though Belknap resigned, the House still impeached him; the Senate acquitted him because he was no longer in office, not because members thought him innocent of the charges. When Grant accepted Belknap's resignation, many critics thought he wanted to cover up the whole affair.[88]

Revisiting Reconstruction

Reconstruction still posed a problem for Ulysses S. Grant in his second term because the problems he faced in the first term, finding a balance between securing black rights and shoring up Republican governments, still existed in the second term. Many southern and northern whites did not want to treat blacks as their equals, and southern Republicans never coalesced into a unified party. Each southern state posed unique challenges for the Grant administration as conservative interests attempted to end Republican rule in the 1870s, and the president seemed undecided whether the federal government should still be involved in the South. Historian William Gillette concluded that "Grant came to the presidency pledging peace, but at the end of his second term, his southern policy had neither brought true peace for the nation, nor secured power for his party, nor increased popularity for his administration."[89] Grant's policy ultimately failed in the end because the president and the people lacked a commitment to Reconstruction.

Support for Reconstruction began to dwindle in 1873 because of the rise of violence in Louisiana. The previous year, the Republican Party split between the regular Republicans and the Liberal Republicans and ran two sets of candidates in the state elections. With the results inconclusive, both groups convened a legislature and inaugurated a governor, meaning the state had two governments. A federal court finally sided with the regular Republicans, and Grant sent federal troops to enforce the decision. Regrettably, the regular Republicans were not particularly popular with most whites or with the Grant administration, for that matter. Those opposed to Governor William P. Kellogg joined White Leagues, paramilitary units that scoured the countryside to terrorize Republican leaders and their supporters. The worst of the violence occurred on April 13, 1873 in Colfax during a clash between the local White League and the black militia. Three whites and over one hundred blacks died. Leaguers killed half of the black victims after they surrendered. The federal government subsequently charged seventy-two whites for their involvement in the Colfax Massacre, but juries convicted only three.[90]

Though the federal government took a tough stand after the Colfax Massacre, the violence did not stop; in fact, it seemed to get only worse as the 1874 elections approached. Democrats made racist appeals to white voters in an attempt to oust the Republican Party, and they backed their statements with violence. In August, White Leaguers assassinated six officials near Shreveport. In September, they marched on New Orleans to oust the Kellogg administration. In the skirmish between the White League and state forces, over thirty-one people died and nearly eighty people suffered wounds. The White League only gave up control of city hall, the state house, and the arsenal when federal troops dispatched by the president arrived. When the elections finally happened, the Democrats appeared to take control of the legislature. However, the certifying board threw out the returns in many parishes because of the intimidation. When the Democrats maneuvered to seat their representatives anyway, the governor asked the federal troops for assistance. The field commander then marched into the state house and forcibly removed the Democrats. Critics of the Grant administration's southern policy abhorred the action because, if the military could act in Louisiana, then it could also act in Michigan or anywhere else.[91]

The ongoing problems in the South, coupled with the Panic of 1873, caused voters to turn against the Republican Party in the midterm elections of 1874. A 110-vote Republican majority in the House turned into a sixty-vote Democratic majority after the election; the Democrats also gained ten seats in the Senate. Democratic victories made it clear that Congress would no longer support additional enforcement measures because the American people clearly indicated they wanted the government to turn its attention to more pressing issues like economic recovery. The election results caused Republican Party leaders to look for ways to repair the damage.

Figure 17.10 "The Union as it Was" | In this political cartoon, Thomas Nast reacts to the efforts by the White Leagues to redeem Louisiana from Republican rule. Grant responded to the situation with force, but it only hurt the prospects of the Republican Party in Louisiana and nationally in 1874.

Author: Thomas Nast
Source: Wikimedia Commons

The most obvious answer seemed to stop propping up southern governments. Before they firmly committed to that policy, in his annual message to Congress in December 1874, Grant reminded members and the American people that if they accepted blacks as citizens then much of the violence would stop. Partially to respond to Grant's rejoinder and partially to pay tribute to longtime antislavery advocate Charles Sumner who recently died, Congress approved the Civil Rights Act of 1875 to prevent racial discrimination in all public venues except schools. Many Democrats, however, only supported the measure because they expected the federal courts to declare it unconstitutional. Beyond that, the federal government's commitment to reconstruction waned in 1875. When Mississippi Democrats launched a campaign of violence to take back the state, Grant's advisers convinced him not to send troops to assist the Republican governor.[92]

While the Supreme Court did not reverse the Civil Rights Act of 1875 until 1883, it did declare the Enforcement Acts unconstitutional in 1876. Grant hoped to protect the government's ability to enforce the Fourteenth and Fifteenth Amendments through his Supreme Court nominations. In the end, three of the four men Grant nominated to serve on the Supreme Court voted against the government's attempts to defend the freedpeople in two important decisions. *U.S. v. Reese* related to a Kentucky tax collector's attempt to prevent blacks from voting in local and state elections by not collecting their poll tax. The Court invalidated the First Enforcement Act when it ruled that the Fifteenth Amendment did not apply to local or state elections, only to national elections. *U.S. v. Cruikshank* stemmed from the government's attempt to prosecute the perpetrators of the Colfax Massacre. This time, the Court ruled that the Fourteenth and Fifteenth Amendment applied only to state actions, not individual actions, and thus the federal government had no right to prosecute individuals for ordinary crimes like assault and murder. The two decisions closed the door to further federal intervention should anyone at the national level have cared to do so, and few did at that point.[93]

17.5.4 The South Redeemed

Frustration with reconstruction set the stage for the presidential election of 1876, and most people realized that the results of that contest would determine the fate of Republican rule in the South. After 1875, only Florida, Louisiana, and South Carolina still had Republican governments, and leaders in all three states needed federal support to maintain their power. Grant spoke fervently about the need to curb political terrorism and protect black rights, but he still lacked a policy to achieve both goals. So, in early 1876, Grant tried to divorce the Republican Party's future from the Civil War and Reconstruction by focusing the public's attention on the possibilities of public education and the importance of the separation of church and state. By then, most Republicans discounted the president's usefulness to help the party recover from the debacle in 1874 because of the numerous scandals swirling around his administration. They were actually happy when Grant squashed the rumors that he might run again.[94]

The Democrats hoped to build on their victories in 1874 by further capitalizing on American frustration with the Grant administration's scandals and reconstruction policies. Therefore, they focused the campaign on the issue of reform. First, they chose Samuel J. Tilden as their presidential nominee. Tilden, the governor of New York, built his reputation in party circles by promoting civil service reform. Second, the party's platform focused on ending the depression and the political corruption in government. The platform suggested only reform could save the Union "from a corrupt centralism" which led to fraud in the central government, misrule in the South, and continued economic misery. The Democrats proposed "to establish a sound currency, restore the public credit and maintain the national honor." Moreover, in the centennial election, they made their support and the American people's support for reform-minded legislation a patriotic venture.[95]

The Republican Party had numerous people to choose from in 1876. Former Speaker of the House, James G. Blaine, looked like the favorite going into the convention. However, allegations of impropriety for selling some railroad stock to the Union Pacific well above market value made him a poor choice in an election focused on government scandals. Benjamin H. Bristow, Grant's secretary of treasury, won support from reformers in the party for his role in taking down the Whiskey Ring, but some wondered whether he had the disposition to be president. Finally, Rutherford B. Hayes, the governor of Ohio, emerged as the most likely favorite son candidate to do well at the convention. Blaine led in the early balloting, but as the convention dragged on, delegates turned to Hayes as a compromise candidate because he came from the crucial state of Ohio, had a reputation for reform, and favored a moderate policy toward Reconstruction. The party's platform pledged "the permanent pacification" of the southern states as well as "the complete protection of all its citizens in the free enjoyment of all their rights." The remainder of the statement focused on political corruption, public education, land grants, tariff revision, immigration restriction, and other issues.[96]

Figure 17.11 The Candidates in 1876 | Frustration with reconstruction set the stage for the presidential election of 1876. The Republicans chose Rutherford B. Hayes (left), while the Democrats chose Samuel J. Tilden (right). Initially both campaigns focused on issues other than reconstruction; however, violence in South Carolina prompted the Republicans to wave the bloody shirt.

Authors: Mathew Brady, Unknown
Source: Library of Congress (both)

The Republicans, more so than the Democrats, struggled to find a cohesive voice during the campaign because their platform seemed at times contradictory. Moreover, Hayes did little to attempt to explain how he would do anything different from Grant when it came to preserving peace and political rights in the South, especially as South Carolina descended into violence in the months before the election. At first, Grant seemed to let South Carolina go the way of Mississippi, but then he changed his mind after the Hamburg Massacre. On July 4, 1876, the black militia in Hamburg held a parade; local authorities arrested them for blocking traffic. At the trial only a few days later, violence broke out outside the courthouse. Outgunned, the black forces surrendered; that night white forces murdered five of them. Grant sent troops in an attempt to prevent more such incidences. The violence, according to Brooks Simpson, proved a blessing in disguise for the Republicans during the campaign. The massacre showed how some white southerners had not really repented allowing the party to wave "the bloody shirt" or reminding voters of the rebellious nature of the southern states. But, to a certain extent, the tactic fell on deaf ears; northerners still were more concerned about the economy.[97]

Polling for the presidential election took place throughout the fall, and as the November deadline approached, Tilden appeared to be ahead of Hayes in the popular and Electoral College votes. The Democrats seemed poised to take the South, and so they only needed to take New York, and Indiana, New York, New Jersey, and Connecticut, or some combination thereof to win. Tilden won the popular vote with 51 percent to 48 percent for Hayes. However, the Electoral College returns were not so clear because both the Democrats and the Republicans claimed Florida, Louisiana, and South Carolina. Given that the sitting Republican governments ultimately determined the accuracy of the voting, all three states declared for Hayes. Democrats charged that Republicans stole the election; Republicans responded that the Democrats had already done so by using violence to keep Republican voters away from the polls. At that point, it became clear that Congress needed to find a solution for dealing with the contested Electoral College returns, and the Constitution only said that Congress should count the returns. It did not specify how to count contested votes. Given that the Republican Senate and the Democratic House did not agree on this point, they could not determine who won the election.[98]

Congress desperately needed to make a decision on the contest votes because rumors spread wildly in the months before the scheduled inauguration that the country was on the verge of another civil war. Finally, Congress decided to create an electoral commission composed of five members from the Senate, five members from the House, and five members from the Supreme Court to determine which returns from Florida, Louisiana, and South Carolina to count. Seven of the members would be Democrats; seven would be Republicans; and one member would be an independent to break the expected tie. Both parties agreed to the composition of the committee and that, unless both chambers voted to overrule the commission, their decision would be final. Democrats expected the independent member to be Supreme Court Justice David Davis, whom they felt would side with them. However, Davis declined to serve because the legislature of Illinois selected him as one of their U.S. senators. That meant the final member from the Supreme Court would be a Republican Joseph Bradley.[99]

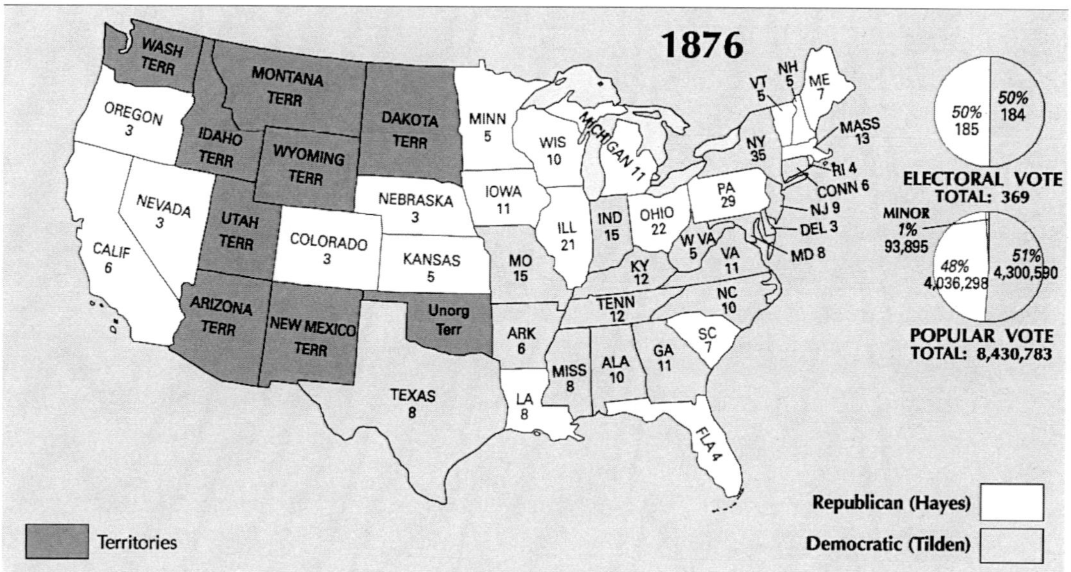

Figure 17.12 Presidential Election Map, 1876 | Samuel J. Tilden won the popular vote suggesting the willingness of the American people to abandon reconstruction. However, the Electoral College returns for Florida, Louisiana, and South Carolina were disputed. Eventually, an impartial electoral commission created by Congress led to Hayes to win the Electoral College. With the Compromise of 1877, Hayes informally agreed to remove federal troops from the South if southern legislators would not filibuster the commission's decision.

Author: National Atlas of the United States
Source: Wikimedia Commons

When the commission met in February, they went through the states in alphabetical order, making Florida the first contested state to come before the members. The Democrats protested that the Republicans illegally declared the state for Hayes; meanwhile, the Republicans countered that the only justification for not accepting the official returns was to review all the local returns. With the inauguration fast approaching, the commission voted eight to seven, with Bradley casting the tie-breaking vote, to accept the returns certified by the Republican governor. They subsequently voted the same way for Louisiana and South Carolina. The Senate quickly accepted the commission's decision. House Democrats thought they could use a filibuster to prevent Hayes from assuming the presidency. If they could hold off a decision until March 4, then, per the Constitution, it would fall to the House to select the president. To ward off this possibility, the Republican Party worked behind the scenes to appease southerners in what became known as the Compromise of 1877. Informally, Hayes agreed to land grants for a southern transcontinental line, federal funding for internal improvements, and the removal of federal troops from Louisiana and South Carolina. Realizing they would likely receive more concessions from Hayes than from Tilden, enough Southern Democrats tilted to Hayes, thus ending the possibility of a filibuster. After Rutherford B. Hayes took office, he attempted to follow through with the promises he made to Southern Democrats. Reconstruction officially ended, and the federal government ceased its efforts to maintain the rights of black citizens.[100]

17.5.5 Before You Move On...

Key Concepts

In 1869, famed Civil War general Ulysses S. Grant became the president of the United States. The American people took to heart his call for peace during the campaign and looked forward to a lessening of sectional tensions in the coming years. However, the Grant administration struggled to define a coherent southern policy to ensure that peace. The president hoped to promote black rights and retain Republican rule. Those two goals, given the racism of many southern whites, seemed an impossible objective. During Grant's first term, the last of the southern states, Virginia, Mississippi, and Texas, reentered the Union. Even before that happened, however, other southern states began the process of redemption, whereby they ousted Republican governments, often by using violence. Grant's failure to bring peace or secure civil service reform caused the Republican Party to split before the election of 1872. Liberal Republicans banded with Democrats to support Horace Greely for president. Grant won the reelection but found his second term more difficult than the first. The depression caused by the Panic of 1873, the concerns about political corruption brought on by a series of scandals tied to the president, and the continued problems in the South resulting from the efforts to redeem Louisiana and Mississippi left the Republican Party vulnerable going into the presidential election of 1876. Republican Rutherford B. Hayes ultimately defeated Democrat Samuel J. Tilden in a heavily contested election, which was decided by a special election commission. The Compromise of 1877 sealed the fate of Reconstruction as the nation looked forward to dealing with new political and economic issues.

Test Yourself

1. The Grant administration supported the adoption of the Enforcement Acts to curb Klan violence against black voters in the South.

   a. True

   b. False

2. Southern redeemers hoped to preserve Republican rule in the South.

   a. True

   b. False

3. Which of the following partially explain Ulysses S. Grant's failure to develop a successful southern policy?

   a. He allowed corruption to develop in his administration.

   b. He proposed to withdrawal federal troops from the South.

   c. He opposed Congressional Reconstruction.

   d. None of the above.

4. Who won the presidential election of 1876?
   a. Ulysses S. Grant
   b. Horace Greeley
   c. Samuel J. Tilden
   d. Rutherford B. Hayes

See page 700 for answers

17.6 Conclusion

During Reconstruction, defined as the period from 1865 when the Confederate troops surrendered to 1877 when the last federal troops withdrew from the South, the United States sought to restore the southern states to the Union and to define the rights of the freedmen in that Union. Conflicting ideas about these issues made the process a difficult one, to say the least. Throughout the period, national leaders struggled to find a policy that would result in political and social harmony. After 1865, Andrew Johnson and Congressional Republicans debated over which branch of government would determine Reconstruction policy. Johnson favored a quick reunion that benefitted the non-slaveholders at the expense of the former slaveholders and the former slaves. Republicans hoped to devise a policy that would punish the former slaveholders and encourage the yeomen and the freedmen to work together to support Republican rule. Congressional Republicans appeared to win the debate, but it certainly was not a lasting victory.

Many white southerners were not ready to accept the equality of the races; conservatives played on the fear of "Negro rule" to weaken the Republican governments in the late 1860s and early 1870s. As conservative southerners began to reassert their authority, the American people elected Ulysses S. Grant as president in 1868 because he promised peace. Northerners tired of the focus on the South, especially after the nation entered a depression in 1873. Meanwhile, southerners wanted to reduce the amount of federal control over political and social issues in their states. Grant never found a policy that could meet the needs of northerners and southerners, further souring people on Reconstruction. Thus in 1876, both presidential candidates, Republican Rutherford B. Hayes and Democrat Samuel J. Tilden, tailored their campaign message to suggest their victory would lead to the end of Reconstruction. While Tilden won the popular vote, a special election commission awarded the Electoral College to Hayes. Southern Democrats in Congress, who had redeemed their states from Republican rule in the 1870s, chose not to block the result because Hayes informally pledged to remove federal troops and to increase federal aid for internal improvements for the South. The Compromise of 1877 effectively ended Reconstruction; however, it failed to protect the rights gained by the former slaves after the war.

17.7 CRITICAL THINKING EXERCISES

- Why did the Lincoln administration's policies on reconstruction fail? What did the problems encountered in the southern states teach national leaders as they prepared for postwar reconstruction, or what should have those problems taught national leaders?
- Why do you think that the Thirteenth Amendment, which abolished slavery in the United States, was necessary when the Emancipation Proclamation and Civil Rights Act addressed the same issue? And why was the Fifteenth Amendment necessary when the right to vote had already been mentioned in the Fourteenth Amendment?
- Sherman's plan for the Sea Islands was a bold move that failed due to political opposition. Do you believe Sherman was right to create the Sea Island homesteads, or Johnson was right to order the properties returned to their original owners?
- What, if anything, could the federal government have done to make white southerners believe that Regulators were not necessary?
- What, in your opinion, should the federal government have done for the newly freed slaves to help ensure their successful transition to life as free people?
- Many historians have been critical of Ulysses S. Grant's leadership. Do you agree or disagree with their view? Be sure to consider what challenges and limitations Grant faced as president in making your assessment.

17.8 KEY TERMS

- Amnesty Proclamation
- Black Codes
- Black Suffrage
- Carpet Baggers
- Charles Sumner
- Civil Rights Act of 1866
- Civil Rights Act of 1875
- Civil Service Reform
- Colfax Massacre
- Compromise of 1877
- Congressional Election of 1866
- Consumption
- Davis Bend
- Frederick Douglass
- Due Process
- Election of 1868
- Election of 1872
- Election of 1876
- Enforcement Acts
- Feud
- Fifteenth Amendment
- First Congressional Reconstruction Act, 1867
- Fourteenth Amendment

- Freedman's Bureau bill
- Ulysses S. Grant
- Horace Greeley
- Rutherford B. Hayes
- Impeachment of Andrew Johnson
- Jim Crow
- Andrew Johnson
- Joint Committee on Reconstruction
- Justice Department
- Ku Klux Klan (KKK)
- Liberal Republicans
- Lynching
- Memphis Race Riot
- New Orleans Race Riot
- Panic of 1873
- Presidential veto
- Radical Reconstruction
- Radical Republicans
- Regulators
- Scalawags
- Sea Islands
- Special Field Order No. 15
- Specie Resumption Act of 1875
- Thaddeus Stevens
- Edwin Stanton
- Alexander Stephens
- Ten Percent Plan
- Tenure of Office Act of 1867
- Thirteenth Amendment
- Samuel J. Tilden
- Tuberculosis
- *U.S. v. Cruikshank* (1876)
- *U.S. v. Reese* (1876)
- Benjamin Wade
- Wade-Davis bill
- Whiskey Ring

17.9 CHRONOLOGY

The following chronology is a list of important dates and events associated with this chapter.

Date	Event
Spring 1862	Union officials began the process of reconstruction on South Carolina's Sea Islands
November 1863	Union officials began the Davis Bend experiment based on the principles of free labor
December 1863	Lincoln issued the "Proclamation of Amnesty and Reconstruction" or the Ten Percent Plan
March 1864	Unionists in Arkansas adopted a new constitution under the Ten Percent Plan

Date	Event
April 1864	Unionists in Virginia adopted a new constitution under the Ten Percent Plan
July 1864	Unionists in Louisiana adopted a new constitution under the Ten Percent Plan; Congress approved the Wade-Davis bill; Lincoln vetoed the measure
January 1865	Sherman met with former slaves in Savannah to discuss the meaning of freedom and then issued Special Field Order No. 15
March 1865	Congress approved and Lincoln signed the Freedmen's Bureau bill
April 1865	Lee surrendered to Grant; Civil War ended Lincoln assassinated; Vice President Andrew Johnson replaced him as President
May 1865	President Johnson issued the Amnesty Proclamation
Summer 1865	Black Codes established in most Southern States
December 1865	Congress created Joint Committee of Fifteen on Reconstruction; Thirteenth Amendment abolished slavery in the United States; Ku Klux Klan formed in Tennessee
February 1866	Powers of Freedmen's Bureau expanded by Congress
April 1866	Civil Rights Act of 1866 passed over Johnson's veto
May 1866	Race Riot occurred in Memphis, Tennessee; Race Riot occurred in New Orleans, Louisiana
June 1866	Fourteenth Amendment to the Constitution approved by Congress
February 1867	House of Representatives voted to impeach President Andrew Johnson
March 1867	First Congressional Reconstruction Act passed over Johnson's veto; Tenure of Office Act passed by Congress
May 1867	Senate voted to acquit President Johnson
July 1867	Addenda to the Reconstruction Act passed by Congress over Johnson's veto
Summer 1868	Ku Klux Klan violence increased in the South as the presidential election neared

Date	Event
July 1868	Fourteenth Amendment ratified by the states
November 1886	Ulysses S. Grant defeated Horatio Seymour in the presidential race
February 1869	Fifteenth Amendment passed by Congress
December 1869	Grant encouraged Congress to readmit Virginia, Mississippi, and Texas, the last of the unreconstructed states; Grant asked Congress to return Georgia to military rule because conservatives in the state legislature refused to seat the black representatives
May 1870	Congress passed the First Enforcement Act
December 1870	Grant asked Congress to consider civil service reform and Congress created a commission to look into the matter in early 1871
February 1871	Second Enforcement Act passed by Congress
April 1871	Third Enforcement Act (the Ku Klux Klan Act) passed by Congress
October 1871	Grant suspended habeas corpus for nine counties in South Carolina and sent federal troops to maintain order
May 1872	Liberal Republicans nominated Horace Greeley for president; the Democrats later endorsed their selection
September 1872	*New York Sun* exposed the Crédit Mobilier affair
November 1872	Ulysses S. Grant defeated Horace Greeley in the presidential race
April 1873	Colfax Massacre occurred
September 1873	Jay Cooke &Co. failed setting off the Panic of 1873
March 1873	Congress voted to increase government salaries touching off the Back Pay Grab scandal
March 1874	Congress approved the inflation bill to infuse money into the American economy, but Grant vetoed the measure
June 1874	Benjamin Bristow took over as the secretary of treasury and began to investigate the Whiskey Ring
September 1874	The White League in Louisiana attempted to overthrow the Republican governor; Grant dispatched federal troops to end the violence

Date	Event
November 1874	Democrats regained control of the House of Representatives
January 1875	Congress passed the Specie Resumption Act
March 1875	Congress passed the Civil Rights Act
September 1875	Mississippi requested federal assistance to fight Klan violence, and the Grant administration refused
March 1876	Grant accepted William Belknap's resignation before the House impeached him for accepting bribes; Supreme Court issued its decision in *U.S. v. Reese* and *U.S. v. Cruikshank*
June 1876	Republicans nominated Ohio Governor Rutherford B. Hayes for president; Democrats nominated New York Governor Samuel J. Tilden for president
July 1876	Violence broke out in South Carolina after the Hamburg Massacre; Grant sent troops to respond to the situation
November 1876	Tilden won popular vote in the presidential election, but the Republicans and the Democrats debated over the Electoral College votes of Florida, Louisiana, and South Carolina
February 1877	Congress agreed to create an electoral commission to review the Electoral College returns; the commission awarded the states to Hayes
March 1877	Hayes took the oath of office, and Reconstruction effectively ended

17.10 BIBLIOGRAPHY

American Black Codes. The George Washington University, June 23, 2012. http://home.gwu.edu/~jjhawkin/BlackCodes/BlackCodes.htm.

Berlin, Ira, Barbara J. Fields, Steven F. Miller, Joseph P. Reidy, and Leslie S. Rowland (Freedman and Southern Society Project). *Slaves No More: Three Essays on Emancipation and the Civil War*. Cambridge University Press, 1992.

Bunting, Josiah. *Ulysses S. Grant*. New York: Times Books, 2004.

Cimbala, Paul A. and Randall M. Miller. *The Freedmen's Bureau and Reconstruction: Reconsideration*. New York: Fordham University Press, 1999.

Civil Rights Act of 1866. Teaching American History.org, June 23, 2012. http://www.teachingamericanhistory.org/library/index.asp?document=480.

Constitution of the State of South Carolina, 1868, Teaching American History in South Carolina, June 23, 2012. http://www.teachingushistory.org/ttrove/1868Constitution.htm.

Cox, LaWanda. *Lincoln and Black Freedom: A Study in Presidential Leadership*. Columbia: University of South Carolina Press, 1981.

Douglass, Frederick. *Appeal to Congress for Impartial Suffrage, January 1867*. University of Oklahoma, College of Law, June 23, 2012. http://www.law.ou.edu/ushistory/suff.shtml.

Foner, Eric. *Reconstruction: America's Unfinished Revolution, 1869-1877*. New York: Harper & Row, 1988.

Foner, Eric. *The Fiery Trial: Abraham Lincoln and American Slavery*. New York: W.W. Norton, 2010.

Freedmen and Southern Society Project. The University of Maryland, July 2, 2012. http://www.history.umd.edu/Freedmen/index.html.

Gallagher, Gary W. *The Confederate War*. Cambridge, Massachusetts: Harvard University Press, 1997.

Gillette, William. *Retreat from Reconstruction, 1869-1877*. Baton Rouge: Louisiana State Press, 1979.

Harris, William C. *With Charity for All: Lincoln and the Restoration of the Union*. Lexington: University of Kentucky, 1997.

History of the Impeachment of Andrew Johnson, Chapter III. Avalon Project, Yale Law School, June 25, 2012. http://avalon.law.yale.edu/19th_century/john_chap_03.asp#ncproc.

Hyslop, Stephen G. *Eyewitness to the Civil War*. Washington, DC: National Geographic, 2000.

Johnson, Andrew. "Proclamation Declaring the Insurrection At An End, 1866." *Modern History Sourcebook*, ed. Paul Halsall, June 23, 2012. http://www.fordham.edu/Halsall/mod/1866endfocivilwar.asp.

Johnson, Andrew. "Proclamation of Amnesty." *The Avalon Project*. Yale Law School, June 23, 2012. http://avalon.law.yale.edu/19th_century/john_chap_03.asp#ncproc.

Long, William R. "Presidential Pardons I (1863-1868): Lincoln First (1863-64)." Legal Essays, July 2, 2012. http://www.drbilllong.com/LegalEssays/Pardons.html.

McPherson, James M. *Ordeal by Fire: The Civil War and Reconstruction*, first edition. New York: Alfred A Knopf, 1982.

McPherson, James M. *Ordeal by Fire: The Civil War and Reconstruction*, third edition. New York: Alfred A Knopf, 2002.

Morison, Samuel Eliot, Henry Steele Commager and William E. Leuchtenburg. *A Concise History of the American Republic*, volume 1. New York: Oxford University Press, 1977.

Perett, Geoffrey. *Ulysses S. Grant: Soldier and President*. New York: Random House, 1997.

Perman, Michael. *The Road to Redemption: Southern Politics, 1869-1877*. Chapel Hill: University of North Carolina Press, 1984.

Phillips, Jason. "Reconstruction in Mississippi." *Mississippi History Now*, Mississippi Historical Society, July 2, 2012. http://mshistorynow.mdah.state.ms.us/index.php?id=204.

Randall, J.G and David Donald. *The Civil War and Reconstruction*, second edition. Boston: D.C. Heath, 1965.

"Reconstruction: The Second Civil War [Transcript]." *The American Experience*, PBS, June 2, 2012. http://www.pbs.org/wgbh/amex/reconstruction/program/index.html.

Report Joint Committee on Reconstruction, 20 June 1866. *From Revolution to Reconstruction...And What Happened Afterwards*, June 25, 2012. http://odur.let.rug.nl/~usa/D/1851-1875/reconstruction/repojc.htm.

Rhodes, James Ford. *History of the United States*, Volume VII. New York: MacMillan, 1906.

Robertson, James. *The Untold Civil War: Exploring the Human Side of War*. Washington, D.C.: National Geographic, 2011.

Ross, Steven Joseph. "Freed Soil, Freed Labor, Freedmen: John Eaton and the Davis Bend Experiment." *The Journal of Southern History* 44, no. 2 (1978): 213-232.

Simpson, Brooks D. *The Reconstruction Presidents*. Lawrence: University of Kansas Press, 1998.

Smith, Jean Edward. *Grant*. New York: Simon & Schuster, 2001.

Stamp, Kenneth M. *The Era of Reconstruction, 1865-1877*. New York: Alfred A. Knopf, 1966.

Stevens, Thaddeus. "Speech of December 18, 1865." *Modern History Sourcebook*, ed. by Paul Halsall, June 25, 2012. http://www.fordham.edu/halsall.

Tenure of Office Act, 1867. *Teaching American History.org*, June 25, 2012. http://teachingamericanhistory.org/library/index.asp?document=1922.

The Reconstruction Acts. *Texas State Archives and Library Commission*, June 25, 2012. https://www.tsl.state.tx.us/ref/abouttx/secession/reconstruction.html.

Thompson, *Clara Mildred. Reconstruction in Georgia: Economic, Social, Political, 1865-1872, Issue 154.* New York: Columbia University, 1915. Google eBooks, July 2, 2012. http://books.google.com/books?id=i5shAQAAIAAJ&dq=reconstruction+narratives&source=gbs_navlinks_s.

U. S. Army. *Army Historical Series, American Military History*, vol. 1. Washington, DC: Center of Military History, 1989, June 25, 2012. http://www.history.army.mil/books/AMH/amh-toc.htm.

U.S. Federal Census Records. Virginia, 1850-1880.

"The Warrenton Tragedy." *New York Times*, March 17, 1869. New York Times Archives, July 2, 2012. http://query.nytimes.com/mem/archive-free/pdf?res=9505EED81731EF34BC4F52DFB5668382679FDE.

Watson, David K. "The Trial of Jefferson Davis: An Interesting Constitutional Question." *The Yale Law Journal*, 24, No. 8 (June 1915): 669-676. http://www.jstor.org/stable/786018.

17.11 END NOTES

1 Eric Foner, *The Fiery Trial: Abraham Lincoln and American Slavery* (New York: W.W. Norton, 2010), 166-170, 176; Ira, Berlin, Barbara J. Fields, Steven F. Miller, Joseph P. Reidy, and Leslie S. Rowland, *Slaves No More: Three Essays on Emancipation and the Civil War* (Cambridge University Press, 1992), 3, 8, 20-24.

2 Eric Foner, *Reconstruction: America's Unfinished Revolution, 1863-1877* (New York: Harper & Row, 1988), 35; James M. McPherson, *Ordeal by Fire: The Civil War and Reconstruction*, third edition (New York: Alfred A Knopf, 2002), 436-437.

3 Foner, *The Fiery Trial*, 212-214; Brooks D. Simpson, *The Reconstruction Presidents* (Lawrence: University of Kansas Press, 1998), 11.

4 McPherson, *Ordeal by Fire*, third edition, 295-297.

5 Foner, *The Fiery Trial*, 217; McPherson, *Ordeal by Fire*, third edition, 293-295.

6 Abraham Lincoln to John A. McClernand, 8 January 1863, *The Collected Works of Abraham Lincoln*, Volume 6 (Ann Arbor: University of Michigan Digital Library Production Services, 2001), June 6, 2012, http://quod.lib.umich.edu/l/lincoln/lincoln6/1:84?rgn=div1;view=fulltext.

7 Foner, *The Fiery Trial*, 268-270; Simpson, *The Reconstruction Presidents*, 21-22, 27.

8 Abraham Lincoln, Proclamation of Amnesty and Reconstruction, 8 December 1863, Freedom & Southern Society Project, University of Maryland, June 7, 2012, http://www.history.umd.edu/Freedmen/procamn.htm; Abraham Lincoln, Third Annual Message, 8 December 1863, The American Presidency Project, ed. Gerhard Peters and John T. Woolley, June 7, 2012, http://www.presidency.ucsb.edu/ws/?pid=29504.

9 McPherson, *Ordeal by Fire*, third edition, 436; Foner, *The Fiery Trial*, 272-274; Foner, *Reconstruction*, 36; Simpson, *The Reconstruction Presidents*, 39-41.

10 Foner, *Reconstruction*, 37; 39-40.

11 Foner, *The Fiery Trial*, 181-184.

12 Foner, *Reconstruction*, 37-38.

13 Foner, *The Fiery Trial*, 275-277.

14 Foner, *Reconstruction*, 41-43.

15 McPherson, *Ordeal by Fire*, third edition, 437.

16 Foner, *The Fiery Trial*, 279.

17 Foner, *Reconstruction*, 43-45.

18 Foner, *Reconstruction*, 47-50; McPherson, *Ordeal by Fire*, third edition, 438-439; William C. Harris, *With Charity for All: Lincoln and the Restoration of the Union* (Lexington: University of Kentucky, 1997), 182-183.

19 Foner, *Reconstruction*, 51-54.

20 Foner, *Reconstruction*, 58-60; Steven Joseph Ross, "Freed Soil, Freed Labor, Freedmen: John Eaton and the Davis Bend Experiment," *The Journal of Southern History* 44, no. 2 (1978): 213-232.

21 Foner, *Reconstruction*, 69-70.

22 Garrison Frazier quoted in "Colloquy with Colored Ministers," *The Journal of Negro History* 16, no. 1 (1931): 91.

23 Foner, *Reconstruction*, 70-71.

24 Foner, *Reconstruction*, 36, 62.

25 Foner, *Reconstruction*, 60; McPherson, *Ordeal by Fire*, third edition, 456-457.

26 McPherson, *Ordeal by Fire*, 439; Simpson, *The Reconstruction Presidents*, 47-48.

27 Foner, *The Fiery Trial*, 301; McPherson, *Ordeal by Fire*, third edition, 440.

28 McPherson, *Ordeal by Fire*, third edition, 440-442, 513-514.

29 McPherson, *Ordeal by Fire*, third edition, 435; Foner, *Reconstruction*, 66-68.

30 Foner, *Reconstruction*, 68-70; Randall M. Miller, "The Freedmen's Bureau and Reconstruction: An Overview," in *The Freedmen's Bureau and Reconstruction: Reconsideration* ed., Paul A. Cimbala and Randall M. Miller (New York: Fordham University Press, 1999), xv.

31 Samuel Eliot Morison, Henry Steele Commager, and William E. Leuchtenburg, *A Concise History of the American Republic*, vol. 1 (New York: Oxford University Press, 1977), 333.

32 Morison, et al., *Concise History,* 333.

33 Quoted in James M. McPherson, Ordeal by Fire: The Civil War and Reconstruction, first edition (New York: Alfred A Knopf, 1982), 498.

34 Quoted in McPherson, *Ordeal by Fire*, first edition, 498.

35 McPherson, *Ordeal by Fire*, first edition, 499.

36 McPherson, *Ordeal by Fire*, first edition, 504.

37 *The American Black Codes, 1865-1866*. The George Washington University, September 26, 2012, http://home.gwu.edu/~jjhawkin/BlackCodes/BlackCodes.htm.

38 McPherson, *Ordeal by Fire*, first edition, 501.

39 Quoted in Morison, et al, *Concise History*, 334

40 Quoted in Morison, et al, *Concise History*, 334.

41 Civil Rights Act of 1866, *Teaching American History.org*, June 23, 2012, http://www.teachingamericanhistory.org/library/index.asp?document=480.

42 Report Joint Committee on Reconstruction, 20 June 1866, *From Revolution to Reconstruction…And What Happened Afterwards*, June 25, 2012, http://odur.let.rug.nl/~usa/D/1851-1875/reconstruction/repojc.htm.

43 J.G Randall and David Donald, *The Civil War and Reconstruction*, second edition (Boston: D.C. Heath, 1965), 587-588.

44 Randal and Donald, *The Civil War and Reconstruction*, 588.

45 Morison, et al., *Concise History*, 338.

46 Quoted in *The Civil War and Reconstruction,* 592.

47 "An act to provide for the more efficient government of the Rebel States" 2 March 1867, *The Reconstruction Acts: 1867*, Texas State Archives and Library Commission, June 25, 2012, https://www.tsl.state.tx.us/ref/.

48 "An act to provide for the more efficient government of the Rebel States."

49 Addendum of July 1867 to "An act to provide for the more efficient government of the Rebel States," *American Military History*, vol. 1, Army Historical Series, June 25, 2012, http://www.history.army.mil/books/AMH-V1/ch13.htm.

50 Randall and Donald, *The Civil War and Reconstruction*, 593.

51 *Constitution of the State of South Carolina, 1868*, Teaching American History in South Carolina, June 23, 2012, http://www.teachingushistory.org/ttrove/1868Constitution.htm.

52 "An act to provide for the more efficient government of the Rebel States."

53 PBS Online. *Reconstruction, the Second Civil War*.The American Experience. http://www.pbs.org/wgbh/amex/reconstruction/activism/sf_rights.html.

54 American Black Codes. http://home.gwu.edu/~jjhawkin/BlackCodes/BlackCodes.htm.

55 Educational Broadcasting Corporation. *The Rise and Fall of Jim Crow.* http://www.pbs.org/wnet/jimcrow/stories_events_kkk.html.

56 A&E Television Networks. History.com. *African-American Leaders During Reconstruction*. http://www.history.com/topics/african-american-leaders-during-reconstruction.

57 Josiah Bunting, *Ulysses S. Grant* (New York: Times Books, 2004), 78-79, 81-83; Simpson, *The Reconstruction Presidents*, 134; McPherson, *Ordeal by Fire*, third edition, 584.

58 McPherson, *Ordeal by Fire*, third edition, 584-585.

59 McPherson, *Ordeal by Fire*, third edition, 585-588.

60 Jean Edward Smith, *Grant* (New York: Simon & Schuster, 2001), 461, 465.

61 Ulysses S. Grant, "Inaugural Address," 4 March 1869, *The American Presidency Project*, ed. Gerhard Peters and John T. Woolley, June 15, 2012, http://www.presidency.ucsb.edu/ws/?pid=25820; Smith, *Grant*, 467-468.

62 Bunting, *Ulysses S. Grant*, 100, 104-106, 117, 121.

63 Simpson, *The Reconstruction Presidents*, 135-136; William Gillette, *Retreat from Reconstruction, 1869-1877* (Baton Rouge: Louisiana State Press, 1979), 166-168.

64 Simpson, *The Reconstruction Presidents*, 140-142; Gillette, *Retreat from Reconstruction*, 81-85.

65 McPherson, *Ordeal by Fire*, third edition, 589; Gillette, *Retreat from Reconstruction*, 85-86.

66 Gillette, *Retreat from Reconstruction*, 87-89; Foner, *Reconstruction*, 423-424.

67 McPherson, *Ordeal by Fire*, third edition, 607; Foner, *Reconstruction*, 425-426; "Reconstruction: The Second Civil War," Episode 2 Transcript, *The American Experience*, PBS, June 18, 2012, http://www.pbs.org/wgbh/amex/reconstruction/filmmore/pt_p2.html.

68 Smith, *Grant*, 544; McPherson, *Ordeal by Fire*, third edition, 607-608.

69 McPherson, *Ordeal by Fire*, third edition, 609; Smith, *Grant*, 544; Simpson, *The Reconstruction Presidents*, 151-153.

70 McPherson, *Ordeal by Fire*, third edition, 609; Smith, *Grant*, 546-547.

71 McPherson, *Ordeal by Fire*, third edition, 609-610; Simpson, *The Reconstruction Presidents*, 155-156.

72 McPherson, *Ordeal by Fire*, third edition, 594, 638; Bunting, *Ulysses S. Grant*, 87, 90-92, 122-124.

73 McPherson, *Ordeal by Fire*, third edition, 594-595; Bunting, *Ulysses S. Grant*, 124-125.

74 Smith, *Grant*, 587-589; Geoffrey Perett, *Ulysses S. Grant: Soldier and President* (New York: Random House, 1997), 433-434.

75 McPherson, *Ordeal by Fire*, third edition, 605-606; Bunting, *Ulysses S. Grant*, 126; Foner, *Reconstruction*, 497-499.

76 Foner, *Reconstruction*, 499-503; McPherson, third edition, *Ordeal by Fire*, 610-613; Michael Perman, *The Road to Redemption: Southern Politics, 1869-1879* (Chapel Hill: University of North Carolina Press, 1984), 58, 108-109.

77 Smith, *Grant*, 549; Foner, *Reconstruction*, 504-505; McPherson, *Ordeal by Fire*, third edition, 613.

78 Smith, *Grant*, 549-552; Bunting, *Ulysses S. Grant*, 127-128.

79 Ulysses S. Grant, "Inaugural Address," 4 March 1873, *The American Presidency Project*, ed. Gerhard Peters and John T. Woolley, June 18, 2012, http://www.presidency.ucsb.edu/ws/index.php?pid=25821#axzz1yArtTlXn.

80 Smith, *Grant*, 481-490.

81 Smith, *Grant*, 575; Jennifer Lee, "New York and the Panic of 1873," *New York Times*, City Room, October 14, 2008, http://cityroom.blogs.nytimes.com/2008/10/14/learning-lessons-from-the-panic-of-1873/.

82 Smith, *Grant*, 576; Lee, "New York and the Panic of 1873;" James Ford Rhodes, *History of the United States*, Volume VII (New York: MacMillan, 1906), 45-51; McPherson, *Ordeal by Fire*, third edition, 629; Foner, *Reconstruction*, 514-517.

83 Rhodes, *History of the United States*, 53, 61-62; Smith, Grant, 577-580.

84 Smith, *Grant*, 581-583; Rhodes, *History of the United States*, 63-64, 70-73; Lee, "New York and the Panic of 1873."

85 Bunting, *Ulysses S. Grant*, 131-132, 134.

86 Smith, *Grant*, 553; Bunting, *Ulysses S. Grant*, 134-135.

87 Smith, *Grant*, 583-584, 590-593; Bunting, *Ulysses S. Grant*, 136-138.

88 Smith, *Grant*, 593-595; Bunting, *Ulysses S. Grant*, 135-136.

89 Gillette, *Retreat from Reconstruction*, 172-174, 180-181, 190-191.

90 McPherson, *Ordeal by Fire*, third edition, 633-634.

91 McPherson, *Ordeal by Fire*, third edition, 634-635; Foner, *Reconstruction*, 550-551.

92 Simpson, *The Reconstruction Presidents*, 173-175, 181; McPherson, *Ordeal by Fire*, third edition, 620-621, 635-637; Foner, *Reconstruction*, 523.

93 McPherson, *Ordeal by Fire*, third edition, 637-638; Simpson, *The Reconstruction Presidents*, 181-182; Smith *Grant*, 562-563.

94 Simpson, *The Reconstruction Presidents*, 188-189.

95 Foner, *Reconstruction*, 568; "Democratic Party Platform of 1876," 22 June 1876, *The American Presidency Project*, ed. Gerhard Peters and John T. Woolley, June 12, 2012, http://www.presidency.ucsb.edu/ws/?pid=29581.

96 McPherson, *Ordeal by Fire*, third edition, 640; Foner, *Reconstruction*, 567; "Republican Party Platform of 1876," 14 June 1876, *The American Presidency Project* ed. Gerhard Peters and John T. Woolley, June 20, 2012, http://www.presidency.ucsb.edu/ws/?pid=29624.

97 Foner, *Reconstruction*, 571.

98 McPherson, *Ordeal by Fire*, third edition, 641-643.

99 McPherson, *Ordeal by Fire*, third edition, 643-644.

100 McPherson, *Ordeal by Fire*, third edition, 644-645.

ANSWER KEY FOR CHAPTER SEVENTEEN: RECONSTRUCTION

Check your answers to the questions in the Before You Move On Sections for this chapter.

Correct answers are **BOLDED**

Section 17.2.6 - p652

1. Which of the following statements best describes Abraham Lincoln's "Proclamation on Amnesty and Reconstruction"?
   a. The policy was consistent in the Union-occupied territories.
   b. The policy was designed to promote the rights of the freedmen, not to help end the war.
   C. THE POLICY WAS FAIRLY LENIENT TOWARD THE SOUTHERN STATES.
   d. The policy was widely supported by the Radical Republicans in Congress.

2. The Border States quickly accepted Lincoln's proposals for gradual compensated emancipation and willingly implemented the Thirteenth Amendment.
   a. True
   B. FALSE

3. Which of the following measures did Republicans in Congress promote in 1864 to counter Lincoln's Ten-Percent Plan?
   a. The Military Reconstruction Bill
   b. The Louisiana Bill
   c. The Civil Rights Bill
   D. THE WADE-DAVIS BILL

4. Congress envisioned the Freedmen's Bureau created in March of 1865 as a permanent solution to dealing with the problems of African Americans after the Civil War.
   a. True
   B. FALSE

Section 17.3.6 - p660

1. The Black Codes passed in most southern states in 1865-1866 were based on the Slave Codes common in the period before emancipation.
   A. TRUE
   b. False

2. The purpose of the Tenure of Office Act was to:
   A. FORCE ANDREW JOHNSON INTO A POSITION THAT COULD LEAD TO HIS IMPEACHMENT.
   b. Allow the presidency greater freedom in appointing officials to his Cabinet.
   c. Limit the number of terms members of the Supreme Court could serve.
   d. Keep previous confederate officials from holding office in southern states.

3. According to the First Reconstruction Act passed in 1867, the South was divided into military districts.
   A. TRUE
   b. False

4. The Fifteenth Amendment specifies that no citizen of the United States will be:
   a. Deprived of the right of due process.
   b. Forced into servitude.
   C. DEPRIVED OF THE RIGHT TO VOTE.
   d. Kept from the occupation of his/her choice.

Section 17.4.7 - p667

1. To whites in the South, all whites were the same.
   a. True
   B. FALSE

2. Jefferson Davis was convicted of treason.
   a. True
   B. FALSE

3. Sharecroppers were tenant farmers who paid their rent with shares of their crops.
   A. TRUE
   b. False

4. Cotton formed a strong economic basis for the South during Reconstruction.
   a. True
   B. FALSE

Section 17.5.5 - p686

1. The Grant administration supported the adoption of the Enforcement Acts to curb Klan violence against black voters in the South.
   A. TRUE
   b. False

2. Southern redeemers hoped to preserve Republican rule in the South.
   a. True
   B. FALSE

3. Which of the following partially explain Ulysses S. Grant's failure to develop a successful southern policy?
   A. HE ALLOWED CORRUPTION TO DEVELOP IN HIS ADMINISTRATION.
   b. He proposed to withdrawal federal troops from the South.
   c. He opposed Congressional Reconstruction.
   d. None of the above.

4. Who won the presidential election of 1876?
   a. Ulysses S. Grant
   b. Horace Greeley
   c. Samuel J. Tilden
   D. RUTHERFORD B. HAYES